THE GOSPEL FOR THE PEOPLE

CHARLES H. SPURGEON

SOLID GROUND CHRISTIAN BOOKS

THE GOSPEL
FOR
THE PEOPLE

CHARLES H. SPURGEON

SOLID GROUND CHRISTIAN BOOKS
BIRMINGHAM, ALABAMA USA

Solid Ground Christian Books
PO Box 660132
Vestavia Hills AL 35266
205-443-0311
mike.sgcb@gmail.com
www.solid-ground-books.com

THE GOSPEL FOR THE PEOPLE
Sixty Short Sermons
Charles Haddon Spurgeon (1834-1892)
Selected by Thomas Spurgeon (1856-1917)

First published in 1895 by Passmore and Alabaster in London

First Solid Ground edition published in April 2013

Cover design by Borgo Design
Contact them at borgogirl@bellsouth.net

ISBN- 978-159925-2841

THE GOSPEL

FOR

THE PEOPLE.

SIXTY SHORT SERMONS

BY

C. H. SPURGEON,

WITH A SKETCH OF HIS LIFE,

AND

FOURTEEN PORTRAITS AND ENGRAVINGS.

WITH A PREFACE

BY

PASTOR THOMAS SPURGEON.

LONDON:

PASSMORE AND ALABASTER,

PATERNOSTER BUILDINGS.

1895.

Yours truly

C. H. Spurgeon

PREFACE.

DEAR READER,

I KNOW not how often it has fallen to my lot to meet with godly men, in out-of-the-way corners of the earth, who do the little they can do for Jesus by calling together their neighbours and friends on the Lord's day, that they may read to them a sermon preached by my late dear father.

It is my joy to know very intimately some thriving churches which were thus commenced, and amongst my personal friends I number not a few earnest-hearted believers who are still toiling on as nonconformist 'lay readers.' I say 'toiling on' because I am well aware that even this form of service has its own difficulties.

One of these difficulties is found in the length of the sermons in their usual form. Reading is slower work than preaching. My friends have told me that they cannot get through one in the allotted time ; and many of their hearers have come great distances, and must hurry home. But when any attempt to excise is made, the reader hardly knows which of the good things to omit. He naturally fears that a mutilated message may miss the mark. What earnest prayer and honest work have I known to be expended by some of these good brethren on Saturday evenings, when the farm work was done, in preparation for the morrow's holy task ! Never was a settled' and salaried minister more careful and prayerful. It was no small concern to know what might be left out, and how the portions which could be read might be fitly joined together.

With this in mind I ventured to suggest the issue of a volume of short sermons, suitable for reading in the bush, and on the sea, and at the fire-side. So here it is !

Of the sermons I need say nought. They are, as all *his* were, full of sound doctrine, saving truth, and heart-moving appeal, combined with brilliant thought, common sense, and quaint humour.

I think I see some of my old friends rejoicing when this goodly store reaches them, for will they not be set up with material for their ministry for many a week to come?

I think I see the members of the little congregations rejoicing as they realise that this special provision has been made for them, and, best of all, I think I see not a few of the country folk yielding to the power of the truth, even as their ripening crops bow before the autumn breeze. God bless the little gatherings, and the faithful readers of the word, and these short sermons of His beloved servant.

So prays,

Yours in the Gospel,

Thomas Spurgeon

METROPOLITAN TABERNACLE,
November, 1895.

TABLE OF CONTENTS

JESUS, THE SUBSTITUTE FOR HIS PEOPLE.

A Sermon

DELIVERED BY

C. H. SPURGEON,

AT THE METROPOLITAN TABERNACLE, NEWINGTON.

"Who is he that condemneth? It is Christ that died, yea rather, that is risen again, who is even at the right hand of God, who also maketh intercession for us."—Romans viii.·34.

THE most dreadful alarm that can disturb a reasonable man is the fear of being condemned by the Judge of all. To be condemned of God now, how dreadful! To be condemned of him at the last great day, how terrible! Well might Belshazzar's loins be loosed when the hand-writing on the wall condemned him as weighed in the balances and found wanting : and well may the conscience of the convicted one be comparable to a little hell when at its lesser judgment-seat the law pronounces sentence upon him on account of his past life. I know of no greater distress than that caused by the suspicion of condemnation in the believer's mind. We are not afraid of tribulation, but we dread condemnation. We are not ashamed when wrongly condemned of men, but the bare idea of being condemned of God makes us like Moses "exceeding fear and quake." The bare possibility of being found guilty at the great judgment-seat of God is so alarming to us that we cannot rest until we see it removed. When Paul offered a loving and grateful prayer for Onesiphorus he could ask no more for him than, "the Lord grant that he may find mercy in that day." Yet, though condemnation is the most fatal of all ills, the apostle Paul in the holy ardour of his faith dares ask, "Who is he that condemneth?" He challenges earth and hell and heaven. In the justifiable venture-someness of his confidence in the blood and righteousness of Jesus Christ he looks up to the excellent glory and to the throne of the thrice holy God, and even in his presence before whom the heavens are not pure, and who charged his angels with folly, he dares to say, "Who is he that condemneth?"

By what method was Paul, who had a tender and awakened conscience, so completely delivered from all fear of condemnation? It

Nos. 1,223-4-5.

certainly was not by any depreciation of the enormity of sin. Amongst all the writers who have ever spoken of the evil of sin none have inveighed against it more heartily, or mourned it more sincerely from their very soul, than the apostle. He declares it to be exceeding sinful. You never find him suggesting apologies or extenuations; he neither mitigates sin nor its consequences. He is very plain when he speaks of the wages of sin and of what will follow as the consequences of iniquity. He sought not that false peace which comes from regarding transgression as a trifle, in fact he was a great destroyer of such refuges of lies. Rest assured, dear hearer, that you will never attain to a well-grounded freedom from the fear of condemnation by trying to make your sins appear little. That is not the way: it is far better to feel the weight of sin till it oppresses your soul than to be rid of the burden by presumption and hardness of heart. Your sins are damnable, and must condemn you unless they are purged away by the great sin-offering.

Neither did the apostle quiet his fears by confidence in anything that he had himself felt or done. Read the passage through and you will find no allusion to himself. If he is sure that none can condemn him, it is not because he has prayed, nor because he has repented, nor because he has been the apostle of the Gentiles, nor because he has suffered many stripes and endured much for Christ's sake. He gives no hint of having derived peace from any of these things, but in the humble spirit of a true believer in Jesus he builds his hope of safety upon the work of his Saviour; his reasons for rejoicing in noncondemnation all lie in the death, and resurrection, the power and the plea of his blessed Substitute. He looks right out of himself, for there he could see a thousand reasons for condemnation, to Jesus through whom condemnation is rendered impossible, and then in exulting confidence he lifts up the challenge, "Who shall lay anything to the charge of God's elect?" and dares to demand of men and angels and devils, yea of the great Judge himself, "Who is he that condemneth?"

Now since it is not an uncommon thing for Christians in a weakly state of mind, exercised with doubts and harassed with cares, to feel the cold shadow of condemnation chilling their spirits, I would speak to such, hoping that the good Spirit may comfort their hearts.

Dear child of God, you must not live under fear of condemnation, for "there is therefore now no condemnation to them which are in Christ Jesus," and God would not have you fear that which can never come to you. If you be not a Christian, delay not till you have escaped from condemnation by laying hold on Christ Jesus; but if you have indeed believed in the Lord Jesus you are not under condemnation, and you never can be either in this life or in that which is to come. Let me help you by refreshing your memory with those precious truths concerning Christ, which show that believers are clear before the Lord. May the Holy Spirit apply them to your souls and give you rest.

I. And first you, as a believer, cannot be condemned because CHRIST HATH DIED. *The believer has Christ for his substitute*, and upon that substitute his sin has been laid. The Lord Jesus was made sin for his people. "The Lord hath made to meet upon him the iniquity of us all." "He bare the sin of many." Now our Lord Jesus

Christ by his death has suffered the penalty of our sin, and made recompense to divine justice. Observe, then, the comfort which this brings to us. If the Lord Jesus has been condemned for us, how can we be condemned? While justice survives in heaven, and mercy reigns on earth, it is not possible that a soul condemned in Christ should also be condemned in itself. If the punishment has been meted out to its substitute, it is neither consistent with mercy nor justice that the penalty should a second time be executed. The death of Christ is an all-sufficient ground of confidence for every man that believeth in Jesus; he may know of a surety that his sin is put away, and his iniquity is covered. Fix your eye on the fact that you have a substitute who has borne divine wrath on your account, and you will know no fear of condemnation.

> " Jehovah lifted up his rod—
> O CHRIST, it fell on thee!
> Thou wast sore stricken of thy God;
> There's not one stroke for me."

Observe, dear brethren, *who it was that died*, for this will help you. Christ Jesus *the Son of God* died, the just for the unjust. He who was your Saviour was no mere man. Those who deny the Godhead of Christ are consistent in rejecting the atonement. It is not possible to hold a proper substitutionary propitiation for sin unless you hold that Christ was God. If one man might suffer for another, yet one man's sufferings could not avail for ten thousand times ten thousand men. What efficacy could there be in the death of one innocent person to put away the transgressions of a multitude? Nay, but because he who carried our sins up to the tree was God over all, blessed for ever; because he who suffered his feet to be fastened to the wood was none other than that same Word who was in the beginning with God, and who also was God; because he who bowed his head to death was none other than the Christ, who is immortality and life:—his dying had efficacy in it to take away the sins of all for whom he died. As I think of my Redeemer and remember that he is God himself, I feel that if he took my nature and died, then indeed my sin is gone. I can rest on that. I am sure that if he who is infinite and omnipotent offered a satisfaction for my sins I need not enquire as to the sufficiency of the atonement, for who dares to suggest a limit to its power? What Jesus did and suffered must be equal to any emergency. Were my sins even greater than they are his blood could make them whiter than snow. If God incarnate died in my stead my iniquities are cleansed.

Again, remember who it was that died, and take another view of him. It was *Christ* which being interpreted means " *the anointed.*" He who came to save us did not come unsent or uncommissioned. He came by his Father's will, saying, " Lo, I come, in the volume of the book it is written of me, I delight to do thy will, O God." He came by the Father's power, " for him hath God set forth to be a propitiation for our sins." He came with the Father's anointing, saying, "The Spirit of the Lord is upon me." He was *the* Messiah, sent of God. The Christian need have no fear of condemnation when he sees Christ die for him, because God himself appointed Christ to die, and if God arranged the plan of substitution, and appointed the substitute, he cannot repudiate the vicarious work. Even if we could not speak as we have done of the glorious person of our Lord, yet if the divine sovereignty and wisdom elected such an one as Christ to bear our sin we may be well satisfied to take God's choice, and rest content with that which contents the Lord.

Again, believer, sin cannot condemn you because Christ *died*. His sufferings I doubt not were vicarious long before he came to the cross, but still the substance of the penalty due to sin was death, and it was when Jesus died that he finished transgression, made an end of sin, and brought in everlasting righteousness. The law could go no further than its own capital sentence, which is death : this was the dire punishment pronounced in the garden,—" In the day that thou eatest thereof thou shall surely die." Christ died physically, with all the concomitants of ignominy and pain, and his inner death, which was the bitterest part of the sentence, was attended by the loss of his Father's countenance and a horror unutterable. He descended into the grave, and for three days and three nights he slept within the tomb really dead. Herein is our joy, our Lord has suffered the extreme penalty and given blood for blood, and life for life. He has paid all that was due, for he has paid his life ; he has given himself for us, and borne our sins in his own body on the tree, so that his death is the death of our sins. " It is Christ that died."

I speak not upon these things with any flourishes of words, I give you but the bare doctrine. May the Spirit of God apply these truths to your souls, and you will see that no condemnation can come on those who are in Christ.

It is quite certain, beloved, that the death of Christ must have been effectual for the removal of those sins which were laid upon him. It is not conceivable that Christ died in vain—I mean not conceivable without blasphemy, and I hope we could not descend to that. He was appointed of God to bear the sin of many, and though he was God himself, yet he came into the world and took upon himself the form of a servant and bore those sins, not merely in sorrow but in death itself, and it is not possible that he should be defeated or disappointed of his purpose. Not in one jot or tittle will the intent of Christ's death be frustrated. Jesus shall see of the travail of his soul and be satisfied. That which he meant to do by dying shall be done, and he shall not pour his blood upon the ground in waste in any measure or sense. Then, if Jesus died for you there stands this sure argument, that as he did not die in vain you shall not perish. He has suffered and you shall not suffer. He has been condemned and you shall not be condemned. He has died for you, and now he gives you the promise— " Because I live you shall live also."

II. The apostle goes on to a second argument, which he strengthens with the word " rather." "It is Christ that died, yea *rather*, THAT IS RISEN AGAIN." I do not think we give sufficient weight to this " rather." The death of Christ is the rocky basis of all comfort, but we must not overlook the fact that the resurrection of Christ is considered by the apostle to yield richer comfort than his death—" yea rather, that is risen again." How can we derive more comfort from Christ's resurrection than from his death, if from his death we gain a sufficient ground of consolation ? I answer, because *our Lord's resurrection denoted his total clearance from all the sin which was laid upon him.* A woman is overwhelmed with debt : how shall she be discharged from her liabilities ? A friend, out of his great love to her, marries her. No sooner is the marriage ceremony performed than she is by that very act clear of debt, because her debts are her husband's, and in taking her he takes all her obligations. She may gather comfort from that thought, but she is much more at ease when her beloved goes to her creditors, pays all, and brings her the receipts. First she is comforted by the marriage, which legally relieves her from the liability, but much more is she at rest when her husband himself is rid of all the liability which he assumed. Our Lord Jesus took our debts ; in death he paid them, and in resurrection he blotted out the record. By his resurrection he took away the last vestige of charge against us, for the resurrection of Christ was the Father's declaration that he was satisfied with the Son's atonement. As our hymnster puts it—

> " The Lord is risen indeed,
> Then justice asks no more ;
> Mercy and truth are now agreed,
> Which stood opposed before."

In his prison-house of the grave the hostage and surety of our souls would have been confined to this very hour, unless the satisfaction which he offered had been satisfactory to God, but being fully accepted he was set free from bonds, and all his people are thereby justified. ".Who is he that condemneth ? Christ is risen again."

Mark further that *the resurrection of Christ indicated our acceptance with God.* When God raised him from the dead he thereby gave testimony that he had accepted Christ's work, but the acceptance of our representative is the acceptance of ourselves. When the French ambassador was sent away from the Court of Prussia it meant that war was declared, and when the ambassador was again received peace was re-established. When Jesus was so accepted of God that he rose again from the dead everyone of us who believe in him was accepted of God too, for what was done to Jesus was in effect done to all the members of his mystical body. With him are we crucified, with him are we buried, with him we rise again, and in his acceptance we are accepted.

Did not his resurrection also indicate that *he had gone right through with the entire penalty,* and that his death was sufficient ? Suppose for a moment that one thousand eight hundred and more years had passed away, and that still he slumbered in the tomb. In such a case we might have been enabled to believe that God had accepted Christ's substitutionary sacrifice, and would ultimately raise him from the dead, but we should have had our fears. But now we have before our eyes a sign and token, as consoling as the rainbow in the day of rain, for Jesus is risen, and it is clear that the law can exact no more from him. He lives now by a new life, and the law has no claim against him. *He* against whom the claim was brought has died, his present life is not that against which the law can bring a suit. So with us : the law had claims on us once, but we are new creatures in Christ

Jesus, we have participated in the resurrection life of Christ, and the law cannot demand penalties from our new life. The incorruptible seed within us has not sinned, for it is born of God. The law cannot condemn us, for we have died to it in Christ, and are beyond its jurisdiction.

I leave with you this blessed consolation. Your surety has discharged the debt for you, and being justified in the Spirit has gone forth from the tomb. Lay not a burden upon yourselves by your unbelief. Do not afflict your conscience with dead works, but turn to Christ's cross and look for a revived consciousness of pardon through the blood washing.

III. I must pass on now to the third point upon which the apostle insists. "WHO IS EVEN AT THE RIGHT HAND OF GOD." Bear in mind still that what Jesus is his people are, for they are one with him. His condition and position are typical of their own. "Who is even at the right hand of God." That means *love,* for the right hand is for the beloved. That means *acceptance.* Who shall sit at the right hand of God but one who is dear to God? That means *honour.* To which of the angels has he given to sit at his right hand? *Power* also is implied! No cherub or seraph can be said to be at the right hand of God. Christ, then, who once suffered in the flesh is, in love, and acceptance, and honour, and power at the right hand of God. See you the force, then, of the interrogation, "Who is he that condemneth?" It may be made apparent in a twofold manner. "Who can condemn me while I have such a friend at court? While my representative sits near to God how can I be condemned?" But next, I am where he is, for it is written, "He hath raised us up together, and made us sit together in heavenly places in Christ Jesus." Can you suppose it possible to condemn one who is already at the right hand of God? The right hand of God is a place so near, so eminent, that one cannot suppose an adversary bringing a charge against us there. Yet there the believer is in his representative, and who dare accuse him? It was laid at Haman's door as his worst crime that he sought to compass the death of queen Esther herself, so dear to the king's heart; and shall any foe condemn or destroy those who are dearer to God than ever Esther was to Ahasuerus, for they sit at his right hand, vitally and indissolubly united to Jesus. Suppose you were actually at the right hand of God, would you then have any fear of being condemned? Do you think the bright spirits before the throne have any dread of being condemned, though they were once sinners like yourself? "No," say you, "I should have perfect confidence if I were there." But you are there in your representative. If you think you are not I will ask you this question, "Who shall separate us from the love of Christ?" Is Christ divided? If you are a believer you are one with him, and the members must be where the head is. Till they condemn the head they cannot condemn the members? Is not that clear? If you are at the right hand of God in Christ Jesus who is he that condemneth? Let them condemn those white-robed hosts who for ever circle the throne of God, and cast their crowns at his feet; let them attempt that, I say, before they lay anything to the charge of the meanest believer in Christ Jesus.

IV. The last word which the apostle gives us is this, "WHO ALSO

MAKETH INTERCESSION FOR US." This is another reason why fear of condemnation should never cross our minds if we have indeed trusted our souls with Christ, for if Jesus intercedes for us he must make a point of interceding that we may never be condemned. He would not direct his intercession to minor points and leave the major unheeded. " Father, I will that they also whom thou hast given me be with me where I am " includes their being forgiven all their sins, for they could not come there if their sins were not forgiven. Rest assured that a pleading Saviour makes secure the acquittal of his people.

Reflect that our Lord's intercession must be prevalent. It is not supposable that Christ asks in vain. He is no humble petitioner at a distance who, with moan and sigh, asks for what he deserves not, but with the breast-plate on, sparkling with the jewels which bear his people's names, and bringing his own blood as an infinitely satisfactory atonement to the mercy-seat of God, he pleads with unquestioned authority. If Abel's blood, crying from the ground, was heard in heaven and brought down vengeance, much more shall the blood of Christ, which speaketh within the veil, secure the pardon and salvation of his people. The plea of Jesus is indisputable, and cannot be put aside. He pleads this,—" I have suffered in that man's stead." Can the infinite justice of God deny that plea ? " By thy will, O God, I gave myself a substitute for these my people. Wilt thou not put away the sin of these for whom I stood ?" Is not this good pleading? There is God's covenant for it, there is God's promise for it, and God's honour involved in it, so that when Jesus pleads, it is not only the dignity of his person that has weight, and the love which God bears to his only begotten, which is equally weighty, but his claim is over-whelming, and his intercession omnipotent.

How safe is the Christian since Jesus ever liveth to make interces-sion for him! Have I committed myself into his dear hands? Then may I never so dishonour him as to mistrust him. Do I really trust him as dying, as risen, as sitting at the Father's right hand, and as plead-ing for me? Can I permit myself to indulge a solitary suspicion? Then, my Father, forgive this great offence, and help thy servant by a greater confidence of faith to rejoice in Christ Jesus and say, " There is therefore now no condemnation." Go away, ye that love Christ, and are resting on him, with the savour of this sweet doctrine on your hearts ; but, oh, you that have not trusted Christ there is present con-demnation for you. Ye are condemned already, because ye have not believed on the Son of God ; and there is future condemnation for you, for the day cometh, the dreadful day, when the ungodly shall be as stubble in the fire of Jehovah's wrath. The hour hasteneth when the Lord will lay justice to the line, and righteousness to the plummet ; and sweep away the refuges of lies. Come, poor soul, come and trust the crucified, and you shall live, and with us you shall rejoice that none can condemn you.

PORTION OF SCRIPTURE READ BEFORE SERMON—Isaiah liii.

HYMNS FROM "OUR OWN HYMN BOOK"—329, 404, 299.

Metropolitan Tabernacle Pulpit.

JESUS, THE STUMBLING STONE OF UNBELIEVERS.

A Sermon

DELIVERED BY

C. H. SPURGEON,

AT THE METROPOLITAN TABERNACLE, NEWINGTON.

"Unto you therefore which believe he is precious: but unto them which be disobedient, the stone which the builders disallowed, the same is made the head of the corner, and a stone of stumbling, and a rock of offence, even to them which stumble at the word, being disobedient."—1 Peter ii. 7, 8.

So it ever is where Jesus comes, he divides the company into believers and unbelievers, the obedient and the disobedient. But why are unbelievers here called disobedient? Is faith a matter of law, and because a man does not believe does he therefore disobey? How can it be otherwise? Is it not a natural duty for every man to believe that which is true? Let the very least among us judge in so simple a matter. It so happens that in the very form and sound of the words, in the original tongue, to believe and to obey are much the same; and certainly to disbelieve and to disobey are things of very near relationship. To disbelieve is in its very essence disobeying, for he who disbelieves the word of the king is disloyal at heart. If I doubt the veracity of God I have assailed his authority, and if when he sets forth his Son to be a propitiation for sin I refuse to accept him, disobedience is included in that rejection. As it were difficult to tell by which form of sin our father Adam fell, for all sins were wrapped up in the taking of the forbidden fruit, so unbelief contains within itself the eggs of all sins possible to men.

Moreover, unbelief of God's word is the root of all other sin. Given a man who does not believe his God and you have a man who casts off the law of God. He has already rejected his gospel, why should he respect the law? If the silken cords of love are broken asunder, how much less is the man likely to bear the bonds of law?

Now, inasmuch as it is painfully certain that a very large proportion of those who hear the gospel are unbelieving and disobedient, it becomes important to consider, What is the result of this disobedience? This disobedience leads them into violent opposition; what effect does their opposition produce? The text tells us *the result of human opposition upon Christ himself,* and, secondly *upon the persons who offer it.*

8

I. Let us consider, in the first place, then, THE RESULT OF THE UNBELIEF, AND THE OPPOSITION OF MEN, UPON THE LORD JESUS CHRIST. We are told that, as far as he is concerned, "the stone which the builders disallowed, the same is made the head of the corner"— in one word, it has not affected him at all. The opposition of mankind has by no means, and in no degree, lessened the glory which God has put upon his dear Son. The builders rejected the stone with disdain: "it shall not be builded," said they, "in the temple of our hope;" but, God has said, "It shall be the top stone," and the top stone it is, and shall be despite all the opposition of earth or hell. The rage of puny man shall no more defeat the Lord than the anger of a gnat can affect the sun, and human opposition shall no more thwart the divine will than a sere leaf cast into Niagara can block the cataract. He that stumbleth upon this stone shall be broken, but the stone itself will not be injured.

Observe how the Lord Jesus has been rejected of man, and yet his cause has stood against all opposition. First came *the Jew*. He had the pride of race to maintain. Were not the Jews the chosen people of God? Was not Israel set apart by the Most High? Jesus comes preaching the gospel to every creature, he sends his disciples even to the Gentiles: therefore the Jews will not have him. They have been looking for a temporal prince, he does not come with the magnificence they expected; he is a root out of a dry ground, without form or comeliness; they see nothing of Solomon's splendour in the poor scion of the dried-up stock of David, therefore, "Away with him! Let him be crucified!" But the opposition of his countrymen did not defeat the cause of Christ; if rejected in Palestine his word was received in Greece, it triumphed in Rome, it passed onward to Spain, it found a dwelling-place in Britain, and at this day it lights up the face of the earth. The persecution of the apostles at Jerusalem hastened the spread of the gospel, for they that were scattered abroad went everywhere preaching the Word, so that Jewish enmity was overruled for good, and the foolish builders were made subservient to the uplifting of the rejected headstone.

Next arose *the philosopher* to be the gospel's foe. Different schools of thought held sway over the more cultivated minds of the period, and no sooner did Paul begin to preach where these philosophies were known than they called him a babbler. They heard what he had to say, and condemned him as a fool. This resurrection from the dead, this doctrine of an incarnate God who suffered for human sin—it was too simple for them, too plain to fit in with their subtle philosophies. But though philosophy made terrible inroads for a while on the church of God, in the form of the gnostic heresy, did it really impede the chariot wheels of Christ? Did it conquer the faith? Oh no, my brethren, for at this day where are these philosophies? Who now believes in the Stoics? Who would care to be called an Epicurean? These philosophies have passed away, the stone cut out of the mountain without hands has broken them in pieces. The stone from the sling of Christ has smitten the heathen philosophy in the forehead; we see its corpse lying headless in many an ancient tome, while the Son of David goes forth conquering and to conquer.

After those days there came against the church of God the determined opposition of *the secular power*. The imperial authorities saw danger in Christianity. These peasants and boors and mechanics set up a new religion, a religion which spoke of another king, one Jesus. They met together on the first day of the week, and sang hymns in his honour as to God ; moreover, they refused to keep the holy days of the gods, nor would they worship the images of the emperors, either departed or living. Everybody else paid homage to these imperial demons except these Christian people ; so the secular power said, "We will put them down. Let them be dragged before the judgment-seat ; let them be imprisoned, let them be stripped of their goods, and if that does not drive them out of this new doctrine, let us try the rack and such like tortures, and if that does not end them let them die. Why cannot men worship the gods of their fathers ? Thus they tried to stamp out the faith of Jesus, crowding their prisons, flooding their theatres with blood, and wearying the executioners. All that cruelty could do was done ; but, my brethren, what was the result ? The more the Christians were oppressed, the more they multiplied ; the scattering of the coals increased the conflagration. The tribunals of judgment became pulpits from which Christianity was preached, and men who stood burning at the stake commanded mighty audiences, among which they proclaimed Jesus Christ as king. The martyr's courage made men enquire, "Is there not something here, the like of which we have never seen before ?" and it was not long before imperial legions bowed before the cross of Christ, and the Galilean had won the day.

Since that period the church has been attacked in various modes. The Arian *heresy* assaulted the deity of Christ, but the church of God delivered herself from the accursed thing, as Paul shook the viper into the fire. Then came popery, the antichrist, the ape of Jesus, and counterfeit of his sacrifice. Now they set up the cross of ivory, hung round with gems, to mimic the King of kings on his cross of shame ; they thrust before us the crucifix of man's making instead of Jesus himself upon the tree. Now we are asked to worship saints, and relics and images, and I know not what beside, and a man is lifted into the throne of the infallible God. Some timid minds fear that Jesus Christ as a stone rejected will be cast out of sight, while high over all the vicar of Christ at Rome shall be made the head of the corner, but the Lord will not suffer it. Brethren, have faith in God and think not so. The differing modes of Popery, Roman and Anglican, shall pass away as all things else have done that withstood the cross and cause of Jesus Christ. Even as a moment's foam dissolves into the wave that bears it and is gone for ever, so shall all these disappear : yet shall Jesus Christ's holy gospel and himself, the Saviour, be set on high as a rock defying the billows. What a day was that when Luther's rough protest broke the silence of the dark ages, when the clear teaching of Calvin followed, and the bold notes of Zwingle were heard, and a thousand voices shouted in chorus ! What a day was that when the nations awoke from their long sleep to lie no longer under priestly domination, resolute to be free ! Cannot God, who sent one Reformation, send another ? Be of good courage, for brighter days are on the way. There shall come yet greater awakenings, the Lord the avenger of his church shall yet arise, and the stone which the builders disallowed, the same shall be the head stone of the corner.

By prophetic vision I see gathering another opposition which will be as difficult to cope with as any that has gone before. I see mustering within the ranks of the church of God men who say they hate all creeds, meaning that they despise all truth, men who would fain be ministers amongst us and yet tread under foot all that we hold sacred, not teaching at first the fulness of their infidelity, but little by little gathering courage to vent their unbeliefs and heresies. Credophobia is maddening many. They appear to fear lest they should believe anything, and to hope that there is something good to be found in atheism, or devil worship,—indeed in all religions except the only true one. We lift our earnest protest, but if it should be lost amidst the general popular clamour, and if the nations should be drunk again with the wine of this fornication and turn aside to error, what matters it to the ultimate success of the eternal cause ? Yet hath Jehovah set his king upon his holy hill of Zion, and yet shall the ancient decree be fulfilled, and the throne of Christ shall stand, and the covenant sealed with blood shall be sure to all the chosen seed. Let us have comfort, for despite all that can be done by men or devils not one elect soul shall be lost, not one soul redeemed by blood shall be snatched out of the Redeemer's hand. Christ shall not lose so much as a grain of glory neither in earth nor in heaven. His people's earnest contention for the faith shall honour him, their patient suffering shall give him praise : heaven shall be the sweeter rest to them, and the brighter place of glory to him when he shall return with them from Edom, with dyed garments from Bozrah, travelling in the greatness of his strength, having trodden the winepress and overcome his foes. Then shall his rest be glorious, and his joy complete.

Thus much, then, upon the effect of human opposition. " The stone which the builders disallowed, the same has become the head stone of the corner."

II. A far more painful subject must now occupy our attention, namely, THE CONSEQUENCE OF THIS OPPOSITION TO THE OPPOSERS, and here let us dwell with great solemnity upon one or two points. When men stumble at the plan of salvation by Christ's sacrificial work, *what is it that they stumble at?* The reply must be a somewhat wide one, but it cannot possibly comprehend all the reasons for man's wicked opposition to his best friend.

Some stumble at the person of Christ. Jesus, they will admit, was a good man, but they cannot accept him as co-equal and co-eternal with the Father. Oh, my hearer, if thou wouldst be saved, stumble not at this, for who but a God could save thee ; and how could the justice of God have been satisfied unless one of infinite nature had become the propitiation for sin ? My soul falls gratefully back upon the doctrine of the deity of Christ for her deepest comfort, and I pray that none of you may reject it, for be assured that apart from it there is no true ground of peace for the conscience.

Some stumble at his work. Many cannot see how Jesus Christ is become the propitiation for human guilt, and we fear that the reason why they cannot see must lie in that word of our Lord, " Ye believe not because ye are not of my sheep." We fell, my brethren, not personally, but in another. It was our first father Adam who first ruined us, not we ourselves. Perhaps it was because we so fell that it was possible for us to be restored. As we fell in another, there was a loophole for mercy, for the Lord having dealt with us under one federal head, could justly deal with us under another federal head ; and thus fallen in another we now rise in another. As by the offence of one the condemnation came upon all men, so by the righteousness of one doth the forgiveness come to as many as believe in him. The doctrine of substitution or representation begins at the fountain of human history and runs through its whole course. I beseech you do not cavil at it. It is rich balm and comfort to us who have received it, it has turned our hell to heaven, the Spirit by its means has renewed our nature, and has made us other than we were, and to-day we have no hope apart from the vicarious sacrifice of Immanuel. Oh that you who are objectors would accept that which to-day ye stumble at.

Some stumble at Christ's teaching; and what is it they stumble at in that ? Sometimes it is because it is too holy : " Christ is too puritanical, he cuts off our pleasures." But it is not so ; he denies us no pleasure which is not sinful, he multiplies our joys ; the things which he denies to us are only joyous in appearance, while his commands are real bliss. " Still," say some, " his teachings are too severe." Yet from others I hear the opposite accusation, for when we preach free grace, objectors cry, " You encourage men in sin." There is little chance of pleasing the sons of men, for what gratifies some offends others ; but truly there is no just reason on either ground to stumble at the gospel, for though it does place good works where they should be placed, as fruits of the Spirit and not as things of merit, yet it is a gospel according to holiness, as those know who have proved its power.

We have found some object to the teachings of Christ, because they are too humbling. He destroys self-confidence, and he presents salvation to none but those who are lost. " This lays us too low," saith one. Yet have I heard from the opposite corner of the house an objection to the gospel, because it makes men proud, for say some, " How dare you speak of being certain that you are saved ? That is a boastful speech, and ill befits a lowly mind." Friend, do not stumble at blessed truth, for believers are certainly saved and may know it, and yet be all the humbler for the knowledge. Thou art humbled, it is true, by Christ, and laid low, but he exalts thee in due time, and when he exalts thee by his grace there is no fear of boasting, for boasting is excluded by grace.

Still I have known others object that the gospel is too mysterious, they cannot understand it, they say. While again, from the other corner of the compass, I have heard the objection that it is too plain. This being saved by simply believing in Christ is too plain for many and too hard for others. Beloved, do not cavil at it for either reason. What if there be mysteries in it ? Canst thou expect to comprehend all that God knoweth ? Be thou teachable as a child, and the gospel will be sweet to thee.

We have known some who have stumbled at Christ on account of his people, and truly they have some excuse. They, have said, " Look at Christ's followers, see their imperfections and hypocrisies." But wherefore judge a master by his servants ? I could weep while I confess how much there is of truth in your accusations, but let me beseech you, lay the fault at our door, not at our Master's, for there is nothing in his teaching that encourages our sinning, and none can be more severe towards hypocrisy than is Christ Jesus our Lord. This stumbling at his people is, however, frequently founded on another reason. The lovers of the gospel, it is said, are generally very poor, and unfashionable ; to unite with them is to lose caste. Now that is true, and it always has been so ; from the first day until now the gospel has flourished most where there has been least care for fashion and honour among men : but, I wot, if ye be men, this will be a small concern with you. Only those who are not men, but mimics of men, care for these small matters. You, if your manhood be as it should be, will feel that to follow truth barefooted through the mire is better than to ride with the lie in all her pomp. Besides, taking the great ones of the earth as a class, is their society so specially desirable ? Are the rich so very virtuous ? Are the great so peculiarly good ? I trow not. We have noble exceptions, there are a few who wear the coronet and yet will wear a crown in heaven, but taking them as a class the honourable among men are no better than they should be. No order of men have more to answer for than kings and princes : at their will human blood has flowed like water, and nations have been consumed by famine and pestilence as the result of their wars. Why, then, account their favour to be so precious a thing ? We can turn the tables upon those who sneer at Christ's servants for their lowness of rank, for before the eye of God the great ones are the meanest of all when they become leaders in iniquity. Now, if these be your objections, I pray God to give you grace to play the man, and bear joyfully the reproach of Christ.

What does this stumbling at Christ cost the ungodly? I answer, it costs them a great deal. Those who make him a rock of stumbling are great losers by it *in this life.* Opposition to Jesus is to many men a kicking against the pricks. When the Eastern husbandman drives his bullock, and it moves amiss he goads it, and if the bullock is not broken in, it kicks against the goad as soon as it is pricked, and the consequence is it drives the goad into itself more deeply, and if it then kicks violently, the goad pierces and wounds it still more. It is so with rebellious men. Their persecutions hurt themselves, they cannot really injure our Lord. The hammer said, "I will break the anvil," and the anvil did not answer, but abode in its place, while the hammer smote it day after day. Month after month, year after year, the anvil patiently received the blows, but after awhile the hammer broke, and though it did not say so, for it was too quiet to speak, the anvil might have said, " I have broken hundreds of hammers before, and I shall break hundreds more by patient endurance." It is so with Christ, and his church, and his gospel ; the persecutor may smite, and smite, and smite, the true Christian makes no reply, but patiently bears, and in the long run that patient endurance will break the persecutor down. What anger it costs ungodly men to oppose Christ ! Some of them cannot let

him alone, they will rage and fume.   Concerning Jesus it is true that
you must either love or hate him, he cannot long be indifferent to you,
and hence come inward conflicts to opposers.   I remember an ungodly
man who was a raving hater of Christ.   A Bible was brought into his
house, he seized it, and destroyed it in his wrath.   He did not know
that when his daughter went to bed her eyes were wet with tears at what
her father had done, and that the next night there was a New Testament
under her head.   When by-and-by he found out that she attended the
house of God, there were great threats, and I do not know what of blus-
tering, but it was done all the same for that, and his anger was patiently
borne.   "Well," he thought, "she is a foolish girl, it will end there,"
but very soon another daughter became pious, and then he was furious.
He took his wife into his counsels, to help him, but by her quivering
manner she betrayed that she did not like his proceedings, and after
awhile he found out that she, when he was away, had slunk into the
little meeting-house, too, and that she was feeling with her daughters
the value of eternal things.   Well, at least he had a boy left; the women
were always fools, he said, but his boy he hoped would show more sense,
and not be deluded.   Like his father, he would never fall into superstition, would he ?   He would see about it and question him.   What was
his surprise to find the boy speak up like a man, and say, "Yes, father,
I believe as my sisters do, and I go to the house of God whenever I
can, and I mean to do so."   To his surprise, he found all his house
inclined to hear the gospel, and most of them believers in it.   It
did him no good to be in a passion about it, but he used to rave
horribly, and I fear he thereby shortened his days.   But the thing went
on for all he could do ; the servants of the house also joined the people
at the meeting, and his labourers went in the same way.   God intended
to bless the family, and the enemy was powerless to prevent it, though
it cost him much anger and wrath.

Ah, what it costs some men *when they come to die!*   In the days
when persecution was more public than it is now, many persons were
guilty of being informers against the Puritans, or the Quakers; their
deaths were in many cases appalling, not because of any peculiar pains
they endured, but because their persecutions came up to their memory
in their last moments, and some of them could not rest for crying out
and making acknowledgment of the injustice that they had done to
good men in hunting them into prisons for worshipping God.   If any
of you do not believe in Jesus, and will not be saved by him yourselves, I would recommend you to let him and his people alone, for if
you oppose him you will be the losers, he will not.   Your opposition
is utterly futile; like a snake biting a file you will only break your
own teeth.   You cannot hurt the church, nor hurt the word of God.
Perhaps your very opposition is one cog in the wheel to urge it on.
If the thing be of God it is in vain that you fight against it.   Be as
wise as Haman's wife when she warned her husband that if Mordecai
was of the seed of the Jews, before whom he had begun to fall, it was
no use to take up the cudgels against him.   This warning he proved
to be true when he was hung upon the gallows fifty cubits high.   To
oppose the seed royal of heaven is of no use whatever, but ensures ruin
to those who engage in it.

Now, suppose a man says, " I am not going to believe that Jesus Christ came into this world and died for the guilty, neither will I have him for my Saviour; I will run the risks." Well, if you do it, it is at your own cost, recollect. Do it if you dare. Many years ago a captain was sent out in one of the Government ships, the *Thetis*, to discover a shoal, a rock, or some other obstruction said to exist in the Mediterranean Sea. The captain was an old salt, who knew little about navigation as a science, and cared less for rules, books, theories, and so on. He always sneered at scientific works. Though he sailed near the spot, he did not discover the rock, and came back; but one of his officers was persuaded that, nevertheless, there was something in the report, and some time after, when he had become himself a first officer in another vessel, he sailed near the spot, and discovered it. It was marked on the charts of the Admiralty, and he received a considerable reward for having made the discovery. The old captain cursed and swore at these new fangled fellows who could find what he could not. He would not believe the shoal was there; one thing he would do, they might call him a liar if he did not drive the *Thetis* right over the spot where the rock was marked, and so prove it to be all nonsense. He had an opportunity some time after, when he was out upon a cruise. He sailed close to the spot marked on the chart, and thinking he had passed over it he cried out to those who were standing round, with many expressions of blasphemy, that he had proved these whipper-snappers to be fools and liars. Just as he uttered his boast there came a crash, the ship was on the rock, and in a few minutes she was sinking. By the good providence of God all on board escaped except the captain; he was in such a desperate state of mind that when last he was seen he was on deck in his shirt sleeves rushing about as if he had gone mad. You see his firm belief that there was no rock there did not alter the case, he was wrecked for his obstinacy. There are a great many who say, " Oh, I do not believe it, I shall not bother my head about it." Well, you are warned! You are warned, remember that! There is a way of salvation by Jesus Christ, the incarnate God, and we implore you to accept it: if you do not, this rock of unbelief will be your eternal shipwreck. I pray God that every one of us may bow before Christ, and accept him as our king. He will shortly come to be our judge! Oh, let us worship him as our Mediator! Look ye to him, look ye to him, on his cross, for ye must soon look to him on his throne. Look to his wounds! Behold the atoning blood! Look to him, and find salvation; for whether ye look to him now or no, ye will have to look to him in that day when heaven and earth shall rock and reel, and the trumpet shall sound, and the dead shall rise, and you among them, and the books shall be opened, and the sentence of eternal wrath shall be uttered against the disobedient and unbelieving. God save us all for Jesus' sake. Amen.

PORTION OF SCRIPTURE READ BEFORE SERMON—1 Peter ii.

HYMNS FROM "OUR OWN HYMN BOOK"—118, 2, 961.

Metropolitan Tabernacle Pulpit.

JESUS, THE DELIGHT OF HEAVEN.

DELIVERED BY

C. H. SPURGEON,

AT THE METROPOLITAN TABERNACLE, NEWINGTON.

"And they sung a new song, saying, Thou art worthy to take the book, and to open the seals thereof: for thou wast slain, and hast redeemed us to God by thy blood out of every kindred, and tongue, and people, and nation; and hast made us unto our God kings and priests: and we shall reign on the earth."—Revelation v. 9, 10.

If you want to know a man's character, it is well to inquire at his home. What do his children and servants think of him? What is the estimate formed by those who are always with him? George Whitefield was once asked his opinion of a person, and his answer was very wise, for he replied, "I never lived with him." Beloved brethren in Christ, see what an estimate is formed of your Lord at home up yonder, where they know him best, and see him most constantly, and in the clearest light. They have discovered no faults in him. The angels who have beheld him ever since they were created, the redeemed who have been with him, some of them for thousands of years, have found no spot in him; but their unanimous verdict expressed freely in joyful song is, "Thou art worthy; thou art worthy; thou art worthy."

If you desire to know a man it will be well to find out what the best sort of people think of him, for the good opinion of bad men is worthless. "What have I done," said one of the Greek philosophers, "that you speak well of me?" when he found himself applauded by a man of evil character. A character that comes from men fitted to judge, who know what purity is, who have had their eyes opened to discriminate between virtue and its counterfeit—such a character is well worth having. One would not like to be thought ill of by a saint. We value the esteem of those whose judgment is sound, who are free from prejudice, and who love only that which is honest and of good repute. Now, beloved, see what your Lord is thought of in the best society, where they are all perfect, where they are no longer children, but are all able to judge, where they live in a clear light, and are

16

free from prejudice. where they cannot make a mistake. See what they think of him. They themselves are without fault before the throne; but they do not think themselves worthy, they ascribe worthiness to Jesus only. None stood up to take the book from the open hand of the great King; but when they saw the Lamb do so they felt that it was his right to take that prominent and honourable position, and with one accord they said, "Thou art worthy to take the book, and to open the seals thereof, for thou wast slain." You and I cannot have too lofty thoughts of Jesus. We err in not thinking enough of him. Let our estimate of him grow, and let us cry with Thomas, "My Lord and my God!" Oh, for great thoughts of Jesus. Oh, to set him on the highest imaginable throne in the conceptions of our soul, and to make every power and faculty of our manhood fall prostrate like the elders before him, while whatever of honour God may put upon us we cast always at his feet, and ever say, with heart and lip and act, "Thou art worthy, Jesus, Emmanuel, Redeemer, who hast purchased us by thy blood. Worthy art thou, worthy for ever and for ever."

It is to the estimate of the perfect spirits that I would call your attention. What think ye of Christ, ye glorified ones with whom we shall so soon unite? We have your answer in the words we have read. "Thou art worthy to take the book, and to open the seals thereof: for thou wast slain, and hast redeemed us to God by thy blood out of every kindred, and tongue, and people, and nation: and hast made us unto our God kings and priests: and we shall reign on the earth."

I. Notice first that the bright ones before the throne adore the Lord Jesus as WORTHY OF THE HIGH OFFICE OF MEDIATOR. They adore him as alone worthy of that office, for there was silence in heaven when the roll was held in God's hand, and the challenge was given, "Who is worthy to take the book, and to open the seals thereof?" Dumb were the four living creatures; silent were the cherubim and seraphim: in mute solemnity sat the four-and-twenty elders on their thrones. They put in no claim for worthiness, but by their silence, and their subsequent song when Christ came forward, they admitted that he alone could unfold the purposes of God, and interpret them to the sons of men. For I take it that one of the meanings of our Lord's taking the book into his hand was this: that he was *the fulfiller* of that mysterious roll so closely sealed. He was come to unfold it, and by transactions in which he should hold the chief place, it was to be fulfilled. The key of the purposes of God is Christ. We do not know what the decrees of God may be until they are fulfilled; but we do know that of him and through him, and to him, are all things, and that everything will begin and end with Jesus, for he is Alpha and Omega, the beginning and the end. He is the initial letter of all history, and he will be the "finis" of it when he shall give up the throne to God even the Father, that God may be all in all. As our Lord Jesus is the fulfiller, so he is *the interpreter*. He has been with the Father, and "No man knoweth the Father save the Son, and he to whom the Son shall reveal him." He is the great interpreter to us of the mind of God. His Spirit dwelling in us takes of his things and shows them unto us, and in the light of the Spirit we see the

glory of God in the face of Jesus Christ. "No man cometh to the
Father," saith he, "but by me;" for no man can expound the Father
to us or conduct us to the Father save Jesus Christ, the sole interpreter of the divine secret. And so I regard the expressions here as
setting him forth as mediator, for he it is who stands between God
and man. He is worthy to take the book in his hand on our behalf,
and grasp for us the indentures of our inheritance beyond the stars. No
one else can go in for us to the august presence of the Most High, and
take the title-deeds of grace into his hand on our behalf; but Christ
can do it, and taking it he can unfold it and expound to us the wondrous purpose of electing love towards the chosen ones. Stand back,
ye sons of anti-Christ, with your brazen foreheads! How dare ye
bring forward a virgin, blessed among women, and cause her very
name to be defiled by styling her our intercessor before God? How
dare ye bring your saints and saintesses and make these to mediate
between God and men? "There is one mediator between God and
man, the man Christ Jesus." The saints in heaven sing of him,
"Thou art worthy"; but they salute none else beside. They reserve
no homage for any other intercessor or mediator or interpreter or fulfiller of the divine grace, for they know of no other. Unto him they
give, and to him alone, the honour to go in unto the King on the
behalf of the sons of men, and to take the book in his hand.

Notice carefully to what they ascribe this worthiness :—"Thou art
worthy to take the book and open the seals thereof, *for thou wast
slain.*" Now, the case stands thus. God has given to us innumerable
blessings in the covenant of grace, but they are given upon a condition.
There are two sides to a covenant. Jesus Christ is our representative
and covenant-head, and the condition which as the mediator he had
to fulfil was this—that in due time he would offer to divine justice an
honourable amend for all the injury done to the honour of God by
our sins. As mediator, our Lord's worthiness did not merely arise
from his person as God and perfect man: this fitted him to undertake the office, but his right to claim the privileges written in the
Magna Charta which God held in his hand, his right to take possession for his people of that seven-sealed indenture lies in this, that
he has fulfilled the condition of the covenant, and hence they sing,
"Thou art worthy, for thou wast slain." Not "Thou art worthy, for
thou wast born on earth, and thou didst live a holy life," but "Thou
wast slain ;" for he must render recompense to incensed justice and
injured holiness, and that he did upon the bloody tree. Whenever we
begin to talk about this, the believers in the modern atonement—which
is no atonement, but a hazy piece of cloudland—say to us, "Oh, you hold
the commercial theory, do you ?" They know right well that we only
use, because the Bible uses them, commercial expressions as metaphors ;
but I venture to say to them, "You may well assert that there is nothing
commercial about your system, for the commercial value of a counterfeit farthing would be too much to pay for the atonement in which
you believe." I believe in an atonement in which Christ literally took
the sin of his people, and for them endured the wrath of God, giving
to justice *quid pro quo* for all that was due to it, or an equivalent for
it : bearing, that we might not bear, the wrath that was due to us.

Jesus himself really " bore our sins in his own body on the tree."
" He was made sin for us who knew no sin, that we might be made
the righteousness of God in him ; " there was a literal, positive, actual
substitution of " the just for the unjust to bring us to God." No
other atonement is worth the breath used in preaching of it. It will
neither give comfort to the conscience nor glory to God. But on this
rock our souls may rest without fear, and it is because of this that they
sing in heaven, " Thou art worthy, *for thou wast slain.* Thou canst
claim our absolution : thou canst take the Magna Charta of thine
elect into thy hand, and unroll the covenant established with them of
old. Thou canst reveal to us the sure mercies of David, for thy part
in the covenant has been fulfilled ; thy substitutionary death has made
thy people heirs with thee." Fain would I fly yonder to join their song,
but till then I'll lisp it forth as best I may,—" Thou art worthy to take
the book and open the seals thereof, for thou wast slain."

II. Secondly, in heaven they adore the Lord as their REDEEMER.
" Thou wast slain, *and hast redeemed us to God by thy blood.*"

The metaphor of redemption, if I understand it, signifies this. A
thing which is redeemed in the strict sense belonged beforehand to the
person who redeemed it. Under the Jewish law lands were mortgaged
as they are now ; and when the money lent upon them, or the service
due for them, was paid, the land was said to be redeemed. An inheritance first belonged to a person, and then went away from him by
stress of poverty, but if a certain price was paid it came back. Now
" all souls are mine " saith the Lord, and the souls of men belong to
God. The metaphor is used, and, mark, these expressions are but
metaphors ; but the sense under them is no metaphor ; it is fact.
Our souls had come under mortgage, as it were, through the sin committed, so that God could not accept us without violating his justice
until something had been done by which he who is infinitely just could
freely distribute his grace to us. Now, Jesus Christ has taken the
mortgage from God's inheritance. " The Lord's portion is his people ; "
that portion was hampered till Jesus set it free. We were God's always,
but we had fallen into slavery to sin. Jesus came to make recompense for our offences, and thus we return to where we were before,
only with additional gifts which his grace bestows. In heaven they
say " thou hast redeemed us ; " and they tell the price, " thou hast redeemed us to God *by thy blood.*" There lay the price, the sufferings and death of Jesus have set his people free from the slavery into
which they were brought. They are redeemed, and they are redeemed
unto God. That is the point : they come back to God as lands come
back to the owner when the mortgage is discharged. We come back
to God again, to whom we always and ever did belong, because Jesus
has redeemed us unto God by his blood.

And please to notice that the redemption they sing about in heaven
is not general redemption. It is particular redemption. " Thou hast
redeemed *us* to God by thy blood *out of* every kindred, and tongue,
and people, and nation." They do not speak of the redemption of
every tongue, and people, and nation, but of a redemption *out of* every
tongue, and people, and nation. I thank God I do not believe that
I was redeemed in the same way that Judas was, and no more. If so,

I shall go to hell as Judas did. General redemption is not worth any-thing to anybody, for of itself it secures to no one a place in heaven : but the special redemption which does redeem, and redeems men *out of* the rest of mankind, is the redemption that is to be prayed for, and for which we shall praise God for ever and ever. We are redeemed from among men. " Christ loved his church and gave himself for it." " He is the Saviour of all men "—let us never deny that—" but specially of them that believe." There is a wide, far-reaching sacrificial atonement which brings untold blessings to all mankind, but by that atonement a special divine object was aimed at, which will be carried out, and that object is the actual redemption of his own elect from the bondage of their sins, the price being the blood of Jesus Christ. Oh, brethren, may we have a share in this particular, efficient redemption, for this alone can bring us where they sing the new song.

This redemption is one which is personally realised. Thou hast redeemed *us* to God. Redemption is sweet, but " thou hast redeemed *us* " is sweeter still. If I can but believe he loved me, and gave him-self for me, that will tune my tongue to sing Jehovah's praise, for what said David ? " Oh that men would praise the Lord for his goodness." He repeated that several times over, but it would never have been car-ried out unless he had said, " Let the redeemed of the Lord say so, whom he hath redeemed out of the hand of the enemy." In vain he called upon others, their tongues were dedicated to their pleasures ; but the redeemed of the Lord are a fit choir to magnify his name.

The pith of what I have to say is this : in heaven they praise Jesus Christ because he has redeemed them,—my dear hearer, has he ever redeemed you ? Oh, says one, I believe he has redeemed everybody. But of what avail is that ? Do not the great mass of mankind sink to perdition ? If you rest upon such a redemption you rest upon what will not save you. He redeemed his own elect ; or, in other words, he redeemed believers. " God so loved the world " is a text much cried up, but pray go on with it. How much did he love the world ? " That he gave his only begotten Son *that whosoever believeth in him* should not perish." There is the specialty of it—" Whosoever believeth in him ;" and if you do not believe in him neither have you part or lot in his redemption, you are slaves to sin and Satan, and so will you live and so will you die : but believing in the Lord Jesus you have the marks of being specially and effectually redeemed by him, and when you get to heaven this will be your song,—" Thou hast redeemed us unto God by thy blood out of every kindred, and people, and tongue." Blessed be God for this. Some of all sorts are saved, some of all colours, ranks, nations, and ages are saved ; some of all conditions of education and morals, some of the poorest, and some of the richest are redeemed : so that when we all assemble in heaven, though we make a motley throng on earth, we shall constitute a united choir, having all our voices tuned to this one note, " Worthy is the Lamb that was slain."

III. Thirdly, and briefly, in heaven they praise Christ, not merely as mediator and as redeemer, but as the DONOR OF THEIR DIGNITIES. They are kings and reign. We too are kings ; but as yet we are not known or recognised, and often we ourselves forget our high descent.

Up there they are crowned monarchs, but they say, "*Thou hast made us* kings." They are priests too, as we are now, every one of us. When a fellow comes forward in all sorts of curious garments, and says he is a priest, the poorest child of God may say, "Stand away, and don't interfere with my office: I am a priest; I know not what you may be. You surely must be a priest of Baal, for the only mention of the word vestments in Scripture is in connection with the temple of Baal." The priesthood belongs to all the saints. They sometimes call you laity, but the Holy Ghost says of all the saints, "Ye are God's *cleros*"—ye are God's clergy. Every child of God is a clergyman or a clergywoman. There are no priestly distinctions known in Scripture. Away with them! Away with them for ever! The Prayer-book says, "Then shall the *priest* say." What a pity that word was ever left there. The very word "priest" has such a smell of the sulphur of Rome about it, that so long as it remains the Church of England will give forth an ill savour. Call yourself a priest, sir! I wonder men are not ashamed to take the title: when I recollect what priests have done in all ages—what priests connected with the church of Rome have done, I repeat what I have often said: I would sooner a man pointed at me in the street and called me a devil, than called me a priest; for bad as the devil has been, he has hardly been able to match the crimes, cruelties, and villainies which have been transacted under the cover of a special priesthood. From that may we be delivered: but the priesthood of God's saints, the priesthood of holiness, which offers prayer and praise unto God—this they have in heaven; but they say of it, "*Thou hast made us priests.*" What the saints are, and what they are to be, they ascribe to Jesus. They have no glory but what they received from him, and they know it, and are perpetually confessing it.

Let our hearts sing with the redeemed—"All for Jesus, for all is from Jesus! All for Jesus, for Jesus has given us all we have." Let us begin that music here.

IV. Once again. They in heaven adore the Saviour as DIVINE.

I am not straining the words of my text at all, but keeping the whole passage before me. If you read the two chapters you will find that while they sing to God, "Thou art worthy, O Lord, to receive honour and glory and power," they sing to the Lamb, "Worthy is the Lamb that was slain, to receive power and riches and wisdom." The ascriptions which are given to the Creator are also offered to the Lamb, and he is represented as sitting on the same throne. Mark carefully that the adoration which they give to him he does not resent. When John fell down to worship one of the angels he received an earnest protest, "See thou do it not." Now, if the worship given to Christ had been wrong, the thrice holy Saviour would have exclaimed most earnestly, "See thou do it not"; but he intimates no objection to the worship, although it is freely rendered by all the intelligent beings before the throne. Depend upon it, my hearer, you never will go to heaven unless you are prepared to worship Jesus Christ as God. They are all doing it there: you will have to come to it, and if you entertain the notion that he is a mere man, or that he is anything less than God, I am afraid you will have to begin at the beginning and learn what true religion means. You have a poor foundation to rest upon. I could not trust my soul with a mere man, or believe in an atonement made by a mere man : I must see God himself putting his hand to so gigantic a work. I cannot imagine a mere man being thus praised as the Lamb is praised. Jesus is " God over all, blessed for ever." When we ever speak at all severely of Socinians and Unitarians you must not be surprised at it, because if we are right they are blasphemers, and if they are right we are idolators, and there is no choice between the two. We never could agree, and never shall while the world standeth. We preach Christ the Son of God as very God of very God, and if they reject him it is not for us to pretend that it makes no difference, when in fact it makes all the difference in the world. We would not wish them to say more than they believe to be true, and they must not expect us to say less than we believe to be true. If Jesus be God, they must believe it, and must worship him as such, or else they cannot participate in the salvation which he has provided. I love the deity of Christ! I preach his humanity with all my might, and I rejoice that he is the son of man ; but oh, he must be the Son of God too, or there is no peace for me.

> " Till God in human flesh I see,
>   My thoughts no comfort find.
> The holy, just, and sacred Three
>   Are terrors to my mind.
>
> " But if Emmanuel's face appear,
>   My hope, my joy begins :
> His name forbids my slavish fear ;
>   His grace removes my sins."

Now I have almost done, only this is the outcome of the subject. You see the opinion they have of Jesus in heaven. My dear friends, are you of the same mind with them ? You will never go there till you are. There are no sects in heaven—no two parties. They hold the same views about Jesus there. Let me ask you then, are you of the same persuasion as the glorified saints ? They praise Jesus *for what he has done.* It is very wonderful to my mind that when they are adoring the Saviour they seem to strike that one key : they praise him for what he has done, and they praise him for what he has done *for them.* They might have praised him for what he is, but in the text they do not. Now, this reason which has such sway in heaven is the very same which moves us here—" We love him because he first loved us," and as if to show that this kind of love is not an inferior love, the love of gratitude seems to be the very sum and substance of the love of heaven— " Thou wast slain, and hast redeemed us." Can you praise him for redeeming you ? Dear hearer, you have heard about Jesus hundreds of times. Has he saved *you?* You know there is a fountain filled with blood, which cleanses from all sin ; has it cleansed you ? You know he has woven a robe of righteousness which covers his people from head to foot : has he covered you with it ? You will never praise him till that is the case, and you cannot go to heaven till you are ready for his praise. " Well, but I go to my place of worship." So you may ; but that will not save you till you get a personal hold on Christ for yourself. "My mother and father were godly people." I am glad they were : I hope they won't have an ungodly son. You must, however, have a personal religion— something done by Jesus Christ *for you.* Young woman over yonder, has Jesus Christ redeemed *you* from among the mass of the people ; brought *you* out from your sins, and separated *you* to himself ? Have you had the blood applied to your soul—the precious blood of sprinkling which speaks peace in the conscience ? Time is flying, and you have been hearers month after month ; will it always be so ? Will you never cry unto God, "Lord, let me know thy redemption ; let me have a share in the precious blood : let me be washed from my sins " ? Recollect you must be able to praise him for what he has done *for you,* or else you are not of the opinion of those in heaven, and into heaven you cannot come.

It is clear from the song I have been reading that in heaven Christ is everybody and everything. Is Christ so with you ? It is a solemn question to put to persons. Is Christ first and last and middle with you, top and bottom, foundation and pinnacle, all in all ? He knows not Christ who does not know that Christ is all. Christ and company will never do. Christ is the sole Saviour, the sole trust, the one prophet, priest, and king to all who accept him. Is he everything to you ? Ah, there are some who think they love Christ ; they think they trust Christ ; but if he were to come to their house he would have a seat at the far end of the table if they treated him as they treat him now. They give him part of the Sabbath-day : they were loafing about all the morning, they were only able to get here this evening, and even now they have not come to worship, but only out of curiosity. A chapter in the Bible—how long is it, young man, since you read one ? Private prayer—ah, I must not go into that ; it is such a sorry story that you would have to tell. If anybody said to you, " You are not a Christian," you would be offended. Well, I will say it, and you may be offended if you like, but remember you should be offended with yourself rather than with me. If you offend my Lord I am not at all afraid of your being offended with his servant, and therefore I tell you, if Christ be anything short of Lord and King in your soul, Christ and you are wide apart. He must be in the front rank, Lord High Admiral upon the sea, and Commander-in-Chief on the land. He is not going to be a petty officer, to come in at your odd times to be a lackey to you. You must take him to be Head, Lord, and Master. Is it so with you ? If not, you differ from those in heaven, for he is all in all to them.

Once more. Can you join with the words of our text and say, " He is worthy, he is worthy " ? I hope there are many here who if they for a moment heard that full burst of song, " He is worthy," would join it very heartily, and say, " Ay, he *is* worthy." I seemed to-night when I was praying as if I could hear them sing, " He is worthy," and I could hardly restrain myself from shouting, " Well sing ye so, ye spirits before the throne ! He *is* worthy !" If we were to loose our silence for a moment, and break the decorum which we have observed through the sermon, and with one unanimous shout cry, " Yes, he is worthy," I think it would be a fit thing to do. Jesus is worthy of my life, worthy of my love, worthy of everything I can say for him, worthy of a thousand times more than that, worthy of all the music and harps on earth, worthy of all the songs of all the sweetest singers, worthy of all the poetry of the best writers, worthy of all the adoration of every knee, worthy of all that every man has or can conceive, or can compass, worthy to be adored of all that are in the earth and under the earth, and in the sea, and in the heavens, and in the heaven of heavens. He is worthy. We say "worthy," because we cannot tell how worthy. I think these good singers in heaven desired to give to the Lamb his due, and then they paused, and said to themselves, "We cannot give him the praise he deserves, but we know that he is worthy. We cannot pretend to give him what he is worthy of, but we will say he is worthy." Yes he *is* worthy. If I had fifty thousand lives in this poor body, he is worthy that they should all be poured out one after another in martyrdom. One should be burned alive, and another should be broken on the wheel, and another should be starved by inches, and another should be dragged at the heels of a wild horse, and he would deserve them all. He is worthy, and if we had all the mines of India— silver and gold and gems, the rarest treasures of all the kings that ever lived, if we were to give it all up to him, and go barefoot, he is worthy. And if, after having done that, we were to abide day and night in perpetual work without rest, all for his sake, and if each one of us were multiplied into a million, and all of us laboured so, he is worthy. Worthy. I would make every drop of dew sparkle with his praise, and every leaf in the forest bear his name. I would make every dell and every mountain vocal with adoration, and teach the stars, and teach the angels above the stars, his praise.

> " Oh for a thousand tongues to sing
> My great Redeemer's praise ! "

Let time and space become one mouth for song, and all eternity sound forth that mighty word, "He is worthy." Do you feel that he is worthy? If you do not, you cannot be admitted where they sing that song, for if you could enter there you would be unhappy. Never hope to enter there until your soul can say, " I have rested in his blood, I am by it redeemed unto God, and the Redeemer is worthy ; and I will bear witness of his worthiness till time shall be no more."

God bless you all, for Jesus' sake. Amen.

PORTION OF SCRIPTURE READ BEFORE SERMON—Revelation iv. v

Hymns from " Our Own Hymn Book "—412, 416, 417.

"THIS YEAR ALSO."

A short Sermon

FOR THE NEW YEAR. FROM THE SICK CHAMBER OF

C. H. SPURGEON.

"This year also."—Luke xiii. 8.

AT the opening of another year, and at the commencement of another volume of sermons, we earnestly desire to utter the word of exhortation: but alas, at this present, the preacher is a prisoner, and must speak from his pillow instead of his pulpit. Let not the few words which we can put together come with diminished power from a sick man, for the musket fired by a wounded soldier sends forth the bullet with none the less force. Our desire is to speak with living words, or not at all. He who enables us to sit up and compose these trembling sentences is entreated to clothe them with his Spirit, that they may be according to his own mind.

The interceding vine-dresser pleaded for the fruitless fig-tree, "let it alone *this year also*," dating as it were a year from the time wherein he spoke. Trees and fruitbearing plants have a natural measurement for their lives: evidently a year came to its close when it was time to seek fruit on the fig-tree, and another year commenced when the vine-dresser began again his digging and pruning work. Men are such barren things that their fruitage marks no certain periods, and it becomes needful to make artificial divisions of time for them; there seems to be no set period for man's spiritual harvest or vintage, or if there be, the sheaves and the clusters come not in their season, and hence we have to say one to another,—"This shall be the beginning of a new year." Be it so, then. Let us congratulate each other upon seeing the dawn of "this year also," and let us unitedly pray that we may enter upon it, continue in it, and come to its close under the unfailing blessing of the Lord to whom all years belong.

I. The beginning of a new year SUGGESTS A RETROSPECT. Let us take it, deliberately and honestly. "*This year also*:"—then there had been former years of grace. The dresser of the vineyard was not for the first time aware of the fig-tree's failure, neither had the owner come for the first time seeking figs in vain. God, who gives us "this year also," has given us others before it; his sparing mercy is no novelty, his patience has already

No. 1,451.

25

been taxed by our provocations. First came our *youthful* years, when even a little fruit unto God is peculiarly sweet to him. How did we spend them? Did our strength run all into wild wood and wanton branch? If so, we may well bewail that wasted vigour, that life misspent, that sin exceedingly multiplied. He who saw us misure those golden months of youth nevertheless affords us " this year also," and we should enter upon it with a holy jealousy, lest what of strength and ardour may be left to us should be allowed to run away into the same wasteful courses as aforetime. Upon the heels of our youthful years came those of *early manhood*, when we began to muster a household, and to become as a tree fixed in its place; then also fruit would have been precious. Did we bear any? Did we present unto the Lord a basket of summer fruit? Did we offer him the firstling of our strength? If we did so, we may well adore the grace which so early saved us; but if not, the past chides us, and, lifting an admonitory finger, it warns us not to let " this year also " follow the way of the rest of our lives. He who has wasted youth and the morning of manhood has surely had enough of fooling : the time past may well suffice him to have wrought the will of the flesh : it will be a superfluity of naughtiness to suffer " this year also" to be trodden down in the service of sin. Many of us are now in the *prime of life*, and our years already spent are not few. Have we still need to confess that our years are eaten up by the grasshopper and the canker-worm? Have we reached the half-way house, and still know not whither we are going? Are we fools at forty? Are we half a century old by the calendar and yet far off from years of discretion? Alas, great God, that there should be men past this age who are still without knowledge! Unsaved at sixty, unregenerate at seventy, unawakened at eighty, unrenewed at ninety! These are each and all startling. Yet, peradventure, they will each one fall upon ears which they should make to tingle, but they will hear them as though they heard them not. Continuance in evil breeds callousness of heart, and when the soul has long been sleeping in indifference it is hard to arouse it from the deadly slumber.

The sound of the words " this year also " makes some of us remember *years of great mercy*, sparkling and flashing with delight. Were those years laid at the Lord's feet? They were comparable to the silver bells upon the horses—were they " holiness unto the Lord"? If not, how shall we answer for it if " this year also " should be musical with merry mercy and yet be spent in the ways of carelessness? The same words recall to some of us our *years of sharp affliction* when we were, indeed, digged about and dunged. How went those years? God was doing great things for us, exercising careful and expensive husbandry, caring for us with exceeding great and wise care,—did we render according to the benefit received? Did we rise from the bed more patient and gentle, weaned from the world, and welded to Christ? Did we bring forth clusters to reward the dresser of the vineyard? Let us not refuse these questions of self-examination, for it may be this is to be another of these years of captivity, another season of the furnace and the fining-pot. The Lord grant that the coming tribulation may take more chaff out of us than any of its predecessors, and leave the wheat cleaner and better.

The new year also reminds us of *opportunities for usefulness*, which have come and gone, and of *unfulfilled resolutions* which have blossomed only to fade; shall "this year also" be as those which have gone before? May we not hope for grace to advance upon grace already gained, and should we not seek for power to turn our poor sickly promises into robust action?

Looking back on the past we lament the follies by which we would not willingly be held captive "this year also," and we adore the forgiving mercy, the preserving providence, the boundless liberality, the divine love, of which we hope to be partakers "this year also."

II. If the preacher could think freely he could wherry the text at his pleasure in many directions, but he is feeble, and so must let it drive with the current which bears it on to a second consideration: the text MEN-TIONS A MERCY. It was in great goodness that the tree which cumbered the soil was allowed to stand for another year, and prolonged life should always be regarded as a boon of mercy. We must view "this year also" as a grant from infinite grace. It is wrong to speak as if we cared nothing for life, and looked upon our being here as an evil or a punishment; we are here "this year also" as the result of love's pleadings, and in pursuance of love's designs.

The wicked man should count that the Lord's longsuffering points to his salvation, and he should permit the cords of love to draw him to it. O that the Holy Spirit would make the blasphemer, the Sabbath-breaker, and the openly vicious to feel what a wonder it is that their lives are prolonged "this year also"! Are they spared to curse, and riot, and defy their Maker? Shall this be the only fruit of patient mercy? The procrastinator who has put off the messenger of heaven with his delays and half promises, ought he not to wonder that he is allowed to see "this year also"? How is it that the Lord has borne with him and put up with his vacillations and hesitations? Is this year of grace to be spent in the same manner? Transient impressions, hasty resolves, and speedy apostasies—are these to be the weary story over and over again? The startled conscience, the tyrant passion, the smothered emotion! Are these to be the tokens of yet another year? May God forbid that any one of us should hesitate and delay through "this year also." Infinite pity holds back the axe of justice, shall it be insulted by the repetition of the sins which caused the uplifting of the instrument of wrath? What can be more tantalizing to the heart of goodness than indecision? Well might the Lord's prophet become impatient and cry, "How long halt ye between two opinions?" Well may God himself push for a decision and demand an immediate reply. O undecided soul, wilt thou swing much longer between heaven and hell, and act as if it were hard to choose between the slavery of Satan and the liberty of the Great Father's home of love? "This year also" wilt thou sport in defiance of justice, and pervert the generosity of mercy into a licence for still further rebellion? "This year also" must divine love be made an occasion for continued sin? O do not act so basely, so contrary to every noble instinct, so injuriously to thine own best interests.

The believer is kept out of heaven "this year also" in love, and not in anger. There are some for whose sake it is needful he should abide in the flesh, some to be helped by him on their heavenward way, and others to be led to the Redeemer's feet by his instruction. The heaven of many saints is not yet prepared for them, because their nearest companions have not yet arrived, and their spiritual children have not yet gathered in glory in sufficient number to give them a thoroughly heavenly welcome: they must wait "this year also" that their rest may be the more glorious, and that the sheaves which they will bring with them may afford them greater joy. Surely, for the sake of souls, for the delight of glorifying our Lord, and for the increase of the jewels of our crown, we may be glad to wait below "this year also." This is a wide field, but we may not linger in it, for our space is little, and our strength is even less.

III.   Our last feeble utterance shall remind you that the expression, "This year also," IMPLIES A LIMIT.   The vine-dresser asked no longer a reprieve than one year. If his digging and manuring should not then prove successful he would plead no more, but the tree should fall. Even when Jesus is the pleader, the request of mercy has its bounds and times. It is not for ever that we shall be let alone, and allowed to cumber the ground; if we will not repent we must perish, if we will not be benefited by the spade we must fall by the axe.

There will come a last year to each one of us: therefore let each one say to himself—Is this my last? If it should be the last with the preacher, he would gird up his loins to deliver the Lord's message with all his soul, and bid his fellow-men be reconciled to God. Dear friend, is "this year also" to be *your* last? Are you ready to see the curtain rise upon eternity? . Are you now prepared to hear the midnight cry, and to enter into the marriage supper? The judgment and all that will follow upon it are most surely the heritage of every living man, blessed are they who by faith in Jesus are able to face the bar of God without a thought of terror.

If we live to be counted among the oldest inhabitants we must depart at last: there must be an end, and the voice must be heard—" Thus saith the Lord, this year thou shalt die." So many have gone before us, and are going every hour, that no man should need any other *memento mori*, and yet man is so eager to forget his own mortality, and thereby to forfeit his hopes of bliss, that we cannot too often bring it before the mind's eye. O mortal man, bethink thee! Prepare to meet thy God; for thou must meet him. Seek the Saviour, yea, seek him ere another sun sinks to his rest.

Once more, "this year also," and it may be for this year only, the cross is uplifted as the pharos of the world, the one light to which no eye can look in vain. Oh that millions would look that way and live. Soon the Lord Jesus will come a second time, and then the blaze of his throne will supplant the mild radiance of his cross: the Judge will be seen rather than the Redeemer. Now he saves, but then he will destroy. Let us hear his voice at this moment. He hath limited a day, let us be eager to avail ourselves of the gracious season. Let us believe in Jesus this day, seeing it may be our last. These are the pleadings of one who now falls back on his pillow in very weakness. Hear them for your souls' sakes and live.

Metropolitan Tabernacle Pulpit.

THE COVENANT PLEADED.

A Sermon

DELIVERED BY

C. H. SPURGEON,

AT THE METROPOLITAN TABERNACLE, NEWINGTON.

"Have respect unto the covenant."—Psalm lxxiv. 20.

HE will succeed in prayer who understands the science of pleading with God. "Put me in remembrance: let us plead together," is a divine command. "Come now, let us reason together" is a sacred invitation. "Bring forth your strong reasons, saith the Lord," is a condescending direction as to the way of becoming victorious in supplication. Pleading is wrestling: arguments are the grips, the feints, the throes, the struggles with which we hold and vanquish the covenant angel. The humble statement of our wants is not without its value, but to be able to give reasons and arguments why God should hear us is to offer potent, prevalent prayer. Among all the arguments that can be used in pleading with God, perhaps there is none stronger than this—"Have respect unto the covenant." Like Goliath's sword, we may say of it, "There is none like it." If we have God's word for a thing we may well pray, "Do as thou hast said, for as a good man only needs to be reminded of his own word in order to be brought to keep it, even so is it with our faithful God; he only needs that for these things we put him in remembrance to do them for us." If he has given us more than his word, namely, his covenant, his solemn compact, we may then with the greatest composure of spirit cry to him, "Have respect unto the covenant," and then we may both hope and quietly wait for his salvation.

I need not tell you, for you are, I trust, well-grounded in that matter, that the covenant here spoken of is the covenant of grace. There is a covenant which we could not plead in prayer, the covenant of works, a covenant which destroys us, for we have broken it. Our first father sinned, and the covenant was broken; we have continued in his perverseness, and that covenant condemns us. By the covenant of works can none of us be justified, for we continue still to break our portion of it, and to bring upon ourselves wrath to the uttermost. The Lord hath made a new covenant with the second Adam, our federal head, Jesus Christ our Lord,—a covenant without conditions, except such conditions as Christ has already fulfilled, a covenant, ordered in all things and sure, which now consists of promises only, which run after this fashion—"I will be to them a God, and they shall be to me a people": "A new heart also will I give them, and a right spirit will I put within them": "From all their transgressions will I cleanse them":—a covenant, I say, which had once conditions in it, all of which our Lord Jesus fulfilled when he finished transgression, made an end of sin, and brought in everlasting righteousness; and now the covenant is all of promise, and consists of infallible and eternal shalls and wills, which shall abide the same for ever.

We shall talk of the text thus, *What is meant by the plea before us—* " Have respect unto the covenant"? Then we will think a little *of whence it derives its force*: thirdly, we will consider *how and when we may plead it*: and we will close by noticing *what are the practical inferences from it.*

I. Let us begin by this—WHAT IS MEANT BY THE PLEA " Have respect unto the covenant"? It means this, does it not? " *Fulfil thy covenant*, O God: let it not be a dead letter. Thou hast said this and that; now do as thou hast said. Thou hast been pleased by solemn sanction of oath and blood to make this covenant with thy people. Now be pleased to keep it. Hast thou said, and wilt thou not do it? We are persuaded of thy faithfulness, let our eyes behold thy covenant engagements fulfilled.

It means again, " *Fulfil all the promises of thy covenant*," for indeed all the promises are now in the covenant. They are all yea and amen in Christ Jesus, to the glory of God by us; and I may say without being unscriptural that the covenant contains within its sacred charter every gracious word that has come from the Most High, either by the mouth of prophets or apostles, or by the lips of Jesus Christ himself. The meaning in this case would be—" Lord, keep thy promises concerning thy people. We are in want: now, O Lord, fulfil thy promise that we shall not want any good thing. Here is another of thy promises: ' When thou passest through the waters, I will be with thee.' We are in rivers of trouble. Be with us now. Redeem thy promises to thy servants. Let them not stand on the book as letters that mock us, but prove that thou didst mean what thou didst write and say, and let us see that thou hast power and will to make every jot and tittle good of all thou hast spoken. For hast thou not said, ' Heaven and earth shall pass away, but my word shall not pass away'? Oh then have respect unto the promises of thy covenant."

In the connection of our text there is no doubt that the suppliant meant, " O Lord, prevent anything from turning aside thy promises." The church was then in a very terrible state. The temple was burnt, and the assemblage broken up, the worship of God had ceased, and idolatrous emblems stood even in the holy place where once the glory of God shone forth. The plea is, " Do not suffer the power of the enemy to be so great as to frustrate thy purposes, or to make thy promises void." So may we pray—" O Lord, do not suffer me to endure such temptation that I shall fall. Do not suffer such affliction to come upon me that I shall be destroyed; for hast thou not promised that no temptation shall happen to us but such as we are able to bear, and that with the temptation there shall be a way of escape? Now have respect unto thy covenant, and so order thy providence that nothing shall happen to us contrary to that divine agreement."

And it means also, " So order everything around us that the covenant may be fulfilled. Is thy church low? Raise up again in her midst men who preach the gospel with power, who shall be the means of her uplifting. Creator of men, Master of human hearts, thou who canst circumcise human lips to speak thy word with power, do this, and let thy covenant with thy church that thou wilt never leave her be fulfilled. The kings of the earth are in thy hand. All events are controlled by thee. Thou orderest all things, from the minute to the immense. Nothing, however small, is too small for thy purpose : nothing, however great, is too great for thy rule. Manage everything so that in the end each promise of thy covenant shall be fulfilled to all thy chosen people."

That, I think, is the meaning of the plea, " Have respect unto the covenant." Keep it and see it kept. Fulfil the promise, and prevent thy foes from doing evil to thy children. Precious plea, assuredly.

II. And now let us see WHENCE IT DERIVES ITS FORCE. " Have respect unto the covenant."

It derives its force, first, from *the veracity of God.* If it be a covenant of man's making we expect a man to keep it ; and a man who does not keep his covenant is not esteemed amongst his fellows. If a man has given his word, that word is his bond. If a thing be solemnly signed and sealed it becomes even more binding, and he that would run back from a covenant would be thought to have forfeited his character among men. God forbid that we should ever think the Most High could be false to his word. It is not possible. He can do all things except this—he cannot lie ; it is not possible that he should ever be untrue. He cannot even change : the gifts and calling of God are without repentance. He will not alter the thing that hath gone out of his lips. When then we come before God in prayer for a covenant mercy we have his truthfulness to support us. " O God, thou must do this. Thou art a sovereign : thou canst do as thou wilt, but thou hast bound thyself by bonds that hold thy majesty ; thou hast said it, and it is not possible that thou shouldst go back from thine own word." How strong our faith ought to be when we have God's truth to lean upon. What dishonour we do to our God by our weak faith ; for it is virtually a suspicion of the fidelity of our covenant God.

Next, to support us in using this plea we have God's sacred *jealousy for his honour.* He has told us himself that he is a jealous God ; his name is jealousy ; he has great respect unto his honour among the sons of men. Hence this was Moses's plea—" What will the enemy say ? And what wilt thou do unto thy great name ?" Now, if God's covenant could be trifled with, and if it could be proved that he had not kept the promise that he made to his creatures, it would not only be a dreadful thing for us, but it would bring grievous dishonour upon his name ; and that shall never be. God is too pure and holy, and he is withal too honourable ever to run back from the word that he has given to his servants. If I feel that my feet have almost gone I may still be assured that he will not suffer me wholly to perish, else were his honour stained, for he hath said, " They shall never perish, neither shall any pluck them out of my hand." He might give me up to mine enemies so far as my deserts are concerned, for I deserve to be destroyed by them—but then his honour is engaged to save the meanest of his people, and he has said, " I give unto them eternal life." He will not, therefore, for his honour's sake, suffer me to be the prey of the adversary ; but will preserve me, even me, unto the day of his appearing. Here is good foothold for faith.

The next reflection that should greatly strengthen us is *the venerable character of the covenant.* This covenant was no transaction of yesterday : or ever the earth was this covenant was made. We may not speak of first or last with God, but speaking after the manner of men the covenant of grace is God's first thought. Though we usually put the covenant of works first in order of time as revealed, yet in very deed the covenant of grace is the older of the two. God's people were not chosen yesterday, but before the foundations of the world ; and the Lamb slain to ratify that covenant, though slain eighteen hundred years ago, was in the divine purpose slain from before the foundations of the world. It is an ancient covenant : there is nothing so ancient. It is to God a covenant which he holds in high esteem. It is not one of his light thoughts, not one of those thoughts which lead him to create the morning dew that melts ere the day has run its course, or to make the clouds that light up the setting sun with glory but which soon have lost their radiance; but it is one of his great thoughts, yea, it is his eternal thought, the thought out of his own inmost soul—this covenant of grace. And because it is so ancient, and to God a matter so important, when we come to him with this plea in our mouths we must not think of being staggered by unbelief, but may open our mouths wide, for he will assuredly fill them. Here is thy covenant, O God, which of thy own spontaneous sovereign will thou didst ordain of old, a covenant in which thy very heart is laid bare, and thy love which is thyself is manifested. O God, have respect unto it, and do as thou hast said, and fulfil thy promise to thy people.

Nor is this all. It is but the beginning. In one sermon I should not have time to show you all the reasons that give force to the plea; but here is one. The covenant has upon it *a solemn endorsement.* There was the stamp of God's own word—that is enough. The very word that created the universe is the word that spake the covenant. But, as if that were not sufficient, seeing we are unbelieving, God has added to it his oath, and because he could swear by no greater, he has sworn by himself. It were blasphemy to dream that the Eternal could be perjured, and he has set his oath to his covenant, in order that, by two immutable things wherein it is impossible for God to lie, he might give to the heirs of grace strong consolation.

But more, that venerable covenant thus confirmed by oath was *sealed with blood.* Jesus died to ratify it. His heart's blood bedewed that Magna Charta of the grace of God to his people. It is a covenant now which God the just *must* keep. Jesus has fulfilled our side of it—has executed to the letter all the demands of God upon man. Our Surety and our Substitute has at once kept the law and suffered all that was due by his people on account of their breach of it ; and now shall not the Lord be true and the everlasting Father be faithful to his own Son ? How can he refuse to his Son the joy which he set before him and the reward which he promised him ? " He shall see his seed : he shall see of the travail of his soul and shall be satisfied." My soul, the faithfulness of God to his covenant is not so much a matter between thee and God as between Christ and God, for now it so stands—Christ as their representative puts in his claim before the throne of infinite justice for the salvation of every soul for whom he shed his blood, and he must have what he has purchased. Oh what confidence is here ! The rights of the Son, blended with the love and the veracity of the Father, makes the covenant to be ordered in all things and sure.

Moreover, remember, and I will not detain you much longer with this, that up till now nothing in the covenant has ever failed. The Lord has been tried by ten thousand times ten thousand of his people, and they have been in trying emergencies and serious difficulties ; but it has never been reported in the gates of Zion that the promise has become naught, neither have any said that the covenant is null and void. Ask ye those before you who passed through deeper waters than yourselves. Ask the martyrs who gave their lives up for their Master, " Was he with them to the end ? " The placid smiles upon their countenances while enduring the most painful death were evident testimonies that God is true. Their joyous songs, the clapping of their hands amidst the fire, and their exultation even on the rack, or when rotting in some loathsome dungeon—all these have proved how faithful the Lord has been.

And have you not heard with your own ears the testimony of God's dying people ? They were in conditions in which they could not have been sustained by mere imagination, nor buoyed up by frenzy, and yet they have been as joyful as if their dying day had been their wedding day. Death is too solemn a matter for a man to play a masquerade there. But what did your wife say in death ? or your mother now with God ? or what your child, who had learnt the Saviour's love ? Can you not recall their testimonies even now ? I think I hear some of them, and amongst the things of earth that are like to the joys of heaven, I think this is one of the foremost,—the joy of departed saints when they already hear the voices of angels hovering near, and turn round and tell us in broken language of the joys that are bursting in upon them— their sight blinded by the excess of brightness, and their hearts ravished with the bliss that floods them. Oh it has been sweet to see the saints depart !

I mention these things now, not merely to refresh your memories, but to establish your faith in God. He has been true so many times and false never, and shall we now experience any difficulty in resting on his covenant ? No, by all these many years in which the faithfulness of God has been put to the test, and has never failed, let us be confident that he will still regard us, and let us pray boldly,—" Have respect unto the covenant." For, mark you, as it has been in the beginning, it is now, and ever shall be, world without end. It shall be to the last saint as it was with the first. The testimony of the last soldier of the host shall be, " Not one good thing hath failed of all that the Lord God hath promised."

Only one more reflection here. Our God has taught many of us to trust in his name. We were long in learning the lesson, and nothing but Omnipotence could have made us willing to walk by faith, and not by sight ; but with much patience the Lord has brought us at last to have no reliance but on himself, and now we are depending on his faithfulness and his truth. Is that thy case, brother ? What then ?

Thinkest thou that God has given thee this faith to mock thee? Believest thou that he has taught thee to trust in his name, and thus far has brought thee to put thee to shame? Has his Holy Spirit given thee confidence in a lie? and has he wrought in thee faith in a fiction? God forbid! Our God is no demon who would delight in the misery which a groundless confidence would be sure to bring to us. If thou hast faith, he gave it to thee, and he that gave it to thee knows his own gift, and will honour it. He was never false yet, even to the feeblest faith, and if thy faith is great, thou shalt find him greater than thy faith, even when thy faith is at its greatest; therefore be of good cheer. The fact that thou believest should encourage thee to say, "Now, O Lord, I have come to rest upon thee, canst thou fail me? I, a poor worm, know no confidence but thy dear name, wilt thou forsake me? I have no refuge but thy wounds, O Jesus, no hope but in thy atoning sacrifice, no light but in thy light: canst thou cast me off?" It is not possible that the Lord should cast off one who thus trusts him. Can a woman forget her sucking child, that she should not have compassion on the son of her womb? Can any of us forget our children when they fondly trust us in the days of their weakness? No, the Lord is no monster: he is tender and full of compassion, faithful and true; and Jesus is a friend which sticketh closer than a brother. The very fact that he has given us faith in his covenant should help us to plead,— "Have respect unto the covenant."

III. Having thus shown you, dear friends, the meaning of the plea, and whence it derives its force, we will now pause a minute and observe HOW AND WHEN THAT COVENANT MAY BE PLEADED.

First, it may be pleaded *under a sense of sin*—when the soul feels its guiltiness. Let me read to you the words of our apostle, in the eighth chapter of the Hebrews, where he is speaking of this covenant at the tenth verse. "For this is the covenant that I will make with the house of Israel after those days, saith the Lord; I will put my laws into their mind, and write them in their hearts: and I will be to them a God, and they shall be to me a people. And they shall not teach every man his neighbour, and every man his brother, saying, Know the Lord: for all shall know me, from the least to the greatest. For I will be merciful to their unrighteousness, and their sins and their iniquities will I remember no more." Now, dear hearer, suppose that thou art under a sense of sin; something has revived in thee a recollection of past guilt, or it may be that thou hast sadly stumbled this very day, and Satan whispers, "Thou wilt surely be destroyed, for thou hast sinned." Now go to the great Father, and open this page, putting thy finger on that twelfth verse, and say, "Lord, thou hast in infinite, boundless, inconceivable mercy entered into covenant with me, a poor sinner, seeing I believe in the name of Jesus, and now I beseech thee have respect unto thy covenant. Thou hast said, *I will be merciful to their unrighteousness:*—O God be merciful to mine. *Their sins and their iniquities will I remember no more:* Lord, remember no more my sins: forget for ever my iniquity." That is the way to use the covenant: when under a sense of sin, run to that clause which meets your case.

But suppose, beloved brother or sister, you are *labouring to overcome inward corruption*, with intense desire that holiness should be wrought in you. Then read the covenant again as you find it in the thirty-first chapter of Jeremiah at the thirty-third verse. It is the same covenant, only we are reading another version of it. "This shall be the covenant that I will make with the house of Israel; after those days, saith the Lord, I will put my law in their inward parts, and write it in their hearts." Now, can you not plead that and say, "Lord, thy commandments upon stone are holy, but I forget them, and break them; but, O my God, write them on the fleshy tablets of my heart. Come now and make me holy; transform me; write thy will upon my very soul, that I may live it out, and from the warm impulses of my heart serve thee as thou wouldst be served. Have respect unto thy covenant and sanctify thy servant."

Or suppose you desire to be *upheld under strong temptation,* lest you should go back and return to your old ways. Take the covenant as you find it in Jeremiah at the thirty-second chapter at the fortieth verse. Note these verses and learn them by heart, for they may be a great help to you some of these days. Read the fortieth verse of the thirty-second chapter of Jeremiah. "And I will make an everlasting covenant with them, that I will not turn away from them, to do them good; but I will put my fear in their hearts, that they shall not depart from me." Now go and say, "O Lord, I am almost gone, and they tell me I shall finally fall, but O, my Lord and Master, there stands thy word. Put thy fear in my heart and fulfil thy promise, that I shall not depart from thee." This is the sure road to final perseverance.

Thus I might take you through all the various needs of God's people, and show that in seeking to have them supplied they may fitly cry, "Have respect unto the covenant." For instance, suppose you were in great distress of mind and needed comfort, you could go to him with that covenant promise, "As a mother comforteth her children, even so will I comfort thee,—out of Zion will I comfort thee." Go to him with that and say, "Lord, comfort thy servant." Or if there should happen to be a trouble upon us, not for yourselves, but for the church; how sweet it is to go to the Lord and say, "Thy covenant runs thus—'the gates of hell shall not prevail against her.' O Lord, it seems as though they would prevail. Interpose thy strength and save thy church." If it ever should happen that you are looking for the conversion of the ungodly, and desiring to see sinners saved, and the world seems so dark, look at our text again—the whole verse—"Have respect unto the covenant, for the dark places of the earth are full of the habitations of cruelty," to which you may add, "but thou hast said that thy glory shall cover the earth, and that all flesh shall see the salvation of God. Lord, have respect unto thy covenant. Help our missionaries, speed thy gospel, bid the the mighty angel fly through the midst of heaven to preach the everlasting gospel to every creature. Why, it is a grand missionary prayer. "Have respect unto the covenant." Beloved, it is a two-edged sword, to be used in all conditions of strife, and it is a holy balm of Gilead, that will heal in all conditions of suffering.

IV. And so I close with this last question, WHAT ARE THE PRACTICAL INFERENCES FROM ALL THIS? "Have respect unto the covenant." Why, that if we ask God to have respect unto it *we* ought to have respect unto it ourselves, and in this way.

Have a grateful respect for it. Bless the Lord that he ever condescended to enter into covenant with you. What could he see in you even to give you a promise, much more to make a covenant with you? Blessed be his dear name, this is the sweet theme of our hymns on earth, and shall be the subject of our songs in heaven.

Next, *have a believing respect for it.* If it is God's covenant, do not dishonour it. It stands sure. Why do you stagger at it through unbelief?

> " His every work of grace is strong
> As that which built the skies ;
> The voice that rolls the stars along
> Speaks all the promises."

Next, *have a joyful respect for it.* Wake your harps, and join in praise with David : " Although my house be not so with God, yet hath he made with me an everlasting covenant." Here is enough to make a heaven in our hearts while yet we are below—the Lord hath entered into a covenant of grace and peace with us, and he will bless us for ever.

Then have a jealous respect for it. Never suffer the covenant of works to be mixed with it. Hate that preaching—I say not less than that—hate that preaching which does not discriminate between the covenant of works and the covenant of grace, for it is deadly preaching and damning preaching. You must always have a straight, clear line here between what is of man and what is of God, for cursed is he that trusteth in man and maketh flesh his arm; and if you have begun with the Spirit under this covenant do not think of being made perfect in the flesh under another covenant. Be ye holy under the precepts of the heavenly Father; but be ye not legal under the taskmaster's lash. Return not to the bondage of the law, for ye are not under law, but under grace.

Lastly, *have a practical respect for it.* Let all see that the covenant of grace, while it is your reliance, is also your delight. Be ready to speak of it to others. Be ready to show that the effect of its grace upon you is one that is worthy of God, since it has a purifying effect upon your life. He that hath this hope in him purifieth himself even as he is pure. Have respect unto the covenant by walking as such people should who can say that God is to them a God, and they are to him a people. The covenant says, " From all their idols will I cleanse them." Don't love idols then. The covenant says, " I will sprinkle pure water upon them, and they shall be clean." Be ye clean then, ye covenanted ones, and may the Lord preserve you and make his covenant to be your boast on earth and your song for ever in heaven. Oh that the Lord may bring us into the bonds of his covenant, and give us a simple faith in his dear Son, for that is the mark of the covenanted ones. Amen and Amen.

PORTION OF SCRIPTURE READ BEFORE SERMON —Psalm lxxiv.

HYMNS FROM " OUR OWN HYMN BOOK."—237, 228, 742.

Metropolitan Tabernacle Pulpit.

THE EMPTY SEAT.

A Sermon

WRITTEN WHEN AWAY FROM HIS PEOPLE, BY

C. H. SPURGEON.

"David's place was empty."—1 Samuel xx. 27.

IT was quite right that David's place should be empty, because Saul sought to slay him, and he could not safely sit in the presence of an enemy who had twice before cast a javelin at him to "smite him even to the wall with it." Self-preservation is a law of nature which we are bound to obey; no man should needlessly expose himself to sudden death. It were well if many a seat were empty for this reason; for there are places exceedingly dangerous to the soul, from which men should rise and flee at once. Where Satan sits at the head of the table no man should tarry. There is the seat of the scorner, of which the Psalmist spoke: God grant that those who have occupied it may leave it in trembling haste. There is the settle of the drunkard, and the chair of the presumptuous, and the bench of the sluggard, from each of which it were wisdom to depart. May the grace of God make such a change in all who have frequented the gatherings of the frivolous and the assemblies of the wicked that they may never be found in them again, but may be missed by their old companions, who shall ask, " Wherefore cometh the son of Jesse, neither yesterday nor to-day ? " The javelin of temptation may soon destroy character, prospects, and life itself, and he is guilty of the grossest folly who exposes himself to it by placing himself where the arch-enemy finds chosen opportunities to work his deadly will.

At this time I shall use David's empty place for quite another purpose, and shall note first that in your assemblies at this time there are SEATS EMPTIED BY DEATH. Before I had left the shores of England for the space of two days I received the grievous intelligence that two out of the membership of my church had been called home in one day. Of a sister, the wife of an earnest and well-beloved deacon it must be said— her place is empty; and of a brother, who had been her friend and mine, the same expression must be employed. Our sympathies must now flow forth to a bereaved husband, and also to a widow, in whose hearts there are places sorrowfully emptied, and in whose homes there will be an empty chair and an empty couch, which will force from their eyes rivers of tears whenever they look upon them. It is our firm hope and confident belief that in these cases the loss of the house of God below is the gain of

Nos. 1,454-5.

the house of God above : they fill other and better places, and even those who loved them best, and miss them most, would not wish to call them back again. Jesus wills that his own should be with him where he is, and we cannot deny that he has a right to have them. Do not their eyes behold the King in his beauty ? Would we deprive them of the vision ? May the thought of the bliss of the departed yield solace to the surviving, and may divine consolations be richly given by the Holy Ghost in the hour of painful bereavement.

Our places will be empty soon, and we shall be missed from our accustomed pews in the house of prayer; let the seats which have been just vacated remind us of this, and silently call to our remembrance the precept, " Be ye also ready." Use well your places for hearing the gospel, for gathering at the communion table, and for meeting for prayer while yet the opportunities remain to you, for the time is short, and an account will have to be rendered. Love well those who are spared to you, and do them all the good you can, for their places will not hold them for ever. Cheer the aged, console the desponding, help the poor, for they will soon be beyond your reach, and when you look for them you will be told that David's place is empty.

Permit me also to remind you that among your assemblies there are SEATS EMPTIED BY SICKNESS for awhile. You will not forget one place, the most conspicuous, which would be empty were it not filled by willing ministers who supply our lack of service. The providence which empties that place is so wise and good that, though we cannot understand its object, we are sure that it will work for good and for the glory of God. May I ask that, often as I am missed, I may have a fresh interest in your prayers; for these are a minister's wealth, a pastor's portion. Many others of the Lord's family are also sick, and detained at home. They sigh as they remember the happy days when they went up to the house of God in company, and mingled in the solemn feasts of Zion ; but for them there are now no more the thunders of our united shouts of praise, nor the deep Amens of our forms of prayer, and they envy the very swallows that build their nests under the eaves of the sanctuary. Many of us have such afflicted ones in our own families, and God forbid that we should cease to sympathize with them in their deprivations. Yet long continuance of health may dry the founts of pity, and lead to forgetfulness of the sorrows of others ; and therefore it is no superfluity when we remind the healthy that there are others far less favoured to whom it is one of their sharpest sorrows that their places at public worship are empty. Let us pray that a portion may be sent to their homes, according to the old law of David, " as his part is that goeth down to the battle, so shall his part be that tarrieth by the stuff : they shall part alike." Let us try to make this rule of battle a matter of fact by carrying home to the Lord's prisoners as much of the sermon as we can. Jacob did not go down at the first to Egypt, for he was aged and infirm, but his sons brought back corn for him none the less. In telling the sick and bedridden the truths which we have heard our own memories will be refreshed. We are bound with those who are in bonds, and we suffer with the suffering, and therefore, if we are living members of our Lord's mystical body, it is to us a matter of personal interest that David's seat is empty.

In every well-ordered congregation there are SEATS EMPTIED BY HOLY SERVICE. Many Christian professors appear to think that their entire religious duty begins and ends with attendance upon the means of grace: no village station receives their ministry, no ragged school enjoys their presence, no street corner hears their voice, but their pew is filled with commendable constancy. We do not condemn such, yet show we unto them a more excellent way. We know scores of brethren and sisters who come to one service on the Sabbath for spiritual food, and then spend the rest of the day in active labour for their Lord. They are not so unwise as to leave their own vineyard untended by neglecting personal edification, but when this is earnestly attended to they hear their Master's call and go forth into the great harvest and use the strength which their spiritual meal has given them. In this way they are even more benefited than if they were always "feeding," for holy exercise helps their mental digestion, and they all the more completely assimilate their sacred food; in addition to which they have struck a blow at the spiritual selfishness which tempts us to enjoy religious feasts and to make ourselves comfortable while sinners are perishing around us. Many are the Christians whose places ought to be empty during part of the Lord's day : they are able-bodied and gifted, and they ought not to eat the fat and drink the sweet all day long, but should be engaged in carrying portions to those for whom otherwise nothing would be prepared. When the great king made a wedding-feast for his son he sent forth his servants into the highways and hedges to compel the wanderers to come in. Did he starve those servants? Assuredly not. Yet he was not content to invite them to the table and leave the outsiders to hunger and faint. His servants found it to be their meat and their drink to do the will of him that sent them, and to finish his work. Even so will believers receive edification while they are seeking the good of others : like swallows, which feed on the wing, they shall find heavenly meat while they fly in the ways of service. The Holy Spirit delights to give more "oil for the light" to those who are diligently shining amid the darkness.

Yet, let me add a warning here : I have known some young believers who have lacked prudence, and have carried a good thing too far. Before they have well learned they have been eager to teach, and to do so they have ceased learning : multiplied engagements have left them no time for their own instruction, and they have left an edifying ministry to enter upon labour for which they were not qualified. Wisdom is profitable to direct. The most of Christians need to fill their seats for a part of the Sabbath, to hear the word of God, and very few can afford to spend the whole day in seeking the good of others. We grieve to meet with some who are absent from the Lord's table for months because of their zealous occupations. This is presenting one duty to God stained with the blood of another. It is the positive duty of every disciple to obey the Lord's command, "This do ye in remembrance of me"; and efforts which necessitate neglect of the divine precept must be curtailed. Often ought we to show his death until he come. School-teaching, street-preaching, sick-visiting, and so forth cannot be regarded as a substitute for hearing the Word, and commemorating the death of the Redeemer. We must have time to sit at the Master's feet with Mary, or soon, like Martha, we shall be cumbered. Nevertheless, despite this word of caution, I am often glad to hear that "David's place was empty."

It is to be feared that too easily we could find SEATS EMPTIED FOR NO GOOD REASON. Ministers in many congregations are distressed by the irregular attendance of their hearers. A little rain, a slight indisposition, or some other frivolous excuse will keep many at home. A new preacher has come into the neighbourhood, and the rolling stones are moved in his direction for a season to the grievous discouragement of the pastor. This evil of irregular attendance is most manifest at week-day services : there often enough David's seat is empty. No, not David's, for he longs to be even a door-keeper in the house of his God : we mean the seat of Didymus, who was not with the apostles when Jesus came; of Demas, who loved this present evil world ; and of many a hearer who is not also a doer of the word. In many a congregation those who gather at meetings for prayer are shamefully few. I have no reason to complain of this as a fault among my own beloved people to any large extent, and yet I cannot shut my eyes to the fact that there are some members of the church who would have to carry their memories a long way back to recollect what a prayer-meeting is like. Little do they know what they have lost by their neglect. Ah, my friend, does that refer to you? Is David's place empty? Then mend your ways and fill it. Of all soul-refreshing seasons I have often found week-night services to be the best. Like oases in a desert, these quiet periods amid the cares of the week wear a greenness peculiar to themselves. Come and try whether your experience will not tally with mine. I believe you will find it good to be there. Children it is said should be fed like chickens, "little and often"; and to my mind, short, lively services coming frequently, on Sabbaths and week-days, are more refreshing than hearing two or even three long sermons on one day in the week only. At any rate it is good for us to keep the feast with our brethren and not to make them ask, "Wherefore cometh not the son of Jesse either yesterday or to-day ?"

I must take the liberty of being very personal to the usual attendants at the Tabernacle. Dear friends, do not let your seats be empty during my absence. I shall be distressed beyond measure if I hear that the congregations are declining. The best preachers we can obtain are selected to address you, and therefore I hope you will see no need to forsake your usual place. If you do so it will reflect but small credit upon your pastor's ministry, for it will be manifest that you are babes in grace, dependent upon one man for edification. "All are yours, whether Paul, or Apollos, or Cephas"; and if you are men in Christ Jesus you will get good out of them all, and will not say, "Our own blunt Cephas is away, and we cannot hear any one else." I beseech you be very regular in your attendance during my absence, lest those who preach to you should be discouraged, and ourselves also. Above all, *keep up the prayer-meetings*. Nelson said, "England expects every man to do his duty," and at this time, which is an emergency in our church history, I would say,—the church expects every member to sustain all meetings, labours, and offerings with unflagging energy, and especially to *keep up the prayer-meetings*. There, at any rate, let it not be said of any one of you, "David's place was empty."

Grace, mercy, and peace be with you all in Christ Jesus. Amen.

Metropolitan Tabernacle Pulpit.

THE POOR MAN'S PRAYER.

A Sermon

DELIVERED BY

C. H. SPURGEON,

AT THE METROPOLITAN TABERNACLE, NEWINGTON.

"Remember me, O Lord, with the favour that thou bearest unto thy people: O visit me with thy salvation; that I may see the good of thy chosen, that I may rejoice in the gladness of thy nation, that I may glory with thine inheritance."— Psalm cvi. 4, 5.

BELOVED, we always reckon it a very hopeful sign when a man begins to think of personal religion. Merely to come with the crowd and professedly to worship is but poor work; but when a man gets to feel the weight of his own sin, and to confess it with his heart before God,—when he wants a Saviour for himself, and begins to pray alone that he may find that Saviour,—when he is not content with being the child of pious parents, or with having been introduced into the church in his childhood after the fashion of certain sects; but when he pines for real godliness, personal religion, true conversion, it is a blessed sign. When the stag separates itself from the herd we reckon that the dart has struck home; the wound is grievous, and the creature seeks solitude, for a bleeding heart cannot bear company. Blessed are God's woundings, for they lead to a heavenly healing!

We are still more glad when this desire for personal salvation leads a man to prayer,—when he begins really to cry out before God on his own account,—when he has done with the prayers he used to repeat by rote like a parrot, and bursts out with the language of his heart. Though that language may be very broken, or consist only of sighs and tears and groans, it is a happy circumstance. "Behold, he prayeth" was enough for Ananias; he was sure that Paul must be converted; and when we find a man praying, and praying earnestly, for personal salvation, we feel that this is the finger of God, and our heart is glad within us.

The passage before us is one of those earnest personal supplications which we love to hear from any lips. I will read it again, and then proceed to use it in two or three ways. "Remember me, O Lord, with the favour that thou bearest unto thy people: O visit me with thy salvation; that I may see the good of thy chosen, that I may rejoice in the gladness of thy nation, that I may glory with thine inheritance."

Now, first, *this is a very suitable prayer for the humble believer*: it was a humble believer who first uttered it. Next, *it would make a very suitable petition for a penitent backslider;* and, thirdly, *it would be a very sweet gospel prayer for a seeker.* May the Spirit of God bless the word to each of these characters.

I. First, then, this is an admirable prayer FOR A POOR HUMBLE CHRISTIAN. I think I can hear him using the very words.

Notice with interest the first fear felt by this poor trembling Christian. *He is afraid that he is such a little one that God will forget him,* and so he begins with, "*O remember me* with the favour which thou bearest to thy people." I know this man well. I think very much of him, but he thinks very little of himself. I admire his humility, but he often complains that he feels pride in his heart. He is a true believer, but he is a sad doubter. Poor man, he often hangs his head, for he has such a sense of his own unworthiness; I only wish he had an equal sense of Christ's fulness to balance his humility. He is on the road to heaven, but he is often afraid he is not, and that makes him watch every step he takes. I almost wish some confident professors were altogether as doubtful as he is if they would be half as cautious. He is afraid to put one foot before another, lest he should go wrong, and yet he mourns his want of watchfulness. He is always complaining of the hardness of his heart, and yet he is tenderness itself. Dear man—you should hear him pray. His prayers are among the most earnest and blessed you ever listened to, but when he has done he is afraid he never ought to have opened his mouth. He is not fit to pray before others, he says. He thinks his prayers the poorest that ever reach the throne of God; indeed, he is afraid they do not get there, but spend themselves as wasted breath. He has his occasional gleams of sunlight, and when he feels the love of God in his soul he is as merry as the cricket on the hearth. There is not a man out of heaven more gay than he when his hope revives. But, oh, he is so tender about sin that when he finds himself growing a little cold, or in any measure backsliding, he begins to flog himself,—at which I am very glad, but he also begins somewhat to doubt his interest in his Lord, of which I am not glad, but pity him much and blame him too, though with much sympathy for him. Now, I am not quite sure about this good man's name,—it may be Littlefaith, or Feeblemind. Or is it Mr. Despondency I am thinking of? Or am I talking of Miss Much-afraid? Or is it Mr. Ready-to-halt? Well, it is some one of that numerous family. This poor soul thinks, "Surely God will forget me!" No, no, dear heart, he will not forget you. It is wonderful how God does think of little things. Mungo Park picked up a little bit of moss in the desert, and as he marked how beautifully it was variegated, he said, "God is here : he is thinking of the moss, and therefore he will think of me." Once upon a time a little plant grew right in the middle of the forest, and the trees stretched for many a mile all around it, and it said to itself, "The sunlight will never get at me. I have a little flower which I would fain open, but it cannot come forth till the sunbeam cherishes me. Alas! it will never reach *me.* Look at the thick foliage: see the huge trunks of those towering oaks and mighty beeches, these will effectually hide the sun from my tiny form." But in due season the sun looked through the trees like a king through the lattices and smiled on the little flower; for there never was a flower that God has not thought of and provided for. Say ye not right well that "each blade of grass hath its own drop of dew," and think you that God will forget you, little as you are? He knows when swallows fly, and when emmets awake and gather their stores, and will he not think of you? Because you are little you must not suspect the love of your heavenly Father. Mother, which child is that which you never do forget? If you ever went to bed at night and left one of the children out of doors, I know which one it was *not*. It was not the babe which lies helpless in your bosom. You never forget that. And ye helpless ones, ye timid trembling ones, if the Lord must forget any, it would be the strong, but certainly not you. As you breathe the prayer, "Remember *me* with the favour that thou bearest to thy people," the Lord answers you, "I do earnestly remember thee still."

Observe next, that this poor trembling heart seems to be in great trouble for fear the Lord should pass it by, but at the same time *feels that every good thing it can possibly receive must come from the Lord, and must be brought to it by the Lord.* Note the words : "O visit me with thy salvation," as if he had said, "Lord, I cannot come to thee : I am too lame to come, I am too weak to come, but visit me. O Lord, I am like the wounded man between Jericho and Jerusalem : I am half dead, and cannot stir. Come to *me*, Lord ; for I cannot move to thee. Visit me, for only thy visitations can preserve my spirit. I am so wounded and sore broken, and undone, that if thou do not visit me with thy salvation even as if I never had been saved before, I must be lost."

Now, poor trembler, let me whisper a half word into thine ear, and may God the Holy Spirit make it a comfort to thee. Thou needest not say, if thou hast a broken heart, "Lord, visit me." Do you not know that he dwells in you, for is it not written, "To this man will I look, and with this man will I dwell, even with him that is poor and of a contrite spirit, and that trembleth at my word"? Are you not the very person? I wish you could rejoice at God's word, but as you cannot, I am glad you tremble at it, for you are the man that God has promised to dwell with. "*Trembleth at my word*,"—lay hold on that, and believe that the Lord looks towards you, and dwells with you.

What a plaintive prayer this is ! Carefully consider that this poor, weak, humble, trembling one *longs to partake in the blessings which the Lord gives to his own people*, and in the joy which he has in store for them. This is the way in which he speaks, "I hear many Christians around me say that they know and are persuaded, O that I had a little of their certainty. I hear them speak so confidently, with such full assurance, and I see the light leap out of their eyes when they talk about their sweet Lord and Master, and all his love to them ; oh, how I wish I could talk so ! Poor I, I am only able to say, 'Lord, I believe : help thou mine unbelief.' I see them sitting at a loaded table, and they seem to feast most abundantly, but as for me, I am glad it is written that the dogs eat the crumbs which fall from the Master's table, for if I get a crumb now and then, I feel so happy with it ; but I wish I could sit and feast where others of God's children do. Oh that I could talk of rapt fellowship and close communion and inward joy, and overflowing bliss! They tell me, some of them, that they sit down on the doorstep of heaven, and look within and see the golden streets, and that sometimes they hear stray notes from the harps of the blessed ones in the far-off country. Oh, how I wish I had a sip of these joys; for, woe is me, I dwell in Mesech and sojourn in the tents of Kedar; and the only music that I hear is the din of a sinful world,—the viols of them that make merry in wantonness. I miss those precious things which the saints delight in." Poor sorrowing heart, let me say to thee, and say in God's name, if thou lovest thy Lord, all things are thine. They *are* thine freely to enjoy even at this moment. The Lord denies thee no covenant blessing. Make bold to appropriate the sacred joys, for if thou be the least child in the family, yet the heritage of God's children is the same for every one. There is no choice thing that God will keep away from thee. Nay, if there be one morsel more dainty than another it is reserved for such as thou art. Make bold, then. If thou be the Benjamin in the family, thou shalt have Benjamin's mess which is ten times larger than any other. He will comfort thee and bless thee. Only be thou of good cheer, and when thou art praying, "Favour me with the favour which thou bearest to thy people," let thy faith hear him say, "I am thy portion." Rejoice in the Lord thy God. Lift up the hands that hang down, and confirm the feeble knees. Is not my text a sweet prayer for thee? Pray it in faith, and be at peace.

II. We will now look another way, and say that OUR TEXT IS A SUITABLE PETITION FOR A POOR PENITENT BACKSLIDER. I know there are backsliders here; though, alas, I am not sure that they are penitent. The Lord alone can read their hearts. But if they are penitent I can hardly conceive a more suitable petition for them than that which is before us.

It is clear that this poor, pleading backslider *feels that he has forgotten his God.* Have *you* done that? You have been a church-member, and you have gone sadly astray; have you quite forgotten his commandments. You thought you loved him. You used to pray at one time: you had some enjoyment in reading and in hearing the Word; but now you find your pleasure somewhere else. You have left your first love and gone after many lovers. But, oh, if the Lord is gracious to you, you are lamenting your forgetfulness; and though you have not remembered him, the prayer leaps to your lips, "Lord, remember me." Blessed be his name, he does not so easily forget us as we forget him. If thou be a truly penitent backslider thy feelings of repentance prove that God remembers thee. It is he that sets thee weeping, and makes thee sorrow for thy sin. If thou hadst been altogether forgotten of God thou wouldst not have any desire to return to him; but those inward pangs, those secret throes, those desires to be restored to the Lord—these prove that he remembers thee with the favour which he has towards his people.

And, then, I think your next trouble will be this: you *feel that you have lost your fellowship with Christ:* and you are right in so feeling, for "How can two walk together except they be agreed?" How could Christ have fellowship with you in the ways of folly? Do you think Christ would come and talk comfortably to you while you are frivolous, or while you are unclean? How could that be? All joyful communion between your soul and God is broken, and well may you pray, "O visit me with thy salvation. Come back to me, Lord. Come and dwell in me again.

> ' Why should my foolish passions rove ?
> Where can such sweetness be
> As I have tasted in thy love,
> As I have found in thee ?'

Come back, my Lord, and visit me with thy salvation." Is not this a prayer made on purpose for you?

And, next, you observe in the text that the poor backslider is *longing to get a sight of the good things which for a long time has been hid from him.* He cries, " That I may see the good of thy chosen." He has been out amongst the swine, but he could not fill his belly with the husks. He has been hungering and thirsting, and now he remembers that in his Father's house there is bread enough and to spare. Backslider, do you remember that to-night? You know you are not happy, and you begin to perceive that you never will be happy while you are living in the far country. If you had not been a child of God you might have made a happy worldling after the sort of happiness that worldlings know ; but you are spoiled for a worldling if you have ever known the love of God ; and you *have* known that, or else you have been indeed a hypocrite. Do you not sigh to the Lord to give you these good things again? Well, he will freely give them to you, and he will not upbraid you. Come and try him. He is ready to press you to his bosom, and to forget and forgive the past, and accept you in the Beloved.

The poor backslider praying in the words of my text *longs to taste once more the joy he used to feel,* and therefore he says, " That I may rejoice in the gladness of thy nation"; and, again, *he wants to be able to speak as he once could*—"that I may glory with thine inheritance." Poor man, he is ashamed to speak to sinners now. He hangs his head in company, for there are some that call him turncoat. He does not like to have it known that he was once a Christian : and therefore he comes stealing in to the assembly of the saints as if he hoped no one would know him. There he is, but he feels half ashamed to be here : and yet he wishes that he were once more with the Christian brotherhood, and could rejoice with them. My poor friend, you used to be bold as a lion for Christ once, and now you turn tail and fly. How can you be bold with all those inconsistencies? There was a time when you might have made a martyr, but now what a coward you are ; and who wonders that you are so when they know that secret sin has sapped and undermined your profession, and made you weak as water? I beg you to pray the prayer—"That I may glory with thine inheritance." You never will again make your boast in the Lord till you are restored, till you come back again as you came at first with the old cry, " Father, I have sinned before thee, and am no more worthy to be called thy son." Come back even now, my brother, and get another application of the blood of sprinkling. Look again to Jesus. Ah, and I may here say, if you have *not* backslidden, look again to Jesus. Those of us who have not fallen had better look to him with our brethren who have fallen, for there is the same blessing wanted by us all. We have all wandered to some extent. Come, let us look to those dear wounds anew. Can ye not see him? Methinks he hangs before me now. The thorn-crown is on his head, and his eyes are full of languid pity and tearful grief. I see his face bestained with spittle, and black and blue with cruel bruises. I see his hands, they are founts of gore. I see his feet, they gush with rivulets of crimson blood. I look upon him, and I cry, "Was ever grief like thine, O King of sorrow?" and as I look I do remember that the Lord hath laid on him the iniquity of all his people; and, looking, my sin departs from me, because it was laid on him. Looking, my heart begins to love, and then begins to leap. Looking, I come back again to where I stood before; and now, once again, Christ is my all, and I rejoice in him. Have you gone through that process, backslider? If you have done so while I have been speaking, let us praise God together.

III. The last use I have to make of my text will, I hope, be beneficial to many here present. It is this: THIS IS A VERY SWEET PRAYER FOR A POOR SORROWING SEEKER. I beg all who desire conversion to remember this prayer. They had better jot it down, and carry it home with them, or, better still, breathe it to heaven at once.

Consider it well. To begin with, it is *a sinner's prayer*. "Remember me, O Lord!" A sinner's prayer, I say, for the dying thief rejoiced to use the words. He could not have reached down a prayer-book and said a collect, poor man, when he was dying, and there was no need he should. This is the best of prayers,—"Lord, remember me when thou comest into thy kingdom." Trembling sinner, what suited the dying thief may well suit you. Breathe it now, "Forget my sins, my Father, but remember me. Forget my delays, forget my rejectings of a Saviour, forget the hardness of my heart, but, oh, remember me. Let everything pass away from thy mind, and be blotted from thy memory; but, dear Father, by the love of the Lord Jesus, do remember me." Sinner, do not go home without presenting that prayer to God.

Note, again, it is *the prayer of a lost one*. "Visit me with thy salvation." Nobody wants salvation unless he is lost. People may talk about salvation who do not feel that they are lost, but they do not know anything about it, and do not really desire it. Lost soul, where art thou? Art thou lost in a thousand ways—lost even to society? Well, here is a fit prayer for thee—"Visit me with thy salvation." Jesus Christ has not come to seek and to save those who do not want saving, but he has come on purpose to seek and to save that which was lost. Thou art the man he came to bless. Look to him, and thou shalt find that he is the Saviour thou dost require. "Visit me with thy salvation"—I cannot get this prayer into your hearts, but God can, and I am praying in my own soul that many of you in the galleries, or down below there, may now be crying, "Visit me with thy salvation."

Further, remark that our text is *the prayer of one who has a dim eye*—"That I may *see* the good of thy chosen." We have told the seeker to look to Jesus, but he complains, "I do try to look, but I cannot see." Beloved seeker, I do not know that you are bidden to see. You are bidden to look; and if you could not see when you looked you would at least have obeyed the gospel command. The *looking*, the *looking* would bring salvation to you. But for dim eyes Christ is the great cure. He can take away the cataract and remove the *gutta serena*. Pray to-night, "Lord, open my blind eyes, that I may see the good of thy chosen."

Then it is a *prayer for a heavy heart.* "That I may rejoice in the gladness of thy nation." The seeking soul moans out, "O that I had a little joy, or even a trembling hope. If it were ever so small a portion of light I should be glad." Pray for joy. The Lord waits to give it, and if you believe in Jesus your joy shall be full.

And in the last place—not to detain you till you are weary—our text is *the prayer of a spirit that is humble and laid in the very dust,* which cries to God to enable it to glory with his inheritance, because it is stripped of all other glory, emptied of its own boastings. Practically its plea is, "Lord, give me to boast in thy mercy and thy goodness, for I have nothing else to boast of."

Now, beloved hearer, this prayer I would most earnestly press upon you, and I would press it upon you for these reasons.

Just think for a moment. Supposing you are living now without seeing the good of God's chosen, without being saved, what a wretched life it is to live! I cannot understand what men do without God: I cannot comprehend how they live. Do you have no cares, men? "Oh," you say, "we have anxieties in shoals." Well, where do you take them? I find I have troubles enough, but I have a God to take them to. What do you do with many troubles and no God? Do your children never distress your mind? How can you live with bad children, and no God? Do you never lose money in your business? Do you never feel distracted? Do you never say, "What shall I do? Which way shall I turn?" I suppose you do. Then what do you do without a helper or a guide? Poor weak thing as I am, I run under the shelter of my Father's wing, and I feel safe enough. But where do you go? Where do you fly? What is your comfort? I suppose you are something like the poor creatures condemned to death in old times to whom they gave a stupefying cup, so that they might die without feeling the horror of death: surely you must be under a strong delusion that you can believe a lie, for if you were in your senses you could not do without a God,—no, not with your beautiful gardens and fine parks, and wealth, and riches, much less—many of you—with your poverty and hard labour. Poor man without a God, how do you keep up your spirits? What comfort is there in your life? No prayer in the morning, no prayer at night: what days, what nights! Oh, men, I could as soon think of living without eating, or living without breathing, as living without prayer. Wretched naked spirits, your souls must be with no God to cover them! But if it be bad to *live* without Christ—and I am sure it is,—what will it be to *die* without him? What will it be to look into the future, and find no light—no light, and nobody that can bring you any? You have sent to the minister, and he has spoken with you, but he cannot help you; you have had the prayers of your family, who are sobbing at the thought of losing you, but you are looking out alone like one that gazes upon an angry sea in a cold winter's storm, and you can see nothing but the palpable dark. Or, to change the metaphor, you are like a man on yonder wreck. See, he is clinging to the mast; he hears the blast go whistling by him, and anon it comes back howling around him, as if hungry for its prey. He can hear the sea mews screaming in the sky and they seem to prophesy his doom. The waves break over him, drenching him with their brine, till he is ready to freeze as he hangs between death's awful jaws. The lifeboat has been and carried off all it can, and it will never come back any more; and, though he clings with desperation, he knows it is a forlorn hope. He will drift out to sea, and his corpse will lie where pearls lie deep, in the caverns where many thousand skeletons have bleached these many years: his case is terrible to the last degree, and yet it is a feeble picture of a soul leaving the body without an interest in Christ's salvation. Before you get into that state, cry to God, "Remember me, O Lord, with the favour that thou bearest unto thy people. O visit me with thy salvation!"

But the mist darkens and the tempest lowers in tenfold fury when we come to think what it must be to rise again from the tomb without Christ. When that last shrill clarion has sounded, and every grave and cemetery shall have given up their sleepers, and the sea has yielded up the dead that are therein, and battle-fields are swarming with the myriad slain that live again, and in the sky shall be seen the great white throne, and upon it the Son of man who bled for sinners now come to judge and to condemn his adversaries; what will men then do if they have no personal religion, no interest in Christ, no portion in his salvation? Scripture tells us that they will ask the rocks to hide them and the hills to cover them: but they have no bowels of compassion, they will yield no shelter. There will be no refuge for the ungodly, and nothing before them except the fiery indignation and wrath of God. "O turn ye, turn ye, why will ye die?"

This is a common scene to many of you, this great gathering in the Tabernacle. I must confess I cannot look upon it without emotion, though I see it twice each Sabbath day. Here are all of you, and I, a lone man, standing here to talk to you in God's name. It is as much as my soul is worth if I am not earnest with you; but ah, I am not half as earnest as I ought to be. Yet hear me once more. I am a true prophet at this hour—when I warn you that you shall see this sight again if you reject the Saviour. Across the flames of hell you will see it, and you will say to yourself, "The preacher did warn us: he did tell us to cry to God for mercy: he did point us to the Saviour. He bade us pray, and pray there and then." You will remember my entreaties, and then you will renew your agony as, with a wail which shall never end, you will cry, "God called, but I refused: he stretched out his hands, but I regarded him not, and now the day of grace is past, and the Christ whom I despised doth laugh at my calamity and mock when my time is come: for there is no hope—no hope. I knocked too late at mercy's door. My lamp went out. I was a foolish virgin, and I am shut out in outer darkness, where there is weeping and wailing and gnashing of teeth." In the name of the everlasting God I pray you submit yourselves to Christ your Lord at once and you shall live. Amen. Amen.

PORTION OF SCRIPTURE READ BEFORE SERMON—Psalm li.

HYMNS FROM "OUR OWN HYMN BOOK"—51, 584, 556.

EVERY MAN'S NECESSITY.

A Sermon

DELIVERED BY

C. H. SPURGEON,

AT THE METROPOLITAN TABERNACLE, NEWINGTON.

"Ye must be born again."—John iii. 7.

WHEN men are perishing all around you it would be cruel to waste time in attempting to interest their minds or to amuse their fancies. We must do something more practical, and give earnest heed to their pressing necessities. Is it famine which slays them ? Let us feed them. Is it cold ? Let us supply them with covering. Is it disease ? Let us administer medicine. When the case is urgent we confine ourselves to necessaries, and attend with our whole heart to that which *must* have our attention. That which *may be* can wait, but that which *must be* demands our immediate care. Now, the spiritual needs of men are urgent, and among them the most pressing is their regeneration : they must be born again, or they are lost. Therefore, at this time, we will dwell on this topic and give it our whole consideration, letting other interesting matters wait till this most weighty business is happily over. This is a *must*, and we must press it upon you at once with our whole heart. Our earnest desire is for a great ingathering of souls to the garner of salvation, but in order to this they must be born again. We have had many of you hovering round about us like birds around the fowler, but you are not as yet taken in the gospel net ; this state of things cannot content us ; we want to see you decided for Christ, and truly born again. You have been hearers long, but, alas, you remain hearers only, and are not " doers of the word." We mean that the fault shall not lie with us ; if you continue unsaved it shall not be because we have not preached the gospel and kept to preaching it, and preached it as a matter of life and death. Again, then, do we aim at the one point, the point of absolute necessity—" Ye *must* be born again." We trust that if one arrow does not reach the mark another may ; at any rate, we will continue driving at the one target—the conversion of your souls. O you who as yet have not been brought to know the Lord, may the Holy Spirit guide the arrow at this hour.

And now we will have a little simple talk about the great experience called regeneration, or the new birth, without which no man can *see* the kingdom of heaven, much less enter it.

I. And we shall remark concerning it in the first place that the change which is wrought in us by the new birth is MOST THOROUGH: "Ye must be *born again*." A new birth is the most sweeping and entire process conceivable. It is, in fact, more than a change, it is a creation. Regeneration is a great deal more than reformation of life, or a becoming religion; for it is not "Ye must be *washed*, ye must be improved, ye must be elevated;" but "ye must be *born*." It is not enough that the present life, as already possessed, should be renovated, that the existing nature should receive fresh vigour and new tone, but "ye must be *born again*": a new life must be received, and no improving the present life will suffice in its stead.

It is a great deal more also than any change of opinion. I am always afraid of those persons who glory in being converted from one set of religious opinions to another. The best converts to a church are those who are brought into it from the world: those who migrate from other sections of Christianity are not often the most valuable acquisitions. Sometimes, like the convicts, who leave their country for their country's good, they benefit their party best by leaving it, and do not come to the newly adopted section of the church as an unmixed gain. The text says not "Ye must change your opinions, and drink in new notions," but "Ye must have a new nature; ye must be born again." Notions may be altered again and again, and yet the man may be no nearer being a child of God; but let the nature be changed by the Holy Spirit, and then the matter is accomplished. This it is, and nothing short of this, that can land a man in heaven; he must become a new creature in Christ Jesus. The process of the new birth is so thorough that it is a great deal more than an alteration of a man's way of thinking, even upon the best of topics. A man may now think it his duty to be religious, whereas once he was debauched: he may now conceive it to be his duty to be sober, whereas before he was drunken: he may feel it his duty now to be diligent, whereas before he was a sluggard: but all these put together would not amount to a new birth. We rejoice in reformation of any sort. The less sin there is in the world the better, but, for all that, the vital point will not have been reached with all the alterations of thought, and even of life, of which a man is capable; for the text remains in force after all the renovations, conversions, and reformations that are possible to unaided flesh and blood, and it cries with stern, unchanging voice—"Ye must be born again."

The person concerned may have passed through a long series of ceremonies. He may have been received with a welcome into a so-called church, and from the hands of those who think themselves priests there may have distilled the aqueous imposture which is said to regenerate the soul: but there is something more wanted than priests can convey, or than water can effect. Our Lord Jesus Christ meant something far other than the hocus pocus of an empty form when he said, "Ye must be born again." I say in the presence of all that have been baptized in infancy, and all that have been baptized in adult age but were not believers:—ye, even ye, baptized infidels—"*Ye* must be born again." If ye have been baptized and re-baptized, but are still unbelievers, and have not the Spirit of God in your souls, "*ye* must be born again."

What meaneth all this? and what is the signification of this change, so thorough? Do not the words evidently mean that *a new nature* must be created in us? For a life, a nature is the production of a birth. At a birth there comes into the world a life which was not there before. There must come into us *a new life* to which by nature we are perfect strangers; something far beyond that which belongs to us as we are born after the flesh, a life that was not latent in the infant, to be gradually developed in the training of the child, but a life which is altogether absent till divine grace implants it there. "Ye must be born again"— ye must be created again, or as the Scriptures say, "Begotten again unto a lively hope." The life within you must be as fresh a creation as was the light when God spoke it, or as was the world when God formed it out of nothing. A work of divine power must be exercised upon you equal to that which raised the Lord Jesus from the dead and gave him glory.

With a new life in the matter of our ordinary birth there begins *a new experience.* To the new-born child everything is new. Every pain, every sensation of pleasure, is all novel to him—he has known nothing of all this before. And though we may have attained to manhood, or even to old age, when we are born again, the spiritual life is all a fresh experience. There are new feelings of contrition, there is a new faith, there is a new joy, a new hope, everything is new—"Old things have passed away, and all things have become new." Though the man may have traversed many paths, and experienced many sensations, yet the moment he is born again he is a stranger in a strange land, and he is led in a way which he knows not, and in paths which he has not seen. All young souls just born to God, however old they may be as to the bodily reckoning, rejoice in the sacred novelty of the new life, and they thank and bless God who has put his hand a second time to the work and quickened them into newness of life.

Now, as there is a new life, and a new nature, and a new experience, so is there to the child born and the man regenerated *a new world.* It is all new to the child—its brothers and sisters surprise it. When it is taken into the open air, and sees the green fields for the first time, it marvels at them. To the little one everything is fresh. It lives in a museum, it is surrounded with wonders. Even the toys which grown-up people look upon with so much contempt are quite marvels to the little one, it is charmed with them all. Now, a Christian, a man born again, lives in a new world. It is all new to him now, as I remember to have heard a young girl say when first she found the Saviour. When she came to confess her faith in Christ she said, "Either I am altogether changed, or else the world is:" and I could not help telling her I hoped it was both—I hoped she herself was changed, and that this change had produced the other, so that all things had become new. There is a new heaven and a new earth reserved for us by-and-by, and even now, while we are in this world, it is no longer to us what it is to the carnal man. To the twice-born the world is turned upside down. The things we once loved we cease to care for, former objects of ambition we count but dross, while things that were contemptible become to us objects of supreme solicitude. The Holy Spirit having changed us, our views of all around us are entirely different. Such must be your experience, dear hearer, or you will live as carnal men and die in your sins. You *must* experience this divine creation, no matter who you may be ; there can be no exceptions, you must know this great change or be lost. You may have been dandled on the lap of piety ; the name of Jesus may have mingled with the hush of your first lullaby, you may scarce at first have heard any music but that of holy hymns, you may have been taught morality and sanctity by the example of many generations of ancestors ; but, be you who you may, or what you may, you must receive a new life, and you must pass through a new experience, and you must live in a new world or be lost. You must live in the spiritual world, where all is new ; you must have converse with God, a thing unknown to you before ; you must converse with his Son, to whom you have been a stranger ; you must feel the power and energy of the Spirit working in you, a matter which you have never known till now ; or there is no hope for you.

Note that every birth brings into operation *a new force*. A new worker is born ; he is feeble as yet, but those little feet will yet be strong for running, and those tiny hands will yet become dexterous at some useful craft. And so, when a soul is born to God it feels a new power within, and itself becomes a new force. It is obedient to a power which it never recognised before, and a power is put forth from it which it had not been able to exercise before, and did not even understand. A new power has come among men when another soul is born to God : the spiritual world is stronger, and the carnal world is all the weaker for the birth of another spiritual man.

I do not know how to put the matter better than this, but I think I have shown you that regeneration is a most thorough change. To be born again is no child's play. It is not enough for a man to rise under a sermon and say, "I have been impressed and touched by it, and I believe I am converted." There is a vast difference between saying "I am born again" and really undergoing the heavenly birth. It is not making a profession, or even maintaining it with credit for years which will suffice, for, alas, some have seemed almost apostles, and yet have been altogether sons of perdition. You must come to know vitally, indeed and of a truth, in your own soul, what it is for the flesh to be crucified with Christ, and for a new life to be implanted in you supernaturally as the work of the Holy Ghost, or else you cannot enter into the kingdom of God. The work is radical, spiritual, marvellous, divine.

II. In the second place it is MOST WONDERFUL. It is most wonderful in the sense of mystery—as to *the manner of it.* It is not easy to preach from this text and attempt to go minutely into details ; for, if we did so, we might venture too far. I have read treatises upon the subject which were far too destitute of delicacy, and calculated to disgust rather than to impress. We do not pry and must not pry into a divine secret. "Thou hearest the sound thereof, but canst not tell whence it cometh, or whither it goeth ; so is every one that is born of the Spirit." Who shall know how the Holy Ghost works ? That he works by means of the word of God we know ; that he blesses the truth read in a book or heard from the minister—this we know, but how it is he enters into the heart, how it is he creates a spirit within us, how he begets in us the spiritual life—who shall tell but God only ? But then we do not want to know ; it is enough for us to be assured of the fact, the manner we need not pry into. "The secret of the Lord is with them that fear him": they know experimentally what it is to be born again, but they themselves could not explain how it is that the sacred wind bloweth, nor how the Spirit operates upon the human heart. Many discussions there have been as to whether the Spirit of God, as it were, comes nakedly into contact with the nature of man, or whether he always works in and by truth and thought, and so on. Into all this it is not necessary for us to go. We would rather admire, wonder, and adore, for these are better than merely to comprehend; since a man may understand all mysteries and yet be as a sounding brass and a tinkling cymbal.

It is a mystery as to *the supernaturalness of the operation*, for evermore true regeneration is always supernatural. There is no doubt that moral suasion does much with men, that the influence of association will often improve men's manners and habits; that great results may flow from education, especially if it be of the right kind; and that much may be developed in mankind that is admirable, honest, lovely, and of good repute. But this is nothing to the purpose, since it is not what our Saviour meant—it falls short of the new birth, and is indeed quite another thing. The Holy Spirit, the third person in the blessed Trinity must as much come to work upon us as God came forth to work upon this world in its creation, or else we are not born again. It is not enough that we of our own selves and in the energy of our old nature begin to pray, repent, and so on; for all that which can come of our flesh will still be flesh; but in regeneration it is the Spirit who begins by infusing the life, and then the new nature begins to pray and repent. That which is born of the Spirit is spirit, and hence the new birth must be a spiritual operation in order to produce that spiritual nature without which we cannot see and enter into the things of God. This is a solemn matter for you, my hearer, if you have been merely an attendant upon the means of grace and a lover of the outward forms of religion. Do I mean to tell you that you must undergo a change which is beyond your own working, which all the men in this world and all the angels in heaven could not work in you, but which God himself must perform? I do mean that—I mean nothing less than that. "Am I to understand," say you, "that almighty power must work upon me as much as in my creation?" I mean all that, and that it needs as much power to cause you to be born again as it did to make a world: ay, and that the same power which raised Jesus Christ from the dead when he had slept three days in the grave is needed in all its fulness to raise you from your death of sin, and must be exerted if ever you are raised at all. It is a wonderful thing that the Spirit of God should condescend to undertake this work, and that the Lord should set himself a second time to the work. It is surprising that when the vessel was marred upon the wheel and spoiled, instead of breaking it up and consigning it to destruction, he should put forth all his power again and fashion the clay to his own model. He stoops to make us twice born, new-created, begotten again, that we might at the last come to wear the image of Jesus, the first-born among many brethren. "Ye must be born again": the infinite Jehovah must deign to be a second time our Creator or we must perish hopelessly.

This work is wonderful because of *the grandeur of the relationship into which it introduces us.* The child that is born has a father from the very fact of its birth, and we that are born from above cry "Abba, Father," from the very fact that we are regenerated. Adoption gives us the *rights* of children, but regeneration alone gives us the *nature* of children. Because we are sons God sendeth forth the Spirit of his Son into our hearts, whereby we cry "Abba, Father." If I have been born again, no matter what my station in life or position in society, then God is my Father, and it follows that Jesus Christ is my brother; and this not merely in form and in name, as men call each other brethren when there is no actual relationship, but there is a real relationship between us and Christ Jesus and the divine Father, for we are made "partakers of the divine nature." We are the sons of God, and if sons of God, then are we brethren of Christ. It must be so, and it follows from this that, if children, then heirs, and if Christ is the heir, we are joint-heirs with him. My brethren, what privileges spring out of the relationship which arises from the new birth, for our Father then pledges himself for our support, for our comfort, for our education, for all that is necessary for our perfection in the day of the home-bringing when we shall see him face to face. What can happen to a man so great as to be born again? Suppose some of the poorest of the earth who have swept the streets for a paltry pittance should suddenly be elevated by royal favour to the peerage, or imagine that by some revolution of the wheel of providence they should become emperors and kings themselves; yet what of that? The change would be extraordinary, and men would wonder at it; for the passages in history which have been thought most noteworthy have been those wherein paupers have mounted from the dunghill to the throne, and fishermen have cast aside their rough garments to put on the imperial purple. But these strides from nothingness to greatness are inconsiderable and trifling compared with rising from being a slave of Satan to become a son of God. To be elevated by God himself from the darkness and degradation and bondage under which we are brought by the fall and by actual sin to the liberty, to the glory, to the eternal blessedness of the children of God—this surpasses all conception. This can only be ours through our being born again. Our first birth makes us sons of Adam, our second birth makes us sons of God. Born of the flesh, we inherit corruption; we must be born of the Spirit to inherit incorruption. We come into this world heirs of sorrow because we are sons of the fallen man: our new life comes into the new world an heir of glory, because it is descended from the second man, the Lord from heaven. Thus I have spoken upon the wonderful character of this work, as well as upon the thoroughness of it.

III. Now, let us remark, in the third place, that, wonderful and mysterious as the new birth must always be, it is MOST MANIFEST. The house knows when a child is born. There are mysteries surrounding its birth, but the fact is apparent enough. You shall soon hear its cry in the nursery, and ere long its prattle in the parlour; you shall see the joy of the parents as they clasp their offspring, and the care with which they watch for its good. So in the new birth, we know not how the Spirit works, but we know that he does work, and we soon see that a marvellous change has come over those whom he has made possessors of the heavenly seed, creatures of the new life. Those who know converted persons best are among the first to perceive the transforming miracle of grace. Do you not think that Elstow knew when John Bunyan had found the Saviour? The bell-ringers knew it, there was no more Sabbath breaking: and the few poor, godly people that used to meet at Bedford knew it, for he crept into their midst and began to ask them about the things which had become the delight of his soul. We sometimes hear of a person being born again and not knowing it—a somewhat singular matter. Yet I suppose that such an event, after a fashion, very commonly happens in the Episcopalian denomination, because if persons are born again in infant baptism there are thousands in London who have undergone the change, but I am sure that they cannot be sure of it, for their own lives would not tell them so, and their own emotions and feelings would not lead them to any such belief. Regeneration is a poor business if these baptized rebels are regenerate. Why, at that rate, our prisons swarm with regenerated thieves, and our streets are infested with regenerated harlots, and occasionally we have regenerate murderers —all born again in their baptism, and made children of God, members of Christ, and inheritors of the kingdom of heaven. The lie is sickening: the devil himself laughs at it. Of all transparent falsehoods surely that of baptismal regeneration is the grossest. It is a marvel that men who live and walk among sane persons should ever fall into it. Ah, sirs, where the true heaven-given life is found there is something to show for it. Does a man say " I am regenerate"? Come, then, sir, what is the difference in you? What life do you lead? Have you a higher object than the ordinary sons of men? Are you swayed by higher motives? Are there diviner impulses pulsing in your soul than those which stir the hearts of worldlings? "for except your righteousness exceed that of the scribes and Pharisees," the best of worldlings, "you cannot enter into the kingdom of God." If the love of Christ within does not make us better than the best of worldly men, we give no evidence of having experienced the renewing work of God the Holy Ghost.

The heavenly life is very manifest: and it is all the more so from the fact that there are certain signs which always attend and attest the new birth. Persons may be born again, and yet they may not be able to see with us in certain points of doctrine; but there are some things which all the regenerate agree about. For first, *every soul that is born again repents of its sin.* If a man lives in his sin as he used to do, he must not pretend that he is a twice-born man, or he will mightily deceive himself. If he can look upon sin in the same light as he did before, if he can find pleasure in it, yea, if he does not unfeignedly turn from it with loathing and seek the mercy of God to blot it out, he knows nothing of what regeneration is. Again *all the regenerate have faith:* they all agree in finding all the sole ground of their hope in the blood and merit of Jesus. Meet them anywhere and they will tell you they have no confidence except in the Saviour's precious blood; he is all their salvation and all their desire. They rest upon this rock, every one of them ; and no matter what high professors they may be, nor what lofty offices they hold in the church, if Christ is not their one and only trust, they know not what it is to be born again.

In addition to this *all that have passed from death unto life pray.* If it really rises from the heart, prayer is an infallible mark of the new birth; and if it can be said of a man " He does not pray," then he is still dead in his sins, the Spirit of God has not renewed his soul. I might mention some other holy signs which are invariable accompaniments of the new birth, but these three will suffice for all practical purposes. You can test yourselves, beloved, by them. Have you repented? Have you faith towards God? Do you rejoice to draw near to God in prayer? If these things be in you they are marks of the new life, for they were never yet found in the spiritually dead. Do you groan over sin? A corpse does not groan : gracious mourning over transgression is one of the surest proofs of inward spiritual life. Trust in Jesus is an equally clear sign of spiritual life, for the dead man does not know what it is to trust; and genuine prayer is equally a certain token of life received from above. A pang of penitential grief, a thought of holy trust, and a yearning of inward prayer are more than all the unregenerate upon earth can compass, even though they should be doctors of divinity or cardinals of the church.

This new life, the new birth, is a very manifest thing from the power that it puts into men after it has had time to develop itself. At first converts are trembling and weak, but if they have received the new life they gather strength, and there is a power in it which the church soon rejoices in, and which the devil trembles at. This power of course can be kept under restraint by unbelief and other follies, but it ought to have full range, and should never be repressed. I often wish our Christian people were a little more natural in their expression of what they feel. If any brother cries " Amen " very heartily after prayer many look at him, and yet in the primitive church it was the universal custom of those who joined in prayer to say " Amen," by way of endorsing it and making it their own. I wonder Christian people have to so large an extent given up the practice. It is a most fit and proper one, and ought to be restored. I read the other day of a good Bible Christian brother who sometimes, when his heart was merry within him with joy in the Holy Ghost, would even leap for joy as he went to the pit to work. Why should he not do so ? Yet you do not like the look of it ; do you ? I would a good deal sooner a man should be as nimble as David before the ark than be as sleepy as some Christians are, who, if they have any joy, repress it and never tell it out : they are afraid of expressing their joy for fear they should be misjudged. Let it not be so with you. If you let the new life within you have its own course, you may be thought eccentric, but in those eccentricities will lie your force. Who is he that shall cramp us and hold us in when the eternal Spirit quickens us ? If God has blotted out our sin we will praise and magnify his name; and if we have been delivered from going down into the pit we will tell others of it and not hold our tongues. Even though our testimony may not be delivered in the most classical style, and our telling forth of the precious Saviour's love may not be all that the educated may wish it to be, yet if we should hold our peace the stones of the street would cry out, and therefore we must and we will speak. He that has a well within him bubbling up must let it gush forth, and he that has the new life within him will in some form or other become a power in the midst of his fellow men, and the secret will ooze out that he is a twice-born man.

I cannot linger longer. Regeneration is a thorough change, and a wonderful change; but it is a manifest change, and in some men it is especially so. Be it our aim to prove to a demonstration that we are born from above.

IV. But now, very briefly, regeneration is a MOST IMPERATIVE change. Ye *must*, ye *must*, ye *must* be born again. Ye may be rich or ye may be poor, but "ye *must* be born again." Ye may be intelligent, ye may be educated, ye may be talented, but "ye *must*, ye *must* be born again." Many things are desirable, but one thing is needful, imperatively needful—ye *must*, ye *must*, ye *must* be born again. This imperative necessity may be seen from many points of view. We cannot mention them all, but just one or two. *If you are not born again, you have no life*, no spiritual life. The first birth gave you bodily life and mental life, but it did not give you spiritual life—it could not do so, for that which is born of the flesh is flesh, and no more. Now, you must have spiritual life or else you are dead in trespasses and sins, and to all that has to do with spiritual blessings—to a spiritual gospel, a spiritual salvation, a spiritual heaven, to all these things you are dead as the corpses in their graves are dead to the business of to-day. There may be great changes taking place in politics; trade may be very prosperous, or it may be depressed, but the dead man has no interest in the nation or its commerce—how can he have? So is it with you; until you are born again, the spiritual world is shut to you, and you are indifferent to it. Angels may be rejoicing, and believers may be rejoicing over saved souls, but you care nothing about it. The Lord Jesus himself may be seeing of the travail of his soul, but it is nothing to you, and it *must be* nothing to you because you are dead. Oh if our bodies could take the shape of our souls, there would be many carcases sitting before me in these pews. Ah, strange and ghastly sight! We thank God that he conceals the spiritual from our eyes, else might we in horror leave the places where we sit, because we should find ourselves in close companionship with the dead. What a horrible thing a dead soul must be, if our spirits could now perceive it as our senses would perceive a corpse. Let us pause here to realise striking facts in this connection. Some of you are linked in marriage with the spiritually dead. Some of you have dwelling in your house the children of your care, who are dead while they live. You will sit to-night at the supper-table with the spiritually dead. Regard them in that light and your hearts will, perhaps, be moved to pray more intensely for them than you have hitherto done. You that sit regularly in this place, I would like you to remember this fact when this house is crowded. Think, "In my pew there are sitting an unconverted man and an unconverted woman, and they are dead." We don't expect them to feel for themselves, but we do expect the living to feel for them. My dear hearers who are unrenewed, do you not see that you must be born again, for unless you are so, you will remain dead to spiritual things?

Furthermore, remember that a man who is not born again *has no spiritual capacity.* We must be receivers first in the spiritual life, and the dead sinner as yet, until God quickens him, can receive nothing. How often are the saints of God spiritually comforted, instructed, enriched under the preaching and hearing of the word ; but it is their spiritual nature that receives the enrichment. The unregenerate have no spiritual nature : they are carnal, sold under sin, and their mental powers, as well as their bodily appetites, are enslaved : hence they have no power to receive the blessing. The gracious and ever blessed rain of the Spirit comes, but they are not like Gideon's fleece ready to drink it in, but like an hard stone upon which the drops may descend, but it cannot be saturated with the moisture, nor softened by it. Unregenerate men are broken cisterns, which it is vain to attempt to fill. Even if God's own grace were to come to them it could not be retained, for they have not the capacity to hold it. Only the spiritual can receive the spiritual. You must then be born again to have a spirit by which spiritual things are discerned and received. Do you not see that you must be born again ?

Once more, ye must be born again, because *without the Spirit of God you are not the children of God, and consequently you have no spiritual inheritance.* The Spirit causes us to be born ; that birth makes us children, and our being children makes us heirs. If we are not born again we are not children, therefore we are not heirs, and we are out of the heritage, for God's heritage of glory is for the heirs of grace and for none others ; and none shall come into the eternal portion but those who are born in his house and are his true sons and daughters. Universal fatherhood, whatever that may be, brings us common mercies ; but it is the special fatherhood which God hath towards the living in Zion which brings us special blessings. Ye must, then, be born again or lose all share in the divine inheritance. No soul can ever cross the threshold of heaven that has not received the new life. No matter how abundant its prayers, nor how multiplied its acts of religiousness, unless it has been born again, the gates of paradise are for ever fastened against it. Banished from the presence of Jehovah's glory, there is only one other place where it can dwell, and that must be where their worm dieth not and their fire is not quenched. "Ye must be born again."

V. I will finish my discourse by saying that this new birth is EMINENTLY PERSONAL. "*Ye* must be born again." The idea of proxy is quite apart from the figure of the text. A man is born himself, *in propria persona* : no other can be born for him ; so here the change which must be wrought in us must be personally experienced and individually known and felt. What delusion it is to fall back upon a parent's godliness or a godfather's promises, or to imagine that the minister or the so-called priest can stand before God for us. "Ye"—"*ye* must be born again," and if ye are not ye shall never enter the kingdom.

Now, I think I hear passing through the congregation at this moment the whisper of many hearts who are saying, "This is very discouraging. We like to hear ' Only believe, and you shall be saved.' We are glad to be told that ' whosoever believeth in the Lord Jesus Christ hath everlasting life,' but this distresses us, for it does not open the door so wide as we could wish." Believe me, I am very glad to tell you of the free and wide gospel of grace. It is joyful work to me to bring that welcome message to you, and I am sure I do bring it as constantly as I come upon this platform. My most frequent note is—"Look unto Christ and be saved all ye ends of the earth." But at the same time God forbid that you should be built up upon a false foundation, or that your faith and confidence should stand apart from the truth as it is in Jesus. It will be found to be wood, and hay, and stubble if it be so. But you say my sermon is discouraging: had you not better ask, "Is it true?" A person has been building a house, and we see him piling up the stones, but he has never digged out the foundation. It is certainly discouraging to him to tell him that it is not the right way to build a house, but it will be a great mercy for him to be discouraged in a work which is so foolish. It will be a great saving to him in the long run if all that he has already built should come down at once, and he should even now begin at the beginning once more, and lay a good foundation and make sure work of it. It would be foolish to cry out, "Do not discourage him": he ought to be discouraged. Yes, indeed, we would discourage all that will end in disappointment. The fact is, your efforts, and your doings, and your merits, all of them, at their very best, must be a failure, and it is a good thing for us to tell you so. "But what am I to do?" saith one. That, permit me to remind you, is not the best question for you to ask, for if the work of salvation were what *you* must do, surely it would be left undone. You may put the question, "What must I do to be saved?" but we will point you away from doing, and we will tell you to believe in the Lord Jesus Christ, that you may be saved. If you persist in saying, "What must I *do*," we will tell you that the sooner you look away from all that you can do the better ; for the work of salvation from sin is the work of the Spirit of God in you, and you must come to look to him through Jesus Christ that he may work in you all those graces and gifts which shall adorn your future life. Faith looks to the blood of Jesus for the pardon of sin, and then looks to him for his Spirit to overcome the power of sin within the heart, nor does she look in vain; but if you look elsewhere you will search till your eyes fail you, but never see your desire. Would to God we could bring you, not only to discouragement, but to despair of yourselves. When you shall feel you are powerless we shall have hope of you, for then you will leave yourselves in the hands of him who can do all things. When self's strength is gone, God's strength will come in.

"Oh, but you tell me I must have divine power working in me." We do tell you that ; we can tell you nothing less, and if that power is ever at work in your soul, its first effect will be to bring you to confess this, and you will fall down before the footstool of divine mercy and say "Lord save me, or I perish. God be merciful to me a sinner." I do not want to rouse your activity, you unconverted people : I want to rouse you to the conviction that you are lost, and I pray God the Holy Spirit may so convince you. I wish, not to make you think "we can cure ourselves," but oh ! that you would feel that you are diseased, and that, though you have destroyed yourselves, your remedy lies in a higher hand—that you must look to Jesus only for healing. To get the supernatural element into the matter is that which we would strive for, and may God the Holy Spirit help us in it. We would have you look away from what is in you or can come from you, and trust to what Christ did on the cross, to what the gracious Father is waiting still to do, and what the Holy Spirit is sent on purpose to work in you that you may be saved. Oh that you may begin to pray for the divine power ! May you never rest in anything short of the divine working in your spirit. It is to this we would bring you.

Now you know all this and have known it for years, the most of you. To know it—ah how great a privilege if not abused ! how great a responsibility if the knowledge shall end here ! Yet to *know* it, oh how sad, unless you *feel* it ! To feel that "I must be born again," and to be wretched till I am renewed in heart is a good beginning. I pray that you may go home and feel "There is no pillow in this world that will suit my head till I have laid it upon the Saviour's bosom ; there is no bliss that can give me solace till I have found pardon in the wounds of my Redeemer." God grant you may sigh and pant in this way, and we shall then believe that you are regenerate. May you receive the Lord Jesus, and he will give you power to become the sons of God, for those who believe in him were born, not of blood, nor of the will of the flesh, nor of the will of man, but of God. Then shall you know the secret of regeneration, and the Lord himself shall be revealed in you. Then shall you know that you are blessed of the Lord, for flesh and blood could not have revealed this unto you. May the Holy Ghost be within you evermore. Amen.

PORTION OF SCRIPTURE READ BEFORE SERMON—John iii. 1—21.

HYMNS FROM "OUR OWN HYMN BOOK"—456, 448, 461.

SATAN'S PUNCTUALITY, POWER, AND PURPOSE.

A Sermon

WRITTEN AT MENTONE, BY

C. H. SPURGEON.

"Then cometh the devil, and taketh away the word out of their hearts, lest they should believe and be saved."—Luke viii. 12.

IT is a great comfort that such multitudes are willing to hear the word of God. Even though many should turn out to be as the rock, the wayside, or the thorny ground, still it is a cheering circumstance that the seed can be sown broadcast over so large an acreage. Yet the thoughts excited by the sight of a vast congregation are not all pleasurable; the question most naturally arises—What will come of all this preaching and hearing? Will the heavenly seed produce a harvest or fall on barren soil? The thoughtful Christian, in considering this question, takes into consideration the condition of the persons addressed, and remembers that many are unprepared for the gospel. So far from being like a field furrowed to receive the seed, they are like a trodden pathway. They hear the gospel, and so far we are hopeful of them, but they have no idea of allowing it to enter their inmost souls. The ground of their hearts is too much occupied already, other feet will tread there and speedily obliterate the sower's footprints, and as for the good seed, it may lie where it falls, entrance into the inner man it can have none. Nor is this all, the anxious observer remembers that there is yet another difficulty: the arch-enemy of God and man is opposed to the salvation of souls, and therefore he is present with destructive power wherever the seed of the Word is being sown. It is of this we shall now speak,—the activity of Satan during the preaching of the gospel. He is out of sight, but we may not allow him to be out of mind: he does all the more mischief if men sleep; let us watchfully turn our eyes towards him, and prove that we are not ignorant of his devices.

Our divine Lord in the words before us reminded his hearers *of the devil's punctuality*,—"*then* cometh the devil"; *of his power*,—"and taketh away the word out of their hearts"; *and of his purpose*, which is the prevention of saving faith,—"lest they should believe and be saved." At this time, when special services are being held, it may be well to bring these points clearly forward that all may be warned against the wicked one, and so by the grace of God his designs may be frustrated.

I. First observe the evil one's PUNCTUALITY. No sooner does the seed fall than the fowls devour it. Our text says "*then*," that is, *there and then*, "cometh the devil." Mark renders it, "Satan cometh immediately." Whoever else may loiter, Satan never does. No sooner does a

Nos. 1,459-60.

camel fall dead in the wilderness than the vultures appear. Not a bird was visible, nor did it seem possible that there could be one within a radius of many miles, yet speedily there are specks in the sky, and soon the devourers are gorging themselves with flesh: even thus do the spirits of evil scent their prey from afar, and hasten to their destroying work. The lapse of time might give opportunity for thought, and thought might lead to repentance, and therefore the enemy hurries to prevent the hearer from considering the truth he has heard. When the gospel has somewhat affected the hearers, so that in some slight degree it is in their hearts, *then* swifter than the flight of the eagle is the haste of the devil to take the word out of their hearts. A little delay might put the case beyond Satanic power, hence the promptitude of diabolic activity. O that we were half as quick and active in the service of our Lord, one half as prompt to seize every opportunity for blessing the souls of men!

No doubt Satan acts at times directly upon the thoughts of men. He personally suggested to Judas the selling of his Master, and many another black insinuation has he cast into men's minds. Like the foul vulture which constantly feasted itself upon the vitals of Prometheus, so does the devil tear away the good thoughts which would be the life of a man's soul. Insatiably malicious, he cannot endure that a single divine truth should bless the heart. Fearful blasphemies, lewd imaginations, gross unbeliefs, or vain frivolities the devil casts into the mind like infernal bombshells to destroy any new-born thought which looks toward Christ and salvation. At one time he fascinates the mind, and anon he terrifies it; his one aim being to distract the man's thoughts from the gospel, and prevent its lodgment in the conscience and heart.

As Satan cannot be everywhere present at one time, he frequently does his evil work by his servants, sending the inferior spirits to act as fowls in devouring the seed, and these again employ various agents. With great cunning are the common incidents of life used in the evil business, so that even by things indifferent in themselves the purposes of the adversary are brought about. The preacher has some speciality in his manner, utterance, or appearance, and this becomes the bird which devours the seed: the hearer is so taken up with a trifling oddity in the minister that he forgets the truth which was spoken. An anecdote was related, an illustration employed, or a word used which awakened a memory in the hearer's breast, and away went the word out of his heart to make room for mere vanity. Or if the sermon was preserved to its close, it then encountered a fresh peril: a lost umbrella, an extra pressure in the aisle, a foolish jest overheard in the crowd, or the absurd dress of an unknown person, may any one of them answer the devil's purpose and snatch away the word. Little does it signify whether the seed is devoured by black crows or white doves, by great fowls or little sparrows: if it does not abide in the heart it cannot bring forth fruit, and hence the devil arranges that somehow he will take away the seed at once. If he never visits a place of worship at any other time, he will be sure to be there when a revival has begun,—"*then* cometh the devil." He lets many a pulpit alone, but when an earnest man begins preaching, "Satan cometh *immediately*."

II. Secondly, we will now for a moment notice his POWER. "And taketh away the word out of their hearts." It is not said that he tries to do it, but that he actually does so. He sees, he comes, and he conquers. The word is there, and the devil takes it away as easily as a bird removes a seed from the wayside. Alas, what a sway has the evil one over the human mind, and how ineffectual is the preacher's work, unless a divine power is put forth with it. Perhaps from the striking manner in which it was stated, a little of the truth abides in the memory, but the enemy takes it quite out of the heart ; and so the main part, the all-important part of our work is undone. *We* may be foolish enough to aim at the head only, but he who is crafty beyond all craft deals with the heart. Who will may win the intellect, if Satan can keep the affections he is quite content. To the man's heart the good seed is lost, the fowls have devoured it; it has become to him a nullity, having no power over him, no life in him. Not a trace is left, any more than there would be a mark remaining of seed cast on the wayside after the birds had taken it away : so effectual is the work of the prince of the power of the air. When Satan thinks it worth his while to come, and come immediately, he means business, and he takes care that his errand shall not fail.

His power is partly derived from his natural sagacity. Fallen as he now is, he was once an angel of light, and his superlative faculties, though perverted, defiled, and dimmed by the blighting influence of sin, are still vastly superior to those of the human beings upon whom he tries his arts. He is more than a match for preacher and hearer united if the Holy Spirit be not there to baffle him. He has also acquired fresh cunning by long practice in his accursed business. He knows the human heart better than anyone, except its Maker ; for thousands of years he has studied the anatomy of our nature, and is conversant with our weaker points. We are all young and inexperienced compared with this ancient tempter, all narrow in our views and limited in our experience compared with this serpent, who is more subtle than all the beasts of the field : what wonder that he takes away the word which is sown in hard hearts.

Moreover, he derives his chief power from the man's condition of soul : it is easy for birds to pick up seed which lies exposed on a trodden path. If the soil had been good and the seed had entered it, he would have had far greater difficulty, he might even have been foiled ; but a hard heart does the devil's work for him in great measure; he need not use violence or craft; there lies the unreceived word upon the surface of the soul, and he takes it away. The power of the evil one largely springs from our own evil. Let us pray the Lord to renew the heart that the testimony of Jesus may be accepted heartily, and may never be taken away. Great is the need for such prayer. Our adversary is no imaginary being, his existence is real, his presence constant, his power immense, his activity indefatigable. Lord, match him, and overmatch him. Drive away this foulest of fowls, break up the soil of the soul, and let thy truth truly live and graciously grow within us.

III. Our short sermon closes with the third point, which is the devil's PURPOSE. He is a sound theologian, and knows that salvation is by believing in the Lord Jesus ; and hence he fears above all things lest men should " believe and be saved." The substance of the gospel lies in those few words, " believe and be saved," and in proportion as Satan hates that gospel we ought to prize it. He is not so much afraid of works as of faith. If he can lead men to work, or feel, or do anything in the place of believing, he is content; but it is believing that he dreads, because God has coupled it with being saved. Every hearer should know this, and be instructed thereby to turn all his attention to the point which the devil considers to be worthy of his whole activity. If the destroyer labours to prevent the heart's believing, the wise will have their wits about them, and regard faith as the one thing needful.

"Lest they should believe and be saved" Satan takes away the word out of their hearts. Here also is wisdom,—wisdom hidden within the enemy's cunning. If the gospel remains in contact with the heart its tendency is to produce faith. The seed abiding in the soil springs up and brings forth fruit, and so will the gospel display its living power if it dwells within the man, and therefore the devil hastens to take it away. The word of God is the sword of the Spirit, and the devil does not like to see it lie near the sinner for fear it should wound him. He dreads the influence of truth upon the conscience, and if he cannot prevent a man's hearing it he labours to prevent his meditating upon it. "Faith cometh by hearing, and hearing by the word of God": to obliterate that which has been heard is the Satanic method of preventing faith. Here, again, is a practical word for the ear of prudence:—let us keep the gospel as much as possible near the mind of the unconverted, let us sow and sow again, if haply some grain may take root. Countrymen were wont in planting certain seeds to put in "one for the worm, and one for the crow, and then a third which would surely grow," and we must do the like. In the book of Jeremiah the Lord describes his own action thus,—"I spoke unto you rising up early and speaking, but ye heard not; and I called, but ye answered not": surely, if the Lord himself has thus continued to speak to an unanswering race we need not murmur if much of our preaching should appear to be in vain. There is life in the seed of the gospel, and it will grow if it can be got into the soil of the heart; let us therefore have faith in it, and never dream of obtaining a crop except by the old-fashioned way of sowing good seed. The devil evidently hates the word, let us then keep to it, and sow it everywhere.

Reader or hearer, you have often heard the gospel, have you heard it in vain? Then the devil has had more to do with you than you have dreamed. Is the thought a pleasant one? The presence of the devil is defiling and degrading, and he has been hovering over you as the birds over the high-road, and lighting upon you to steal away the Word. Think of this. Fellowship with the Father and with his Son Jesus Christ you are missing by your unbelief, and instead thereof you are having fellowship with Satan. Is not this horrible? Instead of the Holy Ghost dwelling in you as he dwells in all believers, the prince of darkness is making you his resort, coming and going at his pleasure into your mind. You remember Jacob's dream of a ladder, and angels ascending and descending from himself to heaven: your life-experience may be set forth by another ladder which descends into the dark abyss, and up and down its rounds foul spirits come and go *to yourself!* Does not this startle you? The Lord grant it may. Do you desire a change? May the Holy Spirit turn your heart into good ground, and then shall the seed of divine grace grow in you, and produce faith in the Lord Jesus.

THE DUAL NATURE AND THE DUEL WITHIN.

A Sermon

DELIVERED BY

C. H. SPURGEON,

AT THE METROPOLITAN TABERNACLE, NEWINGTON.

"But I see another law in my members, warring against the law of my mind, and bringing me into captivity to the law of sin, which is in my members."—Romans vii. 23.

I QUESTION whether any man understands himself, and I am quite certain that no Christian does so. "Great is the mystery of godliness" in more senses than one. The believer is a great riddle to those who observe him; "he is discerned of no man." He is equally an enigma to himself. The frequency of books like Venning's "Orthodox Paradoxes," and good Ralph Erskine's "Believer's Riddle," is not at all wonderful; for a thousand riddles may be made about the Christian, since he is a paradox from beginning to end. As Plato used to say of each man that he was two men, so may we with emphasis say of each Christian that he is two men in one. Oftentimes to himself the evil man within him appears to be uppermost, and yet, by the grace of God, it never can be, for the ultimate victory belongs to the new and spiritual life. We see in every Christian what was seen in the Shulamite in the Song, "as it were the company of two armies." This is not always known by the believer when he commences the new life. He starts knowing that he is a sinner, and that Jesus is his Saviour, but as he proceeds he finds that he is more a sinner than he thought he was. Many surprises await him, and some things which, if he be not prepared for them, will stagger him as though some strange thing had happened to him. Perhaps my discourse on this subject may prevent a new convert from being overwhelmed with unexpected storms, and help him to solve the question which will then arise in his mind, "If I were a child of God, could it be thus with me?"

Our first head will be, THERE ARE IN ALL BELIEVERS TWO PRINCIPLES. The apostle speaks of *the law of his mind*, and then of *another law in his members* warring against the law of his mind. The converted man is a new man in Christ Jesus, but the old nature remains within him.

65

The first life in a Christian in order of time is *the old Adam-nature*. It is there from the first. It is born of and with the flesh; and it remains in us after we are born of the Spirit, for the second birth does not destroy in us the products of the first birth. Regeneration brings into us a new and higher principle, which is ultimately to destroy the sinful nature, but the old principle still remains, and labours to retain its power. Some fancy that the carnal mind is to be improved, gradually tamed down and sanctified; but it is enmity against God, and is not reconciled to God, neither, indeed, can be. The old nature is of the earth earthy, and must be crucified with Christ and buried with him, for it is altogether too bad for mending. This old nature lives in our members; that is to say, its nest is the body, and it works through the body. There are certain appetites of ours which are perfectly allowable, nay, even necessary to existence; but they can be very easily pushed to sinful extremes, and then that which is lawful and right becomes a nest for that which is unlawful and wrong. It is a commendable thing that a man should seek to provide for his own household, yet how many crimes and how much covetousness come into the world from an inordinate indulgence of that desire. A man may eat and drink, yet it is through those appetites that a thousand sins are engendered. A man, when he is in his right condition, puts a bit into the mouth of his desires, and holds them in as with bit and bridle; his higher nature governs his bodily appetites, but not without great effort, for ever since the fall of Adam the machine works irregularly, and is not properly controlled by that which should be the ruling force.

I have heard of some professors who dream that sin is utterly destroyed in them, and that they have no more evil tendencies and desires. I shall not controvert their notion. If it be so, I congratulate them, and greatly wish it were so with me. I have, however, had some little experience of perfect people, and I have generally found them the most disagreeable, touchy, and sensitive persons in the world, and some of them have turned out to be such detestable hypocrites, that I am rather afraid of a person who has no imperfections. As soon as I learn that a brother states that he has lived for months without sin, I wonder whether his secret vice is lewdness, or theft, or drink, but I feel sure that somewhere or other there is a leak in the ship.

The sin which lurks in the flesh, will grow weaker in proportion as the holy principle, of which I have to speak, grows stronger; and it is at no time to be tolerated or excused, but we are to fight against it, and conquer it, and ultimately it is to be destroyed in us, root and branch: yet there it is, and let not the young Christian be staggered when he finds it there.

When we are born again there is dropped into our soul *the living and incorruptible seed* of the word of God, which liveth and abideth for ever. It is akin to the divine nature, and cannot sin, because it is born of God: it has no tendency to sin, but all its appetites are heavenward and Christward. It never stoops from its high position; it is always aspiring towards heaven. It is at deadly enmity with the old nature, which it will in the end destroy; but, as I have said before, it has its work to do, and it is a work which, assisted even by divine strength, will not be accomplished all at once. It is a warfare which, when it seems ended, has often to be renewed, since, after long and victorious campaigns, the routed enemy returns to the field.

Now, I would like each Christian to be assured that he has this second principle in him. It may be weak; it may be struggling for an existence; but it is there, my brother. If thou hast believed in Jesus, thou hast the life which hates sin, and makes thee repent when thou hast fallen into it. That is the life which cries, " Abba, Father," as often as it thinks of God, the life which aspires after holiness, and delights in the law of God. This is the new-born principle which will not permit thee to be at peace if thou shouldst wander into sin, which finds no rest but in the bosom of that God from whom it came, and in likeness to that God from whom it sprang.

These are the two principles which make up the dual man : the flesh and the spirit, the law of the mind and the law of sin, the body of death and the spirit of life.

We notice, secondly, that THE EXISTENCE OF THESE TWO PRINCIPLES IN A CHRISTIAN NECESSITATES A CONFLICT, even as the text says, "Another law in my members *warring against the law of my mind.*" The lion will not lie down with the lamb in us. Fire will not be on good terms with water. Death will not parley with life, nor Christ with Belial. The dual life provokes a daily duel.

I am not sure that the conflict between the new nature and the old is felt by all young Christians at the first. Frequently, Christian life may be divided into three stages : the first period is that of *comfort,* in which the young Christian rejoices in the Lord, and his principal business is to sing, and tell what God has done for him.

The more of this the better. After that, very often comes the stage of *conflict:* instead of being children at home we have grown into men, and therefore we must go to war. Under the old law, when a man was married, or had built a house, he was excused from fighting for a season, but when that was over, he must take his place in the ranks : and so is it with the child of God; he may rest awhile, but he is destined for the war. The period of conflict is often succeeded, especially in old age, by a third stage which we may call *contemplation ;* in which the believer sits down to reflect upon the goodness of the Lord towards him, and upon all the good things which are in store for him. This is the land Beulah, which John Bunyan describes as lying on the edge of the river, and so near to the Celestial City that you can hear the heavenly music across the stream, and, when the wind blows that way, you can smell the sweet perfumes from the gardens of the blessed. That is a stage which we must not expect to reach just now. My young friend, inasmuch as you are at the first weak and tender, the Lord may be pleased to screen you from a great many temptations and from the uprisings of your flesh, but the probabilities are that before long you will put down your harp and take up your sword, and your joy of spirit will give place to the agony of conflict. Sin is in you, lurking in secret places, though it has not as yet leaped forth upon you as a young lion on its prey. You perhaps have thought, " I shall do better than those who have gone before me ; I shall shine as a brilliant saint "; let not him that putteth on his harness boast himself as though he put it off. There are fights before you, and I warn you of them, so that when you remove from the state of content to the state of conflict you may confess, "Before it came to pass I was warned of this, and therefore I am prepared for it." The reason of the fight is this; the new nature comes into our heart, to rule over it, but the carnal mind is not willing to surrender its power. A new throne is set up in the heart, and the old monarch, dethroned, outlawed, and made to lurk in holes and corners, says to himself, "I will not have this. Why should it be? Here am I, who was once this man's king, snubbed and made to hide myself as though I were a stranger. I will get the throne back again." Master Bunyan, in his " Holy War," which is a very wonderful allegory, describes Diabolus, you know, as having his city taken from him. But, after the city had been taken, there lurked, in the holes and corners of that city, certain subjects of Diabolus, and these were always plotting and planning how they could get the city back, by opening the gates at night to let in their old king, or by sowing discontent among the inhabitants. This is the reason for the perpetual strife within our souls. The old lusts that are under ban and curse, and which we are hunting after to crucify them, put their heads together, and labour to regain dominion. The flesh will wait till you are in a very quiet frame of mind and feel very secure, and then it will come down upon you with its evil fascinations. At another time, it may be, you are in great trouble, and you feel ready to sink, and then comes the devil upon you like a roaring lion, hoping to destroy your faith. He knows how to time the temptation, and the flesh knows how to rise in insurrection when we are off our guard, and when surrounding circumstances are all conducive to sin. We cannot be too watchful, for the flesh will rebel all of a sudden. We may get it down, and think we have fettered it securely; but, ah! it finds its hands, it breaks its bonds, and lets fly an arrow at our heart. You said, " I shall never be angry again," and while you were congratulating yourself on the sweetness of your temper you were on a sudden provoked from quite a new quarter, and your wrath boiled over directly. " No," said you, " I never shall be impatient any more," and yet within a few moments you were as full of murmuring as ever you had been in your life. Till the flesh lies in the grave sin will not be dead.

And let me warn you that the flesh may be doing us more mischief when it seems to be doing no mischief at all than at any other time. During war the sappers and miners will work underneath a city, and those inside say, " The enemy are very quiet; we hear no roaring of cannon, we see no capturing of Malakoffs. What can the enemy be at?" They know their business well enough, and are laying their mines for unexpected strokes. Hence an old divine used to say that he was never so much afraid of *any* devil as he was of *no* devil. That is to say, when Satan does not tempt, it is often our worst temptation. To be let alone tends to breed a dry rot in the soul. " He has not been emptied from vessel to vessel," said the prophet of old, " he is settled upon his lees": this spake he of one who was under the divine displeasure. Stagnation is one of the worst things that can happen to us, and so it happeneth that we are never secure.

Thus, dear friends, I have showed you that there is a conflict within; and let me congratulate you if it *be* a conflict. The ungodly know no such inward warfare. They sin, and they love it; but where there is a spiritual conflict the grace of God is present. We do sin, but we hate sin; we fall into it, but we loathe it and fight against it; and every true child of God can say honestly that there is nothing in this world he dreads so much as to grieve his God. If you were dead in sin you would have no trouble about it: but those inward pangs, those deep emotions, those bitter sighs and cries, that exclamation of " Oh, wretched man that I am! who shall deliver me from the body of this death?" all indicate spiritual life. While I sympathise with your sorrow I congratulate you that you feel it, for this is one of the marks of a child of God. Forget not that in renewed men there are two opposing forces, and that these necessitate a life-long war.

Thirdly, we must now note that this warfare SOMETIMES LEADS US INTO CAPTIVITY. Observe, " I see another law in my members warring against the law of my mind, and *bringing me into captivity to the law of sin which is in my members.*" " What does that mean?" says one. It means this, that if you sin it will be captivity to you if you are a child of God. The sinner may find pleasure in sin, but you will not if you are God's son. You will be like a slave in chains, locked up in a horrible dungeon, if you fall into sin. But does the old nature make Christians captives? Yes, in this way. First, many a Christian feels himself in captivity *from the very fact that the old nature has risen within him.* Let me explain myself. Suppose that the old nature suggests to you some sin: you hate the sin and loathe it, and you despise yourself for lying open to be tempted in such a way. The very fact that such a thought has crossed your mind is bondage to your pure spirit. You do not fall into the sin; you shake off the serpent, but you feel its slime upon your soul. Do you not know what it is to have a very violent tendency towards an evil, the very thought of which is detestable to you? Your renewed mind exclaims, "How can I do this great wickedness and sin against God?" but yet the flesh says, " Do it, do it, do it," and pictures the sweetness and the pleasure of it. With your whole soul you set yourself against the temptation, the cold sweat stands upon your brow at the very thought of your falling into so foul a transgression, and you cry to God in prayer; but yet the captivity of your soul is great while the trial lasts, and even in the remembrance of it. You say to yourself, " I am afraid I dallied with the temptation. The bait would not have been so alluring to me if there had not been some consent of my soul to it." You also charge your heart with folly, saying, " Though I did not commit that sin, yet there was a hankering after it in me." Though others could not condemn you, but must even honour your self-denial, yet you condemn yourself for any degree of inclination in the wrong direction, and you feel that the temptation has brought you at once into captivity. What a difference there is between a spot on one thing and a spot on another. A man makes a spot with ink on my coat, and nobody perceives it; but if he were to cast a drop upon this white handkerchief how soon everybody would see it. The old nature is like a black coat, too dark to show a blot; but one spot of temptation falling on the pure white linen of the new nature troubles us exceedingly; we see it, and we loathe it, and we cry out to God that we may get rid of it. The very passing of temptation across a renewed soul brings it into captivity. I stood one day in Rome looking at a very large and well executed photograph of a street and an ancient temple. I had never seen so fine a photograph; but I noticed that right across the middle of it was the trace of a mule and a cart. The artist had done his best to prevent it, but there was the ghost of that cart and mule all the way along, right across the picture. I do not say it spoilt it, but it certainly did not improve it. Even so oftentimes, when our heart is most cleansed and bears best the image of God, right across the fair picture comes the trace of a temptation, and we are grieved. An observer unskilled in art might not notice the mark on the photograph, but a careful artist, with a high ideal, is vexed to see his work thus marred; and so with moral stains, that which the common man thinks a trifle is a great sorrow to the pure-hearted son of God, and he is brought into captivity by it.

Sometimes, too, a Christian's captivity consists in his *losing his joy, through the uprising of the flesh.* I speak what I am sure many of the children of God here know. You are rejoicing in the Lord and triumphant in his name, and by-and-by some corruption struggles for the mastery. "It shall not rise," say you. You put it down, but it strives and you strive too, and in the struggle the joy of the Lord, which was your strength, seems to be taken away from you. A sense of the dreadful fact that the leprosy is in the house of clay in which you live terrifies you, and you are so anxious to get the leprosy out of the walls that you would sooner see the old house moulder into dust than live where evil so readily approaches you. This sight of inbred sin may cast a chill upon your joy. You want to sing the praises of God, but the temptation comes just at that very minute, and you have to battle with it, and the song gives place to the battle-shout. It is time for prayer, and you are in the attitude of devotion, but somehow you cannot control your thoughts; they will roam hither and thither under the force of the flesh. My thoughts frequently seem like a lot of colts let loose, tearing over the fields of my soul without restraint. In holy contemplation you try to concentrate your thoughts upon the subject in hand, and you cannot; very likely somebody knocks at the door at the same time, or a child begins to cry, or a man begins to grind an organ under your window, and how can you meditate? All things seem to be against you. Little outside matters which are trifling to others will often prove terrible disturbers of your spirit, and what others smile at you are made to weep over; for the flesh will lay hold of the most paltry concerns to prevent your coming into communion with the Lord your God. Thus by taking away our joy, and marring our fellowship, the old corruption within us leads us into captivity.

But, ah, brethren, this is not all, for *we do not always escape from actual sin.* We do, in moments of forgetfulness, that which we would willingly undo, and say that which we would willingly unsay. The spirit was willing to be perfect, but the flesh was weak; and then the consequence is, to a child of God, that he feels himself a captive. He has yielded to treacherous blandishments and now like Samson his locks are shorn. He goes out to shake himself as he did aforetime, but the Philistines are upon him, his God is not with him, and it will be a happy thing for him if he does not lose his eyes, and come to grind at the mill like a slave. Oh, what need have we to be on our guard, and to look to the strong for strength, for this old nature within us will bring us into captivity if it can, and will hold us there.

But I must close with this reflection, that THIS WARFARE, AND THIS OCCASIONAL TRIUMPH OF THE FLESH, MAKE US LOOK TO CHRIST FOR VICTORY. The apostle asks, "Who shall deliver me from the body of this death?" And his reply is, "I thank God through Jesus Christ our Lord." Brethren and sisters, I am persuaded that there is no place so safe, and none so proper and fitting for any of us, as a sinner's place at the foot of the cross. I have read a great deal about perfection in the flesh, and I have tried to get it. I have also tried to pray after the fashion which I suppose a perfect man would pray in; but the theory will not hold water as far as I am concerned. When I went up to the temple in that way, and tried to pray, I found a Pharisee at my elbow. A good way off I saw a poor sinner, smiting on his breast, and saying, "God be merciful to me a sinner," and I perceived that he went away justified, while I stood there and envied him. I could not stand it, I went back to my old place at his side, and smote my breast, uttering the old cry, "God be merciful to me a sinner." Then I too felt at ease, and I went home justified and rejoicing in the Lord.

Beloved, whenever there is a question between me and the devil as to whether I am a child of God, I have given over seeking evidence in my own favour, or turning to my experience to prove that I am in a state of grace, for that cunning old lawyer knows more about my infirmities than I do, and can very soon bring two to one against me. My constant way is to tell the accuser, "Well, if I am not a saint I am a sinner, and Jesus came into the world to save sinners, therefore I will go to Christ, and look to him again." The devil himself cannot answer that. You that are oldest in the divine life—and I speak to some who have known the Lord these fifty years—I am sure that you find times in which no mark, evidence, or experience is worth a groat to you by way of comfort, and you are led to adopt the simple expedient which I have recommended to all the tempted ones. It will be wise to live upon Jesus always. Begin again at the foot of the cross, where you began at first, with the old cry,

> " Nothing in my hand I bring :
> Simply to thy cross I cling."

That is the way to conquer sin, as well as to overcome despair; for, when faith in Jesus comes back to your soul, you will be strong to fight with your corruptions, and you will win the victory, which you never will gain if you allow your struggles with your sins to drive you away from your Saviour. Let us resort, then, to Christ who giveth us the victory, and let us, the longer we live, praise Christ the more. You young Christian, you do not know yet what a dear Saviour you have found. You know you have found him, but he is a dearer Christ than you think he is. You were naked and he has clothed you : ay, he has put the armour upon you which will ward off the darts of the arch-enemy. You were hungry, and he has fed you ; ay, but he has fed you with bread immortal, he is nourishing a divine life within your soul. He has given you peace, and you are grateful for it; ay, but he has given you a peace which passeth all understanding, that shall keep your heart and mind. You say it is sweet to find him with you. So it is, but oh, how sweet it will be to have him with you when you pass through the fires and are not burned, when you go through the floods and are not drowned, when you enter upon the final struggle and are not afraid.   Oh, beloved, we may find out, and shall find out, more of our own wants, but we shall also discover more of Christ's all-sufficient fulness.   The storm will become more terrible, but the pilot's power to rule that storm will only be the more displayed.   The ship may rock to and fro till all her timbers are strained, and her keel may threaten to snap in twain, but

> " He will preserve it, he doth steer
> Even when the bark seems most to reel.
> Storms are the triumph of his art."

He will bring his people safely through the howling wilderness and the land of great drought.   Be not afraid, ye that have begun the divine pilgrimage, for his fiery cloudy pillar will attend you.   Dragons there are, but by the sword of the Spirit you shall wound the dragon as of old he was wounded at the Red Sea.   There will be death to fight with, but Christ has died, and you shall be victorious over the grave.   Expect conflict ; be not astonished when it comes, but as confidently expect victory, and shout in prospect of it.   As surely as the Lord has called you to this celestial warfare he will bear you through it.   You shall sing on the other side of Jordan unto him that loved you and washed you from your sins in his blood.   In the haven of the blessed, in the land of the hereafter, in the home of the holy, where the weary are at rest, you shall sing the high praises of God and the Lamb.

I would to God this sermon had a relation to all those who hear or read it, but I fear it has not.   I can only hope that those who have no conflict within may begin to feel one.   May God grant that you may not rest quiet in sin, for to be at peace with sin is to be sleeping yourself into hell.   God arouse you, that you may flee to Christ for mercy at this very hour, and there shall be joy in his presence.   Amen.

Portion of Scripture read before Sermon—Romans vii.

Hymns from "Our Own Hymn Book."—435, 644, 769.

Metropolitan Tabernacle Pulpit.

THE MEAT AND DRINK OF THE NEW NATURE.

A Sermon

DELIVERED BY

C. H. SPURGEON,

AT THE METROPOLITAN TABERNACLE, NEWINGTON.

"For my flesh is meat indeed, and my blood is drink indeed."—John vi. 55.

WE know that the Saviour spoke of spiritual, not of carnal things, and he spoke of himself not as being in any sense meat for our bodies—that could not be—but as being food for our souls. This statement is very plain to us, but those who heard it at the first found it very hard to understand. Nor need we wonder, for men of the schools who play with letters, words, and phrases, frequently meet with difficulties where none exist. The Jews of our Lord's day had fallen into the foolish habit of taking words to pieces and dwelling upon the syllables and letters, until they seemed to have lost all power of getting at the plain meaning which ordinary language was intended to convey. They blinded their own eyes with the pretence of superior wisdom, made puzzles and riddles out of plain words, raised a huge dust, and sat down in it blinded to the end. Our God has taught us more, and given us to understand more clearly, for his Holy Spirit has given us back the childlike spirit, so that we are willing to see the natural sense which words were meant to reveal. Now we see great force and clear expressiveness in that very language which seemed before to conceal the Saviour's meaning. It was a veil to the Jews, and they saw not: it is an instructive parable to us, which, instead of hiding the truth, shadows it out to us, and softens the light for our weak eyes. We see, I fear, even now but dimly, for our spiritual sight is scarcely clear as yet; but yet we see, blessed be God for that, and we see Jesus, and we see something of his loving meaning. We do more than see: we enjoy, and therefore know to the life what it is to feed upon his flesh, which is meat indeed, and to drink his blood, which is drink indeed.

We cannot attempt to explain the deep mysteries of our text, but rather —as the swallow touches the brook with his wing and is away again— we will glance at these crystal waters of this sacred truth, and then up and away. The text teaches us, first, *what Christ must be to us*. We shall consider, secondly, *what is bound up in this*; and, thirdly, *what reflections naturally arise out of it*.

I. WHAT CHRIST MUST BE TO US. The answer from the text is,

73

He must be our meat and drink. He must be everything to us—the one thing needful, the indispensable, necessary, all-sufficient supply. He must be the source of strength, the support of life, and we must feel him to be so. He must, to come back to the figure, be meat and drink to us. Our Lord in speaking to the Jews was doubtless thinking of the paschal lamb, and of the time when Israel came out of Egypt; when they not only had the blood of the lamb sprinkled upon their houses for their security, but the lamb itself within them as their sustenance. They sat down to feed upon it before they enjoyed the fulness of redemption by passing out of Egypt from under the bondage of Pharaoh. They did not understand that symbol, and they little knew what our great Lord and Master meant when he employed it to set forth himself, and said, "My flesh is meat indeed, and my blood is drink indeed."

Our Lord Jesus Christ must be to us, then, our spiritual meat and drink. What mean we by that?

First, that *the doctrine of God incarnate must be the food of our souls.* Brethren, we have no doubt as to the true and proper Deity of our Lord Jesus. We have long since passed out of the region of controversy about that, for he has been God to us in the work of salvation and in the new creation which we have experienced through his power. We have, moreover, no doubt about his humanity, but we do not usually dwell enough upon it. We are bound to adore his Deity, but we must not forget that he is as truly man as if he were not God, and as much a brother to us as if he were not the Son of the Highest. Jesus is assuredly man. Now feed on this. The man Christ Jesus heads up a new race: as the first Adam headed up the race of old, and was our federal head to stand or fall for us, and we were to stand or fall in him, so is there now a new head, who brings us up from the ruin of the first Adam's fall and puts us into a new position before the living God. There is a man who has redeemed us. There is a man who has made all the men in him well pleasing to God. There is a man who represents manhood in perfection in the glory above. There is a man in whom all believers are, even as we read that Levi was in the loins of Abraham when Melchisidec met him. We are in Christ, and we stand now before the eternal throne in that blessed representative man. Feed on this doctrine now. Jesus is a real man, though clothed with all power; he is God, and yet he is the mirror of tenderness; he ruleth all things, and yet is touched with the feeling of our infirmities. You must believe this, and you must receive it, and you must rest upon it, otherwise you have no life in you. Some try to turn this fact into a myth, but indeed it is no parable or figure of speech, for the Christ who spoke these words was there before them—one whom they had often seen eat and drink: he spake of himself with his own lips, and was not a phantom or apparition, but a solid existence of flesh and blood. So then it is upon the historical Christ, whose existence is a matter of fact, that my soul must feed, as I believe him to be both human and divine.

But this is not all: *the food to be fed upon is not merely God incarnate, but Christ suffering.* Notice that he puts it "My *flesh* is meat indeed, and my *blood* is drink indeed": when the flesh and the blood are mentioned separately, death is implied. The two being divided and being named together in one connection are the token and emblem of our Saviour's vicarious sacrifice. We also (I am speaking of the brethren worshipping here) have long ago past beyond the region of controversy as to the substitutionary sacrifice of Jesus Christ our Lord; for if it be not so, then is our preaching vain and our hope is also vain, and we are yet in our sins. We have no hope of eternal life save that which begins, centres, and ends in the sacrifice of Jesus Christ. "This man, when he had offered one sacrifice for sins for ever, sat down at the right hand of God"—that is our sole hope. *He* has made expiation for sin.

> "He bore, that we might never bear,
> His Father's righteous ire."

We are now to build up our souls by feeding upon the suffering, the crucified, the dead, the buried Christ, as having stood as our representative, and as having endured death in our stead. You cannot obtain comfort apart from this if you have felt the weight of sin; and you cannot continue happy apart from this great historical fact if you are conscious of sin. Fly, my hearers, into the wounds of Jesus, and like doves ye shall find shelter in that rock; but with eager wing ye may glide over the waste of human thought without finding a rest for the sole of your weary foot till you light upon the truth of the great substitution. "The Word was made flesh and dwelt among us," is the first bell of heaven's marriage peal, and the second has an equally sweet note of its own—"Christ died for our sins." Ring them both full often. Listen to them as they sound forth—"God *with* us, Christ *for* us." Incarnation, substitution—was there ever better meat and drink for a hungry soul? This surely satisfies the desire of the most hungry spirit—"The blood of Jesus Christ his Son cleanseth us from all sin."

I have, as it were, in those few words set out the viands of the feast. But now I would have you note that our Lord must be to us meat and drink; and *meat is not intended to look at, but to feed on.* I heard the other day that in a certain Socinian place of worship they have gone the length of setting the bread and wine on the table for the people to look at, but they suppose that it is quite unnecessary that they should actually eat and drink. It is fittingly done of them: that is consistent with their creed. They have no Christ to feed upon. There is nothing in their belief which could feed the soul of a mouse, if a mouse had a soul. Why should they attempt to feed the people in figure when really they have no incarnate God or atoning Saviour. If it be indeed true that in one of their places of worship they have exhibited the bread and wine instead of handing it out to be eaten, it is remarkably typical of their bloodless, lifeless gospel, their Christ who is no Deity, their Jesus who is no sacrifice for sin. How can the soul find food there? But we must beware lest we ourselves should ever rest content with merely glancing at Christ and not partaking of him. What is to be done with food, with meat and drink? It is to be received. Food on the table does not nourish; it must be taken into the hand. The cup on the board will never cheer; it must be lifted; it must be appropriated. I know that many of you have by a humble but

brave faith appropriated Christ as he is set before you in the gospel.
He has bidden you come and eat, and you have come pressed by a sore
famine that was in your soul. You have come, and you have said,
" He is mine," and you have taken him to yourselves by simple childlike confidence in him. You have well done, continue to do the same.
"As ye have received Christ Jesus the Lord, so walk ye in him." Go
on receiving him. "To whom coming," says the apostle, "as unto a
living stone"; regard him not as one to whom you have come by one
act and have done with him, but as one to whom you come continually.
" Of his fulness have all we received, and grace for grace," but we are
going on receiving, by continuing to believe in him. Hold on to this.
Having begun in the spirit, do not hope to be perfected by the flesh.
Do not think that you are to be fed afterwards on something other
than Christ, but go on receiving, appropriating, and taking home the
great truths concerning your Lord. Here, my brethren, is the life of
your faith. But even appropriating is not enough to constitute feeding.
After taking the morsel, it is put into the mouth, and received inwardly ;
the draught of wine is poured into the throat and it disappears. Receive
truth not only as a matter of creed, but drink it in as the ox sucks
in the water when he stands up to his knees in the pool. Take Christ
into your very soul—into your *heart's* belief as well as into your mind's
belief. Mental beliefs shift and change : the inward soul's belief never
alters. I reckon that we know nothing rightly till we have absorbed
it, and made it part and parcel of ourselves. The vital truths with
regard to our Lord Jesus must go down into the inward parts of the
soul, as the food descends into the secret parts of the belly to feed the
entire man.

And you know what becomes of the food. It is taken up by the
nature itself, and becomes transmuted into it. After its digestion it
passes through various processes, and ultimately becomes the life-blood,
out of which is built up nerve, muscle, sinew, bone, flesh, heart. Everything comes of it. Now, you must so believe in Jesus that no longer is
it a matter of question with you whether you will retain him or not,
for if you have inwardly received him you cannot lose him for ever.
Oh that blessed " *Quis separabit?* "—" Who shall separate us from the
love of God, which is in Christ Jesus our Lord ?" It is difficult to deprive a person of that which he has received mentally, for facts learned
in childhood are remembered even to old age. No one could compel
another to forget, but yet without such compulsion the memory might
relax its hold through lapse of years : the mind might part with that
which it has received, but no known power could take away from a man
that which he has eaten and assimilated. A person may very readily
pick my pocket of my purse, but what I ate yesterday he cannot steal.
That is mine ; it is joined to myself, and has built me up. I do not
know what portion of my flesh comes of my morning meal, or of my
mid-day repast, but there it is, and there it must be. It has entered into
me, and never can be got away from me again. So when the soul
takes in Christ's truth with that simple childlike faith which is the
mouth, the truth goes into the soul and is thought over, trusted in,
delighted in, and becomes so part and parcel of the inner consciousness
and of the new nature of the man that it would be henceforth utterly

impossible to tear away that truth from him. Pound a true Christian in a mortar and every single atom would say, "I belong to Christ." Grind him finer than the smallest dust of the threshing floor and every minute particle would still say, "Christ is in me." For so it is that the Christ has entered the man, permeated his nature, become his very life, and now it is "I live, yet not I, but Christ liveth in me." Now is the text fulfilled in us, "For ye are dead, and your life is hid with Christ in God. When Christ, who is our life, shall appear, then shall ye also appear with him in glory." "Abide in me," said our Lord, and he gave his own promise to be with us for ever. That is just the result of eating Christ, and to this we must come. Beloved, I have thus explained the matter as well as I can, but as old Rollock says, "The only way to understand feeding upon Christ is to feed upon Christ." This is a practical, personal, experimental business. In learning certain acts you must yourself become a practical scholar, the master cannot teach by merely setting the copy, the scholar must imitate it line by line with his own hand: and so here, I can teach little by words only, you must practise what is spoken. Now feed ye on the Lord Jesus; let each one of you do it. I know what some do: they will not feed on Christ, but they pick over the heavenly bread like dainty folks who have no stomach for their meat. This bit of Christ they would have, but the other does not suit their tooth: justification by faith they would have, but not sanctification,—they do not like that. It is a whole Christ you and I must have—a whole Christ, as to every part of his teaching, character, work, and offices. We must receive him into ourselves without division, rejoicing to take him just as he is. Especially must we receive the spirit of Christ, for "if any man have not the spirit of Christ he is none of his." We must partake in the loving spirit, the self-denying spirit, the generous spirit which lives not within itself, but goes forth in forgiveness of injuries, and in seeking to benefit all mankind. We must have Jesus in us, delighting to take in the whole of him, for he says farther on in this very chapter, "He that eateth *me*"—that is even more comprehensive than his "flesh and his blood"—"He that eateth *me*, even he shall live by me": the entire Christ must be taken into the soul to build up the inner man.

II. Now, secondly, WHAT IS BOUND UP IN THIS EATING OF HIS FLESH AND DRINKING OF HIS BLOOD? Here we will take you back to the context.

And notice, first, that there is for this eating the flesh and drinking the blood of Christ such an essential necessity that *he who has not so eaten and drank has no spiritual life at all.* It is a strong word, "Except ye eat the flesh of the Son of man, and drink his blood, *ye have no life in you.*" He does not mean that they have no natural life; he is speaking about spiritual things. Some that are as foolish as Judaizers in the matter of sticking to the letter, tell us that this means existence, and that no man's eternal existence is certain except that of a believer in Christ. That dogma is not taught here, certainly. Our Lord is not speaking of existence; he is speaking of a far higher thing than existence, namely, *life.* Have you never learned the difference between death and non-existence, and between life and existence? If you have not, you are babes in understanding, and you will often be blundering and losing your way in the midst of texts of Scripture. A man may exist in everlasting death, as, alas, all who die unbelievers must do; but blessed is he who lives! Blessed is he who shall live for ever! Let me repeat the word, "lives"; I did not say exists. What a glorious thing is life. Yet, if I had to explain to you what life is, I might find it far easier by some action of my own to show that I lived than to tell you exactly what life is. He however, who eats Christ has life. He who has not done so has not life. Do you understand this; that unless you have received Christ by faith into your souls you have no life. You can work, you can walk, you can speak; you have all sorts of natural life, but you have not the life everlasting of which Jesus speaks. The life of God is not in you. You are dead, and what a frightful condition that is, and to what horror yet greater does it lead! For wherever there is death the dead thing will go a stage farther on. And what is that stage? Corruption. Only leave a corpse alone long enough, and it must corrupt. Flesh corrupts necessarily. Already there are some signs of corruption about every ungodly man: outward sin, and especially the inward sin of rejecting Christ, are a grievous corruption. Your worm has begun to devour, even the worm that never dies. Then will be reached another stage, for corruption must be cast into the fire. For utter rottenness the end must be burning. O sinner, your fire has begun to burn—the fire that will never be quenched, for sin is the kindling of hell. It is an awful thing to abide in death, and yet he that believeth not on Christ is condemned already, because he hath not believed on the Son of God. It is enough to make you spring from your seats, O ye that are unbelievers, to think that you are not waiting to be tried: you are condemned already. This is not a state of probation, as I often hear it said. Your probation is past. You are condemned already, because you have not believed on the Son of God; and death is upon you now. The sentence has already begun to take effect, and it will go on to the consummation of corruption, till at last the Lord shall say, "Bury my dead out of my sight," and you must be driven from the presence of the Lord and from the glory of his power. There is no life in you unless you have received Christ. Will you think of this, you thinkers? Only think of your being dead. Will you think of this, you ceremonialists, to whom the outward baptism, and the outward Lord's supper, and the church-going and the chapel-going are everything? Unless you have fed on Christ there is no life in you.

Then comes, in the next place, the further truth, namely, that *all who have received Jesus Christ to be to them their meat and drink have eternal life.* "Whoso eateth my flesh, and drinketh my blood, hath eternal life." I do not know how our brethren who doubt the final perseverance of the saints manage to escape from the plain teaching of the text. There are always ways of getting over everything; you can drive a coach and six, they say, through any form of human language. But it does seem to me that if I have eternal life I must eternally live, and cannot possibly die. If I have got eternal life, if words mean anything, I am an eternally saved man. If I have received Jesus Christ into my soul, I have the life in me which will no more die than the life of God, for God's own life is eternal life, and if I have received such life as his, how can I perish? I shall not be slain by sin: the life in me cannot sin, because it is born of God. The life in me will throw off the darts of tempta-tion if it be eternal life. There remains nothing for it but to shake off the death which often surrounds it by reason of the old man, and to mount up like a bird set free from its cage, singing because of its escape, singing in the joy of life, and winging its happy way upward to the throne of God.

Rejoice then, dear friend, that if you have received Christ, you have eternal life in actual possession at this moment. "I do not feel it sometimes," say you. Do not try to live by feeling. It is the most uncertain thing in the world; you might as well try to live by the barometer. Feeling goes up and down, up and down, and changes oftener than the moon. It is hard, uncomfortable living. Live by faith, for it is written, "the just shall live by faith." Your life is a life of trust. Keep to it.

"Ah, but I see so much about me that grieves me." Thank God it grieves you. If you see sin and it does not grieve you, it is a token of death; but if it grieves you, there is life still in you, notwithstanding all the death that surrounds it. You may sometimes have seen a spark in the midst of a heap of autumn leaves which are all damp and will not burn, but only smoulder and smoke, and yet that spark continues to live, and the very smother from the heap proves it is so. There is one who will not quench the smoking flax, but will fan it till it rises to a flame, and then it will devour the leaves which covered it, and dry up the damps which sought to destroy it.

Furthermore, if you believe in Jesus and have received him, you have gathered a life in which Christ giveth us the *victory*, even through his name—a life which will rise, and rise, and rise, and conquer all sin. The believer's inner life must come to absolute perfection, and tread every sin beneath its foot. Very different is this from the doctrine that a man who is a child of God may sin as he pleases and yet be saved. That doctrine is of the devil; but this is quite another doctrine, and ministers to holiness. The quickened man will not willingly and habitually sin, for his seed remaineth in him, and he cannot sin, be-cause he is born of God. The tone and tenor and bearing of his life will be towards holiness and not towards sin, and the Lord who is able to keep him from falling will preserve him to his eternal kingdom and glory, and he that has begun a good work in them will perfect it unto the day of Christ.

Our Lord having thus given us the negative and the positive in our text, tells us that his flesh and blood, or himself, received into the soul, are most efficient nourishment: in it is *satisfaction*. "My flesh is meat *indeed*." The Greek word is "truly," or, some say, "true meat." Now that which we eat for the body is not true meat. As George Herbert says, "When thou art at thy meat eat a bit, and then say, ' Earth to earth I commit.'" It is a deadly business. It is burying earth in earth, and that living grave of earth will be itself buried in earth by-and-by. The eating of material meat is the poor building up of a fabric that must ultimately crumble into nothingness. The meat we eat has all the elements of dissolution about it before we receive it, and it only feeds for a short time,—hence it is not meat indeed.

In the matter of mental food how much there is which is not bread, and can never satisfy the mind. There is nothing in the world that can fill a soul to the full save Jesus. Perhaps I address some thinker who has been trying to satisfy his soul by sniffing up the east wind of speculative philosophy. Ah, well, if you swallow a dose of Kant, or Hegel, Schleiermacher, or any one of those gentlemen, if you do not feel as if you had been eating bubbles and bladders, your mental constitution and mine differ greatly. There is nothing in them all but gas, or vapour less substantial. Why, a man may take down their books—a whole dozen of them—and devour their contents, and then say, "What is it? Is it not much ado about nothing? These thinkings are dreamings, vacuums, airy nothings." All the philosophies that ever were invented could not satisfy a soul. The worst of it is that many do not want to be satisfied. "We," say they, "would sooner be seekers after truth than finders of it." They somewhat differ from men of practical common sense who, ordinarily, would rather have money than earn it, and would rather eat their dinners than hunt for them. Still that is their way, and, if they like it, I suppose they must have it. Every creature after its own order. But if you want to be fed, dear friends, depend upon it nothing will feed you but Christ. There was a man of great appetite who lived many years ago, and he began to feast ravenously. He was such a drinker that I may say of him that he drank up Jordan at a draught, and he was such an eater, that, if you heard the story of what was brought to his table, you would be like the Queen of Sheba, utterly astonished, and say that the half was not told you. His name was Solomon, and he fed his soul with all the arts and sciences, and with all the poetries and luxuries of the age, nor did he refrain from laughter and wantonness. There was not a cup he did not drain, nor a dainty from any land, nor a fruit from any tree, of which he did not eat. Yet when he rose up from that abundant banquet, all he had to say was, "Vanity of vanities; all is vanity." I have seen a poor soul feed on Christ in a very humble cottage, upon a bed in a little room, where she has lain alone almost all day and all night long, year after year, with many aches and pains, and scarcely able to lift her hand to her head, with little but dry bread and a cup of water; and yet I have seen in that bedridden woman's pain-worn face a fulness of satisfaction. I have known her speak like one that had not a wish ungratified, nor a grief worth mentioning. I have beheld her when in her sufferings she could scarcely speak, and yet her every word was essential poetry when she spoke of *him*, her best beloved, who had filled her soul even to overflowing. There is no food *indeed*, no drink *indeed*, for soul and spirit, but that which you find in the incarnate God and in the sacrifice of Christ. O ye hungry, come ye hither and eat ye that which is good and let your soul delight itself in fatness. O ye thirsty, come ye hither, for behold the waters are flowing freely, and the wines on the lees are ready for you in Christ Jesus. That is what is bound up in feeding upon Jesus, there is satisfaction in him.

And then there is bound up with it one other matter, namely, *indwelling*. I go over the same ground again. The Lord Jesus says, "He that eateth my flesh, and drinketh my blood, dwelleth in me, and I in him." When you have eaten the bread, it dwells in you and you in it: it goes into you and it is in you; it becomes part of yourself, and you live by it and in its strength. It is a part of the fabric in which you dwell. Even so he that believes in Christ lives in Christ. He does not merely go to Christ; but he enters into Christ. I delight to remember that I am not merely under the shadow of my Lord, but, as David in the caverns of Engeddi, so does my soul hide herself right away in Jesus. We dwell in him, and are at home. Moreover he enters into us by our feeding upon him, so that he becomes our life, the spring of our being, the object of our desire, the motive force of our service. We are woven together—Christ warp and ourselves woof—woven together in a living loom, and so conjoined that it were hard to tell where *he* ends who has no end, and where we begin who are lost in him. We are less than the least of all saints, and yet members of *his* body who is Lord of all.

We must leave the mystery; remarking that if we have fed on Christ for ourselves, we have proof of what good meat it is we have fed on, and we shall always pray, "Lord, evermore give us this bread."

III. I want your attention for a few minutes while, in the third place, we consider WHAT REFLECTIONS ARISE OUT OF THIS TRUTH. I will simply throw them out for you to turn over for yourselves. They occurred to me when I was hearing a brother preach upon a kindred subject. They took hold of my soul; may they prove useful to you.

And the first was this. If I have a life that feeds on Christ *what a wonderful life it must be.* My bodily life is wonderful, yet it only feeds on the fruits of the earth. My mental life is a marvel, but I know that I can build it up with literature and thought. Above all these I have a life which cannot feed on anything but the flesh and blood of the Son of God. What a life that must be! What a wonderful being a man is when God is in him. I almost reverence the meanest saint when I think of this, for he bears about with him not a Koh-i-noor, but a gem of life, compared with which the queenly diamond pales into a glittering vanity. O love divine, dost thou tabernacle in the sons of men! I have been speaking of mysteries, but I ask you to explain which is the greater mystery, the incarnation of God in Christ or the indwelling of the Holy Ghost in believers? They are two wondrous stoops of Deity, which can only be likened to each other, being each one without other parallel. The spiritual life given to the regenerate must be a life of inconceivable excellence and heavenliness since it can only feed on Christ himself.

The next thought is, if we have the life that feeds on such meat as this, *how strong it must be.* They say of such-and-such men that they may well be strong, seeing what good food they have. Ay, but see what food *we* have; how strong we must be. Do we know our own strength? I do not mean our natural strength, for that is weakness, but I mean the strength which lies in the new nature when it has fed on Christ. O brethren, we are strong to do; we are strong to be; we are strong to suffer. And to take an easy illustration of this—the one that occurs to me first—look at how the saints have suffered. Take down "Foxe's Book of Martyrs": read of Marcus Arethusa, stung to death by wasps without a sigh. Think of Blandina tossed on the horns of bulls, exposed in a red-hot iron chair, and yet never flinching. Give up Christ?

They never dreamed of such a thing. Think of Lawrence on the gridiron, and other heroes innumerable, who were made strong because Christ was in them Ay, and turn to humble men and women, over yonder there in Smithfield, who could clap their hands while every finger burned like a candle, and could shout "None but Christ, none but Christ." Why, they fed on the flesh and blood of Christ, and that made them mighty. They were tortured on the rack like Anne Askew, and yet they scorned to yield. Brave woman! the priests and the friars could not vanquish her. Neither could all the Bishop Bonners in the world burn Christ out of poor Tomkins. When Bonner held the poor man's finger over the candle and said, "How will you like that in every single limb of your body?" Tomkins smiled on the bishop and said that he forgave him the cruelty that he was doing him. Christ in a man makes him a partaker of divine strength. Do you not think, my brethren, that as you are not called to suffer you ought to lay out your strength in the line of doing and giving, and self-denial, and serving Christ by holy living? Certainly you should try to do so, and your strength will be found equal to it. You do not know how strong you are, but Paul shall tell you—"I can do all things through Christ that strengtheneth me." Well may you do all things if you have fed on him who is all, and in all.

Then a third reflection crossed my mind. If we have a life that feeds on this, *how immortal it must be.* We have a text to prove that, and we have given it to you already—"He that believeth on him hath everlasting life." When a man has nothing but bad food, you do not wonder that he dies. It is little marvel that they died by millions in India and China, considering how little nourishment they had during the famine. But if you and I eat Christ, eat the incarnate God and drink his blood, how can we die? What, kill a man that has even a particle of Christ in him! The devil cannot do it: he knows his master. And what does Christ say? "I give unto my sheep eternal life; and they shall never perish, neither shall any man pluck them out of my hand." Oh, blessed truth! We live, not only because our life is itself eternal, but because it feeds on eternal meat. We keep on receiving Christ day by day, for we live upon him: eating is not a work that we finished five-and-twenty years ago, but we continue to feed upon Jesus, and therefore we live. Feeding upon Christ does not mean being converted and then saying, "I am safe, and have no more need to care." Ah, no. It means beginning to receive him in conversion, and continuing to feed upon him evermore; and they who do this may be sure that their life is immortal.

The next thought that struck me was this: if we feed on such meat as this, *how that life must develop.* I do not quite see in myself, and I may say that I do not see in some believers, the full result I should like to see from such food. Has this man been eating such divine food? Let us hear him. He cries, "My leanness, my leanness, woe unto me." He is doing Christ's work spasmodically, feebly, sleepily. He does it without joy, and is soon weary. Is this all he is going to do? Is this all he is going to be? Oh no, brethren, "it doth not yet appear what we shall be." We shall grow; we shall grow. When I hear a man talk about being perfect in the flesh, I hope for the best, and trust that he is not wilfully lying. At any rate, I do not believe him. I would like to *see* his perfection rather than to hear him talk about it. I have generally found that when a cart needs a bell it is a dust cart. I never knew the people of the Bank of England ring a bell when they were going through the streets with bullion, and I do not think it is likely that a man who has much grace will boast of it. Yet I do believe that we can be developed into something very wonderful. A man may grow in grace, and in the knowledge of the Lord till his conversation is in heaven, and he becomes wholly consecrated to the Lord, hating sin, and living like Enoch, who walked with God. There have been such men, and there are such men and women among us still, whose lives glitter with the light of God; why should not we be like them? They are stars in God's firmament, and they shine in the glory of the Most High. The Lord grant us that, feeding on the divine meat, we may develop till the image of Jesus is perfected in us.

And, lastly, he who is thus fed, dear friends, *what company he must keep!* "He that eateth my flesh, and drinketh my blood, dwelleth in me," saith Christ, "and I in him." What heavenly company is this! He goes home at night to his poor family, perhaps, and there is nothing great about his house that you can see; but if your eyes are opened you will see that it is a king's palace, and if you are one of the Lord's, and can step inside, you will see that he has "come to the general assembly and church of the firstborn whose names are written in heaven, and unto God the Judge of all, and unto the spirits of just men made perfect," because he that has Christ in him has heaven around him. All good things are attracted by Christ in man. Put down a little honey, and see how wasps and flies and bees come all around it. What is the sweetest honey in the universe? It is Christ; and if you have Christ in you, his name is as ointment poured forth, therefore do the virgins love him, and they will come where he is. I will tell you yet more,—Christ is never without God, and he that has Christ has the company of the Father. And Christ is never without the Spirit of God, for the Spirit of God is upon him; and he that has Christ is never without the Spirit. What divine society is this! Our Lord Jesus is never unattended by a retinue of sublime intelligences, and so if Christ be in you, he will give his angels charge over you to keep you in all your ways; they shall bear you up in their hands, lest you dash your foot against a stone. O Prince of the blood royal of heaven, O Peer of God's own kingdom, thou art more nearly related to the King of kings than the peers of the realm can be to the Queen, for are you not married to the Prince Imperial? Is he not coming to receive you to himself, that where he is you may be also? If you are feeding on him your union with him is complete. If he is your food, if he is your raiment, if he is your dwelling-place, if he is your all in all, methinks I may compare you to that angel of whom Milton sang, even Uriel, who dwelt in the centre of the sun. It is there we live—in the very substance and essence of all things, and all things move around us like satellites around a central globe, for we are a chosen generation, a royal priesthood, a peculiar people, inasmuch as we have fed on Christ, and Christ dwelleth in us and we in him.

I have not said anything to the unconverted, and yet I have meant it all for them. When you spread a dainty feast, you practically invite the family to come and dine. It is the very best way of enticing them. If they are hungry the meats on the table will make their mouths water, and they will long to partake. Oh, my hearers, whoever you may be, if your mouths water after Christ, come and have him, for he is free to every soul that hungers and thirsts after him.

The Lord give him to you at once, for Jesus's sake. Amen.

PORTION OF SCRIPTURE READ BEFORE SERMON—John vi. 41—71

HYMNS FROM "OUR OWN HYMN BOOK"—260, 820, 761.

THE SEVEN SNEEZES.

A Sermon

WRITTEN AT MENTONE, BY

C. H. SPURGEON,

"*The child sneezed seven times.*"—2 Kings iv. 34.

THE child was dead. Although he had been the special gift of divine promise and was therefore doubly prized by his parents, yet the little lad was not secure from the common hazards of life. He was in the harvest field in the heat of the day, and a sun-stroke smote him down. His father bade one of his young men carry him home, and he died on his mother's knees. The brave woman was heartbroken, but, being full of energy and spirit, she rode off to Elisha, the man of God, to tell him her sorrow, and to upbraid him with the short-lived blessing which had come to her through his prayers. She clung to the prophet in the hour of her bitter sorrow, and he with his whole heart sympathized in her motherly grief. He hastened to the chamber where the dead child was laid upon the bed, and there alone he exercised the sacred power of prayer: again and again he wrestled and at length prevailed, so that in the glad Shunammite's case it was true that "women received their dead raised to life again." Such is the power of faith when it uses the weapon of all prayer: even the gates of the grave cannot prevail against it.

The prophet's mode of operation when he lay upon the child and put his mouth upon the boy's mouth, "and his eyes upon his eyes, and his hands upon his hands," is full of instruction. Spiritual life is the gift of God, but if the dead are to be raised by our means we must enter into hearty sympathy with them; we must create spiritual contact, and become in a great measure identified with those whom we would bless. The Holy Ghost works by those who feel that they would lay down their own lives for the good of others, and would impart to them not only their goods and their instructions, but themselves also, if by any means they might save some. O for more Elishas, for then we should see more sinners raised from their death in sin.

The first clear evidence that the child was restored to life was his sneezing. Doubtless, it greatly rejoiced the prophet's heart. We, too, who are seeking the good of others will greatly exult if we are favoured to see gracious tokens in those for whose good we labour. At all gospel

No. 1,461.

meetings earnest people should be on the look-out for persons convinced of sin, aroused in conscience, or in any other manner made to feel the power of the life-giving Spirit. It will be well if these persons watch with instructed eyes, so that they do not look for what they will never see, nor overlook that which should give them full content. Of natural life we may discern the tokens more readily than those of spiritual life ; we need practice and experience in reference to this more mysterious matter, or we may cause great pain to ourselves and to those whom we would befriend. Possibly we may gather instruction from the signs of life which contented the prophet:—the child sneezed seven times.

This evidence of life was very *simple*. Nothing is freer from art than a sneeze. It is so far from being artificial that it is involuntary. As a rule we sneeze, not because we will, but because we must. No instruction, education, talent, or acquirement is necessary to a sneeze, nor even to a series of seven sneezes ; it is the act of a child, or of an illiterate peasant, quite as much as of a philosopher or a divine. Yet Elisha asked no further evidence of life. He did not require the little lad to repeat a psalm, or walk a mile, or climb a tree ; he knew that he was alive although the act of the newly-given life was of the most elementary kind. Just so let us feel thankful when we hear the first groan of distress or see the first tear of repentance. Hopefulness is a helpful element in the success of those who have to deal with seeking sinners. We ought not to expect too much in enquirers ; we ought not to be satisfied without signs of *life ;* but the faintest sign of life ought to encourage *us* and lead us to encourage *them.* Very little knowledge can be looked for in enquirers ; Elisha did not ask the child to say his catechism. Very little strength will be found in them; Elisha did not bid the child move the table, and the stool, and the candlestick with which the room was furnished. No, the sneeze proved life, though it was inarticulate, and the uninstructed expression of untrained vitality. Repentance for sin, desire after holiness, child-like trust in Jesus, tearful prayer, careful walking, delight in the word of God, and intense self-distrust are among the elementary tokens of life, the sneezes of those freshly raised from the dead. Such tokens are to be seen in all the truly living in Zion, whether old or young, and hence they are not proofs of *growth,* but of life, and it is life that we have to deal with at the first; growth is an after consideration. Elisha did not leave the child upon the bed till he had developed into a man, but as soon as he had heard him sneeze he said to the mother, "Take up thy son"; and we would earnestly say to every church in whose midst a soul has been born unto God, "Take up thy son." Receive the convert, though he be weak in the faith. Carry the lamb in thy bosom, cherish and nurture him till life has girded itself with manly strength.

This evidence of life was *in itself unpleasant.* To the child it was no pleasure to sneeze. We should most of us prefer to be excused from sneezing seven times. Many of the surest marks of the new life are by no means pleasurable. The regenerate are not at once happy; on the other hand, they are often in great bitterness for their sins, and in sore anguish because they have pierced their Saviour. The divine life is not born into the world without pangs. When a man has been nearly drowned, and animation is restored by rubbing, the first movements of the blood within the veins causes tingling and other sensations which are exquisitely painful. Sin causes numbness of soul, and this is attended by an absence of sensation; this is changed when life comes with its look of faith, for the first result is that men look on him whom they have pierced, and mourn for him. Some regard pleasurable emotions as the clearest signs of grace, but they are not so. "I am so happy," is frequently a far less certain token than "I am so grieved because I have sinned." We do not think much of the song of "Happy day," unless it has been preceded by the mournful ditty:

"O that my load of sin were gone!"

A sneeze, again, is not very musical to those who hear it, and so the first signs of grace are not in themselves pleasing to those who are watching for souls. Our minds may be greatly pained to see the sorrow and despondency of the stricken heart, and yet that which we see may be none the less a certain sign of renewed life. We cannot take delight in heart-break and convulsion of soul when considered in themselves; on the contrary, our earnest endeavour is to apply the balm of the gospel and remove such pains; yet are they among the most assured marks of the life of God in the soul in its earlier stages, and we ought to be thankful whenever we see them. That which worldlings condemn as melancholy is often to us a hopeful sign of thoughtfulness; and the self-despair which the ignorant deplore is cause for congratulation among those who pray for conversions. We delight in the sorrows of penitents because of their results, otherwise we take no delight in human grief, but the very reverse.

"The child sneezed seven times," the evidences of life were very *monotonous*. Again and again there came a sneeze and nothing else. No song, no note of music, not even one soft word, but sneeze, sneeze, sneeze, seven times. Yet the noises wearied not the prophet, who was too glad to hear the sounds of life to be very particular about their musical character. The child lived, and that was enough for him. Much of the talk of enquirers is very wearisome; they tell the same melancholy tale over and over again. Answered a score times, they return to the same questions and repeat the same doubts. If one were seeking interest and variety, he would not look for it in the painful repetitions of persons under conviction of sin: though when we are watching for men's souls we do not grow weary, yet in themselves the utterances of the newly awakened are frequently among the most tiresome of communications. They are often difficult to understand, involved, confused, and even absurd; they frequently betray culpable ignorance and sinful obstinacy, combined with pride, unbelief, and self-will; and yet in them there is a secret something which betokens an awakening to the higher life; and therefore we cheerfully lend our ear. After days of exhortation and consolation we find them still floundering in the slough of despond, sticking fast in the mire, out of which they seem half unwilling to be drawn; we must render them the same help over and over again, and point out the stepping stones for the hundredth time. Better that our service should be monotonous than that a soul should perish. The poor child may sneeze seven times if it will, and we will gladly hear it, for it is a joy thus to know that it lives ; and our poor neighbour may repeat his painful story until seventy times seven, if therein we can discover traces of the work of the Spirit upon his soul. Let us not be disappointed because at the first we get so little which is interesting from young converts. We are not examining them for the ministry, we are only looking for evidences of spiritual life : to apply to them the tests which would be proper enough for a doctor of divinity would be both cruel and ridiculous. In preachers of the gospel we expect variety, and wish we could have more of it, but from the babe in grace we are quite content to hear a cry, and a cry is not a subject for musical variations any more than a sneeze.

Yet the sound which entered the prophet's ear was a *sure* token of life, and we must not be content with any doubtful or merely hopeful signs. We want evidences *of life*, and these we must have. We long to see our friends really and truly saved. Do but prove to us that they have passed from death unto life, and we rejoice in the lowest form of that proof, but with less than this we cannot be quiet. Mere resolves to reform, or even reform itself, will not end our anxiety. No fine talk, or expressed emotion, or remarkable excitement will at all content us, we want them to be converted, to be born again from above, to be made new creatures in Christ Jesus. The child might have been washed and dressed in his best clothes, but this would not have fulfilled the prophet's desire ; the lad might have been decked with a chaplet of flowers, and his young cheeks might have been rouged into the imitation of a ruddy blush, but the holy man would have remained unsatisfied : he must have a sign of life. However simple, it must assuredly be a *life-token*, or it would be in vain. Nothing could have been more conclusive than a sneeze. We remember a case in which a loving watcher fancied that a corpse moved its arm, but it was only imagination seconding the wish of affection ; there could, however, be no room for a mistake in a sneeze, much less in seven sneezes ; the prophet might safely call in the mother and commit to her care her undoubtedly living boy. So we also ask for indisputable marks of grace, and till we see them we shall still pray and watch and feel painful anxiety.

So far we have kept to the text, and as our space is limited we can only add these few precepts. Let the Lord's living ones believe that he can raise the spiritually dead. Let them make the ungodly their daily care. Let them bring them where souls are quickened—namely, under the sound of the gospel ; and then let them prayerfully and wisely watch for results. The more watchers in a congregation the better; they will be the preacher's best allies, and greatly increase the fruit of his labours. What sayest thou, dear friend in Christ, canst thou not attempt this service ? It requires graces rather than gifts, affection rather than talent. Rouse thyself to the delightful service, and watch until thou seest the signs of spiritual vitality. However unnoticed by others, let them not escape thine eye and ear and heart, but be ready to take care of the newly-quickened one, even if there be no more to be said of him than that "the child sneezed seven times."

Metropolitan Tabernacle Pulpit.

EYES OPENED.

DELIVERED BY

C. H. SPURGEON,

AT THE METROPOLITAN TABERNACLE, NEWINGTON.

" And God opened her eyes."—Genesis xxi. 19.

THERE was a well of water close to Hagar all the while though she saw it not. God did not cleave the earth and cause new waters to gush forth, nor was there need. The well was there already, but for all practical purposes it might not have been there, for she could not see it. The water was spent in her bottle, her child was dying with thirst, and she herself was ready to faint, and yet the cool spring was bubbling up hard by the spot. It was needful that she should see the well, quite as needful as that the well should be there, and therefore the Lord in great compassion led her to see it, or as the text puts it, " God opened her eyes."

This was a small matter compared with the creation of a new fountain, but our God does very little things as well as very great things when there is need for them. The same God who divides the Red Sea, and makes the Jordan to be dried up, opens a poor woman's eyes. The same God who came with all his chariots of fire to Paran, and with all his holy ones to Sinai, and made the mountain utterly to smoke in his presence, is he of whom we read, "and God opened Hagar's eyes." The infinite Lord is at home in doing little things; he counts the stars, but he also numbers the hairs of our heads. Remember that the same God who moulded the orb on which we dwell also fashions every tiny dewdrop, and he who makes the lightning bolt to fly through the midst of heaven wings every butterfly and guides every minnow in the brooklet. He prepared a great fish to swallow Jonah, but he also prepared a little worm to destroy the gourd. How condescending he is, since he carefully attends to minor matters for his children, and not only kills for them the fatted calf, but puts shoes on their feet. Sometimes very little things become absolutely necessary, for they act as the hinges of history, the pivots upon which the future turns. How frequently the whole course of a man's career has been affected by a moment's thought. The word of a child has affected the destiny of an empire: the chance expression of a speaker, as men talk of chance, has fired races with a new passion, and changed times and shaken kingdoms.

89

The Lord worketh gloriously by agents and events small and despised. God, by opening Hagar's eyes, secured the existence of the Ishmaelitish race, which even to this day remaineth: from the little cometh the great.

There may be persons present who want but very little to enable them to enter into eternal life: they need only that their eyes should be opened. May the Lord grant them that favour. O that he may now bid many a Hagar see his salvation. Why should the thirsty souls wait any longer? Everything is ready: they are on the borders of salvation, but they need that their eyes should be opened. Our subject at this time shall be *the opening of eyes*, taking rather a wide range, because it is a wide subject, and hoping that both to those who see and to those who cannot see there may come a gracious opening of the spiritual eye.

I.   Our first head shall be that IF OUR EYES WERE FURTHER OPENED THE RESULT TO ANY ONE OF US WOULD BE VERY REMARKABLE. We are at present limited in our range of sight. This is true of our natural or physical vision, of our mental vision, and of our spiritual vision; and in each case when the range of sight is enlarged very remarkable discoveries are made. God has been pleased to open the natural eyes of mankind by the invention of optical instruments. What a discovery it was when first of all certain pieces of glass were arranged in connection with each other, and men began to peer into the stars! What a change has come over the knowledge of our race by the invention of the telescope! How much of truly devout, adoring thought, and of deep, intense, unutterable reverence has been born into the world by the Lord's having in this sense opened men's eyes! When he turned his telescope upon the nebulæ, and discovered that these were innumerable stars, what a hymn of praise must have burst from the reverent astronomer's heart. How infinite thou art, most glorious Lord! What wonders hast thou created! Let thy name be had in reverence for ever and ever.

Equally marvellous was the effect upon human knowledge when the microscope was invented. We could never have imagined what wonders of skill and of taste would be revealed by the magnifying glass, and what marvels of beauty would be found compressed within a space too small to measure. Who dreamed that a butterfly's wing would display art and wisdom, and a delicacy never to be rivalled by human workmanship. The most delicate work of art is rough, crude, raw compared with the commonest object in nature; the one is the production of man, the other the handiwork of God. Spend an evening with the microscope, and if your heart be right, you will lift your eye away from the glass to heaven, and exclaim, "Great God, thou art as wonderful in the little as thou art in the great, and as much to be praised for the minute as for the magnificent." While we say, "Great art thou, O God, for thou madest the great and wide sea, and the leviathan whose lot it is to play therein"; we feel that we can also say, "Great art thou, O Lord, for thou madest the drop of water and hast filled it with living things innumerable." Our physical eyes thus opened by either glass reveal strange marvels, and we may infer from this fact that the opening of our mental and spiritual eyes will discover to us equal wonders in other domains, and thus increase our reverence and love towards God.

Suppose, dear brethren, that our eyes could be opened as to all *our past lives*. We have seen them, for we have travelled through them; but it was very cloudy when I went that way; I do not know how it was with you. None of us have our eyes thoroughly opened yet; we have hitherto been travelling through life as men who journey in a mist. Even the things which have come close to us, and have most affected us, have been hidden, as it were, in that which is not light, but darkness visible. And now, if we could look back upon the whole length of life, forty, or fifty, or sixty, or seventy years, with our eyes opened, how singular it would look! Our childhood—how different that period would now appear with God's light upon it. Those early struggles for a livelihood : we thought them hard, but we already begin to see what discipline there was in them, and how necessary they were for us. Those losses and crosses,—why even with our present partial sight we can see how much they were for our good. Yet there remain in life some singular things which we cannot as yet explain. Why was the favourite son taken away just when all our hopes were to have been fulfilled in him? Why was the husband struck down when the little children were so dependent? Why was the wife removed when a mother's care was most needed? Why fell that daughter sick so suddenly? Why were we ourselves balked in the moment of success? If our eyes could be opened so that we could see what would have been if things had gone differently we should all of us thank God that our lives were ordered as they have been. Have you never heard of one who was grievously lamenting the death of his favourite son, and falling asleep dreamed that he saw his boy alive again and that he beheld the life which that son would have led. It was such a life that he wept in his dream, and waking he blessed God that his son could never act according to what he had seen in vision; it was better that he should be dead. Repine no more, my sorrowing friend, for that which you would have kept in your bosom might have turned into a viper, that which you thought a treasure might have burned in your heart like coals of fire. Providence has ordered all things wisely, and if our eyes were opened we should bow in adoring reverence and magnify the God who hath done all things well. Our vision will be strengthened one day, so that we shall see the end from the beginning, and then we shall understand that the Lord maketh all things work together for good to them that love him.

And now suppose, again, our eyes should be opened upon *the future*. Ay, would you not like to spy into destiny? My curiosity is, probably, as great as yours, but still it is balanced by another faculty, and I protest that if I could see into to-morrow I would refuse to look. There is a desire in man to know what lines are written for him in the book of fate—whether they shall be bright or dark. Ah, dear friend, if your eyes could be opened as to all that is to happen, what would you do? If you were wise, and knew your future, you would commit it unto God: commit it to him though you do not know it. If you were wise you would wish to spend that future in his service if you knew it : spend it in his service though it is hidden from you. If you knew what would happen you would feel great need for faith; you do not know what will happen, but your need of faith is precisely the same. Trust you in God, come what may. This thing is certain—that to live unsaved, and unforgiven, is a very dangerous condition; God help you to get out of it at once by flying to Jesus for present salvation, and finding it on the spot. If you knew the future, it might make you idle, but it ought to make you diligent; if you knew the future, it might make you vain, but it should make you humble; if you knew the future, it might make you despondent, but it should make you trust. At any rate, knowing nothing at all about it, obey the voice of the Holy Ghost, who saith, "Commit thy way unto the Lord: trust also in him and he shall bring it to pass: and he shall bring forth thy righteousness as the light, and thy judgment as the noon-day."

If our eyes were opened, again, on another point, as to *the existence of angels*, we should see marvels. We will enter into no speculations; but what a sight would be before us if suddenly we could behold all the creatures that are round about us. The prophet of old prayed for a young man that his eyes might be opened, and immediately he saw horses of fire and chariots of fire round about Elisha. So do angels encircle the people of God. "The angel of the Lord encampeth round about them that fear him." "He shall give his angels charge over thee to keep thee in all thy ways: they shall bear thee up in their hands, lest thou dash thy foot against a stone." "Are they not all ministering spirits sent forth to minister to them that are heirs of salvation?" Millions of spiritual creatures walk this earth, both when we sleep and when we wake, and, if we were more like those pure spirits and more familiar with their Master, we should feel more gratitude to him for setting them round about us. Fear not, you are not alone, O child of God; your Father never calls off your body-guard. The evil spirit comes to tempt you, but the Lord has set his angel-sentinel to keep watch and ward that no ill may approach you. If the Lord opened the eyes of his greatly beloved servants to see how many of these mighty intelligences are silently guarding them, they would cease to complain of loneliness while in the midst of such a thronging ministry of willing friends.

And what, once more, if your eyes could be opened to look into *heaven?* Where it is we do not know. It is not very far away. At any rate, the glorified know what we do here, for they rejoice over one sinner that repents. Evidently, too, it takes not long to travel thither, for it was eventide when Jesus told the thief that he should be with him in paradise that very day, and you may be sure he was there. Oh, that we could see the place of unveiled glory and unmingled bliss as we shall see it in an instant when our Father's messenger, called death, shall strike the scales from our eyes, or rather, remove these dim optics with which we blunderingly see, and let our naked spirit gaze on the reality of things without these hindering eyes, which do but inform us of their outward show. Oh, what glories shall we then see! What splendour, above the light of the sun! What music, sweeter than harpers harping with their harps! What glory! Solomon knew not the like of this. There is the light of all lights, the delight of all delights, the heaven of heavens, the sun of our soul, our all in all,—Jesus upon the throne! What bliss to be with him—with him for ever and ever. Break, thou eternal morning! Break e'en now! Would God that, at least for once, till the day break and the shadows flee away, we had our eyes opened to see the glories beyond; then this poor world would be despised by us, we should forget its pains and pleasures, we should rise superior to all its influences, and we should rise to be heavenly ourselves. Wait awhile, brethren. Wait for a very little while. Wait a "wee and dinna weary," as the Scotchwoman said, and you shall see it all.

> "Just when thou wilt, O Bridegroom, say,
> 'Rise up, my love, and come away!'
> Open to me thy golden gate.
> Just when thou wilt, or soon or late."

So far, I have wandered from the text, but now in my second head I will come back to it.

II. IN SOME THINGS OUR EYES MUST BE OPENED. Those I have spoken about are desirable in a measure, but these are absolutely necessary. For instance, as to the divine salvation, our eyes must be opened. Hagar's case is a strange one. Picture it. She is thirsty, and her boy is dying: her instincts are quickened by her love to her child, and yet she cannot see a well of water. There it is! Close to her! Do you not see it? Just there. She cannot see it till her eyes are opened. It is as plain as a pikestaff, but she does not perceive it. Now, this is a graphic representation of the position of many a seeking sinner. There is the way of salvation, and, if there is anything plain in the world, it is that road of life. The act that twice two make four is not plainer than—believe in the Lord Jesus Christ and thou shalt be saved. Look unto the Son of God and live: what can be more simple? And yet nobody ever did understand the doctrine of "believe and live" till God opened his eyes. The well is there, but the thirsty soul cannot see it. Christ is there, but the sinner cannot see him. There is the fountain filled with blood, but he does not know how to wash in it. There stand the words, "Believe and live," simple words that need no explanation, legible by their own light, and so plain that the wayfaring man, though a fool, may comprehend them; yet, till the eternal light flashes upon the darkened eyeballs of the sinner, he cannot, and he will not perceive the self-evident truth.

Whence this inability to see? I suppose Hagar's eye was somewhat darkened by her grief. She was broken-hearted, poor woman, and therefore her eye was not so clear as usual. So some souls have such grief for sin, such sorrow for having offended God, such fear of wrath to come, that they cannot perceive the truth which would comfort them. What aileth thee, poor soul? What aileth thee? It is well that thou dost grieve for sin, but Christ has come to put it away. It is well that thou dost mourn thy lost estate, but Christ has come to save thee, and there he is right before thee if thou canst but see him.

It was unbelief, too, that darkened Hagar's eyes. God had appeared to her years before, you remember, when she was in very much the same plight, and he had then given her a promise that he would make of her son that was to be born a great nation. She might have reflected that this could never happen unless the boy's life was preserved, and since he could not live without a drink of water, she should have felt confident that water would be forthcoming. She was unbelieving, but it is not ours to judge her; for, alas, we are unbelieving too. Anxious soul, is that thy case? Oh, if thou couldst believe ! Truly, thou hast good cause. It should not be hard to believe what God says, for he cannot lie; but, still, unbelief darkens many an eye.

There are many who cannot see because of self-conceit. When great self feasts his eye upon his own good works or religious performances, of course he cannot see the way of salvation by Christ alone. The Lord take these scales from thy eyes, poor sinner, for self is a great maker of darkness. Nothing more surely holds a soul in gloom than a conceit of its own powers. How I wish I could so put the gospel as to win men from self. I preach the plan of salvation as plainly as ever I can. I use very homely metaphors. I have sometimes even employed what the more refined call vulgar expressions: I would be more vulgar still, if I could thereby help a soul to see Christ. I tell you Jesus is near to you, and within your reach, and that salvation is close at your foot. You have but to trust in the Lord Jesus Christ, and you shall be saved. But I know that, after all is said and done, if you ever see Christ it will be because the Holy Spirit opens your eyes. I cannot open them, nor any other mortal man ; for since the world began it hath not been known that any man has opened the eyes of one that was born blind. Oh, that the Lord would be pleased now to open the eye of every sinner here to see salvation in the atoning blood of Jesus Christ, the Son of God.

III. I must leave that point, and finish with one more. IN OUR PRESENT CASE IT IS VERY DESIRABLE THAT OUR EYES SHOULD BE OPENED. To many it is imperatively needful at this very moment, for if not now recovered from their blindness they will die in their sins. In this great throng there are some to whom it is pre-eminently desirable that their eyes should be opened at once to see what the inevitable result of their present mode of life will be, for their blindness is the source of great peril to them. That young gentleman who is spending his money upon the racecourse and loose society, I should think he might see with half an eye what will come of his conduct. The devil never runs express trains to hell: there is no need for it, for you can go there fast enough by race-horses. The turf has furnished to many an express method of ruining their fortunes and their souls. Get into that line of things, and all it means, and all the society that goes with it, and your future needs no prophet. Many young men do not think till it is too late to think. I wish I could put a cool hand upon that hot brow and stop that young man and make him stand still and consider. O that the Lord would open his eyes. And that young woman who has begun to look (not much, as yet) on what is called gaiety. Ah, the Lord stay thee, my sister, and open thy eyes ere thou goest one step farther, for one step farther may be thy ruin. And that tradesman who has begun—no, he has not quite begun as yet,—but he is thinking about a course of trade which will land him in something more shameful than bankruptcy, I pray the Lord to open his eyes that he may see matters in the true light. I see a man before me who is about to commit moral suicide. O for a gleam of light just now, and a touch of that finger which can open blind eyes. I cannot particularize and go into every case, but I have upon me a strong impression that I am speaking to some young man whose future depends upon his prudent pausing and careful consideration before he puts his foot down again. One step more, and you fall. I beseech you, stand still and hear what God would speak to you now. Turn thee, turn thee from thy sin and seek thy Saviour now, and he will be found of thee at once, and there shall be a life honourable and bright before thee to his glory. But if thou go one step farther in the way in which the tempter's charms, like siren music, would entice thee, thou art lost for ever. God help thee, therefore, to stop, and may it be said of thee, " God opened his eyes."

Now, leaving all these themes of thought, I would remind you that we are about to gather at the communion table and there we would sit with opened eyes. Those who love the Lord cannot endure to sit as blind men in his palace, but they long for all the sight which grace can give them.

First, we would have opened eyes that we may *see Jesus to be very near us*. Do not think of him just now as if he were far away in heaven. He is there in his glorious personality, but his spiritual presence is here also. Did he not say, " Lo, I am with you alway;" and " If I go away I will come again"? He abides with us by his Spirit for ever. Come, let us sit while this sacramental feast is going on, and sing—

> " Amidst us our Belovèd stands,
> And bids us view his piercèd hands ;
> Points to his wounded feet and side,
> Blest emblems of the Crucified.

> "If now with eyes defiled and dim,
> We see the signs but see not *him*,
> Oh may his love the scales displace,
> And bid us see *him* face to face !

> " Our former transports we recount,
> When with him in the holy mount,
> These cause our souls to thirst anew,
> His marr'd but lovely face to view."

We desire that you may have your eyes opened to see *what you are in Christ*. You complain that you are black in yourselves; but you are most fair in him. You lament that you are so wandering: yes, but you are fixed in him. You mourn that you are so weak; yet you are strong in him. A good man went the other day to visit a poor child who was dying, a child whom the Lord had taught many things; and the dear little fellow as he put out his wasted hand said, " So strong in Christ." He could hardly lift a finger, and yet he knew that his weakness was clothed with power in Christ. We are poor puny things, but we can do all things through Christ. We are poor foolish things, but we are wise in Christ. We are good-for-nothing things, but yet we are so precious in Christ, so dear to God in Christ, as to be numbered with his jewels, and known as the Lord's peculiar portion. We are sinful creatures in ourselves, and yet we are perfect in Christ Jesus and complete in him. These are strong expressions, but as they are scriptural, they are assuredly true. How blessed we are in our covenant Head! The Lord open our eyes to see this.

Lastly, dear friend, may the Lord open your eyes to see *what you will be in him.* Ah, what will you be in Christ? In a very little while we shall be with him. Many of our members have gone home to Jesus, and one very earnest brother, very diligent in working for the Master, a young man of whom we expected much, has been swept away by the receding tide while bathing in the sea, but he has gone to his rest, I doubt not. Older friends have also ascended to God just lately, rejoicing to enter into the joy of the Lord. Between now and next month's communion some of us will, probably, have departed to the Father. Let our eyes be opened to behold by faith the glory soon to be revealed. It may almost make you laugh for joy to think of your head wearing a crown—that poor head of yours. These poor aching knees, and weary feet, there will be no more toil for them. That poor scantily furnished room, and hard fare, and narrow means, and weary labour will all be exchanged for mansions of rest, bread of bliss, and new wine of delight. You know each pavement stone between here and your house, for you come so often to the Tabernacle, but you will be walking the streets of gold before long to the eternal temple above. Instead of noisy streets you will traverse paths of rest, amid the songs of seraphs and the psalms of the redeemed, and that, perhaps, within a month. Yes, in less than it takes the moon to fill her horns you shall be where the Lord God and the Lamb are the eternal light. Certain of us are nearer heaven than we think. Let our hearts dance for joy at the bare thought of such speedy felicity. Let us go on our way blessing and magnifying him who has opened our eyes to see the glory which he has prepared for them that love him, which shall be ours ere long.

God bless you for Christ's sake.

PORTION OF SCRIPTURE READ BEFORE SERMON — Genesis xxi. 1—21.

HYMNS FROM "OUR OWN HYMN BOOK."—852, 785.

THE ROES AND THE HINDS.

A Sermon

WRITTEN AT MENTONE, BY

C. H. SPURGEON.

"By the roes, and by the hinds of the field."—Solomon's Song ii. 7.

THE spouse was in the full enjoyment of fellowship with her Beloved. Her joy was so great as almost to overpower her, and yet, so nearly does fear tread upon the heels of joy, she was filled with dread lest her bliss should come to an end. She feared lest others should disturb her Lord, for if he were grieved she would be grieved also, and if he departed the banquet of her delight would be over. She was afraid even of her friends, the daughters of Jerusalem; she knew that the best can interrupt fellowship as well as the worst, and therefore she adjured even Zion's daughters not to sin against Zion's King. Had they aroused her Beloved and broken his sacred peace she would not have found a recompense in their company, but would rather have regarded them with aversion, for having robbed her of her chief delight. The adjuration which she used is a choice specimen of oriental poetry: she charges them, not as we should prosaically do, by everything that is sacred and true, but "by the roes, and by the hinds of the field." So far as we understand her meaning we will endeavour to profit by it during our brief meditation. It touches one of the most mysterious points of the secret life of the believer, and we shall much need the guidance of the Holy Spirit while we endeavour to open up its meaning.

"The roes and the hinds of the field" are creatures of great BEAUTY. Who can gaze upon them as they wander among the bracken without an inward admiration? Now, since nothing can be more lovely than communion with Jesus, the spouse exhorts the daughters of Jerusalem by all the loveliest objects in nature to refrain from disturbing it. No one would wish to drive away the gazelle, but would feast his eyes upon it, and yet its graceful elegance can never be compared with that beauty of holiness, that comeliness of grace which are to be seen in fellowship with Jesus. It is beautiful from both sides; it is a lovely display of condescension for our beloved Lord to reveal himself to us, and on the other hand it is a charming manifestation of every admirable virtue for a believer to enter into fellowship with his Lord. He who would disturb such mutual intercourse must be devoid of spiritual taste, and blind to all which is most worthy of admiration.

As one delights to see the red deer in the open glades of the forest, and counts them the finest ornaments of the scene, so do men whose eyes are opened rejoice in the saints whose high communion with heaven

No. 1,463.

97

renders them beings of superior mould to common mortals. A soul in converse with its God is the admiration of angels. Was ever a lovelier sight seen than Jesus at the table with the beloved disciple leaning on his bosom? Is not Mary sitting at the Master's feet a picture worthy of the choicest art? Do nothing, then, O ye who joy in things of beauty, to mar the fellowship in which the rarest beauty dwells. Neither by worldly care, nor sin, nor trifling make even the slightest stir which might break the Beloved's repose. His restful presence is heaven below, and the best antepast of heaven above; in it we find everything that is pure, and lovely, and of good report. It is good, and only good. Why, then, O daughters of Jerusalem, should ye stir up our Beloved, and cause his adorable excellency to be hidden from us? Rather join with us in preserving a joy so fair, a bliss so comely.

The next thought suggested "by the roes, and by the hinds of the field" is that of TENDER INNOCENCE. These gentle creatures are so harmless, so defenceless, so timid, that he must have a soulless soul who would do them harm or cause them fright. By all, then, that is tender the spouse beseeches her friends not to disturb her Beloved. He is so good, so kind, so holy, harmless, and undefiled, that the most indifferent ought to be ashamed to molest his rest. About him there is nothing to provoke offence, and everything to forbid it. He is a man of sorrows and acquainted with grief; he gave his back to the smiters, and his cheeks to them that plucked off the hair, he hid not his face from shame and spitting. Being reviled he reviled not again, but in his death agonies he prayed for his enemies. Who, then, could find cause for offence in him? Do not his wounds ward off the blows which might be challenged had he been of another character? Who will wish to vex the Lamb of God? Go elsewhere, ye hunters! "The hind of the morning" has already sweated great drops of blood falling to the ground. When dogs compassed him and the assembly of the wicked enclosed him he felt the full of grief—will ye afflict him yet again?

In fellowship with Jesus there is a tenderness which ought to disarm all opposition, and even command respectful deference. A soul communing with the Son of God challenges no enmity. The world may rise against proselyting zeal, or defiant controversy, or ostentatious ceremonialism, for these have prominence and power, and are fair game for martial spirits: but fellowship is quiet, retiring, unobtrusive, harmless. The saints who most abound in it are of a tender spirit, fearful to offend, non-resistant, and patient—surely it would be a superfluity of cruelty to wish to deprive them of their unselfish happiness, which deprives no heart of a drop of pleasure, and costs no eye a tear. Rather let even those who are most indifferent to religion pay a generous respect to those who find their delight in it. Though the worldling may care nothing for the love which overpowers the believer's ravished spirit, let him tread with reverent care when he passes the closet of devotion, or hears a stray note from the song of meditative gratitude. Rough men have paused when they have suddenly come upon a fair gazelle grazing in a secluded spot: charmed at the sight of such tender loveliness they have scarcely dared to move a foot lest they should alarm the gentle roe; and some such feeling may well forbid the harsh criticism or the vulgar laugh when even the infidel beholds a sincere heart in converse with its Lord. As for those of us who know the blessedness of fellowship with Jesus, it behoves us to be doubly jealous of our words and deeds, lest in a single instance we offend one of the Redeemer's little ones, and cause him to lose even for an hour his delight in the Lord. How often are Christians careless about this; till at the sight of some professors the more spiritual may well take alarm, and cry out in anguish, "I charge *you*, O ye daughters of Jerusalem, by the roes, and by the hinds of the field, that ye stir not up, nor awake my love, till he please."

A third thought most certainly had place in the mind of the anxious spouse; she meant to adjure and persuade her friends to silence by everything which sets forth LOVE. The lilies and the roes have always been sacred to love. The poet of the Canticles had elsewhere used the symbol of the text to set forth married love. " Let her be as the loving hind and pleasant roe " (Prov. v. 19). If ever there was true love in all this selfish world, it is the love of Jesus first, and next the love of his people. As for his love, it passeth the love of women, many waters cannot quench it, neither can the floods drown it ; and as for the love of the church, he who best knows it says, " How fair is thy love, my sister, my spouse! How much better is thy love than wine ! and the smell of thine ointment than all spices !" If love, therefore, may plead immunity from war, and ask to have its quietude respected, the spouse used a good argument when she pleaded " by the roes and by the hinds of the field," that her royal Bridegroom's rest of love might not be invaded. If you love, or are loved, or wish to be loved, have a reverent regard for those who commune with Jesus, for their souls take their fill of love, and to drive them from their bliss would be inexcusable barbarity. O ye who have any hearts to feel for others, do not cause the bitterest of sorrow by depriving a sanctified soul of the sweetest of delights. Draw not nigh hither with idle tale, or wanton speech, or empty mirth : the place whereon thou standest is holy ground, for surely God is in that place where a heart enamoured of the altogether Lovely One delights itself in the Lord.

O that all believers were so anxious to retain the enjoyment of divine love that they would warn off every intruder, whoever he might be. The daughters of Jerusalem were welcome to visit the spouse at fitting times, she even on another occasion bade them carry a message for her to her Beloved One, and gave them a full description of his surpassing charms, but when her Lord was with her at the banquet, she only asked of them that they would not come between her and the sunshine of his presence. Nor do we wonder at her jealous fear, for we have had a sip of those sweets which she had tasted, and we would sooner lose all else than lose the luxury of love divine. It is such joy as cannot be imagined by those who have never partaken of it, such joy as can never be rivalled even in the paradise above, if in that place there be any other joy than that which springs from divine love. Let none, then, deprive us of its continued enjoyment. By the sanctities of true love let every friendly mind assist us to preserve the hallowed quiet so essential to communion with our Lord.

Once more, upon the very surface of the figure lies the idea of *delicate sensitiveness.* The roes and the hinds of the field are soon away if anything occurs to disturb them. In this respect they set forth to the life the speediness with which the Beloved departs when he is annoyed by sin. He is as a roe or a young hart, for this quality among many others that while "he comes leaping upon the mountains, skipping upon the hills," he also soon withdraws himself and is gone. Ah, then his spouse bewails his absence, saying, "I sought him, but I could not find him; I called him, but he gave me no answer." The Lord our God is a jealous God. In proportion to the fire of love is the heat of jealousy, and therefore our Lord Jesus will not brook a wandering affection in those greatly beloved ones to whom he manifests himself. It needs constant watchfulness to maintain constant fellowship. Hence the spouse entreats and beseeches those who came near her not to give umbrage to her Lord. They might do this unwittingly, hence she warns them; they might do it in wanton carelessness, hence she "charges" them. She would have them speak softly and move gently, lest he should be disturbed. Should we not feel a like anxiety that nothing in our families, or in any of our relations or connections should be tolerated by us so as to envelope us in the wrong, and grieve our Lord? Should we not specially watch every thought of our mind, desire of our heart, word of our tongue, and deed of our hand, lest any of these should give him umbrage, and break our rapturous intercourse? If we would be favoured above others we must be more on our guard than others are. He who becomes "a man greatly beloved" must needs keep his heart with sevenfold diligence, for to whom much is given of him much will be required. Kings will bear from common subjects behaviour which could not be endured in favourites; that which might cause but slight pain from an enemy will sorely wound if it come from a friend. Therefore the favoured spouse may well use in her entreaty the name of the most tenderly susceptible of love's favourites, and plead "by the roes, and by the hinds of the field."

Dear friend, do you know what intercourse with Jesus means? If so, imitate the spouse whenever you are in the enjoyment of it. Be jealous of yourself and all around you, that the Well-beloved may not be vexed. Aim at the maintenance of life-long communion. Remember how for centuries Enoch walked with God: our lives are but a span compared with his, why should we not always come up from the wilderness leaning on our Beloved? The Holy Ghost has almighty power. Let us ask and receive that our joy may be full.

If you do not understand this precious secret, may the Lord reveal it to you even now. You must first receive the Lord Jesus as your Saviour, or you can never know him as your Bridegroom. Faith must trust him before love can embrace him. You must be brought to be washed, or you can never be brought to be banqueted. Pant after the Redeemer as the hart panteth after the water brooks, and when you have drank of the water of life then shall you be as a hind let loose: then, too, your feet shall be like hinds' feet, and you shall be set upon your high places. When this shall have been made your own by experience you shall understand the text, and shall also breathe the prayer of another verse of the same song—"Make haste, my beloved, and be thou like to a roe or to a young hart upon the mountains of spices."

Metropolitan Tabernacle Pulpit.

THE RISING SUN.

A Sermon

DELIVERED BY

C. H. SPURGEON,

AT THE METROPOLITAN TABERNACLE, NEWINGTON.

"But unto you that fear my name shall the Sun of righteousness arise with healing in his wings; and ye shall go forth, and grow up as calves of the stall."—Malachi iv. 2.

THE Jews expected that the coming of the Messiah would exalt every one of the Israelitish race. Their expectations were great, but they were also carnal and sensuous, since they looked for an earthly king, who would make the despised nation victorious over all its enemies, and enrich every man of Abraham's race. The Scriptures gave them no ground for such universal expectations, but quite the reverse, and in the chapter which is now before us the prophet explains that the coming of Christ would certainly be like the rising of the sun, full of glory and of brightness, but the results would not be the same to all. To those who thought that they were righteous, and despised others, but who were wicked in their conversation, the rising of that sun would bring a burning, withering day. Read the first verse. "The day cometh, that shall burn as an oven; and all the proud, yea, and all that do wickedly, shall be stubble." They shall not be like plants full of sap that would flourish in the tropical heat, but like stubble, which becomes drier and drier, until it takes fire: "and the day that cometh shall burn them up, saith the Lord, that it shall leave them neither root nor stock," for so might it be translated, and then the figure would be congruous throughout. It would scorch up the stubble-field in which there was no life, so intense would be the heat. Now that was the consequence of Christ's coming. The religion of the Jews at his coming was dry and dead, like stubble. The Pharisee thought that he was righteous because he put on a broad phylactery, and tithed anise, and mint, and cummin, and such trifles; the Sadducee thought much of himself because he was a man of common sense, a thinker, a rationalist; and other sectaries of that period found equally frivolous grounds for glorying. The ministry of Christ dried them right up, and they have ceased to be. We use the name of Pharisee and Sadducee to-day, but there is no person in the world who would like to wear

101

either name. The result of Christ's coming, by his Spirit as well as by his personal advent, is always much the same. Should the Spirit of God visit this church with revival it will not have an equally beneficial effect upon all. To some the rising of this sun will bring healing and blessing, but to others it will bring scorching and withering. Know ye not that the summertide which fills the corn and makes it hang its golden head, blushing in very modesty for the blessing which has come upon it, fetches up also the noxious weeds from their secret lairs. Tares gather encouragement from the sun as well as doth the wheat, and so the bad come to their ripeness as well as the good; but the ripeness of that which is bad is only a hurrying on to destruction: the dryness of the stubble is the preparation for its being utterly consumed. We may well pray for revival, but we must not suppose that to the mere formalist a revival will bring a blessing. It may possibly disgust him, and drive him from religion altogether. He will discover that he has no true religion, as he sees the work of the Spirit of God around him, and so the day of the Lord will to him "burn as an oven," and being proud and at the same time doing wickedly, his empty profession of religion will consume like the stubble.

The coming of the Messiah was to bring to another class a fulness of blessing, and it is of these we have to speak. "But unto you that fear my name shall the Sun of righteousness arise," not with scorching, but "with healing in his wings; and ye shall go forth,"—ye shall not be dried up, and burnt, and destroyed, but ye shall "grow up as calves of the stall." You shall obtain great blessings through the presence of your Lord. Two things will take up our attention; the first is, *the description of the people of God*—"Unto you that fear my name"; and the second is, *the blessing which is promised to them*—"the Sun of righteousness shall arise with healing in his wings; and ye shall go forth, and grow up as calves of the stall."

I. Here are TRUE SAINTS DESCRIBED. Let us look at them. The description may be divided into two parts. First, here is their abiding character—they fear the name of the Lord; and secondly, we gather from the text their accidental character, a character which is not always theirs, but into which they sometimes fall, namely, that they need healing, for were they not sick there would be no need of the promise that the Sun of righteousness should arise upon them with healing in his wings.

Notice then, first, *their abiding character*, they fear the name of the Lord. I am delighted to think that this promise is given to this particular character, for it thus comes to beginners in grace. "The fear of the Lord is the beginning of wisdom,"—it is not the highest grace, nor the loftiest attainment of the spiritual nature. Bless the Lord, therefore, ye weak and feeble ones, that the promise is given to you. You do fear the Lord. There are times when we ask ourselves whether we know the rapture of love, and we question greatly whether we ever had the assurance of faith, but even then we know that we have an awe of God. Jonah in the ship was in a very sinful state of mind, and was fleeing away from God, but yet he did not hesitate to say, "I am an Hebrew, and I fear the Lord." This is the abiding character of the saints in their worst state. If they backslide, they still fear the name of the Lord. They fear it at times very slavishly, with the spirit of bondage, but they do fear it. They lose the evidence of their sonship, and they cease to walk in the light, but still they have a fear of the Most High: they do not treat him lightly, they could not sin against him cheaply, there is still within their hearts a sense of his greatness. It generally assumes the form of a reverence of his person. They know there is a God, and they are sure that he made the heavens and the earth; they are equally clear that he is everywhere present, marking the ways of men. Others may blaspheme, but they cannot; others may sin and make merry with it, but sin costs them dear; others may feast themselves without apprehension, but they cannot, for they fear the Lord. I know that this expresses all true religion and has a very comprehensive meaning, but it suits my purpose just now to view it as a description of believers, which is true of them all, into whatever state they may come. They still fear the Lord. Now, soul, dost thou *tremble* before God? There is something in that. I do not ask thee whether thou tremblest at hell. That were no sign of grace, for what thief will not tremble at the gallows? I do not ask thee if thou art afraid of death. What mortal man is not, unless he has a good hope through grace? But dost thou tremble in the presence of God because thou hast offended him, and dost thou tremble in the presence of sin lest thou shouldst again offend him? Does it ever come over thee thus— "How can I do this great wickedness and sin against God?" Just as some men are kept back from crime by the fear of the law art thou kept back from folly by the fear of God? Just as some are impelled to energy by the fear of poverty, so art thou impelled to the divine service by a sense of the fact that not to serve him is to abide under his wrath? It is a low and small matter compared with the higher graces which God worketh in his people, but still it is a precious thing even to tremble at his word. I am glad to think that many of you have lately begun to fear God. I bless his name that you cannot live now as you once did. You are uneasy in your former careless way. I am right glad of it, and though I cannot be sure that this fear may not be a slavish fear, yet I hope for the best, and pray that it may ripen into that real fear of God which is always a work of grace in the soul, so that the promise of our text may belong to you.

Now, beloved, I have said that the description which is here given of the people of God denotes not only their abiding character, that they fear the Lord, but it also mentions *their occasional character*. They sometimes fall into a condition which they deplore, and this the text intimates, first, by the fact that the Sun of righteousness is to arise upon them; for this implies that they were in the dark until then. Whatever other light there may be, we every one of us know that until the sun rises our condition is one of comparative darkness. There are children of God who walk in darkness, dear children of God, too; indeed, I am inclined to think that every child of God gets into the dark sometimes. Some begin with brightness, and then they get a cloudy time in the middle of their experience, while others have their worst darkness at last. Knox and Luther had their sharpest temptations when they came to die. It has been well said that God sometimes puts his children to bed in the dark. It does not matter, for they wake up in the light, in the eternal morning; but a dark season usually happens to us somewhere between the new birth and heaven, perhaps to make the brightness all the brighter when the night shall be for ever ended. Are you in the dark at this moment, dear brother, and are you wondering at it because everybody else seems so lively in their religion? Dear sister, does it seem to you as if, though you have been a believer for years, you were never in a worse state than now, while others are rejoicing? Then ask yourself—Do you fear the Lord still? Is your soul humbled in the presence of his majesty, and have you a desire for his glory? Never despair; the Sun shall rise upon you soon.

Very clear is it from the text, too, that the children of God may sometimes be in ill health, for the Sun of righteousness is to arise upon them with healing in his wings, which would not be so needful a promise if they were not sick. A Christian may be bowed down with grievous spiritual maladies. His pulse may beat slowly, his heart may become feeble; he may be alive, and that may be about all; lethargy may seize him, palsy may make him tremble despondently, he may have wandered from his God. Alas! even an ague fit may be upon him, in which he shakes with unbelief from head to foot. It may be his eyes have become so blinded that he cannot see afar off; and his ears may be dull of hearing, and he may be like the fools in the psalm, whose souls abhorred all manner of meat. He may have put away from him the comforts of the promise, and he may be brought very low; yet he shall not die, but live, and proclaim the works of the Lord, for the soul sickness of a saint is not unto death. He shall be recovered from it, and he shall sing of the Lord whose name is "Jehovah Rophi, the Lord that healeth thee." Oh, child of God, if thou art in a sick and sorrowing state, cry mightily unto thy Lord, and the Sun of righteousness shall arise upon thee with healing in his wings.

Note again, that the children of God, according to our text, may be in a condition of bondage, for it is said that when the Sun of righteousness arises "they shall go forth as calves of the stall." Understand the figure. The calf in the stall is shut up, tied up with a halter at night, but when the sun rises the calf goes forth to the pasture; the young bullock is set free. So the child of God may be in bondage. The recollection of past sins and present unbelief may halter him up and keep him in the stall, but when the Lord reveals himself he is set free. Even true children of God may sometimes have to cry like Paul that they are sold under sin; they may forget the blood of redemption for a season, and think themselves still to be slaves, and yet be the true children of God. Hence the beauty of the promise that they shall go forth.

Yes, and there is more in the text. The children of God may be in such a state that they are not growing, for else we should not have the promise, "Ye shall go forth and grow up" when the Sun of righteousness shall shine. Do you, my dear brother, feel as if you had not grown in grace for months? You need the Sun of righteousness to shine upon you, and you will grow as the plants do. The trees are all bare in winter, and their boughs apparently sear and dead, but bring us the spring sun, and the buds will begin to swell, the leaves will appear, and the trees shall blossom and yield fruit. So shall it be with you.

The Lord has not left you. You may have stayed in your growth awhile, but you shall grow again.

Once more, the child of God may get into such a condition that he has lost his joy, for I will tell you a secret about the text: it might be, and probably ought to be, translated, for the Septuagint has it so, and the Hebrew has that force, "They shall go forth *and leap like calves of the stall.*" The young cattle may have been kept under cover in the winter, but when the sun brings the spring the fields are green, and you let the calves loose. There is joy about the creatures' movements. Even so when the Lord appears to his people, they move with delight, and dance for joy of heart. The Lord's love within them shall make them give expression to their joy. I pray that you may feel this intense delight in gospel liberty and leap for joy. Thus I have described the people to whom the promise comes.

II. My second and most pleasing duty is TO OPEN UP THE PROMISE ITSELF. "The Sun of righteousness shall arise." Child of God in the dark, in prison, ungrowing and unhappy, what a promise is here for you! "The Sun of righteousness shall arise." His rising is to do it all, there is nothing for you to do, no works for you to perform in order to get the needed blessing. The Sun of righteousness shall arise; now, the rising of the sun is one of the most wonderful things in nature, not merely for its grandeur and beauty, but for its sublime display of strength. Who could hold back the horses of the sun? What hand could block the golden wheel of his chariot, or bid him stay his course? The time is come for him to rise, and lo, he delights the world with dawn. Holy Spirit, such is thy power. When it is thy time to work who can stand against thee? As the sun floods the whole earth with his splendour, and no power can hinder his movements, so will the Holy Spirit work, and none can let him. Plead ye then this promise to-night and cry: "O Sun of righteousness, arise upon those that fear thee: come now in all thy majesty and wealth of grace: pour upon us thy light and heat and life, and fill this place with thy glory."

Now mark what will be the result of his rising. As soon as ever this sun is up and Christ begins to shine upon his people, they enjoy a clear light. They were in the dark before, but they are in the light now. I have been living for awhile in a country where the sun is everything. The temperature and the atmosphere are made salubrious and delicious, I had almost said celestial, by his presence. When he shines not the sick pine and the healthy are gloomy, but when clouds no longer veil his face we are as in the garden of the Lord. Everything depends upon the sun. Step down into a valley where he has not shone, and you will find frost; cross the street into the shade, and you shiver in the cold. So clear does the atmosphere become through the removal of all fogs and mists that sometimes we have seen a hundred miles across the sea, rising up like a fair vision, the mountains of distant Corsica. I cannot help using the illustration, because it is so distinctly before me. When the Sun of righteousness arises upon a Christian, and shines full upon him, he does not see islands a hundred miles away, but he sees the golden gates of the celestial city, and the King in his beauty, and the land that is very far off; for the presence of Christ clears the atmosphere, and enables us to see the invisible. Unto you that fear his name may the Sun of righteousness arise and give you just such clearness and light.

But according to the text, the Sun of righteousness, when it rises on those that fear the Lord, gives them healing. There is healing in its wings. By the wings of the sun are meant the beams that shoot up from it into the air, or seem to slant down from it when it is aloft in the sky. There is really healing to men's bodies in the sun. Have we not seen them come to the sunny land consumptive and doubled with weakness, and as they have sat in the sun and warmed themselves for a few weeks, the wound within the lung has begun to heal, and the consumptive man has breathed again, and you have seen that he would live. Some have gone thither who scarce could speak, and beneath the sun they began to speak again, like men whose youth has been renewed. The sun is the great physician. Where he enters not the physician will be needed, but where he shines men speedily revive. As for the Sun of righteousness, oh, how he heals the sick! I would like you sick Christians to sit in his sunlight by the year together, if you did nothing else but bask there, as animals delight to bask in the sun. The flowers know the sun, and they turn their cups to him and drink in of the health he gives them from his golden store. Oh, that we had as much sense to know the Sun of righteousness, that we might by prayer, and meditation, and holy living, bask and sun ourselves in his delicious beams. We shall be strong indeed if he rises upon us with healing in his wings. He has risen, but we wander into the shade: he has risen, but we get into the ice wells of worldliness and sin, and shut out his warmth, and then we wonder we are sick, but sick we always shall be till we come out into the light again, and Jesus shines on us from morn till eve.

I must not enlarge upon any one point, for my time is limited; but I would have you notice how the text says that when the Sun of righteousness shines the Christian gets his liberty. "Ye shall go forth." I have been staying where the invalid does not venture out if the wind blows, and if it is a little chill and the sun is not bright he must stay indoors or lose the benefit he has received; but when the sun is out and the air is calm, then he comes forth and leaves his bedroom, and is all alive once more. There are Christians who have been kept indoors a long time; they have not walked the length of the promise, nor spied out the breadth of the covenant, nor climbed to the top of Pisgah to gaze upon the landscape. O beloved, if the Sun of righteousness, even the Lord Jesus, shall shine upon you, you will go forth not only to enjoy Christian life, but to enter into Christian service, and you will go further afield to bring others to Christ.

Then you will begin to grow. That is another effect of the sun, and how wonderfully the sunlight makes things grow. Here we have in our hot-houses little plants that we think so wonderful that we show them to our friends, and put them on our tables as rarities, but I have seen them in the sunny south ten times as large growing in the open fields, because the sun has looked upon them. The rarities of our country are the common-places of the land of the sun. I have known Christians who have received a little faith and been perfectly astonished at it, and God has blessed them with a little love to Jesus, and they

have felt as though they were splendid saints; but if they lived in the
sunlight they might move mountains by their faith, and their love
would lead them to devote their whole life to Jesus, and yet they would
not be astonished. The Sun of righteousness can produce fruits rich
and rare. Our cold, sunless land, beneath its cloud and fog, what can
it yield in the winter? In more favoured parts of the earth, even in
our winter, the trees are golden with fruits. So is it with the soul.
What can it grow if it lives in worldliness? What can it produce if it
lives to itself? But when it knows the love of Jesus and the power of
his grace, even in its worst estate it brings forth the richest and the
rarest fruit to the glory of his grace.

I shall close by exhorting my fellow church members to live in the
sunlight. Get out of the shadows. There are dreary glens in this
world where the sun never shines : they are called glens of pleasure, and
sometimes the pale moon looks down on them with sickly ray; but the
saint knows the light of the sun from the light of the world's moon.
Get away from those chill places into the clear light. " But," says
one, " I did not know there were joys in religion." My dear friend, do
you know true religion then? for it is " a thing of beauty, and a joy
for ever." He who knows Christ has seen the sun, but till he has
known him he has seen but the glow-worm's glitter. Peace, deep peace,
he never knew who never knew the power of the blood; and joy, real
joy, such as angels call joy, he never knew who never trusted in the
Saviour's atoning sacrifice. Oh, come ye depressed and distressed and
despondent ones, whose religion has been slavery, and whose profession
has been bondage : get a true baptism into Christ by faith in him, and
when you have been plunged into the Godhead's deepest sea then shall
you know a joy and peace which pass all understanding. The world
gives them not: it cannot take them away. "Unto you that fear the
Lord, the Sun of righteousness shall arise with healing in his wings."

I would encourage those who fear the Lord a little, I mean the
seekers. Come ye into the light. Come and welcome, none will question your right. I never heard of anybody yet who said " I must not
sit in the sun; the sun is not mine." The lords of this world have
hedged in every acre, and there is scarce a sterile mountain side which
is not guarded with " trespassers beware." But they cannot hedge
in the blessed sunlight; no, not even for an hour. Through the poor
man's window, though the glass be broken and stuffed up with rags, a
beam of sunlight will pierce its way as gladly as into the halls of
monarchs : it shines on the beggar's rags as well as on the prince's
scarlet : it is free. When Diogenes bade Alexander get out of his sunlight he had a right to do so, for the sunlight belonged as much to
Diogenes in his tub as to Alexander who had conquered a world. O
meanest of the mean in thine own judgment, lowest of the low in thine
own esteem, guiltiest of the guilty as thy conscience calls thee before
God, know thou that the Sun of righteousness has risen, and his light
is free. Come into the sunlight; come into the sunlight! "Oh, but I
shall get better soon: I am sick, but I shall get better soon." Come
into the sunlight, man, for there is healing beneath the wings of the
Sun of righteousness, but nowhere else. "I am kindling a fire, I am
hoping that I may get warm by the sparks of my own kindling."

Come into the sunlight, man. What were all thy fires? Though thou shouldest set Lebanon upon a blaze, and take all the timber that ever grew on Sirion to make a pile thereof, what were it as compared with yonder mighty furnace of the sun, which has burnt on for ages, and will burn on till the last eye of mortal man shall have looked upon it? O soul, go not about with thy whims and thy fancies to save thyself: but come into the sunlight! Come into the sunlight, man! " But perhaps I may not." Who is the poorer if the sunlight shine on thee? There is enough for others even though it pour its floods on thee. The sun is no brighter if thou hast not his beams; he will be no duller though thou and a thousand like thee should lie by the century together basking in his light. So with Jesus. "In him dwelleth all the fulness of the Godhead bodily." If thou take all the mercy that can be wanted to lift thee up from the gates of hell to heaven itself he will have as much mercy left. If all the merit thou canst want to save thy condemned spirit and make thee into a child of God should be thine, as I pray it may, there will be as much merit left in Christ as ever. Why keep back? Why keep back? "But I am so base." Does not the sun shine on dunghills? May not the mercy of God shine on thee, thou dunghill sinner? Thou canst not be too low, thou canst not be too vile; the infinite mercy of God, like the infinite light of the sun, can reach thee. "Alas, I am dark." And what night was too dark for the sun to turn it into day? "Alas, I am cold." But what iceberg was too cold for the sun to thaw it? What winter was too severe for the sun to turn it into summer? Yield thyself up, thou icicle, yield to the sun, and it will melt thee. Yield thyself up, thou dead and shrivelled bough, to that dear sunbeam which waits to kiss thee now, and it will awaken life within thee, and warm thee till thou shalt be laden with rich fruit, to the praise and glory of the Sun of righteousness which has risen upon thee. The Lord grant it may be so with us all, for Jesus' sake. Amen.

PORTION OF SCRIPTURE READ BEFORE SERMON—Malachi iii. iv.

HYMNS FROM "OUR OWN HYMN BOOK"—795, 799, 19.

THE OIL AND THE VESSELS.

A Sermon

WRITTEN AT MENTONE, BY

C. H. SPURGEON.

"And it came to pass, when the vessels were full, that she said unto her son, Bring me yet a vessel. And he said unto her, There is not a vessel more. And the oil stayed."—2 Kings iv. 6.

So long as there were vessels to be filled the miraculous flow of the oil continued, and it only ceased when there were no more jars to contain it. The prophet spoke no word to stay the multiplying process, and the Lord did not set any bound to the bountiful marvel; the poor widow was not straitened in God, but in her supply of empty vessels. Nothing else in the universe restrained the flow of the oil: but the want of vessels to receive it stayed it at once. The vessels failed before the oil; our powers of receiving will give out long before God's power of bestowing.

This is true in reference to OUR PROVIDENTIAL CIRCUMSTANCES. So long as we have needs we shall have supplies, and we shall find our necessities exhausted far sooner than the divine bounty. In the wilderness there fell more manna than the tribes could eat, and there flowed more water than the hosts could drink, and so long as they were in a desert land and required this provision it was continued to them: when they reached Canaan and fed on the old corn of the land the special supplies ceased, but not till then. In the same manner also the Lord will feed his people till they need no more.

The widow's apparent source of supply was only one pot of oil, but this continued to stream forth as vessel by vessel was placed underneath it; so shall the little with which the Lord endows his poor people continue to furnish sufficient from day to day, till the last day of life, like the last vessel, shall have been filled. Some are not content with this, but would have the oil run beyond the last vessel, even after their deaths, never resting till they have hoarded their thousands, and have buried their hearts in gold dust. If the oil will but run till the last vessel is full, what more do we want? If providence secures us food and raiment till we end this mortal life, what more can we require?

Doubtless in the dispensation of wealth and other talents to his servants the Lord considers their capacities. If they had more vessels they should have more oil. The infinitely wise God knows that it is better for some men to be poor than rich; they would not be able to bear prosperity, and so the oil does not flow, because there is not a vessel to fill. If we are able to receive an earthly gift, it will then be a

No. 1,467.

good thing to us, and the Lord has declared that he will not withhold any good thing from those who walk uprightly; but a talent which we could not receive so as to use it properly would be only a curse to us, and hence he does not burden us with it. All that we can hold we shall have : all that we really need, all that we shall be sure to employ to his glory, all that will minister to our highest good, God will pour forth from his inexhaustible fulness, and only when he sees that the gifts would be wasted by becoming superfluities, or burdensome responsibilities, or occasions for temptation, will he restrain his power, and the oil shall be stayed. Rest assured that God's bounty will keep pace with your true capacity, and " verily thou shalt be fed."

The same principle holds good with regard to THE BESTOWAL OF SAVING GRACE. In a congregation the gospel is as the pot of oil, and those who receive from it are needy souls, desirous of the grace of God. Of these we have always too few in our assemblies. Many are the vessels of oil, filled to the brim and fastened down—the full Pharisee, the self-satisfied professor, and the proud worldling are such : for these the miracle of grace has no multiplying power, for they are ready to overflow even now. A full Christ is for empty sinners, and for empty sinners only, and as long as there is a really empty soul in a congregation so long will a blessing go forth with the word, and no longer. It is not our emptiness, but our fulness which can hinder the outgoings of free grace. While there is one soul conscious of sin and eager for pardon, grace will flow ; yea, while there is one heart weary of indifference and anxious to be wounded, grace will flow. " I feel," saith one, " exceedingly unfit to be saved." You are evidently empty, and there is room in you for the oil of grace. " Alas," cries a second, " I feel nothing at all. Even my own unfitness does not distress me." This only shows how utterly empty you are, and in you also the oil will find space for its flow. " Ah," sighs a third, " I have become sceptical, unbelief has made me hard as the nether mill-stone." In you also there is large storage for grace. Only be willing to receive. Stand like the oil-jar with opened mouth, waiting for the oil to pour forth from the miraculous pot. If the Lord hath made thee willing to receive he will not be long before he has given thee grace upon grace. O that we could meet with more emptied souls! Why should the Lord's wonders be cut short for lack of persons who need to have them wrought upon them ? Are there no needy souls about ? Have all men waxed rich, or is it a vain presumption which possesses so many hearts ? Hidden away in corners where they weep their eyes out because they cannot weep, and break their hearts because their hearts will not break, and cry before the Lord because they feel they cannot pray, or feel, or hate sin ; —hidden away in corners, I say, there are truly empty souls, and for these the heavenly oil is running still, is running *now*. " Blessed are they that do hunger and thirst after righteousness, for they shall be filled." No exception in the narrative before us was taken to any vessel so long as it was empty; there was one qualification, and only one, the power to receive indicated by emptiness. Come, then, ye needy souls, come to the eternal fountain and receive a wealth of blessing, freely given because ye need it, and because the Lord Jesus loves to bestow it.

The like is true with regard to OTHER SPIRITUAL BLESSINGS. All fulness dwells in our Lord Jesus, and, as he needs not grace for himself, it is stored up in him, that he may give it out to believers. The saints with one voice confess, " Of his fulness have all we received." The limit of his outpouring is our capacity to receive, and that limit is often set by our straitened prayers; " we have not because we ask not, or because we ask amiss." If our desires were more expanded, our receipts would be more extended. We fail to bring empty vessels, and therefore the oil is stayed. We do not sufficiently see our poverty, and do not therefore enlarge our longings. O for a heart insatiable for Christ, a soul more greedy than the grave itself, which is never satisfied: then would rivers of the heavenly oil flow in upon us, and we should be filled with all the fulness of God.

Frequently we limit the Holy One of Israel by our unbelief. Nothing hinders grace like this impoverishing vice. " He did not many mighty works there because of their unbelief." Unbelief declares it to be impossible that more oil should come from the oil-pot, and so refuses to bring more vessels under the pretence of a humble fear of presumption, thus robbing the soul and dishonouring the Lord. Shame on thee, thou mother of famine, thou drier up of flowing wells! What shall be done unto thee, thou lying traitor! What coals of juniper are fierce enough for thee, thou wicked unbelief? We mourn that our joy is departed, that our graces languish, that our usefulness is restrained. Whose fault is this? Is the Spirit of the Lord straitened? Are these his doings? Nay, verily, we have ourselves stayed the bottles of heaven. May infinite mercy save us from ourselves, and lead us now to " bring hither vessels, even empty vessels not a few."

Pride also has a horrible power to stay the divinely given oil. When on our knees we feel no pressing necessity, no urgent want, no special danger; on the contrary, we are rich and increased in goods, and have need of nothing. Do we wonder, then, that we are not refreshed and feel no delight in the holy exercise? Have we not heard the Lord saying, " Bring me yet a vessel"? And as we have answered, " There is not a vessel more," need we be surprised that the oil is stayed? The Lord save 'us from the parching influence of self-conceit. It will turn an Eden into a wilderness. Soul-poverty leads to fulness, but carnal security creates barrenness. The Holy Spirit delights to comfort every hungry heart, but the full soul loatheth the honeycomb of his consolations, and he leaves it to itself till it is famished and cries out for heavenly bread. Of this one thing let us be sure, that there is abundance of grace to be had so long as we hunger and thirst after it, and never shall a single willing heart be forced to cry, " The oil is stayed," so long as it has an empty vessel to bring.

The same truth will be proved in reference to THE PURPOSES OF GRACE IN THE WORLD. The fulness of divine grace will be equal to every demand upon it till the end of time. Men will never be saved apart from the atonement of our Lord Jesus, but never will that ransom price be found insufficient to redeem the souls that trust in the Redeemer.

"Dear dying Lamb, thy precious blood :
Shall never lose its power,
Till all the ransomed church of God
Be saved to sin no more."

Neither will his intercession lose any of its prevalence for those who come to God by him. To the last hour of time it shall never be said that a single sinner has sought his face in vain, or that an empty vessel has at last been found which Jesus cannot fill.

The power of the Holy Spirit to convict, convert, console, and sanctify shall also abide the same to the end of the age. Never shall there be found a weeping penitent whom he cannot cheer with a lively hope and lead to Jesus for eternal salvation, nor a struggling believer whom he cannot lead on to certain and complete victory. Perfection itself, he shall always be able to work in all the saints, even meetness for their holy heritage above. None of us should despond when we discover anew our own natural inability and deadness. Our hope was never based on created power; a lively hope has its foundation in the omnipotence of the Holy Spirit, and that cannot be the subject of question or of change. For the salvation of all the elect the sacred Trinity will work together till all shall be accomplished.

Whatever remains behind as to the purposes of God he has power to achieve. If there should stand before us a row of empty vessels bearing the names of Babylon overthrown, the Jews converted, the nations evangelized, the idols abolished, and so forth, we must by no means be disheartened, for all these vessels of promise shall be filled in due time. The church of the present day is feeble, and her supplies are quite inadequate to the enterprise before her, yet as out of one oil-pot many vessels were filled which were far greater than itself, so by his poor and despised church, through the foolishness of preaching, the Lord will fulfil his august designs and fill the universe with praise. " Fear not, little flock; for it is your Father's good pleasure to give you the kingdom." With this assurance believing men may boldly go forth among the heathen. The nations are empty vessels, and there are not a few of them; God has given us his blessing upon our cruse of oil, and all we have to do is to pour out and continue to pour out till there is not a vessel more. We are very far from that consummation yet. In our congregations all are not saved; even in our families many are not converted: we cannot say "there is not a vessel more," and, blessed be God, neither may we suspect that the oil will be stayed. With hopeful earnestness let us bring the empty vessels beneath the sacred outflow, that they may be filled.

How glorious will be the consummation when all the chosen shall be gathered in! Then there shall not remain a seeking soul to be saved, nor a praying heart to be comforted, nor a wandering sheep to be sought. Not a vessel shall be found throughout the universe needing to be filled, and then shall the oil of mercy cease to flow, and justice hold her court alone. Woe unto the ungodly in that day, for then the empty vessels shall be broken to shivers; as they would not receive the oil of love they shall be each one filled with the wine of wrath. From which terrible doom may infinite grace preserve each one of us. Amen.

Metropolitan Tabernacle Pulpit.

TWO SORTS OF HEARERS.

A Sermon

DELIVERED BY

C. H. SPURGEON,

AT THE METROPOLITAN TABERNACLE, NEWINGTON.

"But be ye doers of the word, and not hearers only, deceiving your own selves For if any be a hearer of the word, and not a doer, he is like unto a man beholding his natural face in a glass: For he beholdeth himself, and goeth his way, and straightway forgetteth what manner of man he was. But whoso looketh into the perfect law of liberty, and continueth therein, he being not a forgetful hearer, but a doer of the work, this man shall be blessed in his deed."—James i. 22—25.

JAMES has no speculations. "By their fruits ye shall know them," seems to have taken possession of his mind, and he is always demanding practical holiness. He is not satisfied with the buds of hearing, he wants the fruits of obedience. We need more of his practical spirit in this age, for there are certain ministers who are not content with sowing the old seed, the selfsame seed which, from the hand of apostles, confessors, fathers, reformers, and martyrs, produced a harvest unto God; but they spend their time in speculating as to whether the seed of tares grown under certain circumstances may not bring forth wheat; whether, at any rate, good wheat would not be the better for the admixture of just a little sprinkling of tare seed. We want somebody to take these various preachments, put them into a cauldron, boil them down, and see what is the essential practical product of them. Some of you may have seen in the newspapers a short time ago an article which fastened itself upon my mind—an article with regard to the moral state of Germany. The writer, himself a German, says that the scepticism of the professed preachers of the word, the continual doubts which have been suggested by scientific men and more especially by professedly religious men as to revelation, have now produced upon the German nation the most frightful consequences. The picture which he gives makes us fear that our Germanic friends are treading upon a volcano which may explode beneath their feet. The authority of the government has been so severely exercised that men begin to be weary of it; and, meanwhile, the authority of God has been put so much out of the question that the basis of society is undermined. I need not, however, ground my remarks upon that article, for the French revolution at the end of the last century remains in history as an enduring warning as to the dread effects of

113

philosophy when it has cast suspicion upon all religion and created a nation of infidels. I pray God that the like may not happen here; but the party of "modern thought" seem resolved upon repeating the experiment. So greatly is the just severity of God ignored, and so trifling an evil is sin made out to be, that if men were to be doers of what they hear, and to carry out what has been taught from certain professedly Christian pulpits, anarchy would be the result. Free-thinking always leads that way. God keep us from it.

While preachers too often toy with preaching, how much there is among hearers of the same fashion. Hearing is often merely a critical exercise, and the question after a sermon is not "How was that truth fitted to your case?" but "How did you like *him*?" as if that had anything to do with it. When you hear music, do you ask, "How did you like the trumpet?" No, it is the music—not the instrument, that your mind thinks about; yet will persons always consider the minister rather than his message. Many contrast one preacher with another, when they had better contrast themselves with the divine law. Thus hearing the gospel is degraded into a pastime, and judged to be little better than a theatrical entertainment. Such things must not be. Preachers must preach as for eternity, and look for fruit; and hearers must carry out what they hear, or otherwise the sacred ordinance of preaching will cease to be the channel of blessing, and will rather be an insult to God and a mockery to the souls of men. I shall, not at any very great length, but I hope with much earnestness, speak of two classes of hearers, the first, *the unblessed class*, and the second, *the class who*, according to the text, *are blessed in their deed.*

I. First, THE UNBLEST CLASS. They are hearers, but they are described as *hearers who are not doers.* They hear—some of them pretty regularly, others of them only now and then just to while away an hour; and they hear with considerable attention, because they appreciate good speaking. They are interested in doctrine, perhaps, having some little knowledge of the Christian system, and they like to discuss a point or two. Moreover, they are anxious to be able to say that they heard such a one preach, of whom a fame has gone abroad. But as to doing what they hear, that has not entered their minds. They have heard a sermon on repentance, but they have not repented. They have heard the gospel cry, "Believe!" but they have not believed. They know that he who believes purges himself from his old sins, yet they have had no purging, but abide as they were. Now, if I address such, let me say to them,—it is clear that you are and must be unblest. Hearing of a feast will not fill you; hearing of a brook will not quench your thirst. The information that there is gold in the Bank of England will not enrich you; you need cash in your own pocket. The knowledge that there is a shelter from the storm will not save the ship from the tempest. The information that there is a cure for a disease will not make the sick man whole. No: boons must be grasped, blessings must be appropriated and made use of, if they are to be of any value to us. O sirs, you know what you should do, but you have not done it! You have been half inclined to attend to eternal things, but you have let them go, and still you are among those unblest hearers who hear in vain.

Next, these hearers are described as *deceiving themselves*. "Deceiving your own selves," says James. What did they deceive themselves about? Why, probably, they thought they were considerably better for being hearers: much to be commended and sure to get a blessing. They would not have been happy if they had not heard the word on Sunday, and they look with disgust upon their neighbours who make nothing of the Sabbath. They themselves are very superior people because they are regular church-goers or chapel-goers. They have a sitting, and a hymn-book, and a Bible: is not that a good deal? If they stayed away from a place of worship for a month they would be very uneasy; but though they do not believe that going to a place of worship will save them, yet it quiets their conscience, and they feel themselves more at ease. I should like to feed you for a month on your theory. I would rattle the plates in your ears, and see whether you would be fed. I would not accommodate you with a bed at night. Why should I? I would preach you a discourse upon the benefit of sleep. Nor need I even give you a room to occupy: I would read you an eloquent dissertation upon domestic architecture, and show you what a house should be. You would very soon quit my door, and call me inhospitable, if I gave you music instead of meat; and yet you deceive yourselves with the notion that merely hearing about Jesus and his great salvation has made you better men. Or, perhaps, the deceit runs in another line: you foster the idea that the stern truths which you hear do not apply to you. Sinners? Yes, certainly, the preacher addresses sinners, and may they get good out of it; but *you* are not a sinner, at least not in any special sense, so as to need looking after. Repentance? Most people ought to repent, but you do not see any reason why *you* should repent. Looking to Christ for salvation? "Excellent doctrine," you say, "Excellent doctrine!" But, somehow, *you* do not look to him for salvation. Here is the scriptural verdict upon this opinion of yours—"Deceiving your own selves." The gospel does not deceive you; it tells you "Ye must be born again, ye must believe in Jesus Christ, or be lost." The preacher does not deceive you; he never said half a word to support the notion that coming to this place would be of any service to you unless you would yield your hearts to Christ. No, he has learnt to speak plain English about such matters. You deceive your own selves if, being hearers and not doers, you derive comfort from that which you hear.

And then, again, according to our text, *these people are superficial hearers.* They are said to be like to a man who sees his natural face in a glass. Now, even a casual hearer will often find the preaching of the gospel to be like looking in a glass and seeing himself. When a glass is first exhibited to some fresh discovered negro tribe, the chieftain as he sees himself is perfectly astonished. He looks, and looks again, and cannot make it out. So is it in the preaching of the word: the man says, "Why, those are my words: that is my way of feeling." I have often known hearers exclaim, "Why, that is the very expression I used as I was coming along." They feel like her of old who said, "Come, see a man, which told me all things that ever I did." Such a person reads his Bible, and he says, "Come, see a book, which tells me all things that ever I did. Is not this God's book?" The fact is that the word of God is a discerner of the thoughts and intents of the heart. As you have seen hanging up in the butcher's shop the carcases of animals cut right down in the centre, so the word of God is " quick and powerful, piercing to the dividing of soul and spirit, of joints and marrow." It opens up a man to himself, and makes him see himself. He is quite astonished, and cannot make it out. I have no doubt many of you who are unconverted here have felt this under a searching sermon. When you have been reading the Scriptures you have been perfectly astonished at the way in which you have been revealed to yourselves; but it has been superficial work. If a man looks at himself in a glass, and then puts down the mirror and goes his way, he has made but very poor use of it, for it was intended to lead him to remove spots, and improve his personal appearance by washing. Looking in the glass and noticing a black mark on your forehead is mere child's play if you do not wash the spot away. To see yourself as God would have you see yourself in the glass of Scripture is something, but you must afterwards go to Christ for washing or your looking is very superficial work. God grant that if you are made to feel the revealing power of the word of God you may at once come to the practical point and " wash and be clean."

The text accuses these persons of being *hasty hearers*—" he beholdeth himself and goeth his way." They hear a sermon, and they are off. They never give the word time to operate, they are back to business, back to talk and idle chit-chat, the moment the service ends. Enquirers' meetings are often eminently useful, because they give people a little opportunity to think over what they have heard; but much of hearing is not followed up with thought, and so it is ineffectual. We get much more out of meditation than out of hearing. Like the cattle, we must chew the cud, if we would get nutriment from spiritual food: but few do this. It is a great mercy for us, considering the quantity of nonsense there is in the world, that we have two ears so that we can let idle words go in at one ear and out at the other; but it is a great pity that we should use those two ears in such a way in reference to the word of God. Let it have a lodgment, dear friend. Do not let the gospel come in at one ear and out at the other. How are you to prevent it? Why let it come in at both ears. Let it have two roads right down to the soul, and shut your ears when the truth has thoroughly entered in, and compel it to abide in the chamber of your soul. How much of blessing would come to men if they carried the word home with them; if they took the text to pieces, weighed it, and considered it, and prayed for a personal application of it. Then they would become spiritually wise by the teaching of the Holy Ghost. But, alas, they are hasty hearers: they look in the glass and go their way.

One other thing is said about them, namely, that they are *very forgetful hearers*—they forget what manner of men they are. They have heard the discourse, and there is an end of it. You know the story of Donald's coming home a little sooner from kirk than usual, and his wife enquiring, " What! Donald! is the sermon all done?" He replied, " No, no; it is all *said*, but it has not begun to be done yet." But while it has not begun to be done, it often happens that the sermon has ended with many hearers. They have listened to it, but it has run through them like water through a sieve, and they will recollect no more of it till the judgment-day. There is no sin in having a bad memory, but there is great sin in refusing at once to obey the gospel. If you cannot recollect the text, or even remember the subject to-morrow morning, I shall not blame you; but the recollection of the spirit of the whole thing, the drinking in and absorption into yourself of the truth,—that is the main matter, and the carrying of the truth into practice is the essence of the business. That travelling dealer did well who, while listening to Mr. William Dawson, when he was speaking about dishonesty, stood up in the midst of the congregation and broke a certain yard measure with which he had been in the habit of cheating his customers. That woman did well who said that she forgot what the preacher talked about, but she remembered to burn her bushel when she got home, for that too had been short in measure. Never mind about remembering the sermon, if you remember at once to practise it. You may forget the words in which the truth was couched, if you will, but let it purify your life. It reminds me of the gracious woman who used to earn her living by washing wool. When her minister called upon her and asked her about his sermon, and she confessed that she had forgotten the text, he said, "What good could it have done you?" She took him into her back place, where she was carrying on her trade. She put the wool into a sieve, and then pumped on it. "There, sir," she said, "your sermon is like that water. It runs through my mind, sir, just as the water runs through the sieve; but then the water washes the wool, sir, and so the good word washes my soul." David in the hundred and third psalm speaks of those who remember the Lord's commandments *to do* them, and that is the best of memory. Mind that you have it.

Thus I have described certain hearers, and I fear we have many such in all congregations ; admiring hearers, affectionate hearers, attached hearers, but all the while unblest hearers, because they are not doers of the work. We have wondered how it was that they never confessed themselves to be followers of Christ, but we suspect that they have never made such a confession because it would not be true; and yet they are very good, very kind, helpful to the good cause, and their lives are very upright and commendable, but we grieve that they are not decided Christians. One thing they lack—they have no faith in Christ. It does surprise me how some of you can be so favourable to everything that has to do with divine things, and yet have no personal share in the good treasure. What would you say of a cook who prepared dinners for other people and yet died of starvation? Foolish cook, say you. Foolish hearer, say I. Are you going to be like Solomon's friends the Tyrians, who helped to build the temple and yet went on worshipping their idols? Sirs, are you going to look on at the table of mercy and admire it, and yet refuse its provisions? Does it give you a thrill of pleasure to see so many taken from the highways and the hedges and brought in, and will you stand outside and never partake yourself? I always pity the poor little boys on a cold winter night who stand outside a steaming cook-shop window and look in and see others feasting, but have none themselves. I cannot understand you; all things are ready, and you are bidden and persuaded to come, and yet you are content to perish with hunger. I pray you bethink yourselves, and I ask the Spirit of God to make you doers of the word, and not hearers only, deceiving your own selves.

II. But, now, a few minutes for those who are BLESSED HEARERS —those who get the blessing. Who are they? They are described in the twenty-fifth verse,—" But whoso looketh into the perfect law of liberty, and continueth therein, he being not a forgetful hearer, but a doer of the work, this man shall be blessed in his deed."

Now, notice that this hearer who is blest is, first of all, *an earnest, eager, humble hearer.* Note the expression. He does not look *upon* the law of liberty and go his way, but he looketh *into* it. It is the same word which is used in the passage, "which things the angels desire to look into," and the Greek seems to imply a sort of stooping down to look intently into a thing. Thus is it with the hearer who obtains the blessing. He hears of the gospel, and he says, " I will look into this. There is a something here worth attention." He stoops and becomes a little child that he may learn. He searches as men do who are looking after diamonds or gold. " I will look into it," he says. " My mother used to tell me that there was something charming in it, and my father died triumphantly, through the influence of it : I will investigate it. It shall not be for want of examination that I let it slip." Such an individual hears intently and earnestly, laying his soul open to the influences of the truth, desiring to feel its holy power, and to practise its divine commands. That is the right kind of hearer—an earnest listener whose senses are all aroused to receive and retain all that can be learned.

It is implied, too, that he is a *thoughtful, studious, searching hearer*— he looks into the perfect law. I call you back to the figure. As a man will put an insect under a glass, and inspect it again and again through the microscope—looking at the wings, at each joint of the back, and at every part of the creature under his eye—so a hearer who desires a blessing looks closely into the word. He is sacredly curious. He enquires : he pries. He asks all those who should know. He likes to get with old Christians to hear their experience. He loves to compare spiritual things with spiritual, to dissect a text and see how it stands in relation to another, and to its own parts, for he is in earnest when he hears the word. Alas, dear friends, as I have said before, many hearers are too superficial ; they listen to what is said, and there is an end of it, they never search for the marrow of the bones. The hearer who obtains a blessing first gives his whole heart up to attention, and afterwards keeps his heart saturated with the truth by an earnest, diligent, searching study of it, and so by the Spirit's teaching he discovers what is the mind of God to his soul.

Then this hearer goes further. Looking so steadily *he discovers that the gospel is a law of liberty :* and indeed it is so. Blessed is the condition of those who are free from the law of Moses, and have come under law to Christ, who emancipates the soul from every form of bondage. There is no joy like the joy of pardon, there is no release like release from the slavery of sin, there is no freedom like the liberty of holiness, the liberty to draw near to God. He who hears the gospel aright soon discovers that there is that in it which will remove every fetter from his soul. He looks, and looks, and at last loves that perfect law of liberty which sets his heart at large to run in the way of God's commands. Would God that all of you understood it, and had a share in its benefits. This is the man who is blest while he hears.

But it is added that *he continues therein.* If you hear the gospel and it does not bless you, hear it again. If you have read the word of God and it has not saved you, read it again. It *is* able to save your soul. Have you been searching through one gracious, earnest book, and did it not seem to fit your case? Try another. Oh, if men would search for salvation as they search after hidden treasure they would not be long before they found it. I remember, when I was seeking Christ, how I read through Doddridge's "Rise and Progress of Religion" with an avidity such as I showed when as a boy I read some merry tale, for I devoured each page greedily. When I had done with Doddridge I read Baxter's "Call to the Unconverted," which did me good, but yielded me no comfort. I read each page, and drank in every word, though the book was exceedingly bitter to me. I wanted Christ, and if I could find him, and eternal life through him, it did not matter to me how often my eyes grew weary with want of sleep while reading. Oh, if you come to that—that you must have Jesus; *you shall have him.* If your soul is brought to feel that you will search heaven and earth through, if needful, but you will find the Saviour, that Saviour will soon appear to you. The hearer who gains salvation "looketh into the perfect law of liberty," *and continueth therein.*

Lastly, it is added that this man is not a forgetful hearer, but *a doer of the word,* and he shall be blessed in his deed.

Is he bidden to pray? He prays as best he can. Is he bidden to repent? He asks God to enable him to repent. Is he bidden to believe?. He says, "Lord, I believe: help thou mine unbelief." He turns everything that he hears into practice. I wish that we had thousands of hearers of that sort. I remember reading of a certain person who heard of giving a tenth of our substance to God. "Well," said he, "that is right, and I will do it": and he kept his promise. He heard that Daniel drew near to God three times a day in prayer. He said, "That is right; I will do it": and he practised a threefold approach to the throne of grace each day. He made it a rule every time he heard of something that was excellent to practise it at once. Thus he formed holy habits and a noble character, and became a blessed hearer of the word.

Now, dear friends, our text does not say that such a man is blessed *for* the deed, but it says that such a man is blessed *in* the deed. He who does what God bids him shall not be blest *for* it, but he shall be blest *in* it. The happy result will come to us in the act of obedience. May God grant you grace henceforth, whenever the gospel is preached, to stir yourself up with the energy which God's Spirit infuses into you, and say, "I will do it. I will not dream about it, or talk about it, or question about it, or say I will do it and put it off, but now at once the act commanded shall be done."

I finish with this practical suggestion. The remaining portion of life is short with some of you who hear me this day. Grey hairs are upon you here and there, and, according to the course of nature, you must soon stand before your Judge. Would it not be well that you thought about another world, and considered how you shall face your Lord at the last great day? The gospel says, "Believe on the Lord Jesus Christ," which in other words means "Trust him." Repent; confess your sin, forsake it and look to Christ for cleansing. That is the way of salvation,—"He that believeth and is baptized shall be saved." You know all about the way of life. I am telling you a tale which you have heard a thousand times, but the question is, *when is it going to be done?* "Soon, sir," you say. But were you not here when this Tabernacle was opened? "Yes," you say, "I think I was." You said "soon" then, and you say "soon" now. You will say "soon" I expect until that word "soon" will be met with the heavy sentence, "Too late, too late; ye cannot enter now." Take heed that this be not your case before this day has closed. Some men die very suddenly. A sister came to me this morning and said, "My father is dead: he was well in the morning, he came home from the shop, seemed a little ill, and died on a sudden." Seeing that life is so precarious, would it not be best that you should immediately seek the Lord while he may be found, and call upon him while he is near? I would suggest that you do not begin gossiping and talking on the way home to-day, but that you get alone a little while quietly. Do you reply that you have no place where you can be alone: this is not true, you can find some place or other. I recollect a sailor who used to find his prayer closet at the masthead: nobody came up there to disturb him. I knew a carpenter who used to get down a sawpit to pray. There are many such places. The streets of London when crowded are about as lonely as anywhere, and Cheapside may be as good as the mountain side if your heart desires real solitude.

Some of you, I fear, never think at all. As far as thinking goes, if your brains were taken out, many of you would get on almost as well without them. The brains of some people are only useful as a sort of salt, to keep them from rotting by death. Little thinking is done by the great mass of the people except the thought, "What shall we eat and what shall we drink?" Do, I pray you, think a little. Pause and consider what God the Lord sets before you. Be a doer of the work. Do what God bids you. As he bids you repent, repent; as he bids you believe, believe; as he bids you pray, pray; as he bids you accept his grace, God helping you, do it. Oh, that it might be done at once, and to the Lord shall be praise world without end. Amen.

PORTION OF SCRIPTURE READ BEFORE SERMON—James i.

HYMNS FROM "OUR OWN HYMN BOOK"—483, 538, 992.

Metropolitan Tabernacle Pulpit.

THE BEST OF ALL SIGHTS.

A short Sermon

WRITTEN AT MENTONE, BY

C. H. SPURGEON.

"But we see Jesus."—Hebrews ii. 9.

IN holy Scripture faith is placed in opposition to the sight of the eyes, and yet it is frequently described as looking and seeing. It is opposed to carnal sight because it is spiritual sight; a discernment which comes not of the body, but arises out of the strong belief of the soul, wrought in us by the Holy Spirit. Faith is sight in the sense of being a clear and vivid perception, a sure and indisputable discovery, a realising and unquestionable discernment of fact. We see Jesus, for we are sure of his presence, we have unquestionable evidence of his existence, we have an intelligent and intimate knowledge of his person. Our soul has eyes far stronger than the dim optics of the body, and with these we actually *see* Jesus. We have heard of him, and upon the witness of that hearing we have believed, and through believing there has come to us a new life, which rejoices in new light and in opened eyes, and "we see Jesus." In the old sense of sight we speak of him as of one "whom having not seen we love," but in the new sense "we see Jesus." Beloved reader, have you such a renewed nature that you have new senses, and have you with these senses discerned the Lord? If not, may the Holy Spirit yet quicken you; and meanwhile, let us whom he has made alive assure you that we have *heard* his voice, for he saith, "My sheep hear my voice"; we have "*tasted* the good word of God"; we have *touched* him and have been made whole; we have also known the *smell* of his fragrance, for his name to us is "as ointment poured forth"; and now, in the words of our text, "we *see* Jesus." Faith is all the senses in one, and infinitely more; and those who have it not are in a worse case than the blind and deaf, for spiritual life itself is absent.

I. Come, then, brethren beloved, whose eyes have been illuminated, let us muse awhile upon our privileges, that we may exercise them with delight and praise the Lord with them. First, let us regard the glorious sight of Jesus as a COMPENSATION. The text begins with "*but*," because it refers to some things which we do not yet see, which are the objects of strong desire. "We see not yet all things put under him." We do not as yet see Jesus acknowledged as King of kings by all mankind, and

Nos. 1,509-10.

121

this causes us great sorrow, for we would fain see him crowned with glory and honour in every corner of the earth by every man of woman born. Alas, he is to many quite unknown, by multitudes rejected and despised, and by comparatively few is he regarded with reverence and love. Sights surround us which might well make us cry with Jeremiah, "Oh that my head were waters, and mine eyes a fountain of tears"; for blasphemy and rebuke, idolatry, superstition, and unbelief prevail on every side. "But," saith the apostle, "we see Jesus," and this sight compensates for all others, for we see him now, no longer made a little lower than the angels, and tasting the bitterness of death, but "crowned with glory and honour." We see him no more after the flesh, in shame and anguish; far more ravishing is the sight, for we see his work accomplished, his victory complete, his empire secure. He sits as a priest upon the throne at the right hand of God, from henceforth expecting till his enemies are made his footstool.

This is a divine compensation for the tarrying of his visible kingdom, because *it is the major part of it.* The main battle is won. In our Lord's endurance of his substitutionary griefs, and in the overthrow of sin, death, and hell by his personal achievements, the essence of the conflict is over. Nothing is left to be done at all comparable with that which is already performed. The ingathering of the elect, and the subjection of all things, are comparatively easy of accomplishment now that the conflict in the heavenly places is over, and Jesus has led captivity captive. We may look upon the conquest of the kingdoms of this world as a mere routing of the beaten host, now that the power of the enemy has been effectually broken by the great Captain of our salvation.

The compensation is all the greater because our Lord's enthronement *is the pledge of all the rest.* The putting of all things under him, which as yet we see not, is guaranteed to us by what we do see. The exalted Saviour has all power given unto him in heaven and in earth, and with this "all power" he can, at his own pleasure, send forth the rod of his strength out of Sion, and reign in the midst of his enemies. With him are all the forces needful for universal dominion, his white horse waits at the door, and whensoever he chooses he can ride forth conquering and to conquer. At a word from his lips the harlot of Babylon shall perish, and the false prophet shall die, and the idols of the heathen shall be utterly abolished. The empire of wickedness is as a vision of the night, a black and hideous nightmare pressing on the soul of manhood, but when he awaketh he will despise its image, and it shall melt away.

Turn we then, wiping our tears away, from the wretched spectacles of human superstition, scepticism, and sorrow, to the clear vision above us in the opened heaven. There we see "the Man," long promised, the desire of all nations, the deliverer, the death of death, the conqueror of hell; and we see him not as one who girdeth on his harness for the battle, but as one whose warfare is accomplished, who is waiting the time appointed of the Father when he shall divide the spoil. This is the antidote to all depression of spirit, the stimulus to hopeful perseverance, the assurance of joy unspeakable.

II. Nor is this sight a mere compensation for others which as yet are denied us, it is in itself the cause of present EXULTATION. This is true in so many ways that time would fail us to attempt to enumerate them. "We see Jesus," and in him *we see our former unhappy condition for ever ended*. We were fallen in Adam, but we see in Jesus our ruin retrieved by the second Adam. The legal covenant frowned upon us as we beheld it broken by our first federal head ; the new covenant smiles upon us with a whole heaven of bliss as we see it ordered in all things and sure in him who is head over all things to the church. Sin once doomed us to eternal despair, but not now, for he who hath put away sin by the sacrifice of himself hath justified his people by his resurrection. The debt no longer burdens us, for there in eternal glory is the Man who paid it once for all. A sight of Jesus kills each guilty fear, silences each threat of conscience, and photographs peace upon the heart. There remains nothing of all the past to cause a dread of punishment, or arouse a fear of desertion ; for Christ that died ever liveth to make intercession for us, to represent us before the Father, and to prepare for us a place of everlasting rest. We might see ourselves as dead under the law were it not that he has blotted out the handwriting which was against us ; we might see ourselves under the curse were it not that he who was once made a curse for us now reigns in fulness of blessing. We weep as we confess our transgressions, but we see Jesus, and sing for joy of heart, since he hath finished transgression, made an end of sin, and brought in everlasting righteousness.

The same is sweetly true of the present, for *we see our present condition to be thrice blessed by virtue of our union with him*. We see not as yet our nature made perfect, and cleansed from every tendency to evil ; rather do we groan, being burdened, because of the sin which dwelleth in us, the old man which lusteth and rebelleth against the blessed dominion of grace ; and we might be sorely cast down and dragged into despair were it not that "we see Jesus," and perceive that in him we are not what the flesh would argue us to be. He represents us most truthfully, and looking into that mirror we see ourselves justified in Christ Jesus, accepted in the beloved, adopted of the Father, dear to the Eternal heart, yea, in him raised up together, and made to sit together in the heavenlies. We see self, and blush and are ashamed and dismayed ; "but we see Jesus," and his joy is in us, and our joy is full. Think of this, dear brother in Christ, the next time you are upon the dunghill of self-loathing. Lift up now your eyes, and see where he is in whom your life is hid ! See Jesus, and know that as he is so are you also before the Infinite Majesty. You are not condemned, for he is enthroned. You are not despised nor abhorred, for he is beloved and exalted. You are not in jeopardy of perishing, nor in danger of being cast away, for he dwells eternally in the bosom of the Lord God Almighty. What a vision is this for you, when you see Jesus, and see yourself complete in him, perfect in Christ Jesus !

Such a sight effectually *clears our earthly future of all apprehension*. It is true we may yet be sorely tempted, and the battle may go hard with us, but we see Jesus triumphant, and by this sign we grasp the victory. We shall perhaps be subjected to pain, to poverty, to slander, to persecution, and yet none of these things move us because we see Jesus exalted, and therefore know that these are under his power, and cannot touch us except as he grants them his permit so to do. Death is at times terrible in prospect, but its terror ceases when we see Jesus, who has passed safely through the shades of the sepulchre, vanquished the tyrant of the tomb, and left an open passage to immortality to all his own. We see the pains, the groans, and dying strife; see them, indeed, exaggerated by our fears, and the only cure for the consequent alarm is a sight of him who hath said, " He that believeth in me, though he were dead, yet shall he live. And whosoever liveth and believeth in me shall never die." When we see Jesus, past, present, and to come are summed up in him, and over all shines a glorious life which fills our souls with unspeakable delight.

III. Thirdly, "we see Jesus" with gladdest EXPECTATION. His glorious *person* is to us the picture and the pledge of what we shall be: for "it doth not yet appear what we shall be : but we know that, when he shall appear, we shall be like him ; for we shall see him as he is." In infinite love he condescended to become one with us here below, as saith the apostle, " Forasmuch then as the children are partakers of flesh and blood, he also himself likewise took part of the same "; and this descent of love on his part to meet us in our low estate is the assurance that his love will lift us up to meet him in his high estate. He will make us partakers of *his* nature, inasmuch as he has become partaker of *our* nature. It is written, " Both he that sanctifieth and they who are sanctified are all of one : for which cause he is not ashamed to call them brethren." What bliss is this, that we should be like to the incarnate God ! It would seem too good to be true, were it not after the manner of our Lord to do great things for us, and unsearchable.

Nor may we alone derive comfort as to our future from his person, we may also be made glad by a hope as to his *place*. Where we see Jesus to be, there shall we also be. His heaven is our heaven. His prayer secures that we shall be with him where he is, that we may behold his glory. To-day we may be in a workhouse, or in the ward of a hospital, or in a ruinous hovel, " but we see Jesus," and we know that ere long we shall dwell in the palace of the great King.

The glory of Jesus strikes the eye at once, and thus we are made to exult in his *position*, for it, too, is ours. He will give to us to sit upon his throne, even as he sits upon the Father's throne. He hath made us kings and priests unto God, and we shall reign for ever and ever. Whatever of rest, happiness, security, and honour our glorious Bridegroom has attained, he will certainly share it with his spouse ; yea, and all his people shall know what it is to be heirs of God, joint heirs with Jesus Christ, if so be that we suffer with him that we may also be glorified together.

How soon our condition shall rise into complete likeness to the ascended Lord we cannot tell, but it cannot be long, and it may be a very short time. The veil of time is in some cases very thin, another week may be the only separation. And then ! Ah, then ! We shall see Jesus, and what a sight will it be ! Heaven lies in that vision. 'Tis all the heaven our loving hearts desire.

The sight of Jesus which we now enjoy is a foretaste of the clearer sight which is reserved for us, and therefore it will be a happy wisdom to be much in the enjoyment of it. A thousand things tempt us away, and yet there is not one of them worth a moment's thought in comparison.

What are works of art and discoveries of science if compared with our Beloved? What are the gems which adorn the brow of beauty, or the eyes which flash from the face of loveliness, if placed in rivalry with him? Other matters, weighty and important, call for our thought; and yet even these we may place in a second rank when Jesus is near.

We may not be doctors of divinity, much as we would desire to be deeply instructed in the truth; "but we see Jesus." Into many mysteries we cannot pry; "but we see Jesus." Where the divine sovereignty harmonizes with human responsibility is too deep a problem for us; "but we see Jesus." The times and the seasons baffle us, the dispensation of the end is dark to us, "but we see Jesus." Glory over us, ye far-seeing prophets! Deride us, ye deep-glancing philosophers! We leave you to your boastings. We are poor, short-sighted beings, and know but little, but one thing we know, whereas we were once blind, now we see, and " we see Jesus."

This sight has made us unable to see many things which now dazzle our fellow men. They can see priestly power in a certain set of men like themselves. This we cannot see, for "we see Jesus," as ending the line of sacrificing priests, and bestowing a common priesthood upon all the saints. Many see great wisdom in the various schools of doubt, in which we see nothing except pretentious folly, for "we see Jesus," and all human wisdom pales before the wisdom of God, which is perfected in him. Certain of our brethren see perfection in the flesh, "but we see Jesus"; others see the church, and their own sect, "but we see Jesus." A few see nothing but their own separateness from everybody else, and the peculiar excellence of their exclusiveness, "but we see Jesus."

Come, beloved, let us get to our secret chambers of communion, and see Jesus there as from the hill of Pisgah. Let us turn the pages of Scripture, and see Jesus there amid the beds of spices. Let us frequent ordinances, especially the breaking of bread, and see Jesus there. Let us watch in our experience, as we are conformed unto his sufferings, and see him there. Let us go into the field of holy labour, and as we gird ourselves and put on the yoke of service, let us see our Master there. Yea, in all things let us learn to see our Lord, for nature and Providence, experience and Scripture are hung with mirrors which reflect him. Till the day break and the shadows flee away let us continue to gaze upon him, till our eyes shall actually see him for ourselves and not another. Be this the grand distinction of our lives: whatever others may see or not see,

"WE SEE JESUS."

THE HUNGER-BITE.

DELIVERED BY

C. H. SPURGEON,

AT THE METROPOLITAN TABERNACLE, NEWINGTON.

"His strength shall be hunger-bitten."—Job xviii. 12.

BILDAD was declaring the history of the hypocritical, presumptuous, and wicked man; and he intended, no doubt, to insinuate that Job was just such a person, that he had been a deceiver, and that therefore at last God's providence had found him out and was visiting him for his sins. In this Bildad was guilty of great injustice to his friend. All the three miserable comforters of Job were mistaken in the special aim of their discourses, and yet concerning the speeches of each one it may be said that their general statements were, for the most part, true. They uttered truths, but they drew mistaken inferences, and they were ungenerous in the imputations which they cast upon Job. It is true that, sooner or later, either in this world or the next, all conceivable curses do fall upon the hypocrite and the ungodly man, but it is not true that when a Christian is in trouble we are to judge that he is suffering for his sin. It would be both cruel and wicked for us to think so. Nevertheless, because what Bildad said was, in the main, true, though unkindly and wrongly applied, we feel ourselves quite at liberty to take a text out of his mouth.

It is true of many persons that their strength shall be hunger-bitten, and I shall speak concerning these words in three ways, noticing first, that *this is a curse which will surely be fulfilled upon the ungodly.* Secondly, *this is a discipline which God often exercises upon the self-righteous when he means to save them.* And, thirdly—and it is grievous work to have to say it—*this is a form of chastisement upon believers who are not living near to God as they ought to be*—their strength becomes hunger-bitten.

I. First we shall view our text as A CURSE WHICH WILL BE FULFILLED UPON THE UNGODLY. "His strength shall be hunger-bitten."

It is not said that *they* are hunger-bitten merely, but that their *strength* is so; and if their strength be hunger-bitten what must their weakness be? When a man's strength is bitten with hunger, what a hunger must be raging throughout the whole of his nature.

Now, a large proportion of men make their gold to be their strength, their castle and their high tower, and for awhile they do rejoice in their wealth, and find great satisfaction in gathering it, in seeing it multiplied, and in hoping by-and-by that it shall come to great store. But every ungodly man ought to know that riches are not for ever, and often they take to themselves wings and fly away. Men of colossal fortunes have dwindled down to beggars; they made great ventures and realized great failures. None are secure. As long as a man is in this world he is like a ship at sea, he is still liable to be shipwrecked. O you that are boasting in your gold, and calling your treasure your chief good, the day may come to you when your strength will be hunger-bitten, and, like the victims of famine, you will find yourselves helpless,—you whose money aforetime answered all things, and made you feel omnipotent.

But it will be said, of course, that it is not in every case that the ungodly man's strength of wealth is hunger-bitten; and I willingly concede it. But it comes to pass in another fashion. How many there are who keep their wealth, and yet, for all that, are very poor. It is not that the gold goes, but it stays by them and does not comfort them. I do not know which would be the worse of the two—to be hungry for want of bread, or to have abundance of bread, and yet remain hungry eat whatever you might. Thousands in this world are precisely in that condition. They have all that heart could wish, if their heart were right, but it seems nothing to them because they have envy in their spirits. Remember Haman. He is invited to the banquet of wine, he is a chief noble of the empire, he has his monarch's favour, but all that avails him nothing because Mordecai sits in the gate. Envy has cankered his soul, and if he were able to mount to the throne of Ahasuerus himself it would make no difference to him; he would be unhappy there; and all because one poor Jew will not bow to him. There are persons going up and down Cheapside every day who are intolerably wretched about a something which they would hardly like to mention to reasonable men. A wretched trifle frets them like a moth in a garment, and all the glory of their position is eaten away: their strength is hunger-bitten.

Where the canker does not happen to be envy it may come to be a passion akin to it, namely, revenge. Alas, that we should have to talk of revenge as still existing upon this earth after Christ has been here and taught us to pray, "Forgive us our debts as we forgive our debtors." Yet there are ungodly men who even think it right to foster resentments. A word uncourteously spoken, a deed unkindly done, will be laid up, and an opportunity sought for retaliation; or, if not, a hope will be cherished that some blight, or blow from God, may fall upon the offender: and if that offender still bears himself aloft, and lives right merrily, and makes no recompense for the wrong done, the aggrieved one has eaten out his own heart with chagrin, and the strength of his wealth has been hunger-bitten.

Where this has not been the case, it has, perhaps, more frequently happened that persons have been afflicted by avarice. Nothing more tends to impoverish a man than being rich. It is a hard thing to find a rich man who enjoys riches. A rich man is a man who has all he wants, and many a man is rich on a few shillings a week: a poor man is a man who does not get what he wants, and people with twenty thousand a-year are in that list. In fact, where shall you find such poverty as among those poor rich men ? The miser is often pictured as afraid to sleep because thieves may break in ; he rises at midnight to tell over his hoarded treasure, he is afraid lest bonds, securities, mortgages, and the like may, after all, turn out to be mere waste paper ; he frets and stews and mars his life because he has too great a means of living —such a man may not be very common, but it is an easy thing to find people who have very much, and yet are just as careful, just as grasping, just as fretful after more, as if they had but newly started in business, and were almost penniless—their strength is hunger-bitten. If somebody had told them, " You will one day reach to so many thousand pounds," they would have said, " Ah, if ever I get that amount I shall be perfectly satisfied." They have saved that sum long ago, and ten times as much, and now they say, " Ah, you don't know what it is to want money till you have a good portion of it. Now we have so much we must have more. We are up to our necks in the golden stream, and we must needs swim where the bottom cannot be touched." Poor fools ! They have enough water to float them, but they must have enough to drown in. One stick is a capital thing for a lame man, as I know right well, but a thousand sticks would make a terrible load for a man to carry. When any one has a sufficiency let him be thankful for so convenient a staff, but if he will not use what he has until he has accumulated much more, the comfort of his substance is gone, and his strength is hunger-bitten.

There are cases in which the hunger-bite does not take a shape which I could well describe. Instances are met with of persons who have made their gold their strength, who are altogether unrestful. Some have thought that their brain was diseased, but it is likely that the disease was lower down, and in their hearts. We have known wealthy men who believed themselves to be poor, and were haunted with the idea that they should die in the poor-house, even when they were worth a million ; and others who have quarrelled about the division of a farthing, when the loss of ten thousand pounds would have been a fleabite to them. In great substance they have found no substantial rest. They have often wished they could be as cheerful as their own menial servants. As they have lolled in their carriage, and looked at the rosy cheeks of the urchins in the village, they have coveted their health and felt willing to wear their rags if they could possess their appetites. As they have looked upon poor persons with family loves and domestic joys, and felt that their own joys were few in that direction, they have greatly envied them. It is a great mercy when the worldling is made uneasy in this world ; it is a ground for hope that God means to wean him from his idols. But, alas, there are some who do not rest *here*, and yet will not rest hereafter. They have no rest in all that God has given them under the sun, and yet they will not fly to him who is the soul's sure repose.

I need not dwell for another moment upon the failure of the strength which is found in riches. It is the same with all sorts of men who try to find comfort out of Christ and away from God, their " strength shall be hunger-bitten." What a melancholy instance of this is Solomon.

He had an opportunity to try everything in his quest for the chief good, and he did test everything, so that we need not repeat the experiment. He was the great alchemist who tried to turn all manner of metals into gold, but failed with them all. At one time he was building great palaces, and when the building fit was on him he seemed happy; but when once the gorgeous piles were finished he said, "Vanity of vanities: all is vanity." Then he would take to gardening and to the planting of rare plants and trees, and to the digging of fountains, but when he had done enough of this he looked upon his orchard and vineyards and again muttered, "Vanity of vanities: all is vanity." Then he thought he would try laughter and madness: the comic side of human life he would test, as well as the useful; so he plunged into all manner of pleasures, and gathered to himself singing men and singing women, and all delights of the flesh, but after he had drank deep of that cup he said again, "Vanity of vanities: all is vanity." Poor Solomon! He had great strength, but his strength was hunger-bitten. He looked here and there, up and down, on the right hand and on the left, and found no bread for his soul; he snatched at shadows and tried to feed himself with bubbles; he was devoured with hunger in the midst of plenty; and where the humble people of Israel were blessing the God who satisfied their mouth with good things and renewed their youth like the eagles, poor Solomon was complaining that there was nothing new under the sun, and that it was better for a man not to be born than to have lived at all.

Now remark that if this hunger does not come upon the ungodly man during the former part of his life, it will come to him at the close of it. While we have much to do and our minds are occupied we may be able to put off thought, but when, at last, God sends to us that messenger with the bony hand, whose oratory is soul piercing, the dulness of whose eyeless eye darts fire into the soul, then will all human strength be hunger-bitten. When death is left alone with the man, then he perceives that his money bags contain nothing precious, because he must leave them. How now with his broad acres? How now with his large estates? How now with his palatial residence? How now with all that he called dear? How now with his doctor's degree and his learning? How now with his fame and his honour? How now even with his domestic comforts and the joys of life? Hunger-bitten are they all. When he comes to die they cannot help him. The soul that is within him, which he would not allow to speak, now opens its hungry mouth and cries, "Thou hast denied me bread. God, and God alone, could fill me; and thou hast denied me God; and now thou feelest the hunger which has come upon me, and thou *must* feel it, and feel it, too, for ever." Alas, alas, alas, for a man to have spent all his life in earning a disappointment, labouring hard to lose his soul, sweating and straining to lose the race, tugging and toiling to be damned; for that is the case of many a man, and that is whereunto the tide drifteth with all mankind who seek for lasting good apart from God and apart from the blood and righteousness of God's dear Son. Of each one of them it shall be said, "His strength shall be hunger-bitten."

I have said these things mournfully to my own heart; but I would say to any of you who may not be rich, but who are looking for your good in your own little home and the comforts of it—any of you young men who are seeking the great object of life in learning, or the like —if you are not living for God, your strength will be hunger-bitten. If you do not "seek first the kingdom of God and his righteousness," whatever you gain and however satisfied you may be for a little while, an awful hunger must ultimately come upon you, and you will then lament that you spent your money for that which is not bread and your labour for that which satisfieth not.

II.   Briefly, in the second place, we shall speak of our text as indicating A KIND OF DISCIPLINE THROUGH WHICH GOD PUTS THE SELF-RIGHTEOUS WHEN HE MEANS TO SAVE THEM.

Many people are very religious, and yet are not saved.   They are unsaved because they go about to establish their own righteousness, and have not submitted themselves to the righteousness which is of God in Jesus Christ.   Now, these persons may for awhile be very well satisfied with their own righteousness, and if they are not the children of God they will be satisfied with it for life.   Some of them talk in this way,—"I don't know that I ever wronged anybody.   I have always been honest and honourable in my transactions, and I have brought up my children respectably.   I have had a hard fight of it, and for all that nobody could say that I ever disgraced my character." It is not very long ago that I was driven by a cabman, an aged man, and when I got out of his cab I referred to his age, and he remarked upon it himself: I said, "Well, I trust when this life is over you will have a portion in a better world."   "Yes, I think so, sir," he said : "I was never drunk, that I know of, in my life; was always reckoned a civil man; never used bad language; and I go to church *sometimes*." He seemed to be perfectly satisfied, and to be quite astonished that I did not express my assurance of his safety.   His confidence is the common reliance of all classes of Englishmen, and though they may not always put it in that shape, yet that is the notion—that by a sort of goodness, a very poor and mangled goodness, men may after all enter heaven.   Now, when God means to save a man the hunger of the heart comes in and devours all his boasted excellence.   Why, a spiritually hungry soul would take fifty years of self-righteousness and swallow them up like a morsel, and cry for more.   Our goodness is nothing compared with the demands of the law and the necessities of the case. Our fine righteousnesses, how they shrivel up like autumn leaves when the Spirit of God acts as a frost to them.   Our virtues are as a meadow in the spring bedecked with golden kingcups, but when the Spirit of God bloweth upon it the grass withereth, and the flower thereof fadeth, for all flesh is grass, and all the goodliness thereof is as the flower of grass.   It is a part of the operation of the Holy Ghost to wither all the goodliness of human nature, and to destroy all those lovely flowers of natural virtue in which we put such store, cutting them down as with a mower's scythe.   In truth, there is none good, no, not one.   We are all shut up in unbelief and sin by nature.   In the best of natures sin affects the whole body, "the whole head is sick, and the whole heart faint," and it is a great blessing when the Holy Spirit makes us feel this. Painful is the feeling but blessed is the result when, once for all, our strength is hunger-bitten.

Ay, and there are some who are very satisfied because, in addition to a commendable life, they have performed certain ceremonies to which they impute great sanctity. There is a theory abroad nowadays which some persons who are not in either the lunatic or the idiot asylum believe, namely, the theory that sacramental performances convey grace. It is wonderful how a rational being can ever think so, but there are persons, who are apparently rational in other things, who believe that the sprinkling of drops of water upon an infant's brow regenerates it, that the eating of bread and the drinking of wine really convey Christ to the soul, and so on: that aqueous applications and materialistic festivities can bring spiritual good to the heart—a monstrous doctrine, worthy of the priests of Baal, but so foolish as to make one doubt his ears when he hears it stated. Because they have gone through these operations, and have been confirmed, and I do not know what besides, many are content. Others who happen to belong to a dissenting community have passed through the ordeal of joining the church, or have attended class-meetings, and have subscribed to the various societies, think that, therefore, they are saved. Heirs of hell will rest content with such outward things, but heirs of heaven never can. Their strength, if they make external religion their strength, will by-and-by be hunger-bitten, and they will cry out, "My God, my soul panteth for thee as the hart pants for the water-brooks. I cannot be satisfied with outward forms, I want inward grace, and I cannot be content with being told that the grace went with the form. I want to know the grace of God in truth, I long to feel it, I pine to exhibit it in my own life." To be told I was born again when I was a babe will not satisfy *me;* I want to feel the inner life, the new life of God within my spirit. To be told that I did eat Christ when I ate the bread will not content me; my heart longs to know that Christ is really in me the hope of glory, and that I am living upon him. If I cannot have communion with God and with his dear Son for myself in my very soul, I turn with loathing from every substitute, ritualistic, priestly, or otherwise. Beloved, I would have you flee from every sacrament to the Saviour; I would have you fly away from ceremonies to the cross of Christ. There is your only hope. Look to him by faith: for all the rest without this is but outward and carnal, and can minister no good to your spirit. May your strength be hunger-bitten if you are resting in anything which is external and unspiritual.

Many a person has known what it is to have this hunger-bite go right through everything he rested in. I once knew what it was to get a little comfort from my prayers before I found the Saviour, but when the Spirit of God dealt with me I saw that my prayers wanted praying over again. I thought I had some sort of repentance, and I began to be contented with it; but when the Spirit of God came I found that my repentance needed to be repented of. I had felt some confidence in my Bible readings, and hoped that my regular attendance upon public worship would bring me salvation, but I found that I was after all mocking the Word, for I was reading it, but not believing it; hearing it, but not accepting it; was increasing my knowledge and my responsibility, and yet was not rendering obedience to God. Dear soul, if you are resting anywhere short of Christ, may your strength be hunger-bitten. You are at your strongest when you are utter weakness apart from him. When you rest in him completely, and alone, then is salvation accomplished in you, but not till then. May God in his infinite mercy grant that all your strength apart from Christ may be hunger-bitten, and that speedily.

III. Lastly, and very earnestly—and perhaps this last part may have more reference to most of you than anything I have said—I believe THERE ARE MANY OF GOD'S SERVANTS WHOSE STRENGTH IS LAMENTABLY HUNGER-BITTEN. In this age we are all busy, and through being busy we are apt to neglect the soul-feeding ordinances; I mean the reading of Scripture, the hearing of the word, meditation upon it, prayer and communion with God. Some of you do not rise so soon as you might in the morning, and prayer is hurried over; and too often at eventide you are half asleep with the many cares of the day, and prayer is offered in a slovenly way. Nor is this all, for during the day when, if you were as you should be, you would be praying without ceasing, there is this to think of, and that, and the other, and such a pressure of business that ejaculations are few. How can you pray? You did at one time get a text of Scripture in the morning and chew it all day, and you used to get much sweetness out of it, and your soul grew; but now, instead of a text of Scripture, you have pressing engagements as soon as you are out of bed. You would, now and then, steal into a mid-day prayer-meeting, perhaps, or get two or three minutes alone, but you have gradually dropped that habit, and you have felt justified in doing so for "really, time is so precious, and there is so much to do in this age of competition." Dear friend, I am no judge for you, but let me ask you whether you are not becoming hunger-bitten through not feeding upon the word of God. Souls cannot be strong without spiritual meat any more than bodies can be well when meals are neglected. There is a good rule I have heard mothers say about children and chickens—"little and often"; and I think it is true with Christians. They want little and often during the day; not a long passage of Scripture, perhaps memory would fail, but a short passage now and a short passage then, and a little prayer here and a little prayer there. It is wonderful how souls grow in that way. Alas! I fear all this is neglected, and spiritual strength is hunger-bitten. Let us begin from this time forward to give attention to the sustenance of our souls. Let us daily feed upon the word of God, that we may grow thereby; so shall our strength no more be hunger-bitten.

QUESTIONS WHICH OUGHT TO BE ASKED.

DELIVERED BY

C. H. SPURGEON,

AT THE METROPOLITAN TABERNACLE, NEWINGTON.

(This was followed by a farewell address from his son, Thomas Spurgeon.)

"But none saith, Where is God my Maker, who giveth songs in the night; who teacheth us more than the beasts of the earth, and maketh us wiser than the fowls of heaven?"—Job xxxv. 10, 11.

ELIHU perceived the great ones of the earth oppressing the needy, and he traced their domineering tyranny to their forgetfulness of God: "None saith, Where is God my Maker?" Surely, had they thought of God they could not have acted so unjustly. Worse still, if I understand Elihu aright, he complained that even among the oppressed there was the same departure in heart from the Lord: they cried out by reason of the arm of the mighty, but unhappily they did not cry unto God their Maker, though he waits to be gracious unto all such, and executeth righteousness and judgment for all that are oppressed. Both with great and small, with oppressors and oppressed, there is one common fault in our nature, which is described by the apostle in the Romans, "There is none that understandeth, there is none that seeketh after God." Until divine grace comes in and changes our nature there is none that saith, "Where is God my Maker, who giveth songs in the night?" This is a very grave fault, about which we shall speak for a few minutes, and may the Holy Ghost bless the word.

I. And first, LET US THINK OVER THESE NEGLECTED QUESTIONS, beginning with "Where is God my Maker?" There are four questions in the text, each of which reminds us of the folly of forgetting it. First, *Where is God?* Above all things in the world we ought to think of him. Pope said, "The proper study of mankind is man"; but it is far more true that the proper study of mankind is God. Let man study man in the second place, but God first. It is a sad thing that God is all in all, that we owe everything to him, and are under allegiance to him, and yet we neglect him. Some men think of every person but God. They have a place for everything else, but no place in their heart for God. They are most exact in the discharge of other relative duties, and yet they forget their God. They would count themselves mean indeed if

No. 1,511.

133

they did not pay every man his own, and yet they rob God. They rob him of his honour, to which they never give a thought; they rob him of obedience, for his law has no hold on them; they rob him of his praise, for they are receiving daily at his hands, and yet they yield no gratitude to their great Benefactor. "None saith, Where is God?" My dear hearer, do you stand convicted of this? Have you been walking up and down in this great house, and never asked to see the King whose palace it is? Have you been rejoicing at this great feast, and have you never asked to see your Host? Have you gone abroad through the various fields of nature, and have you never wished to know him whose breath perfumes the flowers, whose pencil paints the clouds, whose smile makes sunlight, and whose frown is storm. Oh, it is a strange, sad fact —God so near us, and so necessary to us, and yet not sought for!

The next point is, "None saith, Where is God *my Maker?*" Oh! unthinking man, God made you. He fashioned your curious framework, and put every bone into its place. He, as with needlework, embroidered each nerve, and vein, and sinew. He made this curious harp of twice ten thousand strings: wonderful it is that it has kept in tune so long: but only he could have maintained its harmony. He is your Maker. You are a mass of dust, and you would crumble back to dust at this moment if he withdrew his preserving power: he but speaks, and you dissolve into the earth on which you tread. Do you never think of your Maker? Have you no thought for him without whom you could not think at all? Oh, strange perversity and insanity that a man should find himself thus curiously made, and bearing within his own body that which will make him either a madman or a worshipper; and yet for all that he lives as if he had nothing to do with his Creator— "None saith, Where is God my Maker?"

There is great force in the next sentence: "*Who giveth songs in the night.*" That is to say, God is our *Comforter.* Beloved friends, you that know God, I am sure you will bear witness that, though you have had very severe trials, you have always been sustained in them when God has been near you. Some of us have been sick—nigh unto death, but we have almost loved our suffering chamber, and scarce wished to come out of it, so bright has the room become with the presence of God. Some of us here have known what it is to bury our dearest friends, and others have been short of bread, and forced to look up each morning for your daily manna; but when your heavenly Father has been with you—speak, ye children of God—have you not had joy and rejoicing, and light in your dwellings? When the night has been very dark, yet the fiery pillar has set the desert on a glow. No groans have made night hideous, but you have sung like nightingales amid the blackest shades when God has been with you. I can hardly tell you what joy, what confidence, what inward peace the presence of God gives to a man. It will make him bear and dare, rest and wrestle, yield and yet conquer, die and yet live. It will be very sad, therefore, if we poor sufferers forget our God, our Comforter, our song-giver.

Two little boys were once speaking together about Elijah riding to heaven in the chariot of fire. One of them said, "I think he had plenty of courage. I should have been afraid to ride in such a carriage as that." "Ah!" said the other, "but I would not mind if God drove it."

So do Christians say. They mind not if they are called to mount a chariot of fire if God drives it. We speak as honest men what we do know and feel, and we tell all our fellow-men that as long as God is present with us we have no choice of what happens to us, whether we sorrow or whether we rejoice. We have learned to glory in tribulations also when God's own presence cheers our souls. Why do not they also seek to know the Giver of songs?

And then there is a fourth point. "None saith, Where is God my Maker, who *teacheth us more than the beasts of the earth, and maketh us wiser than the fowls of heaven?*" Here we are reminded that God is our *Instructor.* God has given us intellect; it is not by accident, but by his gift, that we are distinguished from the beasts and the fowls. Now, if animals do not turn to God we do not wonder, but shall man forget? Strange to say, there has been no rebellion against God among the beasts or the birds. The beasts obey their God, and bow their necks to man. There are no sin-loving cattle or apostate fowls, but there are fallen men. Think, O man, it may have been better for thee if thou hadst been made a frog or a toad than to have lived a man if thou shouldst live and die without making peace with thy Maker. Thou gloriest that thou art not a beast: take heed that the beast do not condemn thee. Thou thinkest thyself vastly better than the sparrow which lights upon thy dwelling: take heed that thou do better and rise to nobler things. Methinks if there were a choice in birds, and souls dwelt in them, their minstrelsy would be as pure as now it is: they would scorn to sing loose and frivolous songs, as men do, but they would carol everlastingly sweet psalms of praise to God. Methinks if there were souls in any of the creatures, they would devote themselves to God, as surely as angels do. Why then, O man, why is it that thou with thy superior endowments must needs be the sole rebel, the only creature of earthly mould that forgets the creating and instructing Lord?

Four points are then before us. Man does not ask after his God, his Maker, his Comforter, his Instructor: is he not filled with a fourfold madness? How can he excuse himself?

II. Supposing you do not ask these questions, let me remind you that THERE ARE QUESTIONS WHICH GOD WILL ASK OF YOU.

When Adam had broken God's command he did not say, "Where is God my Maker?" but the Lord did not therefore leave him alone. No, the Lord came out, and a voice, silvery with grace, but yet terrible with justice, rang through the trees, "Adam, where art thou?" There will come such a voice to you who have neglected God. Your Judge will enquire, "Where art thou?" Though you hide in the top of Carmel, or dive with the crooked serpent into the depths of the sea, you will hear that voice, and you will be constrained to answer it. Your dust long scattered to the wind will come together, and your soul will enter into your body, and you will be obliged to answer, "Here am I, for thou didst call me."

Then you will hear the second question, "Why didst thou live and die without me?" And such questions as these will come thick upon you, "What did I do that thou shouldst slight me? Did I not give you innumerable mercies? Why did you never think of me? Did I not put salvation before you? Did I not plead with you? Did I not entreat you to turn unto me? Why did you refuse me?" You will have no answer to those questions: and then there will come another question—ah! how I wish it would come to you while there is time to answer it—"How shall we escape if we neglect so great salvation?" To-night I put it to you that you may propose a way of escape, if your imagination is equal to the task. You will be baffled even in trying to invent an escape *now*, and how much more when your time of judgment really comes! If you neglect the salvation of God in Christ you cannot be saved. In the next world, how will you answer that question—"How shall we escape?" You will ask the rocks to hide you, but they will refuse you that dread indulgence. You will beseech them to crush you, that you may no longer see the terrible face of the King upon the throne, but even that shall be denied you. Oh, be wise, and ere you dare the wrath of the King eternal and dash upon the bosses of his buckler, turn and repent, for why will ye die?

III. Now, if any seek an answer to the grave enquiries of the text, and do sincerely ask, "Where is God my Maker?" let us GIVE THE ANSWERS. Where is *God?* He is everywhere. He is all around you now. If you want him, here he is. He waits to be gracious to you. Where is God your *Maker?* He is within eye-sight of you. You cannot see him, but *he* sees *you.* He reads each thought and every motion of your spirit, and records it too. He is within ear-shot of you. Speak, and he will hear you. Ay, whisper—nay, you need not even form the words with the lips, but let the thought be in the soul, and he is so near you—for in him you live and move and have your being—that he will know your heart before you know it yourself. Where is your *Comforter?* He is ready with his "songs in the night." Where is your *Instructor?* He waits to make you wise unto salvation.

"Where, then, may I meet him?" says one. You cannot meet him —you must not attempt it—except through the Mediator. "There is one God and one Mediator between God and men, the man Christ Jesus." If you come to Jesus you have come to God. "God was in Christ reconciling the world unto himself; not imputing their trespasses unto them, and hath committed unto us the word of reconciliation," which word we preach. Believe in Jesus Christ, and your God is with you. Trust your soul with Jesus Christ, and you have found your Creator, and you shall never again have to say, "Where is God my Maker?" for you shall live in him, and he shall live in you. You have found your Comforter and you shall joy in him, while he shall joy in you. You have also in Christ Jesus found your Instructor, who shall guide you through life, and bring you to perfection in yon bright world above.

May the Holy Ghost use this little sermon as a short sword to slay your indifference; for Christ's sake.

PORTIONS OF SCRIPTURE READ BEFORE SERMON—Psalms xlii., liii.

HYMNS FROM "OUR OWN HYMN BOOK"—550, 711, 606, 522.

LOYAL TO THE CORE.

A Sermon

DELIVERED BY

C. H. SPURGEON,

AT THE METROPOLITAN TABERNACLE, NEWINGTON.

"And Ittai answered the king, and said, As the Lord liveth, and as my lord the king liveth, surely in what place my lord the king shall be, whether in death or life, even there also will thy servant be."—2 Samuel xv. 21.

ALTHOUGH the courage of David appears to have failed him when he fled from his son Absalom, yet certain other noble characteristics came out in brilliant relief, and, among the rest, his large-heartedness and his thoughtfulness for others. A man in such a desperate condition as he was must have earnestly coveted many friends and have been anxious to retain them all, but yet he would not exact their services if they were too costly to themselves, and so he said to Ittai, who appears to have been a Philistine—a proselyte to Israel, who had lately come to join himself to David—"Wherefore goest thou also with us? Thou hast newly come to me, and should I make thee wander with me in my sorrows? Return to thy place and abide with the new king, for thou art a stranger and an exile. May every blessing be upon thee. May mercy and truth be with thee." He did not send him away because he doubted him, but because he felt that he had no claim to the great sacrifices which Ittai might have to make in attending his chequered fortunes. "I do not know what may become of me," he seems to say, "but I do not want to drag you down with myself. Should my cause become desperate, I have no wish to involve you in it, and therefore with the best of motives I wish you farewell." I admire this generosity of spirit. Some men have great expectations: they live upon their friends, and yet complain that charity is cold. These people expect more from their friends than they ought to give. A man's best friends on earth ought to be his own strong arms. Loafers are parasitical plants, they have no root of their own, but like the mistletoe they strike root into some other tree, and suck the very soul out of it for their own nourishment. Sad that men should ever degrade themselves to such despicable meanness! While you can help yourselves, do so, and while you have a right to expect help in times of dire necessity, do not be everlastingly expecting everybody else to be waiting upon you. Feel as David did towards Ittai— that you would by no means wish for services to which you have no

No. 1,512.

137

claim.   Independence of spirit used to be characteristic of Englishmen. I hope it will always continue to be so; and especially among children of God.

On the other hand, look at Ittai, perfectly free to go, but in order to end the controversy once for all, and to make David know that he does not mean to leave him, he takes a solemn oath before Jehovah his God, and he doubles it by swearing by the life of David that he will never leave him; in life, in death, he will be with him.   He has cast in his lot with him for better and for worse, and he means to be faithful to the end.   Old Master Trapp says, "All faithful friends went on a pilgrimage years ago, and none of them have ever come back."   I scarcely credit that, but I am afraid that friends quite so faithful as Ittai are as scarce as two moons in the sky at once, and you might travel over the edge of the world before you found them.   I think, however, that one reason why faithful Ittais have become so scarce may be because largehearted Davids are so rare.   When you tell a man that you expect a good deal of him, he does not see it.   Why should you look for so much?   He is not your debtor.   You have closed at once the valves of his generosity.   But when you tell him honestly that you do not expect more than is right, and that you do not wish to be a tax upon him, when he sees that you consult his welfare more than your own, that is the very reason why he feels attached to you, and counts it a pleasure to serve such a generous-hearted man.   You will generally find that when two people fall out there are faults on both sides: if generous spirits be few, it may be because faithful friends are rare, and if faithful friends are scarce it may be because generous spirits are scarce too.   Be it ours as Christians to live to serve rather than to be served, remembering that we are the followers of a Master who said, "The Son of man came not to be ministered unto, but to minister."   We are not to expect others to serve us, but our life is to be spent in endeavouring to serve them.

I am going to use Ittai's language for a further purpose.   If Ittai, charmed with David's person and character, though a foreigner and a stranger, felt that he could enlist beneath his banner for life —yea, and declared that he would do so there and then—how much more may you and I, if we know what Christ has done for us, and who he is and what he deserves at our hands, at this good hour plight our troth to him and vow, "As the Lord liveth, surely in whatsoever place my Lord and Saviour shall be, whether in death or life, even there also shall his servant be."

And so I shall begin by noticing first *in what form this declaration was made*, that we may learn from it how to make the same declaration.

I.   IN WHAT FORM AND MANNER WAS THIS DECLARATION MADE?

It was made, first, at a time *when David's fortunes were at their lowest ebb*, and consequently it was made unselfishly, without the slightest idea of gain from it.   David was now forsaken of everybody.   His faithful body-guard was all that he had on earth to depend upon, and then it was that Ittai cast in his lot with David.   Now, beloved, it is very easy to follow religion when she goes abroad in her silver slippers, but the true man follows her when she is in rags, and goes through the mire and the slough.   To take up with Christ when everybody cries up his name is what a hypocrite would do, but to take up with Christ when they are shouting, "Away with him! away with him!" is another matter. There are times in which the simple faith of Christ is at a great discount. At one time imposing ceremonies are all the rage, and everybody loves decorated worship, and the pure simplicity of the gospel is overloaded and encumbered with meretricious ornaments; it is such a season that we must stand out for God's more simple plan, and reject the symbolism which verges on idolatry and hides the simplicity of the gospel.

At another time the gospel is assailed by learned criticisms and by insinuations against the authenticity and inspiration of the books of Scripture, while fundamental doctrines are undermined one by one, and he who keeps to the old faith is said to be behind the age, and so on. But happy is that man who takes up with Christ, and with the gospel, and with the truth when it is in its worst estate, crying, "If this be foolery, I am a fool, for where Christ is there will I be; I love him better at his worst than others at their best, and even if he be dead and buried in a sepulchre I will go with Mary and with Magdalene and sit over against the sepulchre and watch until he rise again, for rise again he will; but whether he live or die, where he is there shall his servant be." Ho, then, brave spirits, will ye enlist for Christ when his banner is tattered? Will you enlist under him when his armour is stained with blood? Will you rally to him even when they report him slain? Happy shall ye be! Your loyalty shall be proven to your own eternal glory. Ye are soldiers such as he loves to honour.

Ittai gave himself up wholly to David *when he was but newly come to him*. David says, "Whereas thou camest but yesterday, should I this day make thee go up and down with us?" But Ittai does not care whether he came yesterday or twenty years ago, but he declares, "Surely in what place my lord the king shall be, whether in death or life, even there also will thy servant be." It is best to begin the Christian life with thorough consecration. Have any of you professed to be Christians, and have you never given yourselves entirely to Christ? It is time that you began again. This should be one of the earliest forms of our worship of our Master—this total resignation of ourselves to him. According to his word, the first announcement of our faith should be by baptism, and the meaning of baptism, or immersion in water, is death, burial, and resurrection. As far as this point is concerned, the avowal is just this: "I am henceforth dead to all but Christ, whose servant I now am. Henceforth let no man trouble me, for I bear in my body the marks of the Lord Jesus. The watermark is on me from head to foot. I have been buried with him in baptism unto death to show that henceforth I belong to him." Now, whether you have been baptized or not I leave to yourselves, but in any case this must be true—that henceforth you are dead, and your life is hid with Christ in God. As soon as ever Christ is yours you ought to be Christ's. "I am my Beloved's" should be linked with "My Beloved is mine," in the dawn of the day in which you yield to the Lord.

Again, Ittai surrendered himself to David *in the most voluntary manner*. No one persuaded Ittai to do this; in fact, David seems to have persuaded him the other way. David tested and tried him, but he voluntarily out of the fulness of his heart said, "Where, my lord, the king, is, there also shall his servant be." Now, dear young people, if you believe that the Lord Jesus Christ is yours, give yourselves up to him by a distinct act and deed. Feel that one grand impulse without needing pressure or argument,—"The love of Christ constraineth me"; but do not wait to have your duty urged upon you, for the more free the dedication the more acceptable it will be. I am told that there is no wine so delicious as that which flows from the grape at the first gentle pressure. The longer you squeeze the harsher is the juice. We do not like that service which is pressed out of a man : and certainly the Lord of love will not accept forced labour. No ; let your willinghood show itself. Say—

> "Take myself, and I will be
> Ever, *only*, ALL for thee."

My heart pants after the service of her Lord. With the same spontaneity which Ittai displayed make a solemn consecration of yourselves to David's Lord.

I used a word then which suggests another point, namely, that *Ittai did this very solemnly.* He took an oath which we Christians may not do, and may not wish to do, but still we should make the surrender with quite as much solemnity. In Dr. Doddridge's "Rise and Progress of Religion in the Soul" there is a very solemn form of consecration, which he recommends young men to sign when they give themselves to Christ. I cannot say that I can recommend it, though I practised it, for I fear that there is something of legality about it, and that it may bring the soul into bondage. I have known some write out a deed of dedication to Christ and sign it with their blood. I will neither commend nor censure, but I will say that a complete dedication must be made in some manner, and that it should be done deliberately and with grave thought. You have been bought with a price, and you should, therefore, in a distinct manner own your Lord's property in you, and transfer to him the title-deeds of your body, spirit, and soul.

And this, I think, *Ittai did publicly.* At any rate, he so acted that everybody saw him when David said, "Go over," and he marched in front—the first man to pass the brook. Oh yes, dear friend, you must publicly own yourself a Christian. If you are a Christian you must not try to sneak to heaven round the back alleys, but march up the narrow way like a man and like your Master. He was never ashamed of you, though he might have been: how can you be ashamed of him when there is nothing in him to be ashamed of? Some Christians seem to think that they shall lead an easier life if they never make a profession. Like a rat behind the wainscot they come out after candlelight and get a crumb, and then slip back again. I would not lead such a life. Surely, there is nothing to be ashamed of. A Christian—let us glory in the name! A believer in the Lord Jesus Christ—let them write it on our door plates, if they will. Why should we blush at that? "But," says one, "I would rather be a very quiet one." I will now place a torpedo under this cowardly quietness. What saith the Lord Jesus? "Whosoever shall deny me before men, him will I also deny before my Father which is in heaven ; but he that shall confess me before men, him will I confess also before my Father which is in heaven." Take up your cross and follow him, for "with the heart man believeth unto righteousness, and with the mouth confession is made unto salvation." When our Master ascended up on high he told us to preach the gospel to every creature; and how did he put it? "He that believeth and is baptized shall be saved." There must be, therefore, the believing and the acknowledgment of believing. "But cannot I be saved as a believer if I do not openly confess Christ?" Dear friend, you have no business to tamper with your Master's command, and then say, "Will he not graciously forgive this omission?" Do not neglect one of the two commands, but obey all his will. If you have the spirit of Ittai you will say, "Wheresoever my lord the king is, there also shall thy servant be."

I leave the matter with the consciences of those who may be like Nicodemus, coming to Jesus by night, or who may be like Joseph of Arimathea, who was a disciple, but secretly, for fear of the Jews. May they come out and own their Master, believing that then he will own them.

II. Secondly, WHAT DID THIS DECLARATION INVOLVE? As to Ittai, what did it involve?

First, that *he was henceforth to be David's servant.* Of course, as his soldier, he was to fight for him, and to do his bidding. What sayest thou, man? Canst thou lift thy hand to Christ and say, "Henceforth I will live as thy servant, not doing my own will, but thy will. Thy command is henceforth my rule"? Canst thou say that? If not, do not mock him, but stand back. May the Holy Ghost give thee grace thus to begin, thus to persevere, and thus to end.

It involved, next, for Ittai that *he was to do his utmost for David's cause,* not to be his servant in name, but his soldier, ready for scars and wounds and death, if need be, on the king's behalf. That is what Ittai meant as, in rough soldier-tones, he took the solemn oath that it should be so. Now, if thou wouldst be Christ's disciple, determine henceforth by his grace that thou wilt defend his cause; that if there be rough fighting thou wilt be in it; and if there be a forlorn hope needed thou wilt lead it, and go through floods and flames if thy Master's cause shall call thee. Blessed is the man who will follow the Lamb whithersoever he goeth, giving himself wholly up to his Lord to serve him with all his heart.

But Ittai in *his promise declared that he would give a personal attendance upon the person of his master.* That was, indeed, the pith of it. "In what place my lord the king, shall be, even there also will thy servant be." Brethren, let us make the same resolve in our hearts, that wherever Christ is, there we will be. Where is Christ? In heaven. We will be there by-and-by. Where is he here, spiritually? Answer: in his church. The church is a body of faithful men; and where these are met together, there is Jesus in the midst of them. Very well, then, we will join the church, for wherever our Lord, the King, is, there also shall his servants be. When the list of the redeemed is read we will be found in the register, for our Lord's name is there.

Where else did Jesus go? In the commencement of his ministry he descended into the waters of baptism. Let us follow the Lamb whithersoever he goeth. At the close of his ministry he brake bread, and said,

"This do ye in remembrance of me." Be often at his table, for if there is a place on the earth where he manifests himself to his children it is where bread is broken in his name. Let me now tell a secret. Some of you may have heard it before, but you have forgotten it. Here it is—my Lord is generally here at prayer-meetings on Monday nights, and, indeed, whenever his people come together for prayer, there he is. So I will read you my text, and see whether you will come up to it— "Surely in what place my Lord the King shall be, whether it be in a prayer-meeting or at a sermon, even there also will thy servant be." If you love your Lord, you know where his haunts are; take care that you follow hard after him there.

Where is the Lord Jesus Christ? Well, brethren, he is wherever the truth is, and I pray God that he may raise up a race of men and women in England who are determined to be wherever the truth of God is. We have a host of molluscous creatures about who will always be where the congregation is the most respectable: respectability being measured by clothes and cash. Time was in the church of God when they most esteemed the most pious men; has it come to this that gold takes precedence of grace? Our fathers considered whether a ministry was sound, but now the question is—Is the man clever? Words are preferred to truth, and oratory takes the lead of the gospel. Shame on such an age. O you who have not altogether sold your birthrights, I charge you keep out of this wretched declension.

The man who loves Christ thoroughly will say, "Wheresoever the Lord the King is, there also shall his servant be, if it be with half a dozen poor Baptists or Methodists, or among the most despised people in the town." I charge you, beloved, in whatever town or country your lot is cast, be true to your colours, and never forsake your principles. Wherever the truth is, there go, and where there is anything contrary to truth, do not go, for there your Master is not to be found.

What next? Well, our Master is to be found wherever there is anything to be done for the good of our fellow-men. The Lord Jesus Christ is to be found wherever there is work to be done in seeking after his lost sheep. Some people say that they have very little communion with Christ, and when I look at them, I do not wonder. Two persons cannot walk together if they will not walk at the same pace. Now, my Lord walks an earnest pace whenever he goes through the world, for the King's business requires haste; and if his disciples crawl after a snail's fashion they will lose his company. If some of our groaning brethren would go to the Sunday-school, and there begin to look after the little children, they would meet with their Lord who used to say, "Suffer the little children to come unto me." If others were to get together a little meeting, and teach the ignorant, they would there find him who had compassion on the ignorant and on those that are out of the way. Our Master is where there are fetters to be broken, burdens to be removed, and hearts to be comforted, and if you wish to keep with him you must aid in such service.

Where is our Master? Well, he is always on the side of truth and right. And, O, you Christian people, mind that in everything— politics, business, and everything—you keep to that which is right, not to that which is popular. Do not bow the knee to that which for a little day may be cried up, but stand fast in that which is consistent with rectitude, with humanity, with the cause and honour of God, and with the freedom and progress of men. It can never be wise to do wrong. It can never be foolish to be right. It can never be according to the mind of Christ to tyrannize and to oppress. Keep you ever to whatsoever things are pure and lovely and of good report, and you will so far keep with Christ. Temperance, purity, justice—these are favourites with him; do your best to advance them for his sake.

Above all, remember how Jesus loved secret prayer, and if you resolve to keep with him you must be much at the throne of grace.

I will not detain you over each of these points, but simply say that Ittai's declaration meant also this—that *he intended to share David's condition.* If David was great, Ittai would rejoice. If David was exiled, Ittai would attend his wanderings. Our point must be to resolve in God's strength to keep to Christ in all weathers and in all companies, and that whether in life or death. Ah that word "death" makes it sweet, because then we reap the blessed result of having lived with Christ. We shall go upstairs for the last time and bid good-bye to all, and then we shall feel that in death he is still with us as in life we have been with him. Though our good works can never be a ground of confidence when we are dying, yet if the Lord enables us to follow the Lamb whithersoever he goeth, and so to lead a decided, positive, downright, upright Christian life, our death pillow will not be stuffed with thorns of regret, but we shall have to bless God that we bore a faithful witness as far as we were able to do so. In such a case we shall not when we are dying wish to go back again to rectify the mistakes and insincerities of our lives. No, beloved, it will be very, very sweet to be alone with Jesus in death. He will make all our bed in our sickness; he will make our dying pillow soft, and our soul shall vanish, kissed away by his dear lips, and we shall be with him for ever and for ever. Of those that are nearest to him it is said, " These are they that follow the Lamb whithersoever he goeth. They shall walk with him in white, for they are worthy."

I conclude with this observation. Will our Lord Jesus Christ accept at our hands to-night such a consecrating word? If we are trusting in him for salvation will he permit us to say that we will keep with him as long as we live?

We reply, he will not permit us to say it in our own strength. There was a young man who said, " Lord, I will follow thee whithersoever thou goest," but Christ gave him a cool reception: and there was an older man who said, " Though all men shall forsake thee yet will not I," and in reply his Master prayed for him that his faith should not fail. Now, you must not promise as Peter did, or you will make a greater failure. But, beloved, this self-devotion is what Christ expects of us if we are his disciples. He will not have us love father or mother more than him; we must be ready to give up all for his sake. This is not only what our Master expects from us, but what he deserves from us.

> " Love so amazing, so divine,
> Demands my soul, my life, my all."

This, also, is what the Lord will help us to do, for he will give us grace if we will but seek it at his hands : and this it is which he will graciously reward, and has already rewarded, in that choice word of his in the twelfth of John, where he says of his disciples in the twenty-sixth verse, " If any man serve me, let him follow me ; and where I am, there shall also my servant be : if any man serve me, him will my Father honour." Oh, to be honoured of God in eternity when he shall say, " Stand back, angels ; make way, seraphim and cherubim ; here comes a man that suffered for the sake of my dear Son. Here comes one that was not ashamed of my Only-begotten when his face was smeared with the spittle. Here comes one that stood in the pillory with Jesus, and was called ill names for his sake. Stand back, ye angels, these have greater honour than you." Surely the angels of heaven as they traverse the streets of gold and meet the martyrs will ask them about their sufferings, and say, " You are more favoured than we, for you have had the privilege of suffering and dying for the Lord." O brothers and sisters, snatch at the privilege of living for Jesus ; conse-crate yourselves this day unto him ; live from this hour forward, not to enrich yourselves, nor to gain honour and esteem, but for Jesus, for Jesus alone. Oh, if I could set him before you here ; if I could cause him to stand on this platform just as he came from Gethsemane with his bloody sweat about him, or as he came down from the cross with wounds so bright with glory and so fresh with bleeding out our re-demption, I think I should hear you say, each one of you, " Lord Jesus, we are thine, and in what place thou shalt be, whether in death or life, even there also will thy servants be." So may the Lord help us by his most gracious Spirit who hath wrought all our works in us, for Jesus' sake. Amen.

PORTIONS OF SCRIPTURE READ BEFORE SERMON—2 Samuel xv. 13—23 ; Matthew x. 24—33.

HYMNS FROM " OUR OWN HYMN BOOK "—670, 658, 666.

BELOVED, AND YET AFFLICTED.

Notes of a Sermon

PREACHED BEFORE AN AUDIENCE OF INVALID LADIES AT MENTONE, BY

C. H. SPURGEON.

"*Lord, behold, he whom thou lovest is sick.*"—John xi. 3.

THAT disciple whom Jesus loved is not at all backward to record that Jesus loved Lazarus too: there are no jealousies among those who are chosen by the Well-beloved. Jesus loved Mary, and Martha, and Lazarus: it is a happy thing where a whole family live in the love of Jesus. They were a favoured trio, and yet, as the serpent came into Paradise, so did sorrow enter their quiet household at Bethany. Lazarus was sick. They all felt that if Jesus were there disease would flee at his presence; what then should they do but let him know of their trial? Lazarus was near to death's door, and so his tender sisters at once reported the fact to Jesus, saying, "Lord, behold, he whom thou lovest is sick." Many a time since then has that same message been sent to our Lord, for in full many a case he has chosen his people in the furnace of affliction. Of the Master it is said, "himself took our infirmities, and bare our sicknesses," and it is, therefore, no extraordinary thing for the members to be in this matter conformed to their Head.

I. Notice, first, A FACT mentioned in the text: "Lord, behold, he whom thou lovest is sick." The sisters were somewhat astonished that it should be so, for the word "behold" implies a measure of surprise. "*We* love him, and would make him well directly: *thou* lovest him, and yet he remains sick. Thou canst heal him with a word, why then is thy loved one sick?" Have not you, dear sick friend, often wondered how your painful or lingering disease could be consistent with your being chosen, and called, and made one with Christ? I dare say this has greatly perplexed you, and yet in very truth it is by no means strange, but a thing to be expected.

We need not be astonished that the man whom the Lord loves is sick, for *he is only a man*. The love of Jesus does not separate us from the common necessities and infirmities of human life. Men of God are still men. The covenant of grace is not a charter of exemption from consumption, or rheumatism, or asthma. The bodily ills, which come upon us because of our flesh, will attend us to the tomb, for Paul saith, "we that are in this body do groan."

Those whom the Lord loves are the more likely to be sick, since they are *under a peculiar discipline*. It is written, "Whom the Lord loveth he chasteneth, and scourgeth every son whom he receiveth." Affliction

No. 1,518.

145

of some sort is one of the marks of the true-born child of God, and it frequently happens that the trial takes the form of illness. Shall we therefore wonder that we have to take our turn in the sick chamber? If Job, and David, and Hezekiah must each one smart, who are we that we should be amazed because we are in ill-health?

Nor is it remarkable that we are sick if we reflect upon the great *benefit which often flows from it to ourselves.* I do not know what peculiar improvement may have been wrought in Lazarus, but many a disciple of Jesus would have been of small use if he had not been afflicted. Strong men are apt to be harsh, imperious, and unsympathetic, and therefore they need to be put into the furnace, and melted down. I have known Christian women who would never have been so gentle, tender, wise, experienced, and holy if they had not been mellowed by physical pain. There are fruits in God's garden as well as in man's which never ripen till they are bruised. Young women who are apt to be volatile, conceited, or talkative, are often trained to be full of sweetness and light by sickness after sickness, by which they are taught to sit at Jesus' feet. Many have been able to say with the psalmist, " It is good for me to have been afflicted, that I might learn thy statutes." For this reason even such as are highly favoured and blessed among women may feel a sword piercing through their hearts.

Oftentimes this sickness of the Lord's loved ones is *for the good of others.* Lazarus was permitted to be sick and to die, that by his death and resurrection the apostles might be benefited. His sickness was "for the glory of God." Throughout these nineteen hundred years which have succeeded Lazarus' sickness all believers have been getting good out of it, and this afternoon we are all the better because he languished and died. The church and the world may derive immense advantage through the sorrows of good men : the careless may be awakened, the doubting may be convinced, the ungodly may be converted, the mourner may be comforted through our testimony in sickness ; and if so, would we wish to avoid pain and weakness? Are we not quite willing that our friends should say of us also " Lord, behold, he whom thou lovest is sick "?

II. Our text, however, not only records a fact, but mentions A REPORT of that fact : the sisters sent and told Jesus. Let us keep up a constant correspondence with our Lord about everything.

> " Sing a hymn to Jesus, when thy heart is faint ;
> Tell it all to Jesus, comfort or complaint."

Jesus knows all about us, but *it is a great relief to pour out our hearts before him.* When John the Baptist's broken-hearted disciples saw their leader beheaded, " they took up the body, and went and told Jesus." They could not have done better. In all trouble send a message to Jesus, and do not keep your misery to yourself. In his case there is no need of reserve, there is no fear of his treating you with cold pride, or heartless indifference, or cruel treachery. He is a confidant who never can betray us, a friend who never will refuse us.

There is this fair hope about telling Jesus, that *he is sure to support us under it.* If you go to Jesus, and ask, " Most gracious Lord, why am I sick? I thought I was useful while in health, and now I can do nothing; why is this?" he may be pleased to show you why, or, if not, he will make you willing to bear his will with patience without knowing why. He can bring his truth to your mind to cheer you, or strengthen your heart by his presence, or send you unexpected comforts, and give you to glory in your afflictions. "Ye people, pour out your heart before him: God is a refuge for us." Not in vain did Mary and Martha send to tell Jesus, and not in vain do any seek his face.

Remember, too, that *Jesus may give healing.* It would not be wise to live by a supposed faith, and cast off the physician and his medicines, any more than to discharge the butcher, and the tailor, and expect to be fed and clothed by faith; but this would be far better than forgetting the Lord altogether, and trusting to man only. Healing for both body and soul must be sought from God. We make use of medicines, but these can do nothing apart from the Lord, "who healeth all our diseases." We may tell Jesus about our aches and pains, and gradual declinings, and hacking coughs. Some persons are afraid to go to God about their health: they pray for the pardon of sin, but dare not ask the Lord to remove a headache: and, yet, surely, if the hairs outside our head are all numbered by God it is not much more of a condescension for him to relieve throbs and pressures inside the head. Our big things must be very little to the great God, and our little things cannot be much less. It is a proof of the greatness of the mind of God that while ruling the heavens and the earth, he is not so absorbed by these great concerns as to be forgetful of the least pain or want of any one of his poor children. We may go to him about our failing breath, for he first gave us lungs and life. We may tell him about the eye which grows dim, and the ear which loses hearing, for he made them both. We may mention the swollen knee, and the gathering finger, the stiff neck, and the sprained foot, for he made all these our members, redeemed them all, and will raise them all from the grave. Go at once, and say, "Lord, behold, he whom thou lovest is sick."

III. Thirdly, let us notice in the case of Lazarus A RESULT which we should not have expected. No doubt when Mary and Martha sent to tell Jesus they looked to see Lazarus recover as soon as the messenger reached the Master; but they were not gratified. For two days the Lord remained in the same place, and not till he knew that Lazarus was dead did he speak of going to Judæa. This teaches us that Jesus may be informed of our trouble, and yet may act as if he were indifferent to it. We must not expect in every case that prayer for recovery will be answered, for if so, nobody would die who had chick or child, friend or acquaintance to pray for him. In our prayers for the lives of beloved children of God we must not forget that there is one prayer which may be crossing ours, for Jesus prays, "Father, I will that they also, whom thou hast given me, be with me where I am, that they may behold my glory." We pray that they may remain with us, but when we recognise that Jesus wants them above, what can we do but admit his larger claim and say, "Not as I will, but as thou wilt"? In our own case, we may pray the Lord to raise us up, and yet though he loves us he may permit us to grow worse and worse, and at last to die. Hezekiah had fifteen years added to his life, but we may not gain the reprieve of a single day. Never set such store by the life of any one dear to you, or even by your own life, as to be rebellious against the Lord. If you hold the life of any dear one with too tight a hand, you are making a rod for your own back ; and if you love your own earthly life too well, you are making a thorny pillow for your dying bed. Children are often idols, and in such cases their too ardent lovers are idolaters. We might as well make a god of clay, and worship it, as the Hindoos are said to do, as worship our fellow-creatures, for what are they but clay? Shall dust be so dear to us that we quarrel with our God about it? If our Lord leaves us to suffer, let us not repine. He must do that for us which is kindest and best, for he loves us better than we love ourselves.

Did I hear you say, " Yes, Jesus allowed Lazarus to die, *but he raised him up again*"? I answer, he is the resurrection and the life to us also. Be comforted concerning the departed, " Thy brother shall rise again," and all of us whose hope is in Jesus shall partake in our Lord's resurrection. Not only shall our souls live, but our bodies, too, shall be raised incorruptible. The grave will serve as a refining pot, and this vile body shall come forth vile no longer. Some Christians are greatly cheered by the thought of living till the Lord comes, and so escaping death. I confess that I think this no great gain, for so far from having any preference over them that are asleep, those who are alive and remain at his coming will miss one point of fellowship, in not dying and rising like their Lord. Beloved, all things are yours, and death is expressly mentioned in the list, therefore do not dread it, but rather "long for evening to undress, that you may rest with God."

IV. I will close with A QUESTION—"Jesus loved Martha, and her sister, and Lazarus"—does Jesus in a special sense love you? Alas, many sick ones have no evidence of any special love of Jesus towards them, for they have never sought his face, nor trusted in him. Jesus might say to them " I never knew you," for they have turned their backs upon his blood and his cross. Answer, dear friend, to your own heart this question, " Do you love Jesus?" If so, you love him because he first loved you. Are you trusting him? If so, that faith of yours is the proof that he has loved you from before the foundation of the world, for faith is the token by which he plights his troth to his beloved.

If Jesus loves you, and you are sick, let all the world see how you glorify God in your sickness. Let friends and nurses see how the beloved of the Lord are cheered and comforted by him. Let your holy resignation astonish them, and set them admiring your Beloved, who is so gracious to you that he makes you happy in pain, and joyful at the gates of the grave. If your religion is worth anything it ought to support you now, and it will compel unbelievers to see that he whom the Lord loveth is in better case when he is sick than the ungodly when full of health and vigour.

If you do not know that Jesus loves you, you lack the brightest star that can cheer the night of sickness. I hope you will not die as you now are, and pass into another world without enjoying the love of Jesus : that would be a terrible calamity indeed. Seek his face at once, and it may be that your present sickness is a part of the way of love by which Jesus would bring you to himself. Lord, heal all these sick ones in soul and in body. Amen.

AT SCHOOL.

A Sermon

DELIVERED BY

C. H. SPURGEON,

AT THE METROPOLITAN TABERNACLE, NEW'NGTON.

"Teach me to do thy will; for thou art my God."—Psalm cxliii. 10.

THIS is a prayer about doing, but it is perfectly free from legal taint. The man who offered it had no idea of being saved by his doings, for in the second verse of the psalm he had said, "Enter not into judgment with thy servant: for in thy sight shall no man living be justified." This is not the prayer of a sinner seeking salvation, for salvation is not by doing the will of God but by believing in Christ. It is the prayer of the man who is already saved, and who being saved devotes himself to the service of God, and wishes to be taught in the fear of the Lord. "Teach me to do thy will, O God."

The connection leads us to make the remark that David looked upon the doing of God's will as his best escape from his enemies. He speaks of his cruel persecutors. He declares that though he looked all around he could find none who would help him. Then he prays, "Teach me to do thy will; for thou art my God." And depend upon it, the surest way to escape from harm is to do no ill. If you are surrounded by those who would slander you, your best defence is a blameless life; and if many are watching for your halting and maliciously desiring your fall, your safety lies in holiness. The very best prayer you can pray for your own protection is, "Teach me to do thy will." If you do right none can harm you.

This prayer was suggested by the perplexity of the psalmist's mind. He was overwhelmed, and did not know what to do, and therefore he cried, "Teach me to do *thy* will, O God." He had come to a place where many roads met, and he did not know which path to take; and so he prayed God to guide him in the way appointed. I commend this prayer to all who may be sorely puzzled and anxious. You have exercised your own judgment, and you have, perhaps, too much consulted with friends, and yet your way seems entirely blocked up: then resort to God with this as your heart's prayer, "Teach me to do thy will; for thou art my God."

May the Spirit of God now bless us while we open up this short prayer that we may be helped to understand it, and use it. First, we will speak upon *the prayer;* and then, secondly, upon *its answer.*

I. And, first, THE PRAYER ITSELF—let us notice its character.

No. 1,519.

It is a *holy prayer.* "Teach me to do thy will." The man who utters this language desires to be free from sin, for sin can never be God's will. Under no circumstances whatever may I do wrong and fancy that I am doing God's will therein. I have read of an extremely poor man who wanted fuel for the fire for his children, and the text came to his mind, "All things are yours." Armed with this text, he thought he would take a little wood from his neighbour's wood-pile; but very happily there came to his mind another text, "Thou shalt not steal." He was quite clear about its meaning, and so he let the wood alone; but he recollected afterwards how that text had saved him from a great transgression. Depend upon it, whatever circumstances or impressions may seem to say, it is never God's will that you should do wrong. There are devil's providences as well as God's providences. When Jonah wanted to go to Tarshish, he found a ship going thither; and I dare say he said "How providential!" Yes, but no providence can ever be an excuse for sinning against God. We are to do right, and therefore we pray, "Teach me to do thy will."

It is a *humble prayer*—the prayer of a man of deep experience, and yet, for all that, and perhaps because of that, a man who felt that he needed teaching as to every step he should take. When you do not want teaching, brother, it is because you are too stupid to learn: you may depend upon that. It is only a very young lady fresh from a boarding-school, who has "finished her education," and it is only a great fool of a man who thinks that he can learn no more. Those who know themselves best, and know the world best, and know God best, always have the lowest thoughts of themselves. They have no wisdom of their own except this, that they are wise enough to flee from their own wisdom, and say to the Lord, "Teach me to do thy will." This is a holy prayer and a humble prayer, and commends itself to every holy and humble heart.

It is, dear friends, a *docile prayer*—the prayer of a teachable man. "Teach me to do thy will." It is not merely, you see, "Teach me thy will," but "Teach me to do it." The person is so ignorant that he needs to be taught how to do anything and everything. You may tell a child how to walk, but it will not walk for all that. You must teach it to walk. You must take it by the arms as God did Ephraim. He says, "I taught Ephraim also to go, taking them by their arms," just as a nurse teaches her little ones. "Teach me to do." Lord, it is not enough that thou teach my head and teach my heart, but teach my hands and my feet. "Teach me to do thy will." Such a suppliant is docile, and ready to learn.

It is an *acquiescent prayer* also, which is a great thing in its favour. "Teach me to do *thy* will—not mine. I will put my will on one side." He does not say, "Lord, teach me to do part of thy will, that part which pleases me," but all thy will. If there be any part of thy will which I am not pleased with, for that very reason teach it to me, until my whole soul shall be conformed to thy mind, and I shall love thy will, not because it happens to be pleasing, but because it is thy will. It is a prayer of resignation and self-abnegation, and is, perhaps, one of the highest that the Christian can pray, though it may well befit the learner who stands for the first time at wisdom's door.

And then notice that it is a *believing prayer*—" Teach me to do thy will ; *for thou art my God.*" There is faith in God in this claim. " Thou art my God ; " and there is faith in God's condescension that he will act as a Teacher. Brethren, we have two faults. We do not think God to be so great as he is, and we do not think God can be so little as he can be. We err on both sides, and neither know his height of glory nor his depth of grace. We practically say, " This trial is too mean ; I will bear it without him." We forget that the same God who rules the stars condescends to be a Teacher, and teaches us to do his will. We heard once of a president of a great nation who nevertheless taught in a Sunday-school : it was thought to be great condescension, but what shall I say of him who, while he sits amid the choirs of angels and accepts their praises, comes down to his little children and teaches them to do his will ! The prayer before us is very precious, for it is holy, humble, docile, acquiescent, and believing.

Let us now notice what the actual request is. In so many words it says, " Teach me to do thy will." So, brethren and sisters, it is *a practical prayer*. He does not say merely, " Teach me to know thy will "—a very excellent prayer that ; but there are a great many who stick fast in the knowing, and do not go on to the doing ; these are forgetful hearers, deceiving themselves. An ounce of doing is worth a ton of knowing. The most orthodox faith in the world, if it be accompanied by an unholy life, will only increase a man's damnation. There must be the yielding up of the members and of the mind unto God in obedience, or else the more we know the greater will be our condemnation.

The psalmist does not say, " Lord, help me to talk about thy will," though it is a very proper thing to talk about, and a very profitable thing to hear about. But still doing is better than talking. If *t's* were *w's* there would be more saints in the world than there are ; that is to say, if those who *t*alk uprightly would also *w*alk uprightly it would be well ; but with many the talk is better than the walk. Better a silent tongue than an unclean life. Practical godliness is preferable to the sweetest eloquence.

The prayer is, " Teach me to do *thy will*." There are some who long to be taught in all mysteries ; and truly to understand a mystery aright is a great privilege, but their main thought seems to be to know the deep doctrines, the mysterious points. Many go into prophecy, and a nice muddle they make when they get there. We have had I do not know how many theories of prophecy, each one of them more absurd than the rest, and so it will be, I fear, to the world's end. Truly, it would be a good thing to understand the prophecies, and all knowledge, " and yet show I unto you a more excellent way"; and that excellent way is to live a life of humble, godly dependence and faith, and to show forth in your life the love that was in Christ Jesus. Lord, I chiefly long to know thy will : teach me that, and I am content.

I have already said that this prayer asks that we may do God's will, not our own. Oh ! how naturally our heart prays, " Lord, let me have my own way." That is the first prayer of human nature when it is let alone ; " Who is the Lord that I should obey his voice ? Let me have my own way." That desire will sometimes enter the Christian's heart, though I hope it will not long remain there. We may be praying,

"Lord, not my will, but thine be done," and yet the wicked, rebellious heart may be saying inside, "But do let it be my will, Lord: do let it be my will." Still do we cling to self. May the Lord deliver us from Lord Will-be-will, who is a terrible tyrant wherever he rules; and may this be our prayer, "Teach me to do thy will."

We are not to ask to do other people's will, though some persons are always slaves to the wills of others. Whatever their company is that are they. In Rome they do as Rome does: they try to accommodate themselves to their family; they cannot take a stand, or be decided, but they are ruled and governed, poor slaves that they are, by their connections. They fear the frown of man. Oh that they would rise to something nobler, and pray, "Lord, teach me to do thy will, whether it is the will of the great ones of the earth, or the will of my influential friends, or the will of my loud talking neighbours or not. Help me to do *thy* will, to take my stand, and say, 'As for me and my house, *we* will serve the Lord.'" It is a blessed prayer. The more we look at it the more we see in it.

What does he mean by doing God's will? Does he not mean, "Help me to do as thy word bids me"? For the will of God is put before us very plainly in *his law*, and, especially, in that law as viewed in the hand of Christ. "This is the will of God, even our sanctification." To serve him devoutly, and to love our neighbour as ourselves—this is the will of God. May his Spirit help us. "Teach me to do thy will, O God."

That will also takes the form of *providence*. Out of two courses equally right we sometimes have to ask the question, "Lord, what is thy will here?" There is nothing immoral in either the one or the other, and hence our difficulty, and then we come to the Lord and say, "Here is a case in which thy law does not guide me, otherwise I should decide at once, but wilt thou now show me what thou wilt have me to do?" In another case the will of God may be suggested by *opportunity*. Dear friend, the will of God is that you should speak to that friend sitting near you about soul-matters. The will of God is that your unconverted servant should have your prayers and your instruction. God puts men in our way on purpose that we may do them good. I have no doubt whatever that many a Christian is made to go where he would not choose to go, and to associate with persons that he would not wish to associate with, on purpose that he may be the means of taking light into dark places, and of carrying life from God to dead souls. So that if you pray this prayer, "Teach me to do thy will," and carry it out, you will watch for opportunities of serving the Lord.

The prayer seems to me to have all that compass, and much more.

But I would answer another enquiry. *What is the intention of the prayer as to manner?* It does not say, "Lord, enable me to do thy will," but, "*Teach* me to do thy will," as if there were some peculiar way of doing it that had to be taught, as when a young man goes apprentice to acquire a trade. Lord, I would put myself under indentures to thy grace that thou mayest teach me the art and mystery of doing thy will.

How then ought God's will to be done?

It should be done *thoughtfully.* A great many Christians are not half as considerate as they should be. We should go through life, not flippantly like the butterfly that flits from flower to flower, but like the bee that stays and sucks honey, and gathers sweet store for the hive. We should be seriously in earnest; and one point of earnestness should be

> " With holy trembling, holy fear,
> To make my calling sure,
> Thine utmost counsel to fulfil,
> And suffer all thy righteous will,
> And to the end endure."

Lord, help me to do thy will, seriously bending all my soul to the doing of it; not trifling in thy courts, nor making life a play, but loving thee with my understanding.

The Lord's will should be done *immediately*. As soon as a command is known it should be obeyed. Lord, suffer me not to consult with flesh and blood. Make me prompt and quick of understanding in the fear of God. Teach me to do thy will as angels do, who no sooner hear thy word than they fly like flames of fire to fulfil thy behests.

His will should by done *cheerfully*. Jehovah seeks not slaves to grace his throne. He would have us delight to do his will: yea, his law should be in our heart. Oh! brothers and sisters, you need to pray this: "Teach me to do thy will," or else you will miss the mark.

Teach me to do it *constantly*. Let me not sometimes be thy servant, and then run away from thee. Keep me to it. Let me never weary. When the morning wakes me may it find me ready, and when the evening bids me rest may I be serving thee until I fall asleep.

Teach me to do it also, Lord, *universally*, not some part of it, but all of it, not one of thy commands being neglected, nor one single part of my daily task being left undone. I am thy servant; make me to be what a good servant is to her mistress, neglecting none of the cares of the household. May I be watchful in all points.

Teach me to do thy will *spiritually*, not making the outside of cups and platters clean, but obeying thee within my soul. May what I do be done with all my heart. If I pray, help me to pray in the spirit. If I sing, let my heart make music unto thee. When I am talking to others about thy name, and trying to spread the savour of Jesus, let me not do it in my own strength, or in a wrong spirit, but may the Holy Ghost be upon me.

Teach me to do thy will *intensely*. Let the zeal of thy house eat me up. Oh that I might throw my whole self into it.

This little prayer grows, does it not? Pray it, brothers and sisters, and may the Lord answer you.

Once again, there are necessary qualities which we must seek if we would sincerely pray this prayer, "Teach me to do thy will." Then, you must have *decision of character*, for some never do God's will, though they wish they did, and they regret, they say, that they cannot: they resolve that they will, and there it ends. O you spongy souls! Some of you are sadly squeezable. Whatever hand grips you can shape you. Decision is needed, for you cannot do God's will unless you know how to say, "No," and to put your foot down, and declare that whatever may happen you will not turn aside from the service of your God.

If the Lord shall teach you to do his will, you will also need *courage*. The prayer virtually says, "When my enemies ridicule me, teach me to do thy will. When they threaten me, teach me to do thy will. When they tempt me, teach me to do thy will. When they slander me, teach me to do thy will, to be brave with the bravery which resolves to do the right, and leaves the issues with God."

"Teach me to do thy will." It means—Give me *resignation*, kill in me my self-hood, put down, I pray thee, my pride, make me willing to be anything or to do anything thou wilt.

It is a prayer that necessitates *humility*. No man can pray it unless he is willing to stoop and wash the saints' feet. "Teach me to do thy will." Let me be a scullion in thy kitchen if so I may glorify thee. I have no choice but that thou be all in all.

It is a prayer, too, *for spiritual life*, and much of it, for a dead man cannot do God's will. Shall the dead praise him? Shall they that go down to the pit give him thanks? Oh, no, brothers and sisters; you must be full of life if you are to do God's will. Some professors are not quickened one-third of the way up yet. I hope they have a measure of quickening, but it does not seem to have reached the extremities. There may be a little quickening in the heart, but it has not quickened the tongue to confess Christ, nor quickened the hand to give to Christ, or to work for Christ. They seem to be half-dead. O Lord, fill me with life from the sole of my foot to the crown of my head, for how can I do thy will unless thy Spirit saturates me through and through, till every pulse is consecrated? I would be wholly thine. "Teach me to do thy will."

II. I will not detain you many minutes over the second part of our sermon, in which we are to say a little upon ITS ANSWER. There is the prayer, "Teach me to do thy will." Will it get an answer? Yes, brethren, it will assuredly obtain an answer of peace.

For, first, *there is a reason for expecting it.* "Thou art my God." Oh, yes, if we were asking this of some one else we might fear, but "thou art my God" is blessed argument, because the greater supposes the less. If God has given us himself, he will give us teaching. It is also God's way to teach:—"Good and upright is the Lord, therefore will he teach transgressors in the way." It is a quality of a good man to wish to make others good; it is supremely the quality of the good God to make others good. When I think of what the Lord is, I am certain that he will be willing to teach me to do his will. Moreover, he has promised to do it. "I will instruct thee, and teach thee in the way that thou shalt go. I will guide thee with mine eye." And, again, he is glorified by so doing, for it brings glory to God when his people do his will; therefore may I expect for all these reasons that he will teach me to do his will.

Again, dear friends, *it needs to be answered.* "Teach *me* to do thy will. Lord, there is nobody who can ever teach *me* thy will except thou do it. I shall never learn it of myself. This scholarship I shall never pick up by chance. Lord, unless thou hold me fast, and teach me with thy supremest art, I shall never learn to do thy will as I desire to learn it." You see, he turns away from every other teacher to his God, he puts himself to school to God alone. And there is the prayer, "Teach me to do thy will; for thou art my God." Brother, you must have this teaching, or else you will never do God's will. No strength of nature, no wit of nature, can ever suffice to serve the Lord aright; you must be taught from above.

There are many ways in which God gives his answer to this prayer—"Teach me to do thy will." We have received one wonderful answer to it already. He has given *Jesus Christ to be our Example.* There is no teaching like actual example. If you want to know the will of God study the life of Christ.

The Lord is pleased to give us fainter copies of that same will of his in his saints. Read the sacred biographies of the Scriptures. Watch the *holy lives* of those who are among you, who live near to God, and follow them so far as they follow Christ. They are not complete copies; there are blots and blunders: still, the Lord does teach young people by the godly lives of their parents, and he instructs all of us by the biographies of devoted men and women.

Again, the Lord teaches us by every line of *his word,* and oftentimes when that word is heard, or carefully read, it comes home with great power to the soul, and guides us in the way of life.

Moreover the Lord has a way of teaching us by *his own Spirit.* The Holy Spirit speaks in secret whispers to those who are able to hear him. It is not every professing Christian that has the visitations of the Spirit of God in personal monitions, but there are saints who hear a voice behind them saying, "This is the way, walk ye in it." God guides us with his eye as well as by his word. Opened eyes can see in a moment what the Lord means. He has *gentle* means. His daily dealings in loving tenderness are guides to us. Every mercy is a star to pilot us to heaven. When we are not willing to be guided so easily, he will teach us by *rough means.* The Lord has a bit and a whip for those who need them. He will restrain us by affliction and infirmity, and sometimes chasten us very sore with losses, bereavements, depression of spirit, and the like: but in some way or other he will hear the prayer for teaching, for it is a covenant promise, "All thy children shall be taught of the Lord." Blessed are they to whom the teaching comes sweetly and softly. It can be so if we are willing to have it so ; but surely if we will not be tenderly guided, God will make us to do his will as men compel the bullock to do their will when it is rebellious under ·the yoke, and must be·broken in. The Lord will hear our prayer for instruction; but it may not be quite in the way we should have chosen.

One thing more. I trust we have, all of us who know the Lord, prayed the prayer, "Teach me to do thy will; for thou art my God." Now mind, my dear friend, mind that you do it sincerely, and know what you are at, because after offering such a petition as this, you dare not go into sin. You cannot say, "Teach me to do thy will," and then go off to frivolous amusements, or spend your evenings in vain and giddy society, because that would be an insolent mockery of God. "Teach me to do thy will," you say, and then get up and do what you know to be clean contrary to his mind and will: what defiant profanity is this!

Again, do not offer this prayer with a reserve. Do not say, or mean, "Teach me to do thy will in all points but one. That is a point in which I pray thee have me excused." I am afraid that certain believers do not want to learn too much. I have known them not like to read special passages of Scripture. Perhaps they trouble them doctrinally, or as to the ordinances of the Christian faith, or as to matters of church discipline; if they do not paste those pages together to hide the obnoxious passage yet they do not like them opened too much. They would rather read a verse which looks more to their mind. But, brother, if thou and a text have a quarrel, make it up directly. Thou must not alter the text; alter thy creed, alter thy life, alter thy thought, God the Holy Spirit helping thee; for the text is right, and thou art in the wrong. "Teach me to do thy will," means, if we pray it honestly, "I will search God's book to know what his mind is." Why, there are numbers of you who join with the church you were brought up to, whatever it is. You do not take the trouble to examine as to whether your church is Scriptural or not. This is a blind way of acting. This is not obeying the will of God. Know what God's book teaches. Search the Scriptures. Many Christians believe what their minister preaches because *he* preaches it. Do not believe a word of what I preach unless you can find it in the Word of God. "To the law and to the testimony. If we speak not according to this word it is because there is no light in us." We are all fallible, and though we teach as best we can, and hope that God teaches you much by us, yet we are not inspired, and do not pretend to be. Search you the book of God on your own account, and abide by what you find there, and by nothing else. Where the Bible leads you are bound to follow, and following its guidance you shall not walk in darkness. Seek to know the will of God; and when you know it, carry it out, and pray the Holy Ghost to take away the dearest idol you have known—the thought that pleases you best— out of your mind, if it is contrary to the supreme will of the eternal God. The Lord grant we may thus pray, and thus be heard.

Alas, unconverted people cannot pray after the fashion of my text. They have, first of all, to believe in the Lord Jesus Christ before they can do the will of the Lord. May you all be led to believe in the Saviour, and when you have so done then may the Holy Ghost lead you to pray, "Teach me to do thy will; for thou art my God."

The Lord bless you, for Christ's sake. Amen.

PORTIONS OF SCRIPTURE READ BEFORE SERMON—Psalms cxlii. and cxliii.

HYMNS FROM "OUR OWN HYMN BOOK"—119 (Part I.), 708, 143.

PRESSING QUESTIONS OF AN AWAKENED MIND.

DELIVERED BY

C. H. SPURGEON,

AT THE METROPOLITAN TABERNACLE, NEWINGTON.

"Who art thou, Lord? .... What wilt thou have me to do?"—Acts ix. 5, 6.

PAUL fell to the ground overcome by the brightness of the light which outshone the mid-day sun, and as he lay there he cried, "Who art thou, Lord?" After receiving an answer to his first question, he humbly asked another, "Lord, what wilt thou have me to do?"

This morning I spent all my strength, and I scarcely have any remaining for this evening, but the subject was well worthy of the greatest exhaustion.[*] I tried to show that we must receive the kingdom of heaven as little children, or else we could not in any wise enter into it. I wanted, if I could, to add a sort of practical tail-piece to that subject, something that would enable me, yet more fully, to explain the childlike spirit which comes at conversion, and which is absolutely needful as one of the first marks and consequences of the work of the Spirit of God upon the heart. I cannot find a better illustration of the childlike spirit than this which is now before us.

Paul was a great man, and on the way to Damascus I have no doubt he rode a very high horse. He verily thought that he was doing God service. He was a Pharisee of the Pharisees, and had a very high estimate of his own character; and now that he had letters from the high priest upon his person, he felt himself to be armed with great power, and to be no mean man. He would let those poor Christians in Damascus know! He would worry them out of their fanaticism. He would take care to let them see that Saul of Tarsus was greater than Jesus of Nazareth. But a few seconds sufficed for the Lord to alter the man. How soon he brought him down! The manifestation of Jesus Christ himself from heaven soon subdued the great man into a little child, for the two questions which are now before us are exceedingly childlike. He enquires, with sacred curiosity, "Who art thou, Lord?" and then he surrenders at discretion, crying, "What wilt thou have me to do?" He seems to cry, "I give up my weapons. I submit

---

[*] "Receiving the kingdom of God as a little child." No. 1,439.

No. 1,520.

to be thy servant. I only ask to be taught what I am to do, and I am ready to do it. Thou hast conquered me. Behold, at thy feet I lie; only raise me up and give me something to do in thy service, for I will gladly undertake it." To this spirit we must all come if we are to be saved. We must come to think of Jesus so as to desire to know him; and then we must reverence Jesus so as to be willing to obey his will in all things. Upon those two points I am going to speak with a measure of brevity to-night.

Our first object of thought will be—*the earnest enquirer seeking to know his Lord;* and the second will be *the obedient disciple requesting directions.*

I. First, then, if any one of us would be saved he must be brought by divine grace to be AN EARNEST ENQUIRER AFTER THE KNOWLEDGE OF CHRIST. He must ask the question, "Who art thou, Lord?"

Notice that *he is willing to be taught.* He lies there with the Christ above him, and he asks him a question. He is not only willing to learn, but he is eager to be taught. "Who art thou, Lord?" is the utterance of his inmost soul. He wants to know. And dost not thou want to know, my hearer? There is but one name given under heaven whereby thou must be saved. Dost thou not wish to know something about him whose name it is? Art thou indifferent to thy soul's affairs, careless about what shall become of thy immortal soul? Did Jesus die, and is it nothing to thee? Dost thou pass by his cross as though it were the market cross of a village? Dost thou hear of his death as though it were some common-place event in history to be once read and then forgotten? I pray it may not be so with thee. But since thou must either be lost or saved eternally, come thou and ask with deep anxiety, "Who art thou, Lord? Who art thou by whom I am to be saved? What right, what power hast thou to save? What claim hast thou upon my faith? Oh, tell me, for I long to know." Want of thought ruins half mankind. If men were but anxious to understand the truth they would soon learn it and receive it. If like the Bereans they would search the Scriptures to find the truth, or if like Lydia their hearts were opened to receive it, they would soon know the Lord. Like Paul, we must be willing to learn.

And, next, observe *the subject that he wished to be instructed upon.* "Who art thou, Lord?" You have heard that Christ is the Saviour, let your ambition be to know all about *him.* I will tell you one thing: saints on earth, and even saints in heaven, are always wanting to have this question more fully answered to them,—"Who art thou, Lord?" Those who know him best will tell you that there is a something about him which still surpasses all their knowledge; and I suppose that even when we see him face to face there will remain a mystery in his matchless love, and a depth unsearchable in his divine person, into which even then we shall not be able to dive. "Who art thou, Lord?" may well be the question of a soul that is seeking salvation, since it is still the question of those who have found it.

"Who art thou, Lord?" What is thy person? What is thy nature? How is it that thou art able to save? Learn well that he is divine, yet human; the Son of Mary, and yet the Son of God. He is man, thy brother, touched with the feeling of thy infirmities, yet is he God eternal, infinite, full of all power and majesty, assuredly divine. Learn thou this if thou wouldst be saved, and regard the Lord Jesus as God over all, blessed for ever, yet clothed in the form of a servant, and made in the likeness of sinful flesh. Learn that.

"Who art thou, Lord?" What are thy offices? If my eye could see thee I would ask thee, What titles dost thou bear? What offices dost thou sustain? He is a prophet; thou must be instructed by him, and believe his teaching. He is a priest; thou must be washed by his blood, and he must offer sacrifice for thee; nay, rather, he has offered it, and thou must accept it as being for thee and on thy behalf. He is a King, too, and if thou wilt be saved by him thou must let him govern thee. Thou must yield thyself to him and be his subject, and take up his cross and bear his easy yoke, which is no burden to the neck. Prophet, priest, king, and a thousand other offices does he sustain. Ask, thou craving sinner, ask, "Who art thou, Lord?" till thou shalt discover something about him that exactly suits thee, and then thy faith shall light upon it and thy heart shall cry, "He is all my salvation, and all my desire."

"Who art thou, Lord?" It is a question you may ask about *his relationships*. Who is he? The Son of the Highest, and yet the brother of the lowest. Who is he? King of angels and King of kings, and yet the friend of sinners and the helper of the humblest that will come to him. He stands as the head over all things to the church: his church's husband and the world's ruler, master of providence, sovereign of heaven, conqueror of hell itself. All power is in his hands. The Father has committed it unto him, and now he stands in such relationship to us that if we believe in him he gives us eternal life, and guards us from all ill, for he has said, "I give unto my sheep eternal life, and they shall never perish, neither shall any pluck them out of my hands." O beloved hearer, if thou wouldest be saved, study deeply that question, "Who art thou, Lord?" and be not satisfied till thou knowest Christ and art known of him—till there is a mutual knowledge between thee and himself, for it is only so that thou canst be saved. An unknown Christ is no Christ to you. A Saviour whom you do not know is a Saviour who will not know you in the day of his appearing.

"Who art thou, Lord?" Now, that question, as I have said, concerning Christ should be asked by us all, but it is not at all a speculative question. It is a question of the utmost practical importance to every man, and in proportion as a man knows the answer to that question he will receive its practical result. Hearken and perceive this. "Who art thou, Lord?" What will be the first result of having this question answered?

Why, when Paul knew that he whose face had shone upon him brighter than the sun was Jesus of Nazareth, he was seized with the deepest possible *contrition*. "What!" he seemed to say, "have I persecuted the Lord? When I was hunting down those poor people was I hunting down the Messiah? Was I fighting against the Christ of God?" He had not known that before, but when he knew who the Lord was then his heart was broken within him with a deep sense of sin. Now, come ye hither, some of you; you have been living for years refusing true religion, and despising it, but have you ever thought that you were refusing Jesus Christ the Son of God, and despising the Beloved of God who condescended to come into the world to suffer for love's sake? When they put Jesus to death he was, as our sweet poet puts it—

"Found guilty of excess of love."

It was all that could be laid to his dear charge; but for excess of love he died. And thou hast refused him. Thou hast now these twenty years and more refused that thorn-crowned head, that brow so marred, those wounded hands, that gashed and wounded side! Thou hast refused the matchless Saviour, without whom thou art undone for ever! Hast thou known this? Hast thou done it wilfully? I hope thou canst reply, "But I did it ignorantly in unbelief." Therefore he winks at your ill manners, and he bids you now come to him and he will gladly receive you. He will in no wise cast you out.

To know Christ, then, is a practical knowledge, because it leads to repentance. When Christ is unknown we can go on refusing and even persecuting him; but when we clearly perceive that it is the Son of God and the bleeding Lamb whom we have refused and persecuted, then our hearts melt; we beg his forgiveness, and cast ourselves at his feet.

A second practical result is that then our *hope* is encouraged; for though Paul at the sight of the Lord Jesus must have been full of bitter anguish, it was by that same sight that he was afterwards cheered and comforted. What! Art thou in heaven brighter than the sun? Art thou the man of Nazareth whom I have persecuted? Art thou he who was rejected and despised? O thou bright and shining one, art thou that same Christ to whom the publicans and harlots drew near? Art thou he who came to seek and to save that which was lost? Art thou exalted on high to give repentance unto Israel and remission of sins? Then is there hope for me. It is the sinner's Christ that is in heaven, the same that took the little children and said, "Suffer them to come to me." Oh, then, I will trust him. I feel I may, I can, I must. I yield myself to him because I know him now. I did not before. How practical is this knowledge!

And it had another effect upon Paul. It led him to *complete submission.* He said, "Is this Christ whom I have rejected Lord of all? Then it is indeed hard for me to kick against the pricks. I will not do so any longer. Resist him? That I dare not do! If all power be in his hands, then to oppose him is as hopeless as it is wicked. Behold, I surrender at discretion. O Lord Jesus, be my king. Accept me as thy subject. I oppose thee no longer." How I wish that Jesus would make some here know him who have never known him before—that they may at this very hour yield to him; because if once they knew him it would fire them with *ardour in his service.* There was never a man yet that did really know Christ whom Christ did not fill with an inward flame, so that he felt he could live or die for him. Some human leaders have had such extraordinary influence over their soldiery that they have commanded and have been cheerfully obeyed, even at the cost of life. The Christ of God has a superlative power over all hearts that know him. See how Paul felt his influence, and scoured the world to win Christ's lost ones. Perils of robbers; perils of rivers, the deep sea itself, scourging, stoning; all these were nothing to the apostle from the day when he knew Christ. He had been exceedingly hot against him, but now he burns and blazes with zeal for him. And so will it be with all who know Jesus. Right practical, then, is the question, "Who art thou, Lord?" Oh that the Spirit of God would lead every one to ask that question for himself.

Only once more and I leave the question. It is this. While Paul was willing to learn, and his subject was important, for he wished to learn of Christ, and exceedingly practical, for it moved him to every good thing, it is worthy of remark that *he sought instruction from the best possible Master;* for, my brethren, who can tell us who Christ is but Christ himself? Here is his book. Read it. It is the looking-glass. Jesus is yonder, and he looks into this book, and if you look into it with well-washed eyes, you may see his reflected image in this glass; darkly, however, at the best. So, too, when you hear his faithful servants preach you may see somewhat of Christ; but let me tell you there is no sight of Christ like that which comes personally to your own soul by the Holy Spirit. I do not mean that any men among us will ever see Christ while we are here with these eyes; and if we did, it might not do us good, for thousands saw him who, nevertheless, cried "Crucify him." But I do mean that there are eyes inside these eyes, eyes of the mind and of the soul, to which Christ himself must reveal himself; and I charge you who have never seen him so to fall on your knees and cry, "Show thyself to me." You must have personal dealings with him, each one for himself, and you may have these dealings. He is accessible to-night. He will receive you at once if you seek him. He has declared that he will not cast any out that come to him. Oh, will you not ask him to show himself to you? If you knew he would refuse you, you might be excused the prayer; but since he will manifest himself to every contrite, lowly, seeking soul, will you not seek him? Will you not even now humbly put to him this question, "Who art thou, Lord?" Reveal thyself to me, as thou dost not to the world, but as thou dost reveal thyself to seeking souls.

So then I leave that question to come to the second one. May the Holy Spirit help us while we handle it.

II. "What wilt thou have me to do?" THE OBEDIENT DISCIPLE REQUESTING DIRECTION.

We are always telling you that whosoever believeth in the Lord Jesus Christ has everlasting life. That is the basis-doctrine of the gospel; but recollect that we never told you that you might believe in the Lord Jesus Christ and then live as you liked. That be far from us. He who truly believes in Christ does as Christ bids him, and becomes henceforth Christ's servant and disciple as well as his saved one. Hence the question, "Lord, what wilt thou have me to do?"

You will notice that the apostle here puts himself into the position of a soldier waiting for orders. He will not stir till he has received his officer's command. "Lord, what wilt thou have me to do?" He stands quite ready to do it; but he wants to know what the order may be, and therefore he looks up, and prays, "Lord, direct me. What wouldst thou have me to do?" It is the Lord's will alone that he now means to do. "Lord, what wilt *thou* have me to do?" Before it used to be, "What will Moses have me to do?" And with some now present it has been

"What should I like to do?" for whatsoever their soul lusteth after that have they done, and whatsoever new pleasure, no matter how sinful it might be, if it were within their reach, they followed greedily after it; but he that would be saved must yield up his own will to his Lord. Now, beloved, take heed unto yourselves that Christ be your Master, and nobody else. It would never do to say, "What would the church have me to do?" As far as the church teaches what Christ taught, obey her, but no farther. It would not even be right to say, "What would an apostle have me to do?" Paul said, "Be ye followers of me, even as I also am of Christ." But if Paul does not follow Christ, we must not follow Paul. He says, "Though we, or an angel from heaven, preach any other gospel, let him be accursed;" and so let it stand. I count it to be a sad lowering of a Christian's standard when he takes any mortal man living, or even any man now in heaven, to be his guide and master. "One is your Master, even Christ;" and your question should be, "Lord, what wilt thou have me to do? I see what I am bidden to do in the Prayer Book. I see what I am bidden to do by learned and godly men, but these things have no authority over my conscience. Lord, what wouldst *thou* have me to do? If it be not thy will and thy word I know there can be no light in it, but what I know not, teach thou me."

And, then, see that this childlike obedience of the apostle is *personal.* It is, "Lord, what wilt thou have *me* to do? I have little enough to do with my neighbours. They have their duty and their calling, but, Lord, what wouldst thou have *me* to do? Other persons must follow the light they have; but, Lord, what wilt thou have *me* to do? My father, my brother, my friend, I have no right to judge these: to their own Master they must stand or fall; but, Lord, what wouldst thou have *me* to do?" You that look at your own inability when you come to Christ, must come to him with a personal faith, pleading for strength to do his will. You must yield to Jesus a personal obedience, even should it separate you from all your family. Let it separate the nearest ties, let it cause your past friends to give you the cold shoulder, let it subject you to persecution even unto death; you have nothing to do with these consequences, your business is to say, "Show me what thou wouldst have me to do, and I will do it." I mention a little incident in my own personal history, for which I have always had reason enough to thank God. When I was converted to God after some long time of bitter anguish of spirit I found rest; and the very first thing I did when I found rest in Christ was to read for myself the New Testament, and see what the Lord would have me to do. I found in the word of God the duty of believers' baptism. I had never met with any Baptist friends in my life until I had for myself discovered the truth. I had not even heard of their existence, so negligent had they been in the spreading of their views on that matter; but taking up the New Testament with my lexicon to see what the word meant, I found that the word baptize signified to immerse. When I read the Scriptures I found everywhere that believers were immersed. I did not at first know of the existence of another person who held that opinion, but it did not signify to me the turn of a hair. I was only afraid that I might not find anybody to baptize me, but I meant to attend to the duty in some way or other. I discovered afterwards that there were many who had searched the Scriptures and had come to the same conclusion as myself; but to me, then, it did seem like coming away from all the Christian people that I knew. Have I ever regretted the step? No. Unimportant as some might think it, it gave to my whole spirit and life a tone for which I have reason to thank God. I stood upon my own feet, having read the Bible for myself. I took my own way in obedience to my Lord and Master, and from that day I know not that I have wilfully turned aside from his statutes, either in doctrines or in precept, but I have taught the faith as I have learned it. When I go to my chamber at night with a thousand imperfections to confess, yet I can feel that I have honestly and faithfully followed my Master. If I have erred it has been from want of light, and not from want of will to serve him; but if I had burked that first conviction, and if I had made little nicks in my conscience at first, could I stand before you all this night and declare that I have not shunned both to do and to declare the whole counsel of God? I charge every young man as soon as he believes in Christ to read and search the Bible for himself, and say, "Show me what thou wouldest have me to do." I would rather be right alone than be wrong with all the world: and every honest Christian man ought to feel that he would rather follow Jesus Christ with two or three than run with a multitude after the traditions of men. God help you, beloved, as soon as you are converted to become thoroughly obedient disciples, searching the Word. I do not set so much importance upon the result of your investigation as I do upon the investigation itself. I care less about the result you arrive at than I do for the spirit which would lead you, as a disciple, earnestly to desire to follow your Master, and would lead you to do everything that you believe to be his will—the little as well as the great. The Lord help us to be anxious to know and do his will in all things, fearless of consequences.

Note again, that the apostle not only puts it personally, but he pleads for grace *at once*. "Lord, show me what thou wouldst have me to do?" as much as to say, "I will do it directly." He does not ask to be allowed a little delay, but "What wouldst thou have me to do? Here I. thy willing servant stand." Young man, if you would have salvation you must be ready to follow Christ to-night. To-night, it may be, is the time when the Spirit of God is struggling with you, and if resisted he never may return. Just now the scales hang in an even balance. Which way shall they turn? It may be to-night for death or life the scale shall turn for the last time. O blessed Jesus in heaven, why should we hesitate if thou wilt indeed save us? We may well make a complete surrender and say, "Now, even now, I enlist beneath thy banner, for I thy willing servant am."

And observe, once more, that *he does not make any kind of conditions.* What wouldst thou have me to do? I will do it. If unpleasant to the flesh it shall be pleasant to my heart: and if it appear stern, yet if thou wilt help me I will do it, "What wilt thou have me to do?" Saul little knew when he asked the question what the doing of his Master's will would involve, but he meant at the time that whatever it would involve he was prepared for it. O you that would be Christians, do not suppose that it is just believing something—an article of a creed, or undergoing a ceremony—that will save you; you must, if you are Christ's, yield yourselves up to him. He did not come into this world to lead men to heaven by back roads and crooked paths, but he leads them into the way of righteousness, the end whereof is everlasting peace. Will you be child enough to follow him? Will you have the childlike spirit which only wants first to know who he is and then exclaims—

> " Through floods or flames if Jesus lead
> I'll follow where he goes."

The Lord grant it may be so with us!

I close with just this remark, that it is by knowing Christ that you will learn to obey him, and the more you obey him the more easy it will be: and in obeying him you will find your honour. Paul at this day stands in a most honourable place in the church of God, simply because being called of God to do his will he did it faithfully even to the end. Is it not beautiful to see how Paul in one moment seems to have forgotten all his old Pharisaism? All the hard words and bitter blasphemies that he had spoken against Christ, they have all gone in a moment. What strange changes will come over some beings in an instant. One of my students who has been a sailor has preached the gospel for some long time, but his English was far from grammatical. Having been in college some little time he began to speak correctly, but suddenly the old habit returned upon him. He was in the *Princess Alice* at the time of the lamentable catastrophe, and he escaped in an almost miraculous manner. I saw him some time after, and congratulated him on his escape, and he replied that he had saved his life but had lost all his grammar. He found himself for awhile using the language of two or three years ago: and even now, though he is recovering his spirits,* he declares that he cannot get back what he had learnt. He seems to have drowned his grammar on that terrible occasion. Now, just as we may lose some good thing by a dreadful accident, or occurrence, which seems to sweep over the mind like a huge wave and wash away our treasures, so by a blessed catastrophe, if Christ should meet with any man to-night, much which he has valued will be swept away! You may write on wax, and may make the record fair. Take a hot iron and roll it across the wax, and it is all gone. That seems to me to be just what Jesus did with Paul's heart. It was all written over with blasphemy and rebellion, and he rolled the hot iron of burning love over his soul and the evil inscription was all gone. He ceased to blaspheme, and he began to praise. May the like be done to many here present to the praise and glory of my Master's love and power. Amen and amen.

PORTION OF SCRIPTURE READ BEFORE SERMON—Acts xxvi.

HYMNS FROM "OUR OWN HYMN BOOK"—505, 589, (" Flowers and Fruits " 109).

---

* October 20, 1878.

A PLAIN ANSWER TO AN IMPORTANT ENQUIRY.

A Sermon

DELIVERED BY

C. H. SPURGEON,

AT THE METROPOLITAN TABERNACLE, NEWINGTON.

"Jesus answered and said unto them, This is the work of God, that ye believe on him whom he hath sent."—John vi. 29.

NOTICE the connection, or you will miss the meaning of the words; for at first sight it looks as if our Saviour taught us that it is the work of God for us to believe on him. Now, that would be quite true; and it is very plainly taught in other parts of Scripture that faith is the work of God; but that is not the teaching in this particular instance, as will be very plain if you look at the context. First, our Saviour said to the people, "See how you labour after the bread of your bodies. You have been running all round the coast to find me in order that I might feed you again with loaves and fishes. Now," says he, "let your labour run after something better. Labour not for the meat that perisheth, but for that which endureth to life eternal." He gently rebukes them : "Do not spend all your strength in seeking after temporal good, but think about your immortal natures. Satisfy the hunger of your spirits, the better part of you." They immediately answered, "You tell us to labour after the bread that does not perish. What shall we do that we might work the work of God and so obtain it?" Our translation fails to let us see that they used precisely the same word as the Saviour had done. He said "labour," and they said, "What shall we do that we may labour this labour of God? What is it?" They took him at his word, and they put a question in accordance therewith.

When men begin to be aroused about spiritual things, they naturally cry, "What must we do to be saved? What must we do that we may work the work of God?" It is a faulty question, it is a question very much shaped by their ignorance and error. They suppose that there are works to be done, and merit to be earned, by doing and obeying a law, and so they put it in that shape—"What shall we do? What shall we work that we may work the work of God?" The Saviour did not chide them for the shape of the question. It was not the time to expect accuracy, but he gave them such truth as they could understand, and he replied, "You want to know what work you must do that shall be 'the work of God,' or a work pleasing to God. This then is 'the work of

No. 1,521.

165

God': the work most pleasing to God of all the works that can be done by men, that ye believe on him whom he hath sent." The teaching here is not that faith is wrought in us by God, which I have already said is a great truth, but it is this—that if men desire to work, the first and chief of all work is that they believe on Jesus Christ whom God hath sent. Does any man object to faith being called the work of man? If he does, I ask him wherefore he objects. It is true that faith is the gift of God, but this does not militate for a moment with the other truth that faith is the work of man: for it is and must be the act of man. No one in his senses can deny that. Will you venture to say that man does not believe? Then I venture to tell you that he who does not personally believe in Jesus is a lost man; and if there be such a thing as a faith which is not a man's own act and deed it will not save him. The man must himself believe or perish: this is the plain doctrine of Scripture. Repentance is wrought in us by the Holy Ghost, but we must ourselves repent, or we never shall be saved. Faith is wrought in us by the Holy Ghost, but the Holy Ghost does not believe, or repent: these are a man's own acts. With our hearts we believe unto righteousness. If we do not believe then we are not partakers of the promise which is given to those who do believe. Faith is, therefore, the work of man; and it is the chief of works, the work most pleasing to God, the most godlike work, or, as the text puts it, " This is the work of God, that ye believe on him whom he hath sent.'

To open up this one thought I pray for help from on high: it is just this, that *faith is the most pleasing of all the works that man can do.* It is here called " the work," but not strictly and properly, for it can never be ranged with the works of the law, from which it essentially differs; but the Saviour took up the word which they used, and spoke to their ignorance that he might instruct them.

I. Regarding it as a work, faith is most pleasing to God; for, first, IT IS THE COMPREHENSIVE SUMMARY OF ALL TRUE WORK. *There lies within the loins of faith every possible form of holiness.* As a forest may lie asleep within an acorn, so within the bounds of faith, little though it be, every virtue lies hidden. It may be microscopic in form, but it is certainly there, and only needs development. Repentance dwells in faith, for he that believes in Jesus Christ unto salvation knows that he is a sinner, and he must have some hatred of sin, or else he would not have taken Christ to deliver him from his sin. Love to God is there, for, most assuredly, when I trust a man—completely trust him—it would be impossible for me to do so unless I felt some leaning of my spirit towards him; and the complete trusting of the soul to Christ, which is faith, has had in it no small measure of love to Christ. If I had before me a list of all the graces of the Spirit of God, and I were to take them up one by one, and then analyze faith, I should find some measure of all these good works of the Spirit hidden away in the simple act of believing in Jesus Christ.

I know what some of you have said—" Is that all that I am to do in order to be saved? Am I simply and alone to believe in Christ, that is, trust myself with him?" Yes, that is all, and it is so small an act that the most uneducated heart can perform it, but yet within it there are inconceivable mysteries of goodness. Just as sometimes inside a walnut shell I have seen packed away with careful art all sorts of gems and jewels, "with my lady's gloves to wear," so within this little walnut shell of "believe and live" there will be found by any careful eye all the graces of the Spirit of God.

What is more, *all the graces come out of faith in due time*, for faith sums up the whole of a Christian's life. Now, my brethren, I challenge you to read the eleventh chapter to the Hebrews, and see if you can think of anything noble, brave, glorious, which has not its counterpart in that chapter. But recollect, it is a description of the heroism—not of this virtue or of that, but of faith. In the long list, beginning with Abel and going down to the last, faith wrought all. From faith comes the power that stops the mouths of lions, quenches the violence of flames; out of weakness becomes strong. It is faith that tramples on temptation, it is faith that overcomes the world. It is faith that attains to holiness. Within the compass of that little babe whom you hold in your hand, a slender weight that you can scarcely feel, there are all the elements of yonder man of six feet, who leads the van in the royal host, and so the true Christian man in the perfection of the stature of Christ is all within the babe in grace who cries, "Lord, I believe; help thou mine unbelief."

I can well understand why our Saviour should say, "If you wish to work the work of God, you must believe in Jesus Christ whom he hath sent"; for in that act lie all the virtues, and out of that act will grow all the virtues in due time.

II. But now, secondly, this simple matter of trusting Jesus Christ, which is called FAITH, IS, IN ITSELF, MOST PLEASING TO GOD.

First, *it is the creature acknowledging its God.* While a man says, "I do not care about my soul," he lives in atheism, disowning God, living as if there were no God. When a man says, "I need no saving," that is contradicting God's testimony, wherein he declares that we are all gone out of the way and have altogether become abominable. When a man says, "I may be wrong, but I can get right of myself. My own good deeds will save me"; he is setting himself up in independence of his God; in fact, making himself his own God, and so, practically, setting up another God. But when the man cries, "I have sinned," there is an acknowledgment that the law is good, and holy, and just. When he then adds, "I have so sinned that I deserve punishment, and I submit myself to it," there is a recognition of the court of heaven, and an admission of the righteousness of its sentences. The rebellious heart submits itself to the authority of God. When he further says, "But I have heard, great God, that thou hast given thy Son to bleed and die for sinners, and that he is able to save to the uttermost them that trust him, and I do trust him," the submission of the man to God is complete. Before, he said, "I do not believe it. It does not stand to reason," that is proud reason still a rebel. Or he said, "It may or may not be so, but I do not see the peculiar beauty of an atoning sacrifice." There again is the proud heart kicking against God. But the man comes into his right place when he believes. When he believes in Jesus Christ and accepts mercy through the great sacrifice, God is well pleased because his poor erring *creature has come into its right place*, and God sees in the act of faith the restitution of rectitude.

Again, God is pleased with faith because *it accepts God's way of reconciliation.* God has given Christ that he might reconcile us to himself by him. When a man says, "I take Christ to be my Saviour," he accepts God's way of reconciliation, and then God must be reconciled, for he has promised so to be. As he longs to be reconciled, and willeth not that any should perish, but that they should come to repentance, so does he rejoice when they are willing to make peace with him in his own appointed way. It shows a deference to his wisdom, a confidence in his love, a yielding to his divine will, and that is what he seeks after. All this, I say, is included in faith, and makes it well pleasing to God.

Perhaps the most acceptable element in faith to the eye of God is the fact that *it puts honour upon Jesus Christ*, for he dearly loves his Son. We cannot tell how deep is the love of the Father towards his only begotten Son. That which dishonours Jesus must be very obnoxious to the Father, and your self-confidence, my friend, is a dishonour to the merit and salvation of Christ, and God abhors it; but when you fling that all away, and have no hope but in the great atonement which he has made, then, I say, because your faith honours Jesus, therefore God delights in it, and he will honour your faith. It is not possible that he should cast a soul away that clings to the great High Priest. Oh, if you look to Jesus, that eye of yours shall never lose its sight: if your heart clings to Jesus, that heart of yours shall never lose its life: if your soul joys in Jesus, that soul of yours shall never lose its joy.

The fact is, that faith *puts us into a right relationship with God;* for what is the right relationship of a creature to his God but that of *dependence?* Is it not most suitable that since God made us, and he has all power and all strength, we should depend upon him for our being, as well as for our well-being? See how he hangs the world upon nothing. This round globe never starts nor falters, but is steadily upheld in its mighty march by the unseen hand of God. Yonder stars, mighty worlds though they be, have no power to keep themselves in their places; but the power of God establishes them. All things hang upon him, and the only position for a created being is that of entire dependence; what is that but faith? I believe there is faith in heaven. Do not tell me there is no faith there. I believe it to be the essence of heaven that the glorified exercise unquestioning faith, and never feel a doubt. It will be the joy of every spirit before the throne to depend every moment for its immortality and bliss upon God, and to be quite confident that he will never fail it. Some sorts of faith will be turned to sight; but if faith be confidence in God, I bless God I shall have a great deal more of it in heaven than I can have here. A perfect child must have a perfect faith in a perfect father. Because faith brings the creature back to conscious dependence, therefore God is well pleased with it.

Faith restores us by putting us into a place of *childlike rest.* If a son has fallen into the hands of a malicious individual, who has whispered into his ear that his father hates him—that he is doing all he possibly can to ruin him—at first the youth will not believe the accusation, but perhaps after a while he begins to think it true. From that time forward every action that his father does will be interpreted the wrong way; and if there be anything in the father's life which is more kind than usual, it is highly probable that this poor misled boy will see a deeper subtlety of malice in it than in his father's ordinary actions.

The lad will break his father's commands, and vex and anger his father. What is the first thing to be done to set that youth right? You may make him dread his father, and then he will behave properly in his outward actions, but he will only be waiting his time to break loose. Suppose it to be possible to make him believe in his father, and to be assured that his father loved him, and had all along been the kindest man on earth, he would run into his father's arms. He will be willing enough to obey a parent whom he trusts: it will be his delight to do so.

You have won his confidence, and everything is right now. This is what faith does to us. The devil and our own corrupt nature say, " God is unkind, for he has made an awful hell," and so on. Faith interposes and cries, " He has put away his wrath. He has made full atonement for sin. He is willing to receive us." Then faith says, " Trust him; trust him implicitly"; and when the soul has done that, then faith testifies "He has loved you with an everlasting love. Jesus died for you, and he has provided a heaven for you." Let this be known and felt, and what a change takes place! Oh, then, you hate your sin! Oh, then, you are ready to say, " How could I play the fool against one so kind, so good, so right?" Under this impulse you will serve him, and live for him. That simple matter of believing him has done it all. It is the hinge on which character turns. Hard thoughts of God lead to acts of rebellion, but a childlike confidence in infinite love softens the heart, and sanctifies it, and makes the man to be a true child towards the great Father. Do you wonder, then, that there is much in faith in itself which is pleasing to God? And if you ask what great works you are to do to please God, we shall not tell you to build a row of almshouses, or endow an orphanage, or give your body to be burned; believe in Jesus Christ, and you have done more than all these things put together.

III.   And now a third reason why faith is so great a thing is this— that FAITH IN JESUS CHRIST IS THE TEST OF WORKING FOR GOD, for all the works that ever were, without faith in Jesus Christ, are not works for God at all.

Let me explain and prove my point. Suppose that a person should say, " But I mean to live for the great God, and work for him." Without faith *the spirit of work is wrong.* My friend, suppose you said to me, " I will live for you and spend my life in your service, but I am not going to believe what you say"? There would be a point of disagreement between us, which would render it impossible for you to be of any service to me, or for anything that you did to be of any value to me. You call me a liar to begin with, and then say you serve me. Many of you that have heard the gospel may, perhaps, think that you are serving God, though you have never believed in Christ: but, I tell you, your best actions are nothing but whitewashed sins. All that you do must be destitute of real excellence, because you begin by making God a liar. It is a hard word, say you. I cannot help it; it is the word of John, the most gentle spirit amongst all biblical characters. John says, " He that believeth not hath made God a liar, because he hath not believed on the Son of God." If you begin by calling God a liar, I do not care much what you do after that. I would a great deal rather you should be moral than immoral, and sober than drunken; but, after all, you will be lost in either case if you persevere in calling God a liar. All your holiness will be a sham if you will not believe in Jesus. The test of true work for God is this—"That ye believe on Jesus Christ whom he hath sent."

Without faith *the motive of work fails.* "But," cries another person, "I believe I have deserved well of God; I have kept myself pretty right, and I have performed many good deeds." What have you done them all for? "I have been working for my salvation," says one. In other words, you have been working for yourself. Pay yourself, then! Self is first, and last; your works are selfishness from top to bottom. You have been trying to be good to get to heaven by it. It is a mean, beggarly life that begins and ends with self! Your Maker, whom you were bound to love with all your heart, you have not loved at all, except that you have meanly pretended to love him, in order to save yourself. You had a kind of cupboard love to him, such as an ass or an ox might have to a corn-bin, or a stall, but no real affection. How can you perform a virtuous act, while self is your tyrant lord? When you have once believed in Jesus Christ then you are saved, and henceforth you live to glorify the name of the Lord: you live to work out that which he has worked in you, to will and to do of his own good pleasure, but till you are saved by faith self is necessarily your first thought. No man is capable of virtue as long as self is his object; and every man must make self his object till he is saved. When he is saved he rises into a nobler atmosphere altogether, and then his works are acceptable to God. Do you not see that at least you have to get out of self-righteousness, and to be saved by believing in Christ, before you can begin to do anything that will be really working for God? Up to that point it will be all working for yourself, and that is a poor, poor thing, which cannot please the most high God.

Beloved friends, living by faith in Jesus Christ is the evidence of your sincerity in any work that you do for God, for can there be any real working for God while your own pride is uppermost? God tells you that your best works are imperfect and will not save you, and he hangs his own dear Son upon the cross to save you because you are a sinner. You turn your back to the cross; you say "My own merits are good enough," and then you talk about serving God after that! Can he accept anything at your hands after you have rejected his Son and insulted himself? You have touched the Lord in the very tenderest point when you have taken your own detestable righteousness, which is just a heap of infected rags, a mass of abominable filth in the sight of God, and you have preferred it to the blood and righteousness of his only Son. After such an atrocious crime as this, how dare you talk about doing service to God? It is impossible, sir. There is a lie in the bottom of your heart. Get rid of it. How can you serve the Lord while your pride thus angers him? He tells you that you must bow before his Son and trust in him; but your reply is, "No, I must feel something or do something." That is as much as saying, "I will be saved in my own way." You talk about serving God after that naughty "I will" of yours has been defying him. Suppose that one of your family will not do what you tell him. He brazens you out. He says he will have his own way; and then he goes into the garden and he plucks you a flower, and he expects that the gift will please you. What? Brought in a rebellious hand! While he is in a wilful state and boiling over with bad temper! Does he think to please you by such a trifle? You say, "No, my child, that cannot be. You must first bow before your father and acknowledge that you have done wrong." He may pout his lips, and say he will never obey you, and then ask to kiss you. Will he have his kiss? Assuredly not till first of all he will submit. That is just the condition of many a seeker after God. He has a wicked pride in his heart, and a rebellious will, and if he will believe in Jesus it will be a proof that his pride and rebellion are given up; but if he will not yield and trust neither can he expect that God will save him.

IV. I would say, in the fourth place, that faith in God is a most blessed and acceptable thing, because IT IS THE SEAL OF ALL OTHER BLESSINGS.

Notice that faith in God is the seal—first, of our *election*. Read the thirty-seventh verse, "All that the Father giveth me shall come to me." Now, if you come to Christ, dear friend, you are one that his Father gave him. You are one of his elect. Oh, what a blessing this is. The doctrine of election is full of rich comfort to all who are interested in it, and election itself is the greatest of all favours. "But how am I to know that I am one of God's elect?" By this testimony, "All that the Father giveth me shall come to me." Every elect soul that reaches adult age is brought to believe in Jesus Christ, and as sure as ever you are brought to believe in Jesus Christ, you may be absolutely certain that you are predestinated to eternal life.

In the next place, faith seals our *effectual calling*. If you look a little farther down you will see, "No man can come unto me except the Father which hath sent me draw him; and I will raise him up at the last day." These are the express words of Christ, and they show that every man that comes to Christ must have been drawn by the Father; that is to say, that effectual calling has exerted its divine power upon him. No man need say, "Am I drawn of the Father?" after he is once sure that he has faith in Jesus Christ; for you never could have believed in Jesus Christ except this had been given you from heaven. The forty-fourth verse is as plain as possible, "No man can come to me except the Father which hath sent me draw him." You have come to him, and therefore the Father must have drawn you.

The next thing that faith assures us of is *final perseverance*. Read the forty-seventh verse—"He that believeth on me hath everlasting life." You need not raise the question, "Have I received everlasting life?" Raise this question first: "Have I believed in Jesus Christ? If so, I have everlasting life." Not a life, mark you, that will last you up to the end of the quarter, when you take a new ticket—nor a life that will preserve you to old age, and then leave you to temptation and death. No, "he that believeth on him hath *everlasting* life," and it is not everlasting life if it does not last for ever. Herein he that believes has the guarantee of final perseverance. Did not Jesus say, "I give unto them eternal life; and they shall never perish, neither shall any pluck them out of my hand"? Are we not told of him that believes in Christ that there shall be in him a well of water springing up unto everlasting life"? Or, as Christ puts it in this very chapter, "he shall never hunger and he shall never thirst." He has drunk a draught of eternal life in Christ Jesus, and he shall never thirst again.

This is a great deal for faith to bring to us, but it is not all, for two or three times over we are told here that whosoever believeth in Christ shall be raised up again at the last day: so that faith secures *resurrection*. Read the thirty-ninth verse and then the forty-ninth verse : "This is the will of him that sent me, that everyone which seeth the Son, and believeth on him, may have everlasting life, and I will raise him up at the last day." How do I know that I shall have a blessed resurrection? How can I be certain that though the worms devour this body, yet when Christ shall stand in the latter day upon the earth, in my flesh I shall see God? I may be quite sure of it, because I believe in Jesus Christ whom he has sent.

Beloved, faith is the seal at the bottom of the title deed, which secures all things for time and eternity to the man that hath it. If thou be a believer, all the wheels of providence revolve for thee. If thou be a believer, every angel spreads his wings for thee. If thou be a believer, life is thine, and the death which seems to close it is only the appointed janitor to open the door of another and a brighter chamber. If thou believest, God himself is thine, and Christ, his Son, is thine. If thou believest, heaven, with its eternity and infinity of joy, which thy eye hath not seen, nor thy heart conceived of, is thine ; nothing shall be kept back from the man that believes his God, and trusts his Redeemer. Oh that the Lord would give faith to you all. "Alas," you say, "I do not feel right." Never mind your feelings, trust in Christ. "Oh, but I am such a sinner." "Jesus Christ came into the world to save sinners." "Alas, but I have tried before." Away with all your trials before. Have done with trying, and accept the finished work. Trust Jesus now. "Do you mean that if I now do trust myself with Christ, I shall be saved while sitting in the pew?" I mean even so. Be thou whosoever thou mayest be, this night look to Jesus and be saved.

If thou wilt have done with thyself, and will trust thy soul in the hand of Jesus, who has sworn to save those that rest themselves upon him, thou art saved. Oh, that those who have heard this gospel many times would now for the first time really understand it, and say, "Is this, after all, the greatest of all works—that I do believe in Jesus Christ whom he hath sent. Lord, I believe : help thou mine unbelief, and save me now." O God, help many to breathe the prayer of faith at this moment, for Jesus's sake. Amen.

PORTION OF SCRIPTURE READ BEFORE SERMON—John vi. 25—65.

HYMNS FROM "OUR OWN HYMN BOOK"—289, 551, 533.

EXPECTED PROOF OF PROFESSED LOVE.

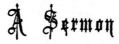

A Sermon

DELIVERED BY

C. H. SPURGEON,

AT THE METROPOLITAN TABERNACLE, NEWINGTON.

"Shew ye the proof of your love."—2 Corinthians viii. 24.

IN every believer's heart there is love to God. He cannot else be a child of God. In every Christian's soul there is love to Jesus Christ. How could he be a Christian otherwise? As a consequence of this, in every Christian's bosom there is a love to the brotherhood:—"We know that we have passed from death unto life because we love the brethren." In every Christian's breast there is also a love to all mankind. He practises that second great commandment, "Thou shalt love thy neighbour as thyself." The spirit of God has cast out the demon of selfishness; and in proportion as that is the case the man possesses the mind of Christ, which is love. As all the law is fulfilled in one word, which is "love," so the outcome of our holy faith is also contained in that one word, "love." Oh that we were saturated with it!

Where there is true love in the heart it becomes a working principle. It does not lie dormant, but it works—works abundantly. It is a vital principle, and where there is life there is movement, and a measure of activity. It is a principle that grows, and out of its growth there comes fruit. For these reasons, and in these ways, true believers give sure proofs of the love that is in their hearts.

I wish to speak to you, at this time, by answering four questions.

I. First, WHAT IS THE EXCELLENCE OF THIS LOVE that we should be so anxious to prove it? This Christian love must have some great worth about it, or else we should not be exhorted by the apostle once and again to prove that we have it.

First remember that true love to God and the saints in the Christian heart is *divine in its origin*. We should never have loved God if he had not first loved us: and unless his Holy Spirit had turned the stream of our affections in that direction, we should have run away from God and have hated God, but we should neither have loved him nor his people. It is the nature of the seed of the serpent to hate the seed of the woman, and as long as we were under condemnation and wrath, and in our natural estate, we were on the serpent's side, and we warred against that which is good.- "The carnal mind is enmity

No. 1,522.

173

against God : for it is not subject to the law of God, neither indeed can be." If, therefore, we have even a spark of love to God, God must have given it to us. It is, therefore, a precious thing because it is of God, and we ought to take heed that we assuredly possess it ; and we also should endeavour so to live that others may be convinced that this divine principle rules our spirits.

As it is divine in its origin, so it is *surpassing in its energy*, for true love to God exceeds all other love. Does not Christ tell us that—that a man must love him better than father or mother, or the dearest relative he has, or else he does not love him at all ? Christ will not be put off with the leavings of our hearts. He must have our whole heart. All human affections, which are natural and proper, are to be held in subservience to this grand and master passion which is to set our soul on a blaze—love to God in Christ Jesus. He loves not Christ at all who does not love him first and best. This affection, like Aaron's rod, must swallow up all others, and our whole heart must belong to the Lord our God.

We must take care that we give proof of an affection which is so surpassing in its energy, for surely if it has such force it must produce its own proof. If it were some minor passion—some little narrow jet of flame that might light up a corner of our being, we might not be so particular about it, but if it is to fire our entire manhood it must produce some effect, or else we may well question whether we possess it.

This love is absolutely *vital in its necessity*. If it can be proved that a man does not love God, love Christ, and love his people, then the life of God does not dwell in him. Life and love are two words singularly alike, and, when we get to the bottom and radical principle of the spiritual nature, we perceive that they are singularly bound up together, insomuch that "he that dwelleth in love dwelleth in God, and God in him." These are some of the apostle John's great little words, which, in their miniature form, contain whole worlds of meaning. Beloved, we must love God, or else we are not in Christ. Hence the importance that the proofs of our love should be very distinct and unmistakeable. We should make our calling and election sure ; and those things never can be sure unless we have abundant proofs of our love. It is vital in its necessity.

However great that love becomes, and I have spoken of it as rising to a superlative degree, it is *warranted by the facts of the case*. Love to God—I will not spend a word in justifying it. Love to Christ—how can it be needful to commend it to you ?

> "Love so amazing, so divine,
> Demands our soul, our life, our all."

And it shall have it, too. Do you not say so, my brethren? Do you not yield to this soft yet mighty bond—soft as silk, yet strong as iron? It holds us fast ; we cannot escape from it. Not love Christ ? Not love his people? Not love the world of sinners lost ? Oh ! sirs, surely we were of all creatures the most brutish if we were to dispute the necessity of love. "Ye know the grace of our Lord Jesus Christ, that, though he was rich, yet for your sakes he became poor, that ye through his poverty might be rich." Go and love Jesus Christ till men call you a fanatic.

Go and love him till you give all your goods to feed the poor. Go and love him till you lie in a prison till the moss grows on your eyelids. Go and love him till you burn to ashes at the stake, and you have not loved him one whit more than he deserves. O our best Beloved, thy deservings warrant us in permitting our zeal for thee to eat us up, and eaten up we would be for thy glory's sake!

This love to Christ has been in all ages very *eminent in its achievements.* Wherever love reigns in a Christian it makes him strong. Faith laughs at impossibilities, and cries, " It must be done"; but love performs the deed, for "faith worketh by love." Love is the right hand of faith. What have not men done out of love to Christ? Truly, the time would fail me to tell of its exploits. What you shall do, dear sister, if you become full of love to Jesus, will astonish you ; and what you shall do, dear brother, if the love of Christ burns through your soul, will far exceed what you have dreamed of as yet. Oh! for more love. Let the martyrs tell you what poor suffering flesh and blood can do when love strengthens it. Let holy women that have debated and disputed, and bled and died for Christ, in all their timidity and weakness made brave as lions for Christ, tell what love has done. Let the walls of the Colosseum at Rome, let the arenas of hundreds of amphitheatres tell how bravely men have played the man: how bravely women have met death for Christ's sake. All that the Church wants is the Holy Ghost to baptize her into the love of Christ, and nothing will be impossible to her.

Thus have I tried to commend this love, and surely we ought to be able to prove that we have it. If we have any question as to whether we have it or not, let us find no rest day or night till the grand debate is ended. We must love Christ or perish. Oh! by the certainty that his saints shall see him face to face and be like him, let us rise to something nobler in the form of love to him than we have ever reached as yet.

This is the love which we are to give proof of.

II. Secondly, WHAT IS THIS PROOF ? The text says, " Show ye to them, and before the churches, the proof of your love." What proof shall we show?

There are so many forms of action which would prove love to Christ that I cannot possibly go through them all, especially as each person, I believe, will give a different proof of his love. There is (to use a difficult word) an idiosyncrasy about each believer. He is a man by himself, and his love, if it is genuine, will take a form peculiar to himself in the proof which it gives. Certain proofs look *towards God and the Lord Jesus.* If you love him, you will keep his commandments, and his commandments are not grievous. If you love him, you will seek to honour him—to spread the savour of his glorious name. If you love God in Christ Jesus, you will be anxious to extend his rule over the hearts of men. If you love God, you will long for communion with him: you will not be satisfied to live for days without speaking with him. If you love him, you will grieve yourself when you grieve him ; your heart will smite you when you have gone astray. If you love God, you will long to be like him ; you will strive after holiness. If you love God, he will reign over you ; Christ will be your King ; your mind will be under subjection to him ; your thoughts will be guided by him ; your opinions will be taken from his word ; your whole life will be seasoned by his Spirit which dwelleth in you.   Do you not see that there are hundreds of ways in which you can show proof of your love towards God ?   Oh, that we may not be found wanting in any of these things !

We may show this love, in the next place, *towards God's ministers.* I cannot help mentioning them because the apostle so distinctly in this chapter speaks of himself and his brethren.   And one special way of showing it is this:—if they speak well of you, do not let them have cause to retract their holy boasting, and to say with tears " I was deceived in these people."   If any have brought you to Christ, be an honour to them and to the gospel that they preach, because, dear friends, the world turns round, and however retired a minister may be, yet worldlings are sure to throw the inconsistencies of his people in his teeth.   They say "That is one of So-and-so's people: see how he acts ;" and our ministry is hindered and our hearts are grieved whenever those who profess to have been brought to Christ walk unworthily. Show us a proof of the love you often express to us as your servants in Christ Jesus, by endeavouring so to walk that when we give in our account we may do it with joy and not with grief, for that would be unprofitable to you.

Next, show proofs of your love *in reference to God's people.*   How can that be done ?   Some of you need to have this thing gone over with you because you have evidently forgotten it.   If you are God's servants you love his people, and the first proof you should give is to go and join with them.   Say, " Where the list of their names is kept I will count it an honour to have my name enrolled."   Certain of you say, " I should count it an honour, but I have hardly the courage to come forward."   What ! have I been sitting these various days to see the timid ones, and have you not all come yet?   We will have another time for you, then, and try if we cannot get you right, for really we are not so frightful as you think we are, and you need not be timid about telling to a poor servant of Jesus Christ that you really love the name of his Master.   He will be glad, and so will you be.   Nay, but you say you are half afraid of yourself.   I wish you were altogether afraid of yourself.   The more afraid of yourself the better, for you are good for nothing in yourself.   But do not be afraid of trusting yourself with Jesus, and when you have so done then the very next thing is to become identified with the visible church of Christ. If you say, " I love the brethren," the brethren may turn round and say, " Give us a proof of your love.   Cast in your lot with us."   Do as she did who, though she had been a heathen, nevertheless clung to one who worshipped the true God, and said, " Whither thou goest, I will go ; and where thou lodgest, I will lodge : thy people shall be my people, and thy God my God."

But when you have joined the church, then surely you should show a proof of your love by a hearty fellowship with the saints.   We do not want you to put your name in the book and to be a professor, and then to sit in one of those pews up in the corner and come in and go out and never speak to anybody.   I meet even now with some who say, " I have been for months at the Tabernacle, and nobody ever spoke to me." Well, I know that there are so many earnest Christians on the watch here to speak with strangers that if you have not been spoken to it must be your own fault. Perhaps you are some dreadfully stiff body, and you have frightened them. I do not know, but it may be so. There are some who look as if they said, "Do not come near me. I do not want any questions asked me." We have some brethren and sisters who will break through your stiffness though, I dare say ; but if it really is so I am very sorry for it, and it need not be so any longer. Speak to somebody at this very service. I do not dislike to hear a low hum of godly conversation before service begins, though some people think it horrible ; neither do I deprecate a little lingering upon the steps and around the building ; you are holding fellowship one with another, and I like that it should be so, for we do not meet too often. It is no desecration of the Sabbath or of the place of worship for Christian people to speak with one another to edification. When you join the church join it in earnest and converse much with the people of God, and by your hearty zeal show them a proof of your love.

And then unite with them in all their service. The school wants Sunday-school teachers. You love Christ, you say, and you love the young : show us a proof of your love. Come and help in that good work. There is something or other that you can do for Jesus, and for his church ; do it, and thus show us a proof of your love.

Show the proof of your love by comforting the saints in affliction ; by helping them as much as you can when they are in need ; by defending their good name whenever you hear them railed at ; by suffering nobody to speak against them falsely when you are by. Stand up for them.

Show them the proof of your love by bearing with their infirmities. The church is not perfect, and if it were it would not be perfect after you had joined it. You who have so many infirmities yourself should patiently bear with the infirmities of others. If the saints are not all you would like them to be, remember, nevertheless, that they are dear to the heart of Christ ; and he, perhaps, sees in them beauties which you would see, too, if you had more beauties yourself. Perhaps your power to find fault arises from your having so many faults yourself; and if you were more sanctified, and more like Christ, you would fix your eye as well upon the beauties of their character as upon their defects. Show us the proof of your love. I am not speaking as though I did not see among you abundant proofs of your love ; but I am speaking to some who perhaps, as yet, have never realized their position of privilege in reference to Christ and to his people ; and they have never let their hearts go out as they should go out towards those whom Christ has purchased with his precious blood.

Show us the proof of your love *to the ungodly*, too—to this great city of four millions. Show us the proof of your love by trying to snatch the firebrands from the flame. Be up and doing. Stand at the street corners, if you can, and preach Jesus Christ. Scatter the printed gospel in every room to which you have access. Talk of Christ to your workpeople. Speak of him to your companions. Endeavour to spread this potent all-heal, this cure for all manner of spiritual diseases, for otherwise, talk as you may, profess as you may, we shall have to say to you, " Show us the proof of your love."

I have only given you a sort of charcoal sketch of what might be the proof of your love: I have not drawn the picture or laid on the colours. Think, dear friends, how you can give such proof at once.

III. But now, in the third place, WHY IS THIS PROOF CALLED FOR? Somebody says, "Why am I called upon to prove my love?" Do not grieve even if I press it very hard upon you, for your case will be something like that of Simon Peter when he too was pressed exceedingly.

Peter was grieved when his Master said to him the third time, "Simon, son of Jonas, lovest thou me?" Now the Lord did not ask it because he doubted him, for he knew Peter's heart. Peter's appeal was a true one, "Thou knowest all things. Thou knowest that I love thee." Do not therefore resent it, and say, "Why should I prove my love?" No, but just listen. *True love always longs to prove itself.* It does not need a command to do it. It is waiting for an opportunity. It is so with your domestic life. You know that it is so. I need not give instances. What a pleasure it is to show love to those we love! In a far higher degree, what a delight it is to a Christian to do something for Jesus! If you have never done anything distinctly for Jesus, what sort of a child of God can you be? I love my Master's service, and I can truly say that I think that I would do anything for his people: but I am not quite so sure about that as I am about the feeling that I would do anything *for him.* When I get a hold of something that is distinctly and undividedly for my Lord's glory, I am so glad to do it. To break an alabaster box of ointment upon his head is a rich delight: truly it might have been given to the poor and have blessed the poor, but Jesus, himself, is best. "It is a waste," somebody murmurs. Yes, yes, but to be wasteful for Christ is the noblest economy. O hearts that love your Lord, never count the silver when you are spending for Jesus! Break the box! Pour out the ointment! The room will be filled with the perfume, and it will not be wasted. Even if there were no nostril to smell it, if Jesus alone had the refreshment of it, it would be all the better. I like to enter the glade of a forest where there are spots unseen of eye of man, and thickets of brake through which nobody but the red deer has ever passed. I delight to sit down by a little rippling brook upon a bank of thyme undesecrated by human foot, and think, "This is God's garden, and every leaf waves for him." How dare the poet say that flowers which were born to blush unseen are wasting their fragrance on the desert air? Why, they are flowering for God, and he delights in them, and they are just the best-used flowers in the world. Oh to be just such a flower as that at times, and to feel that you have got away— away from the gardens where men may come and praise or dispraise, and offer mercenary prizes for flowers and fruits—away where God sees you, and delights in you. We should try to work for Jesus only. Proof is called for, not because Jesus doubts, but because he loves to please us by giving us opportunities of proving our love.

But one reason why we are called upon to prove our love is *that it may become a blessing to other people.* The Corinthians were to prove their love because the poor folks at Jerusalem were starving. It would be of no use for the Corinthians to sing a hymn about charity while the poor saints at Jerusalem had not a loaf to eat. No, they must prove their love, that it might be a benefit to others, and that the influence of that love might spread to others, because the apostle says, "If you Corinthians do not discharge your promise, those people at Macedonia will throw it in my teeth, and do nothing themselves, and therefore, for the sake of the churches in Macedonia, you must be liberal." So, beloved, oftentimes one man, by serving his Master well, stirs up a whole regiment of other Christians, who become ashamed to be doing so little. I may preach a great many sermons, brethren, but they will do very little good compared with what your sermons will do, if, as a church, you live up to the mark as Christians. If in holy love, and concord, and every grace, you abound, other churches will say, "Look at this church." Oh that you may be such saints that others may be encouraged in their work for Christ by you : that is why you are asked to prove your love.

You are asked to prove your love, for *it is reasonable that you should do so.* God did not love you and keep it to himself, and say, "My name is love, but I will *do* nothing." No : he gave his Son from his bosom, his only Son, and that Son he gave to die. God is practical. That which he feels he does : that which he speaks is done. We have many idle words, but the word and mind of God come out in deeds of grace. Is it not right, therefore, that we should give practical proof of our love ?

IV. Time fails me, or I would have dwelt on the fourth point, namely, WHO IT IS THAT CALLS FOR THIS PROOF OF OUR LOVE ?

I will leave out everybody else but one, and say, it is *your Lord,* your own dying, living Saviour who says, "Show me the proof of your love." I will tell you how he is saying it. Affliction has come into your house. There is a dear one dead ; and Jesus says "Now will you kick against me, or will you yield me your treasure ? Simon, son of Jonas, lovest thou me more than these dear ones ? If so, thou wilt part with them and not complain." "Mary, dost thou love me better than mother, or sister, or friend ? If so ; thou wilt bless me when I take them away. Now is thy time ; show me the proof of thy love by bowing before my chastening, and loving me still." Our Lord only takes from us what he gave to us ; let us, therefore, bless his name. Bereaved one, that may be the proof of love to which he is calling *you.*

Perhaps you have had a difference lately with one to whom you ought to be united in friendship, and now your conscience is saying " Christians ought to live in peace and love." But Satan is saying "You were not to blame. Do not humble yourself before such a proud person as your opponent." But my Lord and Master says to you, "Show me the proof of your love. Forgive him for my sake even to seventy times seven ; and if you have wronged him confess the wrong, and humble yourself for my sake. Because I washed my disciples' feet, show me the proof of your love by washing one another's feet." Attend to that admonition, I pray you.

But possibly there are some here who have had in their minds the project of doing something unusual for Jesus, or the church, or the poor, or for missions to the heathen. Satan has said, "You must not give so much as that." Jesus says, "I have prospered you : when others have failed in business I have taken care of you. Show me the proof of your love." Will you not hear his call ? Do not hold back your hand, and do not want anybody to persuade you, because that will spoil it all. It must be spontaneous. It must come from your own heart, moved only by the Spirit of God, if you wish it to be accepted. Perhaps I am addressing a young man who has been for years a member of the church; and it is crossing his mind "What shall I do to show my love?" and it is his ambition to be a missionary in a distant land. Keep not yourself back, my dear young brother. Should it rend a fond connection, or cost you your life, give Jesus such proof of your love as his Spirit suggests to you. Or is it that you ought to speak to people about their souls? The Lord will throw somebody in your way. Give a proof of your love by a holy bravery, and speak right out for Jesus Christ, and do not be ashamed. The Lord invites you to a closer fellowship with himself, to come higher up the mount of God, and to be more thoroughly consecrated. Then show him the proof of your love.

I leave this with you. If you love him, show it. If you do not love him, tremble. I will not repeat what the Scripture says, as though it came from myself, but I would have you recollect it. Paul says, " If any man love not the Lord Jesus Christ, let him be Anathema Maranatha,"—cursed with a curse at the coming of Christ. So it must be if you love not Christ.

Oh! if you do love him, be inventive. Think of a new thing that nobody else ever did for Jesus. Strike out a fresh path. Deny yourselves comforts to have the comfort of proving your love, as his Spirit shall guide and help you; and to his name be praise evermore. Amen and Amen.

PORTION OF SCRIPTURE READ BEFORE SERMON—2 Corinthians viii.

HYMNS FROM " OUR OWN HYMN BOOK "—791, 811, 639.

Metropolitan Tabernacle Pulpit.

MEN BEWITCHED.

DELIVERED BY

C. H. SPURGEON,

AT THE METROPOLITAN TABERNACLE, NEWINGTON.

"O foolish Galatians, who hath bewitched you, that ye should not obey the truth, before whose eyes Jesus Christ hath been evidently set forth, crucified among you?"—Galatians iii. 1.

WITH very great enthusiasm the Galatians received the gospel when Paul preached it to them. They seem to have been a very warm-hearted but fickle people, and Paul found to his great grief that, while he was away from them, certain false teachers came in and turned them aside from the gospel which he had delivered to them. He spake out very plainly about the matter. In this verse he uses very strong terms, while he says to them—"O foolish Galatians, who hath bewitched you, that ye should not obey the truth?" I do not know that any such witchery has fallen upon any of you, but I do know that, being men, we are all subject to like dangers, and I know also that there is a witchery in the very air at this time, so that many are to be found throughout the churches of this land to whom these words might be justly spoken.

We can only hope to escape this evil which Paul so severely condemns by the use of right cautionary means. It is only, in fact, as the Holy Ghost shall keep us that we shall be preserved from the fascinations of error, and kept true to the grand old gospel of the blessed God. At this time I shall very briefly speak, in the first place, upon *the subtle danger* which is hinted at here; "Who hath bewitched you?" Secondly, at more length I shall speak upon *the blessed preservative:* there is no way of being kept from this witchery like having Christ Jesus set forth among us, evidently crucified. And, thirdly, a few words, in closing, upon *the supreme folly* of any who, having tried this divine preservative, nevertheless do become bewitched by error.

I. First, then, let us think of THE SUBTLE DANGER which is ever around us.

It was hard work to preach the gospel at first among the heathen. Men had to lay down their lives to do it. They had to propound new things which the heathen mind did not readily receive. But, by the power of the Spirit of God, converts were made, and churches were formed. And now came another difficulty. Even those that were converted, or appeared to be so, became suddenly, as it were, bewitched

Nos. 1,546-7-8.

181

with error of one kind or another, just as in families children are suddenly taken ill with certain complaints which seem incidental to childhood. If parents had never heard of such things before, they would be astonished. They would suppose that they must lose their children when such unaccountable diseases suddenly appeared in them, and yet they survive. In the family of Christ certain epidemics break out at times. We cannot tell why they should come just then; and at first, perhaps, we are puzzled and perplexed to think that such diseases should come at all; but they do come; and hence it is well to be on our guard against them. Paul calls it being bewitched, because these people fell into strange error, error which had no argument to back it, error surprising and startling. He seems to say, " I cannot make it out. I cannot understand how you should be thus misled." In Paul's day the error was generally that of Judaism. They wanted to go back to circumcision, and to the old sacrifices of the law. Paul was indignant enough about this. " I testify," said he, " to everyone of you, that if he be circumcized he is a debtor to keep the whole law, and he has fallen from grace. If you go back to the old beggarly elements of Judaism, you are leaving Christ, and rejecting Christ, and imperilling your souls." He declares that he could not understand how they should wish to do it. He calls it witchery, for in his day it was believed that men could cast an evil eye upon one another, and thus work evil upon their fellow men. It seemed to Paul to be something like that—as if the devil himself were in it, and came and turned men away from Christ Jesus, to go back to trusting in the law and its obsolete ceremonies.

It was not long before Paul found another kind of error in the church. There came in among the humbler believers certain men of education, who thought themselves highly intelligent—men who knew something about Socrates and Plato; and they said, " These doctrines are too plain. The poor people understand them, and they come into the church; but no doubt they have a deeper meaning, intended only for the initiated." So they began to spiritualize everything, and, in the process, they spirited away the very gospel itself. Paul could not endure it. He said that though he or an angel from heaven should preach any other gospel than that which he had preached it would be a cursed deed. Whether it were Judaism, or Gnosticism, he smote it heavily, and said to those who fell into it, " Who hath bewitched you?"

You who read church history know that in after ages the church fell into Arianism. There were great disputes about the deity of Christ, and the air for a long time was full of that deadly plague. When that battle was over, and such men as Athanasius had settled the question of our Redeemer's Godhead, then came up all the superstitions of Rome—that awful midnight, black with murky clouds, which covered the church for ages. Indeed, if we look back on history, it seems like a witchcraft, that men who had the gospel preached among them in all its glorious simplicity, should after all submit their minds to such debasing falsehoods as those of old Rome, and prostrate themselves before images of of wood and stone after a heathenish manner, even as their pagan forefathers had done.

At this present time it is a marvel to some of us how the churches have been bewitched again. When I was a boy I recollect hearing Mr. Jay say, "Puseyism is a lie!" I remember the words coming just like that from his reverend lips, and everybody, or nearly everybody, thought with him. It was a wonderful event if a high church or ritualistic place was set up. Everybody was astonished at it; and if you said, "This is the church of England, and this is according to her prayer-book," everybody said you were uncharitable, and that it was not so. They pitied our fears, and said that a dozen men were going towards Rome, and that was all. Look ye now, sirs : these things are openly done. Our parish churches are commonly turned into mass houses, and the Church of England is slightly to be distinguished in many parishes from the church of Rome, and yet nobody is astonished; and, if we make a remark about it, we are set down as bigoted. Who hath bewitched this Protestant land? With Smithfield scarcely yet swept of the ashes of her martyrs, they set up the crucifix again! What would Oliver Cromwell say if he and his Ironsides could come back again to see what they are making of this land? I wot some strong things he would say; and, as I cannot speak such vigorous words as he would have uttered, I leave the subject with words borrowed from Paul, which well suit the case, "O foolish Englishmen, who hath bewitched you, that ye should thus turn aside?"

Nor is this all. You see this witchery in another way among our dissenting churches. At a time not yet forgotten Unitarianism and Socinianism gradually crept into Nonconforming congregations, and the pulpits lost their testimony for Christ; the meeting-houses were deserted, and true religion seemed dying out of the land. Then came Whitefield and Wesley, and all their troop of Methodists, and the blessed flame that was almost quenched burned up again, and we, of this generation, have said one to another, "That experiment will never be repeated : the Nonconformist churches will never go in that direction again : they know better. They see the ill-effect of this modern teaching, and they will stick to the grand old gospel now." So I dreamed; but I dream in that way no longer, for scarcely do I look anywhere but I find the gospel of Christ diluted, the milk of the word adulterated, and the grand gospel, as Luther and Calvin would have thundered it out, seldom enough to be heard. O foolish Noncon formists, who hath bewitched you that ye should not obey the truth, but should seek after this novelty and the other—this refinement and the other, and let your God and Saviour go? As for us, if we stand alone, God forbid that we should glory save in the cross of our Lord Jesus Christ.

This is the peril.

II. Our second head is THE ONLY PRESERVATIVE. The apostle says that the Galatians had had Christ set forth before their eyes crucified among them.

Well then, if you want to be kept right and sound in the faith, the first thing is to get the right subject fixed in the centre of your hearts— Jesus Christ crucified. Paul says that he preached *that*. He set Jesus forth. Whatever else he might not have made clear, he did set forth the person and work of Jesus Christ. Beloved, settle this in your soul, that your sole hope and the main subject of your meditation shall always be Jesus Christ. Whatever I do not know, O my Lord, help me to know thee. Whatever I do not believe, enable me to believe thee, and to trust thee, and to take thy every word as the very truth of God. Beloved, away with the religion that has little of Christ in it. Christ must be Alpha and Omega, first and last. The religion that is made up of our doings and our feelings and our willings is a falsehood. Our religion must have Christ for the foundation, Christ as the cornerstone, Christ as the topstone; and if we are not based and bottomed, grounded and settled upon him, our religion is vain. Paul wonders that any to whom Christ has been the chief thing should ever have been bewitched; and I trow that if Christ be really such to your souls, you will not turn aside through error, but Christ crucified will hold you fast.

But Paul says not only that he had preached Christ to them, but that he had set him forth, by which I understand that he had taken pains to make all about Christ clear to them. He had preached his person as man and God. He had preached his work as the atoning sacrifice. He had preached him as risen and pleading before the throne of God. He had preached him as our substitute. He had made this the main doctrine—that, if we are saved, we are saved by the righteousness of Christ, and our sin is put away because Christ bore it in our stead and suffered the penalty due for it, that so the justice of God might be satisfied, and we might be saved. That is what he means by Christ crucified. He had gone into details on this point and set forth the glorious doctrines which cluster about the cross. Brethren, if you want to be kept from the modern witcheries, think much of Christ, and go into detail about him. Be familiar with his divine person. Be well acquainted with his relationships, and his offices: know what he is in the covenant of grace, what he is to the Father, what he is to you. Oh seek to know him! He yet surpasseth knowledge; but be students of Christ. Do not have a mere superficial knowledge of him, but seek to know Christ, and to be found in him. This will keep you free from error.

When the apostle says that he set Christ forth, he means, next, that he had done it with great plainness. The Greek word has to do with a programme or a proclamation; it is as good as to say, " I have set Christ before you as plainly as if I had printed a great bill and stuck it up before your eyes. I have put the letters down in capitals. As a king, when he makes a proclamation, puts it on the walls, and calls attention to it, so," says Paul, " I have set forth Christ before you. I have not talked of him in a mystical way, so that you did not know what I meant, but I have set him forth. I have said of him that he suffered in our stead, and was made a curse for us, as it is written, ' Cursed is every one that hangeth on a tree.' "

Paul set forth Jesus plainly. Now, you know the way in which Jesus Christ is preached by some. It was well described by old Dr. Duncan when he said, " They preach that the death of Christ in some way or other had some sort of connection, in some way or other, with the salvation of men." Yes, that is it—misty, cloudy, foggy—a bottle of smoke. We do not preach Christ in that way, but we just say this, " The Lord hath laid on him the iniquity of us all," and because he was oppressed and he was afflicted in the room and place and stead of the guilty, therefore does God most freely remit the sin of believers and bid them go their way. Substitution—may we never stammer over that—Christ in the sinner's stead.

Beloved, if you will get a hold of that truth, and get it well worked into your soul, you will be more than a match for the ritualism or rationalism of the age. Give up that doctrine? The man who has once drunk it in and knows its sweetness cannot give it up ; for he gets to feel that, having once believed it, it acts in him as a detector by which he discovers what is false doctrine, and it gives to him a taste which makes false doctrine loathsome to him, so that he cries, "Away with it." If anything contrary to this comes before him, he does not timidly say, "Everybody has a right to his opinion"; but he says, "Yes, they may have a right to their opinion, and so have I to mine ; and my opinion is that any opinion which takes away from the glory of Christ's substitutionary sacrifice is a detestable opinion." Get the real atonement of Christ thoroughly into your soul, and you will not be bewitched.

Nor is this all. Paul says that Christ was set forth crucified visibly among them. Did you ever see Christ in this way? I do not ask whether you ever saw a vision. Who wishes for that? I do not ask whether your imagination was so worked upon that you thought you saw the Saviour. There would be no particular use in that, for thousands did actually see him on the cross, and they thrust out the tongue at him and perished in their sins. But let me tell you that it is one of the most strengthening things to our piety to get to feel by faith as though we did behold the Saviour. We do not expect to *see* him until he comes ; yet when we have been alone in our chamber we have as much realized his presence without the use of our eyes as if we had literally seen him. He has been certainly sensibly crucified before us, for this is the point. He says that he had set forth Christ with such vividness—he had word painted so thoroughly well, he had spoken so plainly and so simply, that they seemed to say, "We see it : Christ in our stead, Christ bleeding for our sin." They seemed to see him as if he were before them in their midst. My dear friends, do not say, "Christ died on Calvary. That is thousands of miles off." I know that he did, but what matters it where he died as to locality? He loved you, and gave himself for you. Let him be to you as though he were crucified at Newington Butts, and as though his cross were in the middle of this tabernacle. "Oh, but he died nineteen hundred years ago." I know that he did, but the efficacy of his death is a thing of to-day. "He died unto sin once": and that once pours the splendour of its efficacy all down the ages, and the thing for you to do is to feel as ·if you saw him dying *now*, on the tree *now*—you standing immediately at the foot of the cross, and looking up, and seeing him looking down from off that cross and saying, "I did all this for thee." Cannot you ask the Lord to make it as vivid as that to you? I want, while I am looking upon this great throng, to forget you all, and to see Jesus standing here with the nail prints. Oh, if I could see him how humbly I would throw myself at his feet! With what love would I embrace him! With what reverence would I adore him! But, my Master, I am so sure of the fact that thou didst die in my stead, and that my sins were laid on thee, that even now I see thee discharging all my debts, and bearing all my curse. Though thou art gone to the glory, yet I vividly realize that thou wast here.   This has become a fact to me.

Whenever you get into company where they are talking about the doctrines of grace, and sneering about them, and whenever you get into another class of company, where they say, "Away with your simple worship of God! You must have priests, and incense, and altars, and all": do not argue with them. Get alone, and ask to see Jesus Christ over again. See if there is anything of popish finery about him. See if there is anything of this philosophy, falsely so called, about him. You will determine as soon as you have seen him that you will call all things else vanity and lies, and bind his gospel tó your heart. The cross is the school of orthodoxy. Endeavour to keep there. While I have been alone on the Continent I have, in my quiet moments, had realizations of my Master's presence, and then I have wished that I could borrow the wings of a dove, so that I might there and then stand up and talk to you. I have been very sick and full of pain, and depressed in spirit, and I have judged myself to be of all men most unworthy, and I judged truly. I stand to that judgment still. I felt myself only worthy to be shaken like dust from off the feet of my Lord, and cast into the bottomless pit for ever. Then it was that my Substitute was my hope, and in my lonely chamber at Mentone I clung to his dear skirts; I looked into his wounds; I trusted myself with him again, and I know that I am a saved man. I tell you there is no salvation in any other, but only in Jesus. You will not be led away to any other doctrine if you will return continually to this truth. Some men want a sound pummelling with affliction to get them to love Christ; and some old professors need a touch of poverty sometimes, or a little affliction, or a rack of rheumatism, and that would bring them to their bearings, and they would begin to cry out after realities, and get rid of whims and fancies. When it comes to close dealings between God and your soul, and death stares you in the face, nothing will do but a crucified Redeemer, and no confidence will do but a sinner's childlike reliance upon the finished work of him who suffered in our stead. I speak strongly, but I feel a thousand times more strongly than I can speak.

III. The last point is THE SUPREME FOLLY of those who would leave Jesus for anything else. Suppose that any man should once have trusted in Jesus Christ simply, and have realized the death of Christ, and have come into real contact with the dying, bleeding Master; and suppose that, after that, he should begin to put his confidence in priests and sacraments; or suppose that he should, after that, put on his lavender kid gloves and become a philosopher,—what would he be? Now, do not tell anybody, I pray you. Keep it to yourselves. The apostle Paul did not affect the manners of a gentlemañ, but he spoke very plainly indeed. Do not tell your learned neighbours that I said it, because I did not say it: it is Paul that said it: he says that a man who should do that would be—A FOOL. "Oh, foolish Galatians!" What are you at, Paul? They have been decorating their service; surely you cannot object to that. Don't you know, Paul, that the old Jewish priest used to wear a splendid breastplate wrought with jewels, and he had an ephod adorned with bells and pomegranates? Surely in the worship of God we ought to do things decorously and properly! And on this plea these Galatians have decked themselves out exceedingly. " They are foolish Galatians!" he says. Very rude of him, mark you; very rude of him! I shall not attempt to excuse him, for I fully endorse his verdict.

But here is a gentleman who has been reading Plato, and after reading Plato he has been reading the words of Jesus Christ, and he says that they do not mean what the common people think they mean— that there is a very mysterious philosophical sense hidden within them. For instance, when Jesus Christ says, " These shall go away into ever- lasting punishment," it does not mean at all what the words say. It means that they shall ultimately be restored. Now, Paul, this gentleman is a philosopher; what do you say of him? He says, " He is foolish!" That is all he says, and all that he needs to say, for learned folly is folly at its height. " Oh, foolish Galatians ! Who hath bewitched you ?"

Why do we think these people foolish? Because *we* should be foolish ourselves if we were to do the same. A good many years ago, when I was about fifteen or sixteen years of age, I wanted a Saviour, and I heard the gospel preached by a poor man, who said in the name of Jesus— " Look unto me and be ye saved, all the ends of the earth." It was very plain English, and I understood it, and obeyed it and found rest. I owe all my happiness since then to the same plain doctrine. Now, suppose that I were to say, " I have read a great many books, and there are a great many people willing to hear me. I really could not preach such a com- monplace gospel as I did at the first. I must put it in a sophisticated way, so that none but the *élite* can understand me." I should be—what should I be? I should be a fool, writ large. I should be worse than that, I should be a traitor to my God; for if I was saved' by a simple gospel, then I am bound to preach that same simple gospel till I die, so that others too may be saved by it. When I cease to preach salvation by faith in Jesus put me into a lunatic asylum, for you may be sure that my mind is gone.

There are hundreds of you who feel perfectly happy in Christ. You believe that all your sins are washed away, that you are justified by the righteousness of Christ, and accepted in the Beloved. Now, suppose that you give that up and say, " Instead of believing in Christ's dying once and making an atonement, I am going to believe in the perpetual sacrifice offered by a human being in the mass": you will be very foolish. Suppose that instead of trusting in Jesus Christ for perfect pardon and justification, so that you know that there is no condemnation to you because you are in Christ Jesus, you go back to works, and say, " I am going to work out my own salvation by my own good works": you will be foolish to the last degree, and you will soon discover the fact by the misery that will come over your spirit.

Look again. When you have lived nearest to Christ, and trusted most in him, have you not felt most desire after holiness? Now, tell me, if you have tried the modern views, what state of mind have you been in with regard to your daily walk? I will tell you. You could, with those modern views, frequent the theatre and the music hall, and feel quite easy; and you could do a sharp trick in business and feel comfort- able; but you know that when you have seen Christ you cannot do anything of the kind. You are sanctified by his presence. You feel a strong desire after perfect purity. You feel a horror and a dread of sin.

You walk tenderly and cautiously, and you are bowed down by distress of mind at the thought of your imperfections. Judge then which must be the right doctrine. That which makes you most holy must certainly be true; and if you turn away from your Lord, whose very presence breathes sanctification, and communion with whom is sure to bring holiness, you will be a fool: and we shall have to say, " Oh, foolish Galatians, who hath bewitched you?"

During the late meetings that we have had here, my dear brethren Fullerton and Smith have been preaching the gospel, the straight-out gospel of Jesus Christ, and at one meeting, held afterwards, there were scores of persons who rose up to tell of what that ministry had done for their souls by God the Holy Spirit. There were thieves reclaimed, drunkards reclaimed, harlots reclaimed, great sinners reclaimed. Well, now, suppose that, after all, some of you ladies and gentlemen should say, "We see what the gospel can do, but we are going to try something else," you will be fools. I am always ready to try a new machine: we will try the electric light one of these days instead of gas when we are sure of it; but suppose that it should all go out and leave us in the dark! I will wait till the invention has been tested. So it may happen with the new religious lights that men bring up, which are like dim rushlights compared with the blazing sun of gospel truth; we are not going to try anything new to the risk of our souls. We are going to keep to the old, old gospel until it is worn out. When it gets worn out, and will not save any more, and will not comfort any more, and will not draw us near to God any more, then will be the time for us to think of something fresh. But as that has not come to pass, I beg to say that I will drive another nail into my old colours and fasten them anew to the old mast. What I have preached among you these six-and-twenty years I will preach again; for I am determined to know nothing among men but Christ and him crucified; and may neither the preacher become a fool, nor any of his hearers become fools, by being bewitched, so that they forsake the glorious gospel of Jesus Christ. Oh that you all knew its power, and were all saved by it! God grant that you may be, for Jesus' sake. Amen.

PORTION OF SCRIPTURE READ BEFORE SERMON—Galatians ii. 21; and chapter iii.

HYMNS FROM "OUR OWN HYMN BOOK"—291, 282, 278.

SAMUEL AND THE YOUNG MAN SAUL.

A Sermon

DELIVERED BY

C. H. SPURGEON,

AT THE METROPOLITAN TABERNACLE, NEWINGTON.

"And as they were going down to the end of the city, Samuel said to Saul, Bid the servant pass on before us, (and he passed on,) but stand thou still a while, that I may show thee the word of God."—1 Samuel ix. 27.

THIS was Samuel's third interview with this goodly young man. He had spoken with him and entertained him in his parlour, giving him the place of honour; he had afterwards spent the evening with him in quiet on the house-top, and now they were about to part he took a fresh opportunity of speaking to him. This time he spoke to him with great closeness of personal application, sending the servant out of the way that he might say things to him which nobody else might hear. He tried to speak to the young man's inmost soul. The prophet felt a deep solemnity, his whole heart saying every word that fell from his lip. He knew that this young man was about to be made a king, to take upon him very heavy responsibilities, and he might either be a great curse to Israel or a great blessing, and therefore the man of God, with all the gravity of his years, and all the earnestness of his loving spirit, said, "Stand thou still a while, that I may show thee the word of God." I think I hear his earnest tones, and accents sweetened by a great love, for Samuel loved Saul, and it was his affection which made him speak so earnestly and pointedly. I may have among my hearers at this moment some to whom I have spoken many times, but I should like once more to have a special, personal interview with them. Come, young man, step aside and let me speak with you. Try and think that no one is here except the preacher and yourself, and that he means *you* when he speaks. I long this time to do my Master's work thoroughly with you in the power of the Spirit of God. This time the preacher would hold you fast, as if he said to each one, "I will not let thee go unless thou give thy heart to Christ, and become his servant from this very hour."

There are two things in the text about which I wish to speak. Here is the first: *the attention which he requested;* and the second, on which we shall dwell at greater length, concerns *the subject upon which he spoke.*

I. First, let us think upon THE ATTENTION WHICH HE REQUESTED. *He said to the servant,* "Pass on before us," and he passed on. Will you, also, kindly try to dismiss from your minds any other thoughts besides those which we will try to bring before you. Bid the servant pass on; forget for a while your business, forget your family, forget your joys, forget your sorrows. You have had enough of these, I dare say, all the week. Perhaps you have been haunted by them in your sleep: your dreams have been rendered unhappy by the rehearsal of your trials. By an effort of your mind, in which God will help you, try to make these servants pass on. I wish I could so speak that men would say of my preaching what they said of Whitefield's. One man said, " Whenever I went to church before, I calculated how many looms the church would hold "—for he was a weaver—" but when I heard Whitefield I never thought of a loom." Another said, " While I have been in church I have often built a ship from stem to stern; but when I heard Mr. Whitefield I could not lay a plank; he took my mind right away from such things, and occupied me with higher thoughts." I pray you, help me in my endeavour to engross your attention. Let the ships go, and the loom go, and the kitchen go, and the business go: send on the servant, and be alone now with yourself and your God.

The next point in the attention requested was the desire that he would " stand still a while." They had been walking quietly down the hill till they came to the last house in the town, and when they had come fairly into the fields he said, " Stand thou still a while": as much as to say— I have somewhat important to say, and you will catch it better if you are quiet and motionless as to your body, but especially if your mind can be still. Forget the asses that you sought after, and your father's house, and all home concerns, and calmly listen to me. It is a very desirable thing when we are listening to the gospel to let it have its full effect upon us, to give our minds up to it, and say,—" Let it come like the dew, and soak into my mind as the dew into Gideon's fleece. Let it come like a shower, and let it enter into my very nature as the rain into the clods which are softened by the gentle influence of the showers." I pray you bask in the gospel as men do in the sunlight when they would be warm. Let the gospel have its own legitimate effect upon you. Lay bare your bosom to it. Ask that your soul may have no stone of carelessness laid upon it, as though it were a dead thing in a sepulchre, but that it may come forth in resurrection life through the quickening word of the divine Spirit.

Is not this what the word of God deserves? Should it not have our living, loving attention? When God speaks let all be silent. Hush, ye senators, if God speaks. Sit still, ye princes, if the King of kings lifts up his voice. Quiet, even ye choirs celestial, if Jehovah speaks. An obedient homage should be paid to the voice of God by the deep awe and reverence of the spirit. Do you ever get alone and sit still, and say, as Samuel did, in the dead of night, " Speak, Lord, for thy servant heareth "? If you never do that, the little child Samuel may well rebuke you. He was willing that God should speak to him. But, oh! we are so busy! so busy! so sadly busy! I have heard that the great clock at St. Paul's can scarcely be heard in Cheapside, by reason of the traffic that is going by; and so the most solemn voices are drowned amidst the din and uproar of our business, and we do not often hear God's voice, unless we are accustomed to give ourselves a little quiet and holy stillness, and sit in our chamber alone, and say, "Now, Lord, commune with me. I wish to hear thy voice. I open my Bible. I am about to read a few verses. Oh, speak with me." I do not believe there would be very many persons left unconverted if it were their habit and practice day by day to open the word of God with the desire that God should speak to them. Come then, dear friend, send on your servant, forget your business, and stand still, that I may show you the Word of God.

As the Word of God deserves such quiet attention, *it certainly is only by such attention that it is likely to bless us.* Faith cometh by hearing, but not by such hearing as some men give, for the Word goes in at one ear and out at the other. They hear the gospel as though it were an idle tale, or a merry song, to which they listen at a street corner, and they go their way. Nay, but if thou wouldst get the blessing, thou must hear as for eternity, with all thine ears, and with thy whole heart, praying while thou dost hear, "Lord, bless this to me! Lord, bless this to me!" I remember a child who used to be noted for great attention during sermon, and his mother, noticing his deep earnestness, asked him why. He said, "Because, mother, I heard the preacher once say that if there was a piece of the discourse that was likely to be of good to our souls, Satan would try to make us lose it; and as I do not know which part God will bless me by, I try to hear it all, and to remember it all." Oh, when people come to listen to the preacher with such a spirit as that, it is sweet work to preach. You can easily feed hungry horses, and you can easily feed souls that hunger and thirst after righteousness: "They shall be filled." The Lord help us to give earnest heed to his own saving Word. "Stand thou still a while, that I may show thee the word of God."

But *many things arise to prevent this attention.* You cannot get some folks to be still, they are so frivolous; you cannot make them think. Some men dread the process of thinking, almost as much as they would a touch of the "cat" on their backs. They cannot bear to consider and meditate. God has distinguished them above brutes by giving them the faculty of thought, but this high privilege they try to ignore. Any silly tale, or idle song, or light amusement, or pastime, will entice them, but they have no soul for serious things. They go through life, not as the bee, which sucks honey from every flower, but as the butterfly, which regards the garden as only a place over which it may flit, and where it may occasionally alight, but gather nothing, and so begins and ends its gaudy day, and has nothing in store. Let us not be the fluttering insects of an idle day. God grant we may not follow the fashion of this foolish world. May frivolity and levity be taken away from us, and may we in sober earnestness attend to things eternal. Others, on the other hand, are so exceedingly careful about the things of this world, that you cannot get them to think of the Word of God. What is heaven to them? They know a plan for making a large profit. You shall talk to them of Christ and all his beauties, but they will not afford you a thought: jingle a half-sovereign near them, and you shall excite all their desires. Inform them how they could be rich and famous, they will pay you for the prescription; but tell them about Christ, and you must beg and pray them to read half a page, and as to listening to your sermon,—the thing is dry, they

turn away from it. O you money-grubbers, have you souls at all, or
are you nothing else but bodies? Are you mere leather purses for
holding money? Do you expect to live in the future, to live in eternity,
or do you think that you shall die, like the dog that follows at your
heel? O my hearer, if you be not immortal, I can well excuse you that
you think not of immortality; but if indeed you be a man made in the
image of God, and destined to live for ever, it is but the commonest
common sense that you should begin to prepare for those eternal abodes
in which you are to dwell world without end. Do stand still a while,
and let nothing come in to break the silence of your spirit, while you
listen to the voice of God. I would earnestly persuade every one here
who is not saved to get an hour alone somehow. Make up your mind
to do so. Shut yourself up, and give an hour to solemn, earnest
thought and consideration of your condition before God. I am persuaded that scarcely one would do that solemnly and earnestly but what
it would end well, and we should have by-and-by to bless God for the
happy result of that hour.

II. We leave the point, of the attention to be given, to consider
THE SUBJECT UPON WHICH SAMUEL DISCOURSED with Saul, or rather
the subject about which I would discourse at this time, if I am so happy
as to have secured your ear. He says, "Stand thou still a while, that I
may show thee the word of God." The subject is *the Word of God.*
That God should give us a Word at all is very gracious. It is wonderful
that he should condescend to speak to us, because we cannot understand much: we are like little children at the very best. For our
heavenly Father to bring down the great meanings of his vast mind into
human language is something very wonderful. When he spoke on Sinai
with the accompaniment of tempest and lightning, it was a gracious
thing for God to speak to man anyhow; but in these last days he has
spoken to us by his Son Jesus Christ, who is the Word: Jesus has come
down into this world on purpose to interpret God to man. A man's
mind goes to another man's mind by a word: the word tells what was in
the speaker's thought. So Christ comes from God to us. God says to
us, "You wish me to speak: that is my speech, MY SON; read my love
to you in the fact that I gave my Son; read my justice, for I made *him*
bleed; read my mercy, for in him I pass by transgression, iniquity
and sin." Does God speak in such golden language, does he speak
by his own Son, the eternal Word, and need I ask that he should
have a hearing? Shall it have come to this, that God shall give
up the darling of his bosom to a cruel death and yet we will turn
aside and will not regard it? The Lord grant us deliverance from
such madness and wickedness, and help us to feel, if salvation be
worthy of the death of the Son of God, it must be worthy of our
attending to it. If Jesus thought it worth his while to bleed upon
the cross for man's salvation, it is worth my while to put everything aside till I am saved; it is worth my while to get me to my
chamber, and shut to the door, and feel as if I never would rise from my
knees till I had found peace with God through Jesus Christ. God is
engaged in man's salvation, even the Father; Jesus was engaged in it,
even the blessed Son; and the Holy Spirit is engaged in it, even the
divine Convincer of sin. Surely that which occupies the infinite mind

of the three blessed persons of the divine unity, must surely call to every wise man to lend his ear, and give it all his thoughts that he may receive, obtain, possess, enjoy, and delight himself in the precious things which God gives us freely in Christ Jesus. Then, dear hearer, do be thoughtful, and "Stand still a while, that I may show thee the word of God."

In the particular word of God which Samuel spoke to Saul there was some likeness to the message which I am bound to deliver to you. For, first, Samuel spoke to Saul *about a kingdom*, of which this young man should be the king. He never dreamed of that before. He had thought of his father's asses, but a throne and a crown had never entered his mind. Dost know, O strange young man, thou who hast stolen in to this service, that there is such a thing as the kingdom of God? Jesus said, "Seek ye first the kingdom of God and his righteousness, and all these things shall be added unto you." Dost know, young man, that thou mayest be a king? Yea, if thou givest good heed to the gospel, thou shalt be a king, and sing with us unto the Lord Jesus, for he hath made us kings and priests unto God, and we shall reign with him. Art thou occupied entirely with thy business, with seeking after a degree at the University, with striving to pass an examination or gain a situation? I will not call thee away from such pursuits, yet is there something higher than these. Thou mayest not be contented with such things as these, for God calls thee, he calls thee to a higher destiny, to something noble, so noble that those who share in it rank higher than the kings of the earth. Little did Saul dream that on this day the kingdom should be given him, and little dost thou dream of it perhaps as yet ; but I pray thee let me show thee the word of God, for thou mayest yet find a kingdom there, a kingdom for thee, a crown of life for thee which fadeth not away, and a seat at the right hand of God with Christ in the day of his appearing.

Samuel not only spoke about the kingdom, but he showed him the word of God by *an anointing*. He took out a flask, which contained a little oil, and he poured it on his head. "O my hearer, stand thou still a while," and I will tell thee of an anointing. If thou dost regard this present voice of God, and dost heartily incline thine ear, and come unto Christ that thou mayest live, thou shalt by so doing receive an anointing from the Holy One by which thou shalt know all things that concern thy soul and thy God. Thou sayest, "I know little about religion." Thou shalt be taught of God, for this is the promise : "All thy children shall be taught of the Lord, and great shall be the peace of thy children." Thou sayest, "I am not capable of high and noble things." Thou shalt be made capable, for in the day when God anoints thee thou shalt receive strength,—"To as many as received him, to them gave he power to become the sons of God." Thou shalt receive enlightenment and illumination by the divine unction of the Holy Ghost. Hast thou ever thought of this? There is not only water to wash thee, but oil to anoint thee. Christ can take away thy sin at this moment, and he can also give thee grace so that thou shalt leave off the habits which hitherto have bound thee down, and become a new creature in Christ Jesus. Is not such a gracious visitation worth standing still to receive it?

Samuel spake to Saul about another matter, namely, about *a change that he should undergo*. For as he talked with him he said, "Thou shalt meet a company of prophets, and thou shalt prophesy, and become another man." Little can you tell, my dear friend, what God will do with you. If thou be willing and obedient thou shalt eat the good of the land; if the Spirit of God shall lead thee in penitence to confess thy sin, and in humble, childlike faith to lay hold on Christ, thou shalt become, in a higher sense than Saul ever was, "another man." Thou shalt be born again; thou shalt be a new creature in Christ Jesus. Listen to these words of the blessed covenant, for I would hold thee and show thee the word of God. "I will put a new spirit within you; and I will take the stony heart out of their flesh, and will give them an heart of flesh." "I will put my fear in their hearts, that they shall not depart from me." "I could never be a Christian," says one. No, not as you are, but you shall be made a new man, and the new man is made in the image of Christ, and is a Christian. Hast thou never heard of this? this being changed? this being totally changed? Hast thou never heard that God can create thee for the second time? can destroy in thee the power of sin, and bring thee under another dominion, and make thee as eager after right as thou hast been after wrong, and make thee as happy in the service of Christ as ever thou wast in the service of the devil, ay, and ten thousand times more so?

And oh, I should not wonder, though you think it cannot be, he will open your mouth to talk to others about Christ. Though, young man, you little dream of such a thing at this moment, it may be the Lord has sent me to call you to himself, that you may surrender yourself to Jesus, and then, in some future day, you shall

> "Stand and tell to sinners round
> What a dear Saviour you have found,"

and be as enthusiastic in the service of the Lord Jesus as ever you have been in the frivolities of the world. Does something in your heart say, "I wish that it would so happen to me"? Is there a secret something in your heart echoing to that which I am saying? Oh Lord, grant that it may be so.

This is what we want you to think about, then, the kingdom, the anointing, and the change that God can work in you. If you will come and think well of the Word of God, you will see in it that which will meet all *the past* of your life, whatever it has been. There may be blots upon it, but in the Word of God you will find that which will wash them all away. You may have wept over your life, and yet you cannot wash away its stains; but the Word of God will tell you how you shall be made whiter than snow, and made to start again in life, delivered from every crimson stain. As to *the present*, does it puzzle thee? Ah, well it may, for life is a tangled skein to those who know not God. But thou shalt find the clue of it, thou shalt thread the labyrinth, thou shalt see how even thy afflictions work for thy good, how thy sickness means thy health, how thy being out of work and in poverty is to make thee rich, how even thy lying at death's door is sent to give thee life, and thou shalt so understand the present as to feel that with all its apparent evil it is working for thy good. And as to *the future,* wouldst thou read aright thy destiny? My Lord can tell thee the future by making thee know that, "Surely goodness and mercy shall follow thee all the days of thy life, and thou shalt dwell in the house of the Lord for ever." Oh that men would not neglect the Word of God, either in the hearing of it preached, or in the private reading of it in their homes. For believe me, there is something in the Bible which just suits *you.* Poor fallen woman, have you strolled in here to-night? There is something for you in the Holy Scriptures. Poor despairing man, far gone in desperation, there is something in the Book on purpose for you. I used to think that a certain text in the Bible was written with a special view to my case. It seemed to me that it might have been penned after I had lived, so accurately did it describe me. Even so, dear friend, there is something in the Bible *for you.* Just as when you have lost a key, and you cannot open a drawer, you send for a locksmith, he turns over no end of skeleton keys, till at last he has got the right one, and he moves the bolt for you; so is it with the Scriptures: there is a key for every lock, there is a clue for every difficulty, a help for every trouble, and a comfort for every grief. Only do thou stand still a while, and let us show thee the Word of God. Some Christian brother may find the key for thee, or thou mayest stumble on it whilst searching the Word for thyself, or the Holy Spirit may bring it to thee. There is a word to suit thy case, therefore give the Book a fair opportunity, and stand still and hear the Word of God.

Let me say to thee, thou knowest not the Word, but the Word knows thee. Thou knowest not the Scriptures, but the Scriptures know thee as thou wilt never know thyself, for the Word of God is quick and powerful, and is a discerner of the thoughts and intents of the heart. Many and many a time have persons written to me, or spoken with me, and said, "Did you intend in the sermon to make a personal allusion to me?" I have said, "Yes, I did; most certainly I did; but I never saw you in my life, and never knew anything about your case, only he that sent me bade me say this and that, and he knew who would be there to hear it, and he took care to guide his servant's thought and word, so as to suit your case to a tittle, so that there could be no mistake about it." The letter came to the man's house, as it were, with a full direction, and there was no question that God had sent it to his soul. Now, therefore, my hearer do thou go to the Word of God, and it will speak home to thee, if thou goest with the desire to be personally dealt with.

Dear friends, he who speaks at this time to you can honestly say that he is speaking out the burden of his heart. I came not hither to speak with you, young man, without first earnestly asking to be directed in each word I say; and what motive can I have in all the world in urging you to seek the Saviour's love but your good? Will it concern me, think you, at the last day, whether you are saved or not? If I set Christ before you faithfully, I shall be clear of your blood —fully clear—even if you reject my Lord. But I would put my hand on you, as I do not doubt Samuel did on Saul, and plead with you for your own sake, for the sake of all the future that lies before you, for the sake, perhaps, of some in heaven whose last words were, Follow me; for the sake of a mother who prays for you, and is praying while you are sitting in this house of prayer; above all, for His sake, who loves to save and delights to bless. Oh, by the wounded hand we sung of just now, and by the broken heart, and by the intense affection of the ever-loving Intercessor for sinners, do stand still a while and seek to know the Word of God. It may be that at this moment thou art put into a position in which thou wilt have to make a choice—a choice for eternity; for heaven or for hell. God save thee from making a fatal choice. There is an engagement for to-morrow which, if you follow it, will be your ruin. Do not fulfil it. May God's Spirit lead you to say at once "I am on God's side; I must be, and I will be. It is done, it is done; if he will have me, he shall have me ; if he will wash me, I am ready to be washed ; if he will renew me, I am pleading to be re-newed ; if he will but take me in hand, and bring me to himself, here am I, here am I. 'My Father, I have sinned against heaven and before thee, and am no more worthy to be called thy son.' But receive me, take me back again." Ah, you backslider over there, I pray that you may be led to decide for the kingdom and the anointing, and undergo a change at this very hour. Let this be the time, the set time of mercy to your souls. I should not wonder but that for many years to come, if we are spared, you and I, my friend, who have never spoken together before, may have to rejoice over this present meeting. Samuel was very pleased with Saul for a long time, though unhappily Saul dis-appointed all his hopes ; but I hope I have met with some one anointed of the Lord, whom he intends to bless at this good hour, to whom he will say, "From this day will I bless you. Young heart, thou hast yielded thyself to me, from this day will I comfort thee, bless thee, cheer thee, sanctify thee, instruct thee, cause thee to grow and become strong, and I will use thee in my service, and thou shalt be mine in that day when I make up my jewels." Oh that the clock of destiny would strike to-night, and you would hear it, and solemnly declare,

> "'Tis done! the great transaction's done ;
> I am my Lord's, and he is mine :
> He drew me, and I follow'd on,
> Charm'd to confess the voice divine."

God grant it for Christ's sake.

PORTIONS OF SCRIPTURE READ BEFORE SERMON—1 Samuel ix., x., 1—13.

HYMNS FROM "OUR OWN HYMN BOOK"—512, 507, 505.

JOHN AND HEROD.

DELIVERED BY

C. H. SPURGEON,

AT THE METROPOLITAN TABERNACLE, NEWINGTON.

"For Herod feared John, knowing that he was a just man and an holy, and observed him; and when he heard him, he did many things, and heard him gladly."
—Mark vi. 20.

JOHN sought no honour among men. It was his delight to say concerning our Lord Jesus, "He must increase, but I must decrease." Yet, though John sought no honour of men, he had honour; for it is written, "Herod feared John." Herod was a great monarch, John was but a poor preacher whose garment and diet were of the coarsest kind; but "Herod feared John." John was more royal than royal Herod. His character made him the true king, and the nominal king trembled before him. A man is not to be estimated according to his rank, but according to his character. The peerage which God recognises is arranged according to a man's justice and holiness. He is first before God and holy angels who is first in obedience; and he reigns and is made a king and a priest whom God hath sanctified and clothed with the fair white linen of a holy life. Be not covetous of worldly honours, for you will have honour enough even from wicked men if your lives are "holiness unto the Lord."

Let it be written on John's tomb, if he needs an epitaph, "Herod feared John." Only there is one better testimonial which any minister of the gospel might be glad to receive, and it is this: "John did no miracle, but all things which he spake concerning this man were true." He wrought no marvellous work, which astonished his generation, but he spake of Jesus, and all that he said was true: God grant that our Master's servants may win such praise.

My subject at this time does not lead me to speak so much of John as of Herod. I desire to have no Herod in this congregation, but I am anxious about some of you lest you should be like him; therefore I will speak out of the tenderness of my heart with the desire that none of you may follow the steps of this evil king.

I. I would ask you to consider THE HOPEFUL POINTS IN HEROD'S CHARACTER. First, we find that *Herod respected justice and holiness,* for "Herod feared John, knowing that he was a just man and an holy." I I like to see in every man a respect for virtue even if he himself has it not, for it may be that the next step will be to desire it, and he that

197

desires to be just is almost so. Some have brought their minds to such a pitch of sinfulness that they despise goodness, and ridicule justice and devotion. May God grant that we may never by any process be brought into such a fearful condition as that. When the conscience comes to be so confused as to lose its reverence for that which is good and holy, then is a man in a sad plight indeed. Herod was not in that condition; he honoured justice, honesty, truth, courage, and purity of life. Though he had not these things himself, yet he had a salutary dread of them, which is a near approach to respect for them. I know I am speaking to a great many who respect everything that is good and right; they only wish they were good and right themselves. So far, so good.

The next good point I see in Herod was that *he admired the man in whom he saw justice and righteousness*, and that is a step further; for you may admire an abstract virtue, and yet when you see it actually embodied in a man you may hate him. The ancients recognised justice in Aristides, and yet some of them grew sick of hearing him called "the just." A man may be acknowledged to be just and holy, and for that very reason he may be dreaded. You like to see lions and tigers in the Zoological Gardens, but you would not like to see them in your own room; you would very much prefer to view them behind bars and within cages; and so very many have respect for religion, but religious people they cannot bear. They admire justice! How eloquently they speak of it, but they do not like to deal justly. They admire holiness! but if they come across a saint they persecute him. "Herod feared John," and tolerated John, and went the length of even keeping John for a while out of the hands of Herodias. Many of you like the company of God's people; in fact, you are out of your element when you get with the profane, you cannot endure them, and from those that practise debasing vices you fly at once. You delight in choice company. So far, so good; but that is not enough; we must go much further, or else we may remain like Herod after all.

A third good point about Herod was that *he listened to John*. It is nothing wonderful that you and I should listen to sermons; but it is rather wonderful that a king should do so, and such a king as Herod. Monarchs do not often care for religious discourses, except such as come from court preachers, who wear fine raiment, and use soft speech. John was not the kind of man for a king's palace—too rough, too blunt, too plain-speaking; his words thrust too much home: yet Herod heard him gladly. It was a hopeful point in his character that he would hear a man who preached justice, holiness, and the "Lamb of God that taketh away the sin of the world." It is a fine point and a hopeful point in any man that he will hear and listen to an honest proclamation of God's word, even though it come home to his conscience. Perhaps I address some of you who hear the gospel only now and then; and when you drop into a religious meeting you are like the dog in the library who would gladly have changed all the books for a single bone. There are many such people in London. Religion does not suit them: places of entertainment are much more to their minds. Some say of the preacher, "I won't hear him again, he cuts too closely; he is too personal." John said to Herod that it was not lawful for him to have his brother's wife; but, though he spoke so plainly, Herod listened to him, because "he was a just man and an holy." That was well of Herod, and it is well in you, my friend, if you are willing to hear the gospel, however practically it is spoken. So far, so good.

But there was a better point still in Herod; *he obeyed the word* to which he listened. Herod heard John gladly, "And when he heard him he did many things." Many of our hearers do nothing; they hear, they hear, they hear, and that is the end of it. They learn the way, they know the way, they are expert in the way, but they do not follow the way. They hear the gospel invitation, but they come not to the feast. Some seem to think that religious duty lies in hearing first, and talking afterwards; but they are mistaken. Herod knew better than that. He was not a hearer only, he did *do* something, and it is remarkable that the text tells us that "he did *many things.*" Perhaps these were some of the many things:—he discharged a tax-gatherer who imposed upon the people, or righted the wrongs of a neglected widow, or altered a cruel law which he had promulgated, or changed his habits and manners in certain respects; certainly in many points he was an improved man, for John the Baptist had an influence with him for good, "For Herod feared John, and when he heard him he did many things." I am speaking to some who, when they hear a sermon, put a part of it into practice, and they have done many things since they first attended here, for which we are very grateful. I have known a man become charmed with the gospel, and he has given up his drunkenness, and his Sabbath-breaking, and he has tried, and succeeded, in a great measure, in leaving off profane language, and thus he has greatly improved. And yet, and yet he is only a Herod, after all; for Herod *was* Herod, after he had done many things; and, in his heart, he was still prepared for all sorts of wickedness. Yet he did amend somewhat, and so far, so good.

There was another point about Herod, namely, that *he continued to hear the preacher gladly;* for it is put into the end of the verse as if to indicate that he heard John still. John touched his conscience; but after all, he still *heard him gladly.* He said, "Send for John the Baptist again." Harry the Eighth would listen to Hugh Latimer though he denounced him to his face, and even sent him on his birthday a handkerchief, on which was marked the text, "Whoremongers and adulterers God will judge." Hal cried, "Let us hear honest Hugh Latimer." Even bad men admire those who tell them truth. However unwelcome the warning, they believe it to be honestly spoken, and therefore they respect the preacher. A good point this. You who are present and unconverted have heard most cutting sentences from me, you have heard of "judgment to come," and of that eternal wrath which rests upon those who die in their sins: let me warn you then, that if, after hearing the denunciations of God's Word, you are still willing to hear, I have great hopes of you. So far, so good.

There was yet one other point about Herod, and that is, *his conscience was greatly affected* through the preaching of John; for I am inclined to think that a certain translation, which renders the passage, "Herod did many things," in another way, may be a correct one, "Herod was perplexed," or, "Herod was made to hesitate." Such a sense is found in some manuscripts. He loved his sin, and he could see a "beauty of holiness" in religion, and he wished to be holy; but there was Herodias, and he could not give her up. When he heard a sermon, he was like a relative of his in after days, "almost persuaded," yet he did not give up his lust. He could not go the whole length John would have him go. He could not leave his bosom sin, and yet he felt as if he wished to leave it. There was a halting between two opinions, a hesitating, a wavering: he was inclined to good if he could have good and have his pleasure too; but his pleasure was so very much his master that he could not escape from it. He was like a bird taken with lime-twigs: he wanted to fly; but, sad to say, he was willingly held, limed by his lust. This is the case with many of our hearers. Their consciences are not weaned from their sins; they cannot give them up, and yet they wish they could. They linger on the brink, and fear to launch away. They are almost out of Sodom, have almost escaped the fire shower, and yet in all probability they will stand like Lot's wife, a pillar of salt, because they will look back, and love the sin that lingers in their heart. Consciences nowadays seem to have gone out of fashion; but to have a conscience sensitive to the preaching of the Word is an admirable thing; and if you have such a thing, so far, so good.

II. There were six good points about Herod, then. But now, very sorrowfully, I want to indicate THE FLAWS IN THE CASE OF HEROD. The first flaw was this, that *though he loved John, he never looked to John's Master.* John never wanted anybody to be *his* disciple, but he cried, "Behold the Lamb of God." Herod was, after a sort, a follower of John, but never a follower of Jesus. It is easy for you to hear the preacher and love him and admire him, and yet the preacher's Master may be all unknown to you. I pray you, dear friends, do not let this be the case with any of you. I am the bridegroom's friend, and I shall rejoice greatly when the bridegroom wins your hearts. God forbid that my ministry should ever lead you to myself and cause you to stop there. We are only sign-posts pointing to Christ. Go beyond us. Be ye followers of us as far as we are followers of Christ, but in no other respect. It is to Christ you must go: the end of all our ministry is Christ Jesus. We want you to go to him direct, to seek from him pardon, from him redemption, from him a change of heart, from him a new life; for vain will it be if you have listened to the most faithful of preachers, and have not listened to the preacher's Master and obeyed his gospel. You will be Herods, and nothing more, unless grace leads you to Jesus Christ.

The second flaw about Herod's case was this, that *he had no respect for goodness in his own heart.* He admired it in another, but there was none of it in himself. Our Saviour described Herod admirably. What a master-sketcher of human portraits was Christ! He said of Herod, "Go ye and tell that fox." Herod was a foxy man, selfish, full of tricks; timid when he was in the presence of his superiors, but both cruel and bold when he was in the presence of those who could not defend themselves. We sometimes meet with these foxy people; they want to go to heaven, but they like the road to hell. They will sing a hymn to Jesus; but a good roaring song they like also when they get merry companions together. By all manner of means, a guinea to the church. Oh yes! admirable thing. But how many guineas are spent upon some secret lust? So many try to dodge between God and Satan. They do not want to fall foul of either; they hold with the hare and run with the hounds: they admire all that is good, but they do not want to have too much of it themselves. It might be inconvenient to carry the cross of Christ on their own shoulders and become precise and exact in their own lives, yet they never say a word against other people doing so. It is a fatal flaw to have no root in yourself—a damning flaw, condemning your own self, —to know the right and disregard it, to feel respect for it and yet trample it under foot. I judge that the doom of such will be far more dreadful than that of those who never knew the good, who were trained up in the purlieus of vice, and never had a glimpse of holiness or purity, and therefore never deliberately turned away from them.

Another flaw in Herod's character was that *he never loved the word of God, as God's word.* He admired John, and probably said, "That is the man for me. See how boldly he delivers his Master's message: that is the man I should like to hear." But he never said to himself, "God sent John; God speaks to me through John; oh that I might learn what John is speaking, and be instructed and improved by the word John is uttering, because it is God's word." No, no. I do pray you, ask yourselves, dear hearers, whether this may not apply to you. May it not be that you listen to a sermon because it is Mr. So-and-so's discourse, and you admire the preacher? It will be fatal to you if you treat the word in that way. It must be to you what it is in truth, the the word of God, or it will not save you. It will never impress your soul unless you accept it as the word of God, and bow before it, and desire to feel all its power as coming to you fresh from the lips of God, and sent into your heart by his Holy Spirit.

Now, we know Herod did not receive the word as the word of God because he was a picker and chooser in reference to it. He did not like John's discourse when he spoke of the seventh commandment. If he spoke of the fourth commandment he would say, "That is admirable; the Jews ought to keep it": but when he dealt with the seventh commandment Herod and Herodias would say, "We do not think preachers should allude to such subjects." I have always noticed that people who live in the practice of vice think the servants of God ought not to allude to things so coarse. We are allowed to denounce the sins of the man-in-the-moon and the vices of savages in the middle of Africa; but as to the everyday vices of this city of London, if we put our finger upon them in God's name, then straightway some one cries, "It is indelicate to allude to these things." John dealt with the whole word of God, and he did not only say, "Behold the Lamb of God"; but he cried, "The axe is laid to the root of the trees." He spoke plainly to the conscience. Herod, therefore, had this fatal flaw in his character that he did not attend to *all* that John delivered of the word of God: he liked one part, and did not like another. He resembled those who prefer a doctrinal discourse, but cannot endure the precepts of God's word. I hear one exclaim, "I like practical discourses; I do not want any doctrine." Don't you? There is doctrine in God's word, and you are to receive what God gives you: not half a Bible, but the whole truth as it is in Jesus. That was a great fault in Herod; he did not receive the testimony of John as the word of God.

Next, Herod did *many* things, but *he did not do all things.* He who receives the word of God in truth, does not only attempt to do many things; but he tries to do all that is right. He does not give up one vice, or a dozen vices, but he endeavours to forsake every false way, and seeks to be delivered from every iniquity. Herod did not care for a thorough reformation, for that would call for too great a self-denial. He had one sin he wished to keep, and when John spoke plainly about that he would not listen to him.

Another fault with Herod was that *he was under the sway of sin.* He had given himself up to Herodias. She was his own niece, and had been married to his own brother, and was the mother of children by his own brother, and yet he led her away from his own brother's house that she might become his wife; he, himself, casting off one who had been a good and faithful wife to him for years. It is a mess of filthy incest one hardly likes to think of. The influence of this woman was his curse and ruin. How many men have been destroyed in that way! How many women are ruined daily in this city by coming under the vicious influence of others! My dear men and women, you will have to stand before God on your own account. Do not let anyone cast a spell over you. I pray you, escape for your life; run for it when vice hunts you. I may be sent at this moment with a word on purpose for you, to stir up your conscience, and arouse you to a sense of your danger. It is always perilous to be under the influence of an unconverted person, however moral he may be, but it is supremely dangerous to be under the fascination of a wicked woman or a vicious man. God help you to rise above it by his Spirit, for if you are hearers of the word and doers of evil, you will end in being Herods, and nothing more.

I will only allude to another point in Herod's character, that *his religion,* although it made him do many things, *was rather one of fear than of love.* It is not said that Herod feared God, but that he "feared *John.*" He did not *love* John: he "*feared* John." The whole thing was a matter of fear. He was not a lion, you see; he was a fox—fearful, timid, ready to run away from every barking cur.

There are many people whose whole religion lies in fear. With some it is the fear of men—the fear of what people would say if they did not pretend to be religious—the fear of what their Christian associates would think of them if they were not reputable. With others there is the fear that some awful judgment would come upon them. But the mainspring of the religion of Christ is love. Oh! to love the gospel, to delight in the truth, to rejoice in holiness: this is genuine conversion. The fear of death, and the fear of hell, create a poor, poor faith, which leaves men on Herod's level still.

III. I conclude by showing you very sorrowfully WHAT BECAME OF HEROD. With all his good points he ended most wretchedly. First, *he slew the preacher whom he once respected.* It was he who did it, though the executioner was the instrument. He said, "Go and fetch John the Baptist's head in a charger." So it has happened with many hopeful hearers; they have become slanderers and persecutors of the very preachers before whom they once trembled, and far as they could they have taken off their heads. After a time men dislike being rebuked, and they proceed in their dislike till they scoff at the things they once reverenced, and make the name of Christ a football for their jests. Beware! I pray you, beware! for the way of sin is downhill. Herod feared John, and yet he beheaded him. A person may be evangelical and Calvinistic, and so on, and yet, if he is placed under certain conditions, he may become a hater and a persecutor of the truth he once avowed.

Herod went a step lower, however; for this Herod Antipas was the man who *afterwards mocked the Saviour*. It is said, "Herod with his men of war set him at nought, and mocked him, and arrayed him in a gorgeous robe." This is the man that "did many things" under the leading of John. His course is altered now. He spits on the Redeemer and insults the Son of God. Certain of the most outrageous blasphemers of the gospel were originally Sunday-school scholars and teachers, young men who were "almost persuaded," yet they halted and hesitated, and wavered until they made the plunge and became much worse than they possibly could have become if they had not seen the light of truth. If the devil wants raw material to make a Judas, "the son of perdition," he takes an apostle to work upon. When he takes a thoroughly bad character like Herod, it is necessary to make him plastic as Herod had been in the hands of John. Somehow or other, border men are the worst enemies. In the old wars between England and Scotland, the borderers were the fighting men; and so the border people will do more harm than any until we get them on this side of the frontier. Oh that the grace of God may decide those who now hesitate!

I may mention to you that, before long, Herod *lost all the power he possessed*. He was a foxy man, and always tried to win power, but in the end he was recalled by the Roman emperor in disgrace. That was the end of him. Many a man has given up Christ for honour, and has lost himself as well as lost Christ. Like the man who, in the old Catholic persecuting times, was brought to prison for the faith. He said he loved the Protestant faith; but he cried, "I cannot burn." So he denied the faith, and in the dead of night his house took fire: the man who could not burn was forced to burn, but he had no comfort in that burning, for he had denied his Lord. If you sell Christ for a mess of pottage it will scald your lips; it will burn within your soul like molten lead for ever; for "the wages of sin is death." However bright the golden coin shines, and however musical may be its chink, it will prove an awful curse to the man who sells his Lord to gain it.

To-day the name of Herod is *infamous for ever*. As long as there is a Christian church, the name of Herod will be execrated. And is it not a solemn reflection, that "Herod feared John, and did many things, and heard him gladly"? I know that no young man here believes that he will ever turn out to be a Herod. I might, like the prophet, say, "Thou wilt do this, and do that," and you would answer, "Is thy servant a dog, that he should do this thing?" But you *will* do it, unless you are decided for God.

An appeal like this once startled me. When I was young and tender, there was a hopeful youth who went to school with me, who was held up to me as an example. He was a good boy, and I used to feel no particular affection for his name, because I was so perpetually chided by his goodness, and I was so far removed from it. Being younger than he,

I saw him enter upon his apprenticeship, enter upon the gaieties of a great city and come back dishonoured. It horrified me. Might not I dishonour my character? And when I found that if I gave myself to Christ he would give me a new heart and a right spirit, and when I read that promise of the covenant, " I will put my fear in their hearts, that they shall not depart from me," it seemed to me like a Character Insurance Society. If I believed in Jesus Christ my character was insured; for Christ would enable me to walk in the paths of holiness: this charmed me into desiring an interest in Christ.

If you would not like to be a Herod, be a disciple of Jesus Christ; for there will be no choice for some of you. Some of you are of such powerful natures that you must either thoroughly serve Christ or serve the devil. An old Scotchman was once looking at Rowland Hill, and the good old gentleman said, " What are you looking at ? " He said, "The lines of your face." " What do you think of them?" He replied, " I think that if you had not been a Christian man, you would have been an awful sinner." Some people are of that sort; they are like a pendulum; they must swing one way or the other. Oh that you may swing Christ's way to-night. Cry, " Lord, help me to cleanse my way ; help me to be wholly thine ; help me to possess the righteousness I admire, the holiness I respect. Help me, not only to do *some* things, but everything thou wouldst have me to do. Take me, make me thine, and I will rejoice and joy in him who helps me to be holy." God bless you, dear friends, for Jesus Christ's sake. Amen.

PORTION OF SCRIPTURE READ BEFORE SERMON—Mark vi. 7.—32.

HYMNS FROM "OUR OWN HYMN BOOK"—483, 643, 992.

TAUGHT THAT WE MAY TEACH.

DELIVERED BY

C. H. SPURGEON,

AT THE METROPOLITAN TABERNACLE, NEWINGTON.

"And the man said unto me, Son of man, behold with thine eyes, and hear with thine ears, and set thine heart upon all that I shall shew thee; for to the intent that I might shew them unto thee art thou brought hither: declare all that thou seest to the house of Israel."—Ezekiel xl. 4.

WE learn from this text something concerning Ezekiel himself. He was certainly one of the greatest of the prophets; his visions remind us of those of John, both for their brightness, splendour, and number, and yet this eminent prophet was, nevertheless, styled "son of man." He is continually called by that name. The title is used over and over again throughout the book of his prophecies—"Son of man"— to remind him that even the seer, the prophet, the inspired, the man who was indulged with vision upon vision, was still only a man. The best of men are men at the best. Those eyes that are strengthened to behold the cherubim, and to gaze upon the stupendous wheels of providence, are still only the eyes of a son of man. The title was used to teach him humility, and also to remind him of the condescension of God towards him, and to fill him with awe and wonder that he should be chosen from the rest of mankind, though no more than they, to see such wondrous sights, withheld from other eyes. To us this wears a very promising aspect, for if God can reveal himself to one "son of man," why not to another? And if God can speak, as he did speak, so wonderfully through Ezekiel, one son of man, why not through you? why not through me? for we, too, are sons of men. We have no worthiness or fitness; neither does Ezekiel claim any. He is reminded of his descent: he is still one of the sons of men. Oh, be of good comfort, you who think that God can never use you—you who are poor in spirit, and wish to serve him, but deeply feel your own insignificance. Remember that God is able to do for you exceedingly abundantly above what you ask or even think. He can yet reveal his Son in you, and himself to you, and by you, after such methods as you have never dreamed of; and, possibly, the painful experience through which you are passing even now may be preparing you to stand upon yet loftier mounts, and to behold visions of God, which in happier days

Nos. 1,578-80.

you shall tell out to the house of Israel, by which multitudes shall be blessed through you.

This is our present subject: we will speak upon *the manifestations with which God favours certain of his servants.* Then, secondly, we will dwell upon *their responsibility while they are enjoying such manifestations:* they are bound to behold with their eyes, and hear with their ears, and set their heart upon all that God shall show them. And then, thirdly, we will speak upon *the object which God has in giving these manifestations to his more favoured people.* It is that they may declare all that they see, that the whole house of Israel may, as it were, see by these favoured eyes, and hear by these chosen ears, and may set their hearts upon the word of the Lord because another has first done so.

I. First, I shall have a little to say upon THE MANIFESTATIONS WITH WHICH CERTAIN OF GOD'S SERVANTS ARE FAVOURED.

The Lord Jesus Christ does draw near in a very special manner to some of his people. He did to Ezekiel: for I take it that the man, mentioned in the chapter, whose appearance was like the appearance of brass, is none other than our divine Lord, who, though a man, yet exceeds all men in the brightness of his wondrous person. It was he, doubtless, who appeared to Ezekiel. Long before Christ came on earth to die he appeared to his servants in different ways. He sojourned with Abraham as a wayfarer, for such he found the patriarch to be. He wrestled with Jacob at the brook Jabbok, for Jacob was wrestling with a sore trial. It was he that revealed himself to Moses when the bush was burning; and it was he that stood by Joshua's side as the man having a drawn sword in his hand. In divers ways and forms he proved that his delights were with the sons of men. Or ever the Word appeared in actual flesh and blood, he communed here and there with his chosen servants. He will show himself to any of you who seek him. He will unveil the beauties of his face to every eye that is ready to behold them. There is never a heart that loves him but he will manifest his love to that heart. But, at the same time, he does favour some of his servants who live near to him, and who are called by him to special service, with very remarkable manifestations of his light and glory.

These revelations are not incessant. I suppose that no man is always alike. John was in Patmos I know not how long; but he was " in the Spirit on the Lord's-day " on one occasion, and he specially notes it. I do not suppose that Daniel or Ezekiel saw visions every night, or beheld the glories of God every day. Humanity is scarcely capable of the incessant strain of a perpetual manifestation of God. These things are, as we shall see, " like angels' visits, few and far between." There is a fellowship that can always be kept up, but the flood tide of manifestation —a noon-day revelation—will not last on continually. Ezekiel enjoyed a special manifestation, and he tells us when it was; for men do not see God's face without recollecting it. He knew the date, and recorded it. " In the five and twentieth year of our captivity, in the beginning of the year, in the tenth day of the month, in the fourteenth year after that the city was smitten." Days of heavenly fellowship are red letter days, to be remembered so long as memory holds her seat.

Yes, and it is noteworthy that *the occasion of these manifestations was one of great distress.* Five-and-twenty years of captivity must have been enough to wear down the spirits of God's servants. Hence, he whose feet are as fine brass, as if they burned in a furnace, comes and manifests himself to his people, burning like brass in a furnace, giving them their times of comfort after twenty-five years of captivity. He says, too, that it was fourteen years after the city had been smitten, after it had been laid as a ruinous heap. Then God appeared. Oh, beloved, when you have been long sorrowing you may expect bright days. The coal-black darkness will brighten after all. Nights do not last for ever. Whenever you have much joy, be cautious ; there is a sorrow on the road. But when you have much sadness, be hopeful ; there is a joy on the way to you ; be sure of that. Our blessed Lord reveals himself to his people more in the valleys, in the shades, in the deeps, than he does anywhere else. He has a way and an art of showing himself to his children at midnight, making the darkness light by his presence. Saints have seen Jesus oftener on the bed of pain than in robust health. There were more manifestations of Christ in Scotland among the heather and the hills in the days of bloody Claverhouse than there are now. There was more seen of Christ in France, I do believe, in the days of the Huguenots than ever is seen now. I fear me that our Master has come to be almost a stranger in the land in these days, compared with what he was once, when his people wandered about in sheepskins and goatskins, destitute, afflicted, tormented ; for then he was meeting them at every turn and corner. Let us hope that, if days are gloomy now, and we ourselves are in trouble, our Beloved will come and manifest himself to us as he does not to the world.

It appears, in this case, that *the manifestation to Ezekiel was made when he was put into an elevated condition.* He says, " In the vision of God he brought me into the land of Israel, and set me up upon a very high mountain." God has ways of lifting his people right up, away, away, away from mortal joy or sorrow, care or wish, into the spiritual realm. And then, when the mind has been lifted above its ordinary level, and the faculties are brought up by some divine process into a receptive state, he reveals himself to us. These times come not always, but blessed are they to whom they come at all. When on the mount alone with God their spiritual nature asserts supremacy over the body, till they scarcely know whether they are in the flesh or not, then the Lord reveals himself to them.

When he had elevated him thus it appears that *he conducted him to certain places,* for he says, " For to the intent that I might shew them unto thee art thou brought hither." God's children are brought in experience to unusual places, on purpose that they may get clearer sights of the love and grace and mercy of God in Christ than they could obtain elsewhere. I have sometimes been puzzled to know why I underwent certain states of mind. I have found out the reason occasionally : perhaps as often I have not. I remember preaching to you one Sabbath-day from the text, " My God, my God, why hast thou forsaken me ? " and if ever a minister preached from that text fearing that it was true of himself I did. I was under an awful darkness all the while, and I could not tell why. But on the Monday evening there came to me one who, by his very appearance, I could see was not far from madness ; his eyes were starting from his head, his face was full of terror—and when he was in the room with me alone, he said, "You have delivered me from self-destruction. I am a man that God has forsaken, and no one has ever spoken to my soul or my experience till last Sunday night." By God's great grace and infinite bounty we were able to pilot that brother into smoother waters, and I hope that he now lives to rejoice in God. I felt thankful to the last degree that I had been dragged through all my depression, because I was able to help him. Sometimes our experience is for the good of others, and sometimes it is for our own good. You cannot see the beauty of certain gems unless you place them on black velvet. When you have something black behind, then you see their lustre. So there are promises of God in which you never will discover their very brightest meaning except they are set against some dark soul-trouble. Much of faith's education may be called black-letter learning. Very black the letters are, too, and very ugly-looking, but they must be spelt over. You cannot see the stars in the day-time; you must wait till the sun has gone down. Many promises of God you cannot see till you are in the dark; and when the soul is in gloom it may be that the Lord allows it to get there, that it may gaze upon the starry promises, and value every ray of light that streams from them. So you see, dear friends, God leads his people from one place to another of Christian experience, along hills and dales, ravines and precipices—all in order that, their minds being elevated, they may be prepared to see bright visions of himself, and know him better, love him better, and serve him better.

However, it is not outward circumstances that can affect the divine purpose, *there must always be a movement of the divine Spirit.* In the third verse you read, "He brought me there." When you get home just look through the chapter, and see how this is repeated. "And he brought me to the inner court, and he brought me to the north gate, and he brought me" to this and to that. We never learn a truth inwardly until God brings us to it. We may hear a truth, we ought to be careful that we do not hear anything but the truth; but God must bring that truth home. No truth is known well until it is burnt into us as with a hot iron. Some doctrines we can never doubt. "Oh," said one to me, failing to convince me of some new theories, "no one could get a new idea into your head except with a surgical operation." That witness is true if the new idea be contrary to the old-fashioned gospel. The things I preach are part and parcel of myself. I am sure that they are true. "Are you infallible?" say you. Yes, when I declare what is in God's word. When I declare God's truth, I claim infallibility, not for myself, but for God's word. "Let God be true and every man a liar." It will not do to be saying, "These are our views and opinions." Why, if the doctrines of grace are not true, I am a lost man; if they are not the very truth of God, I have nothing to live for: I have no joy in life, and I have no hope in death. May God bring you, dear friends, into a truth, and I will defy the devil to bring you out of it. If God brings you to it, if he writes it as with his own finger upon your soul, you will know it with solemn certainty. People may say, "Where is your logic? and how does this consist with the progressive development of human thought?" and all that. I reply, "*You* can go and fiddle to what tune you please; as for me, these things are part and parcel of myself, and I have made them my own." I have gripped them, and they hold me fast : I have no choice about them : I do not choose to believe in free grace, I believe it because I cannot help it. When one was asked whether he held Calvinistic doctrine he answered, "No." "Oh," said the other, "I am glad to hear that." "Ay," said he, "but Calvinistic doctrine holds me." There is a great difference between holding truth and truth holding you. You will not hold truth aright unless you can say of it, with all your heart, "The Lord brought me into it ; " "He brought me towards the south ; he brought me into the inner court ; he brought me forth into the outer court ; he brought me to the temple." He did it all. "All thy children shall be taught of the Lord "; and there is no teaching like it, for he that is taught of God is taught infallibly.

Thus I have spoken upon the manifestations with which God favours certain of his people.

II. Now, secondly, let us notice THE RESPONSIBILITY OF THESE CHOSEN MEN WHILE THEY ARE THUS FAVOURED.

"The man said to me, Son of man, behold with thine eyes, and hear with thine ears, and set thine heart upon all that I shall show thee." Did he not mean this—"Use all your senses, all your faculties, all your wits to understand divine truth "? When the Spirit of God favours you with light, mind that you see ; and, when there is a sound of grace, mind that you hear. Be not one of those forgetful hearers who behold their likenesses in a glass, and then go their way and forget what manner of men they are. Oh, how much more we should understand of God's word if we gave our mind to it. We tell our children to learn their lessons "by heart." If we put the full meaning into that expression, that is the way to learn the things of God. Learn them all over ; take them into yourself by every faculty you possess ; strive as God shall help you by his Spirit to get at their innermost meaning by every power that is given you.

First, he says, "See with thine eyes." What are the eyes for but to see with ? He means this,—look, pry, search with your eyes. Do not let the truth flit before you and then say, "Yes, I have seen it." No. Stop it. Hold it by meditation before the mind's eye, and see with your eyes. Look, look, look into it. Remember what is said of the angels : "Which things the angels desire to look into "; not "to look at," but "to look into." Looking to Christ will save you, but it is looking into Christ that gives joy, peace, holiness, heaven. Look into the gospel : let your eyes be intent and steadfastly fixed upon every truth, especially at choice times when God favours you with the noontide light of his face. Then be doubly intent upon his word.

And then he puts it, "Hear with thine ears." Well, a man cannot use his ears for anything else, can he? Ay, but hear with your ears. Listen with all your might. You are to spy out the meaning with the mind's eye ; but, besides that, try to catch the very tone in which the promise or precept has been uttered. Treasure up the exact words, for though cavillers call it folly to speak of verbal inspiration, I believe that we must have verbal inspiration or no inspiration. If any man shall say to you, "The sense of what your Father said is true, never mind his words;" you would reply, "Yes, but I would like to know precisely what he said, word for word." I know that it is so in legal documents. It is not merely the sense that you look to, but every word must be right. God's word, as it came from him, came in such perfection that, even to the syllables in which the sense was clothed, there was infallibility about it. When I get God's word I would desire to hear it with my ears as well as see it with my eyes,—to see its sense and then to love the expressions in which that sense is conveyed to me. He cares little for the sense of the words who is not jealous over the words which convey the sense. Oh, brethren, whenever God does, by his word, open his heart to you, do not lose anything; do not lose a sound —a syllable.

The Lord demands something more. "*Set thine heart upon all that I shall shew thee.*" Oh, but that is the way to learn from God—by loving all that he says—feeling that, whatever God says, it is the thing you want to know. It is well when your whole heart comes to know the truth, and, when it knows it, encompasses it about with warm affections, so that it may be like a fly in amber, the word in the midst of your heart, encased there, enshrined there, never to be taken away from you. Set your whole heart on the word. Some people like to read so many chapters every day. I would not dissuade them from the practice, but I would rather lay my soul asoak in half a dozen verses all day than I would, as it were, rinse my hand in several chapters. Oh, to bathe in a text of Scripture, and to let it be sucked up into your very soul, till it saturates your heart! The man who has read many books is not always a learned man; but he is a strong man who has read three or four books over and over till he has mastered them. He knows something. He has a grasp of thoughts and expressions, and these will build up his life. Set your heart upon God's word! It is the only way to know it thoroughly: let your whole nature be plunged into it as cloth into a dye.

The Lord bids us *do this towards all that he shall show us.* "Set thine heart upon all that I shall shew thee!" We are to be impartial in our study of the word, and to be universal in its reception. Brothers and sisters, do you pick over God's Bible? I pray you, give up the habit. I have known professors who would not read certain chapters. Never read another till you have read that passage which now displeases you. Learn to love it; for, if there is a quarrel between you and a Scripture, it is you that is wrong, not the Scripture; and if there is any part of the word of which you can say "I differ from *that*," the word will never alter: the party to alter is yourself. Try to follow the Lord fully, even though it should cause the revision of cherished sentiments, and even the alteration of your denominational connections. "Are we to be so particular in little things?" says one. Ay, it is in little things that loyalty comes out. A loving and obedient child obeys his father without saying, "This is a great thing, and this is a little thing." "Whatsoever he saith unto you, do it." The habit of trifling with little duties grows very soon into a seared conscience about larger matters. "Oh, but we need not be so particular," says one. Indeed we must be. "Why are you so precise?" said one to a Puritan. "Sir," said he, "I serve a very precise God." "The Lord thy God is a jealous God,"—mind that; and he would have us to be a jealous people as to all his word, whether of doctrine, or of precept, or of promise. Oh, for grace to be willing and ready to see all that he would have us see, and to hear all that he would have us hear, and to receive into our heart all that he would have us receive.

Thus, I have spoken upon the manifestations which God gives to some of his servants, and the responsibility under which they are placed by them.

III. But now, thirdly, what is the practical design of all this? WHAT IS GOD'S REASON FOR MANIFESTING HIMSELF TO HIS SERVANTS?

The object is this,—"Declare thou all that thou seest to the house of Israel."

First, see it yourself, hear it yourself, give your heart to it yourself, and then declare it to the house of Israel. I have lately heard of a minister who said in the pulpit, "The doctrine of atonement,—I have heard a great deal about it, but I do not understand it." He is going to take a holiday that he may solve some of his doubts. If he does not solve his doubts soon I should recommend him to extend that holiday for the term of his natural life. He who does not understand the doctrine of the atonement, should read "The shorter catechism," and pray God to enlighten him. That is a book written for the young and ignorant, and it might be useful to many ministers. God grant us grace that we may know what we do know, and not attempt to declare to others anything but that which we have seen and heard and taken into our own hearts.

But that being done, we are to *tell the truth to others,* especially to those whom it concerns. He had seen the form and vision of a temple and a city; he was to speak of this to the house of Israel. Dear brother, you cannot tell who it may be to whom you are to speak, but this may be your guide:—speak about what you have seen and heard *to those whom it concerns.* Have you been in gloom of mind, and have you been comforted? The first time you meet with a person in that condition, tell out the comfort. Have you felt a great struggle of soul, and have you found rest? Speak of your conflict to a neighbour who is passing through a like struggle. Has God delivered you in the hour of sorrow? Tell that to the next sorrowing person you meet. There is such a thing as casting pearls before swine: that can easily be done by an imprudent talkativeness; but when you find people who are hungry, give them bread; when you find people that are thirsty, offer them water; when you find that they want a blessing from God, tell them of that which has been precious to your own soul.

Ay, but still this is not all your duty. God has shown us his precious word that we may tell it to the house of Israel. Now, the house of Israel were a stiff-necked people, and when Ezekiel went to them, they cast him aside, they would not listen. Yet, he was to go and teach the word to them. We must not say, "I will not speak of Christ to such a one; he would reject it." Do it as a testimony against him, even if you know he will reject it. Go you, my brother, and sow your seed, and recollect that in the parable the sower did not only cast a handful on that fair spot of ground that was all ready for it, but he sowed among thorns and thistles, and he cast seeds even on the highway, from which the birds of the air soon removed it. "Give a portion to seven and also to eight." "In the morning sow thy seed, and in the evening withhold not thy hand, for thou knowest not whether shall prosper, this or that, or whether it shall be alike good." Do thou go and tell what God tells thee. Remember what we read just now. "What I shall show you in secret that reveal ye in the light. What I have spoken to you in closets, that reveal ye upon the housetops." "Are we all to be preachers, then?" Yes, all that have been taught of God are to teach. "Are we all to stand up in public?" says one. I did not say that ; but somewhere or other—perhaps in the pew where you now sit, or on the steps as you go out, or by the roadside, or in the shop to-morrow morning, you can all put in a word edgeways for Jesus Christ. Drop a sentence or two for the honour of his dear name. "I do not know what to say," says some one. Do not say it, then, brother. I would recommend you not to say anything if you do not know what to say ; but if you have seen with your eyes and heard with your ears, and received into your heart, then you know what to say, and the first thing that comes to hand will be the best thing to say, for God, who knows the condition of people's minds, knows how to fit you to their condition, and make your experience as a Christian to tally with the experience of the man who wants the aid of your light. Go, and the Lord be with you.

If there are any here who have never seen the Lord, if they have any desire after him, if they have any sense of sin, if they have any wish for the eternal light, let them remember that gracious word, "Him that cometh unto me I will in no wise cast out," and that precious invitation, "Come unto me, all ye that labour and are heavy laden, and I will give you rest."

May the Holy Spirit bring you to trust in Jesus at once, and to the name of the Lord be the praise for ever and ever. Amen.

PORTION OF SCRIPTURE READ BEFORE SERMON—Matthew x. 16—42.

HYMNS FROM "OUR OWN HYMN BOOK"—720, 814, 764.

Metropolitan Tabernacle Pulpit.

ROADS CLEARED.

A Sermon

DELIVERED BY

C. H. SPURGEON,

AT THE METROPOLITAN TABERNACLE, NEWINGTON.

(Preached on an evening when the Tabernacle was left to strangers.)

"Cast ye up, cast ye up, prepare the way, take up the stumblingblock out of the way of my people."—Isaiah lvii. 14.

WHAT is the way, the way of salvation, the way to heaven? Jesus Christ says, "I am the way." He is the Son of God, and he left the glories of heaven and took upon himself our nature and lived here. In due time he took upon himself our sin, and made atonement for it, and now he has gone up into heaven, and sits at the right hand of God, even the Father, whence he will shortly come to judge the quick and the dead. The way to be delivered from sin, the way to heaven, is simply to trust in Jesus Christ. God has set him forth to be a propitiation for sin, and whosoever believes in Jesus Christ has his sin put away at once, whatever he may have done. Before Christ went to heaven he said to his disciples, "Go ye into all the world, and preach the gospel to every creature. He that believeth and is baptized shall be saved; but he that believeth not shall be damned." This is the way of salvation which we preach, unaltered and unalterable, "Believe in the Lord Jesus Christ, and thou shalt be saved." In other words, trust *him* and you are saved.

This is the entrance into the way of salvation, and this is the track of that way even to the end: trust in Christ "Are not good works needed?" says one. They always flow from faith in Christ. The man that would be saved from sin trusts Christ, and his nature is changed, and so he hates the sin that once he loved, and endeavours to honour the Christ who has saved him; but in the matter of our salvation, the ground and bottom of it is not our works, or tears, or prayers, but simple reliance upon the finished work of Jesus Christ. He is A and he is Z in the alphabet of grace. He is the beginning and he is the ending. "He that believeth in him hath everlasting life." "He that believeth in him is not condemned," and never shall be, for he has passed from death unto life. Such being the way, it is very simple. Straight as an arrow, is it not? And yet in this way there are stumblingblocks.

I. First, LET US SHOW WHY THIS IS.

The first reason is that *the way of believing is such an uncommon way.* Men do not understand the way of trusting. They want to see, to reason, to argue ; but to trust in "God made flesh," dead, buried, risen, gone into heaven, they do not like *that.* Man says, "I cannot trust." How very difficult it would be for a cow, that has always lived by the day the short life that can be fed on grass, if it had to live by reason, as men do. It would be a new, strange way for the poor beast. And when man has to live by faith he is as awkward at it as a cow would be at reasoning. He is out of his element. What, am I to do nothing but trust the Saviour, and will he save me ? Is that to be the top and bottom of it ? It is so. "Then," saith the man, "I cannot get at it ; there are stumblingblocks in the road."

Another reason is that men, when they are really seeking salvation, are *often much troubled in mind.* They are conscious that they have done wrong. Conscience pricks them. They feel that if God be just he must punish them for their wrong-doing. They are well aware that he knows the secrets of their hearts, and this alarms and distresses them, and when they are told that if they believe in Jesus Christ all manner of sin and of blasphemy shall be forgiven, they wonder how it can be ? If we put it very plainly, and say, "However great your guilt, however black your sin, wash in the fountain filled with blood, and you shall be clean,"—it looks plain enough, but they cannot see it. A sense of sin blinds them, and they grope in the noonday, like blind men, for the wall ; stumbling over this and that which has no existence except in their own fears. Conscience makes unbelievers of us all ; and stumblingblocks are created by our trembling condition. I do not know how it is to be otherwise.

Besides this, *men are often ignorant of the way of salvation.* I am not speaking now as though I blamed them. I was brought up myself to attend the house of God regularly. I do not suppose that on any Sabbath day, except through illness, I was ever absent. Yet when I began to seek the Lord, I did not know the way of salvation. I knew the letter of it, but not the real meaning : how can a man know it till the Spirit of God reveals it to him ? The sun itself may shine, but a man will never see till his eyes are open. Until Christ comes, who is the light of the world, men will roam in darkness. Why, in this London of ours, the bulk of people are still without the knowledge that salvation is entirely of grace ; that it is an act of divine mercy that saves a man ; that a man is never saved by his zeal, or his prayers, or his tears, or anything that he does, but is saved entirely by the mercy of God in Jesus Christ. The gospel is not believed or accepted in its real meaning, and so men meet with stumblingblocks.

Satan is always ready to prevent souls from finding peace in Christ. He will inject all sorts of thoughts into men's minds : blasphemies infernal, thoughts incredible he will make to pass through the minds of men who are seeking Christ. He does not meddle with some people ; he knows they are his, and will be his at last, but when a man once shakes himself up, and flees for his life, then the evil one raises all hell about his ears, and by his efforts many souls are made to stumble in a way which is smooth enough to the feet of faith.

II. Thus have I shown why there are so many stumblingblocks.

Now, by God's help, I am going to TRY TO LIFT SOME OF THEM OUT OF THE WAY.

The text says, "Take up the stumblingblocks." Now for a dead lift at some of them.

Here is one of them. One man says, "I would fain believe in this Jesus Christ of whom you tell me, but if I were to come to God through Christ, *would he receive me?*" Ay, that he will. Here is a text: "Him that cometh to me I will in nowise cast out." In all the history of the human race there never has been found a man that came to Jesus Christ whom Christ rejected yet. If you will seek to God in Christ with all your heart, and he shuts the door of mercy in your face you may turn round and say, "I am the first man that Christ refused to help, and now his word is broken, for he said, 'Him that cometh to me I will in nowise cast out,' and he has cast me out." Oh, my friends, some will not come because they are afraid of being rejected; but there is no sense in that fear. Christ cannot, will not, reject a single soul that comes to him, so, out of the way with that stumbling-block!

"But," says another, "I am *a very peculiar person.* I could very well believe that any man in the world who trusted Christ would be saved except myself; but I cannot think that he would save me, for I am so odd." Ah, my friend, I am odd myself, and I had the same feeling that you have. I thought that I was a lot left out of the catalogue. I always had the notion that my brother and my sisters could readily enough find mercy, but I—I could not see how I could be forgiven. I knew more about myself than I should like to tell; and I knew this about myself—that there was a peculiar guilt about me, besides many odd ways that I could not well shake off. Since then I have been the minister of a church that numbers nearly six thousand souls, and that for many years, and I have found out that nearly all of them are about as odd as I am; and so I have cast off the idea of my being so singular. If you knew other people you would find that there are other strange people besides yourself; and if God saves so many strange people, why should he not save you? "I should be a wonder," says one, "If I were saved." Then he will save you, for he delights to do wonders. He will crowd heaven with curiosities of mercy. Heaven will be a museum of prodigies of sovereign grace; and if you are one of that kind, be encouraged. You are the very man that is certain to be received. Go boldly to the gate, it shall not be shut in your face. Look to Jesus and live.

But I hear another say, "Sir, I have *such a horrible sense of sin;* I cannot rest in my bed! I cannot think that I shall be saved." Wait a bit there, my friend; wait a bit; let me speak to this person over here. What is your trouble? "My trouble is, sir, that I have no sense of sin. I know that I am a sinner, and a great sinner; but I do not think that I shall be saved, for I have no horrible thoughts." Will you change with the other man? Will he change with you? I should not advise either of you to make any change; for, in the first place, despairing thoughts are not necessary to salvation; and, in the second place, so long as you know yourself a sinner, and are willing to confess it, such thoughts are untrue. Where is it written in Scripture that we are to despair in order to be saved ? Is not the whole gospel "Believe in the Lord Jesus Christ, and thou shalt be saved"? Where shall you find it recorded in God's word that you are to be driven to remorse in order to find Christ? Repentance is quite another thing. To be sorry for sin, to hate sin, to wish to escape from it—this is a gospel blessing; but remorse—that threatening to destroy yourself, those tortures of mind—this is not desirable; and you may neither wish for it, if you have it not, nor yet despair because you have it, for salvation lies in Christ. Despairing one, look to the cross and live; and thou who dost not despair, look to the same cross and live; for there is salvation for every eye that looks to Jesus crucified.

I see another stumblingblock. A trembler cries, "I am afraid to come and trust Christ, because I do not know whether I am *one of the elect.*" Well, I cannot tell you. I have never been to heaven to search the roll. A young friend over yonder is starting in business. He opened his warehouse last Monday, and he is in hopes that he may prosper in the world. My dear young man, why did you open your shop? Why did you not sit down in idleness and moan, "I would open a shop, but I do not know whether I am predestinated to prosper." If you do not try you will never prosper: that is quite certain. As to secret things we act upon the rule of common sense. When this service is over you will go home, will you not? But if you sit still and say, "I shall not go down the aisle because I do not know whether it is predestinated for me to get home," you will not get home, and some will think that you are predestinated to be a fool. Any man who talks about predestination as if it could be an excuse for living in sin and refusing the Saviour is acting like a fool. If you trust Jesus Christ I will tell you then that you are God's elect, to a certainty; for whosoever believes in Christ is called by the Spirit of God, and none are called in that way but those whom God has chosen from before the foundations of the world.

"Ah," says another person, "I think I have committed *the unpardonable sin.*" Pray, sir, will you tell me what it is, because I have read a large number of books to make that discovery, and I have come to the conclusion that nobody knows what it is. Yet, though I am not sure as to what the crime may be, I can tell you whether you have committed it or not within a little. Do you desire to be saved? Do you long to be delivered from the power of sin? Then you have not committed the unpardonable sin, because it is a sin unto death, and after a man commits it he never has a living wish or desire after God from that moment. His conscience is seared as with a hot iron ; and he learns to defy God, or to be utterly indifferent with regard to eternal things. But as long as there beats within your breast a desire after God, as long as you can heave a sigh of regret because of a wasted life, as long as one tear of penitence can bedew your eye, be not dismayed with the idea that you have committed the sin which is unto death, for you have done nothing of the kind. Let us lift that stumblingblock out of the way altogether.

"Oh, but," says another person, "my stumblingblock is this: that the whole thing *seems too good to be true*—that I, by simply believing in Jesus Christ, shall be saved." I confess that it does seem too good to be true, but it is not. It is good, infinitely good, that your sin should be effectually pardoned, in a moment, freely and without price; but good as it is, it is like our God. God in Christ Jesus is clearly capable of marvellous deeds of grace. Treat God like God, and remember that his ways are as much above your ways, and his thoughts as much above your thoughts, as the heavens are above the earth. All the sins of a whole life he can strike out, as a man cancels a debt in his account-book. With one single mark of red ink he can write "receipted" at the bottom of the tremendous bill, and it is all gone, and gone for ever. There is none like thee, O God! there is none like thee! As Creator, none can make heavens and earth like thine; as Redeemer, none that can fetch a soul up from the pit as thou hast done it; and none can hurl sin into the depths of the sea as thou didst hurl it from the cross. Only trust the Saviour, then, and you shall see his great salvation. This stumblingblock about its being too good need not remain a moment.

I will not stay upon any more of these things, but will just say that there are some stumblingblocks that I cannot remove; they must always stand there, I am afraid.

An objector says to me, " I would believe in Jesus ; I have no fault to find with him, but then, *look at his followers, many of them are hypocrites.*" Yes, we do look at his professed followers, and the tears are in our eyes, for the worst enemies he has are they of his own household. Judas kissed him and sold him. Many are like Judas still. Look here, my friend : what have you to do with that ? Suppose Judas does betray Christ, is Christ any the worse for that ? You are not asked to trust in Judas, you are asked to trust in Christ. " Oh," says one, " but they are all hypocrites." No, no: that will not do. A man takes a bad sovereign—takes half-a-dozen of them in the course of his lifetime. Does he say that all sovereigns are bad? If there were no good ones the bad ones would never pass. The reason why it pays to make bad sovereigns is because good ones are so valuable ; and that is why it pays certain people, as they think, to pass themselves off as Christians. If there were no real Christians, there would be no pretenders to that name. How then can you make the excuse that because there are some hypocrites you will refuse Christ himself? "Ah," says one, " but I know a little about revival meetings and conversions. Don't you know what a lot were converted, and what became of them ? " I know what you are thinking about, but I heard a friend tell a good story in reference to that matter. He said that, notwithstanding that we have to strike off a discount from our converts of those that are not genuine, yet the revivals are worth having, for there is a real gain in them ; for, said he, the objection is something like that of an Irishman who had found a sovereign which was short in weight, so that he could only get eighteen shillings for it. The next time he saw a sovereign lying on the ground he would not pick it up, for, he said, he had lost two shillings by the other. Everybody laughs at him as acting ridiculously. So it is with objectors to revivals and special services. Suppose you do have to strike off the two shillings' worth, yet the eighteen shillings are clear gain ; and *why should you be the bad two shillings,* my friend? Why should *you?* I dare say you know yourself better than I do, and probably you may be the bad two shillings; but I did not say that you were, and I do not wish that you may be. Why should you not be a real convert, a true gain to the church of God? Because there are imposters in the world, is that a reason why I am not to come to Christ? I made you smile just now. It was that you might laugh to scorn this foolery which is so much talked of. Am I to refuse to eat bread because there are bad bakers? Will you never drink milk again because some milk has been adulterated? will you never breathe the air you live in because some air is tainted? Oh, talk not so. That stumblingblock ought not to want moving. If it be any hindrance to you I cannot help it; there it must be.

"But," says another, "here is my stumblingblock: if I were to believe in Christ, and become a Christian, *I should have to alter my whole life."* Just so. I do not dispute that assertion. There would have to be a turning of everything upside down; but then he that sits upon the throne says, "Behold, I make all things new." Perhaps, my friend, you would have to give up your trade, for there are some trades that cannot be followed by a Christian man; and, if yours is such, it is better to give it up than lose your soul. Or you might have to give up the tricks and dodges of your trade. You must give them up, then. If anything you do would keep you out of heaven, it is better that you should become poor than that you should prosper in business by doing wrong and ruining your soul. "What shall it profit a man if he gain the whole world and lose his own soul?" That is putting an extreme case, for nobody gains the whole world. It is only a few fourpences or shillings that men get by cheating. What profit can there be in that, if the soul is to be lost for it?

"Oh, but," says one, "*I should have to run the gauntlet in my family* if I became a Christian." Run the gauntlet, my friend. It is better to go to heaven under all opposition than to go to hell with the flatteries of God's enemies sounding in your ears. If you see a fish floating down the stream, you may know that it is a dead fish. Which way does a live fish go? Why, up-stream; and that is the way a man must go to heaven. "But I could not bear to be laughed at," says one. Poor soul. I have had, upon the whole, about as fair a share of ridicule as anybody living, but I do not recollect that one of my bones ever ached a minute about it; and I think that if I can bear my share, which is tolerably large, you ought to be able to bear yours without being quite overcome by it. Which is the better thing do you think—to be sneered at for doing right or to be commended for doing wrong? Surely it is manly and honourable to say, "I will do the right and follow Christ, whoever may sneer." What matters it? Dogs bark,—let them bark; but in God's name let us not give our souls away to find sops for them. "But my own brethren would be against me." Yes, Christ tells you that. He says, "He that loveth son or daughter more than me he is not worthy of me: a man's foes shall be they of his own household." You will conquer them yet by kindness and love; but I know there will be a wrench. In the higher classes a Christian man gets the cold shoulder, and among the lower orders our working men who talk of liberty are the biggest tyrants alive. The moment a man becomes a

Christian they point him out in the workshop; they jest and jeer at him from morning to night; and then call themselves true-born Englishmen. They may swear as much as they like, and use filthy talk, till you can hardly go down a street without feeling sick at the language you hear; but if a fellow workman chooses to go to a place of worship, and behave himself decently, then he is to be the butt of the workshop. This ought to come to an end, and would if men were men. But, my dear friend, I hope you are not to be cowed and kept down by opposition. If they laugh you into hell they cannot laugh you out again: recollect that. And if to win a few poor smiles, and escape a few silly sneers, you sell Christ, how will you answer for it when you have to stand before him, and he sits upon the great white throne, at last? Look at the martyrs—how they died for Christ. Think of Bunyan when he is brought before the judge, and the judge says, "You! a tinker! to go about preaching! Hold your tongue, sir." "I cannot hold my tongue," says Bunyan. "Then I must send you back to prison unless you promise never to preach again." "If you put me in prison till the moss grows on my eyelids I will preach again the first moment I get out, by the help of God." There is some grit in that man. Oh, that is the man that God loves; the man who against the whole world will do the right, and stand true to his Master. That stumblingblock I would not move away if I could: it is good for us to meet with opposition. I think that even now I see the King upon his throne at the last great day; and as he sits there, surrounded by his courtiers, and the blazing seraphim and mailed cherubim in all their brightness, he rises from his throne and looks afar, and cries, "Who cometh there? That is a man who suffered for me. When I was despised and rejected of men, he was despised and rejected for my sake. Make way, angels; make way, cherubim; make way, seraphim; stand back, and let him come. He was with me in my shame, he shall be with me in my glory. Come and sit even here, at the right hand of God, with me, for thou didst dare to be despised for me; and now shalt thou be with me in all the splendour of my reign." Oh, methinks we can leap over this stumblingblock, and be glad to think that it is there, for it will bring honour and glory and immortality at the last great day.

The last stumblingblock which I cannot move is this. A man will say, "But all this seems so new and strange to me. You want me to lead quite a new life. I do not comprehend it yet. I am to trust Christ whom I never saw!" Yes, that is where you are to begin. "And I am to see God whom I cannot see?" Yes, that is what you are to do. You are to live as in the daily consciousness of God's presence; and that you will do if you begin trusting Christ. "But *I cannot see what effect my trusting Christ would have upon me.*" No, you cannot see it, but it will have a most wonderful effect upon you. You will not be the same man after you have trusted the Saviour; the Spirit of God who gives you faith will change your whole nature. You will be as though you had been born again. "I don't see it," says one. No, but you might see it in this way. Here is a man that has a servant, and that servant believes his master to be everything that is bad; consequently, he does all that he can to annoy him. The master tries to mend the servant. He has spoken to him, and chided him; but he goes on worse and worse. Now, suppose that I could go into the house and say, "My dear man, I beg you to believe in your master. He wishes you well. You have misunderstood him." Suppose that I could induce the servant to believe in his master,—why, my friends, he would be an altered man altogether. Do you not see that the moment he believed in his master he would try to please him? If he said, "My master is a noble man. I love him." From that moment the whole tenor of his life towards his master would be changed. Hence the great power of believing the Lord Jesus. The moment you trust him, you obey his commands, you imitate his example, and you give yourself up to his service.

Thus have I put before you, as best I can, the way of salvation. I thank you for coming on this special occasion. I may never see your faces again; and if I never do, this one thing is true—you have heard the way of salvation, even if you do not follow it. I shall be clear of the blood of every one of you in that great day of account when preacher and hearers will have to answer for how this Sunday night was spent. I have thought that, if I could have been clearly told the way of salvation when I was anxious about my soul, I should have gained peace long before I did; and so I have resolved that I will never let the Sunday pass without preaching the way of salvation; and it is this that for six-and-twenty years and more has held the multitude of people listening to me. I tell nothing but the old, old story. Why do people come? Do we deal in spiceries and nicknacks? No, but in bread; and people always want bread. I have given you to-night no fineries or niceties, but the plain word of salvation. Will you have it, or not? God grant you grace to receive salvation. Believe in the Lord Jesus Christ, and you are saved, and you may go on your way rejoicing in everlasting life.

God grant it, for Christ's sake. Amen.

PORTION OF SCRIPTURE READ BEFORE SERMON—Luke xi. 1 to 27.

HYMNS FROM "OUR OWN HYMN BOOK"—430, 531, 397, 846.

AN INDICTMENT WITH FOUR COUNTS.

A Sermon

DELIVERED BY

C. H. SPURGEON,

AT THE METROPOLITAN TABERNACLE, NEWINGTON.

"She obeyed not the voice; she received not correction; she trusted not in the Lord; she drew not near to her God."—Zephaniah iii. 2.

FOUR heavy counts of a terrible indictment against Jerusalem and the Jewish people. Is it not sad to reflect that Jerusalem was the city of the great king, and yet fell from its high estate? It was the place of the temple; there the light of God shone forth, while other nations were in darkness; there the solemn worship of God was celebrated, whilst false gods were being adored elsewhere; and yet its sin provoked the Lord till he gave it up to the destroyer. It is clear, therefore, that no degree of light, and no amount of privilege, can keep a people alive and right before God. If the heart be not changed, if the grace of God go not with outward ordinances, those who are exalted to heaven may yet be cast down to hell. The putrefaction of the best produces the worst, and when a city which has been favoured as Jerusalem was becomes a den of unclean beasts, then it is a den indeed. Neither Nineveh, nor Babylon, nor Tyre, nor Sidon could equal in criminality this once chosen city of the great king. Let us not, therefore, as a nation begin to exalt ourselves because of our privileges, for if we do not prove worthy of them the candlestick will be taken out of its place, and our darkness will be all the denser because of the light we have lost. If we walk not before the Lord obediently, it may please him to make this island as great a scene of destruction as the mounds of Babel or the rock of Tyre.

We usually take Jerusalem to be the type of a church, and it is one of the fullest types of the one church: "Jerusalem which is above, the mother of us all." We may therefore regard the fate of Jerusalem as being a special warning to churches. In a church is God's dwelling-place, there is the light of knowledge, there is the fire of sacrifice, out of it hath God shined. But a church may sadly decline. There is a church which is now worthy of the name of Antichrist: she went further and further astray, till she has made a man to be her head, and called him infallible, till she set up lords many and gods many, saints and saintesses, and innumerable objects of worship even to cast clouts and rotten rags. There is a church against whom this indictment might be laid to-day : " She obeyed not the voice ; "—she did not hear the gospel. " She received not correction ; "—when reformers came she sought their blood. " She trusted not in the Lord ; she drew not near to her God ;" but she went after others, and set up other intercessors than Christ, and rejected the true Head of the church.

Other churches may fall into like sin unless they are guarded by spiritual power. Remember Laodicea, and how she was spued out of the mouth of Christ, because she was neither cold nor hot. Remember Sardis, which had but a few names in it that were undefiled Where are those cities and those churches now? Let desolation answer. It might be said of them as of Gilgal, of which the Lord said, " Go ye there to the place where my name was at the first, and see if there be one stone left of it upon another which hath not been cast down." Oh that we as a church, and all our sister churches, may walk before the Lord with holy jealousy as to doctrinal correctness, practical holiness, and inner spiritual life ; for, if not, our end will be miserable failure. If the salt of grace be not in a church, it cannot be an acceptable sacrifice to God, nor can it long be kept from the corruption which is natural to all masses of flesh. What are one people more than another? and what is one community more than another? We are men by nature, prone to the same evil, and we shall fall into the same transgression unless the Lord that keepeth Israel shall keep us ; and therein is our confidence, that he doth neither slumber nor sleep.

This text is not only applicable to a nation and to a church, but to individuals among God's own people, though of course only in a degree. Some of God's people follow Christ afar off, their spiritual life is better seen in their fears than in their confidences ; they are trembling always, their hands are slack, their hearts are faint. We trust they are alive unto God, but that is all we can say. I fear it may be said of them, " She obeyed not the voice:" the gentle whisper of divine love falls upon a deaf ear. Oh, how often, brethren, has God spoken and we have not hearkened so as to obey his voice. I fear, too, that there are times when we have not "received correction," when affliction has been lost upon us. We have risen from a sick-bed worse than when we went to it. Our losses and crosses have provoked us to murmuring rather than to heart-searching. We have been bruised as in a mortar among wheat with a pestle, and yet our folly has not departed from us. And this is a very provoking thing, when we despise the rod and the hand that uses it, and turn not at the smiting of the Lord. Yet it is so with some of God's people : they obey not the voice, they receive not correction, and therefore it comes to pass that at times " they trust not in the Lord." They try to bear their trials themselves. They go to friends for advice, and they inherit a curse, for it is written, " Cursed is he that trusteth in man, and maketh flesh his arm." They get into a withered state ; like the heath in the desert, they see not when good cometh, because they trust in man. Must not some of us plead guilty here?

To add to our faults, whenever we have backslidden we have " not drawn near to the Lord our God." The joy and the strength of the Christian life are found in living near to God, living like sheep close to the shepherd, wandering never, but lying down in green pastures to which he leads the way, himself better than the pasture, our joy and our delight. But, alas! it may be said of some, "Thou hast restrained prayer before God." "Are the consolations of God small with thee? Is there any secret thing with thee?" Your transgressions and your iniquities have hidden your God from you. He walks contrary to you because you walk contrary to him. This is too, too often the case, with even those who do trust in Jesus, and have passed from death unto life; and whenever it is the case it means sorrow. He that is no child of God, but a hypocrite, may wander as far from the path of integrity as he chooses without having to suffer for it till the last day; but a child of God cannot sin without smarting for it. Is it not written, "You only have I known of all the families of the earth: therefore I will punish you for your iniquities"? Our Father whips his own children. The boys in the streets may do as they please, but our great Father is sure to chasten those he loves. "As many as I love I rebuke and chasten: be zealous, therefore, and repent."

At this time I do not intend to use the words of our text in any of those ways, but to take it as it may refer to unconverted persons, for it very clearly, without the slightest strain, describes many who are living far away from God, and I shall want you to give me your attention for a little time while I notice *four great sins*. When these are mentioned I shall try to dig into the text, to bring out of it *four hidden consolations*:—they are not apparent on the surface, but when faith applies the microscope and looks into the centre of the text, it discovers four things by which the penitent sinner may be encouraged to come to Christ.

I. First, here are FOUR MANIFEST SINS.

I wonder whether the fact that my text is in the feminine is intended in the providence of God that this sermon may be especially adapted to a woman: I cannot tell, but I should not wonder. I may have been moved to this text on purpose that some poor wandering sister may feel as if God specially directed it to her sex. It says *she*—"She obeyed not the voice." Whatever belongs to any of our race may be taken by all, since in Christ Jesus there is neither male nor female. However, I point out the fact, and pray God that his word may be directed as he wills by the Holy Spirit.

The first sin is *not hearkening to God's voice*. Many have never hearkened to God's voice throughout a long life. They have heard it,—they could not help that; but they have never given heed, they have never lent an attentive ear, saying, "Speak, Lord, for thy servant heareth." He has spoken to many here present in *warnings*. He has said, "My daughter, if thou doest this, it will lead thee to grief and sorrow; if thou remainest hard, and careless, it cannot end well. Nothing can be right at the last which is not right now; wrong must bring woe with it." Sometimes this warning has come home into the heart, but the person of whom I am speaking has stifled it and said, "No, but I will go after mine own way and follow my own pleasure." That warning has come, perhaps, in the silence of the night, or in the very midst of the sin, a something that checked, a pulling of the rein, but the sinner could not be held in, nay, not with bit nor bridle, but he has taken the bit between his teeth, and dashed on in sin. Oh, remember, you that have neglected divine warnings; *you* may have forgotten them, but God has not. When you who love your children have spoken to them and warned them, they may have gone their way and quite forgotten "what mother said," but mother recollected it: her tears flowed, and wrote the memorial of her rebukes upon her face. And God forgets not warnings he has tendered to the sons of men.

I address some, however, who have not only received warning and rejected it, but they have received much *teaching*. You were in a Sabbath school class while yet a girl; you knew the plan of salvation very early in life, and you know it now, but still you have not obeyed the voice. There is Christ, but you have not touched his garment's hem. There is the fountain filled with blood of which you have been accustomed to sing, but you have never washed therein: there is the bread of life, but you have never fed thereon, and in consequence you live not unto God. Oh, it is a sad thing when it can be said, "She obeyed not the voice."

To some who are here present God's voice has come by way of *ex postulation*. There are many expostulations in the word of God such as this—"Turn ye, turn ye; why will ye die, oh house of Israel?" "Come now, and let us reason together: though your sins be as scarlet, they shall be as white as snow." "Come, and let us return unto the Lord: for he hath torn, and he will heal us; he hath smitten, and he will bind us up." "Say unto him, take away all iniquity, receive us graciously, and love us freely." Some of you had many such expostulations addressed to your heart and conscience, but you have not obeyed the voice.

And then at the back of this have come *invitations*, sweet invitations. In the Bible you have read them, in hymns you have sung them, from the pulpit you have heard them, from kind friends you have received them. Oh, how sweetly doth Jesus bid the hungry and the thirsty come to him; the heavy laden and such as are bowed down, to come and find rest in him. You used at one time to feel as if you would yield to these invitations; but you did not, and this sin lieth at your door, a stumblingblock in the way of your peace,—"She obeyed not the voice." When men fail to do right, they usually commit the wrong which is the reverse of it. You have listened to other voices, the siren voice of temptation has enchanted you, the voice of flattery has puffed you up, the voice of Satan has beguiled you, the voice of the flesh has fascinated you, the voice of the world hath wooed you and hath held you captive.

While we lay this indictment before you some of you cannot help saying, "He means me: it is even so with me." The Lord give you repentance, and open your ear: for is it not written, "Incline your ear and come unto me; hear, and your soul shall live, and I will make an everlasting covenant with you, even the sure mercies of David"? Oh divine Spirit, let not men be deaf any longer, but touch them with thy finger, that they may hear the voice of God and live.

That is the first count of the indictment, and the second one is like unto it and groweth out of it—"*she received not correction*." When men refuse God's voice they soon become more hardened still and reject his correction, like a horse which does not answer to the rein, and by-and-by even kicks at the whip, and will not be ruled at all. The Lord's correction comes to us sometimes from *his word*, when he speaks in anger and reminds us that his wrath abideth on the man that believeth not in Christ. Oh, there are heavy tidings from the Lord for you that are impenitent. This book is not a book to play with, it is full of the terrors of the Lord against such as go on in rebellion against him. Perhaps you have been made to tremble as you have read your Bible, and have seen how the Lord pronounces a solemn curse against the man that goeth on in his iniquity.

But the correction may also have come to you from *your own conscience*, quickened by the Word of God. You have come to be uneasy, you start in your sleep with dreams that alarm you. If you are as I once was, everything you look upon seems to have a mouth to accuse you. I remember when the Lord's corrections were very heavy upon me. I could not see a funeral but what I wondered when I too should be carried to the grave; I could not pass a churchyard without the reflection that I should soon be there; and when I heard the passing bell, it seemed to tell me that I should soon be judged, and condemned, for I had no hope of pardon. These are corrections of God, and I pray you regard them.

Possibly, however, you have endured *affliction*. You are not well; you have been made to look into eternity through death's door. Peradventure one or another of your friends has been taken home. You wear the garb of mourning now. God has corrected you. You have had a loss which you thought you could scarce survive, it was so severe. "Despise not thou the chastening of the Lord," but hear his rod, and listen to what he has to say to you in it. Remember, God may smite you worse than he has done; for these few aches and pains he can send something more sharp and smarting. If one child has gone, he can take another, even from your breast; if one relative has died, another may follow, for the great archer hath many arrows in his quiver, and when one sufficeth not he speedily wings another in its painful flight. I pray thee beware, and let it not be said of thee, "She received not correction," or, "He received not correction"; but may you be willing to listen while God is thus dealing with you.

This leads to a third count, in which lies the very essence of deadly sin: "*She trusted not in the Lord.*" She would not come and trust in Christ for salvation; she would believe in her own righteousness. She would not trust in Christ to help her to overcome sin, she said she was quite able to purify herself. Oh, many a young man has started fair for heaven to all appearance, but it has been in his own strength, and, like Pliable, he has no sooner stumbled into the Slough of Despond than he has turned his back on the heavenly city, and returned to the place from which he set out. Beware, I pray you, of having anything to do with a hope that is not based upon trust in God in Christ Jesus. Your religion is vanity, and an insult to high heaven, unless it be based on the atonement of Jesus Christ. Where there is no faith in Jesus peace is presumption. He that dares to hope till he has believed in Christ hopes in vain. But ah, there are some who are driven to do many apparently gracious things, but yet this one thing they will not do, they will not trust in the Lord; and I have known this to be sadly the case with some in great affliction. She did not trust in the Lord: she was a widow, but she did not trust in the Lord. She had many little children, she knew not where to find them bread, but she did not trust in the Lord. She was sick and ill herself, but she trusted not in the Lord. She was laid at death's door, she was in the infirmary, in the hospital, but she trusted not in the Lord. Her heart was very heavy, and she said she wished she could die, but she trusted not in the Lord. Her friends did not help her : those who ought to have been kind were cruel, but she trusted not in the Lord : she was driven into a corner, and yet she did not trust in the Lord.

Ay, but this is a great sin, for surely God takes away our props and dependences on purpose that we may throw our whole weight on himself ; but there are some who will have nothing to do with this trusting, neither for time nor for eternity, neither for body nor for soul. Woe unto any man, be he even a child of God, if he once gets off the pathway of faith, for when we walk by sight we shall see things which shall make us wish we were blind, and only when we trust shall we have to say, "I am not confounded nor ashamed, nor shall I be, world without end." This is sad—" She trusted not in the Lord."

The fourth crime was, " *She drew not near to her God.*" There was no prayer. There was much talk about her trouble, much talk about what she would like to do, but there was no asking of God, no going into the chamber and spreading the case before him, and pleading his mercy. There was no thought of God ; the mind did not get near to him. The desires rambled round in a thousand devious paths, but did not come to God. Oh, it is hard to get some of you to think of God. I try and preach as best I can, and try to find striking words to make you think of God, but, oh, how often do I fail ! The choicest ways I use defeat themselves. May it not be so now ! Let it not be said of you any longer that " she drew not near to her God." We ought to think of him, we ought to seek him, we ought to come to him, as little chicks, when there is a hawk in the air, and they hear the call of the mother hen, soon hide away under her feathers. We ought to run in prayer, that it might be true of us, " He shall cover thee with his feathers, and under his wings shalt thou trust: his truth shall be thy shield and buckler." If you had a child that in its troubles ran out into the street, and when its little heart was heavy went away to strangers, and never told father or mother its sorrow, you would feel much hurt. This is God's quarrel with his rebellious people, that they will go to Satan himself before they will come to him. Nay, think not that I run too far, and use an extravagant expression, for Saul did this ; when God answered him not, he offered no penitent petitions, but resorted to a witch for help. Many would penetrate into the recesses of the unseen world, and tamper with spiritual mysteries sooner than they will go to God. Silly women will believe a fortune teller, but will not trust the Saviour.

Is it so with any of you? Then let this word of accusation sink deep into your spirits, and confess your transgression unto the Lord.

Putting the four sentences together : " She obeyed not the voice ; she received not correction ; she trusted not in the Lord ; she drew not near to God,"—what then? Why, " *woe unto her.*" Read the first verse of the chapter, and there you have it. As I was coming here that word " woe," " woe," " woe " seemed to ring in my ears, and I wondered where it came from. I will tell you. It is a word that goes to be made into a worse word. Let me pronounce it for you—woe; and that leads to something woe-erse—worse; and to the woe-erst—the worst of all. It is bad, lamentable, destructive, ruinous, painful, wretched, miserable woe, worse, worst. I wish I could pronounce the word as my Master did when he said, "Woe unto thee, Bethsaida; woe unto thee, Chorasin; woe unto thee, Capernaum." 1 should hardly like to say as he did, for he had a right to judge which I have not—"Woe unto you scribes and Pharisees, hypocrites," and so on. But that "woe" as he pronounced it must have sounded terribly, softly, sadly, sternly piercing to the heart. Ah, how will the angels sound it at the last? Hear it now, lest ye hear it at the last. "One woe is past, and behold another woe cometh," when the Judge of all the earth shall break the seals and pour out the vials, and the ungodly sons of men shall see the star Wormwood, and shall drink of the bitterness of the wrath of God. Woe. It means sorrow here! No rest! No satisfaction! Woe, woe, even at this day unto the man that trusteth not in God. But what it meaneth in the next world—to be driven from the face of Christ, to be followed with a "woe" which shall have eternal echoes, Woe, woe, woe! I could fain stop and cry with Mr. Whitefield, "The wrath to come! The wrath to come!" Escape from it while yet life lasts and Jesus pleads with you, for otherwise this shall fall like a thunderbolt from the hand of the angry Judge,—"Woe to her. She obeyed not the voice, she received not correction, she trusted not in the Lord, she drew not near to God." Then all this will turn to woe, the voice disregarded will ring again, "Son, remember! Son, remember! Woe, woe." As for the correction which was disregarded, oh how light and gentle it will seem compared with the strokes that will then fall upon the rejecters of Christ! Every correction will then turn to woe. And the not trusting in the Saviour, the unbelief, what woe that will bring! The not drawing near to God, what woe that will cost, when we shall see ourselves afar off, and between us and God a great gulf fixed, so that none can come to us, no, not so much as to bring a drop of water to cool our tongue, neither can any go from us, or escape from the place of woe.

II. To help any who would escape from this woe, I shall spend a minute in noticing THE FOUR HIDDEN CONSOLATIONS WHICH LIE IN THIS TEXT.

I do not intend to enlarge upon them, because I want the previous part of this discourse to abide in your mind : but there are four hidden consolations. The first is, if I have not obeyed his voice yet, it is plain *he does speak*, he speaks to me. My soul, my soul, God is not dumb; canst thou be deaf? Still doth he invite thee, still doth he call thee, still doth his good Spirit strive with thee. This voice of mine to-night I hope will be God's voice to some of you. Be encouraged; he has not given you up, but still calls. When the sentence of death is pronounced there are no warnings given, and since you are having another call, I would encourage you to hope.

The next is, "She received not correction," then *all my troubles and afflictions are meant to bring me to Christ.* They are all sent in love to my soul, and I ought to look at them as such. My friend, where are you? I do not know where you are, or to whom I am speaking, but

I do pray you see that God, who seemeth to have dealt very hardly with you, is only driving you to mercy. His voice has been harsh, and his hand has been heavy, but in love he corrects you. Oh listen to him, come to him. A judge does not correct a criminal doomed to die. God does not correct a soul, with a view to its reclamation, if he has given it up altogether.

Notice the next sentence. "She trusted not in the Lord." Is it a crime, then, that I did not trust in the Lord ? *Then I may trust him,* and I *will,* for that which it is a sin not to do I must have a right to do, and if it be laid to my charge, "She trusteth not in the Lord," oh, sweet mercy, sweet mercy, I may trust ! This is why the Scripture saith, " He that believeth not shall be damned," as if to assure you that you certainly *may* believe, because you will be damned if you do not. Come, then, and let even the black side of the text wear a smile to you, and lead you to trust your God, since he blames you for not doing so.

Then there was the last crime. "She drew not near to God." What, then, does God make it a fault, that I do not draw near to him ? Oh, I wish the Spirit of God would put it into your heart to say, " That shall not be my fault any longer."

> " I'll to the gracious King approach,
>   Whose sceptre pardon gives ;
> Perhaps he may command my touch,
>   And then the suppliant lives."

" I thought I might not come," but now I see I am condemned for not coming; then I will come. I will delay no longer, I will come to Jesus, determined that if I perish I will perish at his feet. Have hope, my friend, for none did ever perish there. May God set his seal to this word of expostulation, for Jesus' sake. Amen.

PORTION OF SCRIPTURE READ BEFORE SERMON—Zephaniah iii.

HYMNS FROM " OUR OWN HYMN BOOK"—515, 509, 514.

TILL WE MEET AGAIN.

DELIVERED BY

C. H. SPURGEON,

AT THE METROPOLITAN TABERNACLE, NEWINGTON.

"The grace of our Lord Jesus Christ be with you all. Amen."—Revelation xxii. 21.

THE first saints could never be long without speaking of their Lord and Saviour. He filled their hearts, and therefore they must needs speak of him. How ingeniously they bring him in! When they commence an epistle the salutation will be sure to bear his name. When they are in the midst of a letter, they lay down their pen and offer a prayer; and when they begin again it is with a benediction in which his name is prominent, or with a doxology ascribing glory unto him, with the Father, and with the Holy Ghost. John's Book of Revelation is full of Christ. Its opening verse rings out the precious name, and the closing line which is now before us repeats the heavenly music. Is not the Lord Jesus the sum and substance, the glory of every vision seen in Patmos? May I not say of the Apocalypse, as John said of the New Jerusalem, "the Lamb is the light thereof"? until he looses the seals and opens the roll, the book of John's prophecy is so folded up that no man shall understand it.

John could not finish his book without mentioning that name which was dearest of all names to him, As he puts aside his pen to write no more, he concludes with an invocation of blessing upon all the saints in every place; and this is the form of it: "The grace of our Lord Jesus Christ be with you all." Paul is thought to have claimed the use of this benediction as his particular token: "in every epistle so I write." I am not sure that it is so, for I suspect that the apostle referred to his own large handwriting, and to the signature which he put to his letters. But still, according to many interpreters, Paul used this particular blessing as his private mark, the seal of the authenticity of a letter. See the end of the epistles to the Corinthians and Thessalonians: "The grace of our Lord Jesus Christ be with you all." Certainly Paul used the words often; but, perhaps, when Paul had been taken up, John deemed it right to adopt Paul's motto, and with it to set, as it were, his stamp and seal upon the last book of Revelation. It was a benediction which could not be engrossed by any one apostle, nor

Nos. 1,628-30.

indeed by all the apostles put together. Paul made it his own, but John had equal right to use it; and it is now all the dearer to us because both these mighties employed it.

Brethren, the benediction before us is not only Paul's word and John's word, and the Bible's last word, but it is now the chosen word of all the ministers of Jesus Christ. Is not this the benediction with which we dismiss the faithful: "The grace of our Lord Jesus Christ, and the love of God, and the communion of the Holy Spirit be with you all"? So shall it remain until the Lord shall come a second time. It is an expression suitable to the most gracious heart, a prayer wherewith the believer may vent his best wishes and express his most devout desires. Over you all at this time, in my own most humble but sincere manner, I would pronounce the benediction, "The grace of our Lord Jesus Christ be with you all."

If the Spirit shall help me, I would at this time first say, let us *consider this benediction;* and then, secondly, let us consider *its peculiar position;* for something can be learned therefrom.

I. First, then, let us CONSIDER THIS BENEDICTION. It divides itself into three parts, under these heads,—What? How? and, To whom?

1. *What?* What is this which John desires when he says,—"The grace of our Lord Jesus Christ be with you all"?

The word is *Charis.* I do not think any better translation could be given than "grace": it is usually translated grace throughout the New Testament. Those who understand the Greek language thoroughly tell us that it has for its root "joy." There is joy at the bottom of *Charis,* or grace. It also signifieth favour, kindliness, and especially love; and I might, without violating the meaning of the Spirit, read the words thus: "The love of our Lord Jesus Christ be with you all." But inasmuch as love to unworthy creatures such as we are can only display itself in free favour—that is, grace, and we know that the term used is an accurate expression, we will let it stand as it is, only putting in a drop or two of the sweet honey of the love which lies within it. John desires that we may have the free favour of Jesus Christ, the love of Jesus Christ, the grace of our Lord Jesus Christ. Jesus Christ himself is generally mentioned in our benedictions as having grace, and the Father as having love; and our usual benediction begins with the grace of our Lord Jesus Christ and the love of God. Is that the proper order? Should we not rather say the Father, the Son, and the Holy Spirit? Brethren, the order observed in the benediction is that of our experience, the order in which we learn, the order in which we receive. We first receive the grace and free favour which are in Christ Jesus, and then from these we learn the love of the Father; for no man cometh unto the Father but by Jesus Christ. The order is correct to our experience, and in an instructive benediction the Holy Spirit intendeth this for our learning.

The Father's love is, as it were, the secret, mysterious germ of everything. That same love in Jesus Christ is grace; his is love in its active form, love descending to earth, love wearing human nature, love paying the great ransom price, love ascending, love sitting and waiting, love pleading, love soon to come with power and glory.

The eternal love which, as it were, did lie in the bosom of the Father, rises up and comes into activity, and is then called the grace of our Lord Jesus Christ.

This grace of our Lord Jesus Christ is therefore the grace of a divine person. We wish you, brethren, as we wish for ourselves, the grace of God himself, rich, boundless, unfathomable, immutable, divine; no temporary grace such as some speak of, which keepeth not its own, but suffereth even the sheep of its own pasture to go astray and perish; but the grace of our Lord Jesus Christ, of whom it is written, " Having loved his own which were in the world, he loved them unto the end"; that grace most potent which said, " None shall pluck them out of my hand." We wish this grace to be with you, the grace which loved you or ever the earth was made,—" I have loved thee with an everlasting love, therefore with lovingkindness have I drawn thee"; the grace which will be with you when this poor world shall have melted back into the nothingness from whence it sprang: infinite, everlasting, unchanging grace—we wish you may have that. May its divine height, and depth, and length, and breadth be enjoyed by you; may you know the loving grace of Christ which passeth knowledge; may you grasp the unsearchable riches of Christ. This is no small treasure,—this grace of a divine person.

Yet is our Lord Jesus also human, as truly human as he is divine, and, believing in him, you have the grace of Jesus Christ the man to be with you all. May you feel his tenderness, his brotherliness, his grace. He is your kinsman, and he graciously favours his own kinsfolk. The man is next of kin unto us, and as Ruth enjoyed all the love of Boaz, so may you possess all the heart of Jesus. May he redeem your inheritance for you, and take you to himself to be his own, in blessed union with himself for ever. May the grace of the Man of Nazareth, the grace of the Son of Mary be with you, as well as the grace of " God over all, blessed for ever," to whom be praise. The grace of that wondrous person who is God and man in one person, and whom we call Lord, is now solemnly invoked upon you.

Read the text again, and pause a while in the middle to enjoy " The grace of our *Lord*." Whatever familiarity we have with him, we call him Master and Lord, and he saith, " Ye do well, for so I am." Let us never forget that. The grace that cometh from his majesty, the grace that cometh from his headship, the grace that cometh from his divinely human supremacy over his church, which is his body—this is the grace which we desire for you all.

Read the next word, " the grace of our Lord *Jesus*": may that be with you; that is to say, the grace of our Saviour, for that is the meaning of the word Jesus. All his saving grace, all that which redeems from guilt, from sin, from trouble, all that which saves us with an everlasting salvation,—may that be yours to the full.

Then comes the other word, " the grace of our Lord Jesus *Christ* be with you"; may he, as the Anointed One, visit you. May the grace of his anointing be with you, may the holy anointing which was poured upon the Head come down upon you, as the sacred nard dropped from Aaron's beard and perfumed all his robes. May you have that anointing from the Holy One which shall make you know all things.

I am tempted to linger over each one of these words, but I may not, for time would forbid. Yet must we tarry on that word " our." " May the grace of *our* Lord." Catch at that sweet word. It may not perhaps be genuine in this case, for it is not in the Sinaitic manuscript, but whether it is so in this particular instance or not, it is in the Word, and stands for ever true. Jesus is *our* Lord,—*our* Lord Jesus Christ: both yours and ours. May the fulness of his grace be with you and with us.

2. Our next division is *How?* " May the grace of our Lord Jesus Christ be with you all." What meaneth this? Our first answer is the wish that the grace of our Lord may rest upon you *as a matter of fact,*—that he may love you truly and intensely; love you, not only as he loves the world, but as he loved his own which were in the world. May you have his redemption, not as a general thing, but according to that word, " He hath redeemed us from among men out of every kindred." May you have the special, peculiar love which Christ hath to those whom his Father gave him, whose names are on his breast-plate, and for whom he has paid an effectual ransom price, that they thereby might be delivered: may such grace be with you. As a matter of fact may it rest upon you as the chosen, adopted, called, and sanctified.

Next, *may you believe that grace,* may you trust that grace, may it be with you because your faith has closed in with it, and you are relying upon it. You believe that Jesus loves you; you believe in his grace, and trust yourself to him, committing your spirit to the keeping of that hand which was pierced and fastened to the cross for you. May his grace be with you in that sense, so that you realize it.

Still further, may his grace be with you *as the object of faith,* so that your belief comes to be full assurance, till you know the love which Christ hath towards you, and no more doubt it than you doubt the love of the dearest friend you have on earth. May his love be a present fact, and not a thing to be questioned, a treasure in which you glory in the secret places of your soul, saying, " He loved me, and gave himself for me." May his grace be with you in the sense that you are confidently assured of it.

And may his grace be with you, next, *as to the favours which flow out of it.* May you enjoy all the blessings which the grace of Christ can yield, the grace of a peaceful conscience, the grace of a cleansed walk, the grace of access to God, the grace of fervent love, the grace of holy expectancy, the grace of self-denial, the grace of perfect consecration, and the grace of final perseverance. May the fountain and well-head be with you, that so the sparkling streams may flow at your feet.

And may grace be with us, next, so as *to produce constant communion between us and Christ,* his favour flowing into our heart, and our hearts returning their gratitude. Oh, to carry on blessed commerce with Christ, exchanging weakness for strength, sin for righteousness, and trust for care. O to give love for love and heart for heart, till my best love loves me, and my best love is all his own. Oh, to come to this pass, that our Well-beloved is with us, and we enjoy sweet mutual intercourse: this is to have the love, or grace, of Jesus with us.

May our Lord Jesus Christ thus in his grace be with us, and may he *work for us all that he can work.* May the grace of our Lord Jesus Christ be with you, brethren, when you desire to pray; then may the great High Priest intercede for you. May the grace of our Lord Jesus Christ be with you, so that when you are downcast he may say, "Let not your heart be troubled." May the grace of our Lord Jesus Christ be with you to check you when you are likely to start aside, to guide you when you know not your way, to inspirit you when you are ready to be cast down, to confirm you when you have almost slipped with your feet. May the grace of our Lord Jesus Christ be with you when heart and flesh are failing you, when the last hour has come, and you are about to appear before God. God grant you to know always all that Christ can do in you, and for you, and with you, and by you. What better benediction could John himself utter?

3. But, now, the third part of our discourse comes under the head of "*to whom.*" "The grace of our Lord Jesus Christ be with you *all.*" Surely if we were to take this in the widest possible sense, and say—may it be with you all, it could not be wrong to wish that all should have the grace of our Lord Jesus Christ with them; yet I know some sound brethren are very jealous of anything that looks like a wide expression, an expression which would wish good to all. For my own part, I do not understand the nature of the orthodoxy which would limit benevolent desires. I should like to be more and more heterodox in the direction of desiring good to all that come in my way. Would to God that the best that could happen to all men did happen to them. I would without the slightest hypocrisy breathe this desire over all mankind, "The grace of our Lord Jesus Christ be with you all." Still, there is no doubt that the connection in which it stands, and also certain versions of it, do confine this benediction to the saints, and practically it must always be confined to them, for the grace of our Lord Jesus Christ is only known and enjoyed by those who have given their hearts to Jesus, and are living by him, in him, and to him. Let us wish the grace of our Lord Jesus Christ to all the saints, at any rate. Some of the saints will hardly own us; but may the grace of our Lord Jesus Christ be with them. They would not let us preach in their pulpits; but may grace be with them. They would not partake of the communion with us; but may grace be with them. They call us sectarians and schismatics, but may "the grace of our Lord Jesus Christ be with them all. Amen," with every one of them, whoever they may be. If they are in Jesus Christ, may the grace of our Lord Jesus Christ be with them. Every now and then you come across a book written by one who is a long way off from understanding all the truth, yet he knows Jesus Christ, and as you read the sweet words that come from his pen concerning the Master you feel your heart knit to him. Your soul feels that it is a pity that the writer was a High Churchman, but if he loves the Lord Jesus Christ we forget his errors, and are delighted with the life of Jesus which we see in him. If a man knows Christ, he knows the most important of matters, and is possessed of a secret quite as precious as any in our own keeping, for what know we more than Christ, and what hope have we but in Christ? If thou lovest Christ, give me thy hand, my friend, notwithstanding thy blunders. If Christ be all thy trust and all thy confidence, I am sorry for thine eyes that thou canst not see a great deal

more, I am sorry for thine head that thou canst not think more straight, but thine heart is in the right place resting on Jesus, reposing on him, and who am I that I should judge thee? There is a life in Christ which a thousand errors cannot kill. There is a life which is the same in all that have it, however diverse they may happen to be upon opinion or outward ceremony. There is a life eternal, and that life is Christ Jesus, and to all that have that life we do with intensity of heart say, "The grace of our Lord Jesus Christ be with you all."

I notice Paul says this in one of his epistles to a church that misbehaved itself dreadfully. It was one of the churches that would not have any minister; a church where they all spoke as they pleased, to whom Paul said, "God is not the author of confusion." They were so depraved a church that they allowed an incestuous person to be present at the communion, but still, after the apostle had rebuked them, he said, "The grace of our Lord Jesus Christ be with you all." Even so must we say to those who err ignorantly, as the Corinthians did. If we differ from brethren, if we have to rebuke them, if sometimes they also rebuke us, and show temper over it, yet may this be the finale of it all, "The grace of our Lord Jesus Christ be with you all." Should we not wish the highest degree of grace to all who are in the body of Christ? Let us not utter this benediction merely because we ought to say it, but because we delight to say it: let us not only wish well to the saints because we are bound to wish them well, but because our hearts cannot do otherwise.

II. So now, not to detain you much longer, I ask your earnest attention for a few minutes to THE POSITION OF THIS BENEDICTION.

First, I draw what I have to say from the fact that *it is the last word of Scripture.* I regard it, therefore, as being the apostle's last and highest wish. We are glad to find that, while the Old Testament finishes with a curse—"Lest I come and smite the earth with a curse," the New Testament concludes with a blessing, "The grace of our Lord Jesus Christ be with you all": as if to show that the very life and spirit of a Christian should be blessing; and this should be to us our last and highest wish for men—that they may receive and retain the grace of our Lord Jesus Christ. I wish this blessing to you all, my dear brothers and sisters. Whatever you may miss, may the grace of our Lord Jesus Christ be always with you. In whatsoever points you or any of us may fail, may we never come short of the grace of our Lord Jesus Christ. What if the preacher should preach to others, and himself be a castaway! Pray that it be not so. What if a deacon or elder should lead the flock of Christ, and yet the grace of our Lord Jesus Christ should not be with him! He would become another Judas or Demas. That would be dreadful. What if you should teach the little ones in the school, and yet not learn yourselves! It would be a sad thing to have come to the Lord's Supper, and yet never to have eaten his flesh and drunk his blood: to be immersed in water, but never to have known the baptism of the Holy Spirit, nor to have been baptized into Christ with the spiritual baptism. What a thing it will be, if, after all our professions, and all our labours, and all our teachings, the grace of our Lord Jesus Christ should not be with us. I pray, brethren, whatever other prayer may not be granted, that this may be, concerning every member of this church, and every member of every church of Jesus Christ, that at any rate the grace of our Lord Jesus Christ may be with us. We cannot do with less than this, and we do not want more than this. If we get grace from Jesus we shall have glory with Jesus, but without it we are without hope.

Standing at *the end of the Book of Revelation* as this does, I next regard its position as indicating what we shall want till the end comes; that is, from now till the descent of our Lord in his second advent. This is the one thing we require, "The grace of our Lord Jesus Christ be with you all." May it be with us daily, hourly! May it be with us, instructing us as to our behaviour in each generation! May it be with us cleansing us from all sin; enabling us to walk in the light as he is in the light! May it be with us, strengthening us to carry our daily burdens, and to bear our witness for his name under the varying circumstances of the ages. May it be with us counselling us when the trials of life distract us! With us transfiguring us from glory to glory, till we shall bear the image of Jesus Christ? May it be with us all-sufficiently! Hath he not said, "My grace is sufficient for thee"? May the grace of our Lord Jesus Christ be with you all in every way in which you shall require it till he cometh! He can furnish you with the whole armour of God; he can equip you with all the necessaries of the pilgrim life. For our labour as gospel-fishermen he supplies all the nets that we shall require, for our work in his vineyard he gives us every tool. May the grace of our Lord Jesus Christ be with us, and we shall be swift of foot as a young roe, and sure of foot as the hart on the mountain side, that slips not, however slippery the crags may be. Only let Christ be with us and we are complete in him; perfect in Christ Jesus. All the equipment that men shall want between earth and heaven to fight against hell, and to trample on the world, and to enter into eternal perfection, is found in Christ. May his grace be with you all. Amen.

Placed as this blessing is at the end of the book there is but this one more thought,—this is what we shall wish for when the end cometh. We shall come to the end of life, as we come to the end of our Bibles. And oh! aged friend, may thy failing eyes be cheered with the sight of the grace of our Lord Jesus Christ, on the last page of life, as thou wilt find it on the last page of thy well-thumbed Bible. Peradventure some of you may come to the last page of life before you get grace: I pray that there you may find it. The grace of our Lord Jesus Christ be with you. Or, suppose we should not die; suppose the Lord should suddenly come in his temple. Oh! then may we have grace to meet him. I am so glad that a benediction closes the Apocalypse; for, as you stand in the book of Revelation, you hear the thunders roll, peal after peal, you see the vials poured forth, darkening the air, and sun and moon turned into blackness and blood! Earth reels beneath your feet, and stars fall like fig leaves from the tree! You are full of confusion and dismay, until you hear this holy whisper, "The grace of our Lord Jesus Christ be with you." Let every star of the firmament fall where it will, the grace of our Lord Jesus Christ is with us. Rock and reel, ye mountains, and be dissolved, O earth, and pass away; if the grace of our Lord Jesus Christ be with us we fear not the end. We can serenely look upon the wreck of matter and the crash of worlds. Let the last august tribunal sit, and men be summoned to stand before it, to receive their final doom, we shall without trembling advance before that great white throne and stand there, if the grace of our Lord Jesus Christ be with us.

> "Bold shall I stand in that great day,
> For who aught to my charge shall lay?
> While through his blood absolved I am
> From sin's tremendous curse and shame."

Oh! happy they, shrouded, and sheltered, and hidden, in Christ their Saviour; to whom his grace shall be like the white robes of Mount Tabor's transfiguration, for they shall be accepted in the Beloved, glorified in the glory of their Master. These are they to whom the text shall be fulfilled—"The grace of our Lord Jesus Christ be with you all."

Finally, brethren, farewell, and as you go out I would like just to take my place at the doorway, to offer my hand of friendship, and say to each one, "Farewell for a little while. This is my best wish for you,—The grace of our Lord Jesus Christ be with you." Will you start back and say, "Sir, I know nothing of this grace"? Then would I ask you to stay a moment while I breathe the prayer, "The grace of our Lord Jesus Christ be with you." May be there is only a tear of penitence in your eye, no light of faith is there as yet. May the grace of our Lord Jesus Christ be with you, poor broken-hearted penitent! May be you do not know Jesus yet, and you are only seeking him. His grace be with you now: may he manifest himself to you! And you, backslider, do you feel as if you cannot receive a blessing? The grace of our Lord Jesus Christ be especially with you, to raise you up, and set you on your feet again, as he did fallen Peter. I would like, if I could, to say to the stranger within our gates to-night, who does not often attend the house of God, it is our heart's desire for you that you may know the grace of our Lord Jesus Christ in truth. To the boys and girls here, the pastor says, "God bless you." Little Mary, or Jane, or John, or Willie, or whatever your name may be, "The grace of our Lord Jesus Christ be with you"; for he saith, "Suffer the little children to come unto me, and forbid them not." As for you, grey-headed friends, you who will soon be home, I wish you this parting blessing, "The grace of our Lord Jesus Christ be with you." Till I see you again, "God bless you." Till the day break, and the shadows flee away, may the Lord Jesus never be absent from you. Amen and amen.

PORTION OF SCRIPTURE READ BEFORE SERMON—1 Thessalonians v.

HYMNS FROM "OUR OWN HYMN BOOK"—951, 1028, 1053.

Metropolitan Tabernacle Pulpit.

TWO GOOD THINGS.

A Sermon

DELIVERED ON THURSDAY EVENING, JUNE 17TH, 1880, BY

C. H. SPURGEON,

AT THE METROPOLITAN TABERNACLE, NEWINGTON.

"It is good for me that I have been afflicted; that I might learn thy statutes."—Psalm cxix. 71.

"It is good for me to draw near to God: I have put my trust in the Lord God, that I may declare all thy works."—Psalm lxxiii. 28.

THERE is an old proverb which says, "When a man is forty he is either a fool or a physician"; that is to say, he either does not know anything, or else he begins to know what is good for him. Some of us who are beyond that age think that we know in some measure what is good for us. We are not inclined to be very positive as to what is good for other people; but there are one or two things in reference to ourselves of which we say very dogmatically, "They are good for *me*." We have undergone such a sufficiency of investigation, experiment, and personal trial, that we are not in any fear of being contradicted; or if we should be, we put our foot down and defy the contradiction.

These two things in my two texts I am certain about, and I believe there are many here who share my positiveness. The first is, that whatever it may be for other people, "it is good *for me* to have been afflicted;" and the second is, that whatever it may be to other people, "it is good *for me* to draw near to God." We assert this, not because we have been told so, but because of personal proof; and we assert it now, not as young beginners who are buckling on their harness, and who think themselves certain; but as those who have gone some distance in the pilgrimage of life, and know by actual test and matter of fact that it is even so.

Brethren, beloved, during our lives we have met with many things which we know were *not* good for us. Some things have been manifestly bad. Sin is always poisonous, whatever form it takes. Error is always injurious, however insidious may be its shape, and however poetic may be the terms in which it is expressed. We pray God that we may have nothing to do with sin or with error, for these things cannot be good; they must be evil. We have also met with certain things which at the time appeared to us to be good, and under some aspects might have been so; but we are not sure at the present moment whether they were good or not. We have enjoyed soft hours of ease which, perhaps, weakened us, or sunshiny times of high delight which in a measure

237

turned our brain. There have been allotted to us times of learning in which we made great acquisitions of knowledge; but "knowledge puffeth up," and we were puffed up, we fear. There have been calms with us when the sea-birds sat upon the waters, and the seas were glassy as a lake, for the winds were hushed; but the calm was treacherous, and it bred ill savour and unhealthiness within our spirit. I am not sure, my friend, though you thought it a fine day when you grew rich—I am not sure that it was a good thing for you to be wealthy; for you have not been half so spiritually-minded or half so happy as you used to be. Yes, you did enter into a much larger sphere, and you thought it a noble thing. You almost rang the bells about it. Are you quite sure that it was good for you? Are you as good a man in the great sphere as you were in the little one? Do you live as near to God now, with that great business to handle, as you did when your hat covered your whole estate, and you went to bed at night with no fear of robbers, for you had nought to lose? Much that seems good is only good in the seeming. As for the two things before us in our texts, we have no question about them. We know that it is good for us that we have been afflicted; we know that it is good for us that we should draw near to God. We will talk about these undoubted jewels, and may God grant that our talk may be profitable.

I. Turning to the hundred-and-nineteenth Psalm, at the seventy-first verse, we will talk of that good thing first: AFFLICTION HAS BEEN GOOD FOR US. "It is good for me that I have been afflicted; that I might learn thy statutes." I repeat what I said just now: every man must speak for himself; we are not sure that affliction is good for everybody. Some persons have been soured by affliction. They fell into trouble and they rebelled against God; and so the trouble did not work in them any permanent good; it rather developed their combative tendencies, and they have ever since remained with their hands against other men, compelling others to lift their hands against them. I have known individuals in a family who seemed to have a spite against everyone they saw, simply because they were disappointed in early life, or had made a venture and sustained a loss. They grew sour, they keep sour, and they grow sourer every day, till one wonders what strength of vinegar will yet flow through their veins. It is not good for some people to have been afflicted at all, and yet it is not the fault of the affliction; it is the fault of the persons afflicted. It might have produced in them a splendid character if all had been right to begin with; but, inasmuch as all was wrong, that very process which should have ripened them into sweetness has hastened them to rottenness. That same thing which in gracious souls has brought forth everything that is pure and lovely, has in others produced everything that is malicious and envious. I hope, however, that I may say of many here present, or that they can say of themselves, "It is good for me that I have been afflicted." The enquiry is,—How has it been good?

First, *it has been good in connection with many other good things.* It has acted as a counteractive with reference to the great blessings which God has bestowed upon us in other ways. We are so constituted that we cannot bear very much prosperity. Some men might have been rich, but God knew they could not bear it, and so he has never suffered them to be tempted above what they are able to bear. Others might have been famous, but they would have been ruined by pride, and so the Lord in tender mercy has withheld from them an opportunity of distinguishing themselves, denying them this apparent advantage for their real good. Where God favours any man with prosperity he will send a corresponding amount of affliction to go with it, and deprive it of its injurious tendencies. I have seen men walking upon the high places of the earth till their brain turned and they fell, and there was woe in the church of God. I have seen others whom God has placed on a lofty pinnacle; but at the same time he has almost crushed them between the upper and the nether millstone of sharp spiritual trouble, or domestic suffering, or physical pain. Many have asked, "Why is this?" and the reason has been that their suffering was a counterpoise to their success. God's servant would have slipped with his feet if it had not been for the secret chastenings that he endured. I put it to some of you whom God has greatly favoured. You have looked upon your prosperity as a boon, but you have wondered why you should be tried at the same time: it was because you could not have borne the favour if you had not received the chastening. You were glad of the sail, and glad of the wind that filled it; but you could not understand why the ballast was put into your hold; you thought it hindered your progress. My friend, you would have been blown out of the water if it had not been for the ballast which kept you where you ought to be. I, for my part, owe more, I think, to the anvil and to the hammer, to the fire and to the file, than to anything else. I bless the Lord for the correctives of his providence by which, if he has blessed me on the one hand with sweets, he has blessed me on the other hand with bitters. To me he has measured out a double blessing—the lamb, and the bitter herbs to eat with it; seldom the one without the other.

Thus "It is good for me to have been afflicted"—good as a corrective for other goods.

It is good, dear friends, to have been afflicted *as a cure for evils existent within our nature.* David says, "Before I was afflicted I went astray; but now I have kept thy word." That is the case with many of God's servants. They were prone to one peculiar temptation, and though they may not have seen it, the chastening hand of God was aimed at that special weakness of their character. We sometimes talk about phrenology, and the bumps on one's head; and *you* may make a great many mistakes over that matter, but God knows your tendencies and faculties. He knows the characteristics of his children accurately —far more accurately than any science can ever tell them, and he deals with extraordinary wisdom and prudence towards each one of his family. I suppose that, when the biographies of the saints are all read by the light of eternity, we, even we, shall be able to see why the painful career of certain Christians could not have been other than it was if they were to get to heaven at last: we shall see why that unusual trial was sent, and sent when they seemed least able to bear it. We shall discover that God interposed the screen of trial against the unseen fiery dart which only his eternal eye discovered, and laid the weight just where Satan was about to put the hand to overthrow, that very weight adding power to stand to the man who, in the lightness of his heart, had else been tripped up. It is all well, brother; it is all well. The surgery which is cutting so deep—the knife which is cutting to the very quick—is only reaching to the point where the mischief lies. That mischief must come out, root and branch. There is a cancer of evil tendency within us, and not a rootlet of it must be left; for, if the least fibre of it be suffered to remain through tenderness it will be an unkind tenderness; for the cancer will shoot again, and fill the heart with its malevolence. Therefore does the Lord out of love cut deep: sharp and cruel are his wounds. Most cruel do they seem when they are in greatest tenderness of grace. We do not know yet all the mischief that is in us. I would undertake in five minutes to make any perfect man prove to himself that he was not perfect. Only let me set certain persons upon him to tease him, and we shall soon see his irritation. Let the devil loose on a man who is hard by the threshold of heaven, and you will soon find that corruption dwells even in the hearts of the regenerate. The Lord would have us aware of this, and therefore he often sends trial to reveal the hidden evil. We are often like a glass of water which has been standing still for hours, and looks very clear and bright; but there is a sediment, and a little stir soon discovers it, and clouds the crystal; that sediment is the old nature. Trial comes and arouses into activity that which had been lying still, and we say, "Dear me, I had no idea that such evil was in my heart." Of course you had not. You who live so comfortably at home among Christian friends do not know how sinful you are; you hear of people out in the world doing this and that, and you say, "What naughty folks they are." They are no worse than you would be if you were put into the same position, only you are at ease and they are sorely tempted. Dogs sleep when no one enters the house; but a knock at the door will set them barking.

The Lord does not wish us to boast of sham holiness, and therefore he sends us trials that we may see the mischief which lurks in our hearts, and that we may be driven to the Holy Spirit for power to conquer our sin, and to the cleansing blood of Jesus Christ for the real taking away of guilt. He who has struggled with his inward sins must know that he has been helped both to discover and to overcome many of them by his afflictions; and so in this sense it is good that he has been afflicted. "Foolishness is bound in the heart of a child; but the rod of correction shall drive it far from him"; if this be so, we may not only bear the rod, but even kiss it.

Affliction is also useful to God's people *as an actual producer of good things in them.* Some virtues cannot be produced in us—at least, I do not see how they can be—apart from affliction. One of them is patience. If a man has no trial, how is he to be patient? We all think ourselves patient when we have nothing to bear. We can all stand on the mountain tops before we have tried those dizzy heights, and we are all brave when the war is over, though things look rather different when bullets whistle about our ears. When we are thrown into the sea our swimming abilities are not quite so extraordinary as we thought they were. We have great notions of what we can do; but trial is the test. Patience, I think, can scarcely be said to be in a man unless he has endured tribulation, "for tribulation worketh patience." A veteran warrior is the child of battles, and a patient Christian is the offspring of adversity.

There is a very sweet grace called sympathy, which is seldom found in persons who have had no trouble. We are told that our dear Lord and Master himself learned sympathy by being tempted in all points like as we are. He had to feel our infirmities, or else he could not have been touched with a fellow feeling towards us. It is surely so with us. I have stayed sometimes with an admirable brother who never had, he told me, an ache or a pain since he was born that he recollects; he is a man of fifty, and in splendid health. Well, he tries to sympathize with people, and he does do it to the utmost of his power, but it makes you smile. It is like an elephant picking up a pin. It is a wonderful feat for him to do. He does not understand it. You know yourself how hard it is to get sympathy out of those who have never endured a trial similar to your own. Someone goes to see a widow, and talks to her about her grief, and she says to herself all the time, "What does he know about it? He has never lost the partner of his life." A bachelor speaks to a dear soul who has just buried her little child. Unless he is a very wise man he is apt to say something about children which will irritate rather than console the bereaved mother. You may try your best, but you have not much of the faculty of sympathy unless you have been in the trial. It is by passing through the fire that we know how to deal with people who are in the furnace. So we may thank God that we have been afflicted, if we are ministers, or if we are teachers of others. We have sometimes to suffer, not for our own sake, but for the sake of others, that we may be enabled to speak a word in season to him that is weary, and say to such, "I know your road. I have been that way before. I know the darkness and weariness of the way." Pilgrims who are enduring the ills of the wilderness take heart when they see a fellow-traveller to whom all these are common things.

Again, it is good for me to have been afflicted because *affliction is a wonderful quickener.* We are very apt to go to sleep; but affliction often wakes us up. A coachman driving a pair of horses was noticed by one who sat upon the box-seat to give a cut of the whip to the off horse. The animal was going on quite regularly and properly, and it seemed a needless cruelty to whip it. Another journey, and he was observed to do just the same just at that place, and the question was put, "I always notice that you give that horse a cut of the whip just here,—why is it?" "Well, sir, he has a nasty habit of shying just at this spot," said the driver, "and I take his attention off by making him think of the whip for a moment." There is something in that, brethren. Every now and then you and I are apt to shy, and an affliction takes off our attention from temptation. There is also another danger in a life of ease : we are far too apt to go to sleep. Like horses, we are apt to get into the way of going on at a regular trot till we move mechanically and pursue our way half asleep. I do not know whether we are all awake even now. Many ministers preach asleep. I am sure they do. Many deacons do all the church business asleep ; and numbers of people come to the prayer-meetings and pray in their sleep. I do not mean physical sleep, but I mean spiritual sleep, which is quite as serious a matter. The whole of some men's religion is a kind of sleep-walking. There is not that vigour in it, there is not that heart in it, there is not that earnestness in it, that there ought to be. They want to be waked up by something startling. Our trials and afflictions are intended to do this. They come like a clap of thunder, and startle us till we ask, " Where am I? What am I at?" And we begin to question ourselves, "Am I really what I profess to be?" Death stares us in the face. We are put into the balance and weighed and tried; we try our hopes and professions, and are less likely to be self-deceived. Realities become realities, and fancies become fancies, when sharp trials befall us. The things of this world become dreams to us when keen affliction comes, and so it is of special benefit to us because, under the Spirit of God, it is awakening and arousing.

Again, according to our text, it is good for us to have been afflicted by way of *instruction*. "It is good for me to have been afflicted; that I might learn thy statutes." Trial is our school where God teaches us on the black-board. This school-house has no windows to let in the cheerful light. It is very dark, and so we cannot look out and get distracted by external objects; but God's grace shines like a candle within, and by that light we see what else we had never seen. I stand on the level of my fellow men in the daylight, and I cannot see the stars; the glare of day hides them; but if I am made to go down the deep well of affliction, I look up, and there are the stars visible above my head. I see what others cannot see. I get the Bible; and its promises seem written as men sometimes write with juice of lemon, in invisible characters; I hold the book before the fire of affliction, and the writing comes out clearly, and I see in the Bible what I never else had seen if it had not been for fiery trials. The word of promise must be precious, for God gave it; but I get into trial myself, and there I test it, and of its preciousness I become personally assured. We learn, I hope, something in the bright fields of joy; but I am more and more persuaded that we do not learn a tenth so much there as we do in the Valley of Death-shade. There the world loses its charms, and we are obliged to look away to God; there illusions and delusions pass away, and we are compelled to rest on the eternal Rock; there we learn the truth in such a way that we never forget or doubt it. I would to God that some young preachers were plagued all the day long, and chastened every morning, that they might become sound in the faith. I could wish that some of God's people were plunged into a sea of tribulation, that they might get rid of the modern nonsense which delights them now, and come back to the old, substantial doctrines of the Puritans, which are the only things worth having when we come to suffer or to die. Yes, it is good for me to have been afflicted. Is it not good for you too, dear friends, in the way of holy education, teaching you God's word, and the value and the preciousness of it?

II. I cannot, however, speak any longer upon the virtues of affliction; for I want two or three minutes to dwell upon the truth that, DRAWING NEAR TO GOD HAS BEEN GOOD FOR US. Turn to the seventy-third psalm at the last verse—" It is good for me to draw near to God."

Here, again, we speak with great certainty. Come, brothers and sisters, is it not good for you to draw near to God? But what does this drawing near to God mean?

First, to feel that God is near us—to be conscious of his presence; to feel, next, that we are perfectly reconciled to him by the death of his Son, and that we are permitted to speak with him as a man speaketh with his friend, and in speaking to him to praise him for what we have received, and to ask him for what we need. We draw near him when we tell him what we feel, and assure him of our belief in his great love. You know what it is to draw near to your friend and to have heart to heart converse with him. Then you and the beloved one are quite alone, and have no secrets. You tell all your own secrets, and you learn all that your beloved has to tell. This is drawing near to God—when the secret of your heart is with God, and the secret of the Lord is with you; when he speaks to you by the Word and you speak to him by prayer; when you confess sin and he grants forgiveness; when you spread your wants before him and he assures you of abundant supplies. Now, is not this good? Is it not pleasant? Is it not enriching? Does it not raise the soul up above the world? Is it not a very good and profitable thing, so that we may say of it emphatically, "It is good for me to draw near to God"?

One good thing that comes out of it is mentioned in the text. Observe: "I have put my trust in the Lord God." The nearer you get to God the more you will be able to trust him. An unknown God is an untrusted God. "They that know thy name will put their trust in thee." Those who have had most dealings with God believe most in him. You that begin with him try to trust him; but those who have dealt with him for long feel that they do trust him, and cannot help it. What is faith in God, brethren, but common-sense? though, like common-sense, it is the most unusual and most uncommon thing in all the world. To trust in one who must be true is a common-sense proceeding; and to trust my God who cannot lie is the dictate of true reason. To make him, who is the greatest fact and the greatest factor, to be in my life both the greatest factor and the greatest fact, and to act as believing him to be real, this is prudence. I pray you, draw near to God, so that faith may become to you the mainspring of your life, the new common-sense of your instructed spiritual nature. I rejoice in a faith that will go with me into everything. Sunday-keeping faith, meeting-going faith, if it ends there, is a pretty piece of confectionery; but faith about my pain, my poverty, my despondency, my old age—that is faith. I want to see a more hardy, practical, workable faith abroad in the land. Look at Abraham's faith. I know it was spiritual, and so do you; but what had it to do with? It had to do with the birth of a child, with seeking a city, with cattle, with land, and the events of every-day life. That is the sort of faith you and I want—Monday faith, and Tuesday faith, and Wednesday faith; faith that will go into the kitchen; faith that will live in the workshop with you that are bookfolders, when the other girls laugh at you; faith that will be with you men that are in the workshop where others use foul language; faith that can cheer a sailor in a storm; faith that can help a dying man in the hospital,—household faith, every-day faith. This is only to be got by drawing near to God. Get right close to him, in deed and in truth, the very life of you living upon the life of God, and then faith will enter into your daily life. You will put your trust in God as your constant helper if you constantly draw near to him.

I desire to bear my witness in the last words of this psalm —"I have put my trust in the Lord God, that I may declare all thy works." My first text, as far as it relates to a preacher, shows how he is taught in private : " It is good for me that I have been afflicted; that I might learn thy statutes " : my second text, so far as it relates to the preacher, shows how he is helped to preach in public,—" It is good for me to draw near to God : I have put my trust in the Lord God, that I may declare all thy works." To be able to speak of God's works to others is no small gift, and you gain it by trusting in God yourself, finding his promise true, and then bearing witness to others. Draw near to God, and have communion with him, and then come down from the mount and speak with the people, believing what you say, and expecting God to bless it to those who hear it. That is the way to preach; and I pray that every one of us who opens his mouth for God may do it in this fashion. It is not merely what is in the Bible that we have to set before the people, but what we ourselves have tasted and felt of the good word of truth experimentally ; declaring Jesus Christ in the power of his resurrection as we know it in our own hearts. We cannot do this except by intimate personal fellowship with God. You, dear friends, who are engaged in teaching, cannot learn the truth without some measure of affliction, and you cannot tell it out in the right spirit without a large measure of drawing near unto God. Then you can say, " This poor man cried, and the Lord heard him." You can say, " One thing I know, whereas I was blind, now I see." You can say, " I sought the Lord, and he helped me." There is a convincing power about such personal testimony. Then it is not only Christ's word that God blesses, but it is your word too. " Oh," say you, " dare you say that ? " Yes, Jesus himself said, " Neither pray I for these alone, but for them also that shall believe on me through *their* word." They themselves took the word from Christ just as they took the bread out of Christ's hands when he fed the multitude : it was Christ's word just as it was Christ's bread till they got it, but as when they had once received the bread it became Peter's bread, and John's bread, and James's bread, and they handed it out, and the people fed thereon ; so did the word become " their word " when they personally accepted it, and afterwards passed it to others. It was all Christ's, and yet it was theirs. And you must get the bread in your own hands; you must taste it yourself; you must break it yourself, or else you will not be likely to be blessed with living power amongst the sons of men. Now, let us join in thanking God, if he has afflicted us, and if he has drawn us near to himself; and let us go forth, not to ask for afflictions—that would be unwise—but to accept them hopefully when they come. Let us draw near to God to-night, and let us not go to our beds till we have seen the face of the Well-beloved. This shall be my vesper song :—

> " Sprinkled afresh with pardoning blood,
>   I lay me down to rest,
> As in the embraces of my God,
>   Or on my Saviour's breast."

PORTION OF SCRIPTURE READ BEFORE SERMON—Psalm lxxiii.

HYMNS FROM " OUR OWN HYMN BOOK "—46 (Vers. II.), 778, 745.

Metropolitan Tabernacle Pulpit.

FOUR CHOICE SENTENCES.

A Sermon

DELIVERED ON THURSDAY EVENING, FEBRUARY 3RD, 1881, BY

C. H. SPURGEON,

AT THE METROPOLITAN TABERNACLE, NEWINGTON.

MY discourse this evening will scarcely be a sermon—it will be expository rather of the life and experience of Jacob upon one point. In order to bring it out I shall want four texts, but lest you should let any one of them slip, I will give them to you one at a time.

I. First, turn to the twenty-eighth chapter of Genesis, at the fifteenth verse, and read of PRESENT BLESSING. The Lord said to his servant Jacob,—

"*Behold, I am with thee.*"

Jacob was the inheritor of a great blessing from his fathers, for this sentence was spoken in connection with the following words, " I am the Lord God of Abraham thy father, and the God of Isaac." It is an inexpressible privilege, dear friends, to be able to look back to father and grandfather, and perhaps farther still, and to say, " We come of a house which has served the Lord as far back as history can inform us." Descended from Christians, we have a greater honour than being descended from princes. There is no heraldry like the heraldry of the saints. Jacob might be very thankful that, as God had blessed Abraham and had blessed Isaac, so he blessed him in the same way, speaking to him in the same terms as he had spoken to them, for he had expressly said to each of them, " I am with thee." Are any of you the children of godly parents, and has the Lord called you by his grace? Then bless his name, and take heed that you do nothing to dishonour an estate so honourable. Try and maintain, as long as you live, the good repute which in infinite love God has put upon your household. Are you, however, a child of godly parents and not yet converted? I would warn you against putting the slightest reliance upon your birth ; for, remember, if Isaac was the child of Abraham, so also was Ishmael, but no blessing came to Ishmael of a spiritual kind. It is in vain to be born of blood, or of the will of the flesh ; we must be born again from above. God is a sovereign, he is not bound to dispense his favours from father to son: and when he does so, we are to admire his grace. Do not imagine that there is such a thing as hereditary piety ; it must be wrought in

245

each individual by the self-same Spirit. Still, it is one of the highest privileges that God has ever been pleased to grant to me that I can rejoice in a father and a grandfather who trained me in the fear of God; and I congratulate every young person who has such a pedigree. God bless you. Be not satisfied unless you yourself obtain such mercy as God gave to your ancestors, and hear the Lord saying, "I am with thee."

This mercy was brought home to Jacob at a time when he greatly needed it. He had just left his father's house, and he felt himself alone. He was coming into special trial, and then it was that he received a fuller understanding of the privilege which God had in store for him. Let me read the words to you,—"I am with thee." I have tried to think them out that I might speak concerning them to you; but they are too full. I defy anybody to measure their height and depth, their length and breadth. That God should give to Jacob bread to eat and raiment to put on was much, but it is nothing compared with "I am with thee." That God should send his angel with Jacob to protect him would have been much; but it is nothing compared with, "I am with thee." This includes countless blessings, but it is in itself a great deal more than all the blessings we can conceive of. There are many fruits that come of it, but the tree that yields them is better than the fruit. "I am with thee." Will God in very deed dwell with men upon the earth? Will God walk with a man, and speak with him? "Lord, what is man, that thou art mindful of him? and the son of man, that thou visitest him?" And yet he says, "I am with thee." Thou art in thy courts above, and thou makest heaven heaven by thy presence, and yet thou sayest, "I am with *thee*." What more couldst thou say to a seraph than this —"I am with thee"?

Why, when God is with a man there is a familiarity of condescension that is altogether unspeakable: *it ensures an infinite love.* "I am with thee." God will not dwell with those he hates. He putteth away the wicked of the earth like dross. He saith to them, "Depart, I never knew you"; but to each one of his people he saith, "I know thee by thy name; thou art mine. And, more than that, I am with thee." As a man delights to be with a friend, so are the delights of Christ with the sons of men, whom he has chosen and redeemed with blood.

"I am with thee,"—*it means practical help.* Whatever we undertake, God is with us in the undertaking; whatever we endure, God is with us in the enduring; whithersoever we wander, God is with us in our wandering. "If God be for us, who can be against us?" If God be with us, can we ever be exiled or banished? If God be with us, what can we not do? If God be with us, what can we not endure? Well said the apostle, as if answering that question, "I can do all things through Christ which strengtheneth me." "I am with thee." Come, brother or sister, if thou wouldst get the fulness of this privilege, believe that God is near thee now, near to thee as he that sits at thy side; nay, nearer; for he is so with thee as to be in thee. And dost thou know that his whole Godhead is with thee? "I am with *thee*:" as if there were not another, the whole Godhead is with *thee*. Thou hast not to cry aloud like Baal's priests, or cut thyself with knives, that thou mayest attract his eye; for he says, "I am with thee." Thy

sighs he hears; thy tears he puts into his bottle. "I am with thee."
And thou hast not his presence only, but *his sympathy:* he means, I am
feeling with thee, suffering with thee. If there be a load, I bear it
with thee; if there be work to do, I will work with thee. Ye are
workers together with God. Beloved, said I not rightly that I can
never open up all this to you? Roll it under your tongue as a sweet
morsel, and if it go down into your inward parts it shall not be bitter
there, but sweeter still. "I am with thee." Oh, the richness of this
special blessing!

How precious it must have seemed as it came to Jacob in that den
of a place, where he lay with the hedges for his curtains, the heavens
for his canopy, the earth for his bed, stones for his pillow, and God for
his companion. "I am with thee. To-morrow when thou shalt open
thine eyes thou wilt look back to the west and say, 'I have left my
father's house and my mother, Rebecca, behind me'; and the tears
will be in thy eyes; and thou wilt look to the east and say, 'I am
going to the house of my mother's kindred, and I know them not,
save that I have heard concerning uncle Laban that he is hard and
grasping; and I know not how he will receive me.'" But is not that
a precious thing to start upon a journey with—"I am with thee"—I,
the ever blessed? Though thy mother is not with thee, "I am
with thee." Is any young friend here who is leaving home? Are
you going away for the first time, and do you feel sad? Or are
you about to emigrate to a distant country, and does your heart feel
heavy? Do not go at all till you can get a hold of this, "I am
with thee." Say unto the Lord, "If thy Spirit go not with me,
carry me not up hence." Wait till he gives the answer, "My Spirit
shall go with thee, and I will give thee rest." This ought to be the
blessing of your opening life, "I am with thee." Is God with you
to-night? Can God be with you? Some come to service after having
quarrelled with their wives and families; God is not with them.
People who are following ill trades, and living ill lives, and rejecting
the gospel, God cannot be with them. "Can two walk together except
they be agreed?" If you are a believer in Christ, and the Spirit of God
has produced in you the true fruits of the Spirit, then you may say,
"He is with me;" but not else.

Now turn to the thirty-first chapter of Genesis, at the third verse,
and read these words,—

"I will be with thee."

We will call this FUTURE BLESSING. It is almost unnecessary to
take this second text; for if it is written, "I *am* with thee," you may
depend upon it that he *will be* with us, for God does not forsake his
people. Some people believe in a God who loves to-day and hates to-
morrow; who pardons sin and yet afterwards condemns. Such a God
is not my God; for mine is unchangeable.

> "Whom once he loves he never leaves,
> But loves them to the end."

"I am God; I change not: therefore ye sons of Jacob are not consumed."

Poor Jacob had been living with Laban, and had passed through many messes and troubles, and it was time that he should receive the word of blessing over again. We read that, "Jacob beheld the countenance of Laban, and, behold, it was not toward him as before." He had begun to take root in the wordling's portion, and was willing to stop away from the promised land, and build up a family among his worldly connections ; but the Lord practically said to him, "This is not your rest." Laban's sons begin to growl as they see how their brother-in-law's flocks have increased, and therefore the time has come for Jacob to go. Jacob does not like it, he never did like moving. Family connections, a host of children, and a mighty crowd of cattle, made a removal a great undertaking. Then the Lord said to him, "I will be with thee ;" as much as to say, "I will be more with thee in Canaan than I ever have been in this place, which is not the land of promise. I will give thee my special presence if thou wilt get away into the place of the separated life ; and walk with me as thy father Isaac did." It was very sweet many years ago to some of us to hear the Lord say, "I am with thee," and to know that it was true ; for "truly our fellowship was with the Father and with his Son, Jesus Christ ;" but it may at this hour be very opportune if the Lord should renew his promise to us by saying, "I will be with thee." You are commencing a new form of life, you are entering on new trials, you are undertaking new duties, and now comes in the new promise, "I will be with thee." If those upon whom you had a right to rely have turned against you, if those who were really indebted to you have become envious of you—" yet, nevertheless," saith God, "I will be with thee."

Jacob's journey was to be a very venturous one. He knew that Laban would not like it, and, probably, would pursue him ; but God says, "Go, and I will be with thee." He knew also that his brother Esau would be pretty sure to take vengeance upon him for the sorry trick he had played him ; and that touched his conscience, and he feared and trembled ; but God said, "I will be with thee." The plainest road in the world is wrong if God does not bid us take it ; and the roughest and most unpromising way will turn out to be safe and right if God commands our journey. Jonah thought it was all right to go to Tarshish ; but God was not with him, and he came back by a route which he never expected to follow. If you go your own road, I wish you may be fortunate enough to meet with as good a return conveyance as Jonah did, for you will certainly have to come back. But if the road be never so rough, if it be God's road, you shall run over it like a young roe ; God will make your feet like hinds' feet, and you shall tread upon your high places. "Thy shoes shall be iron and brass ; and as thy days, so shall thy strength be." Only, mind that you follow a road in which God can be with you ; for there are some ways in which God will never be found. He cannot walk in the ways of sin, or worldliness, or self-seeking : if we choose these we must go alone.

See, then, the promised mercy, and rejoice in it. Go forward, dear child of God, if the pillar of cloud is moving, without the slightest hesitancy, and let this be thy joy and comfort—" Certainly, I will be with thee. In all places whithersoever thou goest I will be with thee."

III. I want to go a step further, and come, in the third place, to

EXPERIENCED BLESSINGS. Let us look at Jacob's experience. Did Jacob find God to be with him? He had a long life and a tried one. He was a man that knew a great deal, and men that know a great deal are doubly likely to meet with great trouble. Cunning, wise, crafty, prudent, self-reliant people frequently flounder out of one slough into another. Above all things, I should dread being partner with a man that is over wise, for such men either make fools of themselves, or else they have to sleep with one eye open. Jacob's cunning was an injury to him in the long run. Abraham was simple as a child; he believed God, and never stooped to a trick: and therefore his life was a noble one. Jacob was a very wise person, the kind of gentleman to have made a financier, or the manager of a company. He was a rare man of business; in fact, he was the father of the Jews, and that is saying a great deal. Yet because of his sharpness he was often robbed, and through his cunning he was overreached; and he did not, after all, so much enjoy life, and was neither so rich nor so happy as his simple-minded grand-father, Abraham.

We will, however, hear what Jacob has to say about these two gracious words of God, " I am with thee," and " I will be with thee." Turn to the thirty-first chapter again, and read the fifth verse. Up to as far as the time that he was about to leave Laban, he says,—

" 𝕿𝖍𝖊 𝕲𝖔𝖉 of my father hath been with me."

I have read that testimony with great joy. I thought of Jacob thus—Well, you certainly were not eminent for grace while with Laban. You were plotting and scheming—you against Laban and Laban against you; and yet your witness is, " The God of my father hath been with me." This is all the more encouraging as coming from you. Jacob seems to say of his God: It was he that gave me my wife and my children; it was he that prospered me in the teeth of those who tried to rob me; the God of my father hath been with me notwithstanding all my shortcomings. I trust that some of you can bear the like witness. Though you have not been all that you could wish in the Christian life, yet you can say, " The God of my father has been with me."

Now, we will look at him a little further on, in the thirty-fifth chapter, and the third verse: there we shall find him saying—" Let us arise, and go up to Bethel; and I will make there an altar unto God, who answered me in the day of my distress, *and was with me in the way which I went.*"

As I have already said, he left Laban's house; and it was a very venturesome journey, but God was with him: Jacob tells us that so it was. Poor Jacob was full of fear when he heard that Esau was coming to meet him. You can see that by the way in which he divided his flocks and his herds, and set apart so large a present for Esau. But God does not leave his people because of their fears. I am so thankful for that. If he were to cast us off because of our unbelief, is there one of us who would not have been cast off long ago? There was Peter walking on the waters with a brave faith: was not Christ with him? Yes, or else he could not have stood on the wave at all. By-and-by his faith failed him, and down went Peter; but did Christ give him up and

say, " You shall die: according to your unbelief shall it be unto you"?
No, there is not such a word as that in the Bible ; but it is written,
" According to thy faith shall it be unto thee." Jesus stretched out his
hand and grasped sinking Peter, saying, "O thou of little faith, wherefore
didst thou doubt ?" So, though you may grieve the Lord by doubting
and fearing, and though you ought to be ashamed of yourself for so
doing, yet, still, he will not forsake you. If there is faith in your heart,
though it be but little, you shall have to say, despite your doubts and
fears, " The Lord was with me in the day of my distress, and was with
me in the way which I went."

There was a night of wrestling with Jacob. His faith enabled
him to draw near to God in mighty prayer, and his fear made him
the more desperate and importunate. He said, " I will not let thee go
except thou bless me." Though he had to be importunate, yet it was
not because God was against him, but because God was with him ; for
he that can exercise importunate prayer proves that God is with him
strengthening him thus to supplicate. His wrestlings ended in his
victory.

On that day, too, I have no doubt, Jacob was very much cast down,
because he remembered his sin. He knew he had ill-treated Esau, and
robbed him of the blessing ; but, for all that, he came with a repentant
heart to submit himself before his brother and to do what he could to .
please him. Because of this, God was with him. Oh, in that day, dear
child of God, when you remember your faults, and your heart is heavy,
do not think that the Lord has left you. It is one token that he is with
you that he makes you confess your sin, and humble yourself before
him. Still believe in him ; still hear his word ; and you shall have to
say, " He was with me in the way which I went."

At the close of his life we find Jacob more fully than ever confessing
that the presence of God had been with him. I read you the passage
where he wished that the God that had been with him might be with
his grandsons in the selfsame way—the forty-eighth chapter, at the
fifteenth and sixteenth verses. " He blessed Joseph, and said, God,
before whom my fathers Abraham and Isaac did walk, the God which
fed me all my life long unto this day, the Angel which redeemed me
from all evil, bless the lads." There is his last testimony to the faithfulness of God.

He had lost Rachel—oh, how it stung his heart; but he says, " God
redeemed me from all evil." There had come a great famine in the
land; but he says that God had fed him all his life long. He had lost
Joseph, and that had been a great sorrow ; but now, in looking back,
he sees that even then God was redeeming him from all evil. He said
once, " Joseph is not, and Simeon is not, and ye will take Benjamin
away ; all these things are against me;" but now he eats his words,
and says, " The Lord hath redeemed me from all evil." He now believes
that God had been always with him, had fed him always, and redeemed
him always, and blessed him always.

Now, mark you, if you trust in God, this shall be your verdict at the
close of life. When you come to die you shall look back upon a life
which has not been without its trials and its difficulties, but you shall
bless God for it all : and if there is any one thing in life for which you will

have to praise God more than for another, it will probably be that very event which seems darkest to you. Did God ever do a better thing for Jacob than when he took Joseph away and sent him to Egypt to preserve the whole family alive? It was the severest trial of the poor old man's career, and yet the brightest blessing after all. Can you not believe it? Inside that hard-shelled nut there is the sweetest kernel that you have tasted. Rest assured of that. Your father's rumbling waggons have woke you out of sleep, and you are frighted at them; but they are loaded with ingots of gold. You never have been so rich as you will be after your great trouble shall have passed away.

IV. It is time for me to conclude, and I do so by bringing before you, in the fourth place, one more word of blessing. We have had present blessing: we have had future blessing: we have had experienced blessing three times over: and now we go to TRANSMITTED BLESSING; for we find Jacob transmitting the blessing to his son and to his grandson. Read in the forty-eighth chapter, at the twenty-first verse,—

"Behold, I die: but God shall be with you."

I commenced by noticing the blessing which passed on from Abraham to Isaac: and now we see that Jacob hands it on to Joseph, to Manasseh, and to Ephraim,—"I die: but God shall be with you." Some of you perhaps are thinking, "We are getting near the end of life; we have children, but they are not all converted yet, and those that are, it may be, are dependent upon us: what will become of them?" Do you think God will leave your children? Cannot you trust them with him? What did your father do with his son? One after another the former generations have passed away, and the Lord has been faithful to their successors. Do you think he will not be faithful to those who come next? You have brought up your children in his fear; you have rested upon his name, and therefore you may say to them, "I die: but God shall be with you." The time will come when we who are ministers shall be taken away from our beloved work on earth, and we cannot help thinking about the dear friends who hang upon our lips and depend upon our ministry. It is well for us to look a little forward and say, "I die: but God shall be with you." My venerated predecessor, Dr. Rippon, many a time prayed for his successor. I am sure he did not know who his successor was to be, for I was born about the time when he was dying; but, doubtless, I inherit that good man's prayers. I am sure I do. "I die," the old man might have said, "but God shall be with you." The church at New Park-street thought it an awful thing for the old gentleman to die; but he would have been of no service to us if he had remained here for ever. And so it will be by-and-by. People say, "What will the Tabernacle people do if they lose their minister?" It will probably be the greatest of blessings when it happens. Many good men have clung to their places longer than they should have done, and have pulled down much that they had built up. It is well when the Lord says to such, "Friend, come up higher." We may look forward each one to leaving our class, or to leaving the church over which we watch, or to leaving the great work over which we preside and we may say, "I die: but God shall be with you." God is not limited to one minister or fifty ministers. When we are gone, God will be with you.

They used to say of our dear friend, George Müller, "What will become of the Orphanage when Mr. Müller is laid aside?" When I was speaking to him, he said to me, "That was a question which I felt George Müller had nothing to do with. God will use George Müller as long as he likes, and when he chooses to put him aside, he will use somebody else." And now, mark, George Müller is not at Bristol. I believe he is at this present moment preaching in America. He has been all over Europe preaching, and the Orphanage has had very little of his personal presence, and yet it has gone on without George Müller, so far. Such a fact tends to answer man's idle questions. Blessed be the everlasting God—if Abraham dies, there is Isaac; and if Isaac dies, there is Jacob; and if Jacob dies, there is Joseph; and if Joseph dies, Ephraim and Manasseh survive. The Lord shall never lack a champion to bear his standard high among the sons of men. Only let us pray God to raise up more faithful ministers. That ought to be our prayer day and night. We have plenty of a sort, but, oh, for more that will weigh out sixteen ounces to the pound of gospel in such a way that people will receive it. We have too much of fine language, too much of florid eloquence, and too little full and plain gospel preaching; but God will keep up the apostolical succession, never fear for that. When Stephen is dying, Paul is not far off. When Elijah is taken up, he leaves his mantle behind him. "I die: but God shall be with you." Take comfort, dear friends, and may his Spirit be with you, through Jesus Christ, his dear Son, whose name is "Emmanuel"—God with us.

PORTION OF SCRIPTURE READ BEFORE SERMON—Genesis xxviii.

HYMNS FROM "OUR OWN HYMN BOOK"—23 (Song III.); 681; 732.

Metropolitan Tabernacle Pulpit.

THE HISTORY OF SUNDRY FOOLS.

A Sermon

INTENDED FOR READING ON LORD'S-DAY, MARCH 1ST, 1885,

DELIVERED BY

C. H. SPURGEON,

AT THE METROPOLITAN TABERNACLE, NEWINGTON,

ON JULY 17TH, 1884.

"Fools because of their transgression, and because of their iniquities, are afflicted. Their soul abhorreth all manner of meat; and they draw near unto the gates of death. Then they cry unto the Lord in their trouble, and he saveth them out of their distresses. He sent his word, and healed them, and delivered them from their destructions."—Psalm cvii., 17—20.

THE psalm contains one picture in four panels. It illustrates a single experience in its main outlines, for in every case it is written, "Then they cry unto the Lord in their trouble, and he saveth them out of their distresses"; and yet each case is very different from any one of the others. We have variety and similarity. It is just so in the case of the people of God. Our fall, our sin, our call by grace, our prayer, the Lord's answer to that prayer by Jesus Christ—in all these, "as face answereth to face, so doth the heart of man to man." We are wonderfully much alike as children of the first Adam, and alike when we become children of the second Adam; and yet no two children of God are quite the same. In human families we meet with great diversity of features among those who are, nevertheless, the offspring of the same parents. In the great family of God the diversity of the features is very wonderful indeed. Look at the four pictures which are so much alike, and which indeed do but represent one, and yet you shall discover in them marked diversity. Learn you this double lesson—that unless your spot is the spot of God's children you are none of his : but also, do not expect to find that spot exactly the same in you as it is in others of his undoubted offspring. As on earth all flesh is not the same flesh, and as in the heavens all glories are not the same glory, for there is one glory of the sun, and another glory of the moon, and another glory of the stars ; so in the ordinary life of Christians here below there is one Spirit, but there are divers operations. Therefore do not judge yourself by any man's biography. Do not condemn yourself if, after reading John Bunyan's "Grace Abounding," you say, "I never went into these dark places." Be glad that you never did. After reading Madame Guyon, do not condemn yourself if you never heard her

Nos. 1824-5-6.

"Torrents," nor felt her ecstasies of divine life. Be sorry that you never have, and aspire after such things, but do not condemn yourself. Here are four pictures, and you may find your likeness in one of the four; but, be not so unwise as to condemn yourself if you are not seen in the other three. "I never went to sea," says one, "this cannot picture me." "I never traversed a Sahara," says another, "this cannot picture me." "I never was in prison in the dark," says a third, "this cannot picture me." But it is possible, dear friend, that you have been a fool, and therefore the sick fool may picture you. When you find yourself in one of the pictures, you may conclude that, as the four are but variations of the same subject, all the four in some degree belong to you. At any rate, if I cannot enter into heaven by twelve gates, I shall be perfectly satisfied to go in at one.

I am only going to bring out two out of the many thousands of things that lie packed away in the wonderful box of my text. There are two things,—*the miserable people*, and *the merciful Lord.*

I. THE MISERABLE PEOPLE, first. I am going to describe them, and my object in the description will be to show what some have been who, nevertheless, have been saved. These people are called fools. They abhorred all manner of meat. They drew near to the gates of death. But they were saved for all that, for they cried unto God in their trouble, and he delivered them out of their distresses. The inference will be that if I—if you—should happen to be just in the same condition as these people, yet we may have hope that God will save us.

To begin with, the first description of them is that *they were fools.* Now, I must not call you fools, but you have all of you liberty to call yourselves so. I find it forbidden in Scripture for any man to call his brother "fool," but I do not find him forbidden to call himself so. Look well to yourself, and see whether you are not a fool now :—at least, if God's grace has saved you, you are bound to own that you were once a FOOL in capital letters ; for every unrenewed and unregenerate man is a fool. We call those fools who have a great want of knowledge of things which it is necessary to know. Where other men find their way, they are lost. Where other men know what to do upon very simple matters, they are quite bewildered and cannot tell how to act. I remember when I did not know the way of salvation. I had heard it from my youth up, and heard it explained very simply, too; but I did not know it. Many must confess that, though now they understand what faith in Jesus is, yet they were very slow in catching the idea. It is an idea which a babe in grace can explain, but which wise men, classically instructed, do not receive. I may stand here, and beat my very heart out in trying to make plain how men are to believe and live, and yet out of my congregation not one will receive God's meaning into his heart unless God the Holy Ghost shall enlighten him ; for we are such fools that the simplest matters of heavenly truth are utterly unknown to us.

He, too, is a fool who, when he does know, does not make right use of his knowledge. He is a greater fool than the former one. He knows all about it, but yet he does not do it. He understands that the only way to be saved is to believe in Christ; but he does not believe. He knows that men must repent of sin if they would find mercy; but he does not repent of sin. He knows that life is uncertain, and yet he is risking his soul upon the chances of his continuing to live. He lives as if he had a lease of his life, and was absolutely certain that he could not die till he chose to be converted. Now this is to be a fool—to act contrary to your own knowledge and better judgment. How many fools there are of this kind!

We call him a fool who hurts himself without any profit—without any justifying cause. The man who flings his life away to save a nation, or even to rescue one solitary person from death, is a hero; but what is he who, for no motive whatever, will maim himself—will take away his own health—will take away his own life? Are there none such here? Look at the drunkard! Look at the man who is guilty of unclean living! Look at such as prefer this world to the world to come, and throw themselves away on trifles! O sirs, there be many men that have injured themselves so that their sin lies in their bones. Even now they feel the result of their transgressions. The moth is foolish that flies into the candle, and, having burnt itself, dashes again into the flame. We count the ox foolish that goes willingly to the shambles; but there are multitudes of men and women who take delight in sin; and, though every cup around them be poisoned, yet they drink at it as though it were nectar. Verily, sinners are fools!

We are great fools when we think that we can find pleasure in sin, or profit in rebellion. We are great fools when we displease our God,—when our best Friend, on whom our eternal future depends, is despised, neglected, and even rejected and hated by us. It is the extreme of folly when a man loses the good will of one who can help him,—when he rejects the love of a tender mother, and the counsel of a wise father. Some men seem resolved to make their enemies their friends, and their friends their enemies. They put darkness for light, and light for darkness. They go to find the living among the dead, and true helpers among those who pander to their sin. Such fools have you and I been. Peradventure, some here are such fools now.

I call that man a fool who throws away jewels that he may gather pebbles, who casts away gold and silver that he may gather up mire and dirt. And what do they do who fling away heaven and eternal life for the sake of a transient joy, a momentary gain? Are there not some men living in this world only to get what will one day turn into smoke? They know that this great world, and all the works of men that are therein, must be dissolved with fervent heat; and yet they labour to build a mansion for their immortal souls in this place, which is to be utterly burned up. And, meanwhile, thou, O Son of God, Immortal Love, art treated as though thou wert a mere fiction! And thou, great Father, fulness of eternal grace, their backs are turned on thee! And O, holiness, and virtue, and immortal blessedness, all of you are suffered to go by while men are hunting for gewgaws and gathering trinkets that shall so soon be taken from them. If haply as you sit here you confess, "I have been a fool; I know I have," then you may gather comfort from the fact that *fools were saved.* He that has gone to the utmost excess of unwisdom may yet hear the invitation of wisdom, and come and learn at Christ's feet all that is needful for eternal life.

The next thing about these people is rather worse : they were not only fools, but *sinners*. The text says that "fools, because of their transgression, and because of their iniquities, are afflicted." You see they had several sorts of sin—transgression and iniquities. They began with one transgression ; they went on to multiplied iniquities. There was first in their heart a transgression against God ; afterwards, there were found in their lives many in-equities, both towards God and towards man. Sin multiplies itself very rapidly. It grows from one to a countless multitude. We will not go into the details of the transgressions and iniquities that you may have committed ; but here is the point,—these people, who were fools, and full of transgression and iniquity, nevertheless cried to God in their trouble, and he delivered them out of their distresses. What form has your sin taken ? Think of it in your own heart. But, whatever form it has taken, God is able to forgive you. "All manner of sin and blasphemy shall be forgiven unto men." "The blood of Jesus Christ, his Son, cleanseth us from all sin." There is no sin which is unpardonable if men repent of it. The sin that is unpardonable is one of which no man ever thought of repenting, for it is a sin which is unto death, and when committed the man is spiritually dead, and never repents. If there be a sin upon you, however black and foul—if it be a horrible sin which I could not mention because it might crimson the cheek of modesty if I did but even hint at it—if you are covered with it, polluted with it beyond all imagination—yet, of the saints in heaven it can be said, "such were some of you, but ye are washed." You are not more astray than certain others, or if you are, so much the greater shall be the glory of God's grace in saving you. It is written of our Lord that he is able to "have compassion on the ignorant, and on them that are out of the way." O you out-of-the-way sinners, what a comfortable word that is for you! No sin shall destroy you if you will come to the sinner's Saviour. No excellence of your own shall save you if you reject that Saviour. Come in all your sin, though it reeks to heaven : though the stench of it be loathsome in your own nostrils, yet, come to Jesus, for "the blood of Jesus Christ, his Son, cleanseth us from all sin."

But we must go on with the picture. These people were not only fools and sinners, which are two bad things ; but they had a third mischief about them : *they were afflicted.* "Fools, because of their transgression, and because of their iniquities, are afflicted." Their affliction was evidently the result of their folly and their transgression. Do I address any who are in that case? I hardly like to say what may have happened to some here. They may be distressed in spirit, and unable to pursue their business with anything like cheerfulness. They may be subject to doleful forebodings and heavy glooms, and all the result of sin in years gone by. They have now got to the core of the apple of sin. It is wonderfully sweet till you get to the core, and then it is bitter, ay, more bitter than death itself.

Once these men were fools and sinners, and now they have to suffer for it. They are afflicted because of their transgression and their iniquities. Some suffer in body. Others suffer in estate : their property is all gone now. They have spent all. Riotously, foolishly, wickedly it has gone. They had money once ; they have none now. They had the means of livelihood and competence, but they have so sinned that they cannot be trusted now. They are waifs and strays on the great ocean, drifting about, nobody wanting them. How I long to say a word of comfort to those who are in that condition! If you repent, if you will arise and come to your Father, why should you not be delivered out of your distresses? Do you not see that God does deliver such as you are? Is not the case before you in the text? They were fools afflicted, they were sinners afflicted, beginning to feel, even on earth, a part of the result of their sin. They began to reap those sheaves of fire which they sowed with such merry-making years ago; and, as they put those sheaves into their bosom, they wondered how they could escape being immediately consumed. But they did escape, and so may you. God has saved such as you now are, and all those saved ones should encourage you to hope that he will save you.

The picture is getting black, but we must put on another coat of colour. In addition to this, these people *had fallen into a soul-sickness.* Through their trouble and their consciousness of sin, they had fallen into such a state of illness that nothing could help them. The best food was brought to them, but they waved it away: their soul abhorred all manner of meat. Some are in such a state that the amusements which once were joys to them are now wearisome. You have been lately to the theatre, and you used to be charmed there. You cannot make out what has come over it: it seems so dull to you. You used to enjoy cheerful evenings with your merry-making friends, but now you would sooner get upstairs alone, for you feel so wretched. When you are alone, there is one person who plagues you: if you could only get away from him, you would be content; but that person happens to be yourself, and there appears to be no rest for you either in company or in solitude. Your soul abhors all manner of meat. I have known souls to get into such a state that books, interesting and instructive, they could not read any longer. They felt no interest in anything of the sort; and poetry, and all the charms of art, which once they very properly enjoyed, could afford them no pleasure. The best mental recreation cannot give such persons any stay from their fierce, self-destroying thoughts. Ay, and they even refuse good spiritual meat. If the preacher tries to give them milk for babes, that is too weak for them: if he brings out strong meat, that is too tough for their teeth. If he brings them "wine on the lees, well-refined," that is too heating; if he offers the water of life, that is too cold. Nothing will suit them. They grumble at all kinds of teaching. Religious books do not cheer them; even the Bible itself seems stale and unprofitable. You are in a frightful condition, my friends, are you not? You are so sick that the meat which best would suit you is that which you least care for. Yet God has saved some who have fallen into this wretched way; and he invites you to come to him, and trust in him, with the promise that he will save even you, though you are as bad as you well can be.

But the case was worse than that, for we read, "They draw near unto the gates of death." This poor creature was *almost dead.* He could see death-gate and hell-gate right before him. He was lying at death's door, expecting every moment to be thrown through the portal into eternal destruction and endless wrath. I remember when I lay in the

bosom of despair in my own apprehension. I knew that I was condemned
on account of sin, and my conscience said "Amen" to the condemnation.
I could not plead any reason why I should not at once be taken out
to endless execution on account of my sin; and I certainly felt the
dread shadow of coming wrath falling upon my soul. AND YET I AM
SAVED, blessed be God! And so shall you, dear hearer, though you be
ready to die, and ready to be damned, be saved by faith in Jesus. Though
you begin to feel the fire-shower falling, and the first of the dread drops
have already burned their way into your soul, yet may you escape.
The Saviour comes to those who

> Buried in sorrow and in sin,
> At death's dark door do lie.

He brings "salvation" to such; and he says to the dying sinner,
"This day has salvation come unto thy house." What a glorious gospel
we have to preach to you miserable people!
But yet we have not quite touched up the picture with the last shade
of black. This man not only lay at death's door, full of trouble, full
of distress, but he was *surrounded by many destructions*. In the twentieth
verse we read, "and he delivered them from their destructions." What!
Are there many destructions to a man? Oh, yes, a great many! I have
known one man destroyed by his shop, another by his wife, another by
his children. Many a woman is destroyed by her clothes; many a man
is destroyed by his eating; millions are destroyed by their drinking.
Everything about us will destroy us unless God saves us. There are
a thousand gates to hell, though there is only one road to heaven.
One man may perish by debauchery; another may perish by respectability One man may be lost in the ale-house; another man may
be lost through his teetotalism, if he makes a god of it. One man
may go down to hell by his want of common decency, and another by
his pride, and prudery, and self-righteousness. Do not deceive yourself
—the way to ruin is easy, and many crowd it. If you want to go to
heaven, well, we shall have to tell you a great deal about what
is to be believed; but if you want to go to hell, I have no need
to tell you anything,—"How shall we escape if we neglect so great
salvation?" A little matter of neglect will land you in hell. But
it is not a little matter of thought that will bring you to heaven;
there must be a stirring up of the entire soul—an awakening of the
whole man to seek after God in Christ Jesus; or else you shall perish.
Surrounded, then, with destructions—snares about your bed, snares about
your table, snares in your solitude, snares in the street, snares in your
shop, snares at dawn of day, and snares at set of sun—you are in awful,
terrible danger; and yet persons surrounded with destructions have
been saved, and why should not you? They have cried to God in their
trouble, and he has delivered them out of their destructions; will he not
do the same at your cry? What a charming word is this for desponding
spirits!
II. I have but a minute or two left, where I should have wished for
an hour, to speak upon THE MERCIFUL LORD.
Very briefly indeed. This merciful Lord appears in this picture
where you do not at first see him. I think I see him in that first

verse: *he sent the affliction.* "Fools, because of their transgression, and because of their iniquities, are afflicted." Ah me! "Are afflicted." Who afflicted them, then? Why, their own Father—their own Shepherd, who saw that they would never come back to him if it were not for affliction. I see you, friend. You are a stray sheep, and I could not get you back. Now you cry, "Alas, I am in trouble!" I am sorry that you should be troubled, but I am not altogether sorry. I can see the black dog is worrying you. It is that he may get you back to the Shepherd. Many will not come back till the black dog has his teeth in their flesh; but if it surely drives you to the good Shepherd, it will be your true friend. I question whether many of us did come to the Lord Jesus Christ until we were afflicted in some way or other. Our bright days led us more and more into sin. Then came a dark day; and then we began to turn. "When he had spent all, there arose a mighty famine in that land." Blessed be God for the famine! "He began to be in want": now he will have to test his gay friends and flatterers. There was a gentleman who had drunk his champagne, and put his feet under his mahogany; and the prodigal said, "Now I have fed that man, I dare say he will entertain me now I am in poverty." "I cannot help you," he replied. "Can you give me some employment?" "No. What are you worth? Well, you can feed my pigs." And he "sent him into his fields to feed swine." That is the black dog again. If the gentleman had said, "Oh, yes, my dear young fellow, you were very generous when you had plenty of money, I am very sorry for you; come and live with me: while I have a crust you shall have part of it;" that would have been the worst thing that could have happened, for the prodigal son would never have thought of going home. I say that your troubles are mercies in disguise. Your sicknesses, your poverty, and your misery—oh, I bless God for them! The heavenly Father has sent this rumbling waggon to bring you home to himself. Oh that you would but come to yourself! Oh that you would but come to him! See, the grace of God appears in the very affliction of these rebellious fools.

But note this, further: *they began to pray;* and here we see the Lord again; for no one seeks after God till God has put the prayer into his heart, and breathed a new life into his spirit.

Then as soon as ever he did pray, *the Lord heard the prayer.* We read, "*He sent his word,* and healed them, and delivered them from their destructions." So, beloved, all that God has to do, in order to save us, is to send us his word. He has done that by sending his dear Son, who is the incarnate Word. He sends us the word in the shape of the Holy Scriptures; he sends us the word in the preaching of his servants; but what we want most of all is to have that word sent home by the power of the Holy Spirit. "He sent his word, and healed them." There is nothing that you want to-night but to have the word which the Lord has spoken sealed home to your heart, so that you accept it, and believe it. "Believe on the Lord Jesus Christ, and thou shalt be saved."

I want you to notice how the Lord rescued these people. You see, they could not eat. They had reached such a state of sickness that they could not take anything; they abhorred all manner of meat, and we do not find that the Lord sent them any meat. No, he sent his word. Did he send his word like a tonic, to give them an appetite? No, he made surer work. Many doctors try to deal with the disease, but God does not. He deals with the patient himself, and his constitution. *He healed them* radically. Then, when he had healed them their appetite came back. They did *not* abhor all manner of meat when once God had healed them. The Lord does not operate upon the symptoms, but upon the person; he does not deliver us from this sin and that sin and the other sin; but he takes away the old heart, out of which the sin comes, and gives a new heart, out of which there come repentance, and faith, and a change of life. If you have a lantern, and it is dark, you may polish the outside of it as long as ever you like, and no light will come out of it: the first thing to be done is to put a candle inside the lantern. This is what the Lord does; and then, when he puts the candle inside the lantern, we say to ourselves, "This lantern looks very dirty, it must be cleaned." Is it any fouler than it was before the light was put into it? It is the same lantern exactly, but, when you put the candle into it, you perceive how dirty it is by the light shining within. It is of no use to try to clean and polish it up till you have placed the lighted candle in it. You know how Mr. Moody puts it. A lady, we will say, takes a looking-glass, and she looks into it; and she sees a spot on her face. That is the use of the looking-glass—to reveal spots; but you never heard of a lady trying to wash her face with a looking-glass, for that is not its use. No, the looking-glass shows the spots, but it cannot take the spots away. First of all, by means of the law, we find out our spots, but we have to go to Jesus Christ, in the gospel, to get those spots taken away. Blessed are those who have gone to him!

"He sent his word, and healed them." With one word, the Lord Jesus at this hour can heal every sin-sick soul before me, for where the word of a King is, there is power. He spake, and the heavens were of old; let him but speak again, and there will be new heavens and a new earth to you. Poor sinner, you are dead, but all that Christ did when he raised the dead in his time was to speak to them; and his word by these lips, through his Spirit, can raise you out of your death in sin. If you are black as the very fiends of hell, and steeped up to the throat in every infamy that God abhors, yet if his word shall come to you, and you receive it into your soul, you shall be saved upon the spot, and delivered from your destructions. Here is a word of the Lord. Obey it, I entreat you. "Look unto me, and be ye saved, all the ends of the earth: for I am God, and there is none else." Here is another; hearken to it, and live:— "Ho, every one that thirsteth, come ye to the waters, and he that hath no money; come ye, buy, and eat; yea, come, buy wine and milk without money and without price." Let all that labour and are heavy-laden come unto Christ, and he will give them rest. The Lord grant that you may come at once, without delay, and to his name shall be the praise. Amen and Amen.

PORTION OF SCRIPTURE READ BEFORE SERMON—Psalm cvii.

HYMNS FROM "OUR OWN HYMN BOOK"—30, 505, 597.

Metropolitan Tabernacle Pulpit.

AN INSCRIPTION FOR THE MAUSOLEUM OF THE SAINTS.

A Sermon

INTENDED FOR READING ON LORD'S-DAY, MARCH 1ST, 1885,

DELIVERED BY

C. H. SPURGEON,

AT THE METROPOLITAN TABERNACLE, NEWINGTON,

ON MAY 8TH, 1884.

"These all died in faith, not having received the promises, but having seen them afar off, and were persuaded of them, and embraced them, and confessed that they were strangers and pilgrims on the earth. For they that say such things declare plainly that they seek a country."—Hebrews xi. 13, 14.

"THESE all died in faith." Believers constitute a class by themselves,— "*These.*" They are the people that dwell alone, and shall not be numbered among the nations. We see a great many distinctions in the world which God takes no notice of : there is neither Jew nor Gentile, bond nor free, in his sight. But there is a distinction which men think little of, which is greatly observed of God ; and that is the distinction between them that believe and those that believe not. Faith puts you across the border most effectually, for it brings you out of darkness into marvellous light, from death to life, and from the dominion of Satan into the kingdom of God's dear Son. It is the most important thing under heaven that we should know that we believe in God. The Holy Spirit puts believers by themselves, and speaks of them as " *These.*"

Believers are a class by themselves, even when they die. It is idle to think that we can mark out a spot in the cemetery where none but saints shall sleep ; but yet there is a truth at the bottom of that folly. There is a separation even in death between the righteous and the wicked. The Lord seems to erect a mausoleum in which lie asleep the bodies of his people, and he writes this epitaph across the front, "THESE ALL DIED IN FAITH." As for those who died without faith, they died indeed ; but, as for his people, a glorious resurrection awaits them.

> " They sleep in Jesus, and are blest,
> How kind their slumbers are."

The characteristics of God's people are peculiar to themselves. They are all alike in this, they all lived and all died in faith. They were not all equally believers, for some were strong in faith, and others were

261

weak ; but yet they all had faith, and it continued in them even to the
end ; so that, without exception,—" these all died in faith."

We will speak, firstly, of *dying in faith;* secondly, of *the faith according to which they died;* thirdly, of *living by faith,* for that is mentioned
in the text, " They confessed that they were strangers and pilgrims on
the earth" ; and then, fourthly, of *the faith by which they lived,*—" For
they that say such things declare plainly that they seek a country."

I.   First, then, here is DYING IN FAITH.   What does it mean ?

Does it not mean that, *when they came to die, they had not faith to
seek,* but having had faith in life, they had faith in death ?   I will
pronounce no opinion upon death-bed repentance.   I have heard
judgments far too sanguine, I have heard verdicts far too severe.
Where we know little, we had better say little ;.but this much I may
say : I would not like to lie upon a sick-bed, much less upon a dying-
bed, and have a Saviour to seek there.   The pains and dying strife are
usually enough to occupy a man's thoughts.   It frequently happens that
the brain is disordered, by disease, and he that was clear of judgment
before is then scarcely able to think.   You must yourself have often
seen men departing out of this life to whom it was useless to speak.   If
conscious at all, they were barely conscious.   Have I not pressed the
hand, and received no token of recognition from a familiar friend?
Have I not spoken into the ear, and yet there has been neither hearing
nor answering ?   Sometimes friends have said, " He seems to know
you, Sir, though he knows nobody else " ; and certainly there has been
a lifting of the eyelid, and a movement of the hand, which made me
feel that my voice had penetrated into those dark recesses into which
the mind had retired.   But what could I say of deep mysteries, or even
of simple faith, when the person has been in such a case ?   It has
been a great joy to feel that we could sing in many instances,

          " 'Tis done, the great transaction's done,"

for there was little hope that it could have been done at that hour.
Dear friends, if any of you are delaying, permit me to warn you not to
do so !   How can it be said of you that you die in faith, if it cannot be said of you that you are living in faith ?   Not long ago, a
friend of mine, who was apparently in robust health, fell dead in the busy
streets of the city ; another came up to our religious meetings, and on
his return died in the waiting-room of the railway-station.   Suppose
that this had happened to any of you.   It might have done so !   Where
would you now have been ?   I bless the name of the Lord that you
are spared, for else you would have been where no voice of warning or of
invitation could have reached you, but where darkness, death, and
despair would have enveloped you for ever.

The saints mentioned in the text had not faith to seek.   They had it
when they came to die.

They did die, however, although they had faith, for faith is not given
to us that we should escape death, but that we may die in faith.   I have
met with one or two friends who have believed that they would never
die, but they have died for all that.   One brother has often favoured
me with a kind letter of protest when I have spoken about believers
dying, for he affirms that he shall never die, and that if a believer does

die it is his own fault, for he must have fallen into sin. It is rather awkward for his theory that all these saints "died in faith." We believe that hundreds, and thousands, and millions of true and strong believers have died; and we expect to follow through the same dark stream of death, unless the Lord shall come.

This proves that God will not in every case hear our prayers for restoration to health. It is not true that if we gather together and pray for a sick man he will always be restored. No believer would die if that were the case, for every Christian man would find some friends in Christ to pray for his recovery. If, therefore, God had thus divested himself of his omnipotence, and put it upon us, we should keep our dear friends here as long as Methuselah, and no one would die. It would be a kind of semi-murder to allow our brother or sister to depart: it would be destroying life by omission to pray, and that would be murder in a degree I thank God that he has not endowed us with any such power, for it would be a very dangerous privilege for any of us to carry about us. Would you have it said that you were the means of the death of your child, or wife, or friend, because you did not pray sufficiently for them? Is a kind of constructive murder to be laid at every man's door when he loses a friend? Is every woman whose child is taken away from her to be charged with want of faith because her child died? This would make her guilty of her child's death. It is atrocious: it is a piece of fanaticism that will not bear thinking of, for, pushed to its legitimate issue, it would be cruel in the extreme, for it would condemn men and women who are perfectly innocent, and who feel that they would have spared the lives of the departed by losing their own, had such a thing been possible.

"These all died in faith." Saints die as well as sinners. David dies as well as Saul. He that leaned on the bosom of Jesus lived long, but died at last—died as surely as Judas did, though in a better style. "It is appointed unto men once to die." Two have entered into glory by another way, but only two. There shall come a day when we that are alive and remain shall not see death; but that day is not yet.

"These all died in faith." I suppose that it means, again, that *these all persevered to the end.* I have often been told that you may be a child of God one day and a child of the devil the next. I do not know upon what Scripture that statement is based. I do not believe a word of it, "He that believeth and is baptized shall be saved." But suppose he apostatizes? You have no business to suppose what God has promised shall not be; for he has promised, "I will put my fear in their hearts, that they shall not depart from me." If a man truly believes, he shall be saved. "The righteous shall hold on his way, and he that hath clean hands shall be stronger and stronger." It has been said that we assert that if a man is once a believer, he may live as he likes, and yet he will never be lost. We never asserted any such thing. It is a caricature of the doctrine that we preach. We believe that God has given to his people eternal life; and that must be true, for he has said, "I give unto my sheep eternal life, and they shall never perish; neither shall any pluck them out of my hand." This means that they shall be kept from sin, and especially shall be preserved from the sin which is unto death. Though they sin through infirmity, they shall not sin fatally,

nor sin finally, but they shall persevere in holiness, and in the love of
God. If they wander they shall be restored. They shall be kept by
the power of God, through faith, unto salvation. The seed which God
puts into the believing soul is a "living and incorruptible seed, which
liveth and abideth for ever." "The water that I shall give him," said
Christ to the woman of Samaria, "shall be in him a well of water,
springing up into everlasting life." He gives no transient salvation, but
he gives one which will hold the believer's soul from the first even to the
last. "These all died in faith": in every one of these instances grace
lived to the last, and triumphed at the close.

Does it not mean, also, that *they never got beyond faith?* These good
people—Abel, Noah, Enoch, Abraham, Isaac, Sarah,—did they never get
beyond faith? We have heard of some who think they have done so.
Having begun in the Spirit, they are afterwards made perfect by the flesh.
First it is the sinner's simple trust; but they get beyond that, and reach
"the second blessing." I wish that they would get beyond that also,
and reach the third blessing, and then they would feel more deeply than
ever the deep depravity of the old nature, and cling still more closely to
Christ. To go on from a second to a third, and a fourth, and a fifth,
and a sixth, and a seventh, and an eighth, and a ninth, and a tenth
blessing, is the thing for a child of God to do ; but to get into a state
of pride, and cry that he has got a second blessing, is a poor way of
growing. There are ten thousand times ten thousand blessings after
which believers are constantly to reach ; but, reach what they may,
"the just shall live by faith " ; he shall never get beyond trusting in
the faithful promise of a gracious God, living out of himself upon
Christ, who must be our all in all. "These all died in faith," the very
best of them. They never got beyond that. How could they? Those
who get above faith are like the man who went up so high on the ladder
that he came down on the other side. They get to be so good that they
trust in themselves instead of resting in him who is the Lord our
Righteousness. The Lord save us from self-conceit !

But then, while they did not get beyond faith, *the mercy is that they
never got below it.* They still had faith. They were sometimes troubled
with suspicions of themselves, and doubts as to whether the Lord had
really wrought a work in their souls ; but they never quite gave up faith.
They had many pains in death, but they did not die in despair. Some
of you cry, "What shall I do when I come to die ?" I will tell you a
more important question, and that is, What will you do now? Take life
and death just as they come, bit by bit. You know how the Spartans
endeavoured to keep back the Persians. They took possession of the
pass of Thermopylæ, and there the brave two hundred stood, and held
the way against myriads. The enemy could only advance one by one.
Now, do not think of all the armies of your troubles that are coming
in the future, but meet them one by one. "Sufficient unto the day is
the evil thereof." Pray—"Give us this day our daily bread." When
you come to die, you shall have dying grace in dying moments ; and if
you have lived in faith do not doubt that you will die in faith. Joyfully,
with all the strength I have, my quivering lips shall sing, instead of
doubting or groaning. Faith shall grow stronger when it is about to be
changed to full fruition. Go on, dear child of God. Though the road

AN INSCRIPTION FOR THE MAUSOLEUM OF THE SAINTS.   265

be dark before you, you can see the next step, and that is all you need
to see, for you cannot take two steps at a time. When you reach the
next step, you will see the next; and so on to the end. He that has
helped you up till now will help you even to the end ; and when you are
laid in the grave, it shall be said of you, as of all believers that went
before you, " these all died in faith."

Thus much upon dying in faith.

II. Now, what was THE FAITH THAT THEY DIED WITH ?

Turn to the text, and you get it. "Not having received the promises."
They had received a great deal, but *they had not received the fulness of
the promises.* Abraham had not beheld his seed so many as the sands
upon the sea-shore. Neither Isaac nor Jacob had ever seen the Shiloh,
in whom all the nations of the earth are blest. No, they had not received
the promises. And you and I have not received all the promises. We
have received a great deal, but there are certain promises which we have
not received yet. The coming, the glorious coming, which is the brightest
hope of the church, when the Lord " shall descend from heaven with a
shout, with the voice of the archangel, and with the trump of God "—
we have not received that as yet.   And heaven itself, with all its
splendour, its white robes and palms of victory, we have not yet received.
We are looking for these. We do not die in the fruition of these. We
die in faith, expecting that we shall enter upon the fulfilment of these
promises.

But, while they did not receive the promises, notice what they did.
They saw them,—saw them afar off. Faith touched their eyes with eye-
salve ; so that Abraham could see his seed in Egypt,—his seed coming
out of the land of Zoan. He could see the people travelling through the
wilderness. He could see them entering upon Canaan, and taking
possession of the land. Yea, our Lord said, "Abraham saw my day."
He saw the babe in Bethlehem. He saw the Son of God, who was the
Son of man, the son of Abraham, too. And you and I, if we have
faith of the kind we ought to have, see already the coming of the
kingdom, the gathering together of the saints, the glory of the better
land, "the general assembly and church of the firstborn, whose names
are written in heaven." By faith we see it. Our faith has such a
realizing power that it is as if we beheld it all. It is better to see it
thus than with the bodily eye, for if we looked upon it carnally we
should begin to doubt our eyes ; but faith is the opposite of doubt, the
evidence of things not seen.

They did more than that. We read that they "*were persuaded of
them.*" "What is your persuasion ? " said one to a Christian man. He
answered, " Well, this is my persuasion : I am persuaded that neither
things present nor things to come shall ever separate us from the love of
God which is in Christ Jesus our Lord." He was persuaded of the
truth of that promise ; and so is every believer when he is in a right
state. He is of that blessed persuasion : he is quite sure about the
promises of God. "Airy nothings," mutters one. " Mere fictions," cries
another. "Absolute certainties," says the saint. He has been persuaded
by an inward persuasion which others know nothing of. The Spirit of
the living God has given him a faith which amounts to full assurance,
and he will not permit a question, or tolerate a suspicion.

It is more than that: *the saints "embraced" the promises.* The Greek word signifies "salutes," as when we see a friend at a distance. In the clear atmosphere of Mentone, I have sometimes stood on quite a lofty mountain, and seen a friend down in the valley, and I have spoken his name; and at first it was greatly to my astonishment when he replied, "Where are you?" I held a conversation with him readily. I could not have actually reached him for a long time, but I saluted him from afar. At times, dear friends, we can see God's promises afar off, and we salute them. We are within hail of the glory-land, and we send up rockets in the dark; or, if it be daylight, we signal to the shore. Do you never do that? Do you never salute the mercies that are to come? Do you never talk to the glory that is to be revealed, ay, and commune with the glorified? This is the faith to live with, and to die with, the faith that sees, and is persuaded, and salutes the promised blessings of a faithful God. The Lord grant us more of that faith from this time forth!

III. Now, with extreme brevity, I want to speak upon THE FAITH TO LIVE WITH—the life of faith.

How do we live if we live by faith? The answer is, they "confessed that they were strangers and pilgrims on the earth." So we are.

We are *strangers by nature.* Born from above, our life differs from those about us. "The world knoweth us not." We do not belong to this world at all. We are in it, but not of it.

We are strangers as to citizenship. Here we are aliens and foreigners, whose privileges are connected with another city, and not with earth.

We are *strangers as to pursuits.* We are wayfaring men hurrying through this Vanity Fair. The men of the fair cry, "Buy! Buy!" but they have no wares that we care to purchase. We buy the truth, and they do not trade in that commodity. We have nothing to do with the business of the fair, but to get through it as quickly as ever we can. Certain things every traveller has to do when he stops in a town: he must seek his inn, and he must take due refreshment; but if he is travelling home from a far country he moves along as fast as he can.

We are *pilgrims in object.* We have not come hither for a pleasure excursion; we are journeying to the temple to behold the face of our Lord. Our faces are set towards Jerusalem, and we are asking the way thither. Our cry is, "Onward! Hinder me not. I must away to the glory-land, where my home is, where my God is!"

We are *pilgrims as to continuance.* We do not expect to be here long. Do any of you? Ah, then you are under a great mistake. We shall soon be gone. Each time we bid each other "good night" we may do it with the suspicion that we shall not all meet again. There never was the same congregation here twice, and there never will be. Almost every week two members of this church depart for the upland country, and leave us in these lowlands. Of late our death-rate has largely increased, and the conscription for the armies of heaven has fallen heavily upon us. How quickly are we gone! Say to yourself, then, next time you are fretting about worldly trouble, "I will not fret about it. It will not last long." Next time you are tempted to rejoice in earthly treasure, say to yourself, "No, I shall not rejoice in this. It is only a shadow. I will rejoice in something more enduring."

Do not wonder if you are found to be *strangers as to usage*, for the world uses foreigners roughly; and they that are really of Christ must expect to be misunderstood and misrepresented. They burned many pilgrims in former days; they cannot do it now; but there are trials of cruel mockings still, and the seed of the serpent still hates the seed of the woman.

This, then, is the way of believers, they live in this world as strangers and foreigners, who are hasting as fast as they can towards their own country, where they shall hear their own language spoken, and shall abide with their own Father for ever. This is the life of faith.

IV. And what is THE FAITH BY WHICH WE ARE ABLE TO ENDURE SUCH A LIFE AS THIS? Why, it is this faith: "They that say such things declare plainly that they seek a country."

Our faith is one which we dare to avow. We declare plainly that we seek a country. We are not ashamed to say that this is not our rest, that we do not expect to find pleasure here. We are speeding over this stormy sea to the Fair Havens, where we shall cast anchor for ever. We are not ashamed to say this, however others may ridicule our hope.

And we say it because we believe it. In that day in which Christ washed away our sins he gave us the token that we should be with him where he is, for this is the mark of the blessed—"They have washed their robes, and made them white in the blood of the Lamb." That day in which we gave ourselves up to Christ, to be his for ever, he gave us a certificate that we should be with him in the glory, for this is his prayer, "Father, I will that they also whom thou hast given me be with me where I am, that they may behold my glory." I trust, beloved, no doubt ever crosses your mind as to the fact that every believer in Christ will certainly be in the glory with Christ for ever and ever. But if you so believe, I pray you to believe it strongly, so that you realize it; and if you do, you will sometimes sit yourself down and laugh; and if a neighbour asks you, "Wherefore do you laugh?" you will say, "I laugh with very delirium of delight to think that this poor aching brow shall one day wear a crown—that I shall exchange these dusty garments for the snow-white robes of perfection—that I, whose voice on earth is so poor and cracked, shall one day sing with seraphim and cherubim." Oh, what joy to the invalid to know that he shall leave his bed on which he has suffered so much, and go where the inhabitant shall no more say, " I am sick." There the poor man shall no longer fight with poverty, and earn his daily bread with toil, for the Lamb that is in the midst of the throne shall feed them, and none shall know a want.

How glad I am that this shall be in so short a time! Some here present may be in heaven before this year is out; ah, perhaps he who speaks to you now may have gone very soon away to his own country! Shall it cost us any regret? It does for others; for we would fain remain to do them good; but for ourselves the contemplation is one of unmingled delight. The change has no loss about it: it is unspeakable gain. We lose nothing by departing to be with Christ, for it is not only better, but, as Paul puts it, it is "far better."

So now let us refresh ourselves with the thoughts of what we have, and forget what we have lost. Let us just think of what is laid up for us, and forget the penury of our estate below. Come; let us revel in the prospect of our ultimate perfection, and thus gather strength wherewith to struggle with our present corruption. Come, let us now rejoice, and ring the joy-bells at the prospect of beholding the Well-Beloved's face without a mist or a veil between; and so let us be content awhile to pass through the darkness, even though we see no light. We will meet; we will meet; we will meet in the glory-land. A dear sister the other day wanted to have a long talk with me, and I did not want she should, for I had twenty more waiting, and she said, "Well, dear pastor, I will have a long talk with you when we both get to heaven." And I said, "Ah, that I will, and I will find you out if I can, or you will find me out; and we will converse without hurry." When we begin to speak up there, she will say to me, "How sweet is your voice!" And I shall look at her, and answer, "How beautiful you have become!" We shall be amazed at one another in the perfect country. "It doth not yet appear what we shall be: but we know that, when *he* shall appear, we shall be like *him*, for we shall see him as he is." My dear aged friend will forget all her rheumatism; and so shall I. You may be bent half double while you are here below, but you will be straight enough up there. Those dim eyes need glasses, but you will want no spectacles before the throne. Limping, and lame, and halt, you are at this hour; but up there you will be able to join with all the happy ones in that music and dancing which shall celebrate the triumph of Christ. Arise, then, and be glad! Lift up your eyes from the dust and the darkness, and gaze upon the light eternal! The gate of heaven is open! If we may not enter yet, we shall enter before it shuts: let us rest assured of that. The day dawns, and until its full light has come let us rejoice in the anticipation of it. Until the day break, and the shadows flee away, let us cry, "Turn, O our Beloved, and abide with us." He will not deny us our fond request.

The Lord bless you, for Christ's sake. Amen.

PORTION OF SCRIPTURE READ BEFORE SERMON—Hebrews xi.

HYMNS FROM "OUR OWN HYMN BOOK"—620, 533, 813.

THE HORNS OF THE ALTAR.

A Sermon

DELIVERED BY

C. H. SPURGEON,

AT THE METROPOLITAN TABERNACLE, NEWINGTON,

ON MARCH 23RD, 1884.

"And he said, Nay; but I will die here."—1 Kings ii. 30.

WE must tell you the story. Solomon was to be the king after David, but his elder brother, Adonijah, was preferred by Joab, the captain of the host, and by Abiathar, the priest; and, therefore, they got together, and tried to steal a march upon dying David, and set up Adonijah. They utterly failed in this; and when Solomon came to the throne Adonijah was afraid for his life, and fled to the horns of the altar at the tabernacle for shelter. Solomon permitted him to find sanctuary there, and forgave him his offence, and said that if he proved himself a worthy man he should live without further molestation. But very soon he began plotting again, and sought to undermine Solomon now that their venerable father was dead. It became therefore necessary, especially according to oriental ideas, for Solomon to strike a heavy blow; and he determined to begin with Joab—the bottom of all the mischief, who, though he had not followed after Absalom in David's time, was now following after Adonijah. No sooner had the king determined upon this, than Joab, conscience-stricken, began to look to himself and fly. Read the twenty-eighth verse. "Then tidings came to Joab: for Joab had turned after Adonijah, though he turned not after Absalom. And Joab fled unto the tabernacle of the Lord, and caught hold on the horns of the altar." I suppose that he thought that, as Adonijah had done this successfully before, Joab might repeat it, and have some hope of his life. Of course, he had no right to enter into the holy place, and lay hold upon the horns of the altar; but being driven to desperation, he knew not what else to do. He was a man of hoary head, who had thirty or more years before committed two atrocious murders, and now they came home to him. He did not know where to fly except he fled to the horns of an altar, which he had very seldom approached before. As far as we can judge, he had shown little respect to religion during his lifetime. He was a rough man of war, and cared little enough about God, or the tabernacle, or the priests, or the altar; but when he was in danger, he fled to that which he had avoided, and sought to make a refuge of that which he had neglected. He was not the only man that had done the

269

same. Perhaps there are some here who before long will be trying to escape from impending woe by like means.

Now, I want you to notice that when Joab fled to the tabernacle of the Lord, and took hold of the horns of the altar, *it was of no use to him.* "And it was told king Solomon that Joab was fled unto the tabernacle of the Lord ; and, behold, he is by the altar. Then Solomon sent Benaiah the son of Jehoiada, saying, Go, fall upon him. And Benaiah came to the tabernacle of the Lord, and said unto him, Thus saith the king, Come forth. And he said, Nay ; but I will die here. And Benaiah brought the king word again, saying, Thus said Joab, and thus he answered me. And the king said unto him, Do as he hath said, and fall upon him, and bury him ; that thou mayest take away the innocent blood, which Joab shed, from me, and from the house of my father. And the Lord shall return his blood upon his own head, who fell upon two men, more righteous and better than he, and slew them with the sword, my father David not knowing thereof, to wit, Abner the son of Ner, captain of the host of Israel, and Amasa, the son of Jether, captain of the host of Judah. Their blood shall therefore return upon the head of Joab. So Benaiah the son of Jehoiada went up, and fell upon him, and slew him : and he was buried in his own house in the wilderness."

I have two lessons which I am anxious to teach at this time. The first is derived from the fact that Joab found no benefit of sanctuary even though he laid hold upon the horns of the altar of God's house, from which I gather this lesson—that *outward ordinances will avail nothing.* Before the living God, who is greater and wiser than Solomon, it will be of no avail to any man to lay hold upon the horns of the altar. But, secondly, there is an altar—a spiritual altar—whereof if a man do but lay hold upon the horns, and say, " Nay; but I will die here," he shall never die ; but he shall be safe against the sword of justice for ever ; for *the Lord has appointed an altar in the person of his own dear Son, Jesus Christ, where there shall be shelter for the very vilest of sinners if they do but come and lay hold thereon.*

I. To begin, then, first, OUTWARD ORDINANCES AVAIL NOT. The laying hold upon the literal horns of an altar, which can be handled, availed not Joab. There are many—oh, how many still!—that are hoping to be saved, because they lay hold, as they think, upon the horns of the altar *by sacraments.* Men of unhallowed life, nevertheless, come to the sacramental table, looking for a blessing. Do they not know that they pollute it ? Do they not know that they are committing a high sin, and a great misdemeanour against God, by coming amongst his people, where they have no right to be ? And yet they think that by committing this atrocity they are securing to themselves safety. How common it is to find in this city, when an irreligious man is dying, that some one will say, " Oh, he is all right ; for a clergyman has been, and given him the sacrament." I often marvel how men calling themselves the servants of God can dare thus to profane the ordinance of the Lord. Did he ever intend the blessed memorial of the Lord's supper to be a kind of superstitious *viaticum,* a something upon which ungodly men may depend in their last hour, as if it could put away sin ? I do not one half so much blame the poor ignorant and superstitious persons who seek after the sacrament in their dying hours, as I do the men who ought to know better, but who pander to what is as downright a superstition as anything that ever came from the Church of Rome, or, for the matter of that, from the fetish worship of the most deluded African tribe. Do they conceive that grace comes to men by bits of bread and drops of wine? These things are meant to put us in memory of the Lord Jesus Christ, and, as far as they do that, and quicken our thoughts of him, they are useful to us; but there is no wizardry or witchcraft linked with these two emblems, so that they convey a form of grace. If you do rely upon such things, I can only say that this error is all of a piece: it is a superstition which begins with, " In my baptism, wherein I was made a member of Christ, a child of God, and an inheritor of the kingdom of heaven"; which statement is altogether false; and then it continues the delusion by prostituting an ordinance meant for the living child of God, and giving it to the ungodly, the ignorant, and the superstitious, as though it could make them meet for entering heaven. I charge you, as before the Lord, cleanse yourselves of this superstition. There is no salvation apart from faith in the Lord Jesus Christ; and you might as well trust in your sins as in sacraments. In fact, the sacraments become sins to men who trust in them, for these men sin against the ordinances of the Lord by putting them where they never ought to be, and making an Antichrist of them, so as to push Christ out of his place with their baptisms and their masses. If ye die with the sacramental bread in your mouths, ye will be lost unless your faith is in the Lord Jesus Christ alone. Your hands, which are superstitiously laid upon the altar's horns, might as well be placed upon your weapons of rebellion. Outward emblems can do you no good whatsoever if you remain unspiritual. Without faith in Christ, even the ordinances of God become things to condemn you. If ye eat and drink unworthily ye eat and drink condemnation to yourselves, not discerning the Lord's body; and, if this be true, how dare any unconverted, unbelieving man put his trust in the outward ordinance of which he has no right to partake?

There are others who put their trust in *religious observances of sundry kinds*. Their visible altar-horn is something which they believe to be very proper and right, and which, indeed, may be so if wisely used, for the thing is good if used lawfully; but it will be their ruin if it be put out of its own place. For instance, there are, doubtless, some who think that they are all right because they frequent *sermons*. They delight to be found hearing the gospel. Now, in this you do well, for, " Faith cometh by hearing, and hearing by the word of God"; but, if you suppose that the mere hearing of a sermon with the outward ear can save you, you suppose what is untrue, and you build the house of your hope upon the sand. " Oh, sir, I have sat to hear the true gospel of our Lord Jesus Christ these many years." Yes, and these many years you have rejected it. The kingdom of God has come nigh unto you, but I fear it will work your damnation through your unbelief; for it will be a savour of death unto you. I fear that in the last great day it shall be seen that I have ministered unto some of you to your hurt. It will not be laid to my charge, but to yours, if I have been faithful in the declaration of the word. Oh, may God grant that no man or woman among you may ever put the slightest faith in the mere hearing of the word! Except ye receive it by faith ye deceive your own souls; if ye are hearers only, what good can come of it?

"Oh, but," says another, "I attend *prayer-meetings.*" I admit that it is not every hypocrite that will regularly come to prayer-meetings, but there are some that do; and, though you are so fond of prayer-meetings, yet, my dear friend, unless it can be said of you, "Behold, *he prayeth,*" you need not make sure of safety. Your being found in the place where prayer is wont to be made may be no true sign of grace. "Ay, but I do more than that, for I have prayers in my own house." Yes, and very proper, too. I would that all did the same; I am grieved that any should neglect the ordinance of *family prayer.* But yet, if you think that the reading of a form of prayer in your household, or even the use of extempore prayer, is a thing to be relied upon for salvation, you do greatly err. "He that believeth in him hath everlasting life"; but he that believes not in the Lord Jesus Christ does but offer unbelieving prayer to God; and what is that but a vain sacrifice which he cannot accept? Oh, do not rely upon the habit of outward worship, or you will lean on a bulrush!

"But I regularly *read a chapter,*" says one. I am extremely glad you do, and God bless that chapter to you! I would that all were in the habit of reading right through the Bible regularly, and endeavouring to understand it; but, if you trust in your Bible-readings as a ground of salvation, you are resting upon a mere soap-bubble which will burst under your weight. Faith in the Lord Jesus Christ, producing in the soul a change of heart, a new birth unto God, this is what is wanted; and, apart from that, all the Bible reading you ever practice can do you no good whatsoever. "Ye must be born again. Ye must be born again"; and if there be not this inward change, then vain is all outward observance. You may wash a corpse, you may clothe that corpse in the purest white shroud that was ever woven, but when all is done it does not live; and what are all the outward devotions of a carnal man but dead things which bring no life with them to men dead in sin?

Some are foolish enough to put their confidence in *ministers.* It would seem to me to be the maddest thing in all the world for anybody to have any confidence in me as to helping him in his salvation; and I trust that nobody is such a fool. I cannot even save myself; what can I do for others? Do not come to me with "Give us of your oil," for I have not enough for myself, except as I keep on begging a supply. When I look at the priests in whom some trust, especially such as I have seen abroad, they may be very fine fellows, but I would not trust some of them with a half-crown, let alone my soul. The very look of most priests makes me wonder how they manage to secure power over people's minds. They may know a great deal, but they do not look as if they were overdone with wit. I would as soon trust my soul in the hands of a gipsy with a red cloak as I would with the best-ordained priest or bishop that ever lived. There is one Mediator between God and men, the man Christ Jesus, and he who sets up another is an enemy of souls. There is but one who can be trusted with our soul affairs, even the Lord Jesus Christ; and woe to us if we put our confidence in men! Ordained or unordained, shaven or unshorn, they cannot help us. Yet I know that people do trust in ministers most foolishly. I remember years ago being at three o'clock in the morning in a house now pulled down, which stood not far from the London Bridge railway-station. A gentleman of considerable means had spent the Sunday at Brighton, had come home, and had been taken with cholera on a sudden, and nothing would do for him, when he was in the pangs of death, but he must send for me. I went, not knowing what was required of me. But when I got there what could I do? There was a little consciousness left to the man, and I spoke to him of Jesus. I asked if he had a Bible. The people of the house searched high and low, but there was no such thing to be found. The mind was soon too beclouded for further comprehension, and as I came away I asked, "Has he ever gone to a place of worship?" No, never—never cared for such a thing; but as soon as he was ill, then, "Oh, send for Mr. Spurgeon!" He must come, and nobody else: and there I stood, and what could I do? There died in the City of London, not long ago, a tradesman of much wealth; and when he came near to die, though I had never seen the man in my life before, he importunately asked for me. I could not go. My brother went to see him, and, after setting before him the way of salvation, he enquired, "What made you wish to see my brother?" "Well," he said, "you know whenever I have a doctor I always like to get the best; and when I employ a lawyer I like a man who is high in the profession. Money is no object. I want the best possible help." Ah me! I shuddered at being so regarded. The best help he could get! That best is nothing—less than nothing, and vanity. What can we do for you, dear hearts, if you will not have our Saviour? We can stand and weep over you, and break our hearts to think that you reject him; but what can we do? Oh, if we could let you into heaven, if we could renew your hearts, how joyfully would we perform the miracle; but we claim no such power, no such influence! Go you to Christ, and lay hold upon the true altar-horn; but do not be so foolish as to put confidence in us or in any other ministers.

"Ah, well," says one, "I am free of that. I am *a professor of religion,* and have been a member of a church now these twenty years." You may be a member of a church fifty years, but you will be damned at last unless you are a member of Christ. It matters not though you are a church-officer, a deacon, an elder, a pastor, a bishop, or even Archbishop of Canterbury, or an apostle, you will perish as surely as Judas, who betrayed his Master with a kiss, unless your heart is right with God. I pray you, put no confidence in your profession. Unless you have Christ in your heart, a profession is but a painted pageantry for a soul to go to hell in. As a corpse is drawn to the grave by horses adorned with nodding plumes, so may you find in an outward profession a pompous way of being lost. God save us from that!

"No," says one, "but I do not trust in a mere profession. I have great reliance upon *orthodoxy.* I will have sound doctrine." That is right, friend, I would have all men value the truth. "My confidence is in my belief in sound doctrine." That is not mine, friend, and I hope that it will not be yours long, for many lost souls have firmly believed orthodox doctrine. In fact, I question whether any one is more orthodox than the devil; for the devils believe and tremble. Satan is no sceptic; he has too much knowledge for that. Devils believe and tremble, and yet they are devils still. Put no confidence in the mere fact that you hold to an orthodox faith, for a dead orthodoxy soon corrupts. You must have faith in Christ, or else this altar-horn of a correct creed, on which you lay your hand, will bring you no salvation.

I will not enlarge upon this topic. Whatever you depend upon apart from the blood and righteousness of Christ, away with it! Away with it! If you are even depending upon your own repentance, and your own faith, away with them! If you are looking to your own prayers or alms, I can only cry again,—Away with them! Nothing but the blood of Jesus; nothing but the atoning sacrifice; but, if you come and lay your hand upon that, blessed shall you be.

II. That assurance is the second part of our discourse, on which I will speak briefly. COMING TO THE SPIRITUAL ALTAR, AND LAYING OUR HAND UPON IT, WILL SAVE US.

Now, notice first, *the act itself.* Joab came within the tabernacle. So, poor soul, come and hide yourself in Christ. Joab took hold of the horns, the projecting corners of the altar, and he would not let go. Come, trembling sinners, and take hold on Christ Jesus.

> " My faith doth lay her hand
> On that dear head of thine ;
> While like a penitent I stand,
> And there confess my sin."

Lean with your hand of faith upon your Lord, and say, " This Christ is mine. This offering for sin is mine. I accept it as the gift of God to me, unworthy though I be."

When that is done, *a fierce demand* may be made upon you. The enemy will probably cry, " Come forth! Come forth!" The self-righteous will say, " What right has such a sinner as you to trust Christ? Come forth!" Mind you say to them, " Nay, but I will die here." Your sins and your guilty conscience will cry to you, " Come forth! Come forth! *You* must not lay hold of Christ. See what you have been, and what you are, and what you are likely to be." Answer to these voices, " Nay, but I will die here. I will never give up my hold of Christ." Satan will come, and he will howl out, " Come forth! What right have you with the Lord Jesus Christ? You cannot think that he came to save such a lost one as you are." Do not listen to him. As often as he howls at you, only say to yourself, " Nay, but I will die here." I pray God that every sinner here may be brought to this desperate resolve, " If I perish, I will perish trusting in the blood and righteousness of Jesus Christ. If I must die, I will die here." For certain, we shall die anywhere else. If we trust in any but Jesus, we must perish. " Other foundation can no man lay than that is laid." " Without shedding of blood there is no remission of sin." " He that believeth on him is not condemned : but he that believeth not,"—whatever else he trusts to,—" is condemned already, because he hath not believed in the name of the only-begotten Son of God." Make, then, this desperate resolve—

> If I must die, here will I die,
> Here at the cross I bide ;
> To whom or whither should I fly?
> Where else can I confide ?

Say to all those who call you away, "Nay, but I will die here"; for nobody ever did perish trusting in Jesus. There has not been through all these centuries a single instance of a soul being cast away that came all guilty and hell-deserving, and took Christ to be its salvation. If you perish, you will be the first that perished with his hand laid upon Christ. His love and power can never fail a sinner's confidence. Wherefore, may God the Holy Spirit lead you to resolve, "If I must die, I will die here." Listen to me, soul, whoever thou mayest be out of this crowd, man or woman, whatever thy life may have been, even though it should have been that of a harlot or a thief, a drunkard or a profligate, if thou wilt now believe in the Lord Jesus Christ, thou shalt be saved ; for, *if not, then God himself will have missed his greatest design.* What did he give Jesus for but to save sinners ? What did he lay sin upon Jesus for, but that he might take it off the sinner, and let him go free, and be pardoned ? If, then, Christ fails, God's grandest expedient has broken down. That method by which the Lord resolved to show what his almighty grace can do has proved to be a failure if a believing sinner is not saved. Dost thou think that such a thing can ever be ? It is blasphemy to think that Jehovah can be defeated. He that believes in Christ shall be saved ; nay, he is saved.

If thou art not saved believing in Christ, then Christ himself is dishonoured. Oh, let them once know, down in the dark abode of fallen spirits, that a man has trusted Christ and yet has not been saved, I tell you that they will make such exultation over Christ as Philistia made over Samson when his eyes were put out. They would feel that they had defeated the Prince of Glory. They would trample on his blood, and ridicule his claim to be the Saviour of men. If any soul can truly say hereafter, "I went to Christ, and he refused me," then Christ does not speak the truth when he says, "Him that cometh to me I will in no wise cast out." Then he has changed his nature, foregone his word, and foresworn himself. But that also can never be. Wherefore, dear heart, cling to Jesus, and say still, "If I die, I will die here."

Moreover, *if thou canst perish trusting in Christ thou wilt discourage all the saints of God;* for if Christ can break his promise to one, then why not to another ? If one promise fails, why not all the promises ? If the blood has lost its power, how can any of us ever hope to enter heaven ? I say it will breed great discouragement in the hearts of all people if this be true ; for what a wet blanket would be thrown over all thy fellow-sinners! If they are coming to Christ, they will start back, and say, "What is the good of it ? Here is one that came to Jesus, and he did not save him. He trusted in the precious blood, and yet his sin was laid to his charge." If one fails, why not the rest ? I must give up preaching the gospel when once I hear of a man trusting Jesus and not being saved ; for I should be afraid to speak with boldness, as I now do.

If one poor soul that puts his trust in Christ should be cast away it would spoil heaven itself. What security is there for glorified spirits that their splendours shall endure except the promise of a faithful, covenant-keeping God ? If, then, looking down from their celestial seats, they behold the great Father breaking his promise, and the Son of God unable to save those for whom he died, then will they say, "We will lay our harps aside, and put our palms away, for we, too, after all, may perish." See, then, O man, heaven and earth, ay, God and his Christ, as to their credit and their glory, do stand and fall with the salvation of every believing sinner. If I were in your stead to-night, I think that I should bless God to have this matter put so plainly to me. I know that years ago, when I was under a sense of sin, if I had heard even such a poor sermon as this I should have jumped for joy at it, and would have ventured upon Christ at once.   Come, poor soul; come at once.   You have heard the gospel long enough; now obey it.   You have heard about Christ long enough; now trust in him.   You have been invited and entreated, and pleaded with; now yield to his grace.   Yield to joy and peace by trusting in him who will give you both of these as soon as you have rested in him.

Look! sinner, look!   A look out of thyself to Jesus will save thee. Look away from all thy works, and prayers, and tears, and feelings, and church-goings, and chapel-goings, and sacraments, and ministers.   Look alone to Jesus.   Look at once to him who on the bloody tree made expiation, and who bids thee look, and thou shalt live.

God make this present hour to be the period of thy new birth. I pray it, and so do his people.   The Lord hearken to our intercessions, for Christ's sake.   Amen.

PORTION OF SCRIPTURE READ BEFORE SERMON—Psalms lxi. and lxii.

HYMNS FROM "OUR OWN HYMN BOOK"—560, 589, 514.

ALL OR NONE; OR, COMPROMISES REFUSED:
A SERMON WITH FIVE TEXTS.

A Sermon

INTENDED FOR READING ON LORD'S-DAY, MARCH 29TH, 1885,

DELIVERED BY

C. H. SPURGEON,

AT THE METROPOLITAN TABERNACLE, NEWINGTON,

ON NOVEMBER 25TH, 1883.

I SHALL have five texts—one of them a good one, the other four bad. The first text is good. It is God's text. Exodus x. 26 :—"*There shall not an hoof be left behind.*" That is God's text, and the whole sermon will illustrate it by exposing the compromises with which it was met.

The other four are Pharaoh's texts, or, if you like, the devil's, for that is exactly what the devil says to men. Exodus viii. 25 :—"*Pharaoh called for Moses and for Aaron, and said, Go ye, sacrifice to your God in the land.*" That is his first proposal. Then we find him saying at the twenty-eighth verse, "*I will let you go, that ye may sacrifice to the Lord your God in the wilderness; only ye shall not go very far away.*" That is the second of his compromises. In the tenth chapter, at the eighth verse, you have the third. He said to them, "*Go, serve the Lord your God: but who are they that shall go?*" Adding, "*Go now, ye that are men, and serve the Lord.*" And Pharaoh's fourth and last proposal is in the twenty-fourth verse of that same tenth chapter :—"*Pharaoh called unto Moses, and said, Only let your flocks and your herds be stayed.*"

Satan is very loth to give up his hold on men. He is quite as loth as Pharaoh, and he must be driven to it by force of arms; I mean by force of divine grace, before he will let God's people go. Having once got them under his power through the fall, through their sin, and through their obduracy of heart, he will not lose his subjects if he can help it; but he will put forth all his craft, and all his strength, if possible to hold them in his accursed sway. Many of Satan's slaves altogether disregard the voice of God. For them there are no Sabbaths, no Bibles, no religion. Practically they say, "Who is Jehovah that we should obey his voice?" Now, when God means to save men—when the eternal purpose so runs, and the divine determination is to be accomplished, he soon puts an end to this. For some reason quite unknown to the man—it may be quite unguessed by him—he feels

Nos. 1830-1-2

uneasy : he is disturbed. He thinks one morning that he will go up to a place of worship ; not that he cares much about it, but he thinks that he shall perhaps be a little easier there. He takes his Bible : he begins to read a chapter. A very striking passage comes before his eye. He is not more easy, for the text has fixed upon him. Like a barbed shaft it has stuck into his soul, and he cannot possibly draw it out again. He is more troubled than ever. He begins to enquire a little about the things of God ; there is some respect now outwardly to religion ; the man is considerably changed.

But do not imagine that the work is accomplished. Our blessed Master has to fight for every inch of ground which he wins in human hearts. With the matchless artillery of his love he drives the enemy back farther and farther, till at last he conquers ; but it is often a long and slow process, and were he not possessed of infinite patience he would give it up. But where it is his resolve that a man shall come out of the world and shall be saved, that resolve must and will be carried into effect ; and the man, though he is only brought so far that he begins to think a little about divine truth and about eternal matters, will have to go a great deal farther than that.

You see him sitting under the word of God, and perhaps Satan says now, " Well, you are a fine fellow. You are beginning to occupy a seat Sunday after Sunday in the house of prayer. You have given up your evil habits to a large extent. You are quite a different man. Now you have done something very pleasing to God. You may rest content with this." And it is a very sad thing when men do rest content with such a paltry hope as can have come out of poor performances like these. But still they will stop just there if they can, for Satan does not mind where he makes men halt so long as they will stay under the dominion of sin, and refuse to come to Christ.

Now the Lord begins to deal with the man perhaps in a way of affliction and trouble. His wife sickens : a child dies : he is himself unhealthy : he fears he is about to die, and his fancied righteousness evaporates before his eyes ; and he thinks that now surely he must seek after something better. Then will Satan come in and say, " There is time enough yet. Do not be in too much of a hurry."

If the Lord drives a man from that by the solemn movements of the Spirit upon his soul, then the devil will say to him, " How do you know that this is all true ? " and he has not to go far before he finds infidels to help his unbelief. I am sorry to say that he can find them in the pulpit pretty plentifully, preaching their infidelities as " advanced thought " ; and so poor souls get bewildered, and scarcely know their right hand from their left, and they begin again to relapse into a condition of indifference, and remain where they were.

Blessed be God, if he means to save such, he will, by push of pike, and point of bayonet, carry the day. They shall not rest where they are. The right hand of the Lord is stretched out still, and he will make the Pharaoh of evil yet know that Jehovah is stronger than he. Grace is mightier than nature, and the eternal purpose more sure of fulfilment than all the resolves of case-hardened consciences ; so at last it comes to this—that the man is driven to yield to God, and when he is driven to that point Satan comes in again with his compromises.

We are going to speak about these four compromises to-night. The first compromise is found in the eighth chapter at the twenty-fifth verse.

" Sacrifice to your God in the land."

" Yes," says the devil, " you must be a Christian, that is evident. You cannot hold out any longer, for you are too uneasy in your sins. You will have to be a Christian." "But," says he, " stop in the world, and be a Christian. Remain where you are. ' Sacrifice to your God *in the land* ' "; by which he sometimes means this: live in sin, and be a believer. Trust yourself with Christ, and then indulge yourself in whatsoever your heart desires. Do you not know that he is a Saviour of sinners? Therefore stop in your sin, and yet trust in him. Oh, I charge you, by the living God, never be duped by such a treacherous lie as this, for it is not possible that you can find any rest or salvation while you live in sin. My dear hearers, Christ came to save us *from* our sins, but not *in* our sins. He has built a hospital of mercy into which he receives the worst possible cases. All are welcome, but he does not receive them that they may continue sick, but that he may heal them, and make sound men of them. When the Lord Jesus Christ takes hold upon a thief, the man is a thief no longer; his inmost heart becomes honest. When the Lord meets with the harlot, he blots out her iniquity, and she is affected with deep repentance for her crimes, and turns unto her Saviour, desiring henceforth to walk in purity all her days. It is impossible that you should serve God and yet continue to indulge in known sin. What a fool that man is who thinks that he may drink and be a Christian, that he may cheat in his business and be a Christian, that he may act like the ungodly world in all respects, and yet be a Christian! It cannot be. Mark Antony yoked two lions together, and drove them through the streets of Rome; but he could never have yoked together the lion of the pit and the lion of the tribe of Judah. There is a deadly hate between these two. The principle of good, if it be yielded to, will destroy the mastery of evil. There cannot be a compromise between them. No man can serve two *masters.* He may serve two, but not two when each determines to be master. Satan will be master if he can, and Christ will be master, and therefore you cannot serve the two. It must be one or the other. If thou art to have thy sin forgiven thee, thou must leave thy sin. Remember that voice which came to Master John Bunyan when he was playing tipcat on Elstow Green on Sunday morning. He thought that he heard a voice say, " Wilt thou leave thy sins and go to heaven, or wilt thou have thy sins and go to hell?" That problem is proposed to you if you are unconverted and undecided. But as to the idea of keeping your sins and going to heaven, shut that out of the question, for it must not, cannot, shall not be: it is a compromise proposed by Satan, but the Lord will not have it.

Yes, but then Satan, retreating a little, says, " Well, now, of course I did not mean that you were not to give up your grosser sins; but I mean to tell you of something better. Love the world, and live with worldlings, and find your company and your joy among them, and yet be a Christian. Surely you are not going to throw up everybody, are you? You know you must not be singular. You must not make yourself an oddity altogether. You have many merry companions of yours, keep to them. They do not, perhaps, do you much good. Well, you must not be too particular, and precise." So he says, "Continue in the world, and be a Christian." Shall I tell you God's word about that? "If any man love the world, the love of the Father is not in him." That is short, though not sweet. A man says, "Well, I shall be a Christian; but I shall find my chief pleasure and my amusement where the world finds it." Will you? "I shall be a Christian; but I shall hold with the hare and run with the hounds. I shall be with the church on Sunday; but nobody shall know that I am not the veriest worldling on the week-day. Can I not put my hymn-book in one pocket and a pack of cards in the other, and so go to heaven and keep friends with the world?" No, it is not possible. "Let my people go, that they may serve me," is God's word. Not, "Let them stop in the land, and still serve you and serve me too." It cannot be. "Know ye not that the friendship of the world is enmity with God?" That text is another sharp, drawn sword cutting to the quick; and there are professors who ought to feel it go to their very hearts, for they are trying all that they possibly can to go as near as ever they can to the border-line, and yet to keep up a hope. What would you think of a man who went as near as he could to burning his house down, just to try how much fire it would stand? Or of one who cut himself with a knife, to see how deep he could go without mortally wounding himself? Or of another, who experimented as to how large a quantity of poison he could take? Why, these are extreme follies; but not so great as that of a man who tries how much sin he may indulge in, and yet be saved. I pray you, do not attempt such perilous experiments. "Come ye out from among them; be ye separate, and touch not the unclean thing." Shun with horror Satan's old compromise: dream not that you can love the world, and yet have the love of the Father in you.

When the enemy cannot get on with that, he harks back a little, and cries, "That is very proper; you are hearing very faithful teaching this time, but listen to me! You can live for yourself, and be a Christian. Do not go out into worldly company, but enjoy yourself at home. You see you want to have your own soul saved. Well, live for *that*." This is only a subtler and uglier form of selfishness. It is nothing better. "Look," says Satan, "I do not ask you to be profligate with your money, be penurious with it: be very thrifty. Everybody will pat you on the back, and say, 'He is taking care of number one, and he is doing the right thing.' Come, now, and make a good thing of religion. Believe in Jesus Christ, of course, in order that you yourself may be saved, and then live all the rest of your life trying to hear sermons that will feed you, and read books that will comfort you, and become a great man among religious folks." Hateful advice! Do you not know, dear friends, that the very essence of Christianity is for a man to deny himself? Self can never properly be the end-all and be-all of a man's existence. Self is to religion, in fact, nothing but the flesh in a pretendedly spiritual form. If a man lives to himself, he is under the dominion of an evil spirit just as much as if he went out into open sin. So you must come out of that. Selfishness will not do. You must love the Lord with all your heart, and you must love your fellow-men. There must be an obedience to that command that thou "love the Lord thy God with all thy heart, and thy neighbour as thyself," or else there is no coming out into safety. Thus the first compromise will not hold at all.

Pushed back from the first compromise, Pharaoh proposes a second, and this is found in the twenty-eighth verse of the eighth chapter :—

"Only ye shall not go very far away."

Satan says, "Yes, I see your conscience tells you that you must come out from the world, and come out from sin, but do not go very far away, for you may want to come back again. In the first place, do not make it public. Do not join a church. Be like a rat behind the wainscot; never come out except it be at night to get a mouthful of food. Do not commit yourself by being baptized, and joining the church; do not go so very far as that. Just try, if you can, and save yourself from the wrath to come by secret religion, but do not let any one know it. There really cannot be any need of actually saying, 'I am a Christian.'" My friend, this is the very depth of Satan. When a soldier goes to the barrack-room, if he is a child of God he may say, "I shall not kneel down to pray because they might throw a boot at me, as they generally do in the barrack-room. I can keep my religion to myself." That man will go wrong. But if he boldly says, "I will fly my flag. I am a Christian, and I will never yield that point, come what may"; he will stand. The beginning of yielding is like the letting out of water; no man knows to what a flood it will come. This is what Satan would have with some of you, that you may fall by little and little. Therefore defeat him: come out boldly. Take up your cross, and follow Jesus. "He that believeth and is baptized shall be saved."

The tempter also says, "Do not be so very precise and exact. The Puritanic saints—well, people point the finger at them. You need not be quite so particular." By which he means this—that you may sin as much as you like so long as you do not violate propriety; and that, after all, you are not to obey God thoroughly, but only to obey him when it pleases you. This is flat rebellion against God. This will never do.

"Well," he says, "if you are to be so precise, yet do not be so desperately earnest. There are some of those friends down there at the Tabernacle who are always looking after the souls of others, and trying to proclaim Christ to everybody. You know they are a very dogmatic lot, and they are a great deal too pushing and fanatical. Do not go with them." Just so. He means, stand and serve the Lord, because you dare not do any other, but never give him your heart; never throw your soul into his cause. That is what Satan says; and do you think that such traitorous service will save you? If Moses had thought that going a little way into the wilderness would have saved Israel, he would have let them go a little way into the wilderness, and there would have been an end of it. But Moses knew that nothing would do for God's Israel but to go clean away as far as ever they could, and put a deep Red Sea between them and Egypt. He knew that they were never to turn back again, come what might, and so Moses pushed for a going forth to a distance; as I would in God's name push for full committal to Christ with everybody who is tempted to a compromise.

"Oh, but," Satan will say, "be earnest too. Yes, be earnest. Of course that is right enough; and be precise in all your actions; but do not be one of those people who are always praying in secret. You can keep an open religious profession going without much private praying, without heart-searching, without communion with God. These are tough things," says he, "to keep up. You will find it difficult to maintain the inward life, and preserve a clean heart and a right spirit. Let these go by default, and attend to externals, and be busy and active; and that will do." But it will not do, for unless the heart and soul be renewed by the Spirit of God, it little matters what your externals may be. You have failed before God unless your very soul is joined unto him by a perpetual covenant that shall never be forgotten. What a blessing it is when a man can say,—I have done with these compromises; I do not want to serve God and win favour with the world. I do not want to go just a little way from the world. I pray God to divide me from the world by an everlasting divorce, just as it was with Paul when he said, "The world is crucified unto me, and I unto the world." "From henceforth let no man trouble me : for I bear in my body the marks of the Lord Jesus." Happy man who has come right out under divine guidance to seek the eternal Canaan! His is the path of safety and acceptance; but they that temporize and parley with sin and Satan will find mischief come out of it.

Pushed back from that, the enemy suggests another compromise in the tenth chapter, at the eighth and eleventh verses :—

" Go, serve the Lord your God : but who are they that shall go ? Go now, ye that are men, and serve the Lord."

Yes, that is his next point. "Yes," he says, "we see what it has come to. You are driven at last to this—that you must be an out-and-out Christian ; but, now," he says, "do not worry your wife with it; do not take it home." Or he says to the woman, "You are to follow Christ. I see you must. You seem driven to *that;* but never say anything to your husband about it." Was not that a pretty idea of Pharaoh's— that all the men were to go, and were to leave the women and children to be his slaves ? And that is just the idea of Satan. "You have plenty to do to look after yourself; but your wife—well, leave her to her own ways. Your husband—leave him to his irreligion." Let us answer him thus,—"As for me and my house, we will serve the Lord." So said Joshua of old; and so let every man here say. Remember Paul's words to the Philippian gaoler, "Believe on the Lord Jesus Christ, and thou shalt be saved, *and thy house.*" Let us pray that we may have the whole house for Christ. Up to your measure of influence over your family, say within yourself, "My Lord, I will never rest until I see all my family brought to thy dear feet. Lord, save my wife : save my husband: save my father : save my brothers and sisters ! Bring these out of bondage !" You cannot be a Christian unless that is your heart-felt desire. He that careth not for his own house is worse than a heathen man and a publican.

And then the children. "Oh," Pharaoh says, "leave the children!" Do you not see he knew very well that, if they did that, they would themselves come back again ? What man among us would go away into the wilderness, and leave his wife and children in slavery? Should we not want to come back to them? Should we not think that we heard their cries? Should we not want to look into their dear faces again? Leave them in slavery? Oh, that cannot be! And yet let me sorrowfully say that there are many professing Christians who seem as though they were themselves determined to be the Lord's, but their children should belong to Pharaoh and to the devil. For instance, the boy is getting of a certain age. Let him be sent to a foreign school, and, preferably, a Roman Catholic school. Will that be useful to his religion? Yet if he should turn out a Papist, his foolish father will almost break his heart. It was all his own doing, was it not? Well, the girls, of course, they must go into society: of course, they must "go into society." And so everything is done to put them into places of danger, where they will not be likely to be converted, and where, in all probability, they will become gay, and vain, and light. Then a situation is looked out for the boy. How often there is no question about the master being a Christian! Is it a business that the lad can follow without injury to his morals? "Nay, it is a fine roaring trade, and it is a cutting house, where he will pick it up in a smart way. Let him go there." Ay; and if he goes to perdition? Alas, there are Christian men who do not think of that! The children of some professors are offered up to the Moloch of this world. We think it a horrible thing that the heathens should offer their children in sacrifice to idols, and yet many professors put their children where, according to all likelihood, they will be ruined. Do not let it be so. Do not let the devil entangle one of you in that compromise, but say, "No, no, no; my house, God helping me, shall be so conducted that I will not put temptation in my children's way. I will not lead them into the paths of sin. If they will go wrong, despite their father's exhortations and their mother's tears, why, they must; but, at any rate, I will be clear of their blood, for I will not put them into places where they would be led astray." I am sure there is a great deal of importance in this remark, and if it cuts anybody very closely, and he says, "I think you are very personal," that is exactly what I mean to be—the precise thing I am aiming at. I desire to put this thing before every individual Christian, that all may see the right and the wrong of it, and may resolve, "Our women and our children shall go with us to worship God. They as well as ourselves shall leave this Egypt, as far as God's grace can help us to accomplish it."

Now the devil is getting pushed into a corner. Here is the man's whole house to go right for God, and the man gives himself up to be a Christian out and out. What now? "Well," says the enemy in the twenty-fourth verse of that tenth chapter,

"*Go ye, serve the Lord; only let your flocks and your herds be stayed.*"

Just so. What does Moses say to that? "Thou must give us also sacrifices and burnt-offerings, that we may sacrifice unto Jehovah our God. Our cattle also shall go with us; *there shall not a hoof be left behind;* for thereof must we take to serve the Lord our God; and we know not with what we must serve the Lord, until we come thither." This was the divine policy of "No surrender," and I plead for it with you. Satan says, "Do not use your property for God. Do not use your talents and your abilities; especially, do not use your money for the Lord Jesus. Keep that for yourself. You will want it one of these days, perhaps. Keep it for your own enjoyment. Live to God in other things, but, as to that, live to yourself." Now, a genuine Christian says, "When I gave myself to the Lord I gave him everything I had. From the crown of my head to the sole of my foot I am the Lord's. He bids me provide things honest in the sight of all men, and care for my household; and so I shall; but yet I am not my own, for I am bought with a price; and therefore it becomes me to feel that everything I have, or ever shall have, is a dedicated thing, and belongs unto the Lord, that I may use it as his steward, not as if it were mine, but at his discretion, and at his bidding. I cannot leave my substance to be the devil's. That must come with me, and must be all my Lord's; for his it is even as I am." The Christian takes the line which Moses indicated: "I do not know what I may be required to give. I know that I am to sacrifice unto the Lord my God, and I do not know how much. I cannot tell what may be the needs of the poor, the needs of the church, the needs of Christ's church all over the land. I do not know, but this I know, that all that I have stands at the surrender point. If my Redeemer wants it he shall have it. If Satan wants it he shall not have a penny of it. If there be anything that is asked of me that will not conduce to good morals—that will not conduce to the promotion of that which is right in the sight of God—I withhold it. But if there be anything that is for Christ's glory and for the good of men, then, as the Lord shall help me, it shall be given freely, and not be begrudged as if it were a tax. It shall be my joy and my delight to devote all that I am, and all that I have, to him who bought me with his precious blood."

Now, brothers and sisters, you that profess to be Christians, come you, stand right square out, and own yourselves wholly and altogether the Lord's.

> " 'Tis done! the great transaction's done;
> I am my Lord's, and he is mine."

"My house is his, and my all is his. Whether I live or die—whether I work or suffer, all that I am, and all that I have, shall be for ever my Lord's." This is to enter into peace: this indeed is to be clean delivered from the power of Satan; this is to be the Lord's free man; and what remains but with joyful footsteps to go onward toward Canaan, shod with shoes of iron and brass, fed with heavenly bread, guarded by the Lord himself, guided by his fiery-cloudy pillar, enjoying all things in him, and finding him in all things? This is to be a Christian of the true order. The Lord make you so by faith in his dear Son! Amen and Amen.

PORTIONS OF SCRIPTURE READ BEFORE SERMON—Selections from the eighth and tenth chapters of Exodus.

HYMNS FROM "OUR OWN HYMN BOOK"—645, 656, 658.

SMOKING FLAX.

DELIVERED BY

C. H. SPURGEON,

AT THE METROPOLITAN TABERNACLE, NEWINGTON,

ON JUNE 1st, 1884.

"The smoking flax shall he not quench."—Isaiah xlii. 3.

I BELIEVE that the first sense of these words is not the one usually given to them, nor yet the one upon which I intend to preach to-night. We read in the 12th of Matthew that our divine Lord was assailed by the scribes and Pharisees, but he did not enter at that time into controversy with them, neither did he make them the perpetual target of his observations. Considering what hypocrites they were, and what boundless mischief they were doing, he treated them very gently indeed. They were, compared to him, but as bruised reeds, and as the smoking flax, and he could, if he had pleased, have broken them up altogether, or have altogether quenched them; but he did not come to be a mere controversialist. He was, in truth, the greatest of all reformers, but he was not so much a breaker-down as he was a builder-up. He came not so much to drive out error by reason, as to expel it by the natural and efficient process of putting truth into its place. So, to a large extent, he left these scribes and Pharisees, and other opponents, alone, and he went quietly on with his own work of healing the sick, and saving the sinful—a very good lesson to us. We get a little pugnacious sometimes, and seek religious controversy; but our Saviour did not strive, nor cry, nor cause his voice to be heard in the streets; a bruised reed he did not break, and a smoking flax he did not quench. The best way to put out the twinkling light of a smoking flax was to let the sun shine. Nobody could see it then. Instead of talking down these bruised reeds, he set up the higher claim of sure and certain truth; for men would not care to trust in bruised reeds when they had once seen something more stable and worthy to be relied upon. You and I will best put down error by preaching truth. If we preach up Christ, the devil goes down. If a crooked stick is before you, you need not explain how crooked it is: lay a straight one down by the side of it, and the work is well done. Preach the truth, and error will stand abashed in its presence.

That is, no doubt, the first meaning of this passage, as you will see by the connection in Matthew. It is said, "A bruised reed shall he not break, and smoking flax shall he not quench, till he send forth judgment unto victory." When the Lord sends forth judgment unto victory, then it will be all over with the bruised reed and the smoking flax of the hypocrite, the Pharisee, the formalist, the legalist, and every other opponent.

Usually these words are understood to mean that Jesus Christ will deal very gently with timid believers, and this meaning is not to be rejected; for in the first place, it is true; and, in the second place, it is true out of this text also, for if our Lord Jesus in his lifetime was gentle even to hypocrites, how much more will he be gentle to sincere but timorous spirits; if it be true that he will not quench the smoking flax even of a Pharisee, how much more true must it be that the smoking flax of a penitent shall not be quenched! So that, if the text does not *say* what is generally understood by it, it implies it, and the words so clearly run into the meaning that is commonly given to them.

I take it that there is a kind of instinct in the church, so that even when judged according to criticism she may seem to misapply a passage of Scripture, she generally does not misapply it, but only brings out a second light which was always behind the first, and which shines none the less brightly, but all the more so, because the first was there. I shall therefore take the text to mean something other than I have stated. "The smoking flax shall he not quench," is a text for you timorous, desponding, feeble-minded, and yet true-hearted believers, and you may appropriate it to yourselves. May the Holy Spirit help you so to do!

I. In talking of it, at this time, I shall first enquire, WHAT STATE THIS METAPHOR REPRESENTS.

A smoking flax represents *a state in which there is a little good.* The margin is "dimly burning flax." It is burning; but it is burning very dimly. There is a spark of good within the heart. You, my dear friend, have a little faith; it is not much bigger than a grain of mustard-seed, but faith of that size has great power in it. I wish that your faith would grow to a tree, but I am very glad that you have any, even though it be minute as the mustard-seed. You have a desire, too, after better things: you are always wanting to be more holy. You love to be among God's people, and though sometimes you are afraid that you are not one of them, you would give all that you have to be sure that you were, for you love their conversation. Having those desires, you do pray. "O sir," say you, "it is not worth calling prayer!" Well, we will not call it prayer, then, but it is prayer; for sometimes, when not even a word is spoken, the desire of the heart is a most acceptable pleading with God. "O sir," you say, "but I do not always desire alike!" I am very sorry that it is so. I wish you always had a strong desire after Christ. Still, you do desire. There is a longing, a desiring, a panting, a hungering, a thirsting; therefore there is some little good in you. "Do not praise me," you say. Oh, no, dear friend, I will not praise you! I know that you would not like it; for you have a modest estimate of yourself, and like the publican you cry, "God be merciful to me a sinner." That tune suits you, does it not? I can see somewhat of good in you since you do not think well of yourself. If you did, we might think ill of you; but inasmuch as you even repent over your repentance, and feel as if your tears want weeping over, I am glad of it. Lowliness of heart is a grace very much despised in these days, but very much valued by the King of heaven. "To this man," says he, "will I look, even to him that is poor and of a contrite spirit, and trembleth at my word." There is some little good in you *put there by the Spirit of God.* "Ah," say you, "I like that word, sir; I am sure there was no good in me by nature." Friend, I am sure of it too, if you are at all like me. The grace of God has put in us our first desire, our first loathing of sin, our first wish to be forgiven, our first desire to return to our Father from whom we have wandered. The Spirit put it there, and you are like the smoking flax, because there is a little living fire in you.

You are like smoking flax, again, because *your good is too little to be of much use to anybody.* What could we do with a smoking flax if we had it here to-night, and the gas was all out? You would, perhaps, see a glimmer, but you would say, "It is not light, but darkness visible." I like a soul in darkness to find that darkness visible. There is a good point about that. Alas, you are such a poor timid creature, you could not comfort a child of God; you cannot even comfort yourself! You could not strengthen the weak, for you want all the strengthening for your own self. You are not much of a soldier; you could not march in rank: we have to carry you about in the ambulance. Well, we are not tired of carrying you, nor is God either. You are still a soldier, for you would fight if you could. Though you are invalided, yet whenever the trumpet sounds you wish to be in the thick of the fight. Poor thing that you are, you would soon be trampled down; but you have spirit enough for it, for which I thank God. Though your courage is of no great use to anybody, yet it is of use to you, for it proves you to be a soldier of the cross, a follower of the Lamb. I would to God that you had more light, that you might light your brother on his dreary way. I wish you had more faith, more joy, more hope, more rest, for you might then be of service to the Lord's household, and the King might find in you a willing helper. But as you cannot do that, you are like the smoking flax: there is a little good, but that good is not great enough to make you very useful. Yet I will tell you one thing you can do. When you meet with another poor soul that is like you, you can sympathize, can you not? You see, when bright and shining lights come near those who are dim, they are apt rather to shame them than to comfort them; but you will not do that. So far you may even help the despondent; at least, you will do so one of these days.

Smoking flax, then, has a little fire, but it is so little that it is of small service, and, what is worse, *it is so little that it is rather unpleasant.* No one delights in the smell of a candle that is dying out. Smoking flax does not yield a sweet savour; neither does a Christian when he is in a mournful condition. There is a little good in him, but there is a great deal of wrong about him, and that wrong has an ill savour. Sometimes these smoking-flax people believe a great many errors. They do not hold the true and solid doctrine of God's everlasting love: they favour notions that are not scriptural; and error is never sweet to Christ, nor to any of his own people. Besides, they have a great smoke of doubts. They doubt this, and they question that, and they suspect the other thing. There is nothing more obnoxious to our divine Lord than distrust of him. It is a gracious act on his part that he puts up with it. One said to Christ, "If thou canst" ; and that was a shocking thing to say to an almighty Lord : another said to him, "If thou wilt" ; and that was a shameful thing to say to one so kind ; and yet he bore with them both. Doubting hearts will cry, "If thou wilt, and if thou canst," and do anything sooner than believe. This is to make an ill savour in the presence of the Lord Jesus Christ; for, though *we* may reckon our doubts to be trifling, they are no trifle to him, but exceedingly grievous and provoking to his heart. A dear sister came in after service this morning, and told me that she was fifty years old on the same day as myself, so she came to shake hands with me; and she added, "I am like you in that ; but I am the very reverse of you in other things." I replied, "Then you must be a good woman." "No," she said, "that is not what I mean." "But are you not a believer ?" "Well," she said, "I—I will try to be." I got hold of her hand, and I said, "You are not going to tell me that you will try and believe my Lord Jesus Christ, for that means unbelief of him who must be true ;" and I held her fast while I added, "When your mother was about, did you say to her, 'Mother, I will try and believe you'? No, you would believe her because she was true; and I must have you believe Jesus Christ." She said, "Sir, do pray for me." "No," I said, "I am not inclined to do that. What should I pray for you about? If you will not believe my Lord, what blessing can he give you? What has he ever done that you should say, 'I cannot believe him'?" She again answered, "I will try." I was not content till I had reminded her of the word, "He that believeth in him hath everlasting life," and I pressed her to a full faith in the risen Lord. The Holy Spirit enabled her to trust, and then she cried, "I have been looking to my feelings, sir, and this has been my mistake." I have no doubt that she had done so ; and a great many others are doing the same ; and their doubts are just that horrible smoke which comes from smoking flax. O, ye poor doubters, believe the Lord Jesus Christ ! To say, "I cannot believe him," is to say in other words that he is a liar, and we cannot allow you to say *that*.

Dear friend, if you are like the smoking flax, there is something good in you ; but that is so sadly little that there is a great deal that is trying about you ; yet the Lord will not quench you. You are full of all sorts of fears ; you are afraid of a shadow ; you are trembling at nothing at all. Why is this? You are troubled when you ought to be glad, and you make your whole family sad when there is no earthly reason for it. May the Lord deliver you ! Those that are highest in faith have tried to comfort you, and you have pulled them down, instead of their being able to draw you up. Come, friend, I would be as gentle as ever I can : my text bids me be so. I have no extinguisher for your smoking flax, for my Lord has said, "The smoking flax shall he not quench."

I must add one more thing about this state, and it is this, though the good of it is so little that it is of very little use to other people, and sometimes is very obnoxious, yet there is *enough good in you to be dangerous in Satan's esteem.* He does not like to observe that there is yet a little fire in you, for he fears that it may become a flame. If any of you were to see a man standing at the back of one of our public buildings lighting his pipe, I will be bound to say that you would be half afraid of an explosion, for he might be applying dynamite. There are times when the smallest smoke would fill the bravest men with fear. Even so

"Satan trembles when he sees
The weakest saint upon his knees."

If he hears you groaning about your sin, he is frightened at it. "Oh," says he, "they have begun to feel : they have begun to mourn : they have begun to desire : they have begun to pray : and soon they will leave me." Let a farmer perceive a little smoke coming out of one of his ricks, and I am sure that he will not say that there is nothing at all in a smoking flax, but he will hasten to prevent a conflagration. So the little grace that is in you, dear friend, Christ sees, and he approves of it, for he knows the possibilities of it—how little faith can grow into strong faith—how the grain of mustard-seed can become a tree, and the birds of the air may yet lodge in the branches thereof; and Satan, also, knows what may come of it, and he is moved to quench it if he can. We, therefore, would encourage you, and fan your spark to a flame.

There is the first question answered. What state does this represent ?

II.   Secondly, WHEN ARE SOULS IN THAT STATE ?

Some are in that state when they are newly saved—*when the flax has just been lighted.* Those that are to be received into the church to-night I welcome very heartily, but they are very newly lit, and some perhaps would have said, "Let them wait a bit." Ay, but then our Lord does not quench the smoking flax because it is newly lighted, nor will I. No place in the world is so good for the lambs as the fold. No place is so good for babes as their own home. No place is so good for young Christians as the church of God. So let them come.

Being newly converted, they are strange to many things. You have made a host of discoveries. You find more depravity in your heart than you thought was there ; you find enemies where you expected to meet with friends. All this is apt to damp your courage ; but do not be cast down ; for though it be but a little that you are lighted, yet the loving Jesus will not quench the smoking flax.

Sometimes a candle smokes, not because it is newly lit, but because it is *almost extinguished.* I know that I speak to some Christians who have been alight with the fire of grace for many years, and yet they feel as if they were near the dark hour of extinction. But you shall not go out. The Lord will not quench you himself, nor will he permit the devil to quench you. He will keep you alight with grace. "Oh," but you say, "I am so depressed in spirit !" Yes, some of God's best servants have been of a sorrowful spirit. Remember Hannah, whom Eli cruelly rebuked, but who, nevertheless, got a blessing. David had to say, "Why art thou cast down, O my soul ? and why art thou disquieted within me ? " and yet he was a man after God's own heart. Perhaps you are not well, or you have had an illness that has told much upon your nervous system, and you are depressed; and therefore it is that you think that grace is leaving you, but it will not. Your spiritual life does not depend upon nature, else it might expire : it depends upon grace, and grace will never cease to shine till it lights you into glory. Therefore be not cast down. You may think that your light will go out in eternal darkness, but it never shall, for the Lord Jesus Christ will preserve the flame.

Sometimes the wick smokes when *worldliness has damped it.* If some of you never have any holy joy, I am not surprised, for you are so taken up with the world, and so fond of it. The life of God is in you, but it is smothered. You are like an autumn fire out in the garden when they are burning the weeds : there *is* a fire, but all you can see is smoke. Yes, you smother up your piety with the things of this world, and no wonder that it smokes ; but what a mercy it is that the Lord does not allow even you to perish ! He keeps the dying flame alive though hidden away.

At times a wick burns low because *a very strong wind has blown upon it.* Many men and women are the subjects of very fierce temptations. The place in which they live is a trial to them, and their natural constitution furnishes them with a host of temptations ; and so the flax scarcely burns, but smokes and smoulders. We do not wonder that it should be so.

There are many other reasons why we grow dim at times—reasons, but none of them sufficient to be an excuse. If we were what we ought to be, we should be burning and shining lights always, and there would be no times in which we should be like the smoking flax ; but then we are not what we ought to be, we fall short of the true standard, and we become feeble believers.

III. I desire to finish with a word of promise. WHAT DOES JESUS DO WITH THOSE WHO ARE IN THIS STATE ? He says that he will not quench the smoking flax. What a world of mercy lies in that word ! Everybody else would quench us but Christ. I am sure that some Christians get into such a state that the most loving Christian friends find it hard to bear with them ; and fear that such a state of mind cannot be consistent with grace at all. Thus your friend would give you over as lost. But Jesus Christ says that he will not do so.

He will not quench you, first, *by pronouncing legal judgment upon you.* He will not say, " You have broken my laws, and I have done with you." If he did, our only answer could be, " Enter not into judgment with thy servant, for in thy sight shall no man living be justified." If the Lord were once to come to that, he would quench us all. Not only some few of the tremblers, but the strongest among us must go to the wall. The Lord Jesus Christ has not come to condemn, but to save.

He will not quench you, dear friend, *by setting up a high experimental standard.* Certain deep divines will say, " You must have felt so much of this, and so much of the other, or else you cannot be a child of God." Who told the good man so ? Who made him to be a judge ? The Lord Jesus Christ does not quench even the feeble, faint desire, or the trembling faith of his servants, though they do fall far short of that experience which ought to belong to a child of God.

He will not judge you, dear friend, *by a lofty standard of knowledge.* I have known persons who have thought, " If that convert is not better instructed in the doctrines, he is no child of God." The Lord has some of his children whose heads are in a very queer state ; and if he first puts their hearts right he afterwards puts their heads right. But for you and for me to say that a man is not a child of God, because he does not know all that the advanced saints know, is a very wicked thing. I am sure that your little child, who cannot read or write, is pressed to your bosom, dear mother, with just as much affection as that brave son of yours who has just been winning the first prize at school. You do not say, " I will not love the little one because he is not a man ; " or, " I will not love my little daughter because she is not grown up to woman-hood." Oh, no ! The Lord loves the little ones. If you can say, " One thing I know, whereas I was blind, now I see," you are taught of God. If you know these two things—yourself a sinner, and Christ a Saviour—you are scholar enough to go to heaven.

And the Lord Jesus Christ will not quench you *by setting up a standard by which to measure your graces.* It is not, " So much faith, and you are saved. So little faith, and you are lost." Oh, no ; if thou hast faith as a grain of mustard-seed it will save thee. If thou dost believe in Christ, thou art saved. That woman who touched the hem of Christ's garment with her finger, and then tremblingly slunk back, was truly healed, slight as her touch was. Even Simeon, who took the Saviour up into his arms, and said, " Lord, now lettest thou thy servant depart in peace," cannot more surely be said to have had a saving faith than that poor woman who came behind, and touched the hem of the Master's garment.

Come along, you little ones,—you trembling ones ! Be not afraid ! Jesus will not quench you by any of these means. I will tell you what he will do with you ; and that is, instead of quenching you, *he will protect you.* He will blow upon you with the soft breath of his love till the little spark will rise into a flame. You young folks do not know what trouble some of us used to have, forty-five years ago, when we got up of a morning and had to strike a light in the old-fashioned way. There we were with a flint and a steel, striking away in a tiresome manner till we spied a little spark down in the tinder—oh, such a little one, and then we gently tried to blow it into a flame ! How we used to prize a spark on a cold, frosty morning, when our fingers were pretty well frozen ! We never put out the sparks by shutting the lid on the top of the tinder, but we tried if we could to light our match.

Now, the Lord Jesus Christ will blow softly upon you with his gentle Spirit. He will bring to your mind exceeding great and precious promises. He will bring to you kind friends, who shall tell you their experience, and try to comfort you. I should not wonder, my dear brother, that one of these days I shall hear you pray a strong, brave prayer ; I should not wonder if you before long come forward, and made an open profession ; and if you have done so already, I feel pretty sure that you will honour it, and grow stronger, till one day we shall say, " Who is that bold witness for Christ ? Who is that burning and shining light ? " He is the man who was once likened to the smoking flax. I have had the portraits of my two boys taken on their birth-days, from the first birthday till they were twenty-one. The first year the little fellows are sitting, two of them in one perambulator. At twenty-one they are doing nothing of the sort : they are men full-grown. Yet I can trace them all along, from the time when they were babes, till they became little boys, and then youths, and then young men. I should not have been pleased to have seen them wheeled about in the perambulator for twenty-one years. In that case, I should have thought myself a most unfortunate father. And so I do not want to have any of you remaining in spiritual infancy : we long to see you come to the fulness of the stature of perfect men in Christ Jesus. Life is precious, but we look for growth : a spark is fire, but we expect flame : grace is priceless, but we long to see it daily increased by going on unto perfection. Despise not the day of small things, but yet advance to greater things than these. Be comforted, but not self-satisfied; rest, but do not loiter.

The table of the Lord is spread, and it is a feast not for men alone, but for babes in grace. Come hither you that love the Lord, and you that trust him, however feeble your trust. However faint your courage, come and welcome! My Lord's table is not for giants only, but for infants also. The viands are not strong meat, but bread and wine, fit food for the faint and feeble. Examine yourselves, ye sincere tremblers; but do not let the examination end in your staying away; but rather mark how the text says, "let a man examine himself, and *so let him eat*": not so let him refrain from eating. Ho, you that hope in his mercy, your Lord invites you to his own feast of love! You may come and welcome. If you have come to Christ himself by faith, come to his table, and remember him to-night.

The Lord bless you, for Jesus' sake. Amen.

PORTION OF SCRIPTURE READ BEFORE SERMON.—Isaiah li.

HYMNS FROM "OUR OWN HYMN-BOOK"—734, 682.

Metropolitan Tabernacle Pulpit.

ELIJAH'S PLEA.

A Sermon

DELIVERED BY

C. H. SPURGEON,

AT THE METROPOLITAN TABERNACLE, NEWINGTON,

ON NOVEMBER 9TH, 1884.

"Let it be known that I have done all these things at thy word."—1 Kings xviii. 36.

THE acts of Elijah were very singular. It had not been known from the foundations of the earth that a man should shut up the doors of the rain for the space of three years. Yet Elijah suddenly leaped upon the scene, announced the judgment of the Lord, and then disappeared for a time. When he reappears, at the bidding of God, he orders Ahab to gather the priests of Baal; and to put to the test the question as to whether Baal or Jehovah was indeed God. Bullocks shall be slain and laid upon the wood without fire; and the God who shall answer by fire shall be determined to be the one living and true God, the God of Israel. We might question within ourselves what right the prophet had to restrain the clouds, or to put God's honour under test. Suppose the Lord had not willed to answer him by fire; had he any right to make the glory of God hang upon such terms as he proposed? The answer is that *he had done all these things according to God's word.* It was no whim of his to chastise the nation with a drought. It was no scheme of his, concocted in his own brain, that he should put the Godhead of Jehovah or of Baal to the test by a sacrifice to be consumed by miraculous fire. Oh, no! If you read the life of Elijah through, you will see that whenever he takes a step it is preceded by, "the word of the Lord came unto Elijah the Tishbite." He never acts of himself; God is at his back. He moves according to the divine will, and he speaks according to the divine teaching; and he pleads this with the Most High,—"I have done all these things at thy word; now let it be known that it. is so." It makes the character of Elijah stand out, not as an example of reckless daring, but as the example of a man of sound mind. Faith in God is true wisdom: childlike confidence in the word of God is the highest form of common-sense. To believe him that cannot lie, and trust in him that cannot fail, is a kind of wisdom that none but fools will laugh at. The wisest of men must concur in the opinion that it is always best to place your reliance where it will certainly be justified, and always best to believe that which cannot possibly be false.

Elijah had so believed, and acted on his belief, and now he naturally expects to be justified in what he has done. An ambassador never dreams that his authorized acts will be repudiated by his king. If a man acts as your agent and does your bidding, the responsibility of his acts lies with you, and you must back him up. It were, indeed, an atrocious thing to send a servant on an errand, and, when he faithfully performed it to the letter, to repudiate your sending him. It is not so with God. If we will only so trust him as to do as he bids us, he will never fail us ; but he will see us through, though earth and hell should stand in the way. It may not be to-day, nor to-morrow, but as surely as the Lord liveth, the time shall come when he that trusted him shall have joy of his confidence.

It seems to me that Elijah's plea is to obedient saints *a firm ground for prayer*, and to those who cannot say that they have acted according to God's word, it is *a solemn matter for question*.

I. To begin with, this is A FIRM GROUND FOR PRAYER. You are *a minister of God, or a worker in the cause of Christ*, and you go forth and preach the gospel with many tears and prayers, and you continue to use all means, such as Christ has ordained : do you say to yourself, "May I expect to have fruit of all this ?" Of course you may. You are not sent on a frivolous errand : you are not bidden to sow dead seed that will never spring up. But when that anxiety weighs heavily upon your heart, go you to the mercy-seat with this as one of your arguments, " Lord, I have done according to thy word. Now let it be seen that it is even so. I have preached thy word, and thou hast said, ' It shall not return unto me void.' I have prayed for these people, and thou hast said, ' The effectual fervent prayer of a righteous man availeth much' ; let it be seen that this is according to thy word." Or, if you are a teacher, you can say, " I brought my children in supplication before thee, and I have gone forth, after studying thy Word, to teach them, to the best of my ability, the way of salvation. Now, Lord, I claim it of thy truth that thou shouldest justify my teaching, and my expectation, by giving me to see the souls of my children saved by thee, through Jesus Christ, thy Son." Do you not see that you have a good argument, if the Lord has set you to do this work ? He has, as it were, bound himself by that very fact to support you in the doing of it ; and if you, with holy diligence and carefulness, do all these things according to his word, then you may come with certainty to the throne of grace, and say unto him, " Do as thou hast said. Hast thou not said, ' He that goeth forth and weepeth, bearing precious seed, shall doubtless come again with rejoicing, bringing his sheaves with him' ? Lord I have done that. Give me my sheaves. Thou has said, ' Cast thy bread upon the waters, for thou shalt find it after many days.' Lord, I have done that ; and therefore I entreat thee fulfil thy promise to me." You may plead in this fashion with the same boldness which made Elias say in the presence of all the people, " Let it be known this day that thou art God in Israel, and that I have done all these things at thy word."

Next, I would apply this teaching *to a whole church*. I am afraid many churches of Christ are not prospering. The congregations are thin, the church is diminishing, the prayer-meeting scantily attended, spiritual life low. If I can conceive of a church in such a condition which, nevertheless, can say to God, "We have done all these things at thy word," I should expect to see that church soon revived in answer to prayer. The reason why some churches do not prosper is, because they have *not* done according to God's word. They have not even cared to know what God's Word says. Another book is their standard. A man is their leader and legislator, instead of the inspired Word of God. Some churches are doing little or nothing for the conversion of sinners. But any man, in any church, who can go before God, and say, "Lord, we have had among us the preaching of the gospel; and we have earnestly prayed for the blessing; we have gathered about thy minister, and we have held him up in the arms of prayer and faith; we have, as individual Christians, sought out each one his particular service, we have gone forth each one to bring in souls to thee, and we have lived in godliness of life by the help of thy grace, now, therefore prosper thy cause," shall find it a good plea. Real prosperity must come to any church that walks according to Christ's rules, obeys Christ's teaching, and is filled with Christ's Spirit. I would exhort all members of churches that are in a poor way just now, to see to it that all things are done at God's word, and then hopefully wait in holy confidence. The fire from heaven must come: the blessing cannot be withheld.

The same principle may be applied also *to any individual believers* who are in trouble through having done right. It happens often that a man feels, "I could make money, but I must not; for the course proposed would be wrong. Such a situation is open, but it involves what my conscience does not approve. I will rather suffer than I will make gain by doing anything that is questionable." It may be that you are in great trouble distinctly through obedience to God. Then, you are the man above all others who may lay this case before the Most High: "Lord, I have done all these things at thy word, and thou hast said, 'I will never leave thee nor forsake thee.' I beseech thee interpose for me." Somehow or other God will provide for you. If he means you to be further tried, he will give you strength to bear it; but the probabilities are that now he has tested you, he will bring you forth from the fire as gold.

> "Do good and know no fear,
> For so thou in the land shalt dwell,
> And God thy food prepare."

Once again. I would like to apply this principle *to the seeking sinner.* You are anxious to be saved. You are attentive to the word, and your heart says, "Let me know what this salvation is, and how to come at it, for I will have it whatever stands in the way." You have heard Jesus say, "Strive to enter in at the strait gate." You have heard his bidding, "Labour not for the meat which perisheth, but for that which endureth to life eternal." You long to enter the strait gate, and eat of the meat which endureth; you would give worlds for such a boon. Thou hast well spoken, my friend. Now, listen:—thou canst not have heaven through thy doings, as a matter of merit. There is no merit possible to thee, for thou hast sinned, and art already condemned. But God has laid down certain lines upon which he has promised to meet thee, and to bless thee. Hast thou followed those lines? For if thou hast, he will not be false to thee. It is written,—" He that believeth and is baptized shall be saved"—can you come before God, and say, "I have believed and have been baptized"? then you are on firm pleading ground. It is written again,—" Whoso confesseth and forsaketh his sins shall have mercy." When you have confessed them, and forsaken them, you have a just claim upon the promise of God, and you can say to him, "Lord, fulfil this word unto thy servant, upon which thou hast caused me to hope. There is no merit in my faith, or my baptism, or my repentance, or my forsaking of sin; yet as thou hast put thy promise side by side with these things, and I have been obedient to thee therein, I now come to thee, and say, ' Prove thine own truth, for I have done all these things at thy word.' " No sinner will come before God at last, and say, " I trusted as thou didst bid me trust; and yet I am lost." It is impossible. Thy blood, if thou art lost, will be on thine own head; but thou shalt never be able to lay thy soul's damnation at the door of God. *He* is not false: it is *thou* that art false.

You see, then, how the principle can be applied in prayer : " I have done these things at thy word ; therefore, O Lord, do as thou hast said."

II. We shall go a little over the same ground while I ask you to put yourselves through your paces by way of SELF-EXAMINATION as to whether or not you have done all these things at God's word.

First, let every *worker* here who has not been successful answer this question—Have you done all these things at God's word? Come. *Have you preached the gospel?* Was it the gospel ? Was it Christ you preached, or merely something about Christ ? Come. Did you give the people bread, or did you give them plates to put the bread on, and knives to cut the bread with? Did you give them drink, or did you give them the cup that had been near the water ? Some preaching is not gospel ; it is a knife that smells of the cheese, but it is not cheese. See to that matter.

If you preached the gospel, *did you preach it rightly?* That is to say, did you state it affectionately, earnestly, clearly, plainly ? If you preach the gospel in Latinized language, the common people will not know what it means ; and if you use great big academy words and dictionary words, the market people will be lost while they are trying to find out what you are at. You cannot expect God to bless you unless the gospel is preached in a very simple way. Have you preached the truth lovingly, with all your heart, throwing your very self into it, as if beyond everything you desired the conversion of those you taught? Has prayer been mixed with it? Have you gone into the pulpit without prayer? Have you come out of it without prayer ? Have you been to the Sabbath-school without prayer ? Have you come away from it without prayer ? If so, since you failed to ask for the blessing, you must not wonder if you do not get it.

And another question—*Has there been an example to back your teaching?* Brethren, have we lived as we have preached? Sisters, have you lived as you have taught in your classes ? These are questions we ought to answer, because perhaps God can reply to us, "No, you have not done according to my word. It was not my gospel you preached: you were a thinker, and you thought out your own thoughts, and I never promised to bless your thoughts, but only my revealed truth. You spoke without affection; you tried to glorify yourself by your oratory; you did not care whether souls were saved or not." Or suppose that God can point to you, and say, " Your example was contrary to your teaching. You looked one way, but you pulled another way." Then there is no plea in prayer: is there ? Come, let us alter. Let us try to rise to the highest pitch of obedience by the help of God's Spirit: not that we can merit success, but that we can command it if we do but act according to God's bidding. Paul planteth, and Apollos watereth, and God giveth the increase.

And now let me turn to *a church*, and put questions to that church. A certain church does not prosper. I wish that every church would let this question go through all its membership: do we as a church acknowledge the headship of Christ ? Do we acknowledge the Statute-Book of Christ—the one Book which alone and by itself is the religion of a Christian man ? Do we as a church seek the glory of God ? Is that our main and only object ? Are we travailing in birth for the souls of the people that live near us ? Are we using every scriptural means to enlighten them with the gospel ? Are we a holy people ? Is our example such as our neighbours may follow ? Do we endeavour, even in meat and drink, to do all to the glory of God ? Are we prayerful ? Oh, the many churches that give up their prayer-meetings, because prayer is not in them ! How can they expect a blessing ? Are we united ? Oh, brothers, it is a horrible thing when church members talk against one another, and even slander one another, as though they were enemies rather than friends. Can God bless such a church as that ? Let us search through and through the camp, lest there be an Achan, whose stolen wedge and Babylonian garment, hidden in his tent, shall bind the hands of the Almighty so that he cannot fight for his people. Let every church see to itself in this.

Next I speak to *Christian people* who have fallen into trouble through serving God. I put it to them, but I want to ask them a few questions. Are you quite sure that you did serve God in it ? You know there are men who indulge crotchets, and whims, and fancies. God has not promised to support you in your whims. Certain people are obstinate, and will not submit to what everybody must bear who has to earn his bread in a world like this. If you are a mere mule, and get the stick, I must leave you to your reward; but I speak to men of understanding. Be as stern as a Puritan against everything that is wrong, but be supple and yieldable to everything that involves self-denial on your part. God will bear us through if the quarrel be his quarrel; but if it is our own quarrel, why then we may help ourselves. There is a deal of difference between being pig-headed and being steadfast. To be steadfast, as a matter of principle in truth which is taught by God's Word, is one thing; but to get a queer idea into your heads is quite another.

Besides, some men are conscientious about certain things, but they have not an all-round conscience. Some are conscientious about not taking less, but they are not conscientious about giving less. Certain folks are conscientious about resting on the Sabbath; but the other half of the command is, " Six days shalt thou labour," and they do not remember that portion of the law. I like a conscience which works fairly and impartially : but if your conscience gives way for the sake of your own gain or pleasure, the world will think that it is a sham, and they will not be far from the mark. But if, through conscientiousness, you should be a sufferer, God will bear you through. Only examine and see that your conscience is enlightened by the Spirit of God.

And now to conclude. I want to address *the seeking sinner.* Some are longing to find peace, but they cannot reach it; and I want them to see whether they have not been negligent in some points so that they would not be able to say with Elijah, " I have done all these things at thy word."

Do I need to say that you cannot be saved by your works? Do I need to repeat it over and over again that nothing you do can deserve mercy? Salvation must be the free gift of God. But this is the point. God will give pardon to a sinner, and peace to a troubled heart, on certain lines. Are you on those lines wholly? If so, you will have peace; and if you have not that peace, something or other has been omitted. To begin with, the first thing is *faith.* Dost thou believe that Jesus Christ is the Son of God? Dost thou believe that he has risen from the dead? Dost thou trust thyself wholly, simply, heartily, once for all, with him? Then it is written,—" He that believeth in him hath ever-lasting life." Go and plead that. " I have no peace," says one. Hast thou unfeignedly *repented* of sin? Is thy mind totally changed about sin, so that what thou didst once love thou dost now hate, and that which thou didst once hate thou dost now love? Is there a hearty loathing, and giving up, and forsaking of sin? Do not deceive yourself. You cannot be saved *in* your sins; you are to be saved *from* your sins. You and your sins must part, or else Christ and you will never be joined. See to this. Labour to give up every sin, and turn from every false way, else your faith is but a dead faith, and will never save you. It may be that you have wronged a person, and have never made *restitution.* Mr. Moody did great good when he preached restitution. If we have wronged another we ought to make it up to him. We ought to return what we have stolen, if that be our sin. A man cannot expect peace of conscience till, as far as in him lies, he has made amends for any wrong he has done to his fellow-men. See to that, or else perhaps this stone may lie at your door, and because it is not rolled away you may never enter into peace.

It may be, my friend, that you have neglected *prayer.* Now, prayer is one of those things without which no man can find the Lord. This is how we seek him, and if we do not seek him how shall we find him? If you have been neglectful in this matter of prayer, you cannot say, " I have done all these things at thy word." May the Lord stir you up to pray mightily, and not to let him go except he bless you! In waiting upon the Lord he will cause you to find rest to your soul.

Possibly, however, you may be a believer in Christ, and you may have no peace because you are associated with ungodly people, and go with them to their follies, and mix with them in their amusements. You see you cannot serve God and Mammon. Thus saith the Lord, " Come out from among them: *be ye separate:* touch not the unclean thing, and I will be a Father unto you, and ye shall be my sons and daughters, saith the Lord Almighty." I know a man who sits in this place: he is probably here to-night: and concerning him I am persuaded that the only thing that keeps him from Christ is the company with which he mingles. I will not say that his company is bad in itself, but it is bad to him; and if there be anything that is right in itself, yet if to me it becomes ruinous, I must give it up. We are not commanded to cut off warts and excrescences, but Jesus bids us cut off right arms, and pluck out right eyes—good things in themselves,—if they are stumbling-blocks in our way so that we cannot get at Christ. What is there in the world that is worth the keeping if it involves me in the loss of my soul? Away with it. Hence many things which are lawful to another man, perhaps, to you may not be expedient because they are injurious. Many things cause no harm to the bulk of men, and yet to some one man they would be the most perilous things, and therefore he should avoid them. Be a law to yourselves, and keep clear of everything that keeps you away from the Saviour.

Perhaps, however, you say, "Well, as far as I know, I do keep out of all ill associations, and I am trying to follow the Lord." Let me press you with a home-question,—*will you be obedient to Jesus in everything?*

> "For know—nor of the terms complain—
> Where Jesus comes he comes to reign."

If you would have Christ for a Saviour, you must also take him for a King. Therefore it is that he puts it to you "He that believeth and is baptized shall be saved." Will the baptism save me? Assuredly not, for you have no right to be baptized until you are saved by faith in Jesus Christ; but remember, if Christ gives you the command—if you accept him as a King—you are bound to obey him. If instead of saying "Be baptized" he had simply said, "Put a feather in your cap," you might have asked, "Will putting a feather in my cap save me?" No, but you are bound to do it because he bids you. If he had said, "Put a stone in your pocket, and carry it with you"; if that were Christ's command, it would be needful that you take the stone, and carry it with you. The less there seems to be of importance about a command, often the more hinges upon it. I have seen a rebellious boy, to whom his father has said, "Sir, pick up that stick. Pick up that stick." There is no very great importance about the command, and so the youth sullenly refuses to obey. "Do you hear, sir? Pick up that stick." No: he will not. Now, if it had been a great thing that he had been bidden to do, which was somewhat beyond his power, it would not have been so clear an evidence of his rebellion when he refused to do it, as it is when it is but a little and trifling thing, and yet he refuses to obey. Therefore, I lay great stress upon this—that you who do believe in Jesus Christ should do according to his word. Say, "Lord, what wouldest thou have me to do? Be it what it may, I will do it, for I am thy servant." I want you, if you would be Christ's, to be just like the brave men that rode at Balaclava.

> "Yours not to reason why;
> Yours but to do and die"—

if it need be, if Jesus calls you thereto. Be this your song—

> "Through floods and flames if Jesus lead,
> I'll follow where he goes."

That kind of faith which at the very outset cries, "I shall not do that, it is not essential"; and then goes on to say, "I do not agree with that, and I do not agree with the other"; is no faith at all. In that case it is you that is master, and not Christ. In his own house you are beginning to alter his commands. "Oh," says one, "but as to baptism: I was baptized, you know, a great many years ago, when I was an infant." Say you so? You have heard of Mary when her mistress said, "Mary, go into the drawing-room, and sweep it and dust it." Her mistress went into the drawing-room, and found it dusty. She said, "Mary, did you not sweep the room, and dust it?" "Well, ma'am, yes I did: only I dusted it first, and then I swept it." That was the wrong order, and spoiled the whole; and it will never do to put Christ's commands the other way upwards, because then they mean just nothing. We ought to do what he bids us, as he bids us, when he bids us, in the order in which he bids us. It is ours simply to be obedient, and when we are so, we may remember that to believe Christ and to obey Christ is the same thing, and often in Scripture the same word that might be read "believe," might be read "obey." He is the Author of eternal salvation to all them that obey him, and that is to all them that believe on him. Trust him then right heartily, and obey him right gladly. You can then go to him in the dying hour, and say, "Lord, I have done all these things at thy word. I claim no merit, but I do claim that thou keep thy gracious promise to me, for thou canst not run back from one word which thou hast spoken."

God bless you, beloved, for Christ's sake.

PORTION OF SCRIPTURE READ BEFORE SERMON—1 Kings xviii. 17—40.

HYMNS FROM "OUR OWN HYMN BOOK"—417, 515, 514.

BUT A STEP.

A Sermon

INTENDED FOR READING ON LORD'S-DAY, NOVEMBER 29TH, 1885,

DELIVERED BY

C. H. SPURGEON,

AT THE METROPOLITAN TABERNACLE, NEWINGTON,

ON SEPTEMBER 13TH, 1885.

"There is but a step between me and death."—1 Samuel xx. 3.

THIS was David's description of his own condition. King Saul was seeking to destroy him. The bitter malice of that king would not be satisfied with anything short of the blood of his rival. Jonathan did not know this. He could not believe so badly of his father as that he could wish to kill the champion of Israel, the brave, true-hearted young David; and so he assured David that it could not be so—that he had not heard of any plots against him. But David, who knew better, said, "It is certainly so. Your father seeks my blood, and there is but a step between me and death."

Now, it was by knowing his danger that David escaped. Had he remained as ignorant of his own peril as his friend Jonathan had been, he would have walked into the lion's mouth, and he would have fallen by the hand of Saul. But to be forewarned is to be forearmed; he was, therefore, able to save his life because he perceived his danger. It would have been a very unwise person who should have said, "Do not tell David about it. You see that he is very happy in Jonathan's company. Do not disturb him. It will only make him fret. Do not tell him about Saul's anger." But a true and wise friend would acquaint David of his danger, in order that he might seize the opportunity to escape. So also to-night somebody might say, "Many people now present are in great danger, and do not dare to think about death; do not mention the unpleasant subject to them." Well, sirs, if my object were to please you, if my desire were to seem as one who playeth a merry tune upon a goodly instrument, I certainly should not speak to you of death and danger. But, then, it would be infamous to allow men and women to stand in infinite jeopardy and not to warn them; and it is kindness to speak to those who are carelessly at ease and tell them salutary truth. It will not put them in danger; but it may, God blessing it, be the means of their escaping from eternal ruin. So, I pray you, while I talk

No. 1,870-1-2.

upon this theme, which may seem to be a sad one, ask God to make it so great blessing to those who hitherto have been sporting upon the brink of fate without thinking of the solemnities of eternity.

It is rather a notable state of things, is it not, for David to be conscious of danger, and to be telling his friend Jonathan that he is in danger? I do not often meet with the case now. If I am the Jonathan, I have to keep on warning David of his danger, and I find it very difficult to wake up my friend to a sense of that danger. I should like to live to see the day in which David would come to Jonathan—I mean in which men in danger would come to me—and say, "There is but a step between me and death." We love to see care for the soul, and concern about a future state. Whenever God's Holy Spirit is at work we do see it: sinners begin to be aware of their condition, and they come and tell us of their danger, and enquire for the way of escape. It is the simplest thing in the world to tell the awakened sinner how he may find peace; the difficulty lies in awakening the sinner. To cheer those who are alarmed is such good work that we would sit up all night at it. We can never have too much of it. To bind up the broken in heart when the Master gives us his gospel, is the most pleasant duty out of heaven. The worst of it is, that we cannot persuade them that they need to be broken in heart, or lead them to feel that they are in peril; but still shutting their eyes to all the truth they will go wildly on, determined not to know. Too many act as if it were folly to look a few days ahead, as if it were a work of supererogation to foresee the evil, a needless sorrow to think of eternity.

To-night I want to press the truth home, as far as it is truth, upon each person here present, that there is, or there may be, but a step between him and death.

First, *in some sense this is true of everybody*, "There is a step, and but a step, between me and death." Secondly, *to some it is peculiarly true.* There are many persons—and some of them are here to-night—who might say with emphasis, "There is but a step between me and death." When I have spoken upon those two things, I shall then say, "*Suppose that it is not so*"; and conclude by saying, "*Suppose that it is so.*"

I. First, then, there is a sense in which this text is no doubt literally TRUE OF EVERY MAN—"There is but a step between me and death"; for *life is so short* that it is no exaggeration to compare it to a step. Suppose that we should live to threescore years and ten, or even fourscore years, or to be, as some few of our friends are here to night, even past their fourscore years, yet life will occupy a very short time. Life is long to look forward to; but I appeal to every aged person whether it is not very short to look back upon. I confess to my own experience that a week is now a hardly appreciable space of time to me. There seems to be very little breathing room between one Sunday and another. One has scarcely preached before one has to prepare again some other word with which to address you. As we grow older time very sensibly quickens its pace. I know that this is an exceedingly trite observation, but I mention it all the more earnestly because the certainty of it should force it home with power upon our minds. You young people look to a mo. th as being quite a period of time, but when you are getting forty, or fifty, or sixty, you will look upon a whole year as no more than a brief interval. Indeed, I do not wonder that Jacob said his years were few. Because he was an old man he thought life short. If he had been a young man he would have said that his days were comparatively many, and would have tried to make himself feel that he had lived a long while ; but when a man grows old his days seem fewer than they were, and the older he gets the shorter his life seems to have been. There are many ways of calculating time, and its length or brevity lies more in idea than in fact. I have sometimes noticed it—I dare say you have— that an hour has seemed to me very long indeed. In certain states of mind I have looked to the clock again and again, and I have thought that I never lived such a long hour. . But often and often does it occur to me that I sit down to write, and that I go on writing, and when I lift up my head an hour has passed, and I think to myself, " It cannot be. There is a mistake. That clock has made a mistake somehow." I have even referred to my watch, and I have found that it was even so ; but where that hour went I do not know. When one is very busy the hours glide away, so that you say, "Time is, after all, only a dream." Time may appear to be long while it is short, and it may be really short when according to human calculation it is long. But all men when they come to die confess that their life has been brief—that it was but a step. Yesterday I was born : to-day I live : to-morrow I must die. Ephemera are born and die in the space between the rising and the setting sun ; their life is a fair picture of our own. We are shadows, and we come and go with the rising and the setting sun. Truly "there is but a step between me and death." O my God, if my life be so short, prepare me for its end ! Help me to stand ready for its close, so that I may give in my final account with joy.

But, in another sense, there is but a step between us and death, namely, that *life is so uncertain.* How unexpectedly it ends ! Strong and hearty men, if I might make a judgment from observation, seem to be among the first to fall. How often have I seen the invalid, who might almost 'long for death, draw out a long existence of continuous pain ; while the man who shook your hand with a powerful grip, and stood erect like a column of iron, is laid low of a sudden and is gone ! No man can reckon upon the full term of life : not one among us can be sure of reaching threescore and ten. We cannot be sure that we shall see old age. A bubble is more solid than human life, and a spider's web is as a cable compared with the thread of our existence. There is but a step between us and death.

And this is all the more true when we consider that *there are so many gates to the grave.* We can die anywhere, at any time, by any means. Not alone abroad are we in danger, but at home in security we are still in peril. I am in my pulpit now, but I am not secure in this citadel from all-besieging death. I remember a dear servant of God in a country town, on a certain Sabbath morning, stood up and repeated as the first hymn of the morning, the sacred song which I gave out just now :

> " Father, I long, I faint to see
> The place of thine abode :
> I'd leave thine earthly courts and flee
> Up to thy seat, my God ";

and he fell back and was gone. His wish was granted. He saw the place of God's abode, I do not doubt. There is no safety from death in the pulpit, nor in your own house. Dr. Gill, who was noted for always being in his study, said one day to a friend, " Well, at least, if a man is in his study he is safe." Some one had been killed in the street through a falling chimney-pot or tile, and this gave emphasis to the doctor's pleasantry. But it so happened that, soon after, the doctor went to visit a member of his church, and while he was away a stormy wind blew, and blew down a stack of chimneys into his study, into the very place where he would have been sitting if he had not been called away. So he said to his friend, " Verily, I see I must not boast of being safe in my study, for we are secure nowhere." In times of battle men may shelter behind trees or walls, and so escape rifle-shot : but where can you get to escape from the arrows of death? Wherever you be, not alone in the crowded, thronging streets, but up there in your own chamber, or on the edge of your bed, you may slip, you may fall, and suffer fatal injury. At your table you may eat and drink and die. Wherever you are, you may well feel, " There is but a step between me and death."

> " Dangers stand thick through all our path
> To push us to the tomb ;
> And fierce diseases wait around
> To hurry mortals home."

Therefore, I would say, as I leave this point, let nobody here reckon upon life. Let him never postpone what ought to be done at once to some future time. I do not know whether any brother here recollects old Mr. Timothy East. I knew him well in his old age. He was a man of careful observation and retentive memory, and in his later days he was full of stories which had happened in his pastoral experience; and he used to tell this one :—A certain woman was very much attached to his ministry, but still a very foolish woman. She used to sit regularly on the pulpit stairs, and she did so for many years, while Timothy East preached the gospel. One thing seemed to shut her heart against all his appeals. She told a neighbour that if she had five minutes before she died, she so understood the way of salvation that she would get all right in that time. She told her minister that, and Timothy said to her, " Oh, that will never do. You may not have that five minutes in which to set things right. Be right at once." Singularly enough, one day, as Mr. East went down the street, a child came to him, and said, " Please, sir, come and see grandmother. Come and see grandmother." He turned in, and there was grandmother struck for death. She looked at him with an entreating glance, and said, " I am lost ! I am lost ! " She died there and then, ere Mr. East could say a word to her about her salvation. Dear friend, I do beseech you not to imitate her folly, but rather say to yourself, " There is but a step between me and death. Therefore, now, God help me, I will lay hold upon eternal life, and seek and find in Christ the salvation that shall fit me to live, and fit me to die, and fit me to rise again, and fit me for the judgment-day, and fit me for eternal glory. " There is but a step between me and death "; there shall not be a step between me and Christ.

II. But, dear friends, I now turn to further remark that TO SOME THIS IS SPECIALLY TRUE. Will you bear with me when I remark that to persons who have reached a ripe old age this is most certainly true: "There is but a step between me and death"? It is inevitable in the order of nature that you should not live long. Now, do not object to think about it and talk about it. It is only foolish persons who will not mention death. If you are all right with God, it can be no trouble to you to remember that as your years multiply, there must be so many the fewer in which you are to abide here below. Those also have but a step between them and death who are touched with some incurable disorder. Some are warned that they have a heart complaint. If that be the case I may fairly say, "There is but a step between you and death." If you are consumptive, and are gradually melting away, you are in like case. What a blessing it is that this form of death gives us notice of its approach, and does not impair the mind, so that a person may calmly seek and find eternal life if that disease has marked him for its own! But there is only a step between the consumptive and death. Those who follow dangerous trades are in a similar condition. The traveller across the deep, the fisherman, the soldier, the miner, and others are frequently at death's door. I need not go into the details of all those various processes by which men earn their bread, which have so much danger about them that there is but a step between those who follow them and death.

Besides this, there are some—and probably some in this congregation—who, whether it be by disease or not, will die in the course of a few weeks. The probabilities, if they are calculated, will show that out of six or seven thousand persons gathered here, there are certainly some, beyond all guesswork, who will not see the month of November, who certainly will never pass into the next year. There is but a step between such and death.

I should like you to be able to think about death. If you do not like to think about it at all, my dear friends, I think that there is something wrong in you, and you ought to take warning from your own dislike. He that is afraid of solemn things has probably solemn reason to be afraid of them. It is greatly wise to talk with our last hours. A man who is going to a certain place should think about the place to which he is going, and make some preparation for it. If he be a wise man he will do so. I should like you to attain to such a state that you could feel as Dr. Watts did. He said to a friend when he was an old man, "I go to my bed each night with perfect indifference as to whether I shall wake up in this world or the next." That is a beautiful state of mind to be in. Or, as the old Scotch minister said when some one asked him, "Is this disease of yours fatal"? and he replied, "I do not know, and I do not wish to know, for I do not think that it can make much difference to me; for if I go to heaven I shall be with God, and if I stop here God will be with me." Oh! is not that a sweet way of putting it? There is not so much difference, after all, between being with God and God's being with us. Old George the Third, who, whatever the faults of his early days, was undoubtedly a godly man in his old age, would have a mausoleum prepared for himself and family; and when Mr. Wyatt, the architect, went to see him by his own order he did not know how to speak to the old king about his grave; but George said, "Friend Wyatt, do not mind speaking about my tomb. I can talk as freely to you about the preparation of a place for me to be buried in, as I could about a drawing-room for me to hold my court in; for I thank God that I am prepared to do my duty if I live, and to sleep in Jesus if I die." There are but few, I think, of his rank who could talk so; but every wise man ought to see to it that, as he must die, he is ready for it—ready for the bar of God. "Ready, ay, ready," says the sailor as he grinds his cutlass; and let the Christian say the same. Ready, ay, ready, to live to an extreme old age patiently waiting, or to depart out of the world unto the Father, which is far better; in any case finding it heaven enough to do the will of God, and to trust in Jesus Christ, whom he hath sent.

Thus I have mentioned the cases of those of whom it may specially be said, "There is but a step between me and death." "Oh," said some one, "you are the wrong side of sixty, Mr. Jones." "No," answered Jones, "I am on the right side of sixty, for I am the heaven side of it"; and that is the way to look at our age. We say,

"Nearer, my God, to thee,"

and then we do not like to grow old: that is absurd. Nay, let us rather rejoice that we are getting nearer the desired haven, nearer our everlasting rest.

III. I am to close by saying first, SUPPOSE IT IS NOT SO. Young friends, you that are here, suppose it is not true that there is only a step between you and death. Suppose it is not so. There may be some here that will live to a very great age. I may be addressing some persons who will rival Sir Moses Montefiore. Possibly you may. Well, what then? If so, I should recommend you to follow the Scriptural advice, "Seek ye first the kingdom of God, and his righteousness." The first things should come first: the best things should have the best of our thoughts. A prince who had been warned of assassination, gaily exclaimed, "Serious things to-morrow"; but before to-morrow he was slain. Yet had he not been slain, his speech would have been an unwise one; for, however long we live, we ought not to push serious matters into a corner. If we are to live, let us live to noble purpose. It would be a great pity to lose a single year, much less a long life. If you are going to live a hundred years, begin them with God. If you are going to have long life, why not spend it for him? There was a storm at sea once, and there was a young man on board who was not used to storms, and he fell into a great state of mind. He was not of much use on board the ship through his fears. He crept into a corner and knelt down to pray; but the captain, on coming along, could not stand that. He shouted, "Get up, you coward, *say your prayers in fine weather*." He did get up, saying to himself, "I only hope that I shall see fine weather to say my prayers in." When he landed, the words the captain said remained in his mind. He said, "That is quite correct, I will say my prayers in fine weather." I would say to you who hope to live a hundred years, *say your prayers in fine weather*. The young man was so impressed with those words that he went to hear the gospel, was converted, and became a minister of Christ.

One Sunday morning, while he was preaching in one of the most notable pulpits in New York, that captain came into the chapel, and the preacher looked him in the face and said, " Say your prayers in fine weather." The captain was astonished, as he perceived that the very man whom he had addressed as a coward was now preaching from the pulpit, and giving out at the commencement of his sermon the advice which he had given him. I trust the captain took his own medicine. I want to give that advice to all who do not think that they are going to die yet. *Say your prayers in fine weather.* Begin with God now. Oh, come and give my Lord Jesus the prime of your youth, the best of your days. I came to Christ when I was fifteen. I was a minister of the gospel when I was sixteen years of age. I have gone on preaching Christ ever since. I wish that I could have begun sixteen years before. I do not repent of coming to him too early; but I urge upon you, young friends, while yet the marrow is in your bones, and your brain is clear, and your eye is true; ere yet you have dishonoured yourself, and weakened your body by sin, come and yield yourselves up to Jesus Christ, that you may spend a whole life in that blessed service which is joy and peace. May the Holy Spirit of his great love make it so with many here present !

Suppose that it is not true that there is but a step between you and death ; nevertheless, while death is at a distance, health and strength furnish the best time for coming to Christ. Do not imagine that when you are ill and near to die, it will be the best time to turn. I remember the striking words of Philip Henry, the father of the famous Matthew Henry. When he was dying, his friends stood round about his bed, and he said, "What a blessing it is, Matthew, that I have not to make my peace with God now ! My body is full of pain, and my mind is greatly disturbed by reason of it. Oh ! " said he, "if that were undone and had now to be done, how could it be done ? " What a mercy when that great transaction is complete ! Now, come pain or weakness, come long sleep, come broken-down spirit, what does it matter ? It is all well ; it is all well. That having *to make our peace with God* when we die is a poor business. I do not like the expression. I like far better the language of a poor bricklayer who fell from a scaffold, and was so injured that he was ready to die. The clergyman of the parish came, and said, " My dear man, I am afraid you will die. You had better make your peace with God." To the joy of the clergyman the man said, " Make my peace with God, sir ? That was made for me upon Calvary's cross eighteen hundred years ago; and I know it." Ah ! that is it—to have a peace that was made by the blood of Christ all those years ago—a peace that never can be broken. Then, come life, come death, ay, or come a lengthened life, and ripe old age, the best preparation for a lengthened life is to know the Lord. The best encouragement and comfort for the decrepitude of extreme old age is to have a good hope through Christ. There is nothing like it. Why, some old folks that I have known, so far from being unhappy, have been the very happiest people that I have ever met with, and though they have lived long, they have come, not to court long life, but they have been willing to depart. Dr. Dwight, the famous tutor, had a mother who lived to be over a hundred years of age ; and one day, when the son heard the bell toll for a neighbour, the old lady said with tears in her eyes, "Won't it soon toll for me? Will they not soon toll for me?" Dear Mr. Rowland Hill used merrily to say, when he got old, that he hoped that they had not forgotten him. That is how he came to look at death; and he would go to some old woman if he could, and sit down and say, "Now, dear sister, if you go before I go, mind that you give my love to John Bunyan and the other Johns. Tell them that Rowley is stopping behind a little while, but he is coming on as fast as he can." Oh! it is a sweet thing gradually to melt away and have the tenement gently taken down, and yet not to feel any trouble about it, but to know that you are in the great Father's hands, and you shall wake up where old age and infirmities will all have passed away, and where, in everlasting youth, you shall behold the face of him you love.

That is, suppose that it is not so.

IV. But now SUPPOSE THAT IT IS SO. Suppose that it is so, and suppose, as yet, that you have no good hope. Dear friend, there is a word that I would like to drop into your ear. If there is but a step between you and death, yet there is only a step between you and Jesus. There is only a step between you and salvation. God help you to take that step to-night. You know the description of the way to heaven: "Take the first on the right by the cross, and keep straight on." May you take that step to-night! It is not a step even; it is only a look.

<blockquote>"There is life in a look at the Crucified One."</blockquote>

Why delay it? Since faith in Christ will put you beyond danger, and will put you beyond the dominion of sin, so that you will live a godly life which shall continue to the end, why not believe in Jesus now? Why not cast yourself upon him now? For suppose it is so? suppose that it is written in the book, "Thou shalt die, and not live"; then is it not your wisdom that you should at once close in with Christ and find eternal salvation in him?

Suppose that it is so, that you are soon to die; then set your house in order. Get everything ready with regard to your temporal affairs. Mind that. A world of sorrow comes through people not having made their wills. Have everything in order. Trim the ship when a storm is expected. Be ready, for you are about to die. Now sit loose by all earthly things. You must assuredly part with them soon; do not hold them tightly. "Set not your affection upon things on earth," or you will weep when you lose your idols. If you harbour any anger in your heart, turn it out directly, for you are going to die. If there is any quarrel between you and anybody else, go home and settle it. Whether you are going to live or die, I advise you to do that. Hold no ill-will to any one, for you are so soon to die. I remember well the story of a husband who had grieved his wife. I do not know what had happened, —some little awkward word or deed. He went out of the house. He had to fell timber that day, and he turned back and said, "Wife, I am very sorry. Let us part good friends. Give me a kiss." Alas, she turned away! All day long she sorrowed, for she loved him well, and she grieved to think that he was gone without that kiss of love. He never came back again alive. Four men brought him home a corpse. She would have given a thousand worlds if they had not parted so. Now, do not part with anybody that you love with any kind of tiffs or quarrellings. End all that, for death is near. If there is but a step between you and death—if the Judge is at the door—go and wind up your little difficulties. You that have family quarrels, wipe them out. You that have got any malice in your heart, turn it out.

Oh, if it is only a step between us and death, then you that are unprepared, it is only a step between you and hell! Escape, I pray you, by the living God. As you love your souls, flee for your lives, and lay hold on Christ.

But if you are in Christ, it is only a step between you and heaven. You may well desire that you might take that step right speedily. I shall never forget one summer afternoon, when I was preaching in a village chapel about the joys of heaven, that an elderly lady sitting on my right kept looking to me with intense delight. Some people's eyes greatly help the preacher. A telegraph goes on between us. She seemed to say to me, "Bless God for that. How I am enjoying it!" She kept drinking in the truth, and I poured out more and more precious things about the eternal kingdom and the sight of the Well-beloved, till I saw what I thought was a strange light pass over her face. I went on, and those eyes were still fixed on me. She sat still as a marble figure; and I stopped and said, "Friends, I think that yon sister over there is dead." They said that it was even so, and they bore her away. She had gone. While I was telling of heaven, she had gone there; and I remember saying that I wished that it had been my case as well as hers. It was better not, perhaps, for many reasons; but oh, I did envy her! I am always looking for the day when I shall see her again. I shall know those eyes, I am sure I shall. I shall recollect that face, if in heaven she is anything like what she was here, or bears any marks of identification. I shall not forget that inward fellowship which existed between a soul that stood with wings outspread for glory, and the poor preacher who was trying to talk of that which he knew but little of compared with her. Well, well, it will soon be my turn. Good night, poor world! It will soon be your turn, and then you shall say, "Good night." Let us meet in glory. Let us meet in glory, for Jesus Christ's sake. Amen.

PORTION OF SCRIPTURE READ BEFORE SERMON—Psalm xc.

HYMNS FROM OUR "OWN HYMN BOOK"—853, 854, 846.

LOVE'S TRANSFORMATIONS:

A COMMUNION MEDITATION.

DELIVERED BY

C. H. SPURGEON,

AT THE METROPOLITAN TABERNACLE, NEWINGTON,

ON SEPTEMBER 4TH, 1881.

'If ye loved me, ye would rejoice, because I said, I go unto the Father."—John xiv. 28.

THE loving Jesus saw a shade of sadness fall upon the faces of the twelve while he talked to them of his departure. Though he was himself to die, with his usual self-forgetfulness he only thought of them, and he desired to comfort them—to comfort them about the present sorrow of his departure. See how adroitly, how wisely, he drew upon their love for their comfort. The most common and usual source of comfort is Christ's love to us, but in this instance the most applicable and the most influential source of comfort was their love to him. He said, therefore, to them, "If ye loved me, ye would rejoice, because I said, I go unto the Father." It was well and wisely spoken, for he touched them upon a point in which they were very tender; if anything could move them to comfort, it would be his appeal to their loyal love. He had appealed to that before, when he said, "If ye love me, keep my commandments"; but now, in softer, sweeter, tenderer tones, he seems to say, "If ye love me, cease your sorrow, and begin to rejoice." The Lord may give *us* drink from that same spring. It is a lower spring compared with the upper spring of his own sweet love; but he may cause it to flow most preciously, so that when we are not bold enough to drink of the higher stream, we may taste of this. If we are able to say, "Thou knowest all things: thou knowest that I love thee," we may be cheered by that truth. "So surely as you do love me," says Christ, "you will rejoice rather than sorrow, because I said, I go unto my Father." Oh, what a blessed Master we serve, who quotes our love, not to blame us for its feebleness, but to draw a happy inference from it! So much does he desire our peace, our restfulness in his own dear self, that even the love we give to him he gives back to us, and bids us find comfort in it.

Let that stand as a preface ; and now I shall deal with the text by way of making some three or four observations upon it.

No. 1,871,

I. And the first is this: IT WILL BE MUCH FOR OUR COMFORT TO TRY TO SEE THINGS IN CHRIST'S LIGHT. Notice the expression, "If ye loved me, ye would rejoice, because I said, I go unto the Father."

Christ had told them that he was about to die. He had said in very plain language on a former occasion, "The Son of man shall be betrayed unto the chief priests and unto the scribes, and they shall condemn him to death, and shall deliver him to the Gentiles to mock, and to scourge, and to crucify him." But now he looks at the matter in another light. His present view of it is, "I go unto the Father." Their view of it was, "Jesus is to die;" his view of it was, "I go unto my Father." Oh, how often our hearts would grow happy if we could but see things in Christ's light! Let us try to do so.

For, here observe, that *Christ sees through things.* You and I look *at* them, and we see Pilate, Herod, the judgment-seat, the scourge, the cross, the spear, the sepulchre; but Jesus looks *through* them, and he sees the Father's throne and himself exalted upon it. Could we not sometimes try to see affairs in Christ's light by looking through them? Come, brother, that present affliction which seemeth not to be joyous but grievous, nevertheless, afterward, yieldeth the peaceable fruits of righteousness. Canst thou not look at the "afterward," and thus discern the end of the Lord? Thy present estate is tossed about and troubled, for thou art on a stormy sea; but thou art being tossed towards the port, and driven even by the storm towards thy desired haven. Canst thou not see through matters as Jesus did? Why dwell always on this life? Canst thou not see what it leads to? "The way may be rough, but it cannot be long;" and then comes an eternity of joy. Canst thou not spy out this? Thy Lord did so; for though his passage into glory was infinitely rougher than thine, though he had to swim through seas of blood, and breast the breakers of hell itself in his death-pangs, yet he looked beyond all, and said, "I go unto the Father." See things in Christ's light. See the end as well as the beginning and the middle, and thou wilt be comforted!

Do you not see, too, that the light in which Christ sees things is such that *he notices the bearing of things?* He says, in effect, "If ye could see my death as I see it—as a going unto the Father—ye would rejoice." He sees the ultimate result and bearing of things. Oh, if we could always do the same, and perceive what will come of our present sorrow, and what it tends to, and what God means to bring out of it all, then we should not so much see the fire as the pure ingot that comes forth of it! Then we should not so much see the ploughing, and the scattering of the seed to be buried beneath frost and snow, but we should hear the shouts of harvest, and see the yellow sheaves gathered into the garner. Oh, to see providences in Christ's light!

But I do not mean to dwell upon this. I only want to throw out the thought, that every troubled one may now think of his own case as Christ would think of it. If you have a sorrow, how would Jesus deal with this sorrow if it were his own? If you are just now in darkness, what would be Christ's outlook from the window of faith? What would he see as coming out of this affliction? There is no better rule for Christian conduct than, "What would Jesus do?" I was much struck when I saw that question hanging up in our Orphanage girls'

school—" What would Jesus do?" Friend, this is what you should do.
What does Jesus think about trial ?—for, according to the measure of
your capacity, my brother, that is what you should think of it. Try
this holy rule, and you will find the major part of your sorrows trans-
formed into joys. A clear understanding of the nature of our trial
would lead us to glory in tribulation. All that has to do with Jesus is
joyous when seen in his light! If you understood his passion, you
would see his glory; if you understood his tomb, you would see his
resurrection; if you understood his death, you would see his throne.

II.   Our second observation is this: OUR LOVE OUGHT TO GO TO-
WARDS OUR LORD'S PERSON. "If ye loved *me*, ye would rejoice."
Come, my dear friends, gather up your thoughts a minute while I
remind you that the chiefest love that we have should go to Jesus
Christ himself: not so much to his salvation, as to himself, should
our hearts fly. "If ye loved *me*, ye would rejoice." We do well to
love Christ's house, and his day, and his book, and his church, and
his service, and his blood, and his throne; but we must, above all these
things, love his person. That is the tender point; " we love *him*," and
other things in him. We love his church for his sake; his truth
because it is his truth; his cross because he bore it for us; and his
salvation because purchased by his blood. I counsel you to pull up the
sluices of your love, and let the full tide flow towards Jesus. Love HIM.

For, first, he is the source of all benefits; therefore, in loving him
you value the benefits, but you trace them to their fountain-head.
Should we love the gift better than the giver? Should the wife love
her jewels better than the beloved one who gave them? It must not be
so. Love the very person of Jesus—the God, the man, Emmanuel, God
with us. Realize him as a distinct existence. Let him stand before
you now " with scars of honour in his flesh, and triumph in his eyes,"
as we sang just now. Love him as the source of your hope, your pardon, your life, your future glory.

Loving him we learn to prize all his gifts the more, for he that loves
the giver values the smallest gift for the giver's sake. Your love to
the person of Jesus will not make you think less of the benefits which
he bestows, but infinitely more. Shoot at the centre of the target.
Love him, and, loving him, you will value all that he gives.

Loving Jesus we have him for our own, and that is a great blessing.
A man may love gold and not have it. A man may love fame and not
have it. But he that loves Christ has Christ; for certainly there was
never yet a hand of love stretched out to embrace him unlawfully. He
is the property of all who lay hold of him with their hearts.

Love him, and then you will sympathize with him. His work will
arouse your greatest interest. When his cause seems to decline, you will
grieve with him; and when he wins the day, you will shout the victory
with him. Love him, and you will love the souls of men. Love Jesus,
and you will seek to bring sinners to him. Nothing, can do you so
much good, and fit you so well for his service, as to love himself. Love
him, and you will love his people, for never heart did love Christ and
hate his church. He that loves the Head loves the members. "Everyone that loveth him that begat loveth him also that is begotten of him."
We know that we love Jesus when we love the brethren.

Love Christ, and you will have a possession which will last for ever ; for other things expire, but love never fails. "Whether there be prophecies, they shall fail; whether there be tongues, they shall cease;" but he that loves possesses a coin that is current in the skies. He shall go on to love for ever. When the sun shall be darkened, and the stars shall fall from heaven, like withered leaves, he that loves Jesus shall still go on to love, and find in that love his heaven.

Remember, if you love the Son, the Father will love you. That is a precious word of his which you will find in the sixteenth chapter of John, at the twenty-seventh verse. There is a common object of love between the believer and the Father. When you glorify Christ, the Father says "Amen" to what you do. There is no lover of the Christ equal to the Father. "The Father loveth the Son, and hath given all things into his hand." Therefore love the Son, and yield all honour to him, even as the Father doth.

If you love him you may well do so. It is necessary—absolutely necessary—that you should love your own Lord, for I will tell you a secret thing, only to be whispered in the believing ear—you are married to him ; and what is the marriage-state without love ? What, then, would the church be to Christ if she loved him not? What a wretched farce this union would be if there were no love between the soul and Christ to whom it is united! You are a member of his body ; shall not the hand love the Head ? Shall not the foot love the Head ? God forbid that we should be without love to Jesus Christ ; love to his own altogether lovely self. May God the Holy Spirit work in us abundantly to love Jesus, who tenderly says, "If ye loved me, ye would rejoice" !

III. My third observation is, that SOMETIMES OUR SORROWS PUT A QUESTION ON OUR LOVE. Do you not notice that it was because they were very sorrowful, not seeing things in the Master's light, that Jesus said, "If ye loved me, ye would rejoice"? Let us try to-night to check the sorrow which may be in our bosoms at this hour, since it may cast an "if" upon our love to Christ.

Notice that if sorrow about the loss of an earthly thing eats into your heart, it puts an "if" upon your love to Christ. Many are the cries of woe : "Alas! I have lost my property; I have lost the old house in which my fathers lived; I have lost my situation ; I have lost my dearest friend !" Is it therefore true that, because of this loss, you have no joy left ? Have you lost your Saviour? I thought you called him your Best-Beloved, and you said that he was your all : is he also gone ? Did I not hear you say, "Whom have I in heaven but thee ? And there is none upon earth that I desire beside thee"? Is that true ? Oh, over-burdened heart ! Oh, heavy spirit ! Dont thou love Jesus ? Then why disconsolate ? An "if" comes up when we think of your despair.

So, too, when we too much repine under personal affliction, a question is suggested. You may be ill to-night ; or you may be fearing that an illness is coming; or you may be in pain or weakness. Because you fear that consumption is upon you, your heart is very heavy. Truly, it is a sad thing to be diseased ; but who sent you this ? Whose will is it that it should be so ? Who is the Lord of the house ?

Is not the grief your Lord's will, your Saviour's will? You say you love him, and yet you will not let him have his way, and are in a pet with him, and would dispute his love in sending this affliction! Is that so, my brother? Does not that murmuring of yours put an " if" of question upon your love to his blessed person?

You say, too, that you have been trusting him, and yet you have fallen into difficulties and straits. You do not know which way to turn; and you suspect that his providence is not wise. Do you think so? If you loved him as you should, would you think so? Is there not an " if" somewhere? I do not mean an " if" about your loving him, but about your loving him as you ought. Methinks, if you loved him as he deserves, you would say, " The King can do no wrong. My King is kind, wise, loving. I yield everything into his blessed hands."

And so your sorrow is occasioned by the fear of death! You go burdened every day about death, do you? That is a poor compliment to the Well-Beloved. I thought you loved him! Love him—and not wish to see his face? It is a dark passage, is it? Oh, if the way were darker still, since he is on the other side, let us pass through it with a song. To be with him where he is—are you reluctant? Reluctant to behold his face? Reluctant to be in his bosom for ever? Is there not an " if" somewhere?

No, your grief is not about your death; it is about those that have died whom you loved. You cannot forgive God for taking away those you loved so well. Who has them, friend? Who has them? I will tell you. It is One who, when he was here, said, " Father, I will that they also, whom thou hast given me, be with me where I am." He prayed for them; he died for them; and now he has his own, and you are displeased! Do you stand fretting because Christ has his own? What! Are you pettish because what he lent you for a while he has taken back? Were not your dear ones always more his than yours? Do you love him, then, and grudge your child, your babe, to Jesus? Do you grudge your mother, your brother, your wife, your husband, to him that bought them with his blood? Oh, I say again, it puts an " if" upon your love—not on the existence of it, but on the degree of it. If you loved him, you would rejoice that he sees of the travail of his soul, and has his saints with him in glory.

IV. That brings me to the closing remark, which contains the gist of the text, and all the rest is meant to lead up to it, namely, this: that OUR LOVE TO OUR DIVINE LORD OUGHT TO BE SUCH THAT HIS EXALTATION, THOUGH IT SHOULD BE OUR LOSS, SHOULD, NEVERTHELESS, GIVE US UNFEIGNED DELIGHT. I will put this very simply before you. There is a daughter of yours in Christ, and she is fading away by consumption. She is very happy in the Lord, and full of joyful expectation. She is about to die, and you are all round the bed: you, her dear mother, stand there weeping most of all. Now, your dear girl shall give you an explanation of my text. She says, " Mother, do you not know that I shall soon be with the angels, and shall see the face of God, without fault? If you loved me, mother, you would rejoice to think that I shall be away from all this weakness and this pain. If you love me, you will be glad to think that your child shall be in glory." Your girl's sweet words shall tell you what Jesus meant. He meant, " If you loved me very much—if you loved *me*—not merely my presence and the comforts that I bring you, and the charm with which I invest your earthly life; but if you loved *me*, you would say, ' Blessed Lord, we readily deny ourselves thy company and all the joy it brings, because it is better for thee to be gone unto the Father. It is more glorious for thee to be in heaven than here; and therefore we do rejoice in thy exaltation.' " You see how it was with those disciples. I need not enlarge upon their case. When Jesus had died and risen again, and had gone away from his disciples, he took upon himself the glory which he had laid aside. The glory which he had with God before the world was, he re-assumed at the time when he entered heaven. Then, too, as the God-Man, he was invested with a new splendour. The Father said, " Let all the angels of God worship him "; and they adored him. New songs went up from every golden street, and all heaven rang with "Hosanna! Hosanna! Hosanna!" as Christ ascended to his throne, To the throne he ascends and there he sits, King and Priest for ever, enthroned until his enemies are made his footstool. No more the bloody sweat: no more the cruel spear : no more the dark and lonesome tomb. He is exalted above all exaltation, higher than the kings of the earth, far above all principalities and powers and every name that is named. We ought to be glad of this—exceeding glad. These disciples were bound to be glad if they loved Christ, for though they could no more enjoy his company, could not sit at the table with him, could not walk through the streets with him any more, yet it was good *for him* to be gone to his glory ; and therefore they were constrained to rejoice.

I want, in conclusion, to draw one or two parallel cases which may be practically applicable to yourselves.

Suppose, beloved, that it should ever be for Christ's glory to leave you in the dark, would you not rejoice to have it so ? A little while ago it was so with me. A few years ago I remember preaching to you from the text, "My God, my God, why hast thou forsaken me ? " and I think that if ever soul of mortal man did know the bitter meaning of that cry I did. I preached, hearing the clanking of my own fetters while I spoke to you. It was sad work. That night, ere I went home, I knew the reason. There came into the vestry a man as nearly insane as man could be. Despair hung like a cloud over his countenance ; and as he took my hand, he said, " I have never met a man before that seemed to know where I am. Talk with me." I saw him the next day, and several days, and saved him, by God's help, from self-destruction. Then did I rejoice because I saw that Christ was glorified. I would lose my Master's company, dark as the day would be to me without it—lose it, ay, by the month together—if it would make him glorious in the heart of one poor downcast man, or bring a single sinner to his feet. Be willing to say the same, brethren. Love Christ, and be willing for him to give you the cold shoulder instead of the kiss of his lips, if he might the more be glorified. God bring us to reach that state of self-denial, to be willing to forego that greatest luxury of heaven, for which angels themselves do pine—the presence of the Lord, if thereby Jesus may be the better served.

Well, now, suppose that you are going to be laid aside, and afflicted, and troubled, and it should be God's intent that by this you should become more useful and more fitted for his service. If you love him, you will rejoice at this. You will accept chastisement with thankfulness, and say, "Lay on the stripes! Multiply the pains! Only fashion me so that I can glorify thee! Make no account of anything else but this—that thou mayest be exalted in my mortal body whether I live or whether I die!"

It is possible, dear friend, that you are going to be eclipsed by one who has a brighter light than any God has yet given you. None of us like this. Somebody is coming forward who will preach better than you. That Sunday-school teacher is going to teach better than you. Somebody near you will display more grace and more gift than you. What then? If you love Jesus you will rejoice that it should be so. You recollect how Paul did. There were some who preached Christ out of contention and ill-will, and wanted to get the better of Paul, and have their names cried up above the apostles. "Ah!" says Paul, "so long as Christ is preached I do rejoice, yea, and will rejoice." Well spoken, Paul! I like the valour of the soldier who helped to fill the ditch with his dead body that his captain might march to victory. Throw yourselves into oblivion that Jesus may triumph. It were a small sacrifice for all the church to die a martyr's death if Jesus were but raised one inch the higher among men. Let us exhibit the self-denying spirit which is born of love. "If ye loved me, ye would rejoice, because I said, I go unto the Father."

Suppose that it should also happen that some of you are going to be deprived of all the privileges of hearing the gospel, because you are going away to a foreign land. You are extremely sorry; but suppose that Jesus means to make use of you to advance his glory among the heathen—by naming his name where it was never known before: then you may rejoice in banishment, rejoice to deny yourselves gospel privileges, rejoice to be scattered far and wide by mount, and stream, and sea, so that you may bring forth a harvest to his glory.

Brethren, if you should be sinking lower and lower in your own esteem, be not sorry for it. If Christ is rising higher and higher in your esteem, count it all gain. Sink, O self, down to death, and the abyss. Sink, sink, till there is nothing left of thee! Go down, pride, self-conceit, self-trust, self-seeking! Go even though your going should cause despondency, so long as Christ is crowned! Sink, sink, soul, if Jesus rises! If thou canst trust him better, love him better, and admire him more, so let it be. As you come to his table, say in your hearts, "Lord, make me glad, or make me sad, so long as thou art exalted! Lord, let me have thy presence, or even let me be without it, so long as thou art exalted and extolled!"

PORTIONS OF SCRIPTURE READ BEFORE SERMON—John xiv. (parts).

HYMNS FROM "OUR OWN HYMN BOOK"—313, 317, 786.

Metropolitan Tabernacle Pulpit.

MY COMFORT IN AFFLICTION.

DELIVERED BY

C. H. SPURGEON,

AT THE METROPOLITAN TABERNACLE, NEWINGTON,

On July 7th, 1881.

"This is my comfort in my affliction: for thy word hath quickened me."—Psalm cxix. 50.

It is almost needless for me to say that, in some respects, the same events happen unto all men alike—in the matter of afflictions it is certainly so. None of us can expect to escape trial. If you be ungodly, "many sorrows shall be to the wicked." If you be godly, "many are the afflictions of the righteous." If you walk in the ways of holiness, you shall find that there are stumbling-blocks cast in the way by the enemy. If you walk in the ways of unrighteousness, you shall be taken in snares, and held therein even unto death. There is no escaping trouble; we are born to it as the sparks fly upward. When we are born the second time, though we inherit innumerable mercies, we are certainly born to another set of troubles, for we enter upon spiritual trials, spiritual conflicts, spiritual pains, and so forth; and thus we get a double set of distresses, as well as twofold mercies. He who wrote this one hundred and nineteenth Psalm was a good man, but assuredly he was an afflicted man. Many times did David sorrow, and sorrow sorely. The man after God's own heart was one who felt God's own hand in chastisement. David was a king; and therefore it would be folly on our part to suppose that men who are wealthier and greater than we are, are more screened from affliction; it is quite the reverse. The higher up the mountain the more boisterous the winds. Depend upon it, that the middle state for which Agur prayed, "Give me neither poverty nor riches," is, upon the whole, the best. Greatness, prominence, popularity, nobility, royalty bring no relief from trial, but rather an increase of it. Nobody who consulted his own comfort would enter upon dignities attended with so much labour and sore travail. Child of God, remember that neither goodness nor greatness can deliver you from affliction. You have to face it, whatever your position in life; therefore face it with dauntless courage, and extort victory from it.

Yet, even if you do face it, you will not escape it. Even if you cry to God to help you, he will help you through the trouble, but he will

No. 1,872.

317

probably not turn it aside from you: he will deliver you from evil, but he may yet lead you into trial. He hath promised that he will deliver you in six troubles, and that in seven there shall no evil touch you; but he does not promise that either six or seven trials shall be kept off from you. One like unto the Son of God was with the three holy children in the fire, but he was not with them till they were in the fire—at least not visibly; and he was not so with them as either to quench the flame, or to prevent their being cast into it. "I am with thee, Israel, passing through the fire," may well describe the covenant assurance. May we realize the fire if only thus we can realize the divine presence! Gladly may we accept the furnace, if we may but find the company of the Son of God with us therein. Every child of God among you can, with the Psalmist, speak of *my* affliction. You may not be able to speak of *my* estate, *my* heritage, *my* wealth, *my* health, but you can all speak of *my* affliction. No man is a monopolist of misery. A portion of the black draught of sorrow is left for others. Of that cup we must all drink, little or much; and we must drink of it as God ordains. So far, then, one event happeneth to all.

My object at this time is to show the difference between the Christian and the worldling in his affliction. First, believers have in their affliction *a peculiar comfort:* "This is my comfort in my affliction." Secondly, that comfort comes from *a peculiar source:* "For thy word hath quickened me." And, thirdly, that peculiar comfort is valuable under very *special trials*, such as are mentioned in the context.

I. First, then, believers have their PECULIAR COMFORT under affliction. "This," says David, "is my comfort in my affliction." "*This*" —dwell on the word "*this*," *as different from the consolations of other men*. The drunkard takes his cup and he quotes Solomon, "Give strong drink unto him that is ready to perish, and wine unto those that be of heavy hearts"; and as he quaffs his cup, he says, "*This* is my comfort in my affliction." The miser hides his gold, takes down his purse, and chinks it. Oh, the music of those golden notes! And he cries, "*This* is my comfort in my affliction." Men mostly have some comfort or other. Some have allowable comforts, though they be but of minor quality; they find comfort in the sympathy of men, in domestic kindness, in philosophic reflection, in homely content; but such comforts generally fail, always fail, when the trial becomes exceedingly severe. Now, just as the wicked man and the worldly man can say of this or that, "*This* is my comfort," the Christian comes forward, and bringing with him the Word of God brimming with rich promises, he says, "*This* is my comfort in my affliction." You put down your comfort, and I put down mine. "*This* is my comfort"—he is evidently not ashamed of it; he is evidently ready to set forth his solace in preference to all others; and while others say, I derive consolation from *this*, and I from *that*, David opens the Holy Scripture, and cheerfully exclaims, "*This* is my comfort." Can you say the same? "*This*" in opposition to everything else—this promise of God, this covenant of his grace, "*This* is my comfort."

Now read "*this*" *in another sense, as indicating that he knew what it was.* "*This* is my comfort." He can explain what it is. Many Christian people get a comfort out of God's Word, and out of believing in Christ, and out of religious exercises, but they can hardly tell what the comfort is. A rose smells sweetly to a man who does not know the name of the rose. A rose-grower tells me, "This is the Marshal Niel." Thank you, dear sir; but I do not know who Marshal Niel is, or was, or why the flower bears his military name; but I can smell the rose all the same. So, many people cannot explain doctrines, but they enjoy them. After all, experience is better than exposition. Yet it is a splendid thing when the two go together, so that the believer can say to his friend, "Listen, I will tell you, '*This* is my comfort.'"

"I saw how happy you were, dear friend, when you were in trouble. I saw you sick the other day, and I noticed your patience. I knew you to be slandered, and I saw how calm you were. Can you tell me why you were so calm and self-contained?" It is a very happy thing if the Christian can turn round, and answer such a question fully. I like to see him ready to give a reason for the hope that is in him with meekness and fear, saying,—"*This* is my comfort in my affliction." I want you, if you have enjoyed comfort from God, to get it packed up in such a form that you can pass it on to a friend. Get it explained to your own understanding, so that you can tell others what it is, so that they may taste the consolation wherewith God has comforted you. Be ready to explain to young beginners,—"*This* is my comfort in my affliction."

Again "*this*" is used in another sense, that is, *as having the thing near at hand.* I do not like speaking of my comfort from God, and saying, *that* is my comfort, *that* is the solace which I enjoyed long ago. Oh, no, no! you need a comfort that you can press to your bosom, and say, "*This* is my comfort," *this* which I have here at this present! "*This*" is the word which indicates nearness. "*This* is my comfort." Do you enjoy it now? You were so happy once. Are you as happy now?

> "What peaceful hours I once enjoyed!
> How sweet their memory still!"

Yes, that is very well, Cowper, but it would be better to sing—

> "What peaceful hours I now enjoy!
> How sweet the present hour!"

"*This* is my comfort"; I have it still with me; as my affliction is present with me, so my consolation is present with me. You have heard the classic story of the Rhodian, who said that at such and such a place he had made a jump of many yards. He bragged till a Greek, who stood by, chalked out the distance, and said, "Would you mind jumping half that length now?" So I have heard people talk of what enjoyments they once had, what delights they once had. I have heard of a man who has the roots of depravity dug out of him; and, as for sin, he has almost forgotten what it is. I would like to watch that brother when under the influence of rheumatism. I do not want him to have it long, but I should like him to have a twinge or two, that I might see whether some roots of corruption do not remain. I think that when he was tried in that way, or if not just in that way, in some other, he would find that there was a rootlet or two still in the soil. If a storm were to come on, perhaps our brave dry-land sailor might not find his anchor quite so easy to cast overboard as he now thinks it is. You smile at the talk of modern perfection, and so do I; but I am sick of it. I do not believe in it; it is so utterly contrary to that which I have to learn every day of my own unworthiness, that I feel a contempt for it. Do have your comforts always handy; pray God that that which was a consolation years ago may be a consolation still, so that you may say, "*This* is my comfort in my affliction."

Again, I think the word "this" *is meant as pleading it in prayer.* Let me read the previous verse, "Remember the word unto thy servant upon which thou hast caused me to hope." That is thy promise which thou hast made me to hope upon; Lord, fulfil it to me; for this thy promise is my comfort in my affliction, and I plead it in prayer. Suppose, brethren, you and I are enabled to take comfort out of a promise, we have in that fact a good argument to plead with God. We may say, "Lord, I have so believed this promise of thine that I have been persuaded that I had in my possession the blessing therein promised to me. And now shall I be ashamed by this my hope? Wilt thou not honour thy word, seeing thou hast caused me to rest upon it?" Is not this good pleading? "Remember the word unto thy servant, upon which thou hast caused me to hope, for this is already my comfort; and thou wilt have given me a false comfort, and led me into error if thy word should fail. O my Lord, since I have sucked my comfort out of the expectation of what thou art about to do, surely by this thou art pledged and bound to thy servant—that thou wilt keep thy word!" Hence the word "this" is seen to be a very comprehensive word. May the Spirit of God teach us each to say of our priceless Bible, "This is my comfort in my affliction."

We pass on to note, secondly, that this comfort comes from A PECULIAR SOURCE—"This is my comfort, *for thy Word hath quickened me.*" The comfort, then, is partly outward, coming from God's Word; but it is mainly, and pre-eminently inward, for it is God's Word experienced as to its quickening power within the soul.

First, *it is God's Word that comforts.* Why do we look anywhere else for consolation but to God's word? Oh, brothers and sisters, I am ashamed to have to say it, but we go to our neighbours, or relatives, and we cry, "Have pity upon me, have pity upon me, O my friends!" and it ends with our crying, "Miserable comforters are ye all." We turn to the pages of our past life, and look there for comfort; but this may also fail us. Though experience is a legitimate source of comfort, yet when the sky is dark and lowering, experience is apt to minister fresh distress. If we were to go at once to God's Word, and search it till we found a promise suitable to our case, we should find relief far sooner. All cisterns dry up: only the fountain remains. Next time you are troubled, reach down the Bible. Say to thy soul: "Soul, sit thou still, and hear what God the Lord will speak, for he will speak peace unto his people." You read one promise, and you feel, "No, that hardly meets the case. Here is another; but it is made to a special character, and I am afraid I am not that character. Here, thank God, is one that just fits me, as a key fits the wards of a lock." When you find such a promise, use it at once. John Bunyan beautifully pictures a pilgrim, laid by the heels in Giant Despair's castle, and there beaten with a crabtree cudgel till one morning he puts his hand into his bosom, and cries to his brother Christian, "What a fool have I been to lie rotting in this noisome dungeon, when all this time I have a key in my bosom which will open every door in Doubting Castle!" "Sayest thou so, my brother," says Christian, "pluck it out, and let us use it at once." This key, which is called Promise, is thrust into the first lock, and the door flies open; and then it is tried upon the next and the next, with quick result. Though the great iron gate had a rusted lock, in which the key did terribly grate and grind, yet it did open, and the prisoners were free from the durance vile of their mistrust. The Promise always has opened the gate, and every gate—ay, the gates of despair shall be opened with that key called Promise, if a man does but know how to hold it firmly, and turn it wisely, till the bolt flies back. "This is my comfort in my affliction," says the Psalmist—God's own Word. Dear friends, fly to this comfort with speed in every time of trouble; get to be familiar with God's Word, that you may do so. I have found it helpful to carry "Clarke's Precious Promises" in my pocket, so as to refer to it in the hour of trial. If you go into the market, and are likely to do a ready-money business, you always take a cheque-book with you; so carry precious promises with you, that you may plead the word which suits your case. I have turned to promises for the sick when I have been of that number, or to promises to the poor, the despondent, the weary, and such like, according to my own condition, and I have always found a Scripture fitted to my case. I do not want a promise made to the sick when I am perfectly well; I do not want balm for a broken heart when my soul is rejoicing in the Lord; but it is very handy to know where to lay your hand upon suitable words of cheer when necessity arises. Thus the external comfort of the Christian is the Word of God.

Now for the internal part of his consolation. "This is my comfort in my affliction, *for thy Word hath quickened me.*" Oh, it is not the letter, but the spirit, which is our real comfort. We look not to that Book, which consists of so much binding, and so much paper, and so much ink; but to the living Witness within the Book. The Holy Ghost embodies himself in these blessed words, and works upon our hearts, so that we are quickened by the Word. It is this which is the true comfort of the soul.

When you read the promise, and it is applied with power to you; when you read the precept, and it works with force upon your conscience; when you read any part of God's Word, and it gives life to your spirit —then it is that you get the comfort of it. I have heard of persons reading so many chapters a day, and getting through the Bible in a year, —a very admirable habit, no doubt; but it may be performed so mechanically that no good whatever may come of it. You want to pray earnestly over the Word, that it may quicken you, or otherwise it will not be a comfort to you. Let us think of what our comfort is in the time of affliction from our soul's being quickened by the Word. Comfort comes thus: God's Word has in past days quickened us. It has been a word of life from the dead. In our affliction, we therefore remember how God has brought us out of spiritual death, and made us alive, and this cheers us. If you can say, "Whatever pain I suffer, whatever grief I endure, yet I am a living child of God," then you have a well-spring of comfort. It is better to be the most afflicted child of God than to be the gayest worldling Better be God's dog than the devil's darling. Child of God, comfort yourself with this: if God has not given me a soft bed, nor left me a whole skin, yet he has quickened me by his Word; and this is a choice favour. Thus our first quickening from spiritual death is a sunny memory.

After we are made alive we need to be quickened in duty, to be quickened in joy, to be quickened in every holy exercise; and we are happy if the Word has given us this repeated quickening. If, in looking back, dear friend, you can say, "Thy Word hath quickened me; I have had much joy in hearing thy Word; I have been made full of energy through thy Word; I have been made to run in the way of thy commandments through thy Word;" all this will be a great comfort to you. You can then plead—"O Lord, while thou mayest have denied me much of the joy that some people have, yet thou hast often quickened me! Oh, be it so again, for *this* is my comfort!" I hope I am speaking to many experienced Christians, who can say that God's Word has very frequently refreshed them when they have been in the depths of distress, and fetched them up from the gates of the grave; and if they can bear this testimony, they know what comfort there is in the quickening of the Word of God, and they will ask to feel that quickening influence again, that so they may be of good comfort.

Brothers and sisters, it is a very strange thing that when God wills to do one thing he often does another. When he wants to comfort us, what does he do? Does he comfort us? Yes, and no: he quickens us, and so he comforts us. Sometimes the roundabout way is the straight way. God does not give the comfort we ask for by a distinct act, but he quickens us, and so we obtain comfort. Here is a person very low and depressed. What does a wise doctor do? He does not give strong drink to act as a temporary fillip to his spirits, for this would end in a reaction in which the man would sink lower; but he gives him a tonic, and braces him up, and when the man is stronger, he becomes happier, and shakes off his nervousness. The Lord comforts his servants by quickening them: "This is my comfort in my affliction; for thy Word hath quickened me."

I speak to some of you who have endured long affliction, and it is a joy to see you out again to-night. Has not God's Word often quickened you in affliction? Perhaps you have been sluggish when in health, but affliction has made you feel the value of the promise, the value of the covenant blessing, and then you have cried to God for it. You may have been worried about worldly cares before, but you have been obliged to drop them in the time of affliction, and your only care has been to get nearer to Christ, and to creep into your Lord's bosom.

Sometimes in prosperity you could hardly pray; but I warrant you you prayed when you were ready to perish, and pined at death's door. Your affliction quickened your prayers. There is a man trying to write with a quill pen; it will not make anything but a thick stroke; but he takes a knife and cuts fiercely at the quill till it marks admirably. So we have to be cut with the sharp knife of affliction, for only then can the Lord make use of us. See how sharply gardeners trim their vines; they take off every shoot till the vine looks like a dry stick. There will be no grapes in the spring if there is not this cutting away in the autumn and winter. God quickens us in our afflictions through his

Word. Our sorrows are made to have a salutary action on our souls; we receive by them spiritual revival and health, and thus comfort flows in to us. It would not be wise to pray to be altogether delivered from trial, though we should like to be. It would be a pleasant thing to have a grassy path all the way to heaven, and never to find a stone in the road; but though pleasant, it might not be safe. If the way were a fine turf, cut every morning with a lawn-mower, and made as soft as velvet, I am afraid we should never get to heaven at all, for we should linger too long upon the road. Some animals' feet are not adapted for smooth places; and, brethren, you and I are of a very slippery-footed race. We slip when the roads are smooth: it is easy to go down hill, but it is not easy to do so without a stumble. John Bunyan tells us that when Christian passed through the Valley of Humiliation, the fight he had there with Apollyon was very much due to the slips he made in going down the hill which descended into the valley. Happy is he who is in the Valley of Humiliation, for "he that is down need fear no fall"; but his happiness will largely depend upon how he came down. Gently, you that are on the hill-tops of delight and prosperity. Gently, lest peradventure you slip with your feet, and mischief come of it!

Quickening is what we want; and if we get it, even if it comes to us by the sharpest tribulation, we may gladly accept it. "This is my comfort in my affliction: for thy Word hath quickened me."

III. Lastly, and very briefly, there are certain PECULIAR TRIALS of Christians in which this peculiar comfort is specially excellent.

Kindly look at the psalm, and notice, in the forty-ninth verse, that the Psalmist suffered from *hope deferred*. "Remember thy Word unto thy servant, upon which thou hast caused me to hope." Long waiting for the promise to be fulfilled may make the soul grow weary; and hope deferred makes the heart sick. At such a time this is to be our comfort: "Thy Word hath quickened me." I have not yet obtained that which I prayed for, but I have been quickened while I have been praying. I have not found the blessing I have been seeking; but I am sure I shall have it, for already the exercise of prayer has been of service to me: *this* is my comfort under the delay of my hope, that thy Word has already quickened me.

Notice the next verse, in which the Psalmist was suffering the great trial of *scorn*. "The proud have had me greatly in derision." Ridicule is a very sharp ordeal. When the proud are able to say something against us that stings; when they laugh, ay, and laugh greatly, and treat us like the mire in the streets, it is a severe affliction, and under it we need rich comfort. If at that time we feel, that if man's word stings, yet God's Word quickens, then we are comforted. If we are driven more to God by being scorned by men, we may very cheerfully accept their contempt, and say, "Lord, I bless thee for this persecution which makes me a partaker of Christ's sufferings." I say it becomes a comfort to us to be quickened by the Word when the ungodly are despising us.

At the fifty-third verse you will see that David was under the trouble of *living among great blasphemers* and doers of open wickedness. He says, "Horror hath taken hold upon me, because of the wicked that forsake thy law." He was horrified at their vices: he wished that he could get away from their society, and never see or hear that which distressed him so much. But if the very sight and sound of sin drive us to pray, and force us to cry to God, the result is good, however painful the process may be. If men never swore in the streets, we should not so often be driven to cry to God to forgive their profanity. If you and I could always be shut up in a glass case, and never see sin or hear of it, it might be a bad thing for us; but if, when we are compelled to see the wickedness of men, and hear their curses and revilings, we can also feel that God's Word is quickening us, even by our horror at sin, it is good for us. We have great comfort in this peculiar species of affliction, though it is exceedingly grievous to tender-hearted, pure, and delicate minds, who dwell near to God.

Just read the fifty-forth verse, and you will see another of David's trials indicated. "Thy statutes have been my song in the house of my pilgrimage." *He had many changes;* he had all the trials of a pilgrim's life—the discomforts of journeying in places where he had no abiding city. But "*this,*" he says, "has been my comfort in my affliction." Thy Word has told me of a city that hath foundations; thy Word has assured me that if I am a stranger upon earth, I am also a citizen of heaven. "Thy Word hath quickened me"; I have felt myself so strengthened by thy Word that I have been glad to feel that this is not my rest. I am glad to feel that I must be away to a better land, and so my heart has been happy, and "thy statutes have been my songs in the house of my pilgrimage."

Lastly, in the fifty-fifth verse, you see David was *in darkness.* He says, "I have remembered thy name, O Lord, in the night, and have kept thy law." Even in the night he could derive comfort from the quickening influence which often comes to the soul from the Scriptures even when we are surrounded by darkness and sorrow. I will not go over that ground again, but certain it is that when our soul is shrouded in distress it often becomes more active and gracious than when it is basking in the sunlight of prosperity. All along then, dear friends, your comfort and mine is the Word of God, laid home by God the Holy Ghost to our hearts, quickening us to an increase of spiritual life. Do not try to flee from your troubles; do not fret under your cares; do not expect this world to bring forth roses without thorns; do not hope to prevent the upspringing of briers and thistles; but ask for quickening; ask for that quickening to come, not by new revelations nor by fanatical excitement, but by God's own Word quietly applied by his own Spirit. So shall you conquer all your troubles, and overcome your difficulties, and enter into heaven singing hallelujahs unto the Lord's right hand and holy arm which have gotten him the victory.

PORTION OF SCRIPTURE READ BEFORE SERMON—Psalm cxix. 49—64.

HYMNS FROM "OUR OWN HYMN BOOK"—481, 119 (Song III.), 482.

"WHERE ARE THE NINE?" OR, PRAISE NEGLECTED.

A Sermon

INTENDED FOR READING ON LORD'S-DAY, DECEMBER 26TH, 1886,

DELIVERED BY

C. H. SPURGEON,

AT THE METROPOLITAN TABERNACLE, NEWINGTON,

On Thursday Evening, October 7th, 1886.

> "And one of them, when he saw that he was healed, turned back, and with a loud voice glorified God, and fell down on his face at his feet, giving him thanks: and he was a Samaritan. And Jesus answering said, Were there not ten cleansed? but where are the nine? There are not found that returned to give glory to God, save this stranger. And he said unto him, Arise, go thy way: thy faith hath made thee whole."—Luke xvii. 15—19.

You have often heard the leprosy described: it was a very horrible disease, I should think the worst that flesh is heir to. We ought to be much more grateful than we are that this fell disease is scarcely known in our favoured country. You have also heard what an instructive symbol it is in human flesh of what sin is in the human soul, how it pollutes, how it destroys. I need not go into that sad subject. But here was a sight for the Saviour—ten men that were lepers! A mass of sorrow indeed! What sights our Lord still sees every day in this sin-defiled world! Not ten men that are sinners, nor even ten millions merely, are to be found all the world over, but on this earth there are a thousand millions of men diseased in soul. It is a miracle of condescension that the Son of God should set foot in such a lazar-house as this.

Yet observe the triumphant grace of our Lord Jesus to the ten men that were lepers. It would make a man's fortune, it would crown a man with lifelong fame, to heal one leper: but our Lord healed ten lepers at once. So full a fountain of grace is he, so freely doth he dispense his favour, that the ten are bidden to go and show themselves to the priests because they are healed, and on the way to the priests they find it is so. None of us can imagine the joy they felt when they perceived that they were healed. Oh, it must have been a sort of new birth to them to find their flesh made fresh as that of a little child! It would not have been wonderful if the whole ten had hurried back, and fallen at Jesus' feet, and lifted up their voices in a tenfold psalm. The sad thing about it is that nine of them, though they were healed, went on their way to the priests in the coolest possible manner : we never hear of their return, they drop out of the story altogether. They have obtained a blessing, they go their way, and there is an end of them.

Nos. 1,935-6-7.

Only one of them, a Samaritan, returned to express his thanks. Misery has strange bedfellows; and so the nine lepers of the seed of Israel consorted with an outcast Samaritan : and he, strange to tell it, was the only one, who, seized by a sudden impulse of gratitude, made his way to his Benefactor, fell down at his feet, and began to glorify God.

If you search the world around, among all choice spices you shall scarcely meet with the frankincense of gratitude. It ought to be as common as the dew-drops that hang upon the hedges in the morning; but, alas, the world is dry of thankfulness to God ! Gratitude to Christ was scarce enough in his own day. I had almost said it was ten to one that nobody would praise him; but I must correct myself a little : it was nine to one. One day in seven is for the Lord's worship; but not one man in ten is devoted to his praise. Our subject is *thankfulness to the Lord Jesus Christ.*

I.   I begin with the point that I have already touched upon, namely, THE SINGULARITY OF THANKFULNESS.

Here note : *there are more who receive benefits than ever give praise for them.* Nine persons healed, one person glorifying God; nine persons healed *of leprosy,* mark you, and only one person kneeling down at Jesus' feet, and thanking him for it ! If for this surpassing benefit, which might have made the dumb to sing, men only thank the Lord in the proportion of one to nine, what shall I say of what we call God's common mercies—only common because he is so liberal with them, for each of them is inestimably valuable ?   Life, health, eyesight, hearing, domestic love, the continuance of friends—I cannot attempt a catalogue of benefits that we receive every day; and yet is there one man in nine that praises God for these ?   A cold " Thank God ! " is all that is given. Others of us do praise him for these benefits, but what poor praises ! Dr. Watts's hymn is sadly true,

> " Hosannas languish on our tongues,
> And our devotion dies."

We do not praise the Lord fitly, proportionately, intensely.   We receive a continent of mercies, and only return an island of praise.   He gives us blessings new every morning, and fresh every evening, great is his faithfulness; and yet we let the years roll round, and seldom observe a day of praise.   Sad is it to see God all goodness, and man all ingratitude !   The tribe who receive benefits may say, " My name is legion "; but those who praise God are so few that a child may write them.

But there is something more remarkable than this : *the number of those who pray is greater than the number of those who praise.*   For these ten men that were lepers all prayed.   Poor and feeble as their voices had become through disease, yet they lifted them up in prayer, and united in crying : " Jesus, Master, have mercy on us !" They all joined in the Litany, " Lord, have mercy upon us !   Christ, have mercy upon us !"   But when they came to the Te Deum, magnifying and praising God, only one of them took up the note.   One would have thought that all who prayed would praise, but it is not so.   Cases have been where a whole ship's crew in time of storm has prayed, and yet none of that crew have sung the praise of God when the storm has become a calm.   Multitudes of our fellow-citizens pray when they are sick, and near to dying; but when they grow better, their praises grow sick unto death.   The angel of mercy, listening at their door, has heard no canticle of love, no song of thankfulness.   Alas, it is too sadly true that more pray than praise !

I put it in another shape to you who are God's people—*most of us pray more than we praise.*   You pray little enough, I fear ; but praise, where is that ?   At our family altars we always pray, but seldom praise.   In our closets we constantly pray, but do we *frequently* praise ?   Prayer is not so heavenly an exercise as praise; prayer is for time, but praise is for eternity.   Praise therefore deserves the first and highest place ; does it not ?   Let us commence the employment which occupies the celestials.   Prayer is for a beggar ; but methinks he is a poor beggar who does not also give praise when he receives an alms.   Praise ought to follow naturally upon the heels of prayer, even when it does not, by divine grace, go before it.   If you are afflicted, if you lose money, if you fall into poverty, if your child is ill, if chastisement visits you in any form, you begin to pray, and I do not blame you for it ; but should it be all praying and no praising ?   Should our life have so much salt, and so little sweet in it ?   Should we get for ourselves so often a draught from the rock of blessing, and so seldom pour out a drink-offering unto the Lord Most High ?   Come, let us chide ourselves as we acknowledge that we offer so much more prayer than praise !

On the same head, let me remark that *more obey ritual than ever praise Christ.*   When Jesus said, "Go shew yourselves to the priests," off they went, all ten of them ; not one stopped behind.   Yet only one came back to behold a personal Saviour, and to praise his name.   So to-day—you will go to church, you will go to chapel, you will read a book, you will perform an outward religious action : but oh, how little praising God, how little lying at his feet, and feeling that we could sing our souls away for gratitude to him who hath done such great things for us !   External religious exercises are easy enough, and common enough ; but the internal matter, the drawing out of the heart in thankful love, how scarce a thing it is !   Nine obey ritual where only one praises the Lord.

Once more, to come yet closer home, *there are more that believe than there are that praise :* for these ten men did believe, but only one praised the Lord Jesus.   Their faith was about the leprosy ; and according to their faith, so it was unto them.   This faith, though it only concerned their leprosy, was yet a very wonderful faith.   It was remarkable that they should believe the Lord Jesus though he did not even say, " Be healed," nor speak a word to them to that effect, but simply said, " Go shew yourselves to the priests."   With parched skins, and death burning its way into their hearts, they went bravely off in confidence that Jesus must mean to bless them.   It was admirable faith ; and yet none of the nine who thus believed ever came back to praise Christ for the mercy received.   I am afraid that there is much of faith, better faith than theirs, which concerns spiritual things, which has yet to flower into practical gratitude.   Perhaps it blooms late in the year, like the chrysanthemum ; but certainly it has not flowered in spring-time, like the primrose and the daffodil.   It is a faith which bears few blossoms of praise.   I chide myself sometimes that I have wrestled with God in prayer, like Elias upon Carmel, but I have not magnified the name of the Lord, like Mary of Nazareth. We do not laud our Lord in proportion to the benefits received. God's treasury would overflow if the revenue of thanks were more honestly paid. There would be no need to plead for missions, and stir up God's people to self-denial, if there were praise at all proportionate even to our faith. We believe for heaven and eternity, and yet do not magnify the Lord as we should for earth and time. It is real faith, I trust—it is not for me to judge it, but it is faulty in result. Faith was only real in these lepers so far as their leprosy was concerned; they did not believe in our Lord's divinity, or believe for eternal life. So also among ourselves, there are men who get benefits from Christ, who even hope that they are saved, but they do not praise him. Their lives are spent in examining their own skins to see whether their leprosy is gone. Their religious life reveals itself in a constant searching of themselves to see if they are really healed. This is a poor way of spending one's energies. This man knew that he was healed, he had full assurance upon that point; and the next impulse of his spirit was to hie him back to where *he* stood who had been his glorious Physician, to fall at *his* feet, and praise *him* with a loud voice, glorifying God. Oh, that all my timorous, doubting hearers may do the same!

I have said enough, I think, upon the scantiness of thanksgiving. Let us go over those points again. More receive benefits than praise God for them; more pray than praise; more obey ritual than praise God with the heart; and more believe, and receive benefits through faith, than rightly praise the Giver of those benefits.

II. I have a great deal to say, and little time to say it in; therefore, briefly let us note THE CHARACTERISTICS OF TRUE THANKFULNESS. This man's simple act may show the character of praise. It does not take the same shape in everybody. Love to Christ, like living flowers, wears many forms; only artificial flowers are all alike. Living praise is marked by *individuality*. This man was one of ten when he was a leper; he was all alone when he returned to praise God. You can sin in company, you can go to hell in company; but when you obtain salvation, you will come to Jesus all alone; and when you are saved, though you will delight to praise God with others if they will join with you, yet if they will not do so, you will delight to sing a solo of gratitude. This man quits the company of the other nine, and comes to Jesus. If Christ has saved you, and your heart is right, you will say, "I *must* praise him ; I *must* love him." You will not be kept back by the chilly state of nine out of ten of your old companions, nor by the worldliness of your family, nor by the coldness of the church. Your personal love to Jesus will make you speak even if heaven, and earth, and sea are all wrapt in silence.

You have a heart burning with adoring love, and you feel as if it were the only heart under heaven that had love to Christ in it ; and therefore you must feed the heavenly flame. You must indulge its desires, you must express its longings ; the fire is in your bones, and must have vent. Since there is an individuality about true praise, come, brothers in Christ, let us praise God each one in his own way!

" Oh, may the sweet, the blissful theme,
  Fill every heart and tongue,
  Till strangers love thy charming name,
  And join the sacred song ! "

The next characteristic of this man's thankfulness was *promptness*. He was back to Christ almost immediately ; for I cannot suppose the Saviour lingered at the village-gate for hours that day. He was too busy to be long on one spot : the Master went about doing good. The man was back soon ; and when you are saved, the quicker you can express your gratitude the better. Second thoughts are best, they say ; but this is not the case when the heart is full of love to Christ. Carry out your first thoughts ; do not stop for the second, unless indeed your heart is so on flame with heavenly devotion that second ones consume the first. Go at once, and praise the Saviour. What grand designs some of you have formed of future service for God ! What small results have followed ! Ah, it is better to lay one brick to-day than to propose to build a palace next year ! Magnify your Lord in the present salvation. Why should his mercies lie in quarantine? Why should your praises be like aloes, which take a century to flower? Why should praise be kept waiting at the door even for a night ? The manna came fresh in the morning ; so let your praises rise betimes. He praises twice who praises at once ; but he who does not praise at once praises never.

The next quality of this man's praise was *spirituality*. We perceive this in the fact that he paused on his way to the priests. It was his duty to go to the priests : he had received a command to do so ; but there is a proportion in all things, and some duties are greater than others. He thought to himself : I was ordered to go to the priests ; but I am healed, and this new circumstance affects the order of my duties : the first thing I ought to do is to go back, and bear witness to the people, glorifying God in the midst of them all, and falling down at Christ's feet. It is well to observe the holy law of proportion. Carnal minds take the ritualistic duty first ; that which is external outweighs with them that which is spiritual. But love soon perceives that the substance is more precious than the shadow, and that to bow at the feet of the great High Priest must be a greater duty than to go before the lesser priests. So the healed leper went first to Jesus. In him the spiritual overrode the ceremonial. He felt that his main duty was in person to adore the divine person who had delivered him from his fell disease. Let us go first to Jesus. Let us in spirit bow before HIM. Ah, yes ! Come to our services, join in our regular worship : but if you love the Lord, you will want something besides this : you will pine to get to Jesus himself, and tell him how you love him. You will long to do something for him by yourself, by which you can show forth the gratitude of your heart to the Christ of God.

True thankfulness also manifests itself in *intensity*. Intensity is perceptible in this case : he turned back, and with a loud voice glorified God. He could have praised, could he not, in a quieter way ? Yes, but when you are just cured of leprosy, and your once feeble voice is restored to you, you cannot whisper out your praises. Brethren, you know it would be impossible to be coolly proper when you are newly

saved! This man with a loud voice glorified God ; and you, too, feel
forced to cry—

> "Fain would I sound it out so loud
> That earth and heaven should hear."

Some of our converts are very wild at times, they grow extravagant.
Do not blame them. Why not indulge them? It will not hurt *you*.
We are all of us so very proper and orderly that we can afford to have
an extravagant one among us now and then. Oh, that God would send
more of that sort to wake the church up, that we, also, might all begin
to praise God with heart and voice, with soul and substance, with
might and main! Hallelujah! My own heart feels the glow.

In true thankfulness, next, there is *humility*. This man fell down at
Jesus' feet : he did not feel perfectly in his place until he was lying
there. "I am nobody, Lord," he seemed to say, and therefore he fell
on his face. But the place for his prostration was "at his feet." I
would rather be nobody at Christ's feet than everybody anywhere else!
There is no place so honourable as down at the feet of Jesus. Ah,
to lie there always, and just love him wholly, and let self die out! Oh,
to have Christ standing over you as the one figure overshadowing your
life henceforth and for ever! True thankfulness lies low before the Lord.

Added to this there was *worship*. He fell down at Jesus' feet,
glorifying God, and giving thanks unto him. Let us worship our Saviour.
Let others think as they like about Jesus, but we will put our finger
into the print of the nails, and say, "My Lord and my God!" If
there be a God, he is God in Christ Jesus to us. We shall never cease
to adore him who has proved his Godhead by delivering us from the
leprosy of sin. All worship be to his supreme majesty!

One thing more about this man I want to notice as to his thankfulness,
and that is, *his silence as to censuring others*. When the Saviour said,
"Where are the nine?" I notice that *this man did not reply*. The
Master said, "Where are the nine? There are not found that returned
to give glory to God, save this stranger." But the adoring stranger
did not stand up, and say, "O Lord, they are all gone off to the
priests : I am astonished at them that they did not return to praise
thee!" O brothers, we have enough to do to mind our own business,
when we feel the grace of God in our own hearts! If I can only get
through my service of praise, I shall have no mind to accuse any of you
who are ungrateful. The Master says : "Where are the nine?" but
the poor healed man at his feet has no word to say against those cruel
nine, he is too much occupied with his personal adoration.

III. I have not half done, and yet you cannot possibly stay beyond
the appointed hour of closing : therefore I must compress my third
division as closely as I possibly can—let us consider THE BLESSEDNESS
OF THANKFULNESS. This man was more blessed by far than the nine.
They were healed, but they were not blessed as he was. There is a
great blessedness in thankfulness.

First, *because it is right*. Should not Christ be praised? This man
did what he could : and there is always an ease of conscience, and a rest
of spirit, when you feel that you are doing all you can in a right cause,
even though you fall far short of your own desire. At this moment, my
brethren, magnify the Lord.

> " Meet and right it is to sing,
> In every time and place,
> Glory to our heavenly King,
> The God of truth and grace.
> Join we then with sweet accord,
> All in one thanksgiving join !
> Holy, holy, holy Lord,
> Eternal praise be thine."

Next, there is this blessing in thankfulness, that *it is a manifestation of personal love*. I love the doctrines of grace, I love the church of God, I love the Sabbath, I love the ordinances ; but I love Jesus most. My heart never rests until I can glorify God personally, and give thanks unto the Christ personally. The indulgence of personal love to Christ is one of the sweetest things out of heaven ; and you cannot indulge that personal love so well as by personal thankfulness both of heart and mouth, and act and deed.

There is another blessedness about thankfulness : *it has clear views*. The thankful eye sees far and deep. The man healed of leprosy, before he went on glorifying God, gave thanks to Jesus. If he had thanked Jesus and stopped there, I should have said that his eyes were not well open ; but when he saw God in Christ, and therefore glorified God for what Christ had done, he showed a deep insight into spiritual truth. He had begun to discover the mysteries of the divine and human person of the blessed Lord. We learn much by prayer. Did not Luther say, " To have prayed well is to have studied well " ? I venture to add a rider to what Luther has so ably said : To have praised well is to have studied better. Praise is a great instructor. Prayer and praise are the oars by which a man may row his boat into the deep waters of the knowledge of Christ.

The next blessedness about praise is that *it is acceptable to Christ*. The Lord Jesus was evidently pleased ; he was grieved to think the other nine should not come back, but he was charmed with this one man that he did return. The question, " Where are the nine ? " bears within it a commendation of the one. Whatever pleases Christ should be carefully cultivated by us. If praise be pleasant to him, let us continually magnify his name. Prayer is the straw of the wheat, but praise is the ear. Jesus loves to see the blade grow up, but he loves better to pluck the golden ears when the harvest of praise is ripe.

Next, notice, that the blessedness of thankfulness is that *it receives the largest blessing*, for the Saviour said to this man what he had not said to the others, " thy faith hath made thee whole." If you would live the higher life, be much in praising God. Some of you are in the lowest state as yet, as this man was, for he was a Samaritan : but by praising God he rose to be a songster rather than a stranger. How often have I noticed how the greatest sinner becomes the greatest praiser ! Those that were farthest off from Christ, and hope, and purity, when they become saved, feel that they owe the most, and therefore they love the best. May it be the ambition of every one of us, even if we be not originally among the vilest of the vile, yet to feel that we owe Jesus most ; and therefore we will praise him most : thus shall we receive the richest blessedness from his hands !

I have done when I have said three things. Let us learn from all this to *put praise in a high place.* Let us hold praise-meetings. Let us think it as great a sin to neglect praise as to restrain prayer.

Next, *let us pay our praise to Christ himself.* Whether we go to the priests or not, let us go to *him.* Let us praise him personally and vehemently. Personal praise to a personal Saviour must be our life's object.

Lastly, if we work for Jesus, and we see converts, and they do not turn out as we expected, do not let us be cast down about it. *If others do not praise our Lord, let us be sorrowful, but let us not be disappointed.* The Saviour had to say, " Where are the nine ? " Ten lepers were healed, but only one praised him. We have many converts who do not join the church ; we have numbers of persons converted who do not come forward to baptism, or to the Lord's Supper. Numbers get a blessing, but do not feel love enough to own it. Those of us who are soul-winners are robbed of our wages by the cowardly spirits who hide their faith. I thank God of late we have had many avowing their conversion ; but if the other nine would come, we should need nine Tabernacles. Alas for the many who have gone back after professing their faith ! Where are the nine?

So you that hold cottage-meetings, you that go round with tracts, you are doing more good than you will ever hear of. You do not know where the nine are, but even if you should only bless one out of ten, you will have cause to thank God.

" Oh," says one, " I have had so little success ; I have had only one soul saved ! " That is more than you deserve. If I were to fish for a week, and only catch one fish, I should be sorry ; but if that happened to be a sturgeon, a royal fish, I should feel that the quality made up for lack of quantity. When you win a soul it is a great prize. One soul brought to Christ—can you estimate its value ? If one be saved, you should be grateful to your Lord, and persevere. Though you wish for more conversions yet, you will not despond so long as even a few are saved ; and, above all, you will not be angry if some of them do not thank you personally, nor join in church-fellowship with you. Ingratitude is common towards soul-winners. How often a minister has brought sinners to Christ, and fed the flock in his early days ! but when the old man grows feeble they want to get rid of him, and try a new broom which will sweep cleaner. " Poor old gentleman, he is quite out of date ! " they say, and so they get rid of him, as gipsies turn an old horse out on the common to feed or starve, they care not which. If anybody expects gratitude, I would remind them of the benediction, " Blessed are they that expect nothing, for they will not be disappointed." Even our Master did not get praise from the nine : therefore do not wonder if you bless others, and others do not bless you. Oh, that some poor soul would come to Christ to-night, some leper to be healed of sin-sickness ! If he does find healing, let him come out, and with a loud voice magnify the Lord who has dealt so graciously with him.

PORTION OF SCRIPTURE READ BEFORE SERMON—Luke xvii. 1—19.

HYMNS FROM " OUR OWN HYMN BOOK "—103 (Ver. III.), 566, 415.

THE UNKEPT VINEYARD; OR, PERSONAL WORK NEGLECTED.

A Sermon

DELIVERED ON LORD'S-DAY EVENING, SEPTEMBER 19TH, 1886, BY

C. H. SPURGEON,

AT THE METROPOLITAN TABERNACLE, NEWINGTON.

"They made me the keeper of the vineyards; but mine own vineyard have I not kept."—Song of Solomon i. 6.

The text is spoken in the first person singular; "They made me." Therefore let the preaching to-night be personal to you, dear friends: personal to the preacher first, and then to each one of this mixed multitude. May we at this hour think less of others than of ourselves! May the sermon be of practical value to our own hearts! I do not suppose that it will be a pleasing sermon: on the other hand it may be a saddening one. I may bring unhappy memories before you; but let us not be afraid of that holy sorrow which is health to the soul. Since the spouse in this text speaketh of herself, "They made me the keeper of the vineyards; but mine own vineyard have I not kept": let each one of us copy her example, and think of our own selves.

The text is the language of complaint. We are all pretty ready at complaining, especially of other people. Not much good comes of picking holes in other men's characters; and yet many spend hours in that unprofitable occupation. It will be well for us, at this time, to let our complaint, like that of the text, deal with ourselves. If there is something wrong at home, let the father blame himself; if there is something ill with the children, let the mother look to her own personal conduct as their instructor. Do not let us lend out our ears, but let us keep them at home for our own use. Let us clear out an open passage to the heart, so that everything that is said shall go down into the spirit, and purify our inner man. Let us from the heart make the confession—"They made me the keeper of the vineyards; but mine own vineyard have I not kept."

Let us make the text practical. Do not let us be satisfied to have uttered the language of complaint; but let us get rid of the evils which we deplore. If we have been wrong, let us labour to be right. If we have neglected our own vineyard, let us confess it with due humiliation; but let us not continue to neglect it. Let us ask of God that holy results may flow out of our self-lamentations, so that before many days we may begin to keep our own vineyards carefully by the grace of God ; and then we shall better carry out the office of keeper of the vineyards of others, if we are called to such an employment.

There are two things upon which I am going to dwell at this time. The first is, that there are many Christian people—I hope they are Christian people—who will be compelled to confess that the greater part of their life is spent in labour which is not of the highest kind, and is not properly their own. I shall find out *the worker who has forgotten his heavenly calling.* And when I have done with this case—and I am afraid that there will be much about it that may touch many of us—I shall then take a more general view, and deal with *any who are undertaking other works, and neglecting their own proper vocation.*

I. First, then, let me begin with THE CHRISTIAN MAN WHO HAS FORGOTTEN HIS HIGH AND HEAVENLY CALLING. In the day when you and I were born again, my brethren, we were born for God. In the day when we saw that Christ died for us, we were bound henceforth to be dead to the world. In the day when we were quickened by the Holy Ghost into newness of life, that life was bound to be a consecrated one. For a thousand reasons it is true that, " Ye are not your own: ye are bought with a price." The ideal Christian is one who has been made alive with a life which he lives for God. He has risen out of the dominion of the world, the flesh, and the devil. He reckons that " if one died for all, then were all dead : and that he died for all, that they which live should not henceforth live unto themselves, but unto him which died for them, and rose again." This you will not deny. Christian friends, you admit that you have a high, holy, and heavenly calling !

Now let us look back. *We have not spent our life idly :* we have been forced to be keepers of the vineyards. I hope I am not addressing anybody here who has tried to live without employment and labour of some kind. No, we have worked, and we have worked hard. Most men speak of their wages as "hard-earned," and I believe that in many cases they speak the bare truth. Many hours in the day have to be spent upon our occupations. We wake up in the morning, and think of what we have to do. We go to bed wearied at night by what we have done. This is as it should be, for God did not make us that we might sport and play, like leviathan in the deep. Even in Paradise man was bidden to dress the garden. There is something to be done by each man, and specially by each Christian man.

Come back to what I began with. In the day when we were born again, as many of us as are new creatures in Christ Jesus, we began to live to God, and not to ourselves. Have we carried out that life ? We have worked, we have even worked hard ; but the question comes to us—What have we worked for ? Who has been our master ? With what object have we toiled ? Of course, if I have been true to my profession as a Christian, I have lived and worked for God, for Christ, for the kingdom of heaven. But has it been so ? And is it so now ? Many are working very hard for wealth, which means, of course, for self, that they may be enriched. Some are working simply for a competence, which means, if it goes no farther, still for self. Others work for their families, a motive good enough in its way, but still only an enlargement, after all, of self. To the Christian there must always be a far higher, deeper, purer, truer motive than self in its widest sense; or else the day must come when he will look back upon his life, and say, " They made me the keeper of the vineyards; but mine own vineyard "—that is, the service of Christ, the glory of him that bought me with his blood—" have I not kept." It seems to me to be a terrible calamity to have to look back on twenty years, and say, " What have I done in all those twenty years for Christ? How much of my energy has been spent in striving to glorify *him*? I have had talents : how many of those talents have been used for him who gave them to me? I have had wealth, or I have had influence. How much of that money have I spent distinctly for my Lord? How much of that influence have I used for the promotion of his kingdom?" You have been busy with this notion, and that motive, and the other endeavour; but have you lived as you will wish to have lived when you stand at his right hand amidst his glories? Have you so acted that you will then judge yourself to have well lived when your Lord and Master shall come to call you to account? Ask yourself, " Am I an earnest labourer together with God, or am I, after all, only a laborious trifler, an industrious doer of nothing, working hard to accomplish no purpose of the sort for which I ought to work, since I ought to live unto my Lord alone ?" I invite all my fellow-servants to take a retrospect, and just to see whether they have kept their own vineyards. I suppose that they have worked hard. I only put the question—Have they kept their own vineyards? Have they served the Lord in all things ?

I am half afraid to go a step farther. To a very large degree we have not been true to our own professions : *our highest work has been neglected,* we have not kept our own vineyards. In looking back, how little time has been spent by us in communion with God ! How little a part of our thoughts has been occupied with meditation, contemplation, adoration, and other acts of devotion ! How little have we surveyed the beauties of Christ, his person, his work, his sufferings, his glory ! We say that it is " heaven below " to commune with Christ ; but do we do it ? We profess that there is no place like the mercy-seat. How much are we at that mercy-seat ? We often say that the Word of God is precious—that every page of it glows with a heavenly light. Do we study it ? Friends, how much time do you spend upon it ? I venture to say that the bulk of Christians spend more time in reading the newspaper than they do in reading the Word of God. I trust that I am too severe in this statement, but I am afraid, greatly afraid, that I am not. The last new book, perhaps the last sentimental story, will win attentive reading, when the divine, mysterious, unutterable depths of heavenly knowledge are disregarded by us. Our Puritan forefathers were strong men, because they lived on the Scriptures. None stood against them in their day, for they fed on good meat, whereas their degenerate children are far too fond of unwholesome food. The chaff of fiction, and the bran of the Quarterlies, are poor substitutes for the old corn of Scripture, the fine flour of spiritual truth. Alas, my brethren, too many eat the unripe fruit of the vineyards of Satan, and the fruits of the Lord's vines they utterly despise !

Think of our neglect of our God, and see whether it is not true that we have treated him very ill. We have been in the shop, we have been on the exchange, we have been at the markets, we have been in the fields, we have been in the public libraries, we have been in the lecture-room, we have been in the forum of debate; but our own closets and studies, our walk with God, and our fellowship with Jesus, we have far too much neglected.

Moreover, the vineyard of holy service for God we have too much left to go to ruin. I would ask you—How about the work your God has called you to do? Men are dying; are you saving them? This great city is like a seething caldron, boiling and bubbling up with infamous iniquity; are we doing anything by way of antidote to the hell-broth concocted in that caldron? Are we indeed a power working towards righteousness? How much good have we done? What have I done to pluck brands from the burning? What have I done to find the lost sheep for whom my Saviour laid down his life? Come, put the questions, and answer them honestly! Nay, do not back out, and say, "I have no ability." I fear you have more ability than you will give an account of with joy at the last great day. I remember a young man who complained that the little church over which he presided was so small. He said, "I cannot do much good. I have not above two hundred hearers." An older man replied, "Two hundred hearers are a great many to have to give an account of at the last great day." As I came in at yonder door this evening, and looked into these thousands of faces, I could not help trembling. How shall I answer for this solemn charge, for this enormous flock, in that last great day? You have all a flock of some kind, larger or smaller. You have all, as Christian people, somebody for whom you will have to answer. Have you done your Master's work in reference to those entrusted to you? O men and women, have you sought to save others from going down into the pit? You have the divine remedy: have you handed it out to these sick and dying ones? You have the heavenly word which can deliver them from destruction: have you spoken it in their ears, praying all the while that God might bless it to their souls. Might not many a man among you say to himself, "I have been a tailor," or "I have been a shop-keeper," or "I have been a mechanic," or "I have been a merchant," or "I have been a physician, and I have attended to these callings; but mine own vineyard, which was my Master's, which I was bound to look to first of all, I have not kept"?

Well, now, *what is the remedy for this?* We need not talk of our fault any more; let us make each one his own personal confession, and then seek amendment. I believe the remedy is a very sweet one. It is not often that medicine is pleasant, but at this time I prescribe for you a charming potion. It is that you follow up the next verse to my text. Read it—"Mine own vineyard have I not kept. Tell me, O thou whom my soul loveth, where thou feedest, where thou makest thy flock to rest at noon; for why should I be as one that turneth aside by the flocks of thy companions?" Get to your Lord, and in him you will find recovery from your neglects. Ask him where he feeds his flock, and go with him. They have warm hearts who commune with Christ. They are prompt in duty who enjoy his fellowship. I cannot help reminding you of what I have often spoken of, namely, our Lord's language to the church at Laodicea. That church had come to be so bad that he said, "I will spue thee out of my mouth." And yet what was the remedy for that church? "Behold, I stand at the door, and knock: if any man hear my voice, and open the door, I will come in to him, and will sup with him, and he with me." After supping with Christ you will not be lukewarm. Nobody can say, "I am neither cold nor hot" when they have been in his company. Rather they will enquire, "Did not our heart burn within us, while he talked with us by the way?" If there be an angel, as Milton sings, whose name is Uriel, who lives in the sun, I will warrant you he is never cold; so he that lives in Christ, and walks with him, is never chill, nor slow in the divine service. Away to your Lord, then!

Hasten to your Lord, and you will soon begin to keep your vineyard; for in the Song you will see *a happy change effected.* The spouse began to keep her vineyard directly, and to do it in the best fashion. Within a very short time you find her saying, "Take us the foxes, the little foxes, that spoil the vines." See, she is hunting out her sins and her follies. Farther on you find her with her Lord in the vineyard, crying, "Awake, O north wind; and come, thou south; blow upon my garden, that the spices thereof may flow out!" She is evidently keeping her garden, and asking for heavenly influences to make the spices and flowers yield their perfume. She went down to see whether the vines flourished, and the pomegranates budded. Anon, with her beloved, she rises early to go to the vineyard, and watch the growth of the plants. Farther on you find her talking about all manner of fruits that she has laid up for her beloved. Thus you see that to walk with Christ is the way to keep your vineyard, and serve your Lord. Come and sit at his feet; lean on his bosom; rest on his arm; and make him to be the joy of your spirit. The Lord grant, dear brethren, that this gentle word, which I have spoken as much to myself as to you, may be blessed to us all!

II. Now, I turn to the congregation in general, and speak with THE MAN WHO IN ANY PLACE HAS TAKEN OTHER WORK, AND NEGLECTED HIS OWN. He can use the words of the text—"They made me the keeper of the vineyards; but mine own vineyard have I not kept."

We know many persons who are always doing a great deal, and yet do nothing; fussy people, people to the front in every movement, persons who could set the whole world right, but are not right themselves. Just before a general election there is a manifestation of most remarkable men—generally persons who know everything, and a few things besides, who, if they could but be sent to Parliament, would turn the whole world upside down, and put even Pandemonium to rights. They would pay the National Debt within six months, and do any other trifle that might occur to them. Very eminent men are these! I have come across impossibly great men. None could be so great as these feel themselves to be. They are an order of very superior persons: reformers, or philosophers, who know what nobody else knows, only, happily, they have not patented the secret, but are prepared to tell it out to others, and thereby illuminate us all.

I suggest to our highly-gifted friends that it is possible to be looking after a great many things, and yet to be neglecting your own vineyard. There is a vineyard that a great many neglect, and that is *their own heart*. It is well to have talent ; it is well to have influence ; but it is better to be right within yourself. It is well for a man to see to his cattle, and look well to his flocks and to his herds ; but let him not forget to cultivate that little patch of ground that lies in the centre of his being. Let him educate his head, and intermeddle with all knowledge ; but let him not forget that there is another plot of ground called the heart, the character, which is more important still. Right principles are spiritual gold, and he that hath them, and is ruled by them, is the man who truly lives. He hath not life, whatever else he hath, who hath not his heart cultivated, and made right and pure. Have you ever thought about your heart yet ? Oh, I do not mean whether you have palpitations ! I am no doctor. I am speaking now about the heart in its moral and spiritual aspect. What is your character, and do you seek to cultivate it ? Do you ever use the hoe upon those weeds which are so plentiful in us all ? Do you water those tiny plants of goodness which have begun to grow ? Do you watch them to keep away the little foxes which would destroy them ? Are you hopeful that yet there may be a harvest in your character which God may look upon with approval ? I pray that we may all look to our hearts. " Keep your heart with all diligence ; for out of it are the issues of life." Pray daily, " Create in me a clean heart, O God ; and renew a right spirit within me " ; for if not, you will go up and down in the world, and do a great deal, and when it comes to the end you will have neglected your noblest nature, and your poor starved soul will die that second death, which is the more dreadful because it is everlasting death. How terrible for a soul to die of neglect ! How can we escape who neglect this great salvation ? If we pay every attention to our bodies, but none to our immortal souls, how shall we justify our folly ? God save us from suicide by neglect ! May we not have to moan out eternally, " They made me the keeper of the vineyards ; but mine own vineyard have I not kept " !

Now, pass over that point, and think of another vineyard. Are not some people neglecting *their families?* Next to our hearts, our households are the vineyards which we are most bound to cultivate. I shall never forget a man whom I knew in my youth, who used to accompany me at times in my walks to the villages to preach. He was always willing to go with me any evening ; but I did not need to ask him, for he asked himself, until I purposely put him off from it. He liked also to preach himself much better than others liked to hear him ; but he was a man who was sure to be somewhere to the front if he could. Even if you snuffed him out, he had a way of lighting himself up again. He was good-natured and irrepressible. He was, I believe, sincerely earnest in doing good. But two boys of his were well known to me, and they would swear horribly. They were ready for every vice, and were under no restraint. One of them drank himself into a dying state with brandy, though he was a mere boy. I do not believe his father had ever spoken to him about the habit of intoxication, though he certainly was sober and virtuous himself. I had no fault to find with him except this grave fault—that he was seldom at home, was not master of the house, and could not control his children. Neither husband nor wife occupied any place of influence in the household; they were simply the slaves of their children: their children made themselves vile, and they restrained them not! This brother would pray for his children at the prayer-meeting, but I do not think he ever practised family prayer. It is shocking to find men and women speaking fluently about religion, and yet their houses are a disgrace to Christianity. I suppose that none of you are as bad as that; but, if it be so, please spell this text over: "They made me the keeper of the vineyards; but mine own vineyard have I not kept." The most careful and prayerful father cannot be held accountable for having wicked sons, if he has done his best to instruct them. The most anxious and tearful mother cannot be blamed if her daughter dishonours the family, provided her mother has done her best to train her up in the right way. But if the parents cannot say that they have done their best, and their children go astray, then they are blameworthy. If any of them have come to the Tabernacle to-night, and their boys and girls are—they do not know where, let them go home quickly, and look them up. If any of my hearers exercise no parental discipline, nor seek to bring their children to Christ, I do implore them to give up every kind of public work till they have first done their work at home. Has anybody made you a minister, and you are not trying to save your own children? I tell you, sir, I do not believe that God made you a minister; for if he had, he would have begun with making you a minister to your own family. "*They* made me the keeper of the vineyards." "They" ought to have known better, and you ought to have known better than to accept the call. How can you be a steward in the great household of the Lord when you cannot even rule your own house? A Sunday-school teacher, teaching other people's children, and never praying with her own! Is not this a sad business? A teacher of a large class of youths who never has taken a class of his own sons and daughters! Why, what will he do when he lives to see his children plunged into vice and sin, and remembers that he has utterly neglected them? This is plain dealing; but I never wear gloves when I preach. I know not where this knife may cut; but if it wounds, I pray you do not blunt its edge. Do you say that this is "very personal"? It is meant to be personal; and if anybody is offended by it, let him be offended with himself, and mend his ways. No longer let it be true of any of us, "They made me the keeper of the vineyards; but mine own vineyard have I not kept."

Besides that, every man who knows the Lord should feel that his vineyard lies also *round about his own house*. If God has saved your children, then, dear friend, try to do something for your neighbours, for your work-people, for those with whom you associate in daily labour. God has appointed you to take care of those nearest home. They say the cobbler's wife goes barefooted. Do not let it be true. Begin at home, and go on with those nearest home. Manifest Christian love to your neighbours. It is a great pity that yonder Christian man, living in a very dark part of London, comes to the Tabernacle, and does good in our societies but never speaks a word for Jesus in the court where he lives. Poor stuff, poor stuff, is that salt which is only salt when it is in the salt-box! Throw that kind of salt away. We want a kind of salt that begins to bite into any bit of meat it touches. Put it where you like, if it is good salt, it begins to operate upon that which is nearest to it. Some people are capital salt *in the box:* they are also good in the cake, they are beautifully white to look at, and you can cut them into ornamental shapes ; but they are never used; they are merely kept for show. If salt does not preserve anything, throw it away. Ask the farmer whether he would like it for his fields. "No," he says, "there is no goodness in it." Salt that has no saltness in it is of no use. You can make the garden path of it. It is good to be trodden under foot of men; but that is all the use to which you can put it. O my beloved fellow Christians, do not let it be said that you reside in a place to which you do no good whatever. I am sure if there were individual, personal work on the part of Christians in the localities where they reside, God the Holy Ghost would bless the unanimous action of his earnest, quickened church, and London would soon know that God has a people in the midst of it. If we keep away from the masses—if we cannot think of labouring in a district because it is too low or too poor—we shall have missed our vocation, and at the last we shall have to lament, "They made me the keeper of the vineyards; but mine own vineyard have I not kept."

You and I must cry mightily to the Holy Spirit to help us to live really and truly the lives which our professions demand of us. A day will come when all church-goings, and chapel-goings, and preachings, and singings, and sacraments, will seem fluff and useless stuff, if there has not been the substance of real living for Christ in all our religiousness. Oh that we would rouse ourselves to something like a divine earnestness ! Oh that we felt the grandeur of our heavenly surroundings! We are no common men! We are loved with no common love! Jesus died for us! He died for us ! He died for us ! And is this poor life of ours, so often dull and worldly, our sole return ? Behold that piece of land ! He that bought it paid his life for it, watered it with bloody sweat, and sowed in it a divine seed. And what is the harvest? We naturally expect great things. Is the poor starveling life of many a professor a fit harvest for Christ's sowing his heart's blood ? God the Father, God the Son, and God the Holy Ghost, all in action—what is the result? Omnipotence linking hands with love, and working out a miracle of grace! What comes of it? A half-hearted professor of religion. Is this all the result? O Lord, was there ever so small an effect from so great a cause? You might almost need a microscope to discover the result of the work of grace in some people's lives. Ought it to be so? Shall it be so? In the name of him that liveth and was dead, dare you let it be so? Help us, O God, to begin to live, and keep the vineyard which thou thyself hast given to us to keep, that we may render in our account at last with joy, and not with grief! Amen.

PORTION OF SCRIPTURE READ BEFORE SERMON—Matthew v. 1—20.

HYMNS FROM "OUR OWN HYMN BOOK"—672, 649, 454.

Metropolitan Tabernacle Pulpit.

A MINGLED STRAIN.

A Sacramental Sermon

BY

C. H. SPURGEON,

AT THE METROPOLITAN TABERNACLE, NEWINGTON.

"Purge me with hyssop, and I shall be clean: wash me, and I shall be whiter than snow."—Psalm li. 7.

IN what state of heart should we come to the communion-table? It is no light matter: in what manner shall we come before the Lord in so sacred an ordinance? By the very nature of the sacred supper we are taught that there should be a mixture of emotions. The bitter and the sweet, the joyful and the sorrowful, are here intermingled. The sacrifice of Christ for sin—is it more a subject of sorrow or of joy? Can we look to the cross without mourning for sin? Can we look at it without rejoicing in pardon bought with blood? Is not the most suitable state of heart for coming to the communion-table just this— mourning for our transgression, and joy because of the great salvation? There is a double character about this holy rite: it is a festival of life, and yet it is a memorial of death. Here is a cup; it is filled with wine; this surely betokens gladness. Hearken to me; that wine is the symbol of blood! This as surely betokens sorrow. In my hand is bread—bread to be eaten, bread which strengtheneth man's heart; shall we not eat bread with thankfulness? But that bread is broken, to represent a body afflicted with pain and anguish: there must be mourning on account of that agony. At the Paschal supper, the lamb of the Lord's Passover had a special sweetness in it: yet the commandment expressly ran—"with bitter herbs they shall eat it." So is it at this table. Here we with joy commemorate the Lamb of God which taketh away the sin of the world, but with deep sorrow we recall the sin which, though taken away, causes us in the recollection of it to repent with great bitterness of heart.

Our text is the expression of one who is deeply conscious of sin, and yet is absolutely certain that God can put away that sin. Thus it holds in one sentence a double thread of meaning. Here is a depth of sorrow, and a still greater deep of hopeful joy: "deep calleth unto deep." I thought that this expression of mixed feeling might guide us as to our emotions at this holy festival.

I. I shall handle the text by making three observations. The first will be this: THERE ARE TIMES WHEN THE LANGUAGE OF A SINNER IS MOST SUITABLE TO A CHILD OF GOD. There are seasons when it is

341

about the only language that he can use, when he seems shut up to it, and he uses it without the slightest suspicion that it is out of place upon his lips ; and, indeed, it is not out of place at all. I suppose that everybody will agree that the language of David in this psalm was most suitable to his condition. When he prayed, "Purge me with hyssop, and I shall be clean : wash me, and. I shall be whiter than snow," he prayed a proper prayer, did he not ? Surely no one is going to cavil with David over this petition ; and yet I cannot be sure. The modern way of handling the Bible is to correct it here, and amend it there ; tear it to pieces, give a bit to the Jews, and a bit to the Gentiles, and a bit to the church, and a bit to everybody, and then make it out that sometimes the old servants of God made great blunders. We, in modern times, are supposed to be more spiritual, and to know a great deal better than the inspired saints of the Old and New Testaments. But still, I should not think that anybody would say that David was wrong ; and if he did, I should reply : This is an inspired psalm, and there is not half a hint given that there is any incorrectness in the language of it, or that David used language under an exaggerated state of feeling, which was not truly applicable to a child of God. I think that nobody will doubt that David was a child of God, and that, even when he had defiled himself, he was still dear to the great Father's heart. I gather, therefore—I feel sure of it—that he was quite right in praying the language of this fifty-first psalm, and saying, "Have mercy upon me, O God, according to thy lovingkindness ; according unto the multitude of thy tender mercies blot out my transgressions ; wash me throughly from mine iniquity, and cleanse me from my sin ! " Yet this is precisely the way in which an unconverted man ought to pray, just the way in which every soul that comes to God may pray. It is only an enlargement of the prayer of the publican, "God be merciful to me a sinner !" This language, so suitable to the sinner, was not out of place in the mouth of one who was not only a believer, but an advanced believer, an experienced believer, an inspired believer, a teacher of others, who, with all his faults, was such a one as we shall rarely see the like of again. Yes, amongst the highest of saints, there was a time with one of them, at least when the lowliest language was appropriate to his condition. There is a spirit abroad which tells us that children of God ought not to ask for pardon of their sins, for they have been pardoned ; that they need not use such language as this, which is appropriate to sinners, for they stand in a totally different position. What I want to know is this : where are we to draw the line ? If, on account of a certain sin, David was perfectly justified in appealing to God in the same style as a poor, unforgiven sinner would have done, am I never justified in doing so ? Is it only a certain form of evil which puts a man under the necessities of humiliation ? It may be that the man has never fallen into adultery, or any other gross sin ; but is there a certain extent of sin to which a man may go before, as a child of God, he is to pray like this ? And is all that falls below that high-water mark of sin a something so inconsiderable that he need not go and ask any particular forgiveness for it, or pray like a sinner at all about it ? May I under most sins speak very confidently as a child of God, who has already been forgiven, to whom it is a somewhat remarkable circumstance that he should have done wrong, but still by no means a serious disaster? I defy anybody to draw the line; and if they do draw it, I will strike it out, for they have no right to draw it. There is no hint in the Word of God that for a certain amount of sin there is to be one style of praying, and for a certain lower amount of sin another style of praying.

I venture to say this, brethren, going farther—that, as this language is certainly appropriate in David's mouth, and as it would be impossible to draw any line at which it would cease to be appropriate, the safest and best plan for you and for me is this—seeing that we are sinners, if we have not been permitted to backslide so much as David, yet *we had better come in the same way:* we had better take the lowest place, urge the lowliest plea, and so make sure work of our salvation. It is safest to assume the greatest supposable need. Let us put ourselves into the humblest position before the throne of the heavenly grace, and cry, "Have mercy upon me, O God, according to thy lovingkindness: according unto the multitude of thy tender mercies blot out my transgressions!"

But is not a man of God forgiven? Ay, that he is! Is he not justified? Ay, that he is. "Who shall lay anything to the charge of God's elect?" Let that all stand true in the highest sense that you can give to it; but, for all that, the sinner's cry is not thereby hushed into silence. True children of God cry, and let me tell you they cry after a stronger fashion than other children. They have their confessions of sin, and these are deeper and more intense than those of others. Whatever our confidence may be, our Lord Jesus Christ never told us to pray, "Lord, I thank thee that I am forgiven, and therefore have no sin to confess: I thank thee that I need not come to thee as a sinner!" But he put into the mouth of his disciples such words as these: "Our Father, which art in heaven, forgive us our trespasses, as we forgive them that trespass against us." I reckon that the Lord's Prayer is never out of date. I expect to be able to pray it when I am on the brink of heaven; and if I should ever be sanctified to the fullest extent, I shall never turn round to the Saviour, and say, "Now, my Lord, I have got beyond thy prayer! Now, Saviour, I can no more address my Father who is in heaven in this language, for I have outgrown thy prayer!" Brethren, the notion sounds to me like blasphemy. Never shall I say to my Saviour, "I have no necessity now to come to thy precious blood, or to say to thee, 'Wash me, and I shall be whiter than snow.'" Listen, brethren: "If we walk in the light, as he is in the light, we have fellowship one with another," and what then? Why, even then "the blood of Jesus Christ his Son cleanseth us from all sin." We still want the blood when walking in the light, as God himself is in the light.

While we are here below we shall need to use just such language as David did. Appropriate as our text is to the sinner, it is equally appropriate to the saint, and he may continue to use it till he gets to heaven. Remark, brethren, that when our hearts cannot honestly use such language, we may think that we are upraised by faith, but it is possible that we may be upblown by presumption. When we do not bow into the very dust, and kiss the Saviour's feet, and wash them with our tears, we may think that it is because we are growing in grace, but it is far more likely that we are swelling with self-esteem. The more holy a man is, the more humble he is. The more really sanctified he is, the more does he cry about his sin, whatever it may be—"Oh, wretched man that I am! who shall deliver me from the body of this death?" When you get the clearest possible view of God, what will be the result? Why, the deepest downcasting in your own spirit. Look at Job. He can answer his wretched accusers, but when he sees God—ah, then he abhors himself in dust and ashes! Was Job wrong in heart? I question whether any of us are half as good as Job. I am sure few of us could have played the man as he did under his sorrows. With all the failure of his patience, the Holy Ghost does not call it a failure, for he says, "Ye have heard of the patience of Job." He says not "of his impatience", but "of his patience"; and yet this blessed, patient man, patient even by God's own testimony, when he saw God, abhorred himself. Look at Isaiah, again. Was there ever a tongue more eloquent, more consecrated, more pure? Were there ever lips more circumcised to God than those of that mighty evangelical prophet? And yet, when he beheld the glory of the Lord, the train of the Lord filling the temple, he said, "Woe is me! for I am a man of unclean lips, and I dwell in the midst of a people of unclean lips." Those of you that can do so may come to my Master's table to-night as saints: I shall come as a sinner. You that feel that you can come there glorying in your growth in grace may so come if you like: I shall come feeling that I am nothing, less than nothing. I shall endeavour to come to the cross just as I came at first, for I find that if I get beyond the position of a believing sinner, I get into a dangerous condition. Safety lies in conformity to truth, and truth will not allow any of us to glory before God. The more I know the Lord, and the more I live in communion with him, the more do I feel happy in lying at his feet, and looking up to him to be my all in all. I would be nothing, and let Christ be everything. Take this from one who has been a preacher of the gospel for more than thirty-five years, and a soul-winner who needs not to be ashamed—I am as entirely dependent upon the free mercy of the Lord this day as ever I was, and I look to be saved in the same manner as the thief upon the cross.

II. Secondly, let me make another observation. It shall be this: AN EXTRAORDINARY SENSE OF GUILT IS QUITE CONSISTENT WITH THE STRONGEST FAITH. It is a blessed thing when the two go together. David was under an extraordinary sense of sin, and right well he might be, for he had committed an extravagant transgression. He had done a very grievous wrong to man, and committed great lewdness before the Lord; and when the Spirit of God at last aroused his conscience, through the rebuke of Nathan, it is not at all wonderful that he should have bowed down under a deeply humiliating sense of his own guiltiness. He was guilty, deeply guilty—more guilty than even he himself knew. You and I, perhaps, may also be by God's grace favoured with a deep sense of sin. But I hear some people say, "Did I understand you rightly, sir, or did my ears deceive me? *Favoured with a deep sense of sin?*" Yes, I said that; for while sin is horrible, a thorough sense of it, bitter as it is, is one of the greatest favours with which God blesses his chosen. I am sure that there are some of God's children whose experience is shallow and superficial, for they do not know the heights and depths of redeeming love, neither are they established in the doctrines of grace, and all because they never were deeply ploughed with a sharp sense of sin. These know nothing of subsoil ploughing, so as to turn their very hearts up under the keen ploughshare of the law. But that man who knows what sin means, and has had it burned with a hot iron into the core of his spirit, is the man who knows what grace means, and is likely to understand its freeness and fulness. He who knows the evil of sin is likely to know the value of the precious blood. I could scarcely ask for any of you a better thing than that you should fully know in your own spirit the horribleness of sin as far as your mind is capable of bearing the strain.

David was so conscious of his guilt that *he compares himself to a leper.* The language of the text refers, I believe, to the cleansing of lepers. Hyssop was dipped in blood, and then the sacrificial blood was sprinkled upon the polluted individuals to make them clean. David felt that he had become a leprous man. He felt like one who has contracted the horrible, the polluting, the incurable disease of leprosy. He felt that he was not fit to come near to God, nor even to associate with his fellow-man. He confessed that his guilt was such that he ought to be put away, shut out from the assembly of the people. His guilt had polluted a whole nation, of whom he was the representative, and to whom he was the example. Did you ever feel like that? I tell you that you do not know all the pollution of sin unless you have been made to feel yourself to be a polluted thing. If you had fifty leprosies, they would not pollute you like sin, for a poor leper is not really polluted : he may bear a grand and noble soul within that rotting body. Sin alone is real pollution, hellish pollution, abominable pollution. There is nothing in hell that is worse than sin ; even the devil is only a devil because sin made him a devil : so that sin is the most horrible and intolerable evil that can fall upon the spirit of man. David felt that dreadful truth. But yet, mark you, though he felt the horror of the disease of sin, his faith was strong enough to make him use the confident language of the text, " Purge me with hyssop, and I shall be clean." Black as my sin is, filthy as it is, if thou do but purge me, O my God, I shall be clean.

Yes, David is sure that God can cleanse him. He pleads as one who has no question upon the matter towards God. His prayer is—" Do thou purge me, and I shall be clean ! Apply the precious blood of the great Sacrifice to me, O God, and I shall be whiter than snow!" There is about the Hebrew a sense which I could hardly give you, except I were to put it thus : " Thou wilt un-sin me." As though God would take his sin right away, and leave him without a speck of sin, without a single grain of it upon him. God could make him as if he had never sinned at all. Such is the power of the cleansing work of God upon the heart that he can restore innocence to us, and make us as if we had never been stained with transgression at all. Believest thou this ? Believest thou this ? Oh, thou art a happy man, if, under the deepest conceivable sense of sin, thou canst still say, " Yes, I believe that he can wash me, and make me whiter than snow ! "

But will you follow me while I go a step farther ? The words of our text are in the Hebrew in the future tense, and they might be read, " Thou shalt purge me, and I shall be clean ; " so that David was not only certain about the power of God to cleanse him, but about the fact that God would do it : "Thou shalt purge me." He cast himself, confessing his sin, at the feet of his God, and he said, "My God, I believe that, through the great Atonement, thou wilt make me clean !" Have you faith like that of David ? Believest thou this ? Beloved, some of us can boldly say, "Ay, that we do ; we believe not only that God can pardon us, but that he will, ay, that he has pardoned us ; and we come to him now, and plead that he would renew in us the cleansing work of the precious blood, and of the water, which flowed from the side of Christ, and so make us perfectly clean ! Yea, we believe that he will do it ; we are sure that he will : and we believe that he will continue to cleanse us till we shall need no more cleansing. Hart's hymn sings concerning the precious blood—

> "If guilt removèd return and remain,
> Its power may be provèd again and again."

This witness is true, and we set our seal to it.

The Psalmist David believed that, although his sin was what it was, yet God could make a rapid cleansing of it. He speaks of the matter as wrought promptly, and speedily. It took seven days to cleanse a leper ; but David does not follow the type when the reality excels it. He says, "Purge me with hyssop, and I shall be clean." It is done directly, done at once ;—washed, and whiter than snow. It will not take seven days to wipe out the crimes of seven years ; nay, if a man had lived seventy years in sin, if he did but come to his God with humble confession, and if the precious blood of Jesus were applied to him, his sins would vanish in the twinkling of an eye. The two facts come together. "Purge me : I shall be clean. Wash me : I shall be whiter than snow." It is done at once. Note the rapidity of the cleansing.

Mark the effectual character of the purgation. "Purge me, and I shall be clean." Not "I shall think that I am," but "I *shall* be. I shall be like a man perfectly healed of leprosy." Such a man was not purged in theory, but in reality ; so that he could go up to the court of the Lord's house, and offer his sacrifice among the rest of Israel. So, if thou wash me, Lord, I shall be really clean ! I shall have access to thee, and I shall have fellowship with all thy saints.

Once more—David believed that God could give him internal cleansing. "In the hidden parts," says he, "thou shalt make me to know wisdom." I do like that about the text. It is "Purge *me* with hyssop, and *I* shall be clean." Where ?—Hands ? Yes. Feet ? Yes. Head ? Yes. All this is good ; but what about the heart ? There is the part that you and I cannot cleanse, but God can. Imagination, conscience, memory, every inward faculty, the Lord can purge us in all these. "Purge me with hyssop, and I shall be clean." This includes the whole man. And this declaration falls from the lip of a man who knew himself to be as defiled as he could be, a very leper, only fit to be put away into his own several house, and shut up there for fear of contaminating the rest of mankind. He boldly says, "If the Lord wash me, I shall be clean, I am certain of it. I shall be perfectly clean, and fit to have communion with himself."

Notice one more remark on this point, namely, that David, while thus conscious of his sins, is so full of faith towards God that *he appropriates all the cleansing power of God to himself.* "Wash *me*, and *I* shall be whiter than snow. Purge *me* with hyssop, and *I* shall be clean." There are four personal words in one verse. It is easy to believe that God can forgive sin in general, but that he can forgive mine in particular—that is the point. Ay, it is easy to believe that he can forgive man, but to believe that he will forgive such a poor specimen of the race as I am is quite another matter ! To take personal hold upon divine blessings is a most blessed faculty. Let us exercise it. Can you do it ? Brothers and sisters, can you do it ? You that cannot call yourselves brothers and sisters, you far-away ones, can you come to Christ, all black and defiled as you are, and just believe in him, that you shall be made whole ? You will not be believing too much the Great Sinners' Friend. According to your faith be it unto you.

III. This brings us to our third and last point, upon which I will speak with great brevity. Notice that A DEEP SENSE OF SIN AND A CONFIDENT FAITH IN GOD MAKE THE LORD'S NAME AND GLORY PRE-EMINENTLY CONSPICUOUS. God is the great actor in the text before us. He purges and he washes, and none but he. The sins and the cleansing are both of them too great to allow of any inferior handling.

"*Purge me.*" He makes it all God's work. He does not say anything about the Aaronic priest. What a poor miserable creature the priest is when a soul is under a sense of sin ! Have you ever met with a person who has been really broken in heart who has gone to a priest ? If so, he has been made ashamed of his looking to man, for he has found him to be a broken cistern that can hold no water. Why, my brethren, if we had this platform full of popes, and one poor soul under a sense of sin to be comforted, the whole lot of them could not touch the sinner's wound, nor do anything to stanch the bleeding of his heart! No, no, the words of the best of men fall short of our need. As the dying monk said, "*Tua vulnera, Jesu!*"—"Thy wounds, Jesus !" These can heal, but nothing else can. God must himself wash us. Nothing short of his personal interposition will suffice.

Now, notice the next word, "Purge me *with hyssop.*" We must have faith, which is represented by hyssop. How little David makes of faith ! He thinks of it only as the poor "hyssop." Many questions have been raised as to what hyssop was. I do not think that anybody knows. Whatever it may have been, it was a plant that had many little shoots and leaves, because its particular fitness was that the blood would cling to its many branches. Its use was that it stored the blood, and held it there in ruby drops upon each one of its sprays : and that is the particular suitability of faith for its peculiar office. It is an excellent thing in itself ; but the particular virtue of faith lies in this —that it holds the blood so as to apply it. Scarlet wool was used in the ceremony of cleansing, and the scarlet wool was useful because it soaked in the blood, and held it within itself : but the hyssop was still more useful because, while it held the blood, it held it ready to drop. That is how faith holds the great Sacrifice : it holds the atoning blood upon every spray, ready to drop upon the tortured conscience. Faith is the sprinkling hyssop : it is nothing in itself, but it applies to the soul that which is our cleansing and our life.

David, moreover, seems to me to say, "Lord, if thou wilt purge me with the blood of the great Sacrifice, it does not matter how it is done! Do it with the little hyssop from off the wall. However tiny and insignificant the plant may be, yet it will hold the precious drops, and bring them to my heart, and I shall be whiter than snow." It is God, you see—it is God all the way through.

"*And I*"—there is just that mention of himself; but what of himself? Why, "I shall be the receiver. I shall be clean." "I." What about that intensive "I"? "I shall be whiter than snow";—I shall be the material on which thou workest—the guilty pardoned—the polluted made clean—the leper made whole, and permitted to come up to thy house.

That is all I ask my Lord to-night—that he will let me come to his table, and be the receiver, the eater, the drinker, the cleansed one, the debtor, the bankrupt debtor, plunged over head and ears in debt to the heavenly Creditor. Oh, to be nothing; to lie at his feet! Oh, to be nothing, but washed—washed in the blood! How sweet it is no longer to ride on horses, but to have God for your all in all; no longer to go forth sword in hand, boasting our strength, and glorying in what we can do, but to sit down at Jesus' feet, and sing the victory which he alone has won! Come, let us pray from our very hearts, "Purge me with hyssop, and I shall be clean: wash me, and I shall be whiter than snow." God bless you, for Jesus' sake! Amen.

PORTION OF SCRIPTURE READ BEFORE SERMON—Psalm li.

HYMNS FROM "OUR OWN HYMN BOOK"—406, 375.

Metropolitan Tabernacle Pulpit.

GRACE FOR COMMUNION.

A Short Address

To a few Friends at Mentone, at the Breaking of Bread,

on Lord's-day afternoon, January 2nd, 1887, by

C. H. SPURGEON.

"Awake, O north wind; and come, thou south; blow upon my garden, that the spices thereof may flow out. Let my beloved come into his garden, and eat his pleasant fruits."—Song of Solomon iv. 16.

THE soul of the believer is the garden of the Lord. Within it are rare plants, such as yield "spices" and "pleasant fruits." Once it was a wilderness, overgrown with thorns and briars; but now it is "a garden enclosed," an "orchard of pomegranates."

At times within that garden everything is very still and quiet; indeed, more still than could be wished. Flowers are in bloom, but they seem scentless, for there are no breezes to waft the perfume. Spices abound, but one may walk in the garden, and not perceive them, for no gales bear their fragrance on their wings. I do not know that, in itself, this is an evil condition: it may be that "So he giveth his beloved sleep." To those who are worn with labour, rest is sweet. Blessed are they who enjoy a Sabbath of the soul!

The loved one in the text desired the company of her Lord, and felt that an inactive condition was not altogether suitable for his coming. Her prayer is first about her garden, that it may be made ready for her Beloved; and then to the Bridegroom himself, that he would come into his garden, and eat its pleasant fruits. She pleads for *the breath of heaven*, and for *the Lord of heaven.*

First, she cries for THE BREATH OF HEAVEN to break the dead calm which broods over her heart. She cannot unlock the caskets of spice, nor cause the sweet odours to flow forth: her own breath would not avail for such an end. She looks away from herself to an unseen and mysterious power. She breathes this earnest prayer, "Awake, O north wind; and come, thou south; blow upon my garden!"

In this prayer there is an evident sense of *inward sleep.* She does not mean that the north wind is asleep: it is her poetical way of confessing that she herself needs to be awakened. She has a sense of *absent-mindedness,* too, for she cries, "Come, thou south." If the south wind would come, the forgetful perfumes would come to themselves, and sweeten all the air. The fault, whatever it is, cannot lie in the winds; it lies in ourselves.

No. 1,941.

Her appeal, as we have already said, is to that great Spirit who operates according to his own will, even as the wind bloweth where it listeth. She does not try to "raise the wind"—that is an earthly expression relating to worldly matters; but, alas, it might fitly be applied to many imitations of spirituality! Have we not heard of "getting up revivals"? Indeed, we can no more command the Holy Spirit than we can compel the wind to blow east or west. Our strength lies in prayer. The spouse prays, "Awake, O north wind; and come, thou south!" She thus owns her entire dependence upon the free Spirit. Although she veiled her faith in a divine Worker under the imagery of her song, yet she spoke as to a person. We believe in the personality of the Holy Ghost, so that we ask *him* to "Awake" and "Come." We believe that we may pray to him; and we are impelled to do so.

Notice that the spouse does not mind what form the divine visitation takes so long as she feels its power. "Awake, O north wind;" though the blast be cold and cutting, it may be that it will effectually fetch forth the perfume of the soul in the form of repentance and self-humiliation. Some precious graces, like rare spices, naturally flow forth in the form of tears; and others are only seen in hours of sorrow, like gums which exude from wounded trees. The rough north wind has done much for some of us in the way of arousing our best graces. Yet it may be that the Lord will send something more tender and cheering; and if so, we would cry, "Come, thou south." Divine love warming the heart has a wonderful power to develop the best part of a man's nature. Many of our precious things are brought forth by the sun of holy joy.

Either movement of the Spirit will sufficiently bestir our inner life; but the spouse desires both. Although in nature you cannot have the north wind and the south blowing at the same time; yet in grace you can. The Holy Ghost may be at one and the same time working grief and gladness, causing humiliation and delight. I have often been conscious of the two winds blowing at once; so that, while I have been ready to die to self, I have been made to live unto God. "Awake, O north wind; and come, thou south!" When all the forms of spiritual energy are felt, no grace will be dormant. No flower can keep asleep when both rough and gentle winds arouse it.

The prayer is—"blow," and the result is—"flow." Lord, if thou blowest, my heart floweth out to thee! "Draw me, we will run after thee." We know right well what it is to have grace in our souls, and yet to feel no movement of it. We may have much faith in existence, yet none in exercise, for no occasion summons it into action. We may have much repentance, yet no conscious repenting; much fire of love, yet no love flaming forth; and much patience in the heart, though at the moment we do not display it. Apart from the occurrences of providence, which arouse our inward emotions one way and another, the only plan by which our graces can be set in active exercise is by the Holy Spirit breathing upon us. He has the power to quicken, arouse, and bestir our faculties and graces, so that holy fruits within us become perceptible to ourselves, and to others who have spiritual discernment. There are states of the atmosphere in which the fragrance of flowers is much more diffused than at other times. The rose owes much to the zephyr which wafts its perfume. How sweet is even a field of beans after a shower! We may have much spice of piety, and yet yield small fragrance unless the living power of the Holy Spirit moves upon us. In a wood there may be many a partridge, or gay pheasant, and yet we may not see so much as one of them until a passing foot tramples down the underwood, and causes the birds to rise upon the wing. The Lord can thus discover our graces by many a messenger; but the more choice and spiritual virtues need an agent as mysterious and all-pervading as the wind—need, in fact, the Spirit of the Lord to arouse them. Holy Spirit, thou canst come to us when we cannot come to thee! From any and every quarter thou canst reach us, taking us on our warm or cold side. Our heart, which is our garden, lies open at every point to thee. The wall which encloses it does not shut thee out. We wait for a visitation. We feel glad at the very thought of it. That gladness is the beginning of the stir; the spices are already flowing forth.

The second half of the prayer expresses our central desire : we long for THE LORD OF HEAVEN to visit us. The bride does not seek that the spices of her garden may become perceptible for her own enjoyment, nor for the delectation of strangers, nor even for the pleasure of the daughters of Jerusalem, but for her Beloved's sake. *He* is to come into his garden, and eat his pleasant fruits. We are a garden for his delight. Our highest wish is that Jesus may have joy in us. I fear that we often come to the table of communion with the idea of enjoying ourselves ; or, rather, of enjoying our Lord ; but we do not rise to the thought of giving *him* joy. Possibly that might even seem presumptuous. Yet, he says, "My delights were with the sons of men." See how joyfully he cries in the next chapter: "I am come into my garden, my sister, my spouse : I have gathered my myrrh with my spice ; I have eaten my honeycomb with my honey ; I have drunk my wine with my milk." Our heavenly Bridegroom rests in his love, he rejoices over us with singing. Often he takes more delight in us than we do in him. We have not even known that he was present, but have been praying him to come ; and all the while he has been near us.

Note well the address of the spouse to her Beloved in the words before us. *She calls him hers*—"My Beloved." When we are sure that he is ours we desire him to come to us as ours, and to reveal himself as ours. Those words "My Beloved" are a prose poem: there is more music in them than in all the laureate's sonnets. However slumbering my graces may be, Jesus is mine. It is as mine that he will make me live, and cause me to pour forth my heart's fragrance.

While he is hers she owns that *she is wholly his*, and all that she has belongs to him. In the first clause she says, "Awake, O north wind ; and come, thou south ; blow upon *my* garden" ; but now she prays, "Let my Beloved come into *his* garden." She had spoken just before of *her* fruits, but now they are *his* fruits. She was not wrong when she first spoke ; but she is more accurate now. We are not our own. We do not bring forth fruit of ourselves. The Lord saith, "From me is thy fruit found." The garden is of our Lord's purchasing, enclosing, planting, and watering ; and all its fruit belongs to him. This is a powerful reason for his visiting us. Should not a man come into his own garden, and eat his own fruits? Oh, that the Holy Spirit may put us into a fit condition to entertain our Lord!

The prayer of the spouse is—"*Let my Beloved come.*" Do we not say, "Amen, let him come"? If he does not come in the glory of his Second Advent at this moment, as, perhaps, he may not, yet let him come. If not to his judgment-seat, yet let him come into his garden. If he will not come to gather before him all nations, yet let him come to gather the fruit of his redemption in us. Let him come into our little circle; let him come into each heart. "Let my Beloved come." Stand back, ye that would hinder him! O my Beloved, let not my sinful, sluggish, wandering thoughts prevent thee from coming! Thou didst visit the disciples, "the doors being shut"; wilt thou not come where every opened door bespeaks thy welcome? Where shouldst thou come but to thy garden? Surely my heart hath great need of thee. Many a plant within it needs thy care. Welcome, welcome, welcome! Heaven cannot welcome thee more heartily, O my Beloved, than my heart shall now do! Heaven doth not need thee so much as I do. Heaven hath the abiding presence of the Lord God Omnipotent; but if thou dwell not within my soul, it is empty, and void, and waste. Come, then, to me, I beseech thee, O my Beloved!

The spouse further cries—"*Let him eat his pleasant fruits.*" I have often felt myself overcome with the bare idea that anything I have ever done should give my Lord pleasure. Can it be that any offering I ever gave him should be thought worthy of his acceptance; or that anything I ever felt or said should be a joy to him? Can he perceive any perfume in my spices, or taste any flavour in my fruits? This is a joy worth worlds. It is one of the highest tokens of his condescension. It is wonderful that the King from the far country should come from the glory land, where all choice fruits are at their best, and enter this poor enclosure in the wilderness, and there eat such fruits as ours, and call them pleasant, too! O Lord Jesus, come into our hearts now! O Holy Spirit, blow upon our hearts at this moment! Let faith, and love, and hope, and joy, and patience, and every grace be now like violets which betray themselves by their perfume, or like roses which load the air with their fragrance!

Though we are not content with ourselves, yet may our Lord be pleased with us! Do come to us, O Lord! That thou art our Beloved is a greater wonder than that thou shouldst come to us. That thou hast made us thy garden is a greater favour than that thou shouldst eat our fruits. Fulfil to us that gracious promise, "I will sup with him, and he with me," for we do open to thee. Thou saidst unto the woman of Samaria, "Give me to drink," and wilt thou not now accept a draught of love from us? She had no husband, but thou art our Husband; wilt thou not drink from the cup which we now hold to thee? Receive our love, our trust, our consecration. Delight thyself also in us, as we now delight ourselves in thee. We are asking a great thing of thee, but thy love warrants large requests. We will now come to thy table, where thou shalt be our meat and drink; but suffer our spices to be the perfume of the feast, and let us each say, "While the King sitteth at his table my spikenard sendeth forth the smell thereof." Fulfil this wish of our soul, divine Lord and Master! Amen.

SALT FOR SACRIFICE.

A Sermon

INTENDED FOR READING ON LORD'S-DAY, JANUARY 23RD, 1887,

DELIVERED BY

C. H. SPURGEON,

AT THE METROPOLITAN TABERNACLE, NEWINGTON.

"And every oblation of thy meat offering shalt thou season with salt; neither shalt thou suffer the salt of the covenant of thy God to be lacking from thy meat offering: with all thine offerings thou shalt offer salt."—Leviticus ii. 13.

IT is taken for granted that all true Israelites would bring many oblations and offerings of different kinds to God. And so they did who were truly devout and really grateful. I am sure that, if the Lord has set our hearts on fire with his own love, we also shall be frequently saying "What shall I render unto the Lord for all his benefits toward me?" It will be the habit of the Christian, as it was the habit of the devout Israelite, to be continually bringing oblations to his God.

How is this to be done? There is the point. We have need each of us to say with Paul, "Lord, what wilt thou have me to do?" and we may add another question, "How wilt thou have me do it?" for will-worship is not acceptable with God. If we bring to God what he does not ask, it will not be received. We must only present to him that which he requires of us; and we must present it to him in his own way, for he is a jealous God.

I call your attention to the fact that, in this verse, the Lord three times expressly commands that with the meat offerings and all other offerings they were to offer salt. Does the great God that made heaven and earth talk about salt? Does he condescend to such minute details of his service as to enact that the absence of a handful of salt shall render a sacrifice unacceptable, and the presence of it shall be absolutely necessary to its being received by him? Then, my brethren, nothing in the service of God is trifling. A pinch of salt may seem to us exceedingly unimportant, but before the Lord it may not be so. In the service of God the alteration of an ordinance of Christ may seem to be a pure matter of indifference, and yet in that alteration there may be the taking away of the very vitals of the ordinance, and the total destruction of its meaning. It is yours, and it is mine, to keep to the letter of God's Word, as well as to the spirit of it, remembering that it

No. 1,942.

is written, "Whosoever shall break one of these least commandments, and shall teach men so, he shall be called the least in the kingdom of heaven." It is not for the servant to say, "This order of my master is unimportant, and the other is binding." The servant's duty is to act in all things exactly as he is bidden. Since our Master is so holy and so wise, it is impossible for us to improve upon his commandments. Yes, God enters into detail with his servants, and even makes orders about salt.

If you will read the chapter through, you will note that other things were needed in connection with the sacrifices of the Israelites. Their sacrifices were of course imperfect. Even on the low ground which they occupied as symbols and emblems they were not complete; for you read, in the first place, that they needed frankincense when they offered their sacrifice to God: God did not smell sweet savour in the bullock, or the ram, or the lamb, unless sweet spices were added. What does that teach us but that the best performances of our hands must not appear before his throne without the merit of Christ mingled therewith? There must be that mixture of myrrh, and aloes, and cassia, with which the garments of our Prince are perfumed, to make our sacrifice to be a sweet savour to the Most High. Take care in your sacrifices that you bring the sacred frankincense.

Another thing that was enjoined constantly was that they should bring oil; and oil is ever the type of the blessed Spirit of God. What is the use of a sermon if there is no unction in it? What is unction but the Holy Ghost? What is prayer without the anointing that cometh of the Holy Spirit? What is praise unless the Spirit of God be in it to give it life, that it may rise to heaven? That which goes to God must first come from God. We need the oil: we cannot do without it. Pray for me that I may have this oil in the sacrifice of my ministry, as I do pray for you that in all that you do for the Lord Jesus your sacrifice may continually have the sacred oil with it.

Then came a third requisite, namely, salt. If you read the preceding verses, you will see that the Lord forbids them to present any honey. "No meat offering, which ye shall bring unto the Lord, shall be made with leaven: for ye shall burn no leaven, nor any honey, in any offering of the Lord made by fire. As for the oblation of the firstfruits, ye shall offer them unto the Lord: but they shall not be burnt on the altar for a sweet savour." Ripe fruits were full of honey, full of sweetness; and God does not ask for sweetness, he asks for salt. I shall notice that as we go on further. Not honey, but salt, must be added to all the sacrifices which we present before the living God.

What is the meaning of all this? We may not pronounce any meaning of the types with certainty unless we have Scripture to direct us; but still, using our best judgment, we do, first of all, see that the text explains itself. Observe, "neither shalt thou suffer *the salt of the covenant of thy God* to be lacking from thy meat offering."

I. It appears, then, that salt was THE SYMBOL OF THE COVENANT. When God made a covenant with David, it is written, "The Lord gave the kingdom to David for ever by a covenant of salt"—by which was meant that it was an unchangeable, incorruptible covenant, which would endure as salt makes a thing to endure, so that it is not liable to putrefy or corrupt. "The salt of the covenant" signifies that, whenever you and I are bringing any offering to the Lord, we must take care that we remember the covenant. Standing at the altar with our gift, serving God with our daily service, as I trust we are doing, let us continually offer the salt of the covenant with all our sacrifices. Here is a man who is doing good works in order to be saved. You are under the wrong covenant, my friend, you are under the covenant of works, and all that you will gain in that way is a curse, for " Cursed is every one that continueth not in all things which are written in the book of the law to do them." " Therefore," says the apostle, " as many as are of the works of the law are under the curse." Get away from that, and get to that other covenant which has salt in it, namely, the covenant of grace, the new covenant of which Christ is the Head. We must not come to God without the salt of faith in Christ, or our offerings will be a sort of antichrist. A man who is trying to save himself is in opposition to the Saviour. He that thinks of the merits of his own good works despises the merit of the finished work of Christ. He is offering to God that which has no salt with it, and it cannot be received.

We want this salt of the covenant in all that we do, in the first place, *to preserve us from falling into legality.* He that serves God for wages forgets the word—" The gift of God is eternal life." It is not wage, but gift, by which you are to live. If you forget that you are under a covenant of pure grace, in which God gives to the unworthy, and saves those who have no claim to any covenant blessing, you will get on legal ground; and, once on legal ground, God cannot accept your sacrifice. With all thine offerings thou shalt offer the salt of the covenant of grace, lest thou be guilty of legality in thy offering.

The covenant is to be remembered also *that it may excite gratitude.* Whenever I think of God entering into covenant that he will not depart from me, and that I shall never depart from him, my love to him overflows. Nothing constrains me to such activity, and such zeal in the cause of God, as a sense of covenant love. Oh, the gratitude one feels for everything which comes to us by the covenant of grace! Remember the old Scotch wife, who thanked God for the porridge, and then thanked him that she had a covenant right to the porridge, since he had said, " Verily, thou shalt be fed." Oh, it makes life very sweet to take everything from the hand of a covenant God, and to see in every mercy a new pledge of covenant faithfulness! It makes life happy; and it also inspires a believer to do great things for his gracious God. Standing on covenant ground we feel consecrated to the noblest ends.

This tends *to arouse our devotion to God.* When we remember that God has entered into covenant with us, then we do not do our work for him in a cold, chilly, dead way; neither do we perform it after a nominal, formal sort ; for we say, " I am one of God's covenanted ones." He hath made with me an everlasting covenant, ordered in all things and sure; therefore my very soul goes after him, and this which I am about to do, though it be only to sing a hymn, or to bow my knee in prayer, shall be done intensely, as by one who is in covenant with God, who is, therefore, bound to serve with all his heart, and with all his soul, and with all his strength. Covenanted service should be the best of service. The covenanting saints of old stopped not at death itself for him to whom they were bound.

My time will not allow me to enlarge, but I do pray the people of God always to keep the covenant in view. That covenant will claim the last accent of our tongues on earth. It shall employ the first notes of our celestial songs. Where are you if you are out of covenant with God? You are under the curse of the old covenant if you are not under the blessing of the new; but if the Lord Jesus Christ has stood Surety on your behalf, and made the covenant sure to you, you will serve God with alacrity and delight, and he will accept your service as a sweet-savour offering in Christ Jesus. That is the first meaning of the text.

II. But, secondly, salt is THE TOKEN OF COMMUNION. In the east, especially, it is the token of fellowship. When an Oriental has once eaten a man's salt, he will do him no harm.

Whenever you are attempting to serve God, take care that you do it in the spirit of fellowship with God. Take care that you suffer not this salt to be lacking from your meat-offering. Offer it in fellowship with God.

And this is a very important point, though I cannot dwell upon it at any length. Beloved, we never serve God rightly, joyfully, happily, if we get out of fellowship with him. "His servants shall serve him, and they shall see his face:" there is no serving God acceptably unless you see his face. Once you feel your love to God dying out, and the presence of God withdrawn from you, you can live by faith, but you cannot work with comfort. You must feel a sweet friendship with God, or else you will not so heartily give yourself to God's service as the saints of God ought to do. I want you to live always in the sense of God's nearness to you. Live always in the delightful conviction that God loves you. Never be satisfied to have a doubt about your being one with Christ, or that you are dear to the heart of God. You cannot sing, you cannot pray, you cannot teach a Sunday-school class, you cannot preach in a fit and proper style, if you lose this salt of communion. You may limp, but you cannot run in the ways of God if your fellowship is broken. "The joy of the Lord is your strength." Have plenty of this salt of fellowship to heap upon every oblation.

Then, feel fellowship with God as to all his purposes. Does God wish to save souls? So do I. Did Christ die to save souls? So would I live to save them. Can you say that? Does the Holy Spirit strive against sin? So would I strive against sin. Feel all this. Endeavour to run on parallel lines with God as far as the creature can keep pace with the Creator; and when you do so—when all your aims and designs are the aims and designs of God—then, brother, you will plough, and you will sow, and you will reap, with joy and gladness of heart. There must be this fellowship with God in his designs; this is the essential salt of sacrifice.

I would have you especially have fellowship with God in Christ Jesus. Does God love Jesus? So do we. Does God desire the glory of his Son? So do we. Does God determine that his Son shall put down all power, and authority, and rule, and be King? We too wish him to reign over us, and over all mankind. "Thy kingdom come" is our prayer, even as it is God's will that the kingdoms of this world should become the kingdoms of our Lord and of his Christ.

Now, if you can work always in fellowship with God, what a grand thing it will be! For want of this, many workers know not their position, and never realize their strength. We are labourers together with God. If we are in our right state, we take a brick to lay it on the wall, and a divine hand has lifted that brick. We use the trowel, and it is the great Master Builder that grasps the tool. We wield the sword, and the Captain of the Lord's host is strengthening our arm, and guiding our hand, that we may do valiantly in the day of battle. What an honour to have the Lord working with us, and by us!

But oh, beloved, do not get out of fellowship with God; and if you have done so, before you do another stroke of work for him, go and get into fellowship with him. If I were captain of the host, and I saw that you were out of fellowship, and yet you were marching to the battle, I would say, "Brother, go back." When we bring our sacrifice, we are to leave it till we are reconciled to our brother; and much more must we leave it till we have a sense of being reconciled to God. I cannot go on serving God if I do not know that I am his child. I cannot go on preaching to you if I have any doubt of my own salvation. At any rate, it would be very wretched work to preach of freedom while myself in chains. He preaches best who is at liberty, and can in his own person tell the captives how Christ makes men free. When you know that you are in covenant with God, and when your heart feels a blessed friendship to him, then it is, dear friends, that your oblation will come up acceptably before him, and you can do your work as it ought to be done before him.

III. But I must get your minds to another point. Salt is THE EMBLEM OF SINCERITY. "With all thine offerings thou shalt offer salt." There must be an intense sincerity about all we do towards God.

I bade you note that you were not allowed to present honey before the Lord. I really wish that some of our brethren who are over-done with honey would notice that. There is a kind of molasses godliness which I can never stomach. It is always, "Dear this," and "Dear that," and "Dear the other," and "This dear man," and "That dear woman." There is also a kind of honey-drop talk in which a person never speaks the plain truth. He speaks as familiarly as if he knew all about you, and would lay down his life for you, though he has never set eyes on you before, and would not give you a halfpenny to save your life. These people avoid rebuking sin, for that is "unkind." They avoid denouncing error; they say, "This dear brother's views differ slightly from mine." A man says that black is white, and I say that it is not so. But it is not kind to say, "It is not so." You should say, "Perhaps you are right, dear brother, though I hardly think so." In this style some men think that our sacrifice is to be offered. If they hear a sermon that cuts at the roots of sin, and deals honestly with error, they say, "That man is very narrow-minded." Well, I have been so accustomed to be called a bigot that I by no means deny the charge. I feel no horror because of the accusation. To tell a man that, if he goes on in his sin, he will be lost for ever, and to preach to him the hell which God denounces against the impenitent, is no unkindness. It is the truest kindness to deal honestly with men. If the surgeon knows very well that a person has a disease about him that requires the knife, and he only says, "It is a mere trifle: I dare say that with a little medicine and a pill or two we may cure you," a simpleton may say, "What a dear kind man!" but a wise man judges otherwise. He is not kind, for he is a liar. If, instead of that, he says "My dear friend, I am very sorry, but I must tell you that this mischief must be taken out by the roots, and, painful as the operation is, I beg you to summon courage to undergo it, for it must be done if life is to be saved." That is a very unpleasant kind of person; and a very narrow-minded and bigoted person; but he is the man for us. He uses salt, and God accepts him: the other man uses honey, and God will have nothing to do with him. When honey comes to the fire, it turns sour. All this pretended sweetness, when it comes to the test, turns sour; there is no real love in it. But the salt, which is sharp, and when it gets into the wound makes it tingle, nevertheless does sound service.

Whenever you come before God with your sacrifices, do not come with the pretence of a love you do not feel, nor with the beautiful nonsense of hypocrites; but come before the Lord in real, sober, earnest truth. If you are wrong and feel it, say so, and out with it; and if God has made you right through his Spirit, do not deny it, lest you be denying the work of the Holy Ghost, and so dishonouring him.

What is meant is that in all our sacrifices we ought to bring our hearts with us. If we sing, let us sing heartily as unto the Lord; not with our voices only, but with our very souls. If we preach, let us preach with all our might: we have such precious truth to handle that it ought not to be dealt with in a trifling manner. If we try to win a soul, let us throw our whole strength into the work. Though we would not scheme, like the Pharisees, to make a proselyte to our sect, yet let us compass sea and land to bring a man to Christ, for such we should do.

And when we bring our heart, and throw it intensely into the service of God, which is one form of the salt, let us take care that all we do is spiritually performed; not done with the external hand, or lip, or eye, but done with the soul, with the innermost heart of our being. Otherwise it will be mere flesh, and without salt it will be viewed as corrupt, and rejected at God's altar.

When you attempt to pray, and rise from your knees feeling that you have not prayed, then do not leave the mercy-seat, but pray till you pray. When you are singing a hymn, and do not feel quite in tune for singing, sing yourself into tune. Do not leave an ordinance till you have tasted the salt of that ordinance. I admire that resolution of John Bradford the martyr. He said that he made a rule that he never ceased from a holy engagement till he had entered into the spirit of it. Too often we treat these things slightingly. There is no soul in them, and yet we are satisfied with them. We eat our unsavoury devotions without salt; but the Lord rejects them. We have had a few minutes in prayer in the morning, and perhaps just a few weary minutes at midnight, we have run through a chapter, or perhaps we have taught a class on the Sabbath afternoon, and taught it perfunctorily without any life, and yet we have been content; or we have preached, but it has been a mere saying of words; there has been no life or vigour in it. Oh, do not so! Bring not to God your unsalted sacrifices, but let the salt of sincerity savour all. It is better to say, " I did not pray," than it is to say, " I did pray," and yet only to have gone through a form. It is better to have to confess, " I did not sing," than to follow the tune when your heart is not in it. You had better leave off the external form than keep it up if your soul be not in it, lest you be found to mock the Most High God. Pile on the salt! Let it season the whole of your sacrifice through and through. Be sincere before the heart-searching God.

IV. Lastly, salt is THE TYPE OF PURIFYING POWER ; and with all our sacrifices we have need to bring a great deal of this salt. The salt eats into the meat ; it drives away corruption; it preserves it. We require a deal of this. Brethren, if we come before God with holy things while we are living in sin, we need not deceive ourselves, we shall not be accepted. If there be any man, of whom it can be said that he is a saint abroad and a devil at home, God will estimate him at what he is at home, and not at what he is abroad. He may lay the sacrifice upon the altar, but if it is brought there with foul hands, and an unholy heart, God will have nothing to do with it. " Without holiness no man shall see the Lord," and, certainly, without holiness can no man serve the Lord. We have our imperfections; but known and wilful sin God's people will not indulge. From this God keeps them. As soon as they know a thing to be sin, and their attention is called to it, that which they have committed in inadvertence causes them grief and sorrow of heart, and they flee from it with all their souls. But do not be deceived. You may be a great man in the church of God, and hold office there, and even be a leader ; but if you lead an unholy life, neither yourself nor your sacrifice can ever be accepted with the Most High. God abhors that his priests should serve him with unwashed hands and feet. " Be ye clean that bear the vessels of the Lord." I constantly preach to you free, rich, and sovereign grace, without the slightest condition; and I preach the same at this time ; but remember that the grace of God brings sanctification with it, and that the gift of God is deliverance from sin ; and that, if we abide in sin, and remain in it, we cannot be the children of God. We must, dear friends, bring with all our oblations that salt in ourselves which shall purify our hearts from inward corruption, and which shall have a power about it to purify others. Know ye not that the saints are the salt of the earth ? And if we are salt to others, we must have salt in ourselves. How can we conquer sin in others if sin be unconquered in ourselves? How can we give a light we have never seen ? How can we have seed as sowers if we have never had bread as eaters ? You know what the woman said concerning the well,—"Father Jacob," she said, "gave us the well, *and drank thereof himself.*" You cannot give other people wells if you do not drink thereof yourself. You cannot benefit a man by grace if you are not first benefited by grace yourself. Can anything come out of a man that is not in him ? There must be a holy, sanctifying power about the child of God, making him to be as salt, or else he cannot act upon the putrid masses round him as the salt ought to do.

With all thine oblations, then, bring this salt. God give it to us!

Let us cry to him for it. I do bless God for this church that God has made you a power in the neighbourhood—that God is making you a power all over this country. Those hundreds of ministers who came up this week, whom we have educated here, and whom all of you have helped to educate, are not these a purifying salt? Our brethren and sisters by thousands are scattered all over the world. Not a week passes without some of our number going far away; and I always say, "Yes, go, dear brethren. Salt should not remain in the box. It ought to be scattered all over the meat. Wherever you go, mind that you are salt, so that people do not say, 'Is this one of the Tabernacle people? He is a poor, lukewarm creature.'" Do not have it so, but do, now that God blesses you so largely, take care that the salt is in you all. "I have no greater joy than to hear that my children walk in truth;" and I have no greater sorrow than this—that there are some among you who are no credit to your profession. There are some among you who do not live even as well as the world expects you to live. I mean not only poor ones, but rich ones among us are a dishonour to us. There are a few of all degrees among us who are not spiritually-minded, but are worldly and carnal: they come to this place, and sit among us, with their faces turned towards heaven, while they themselves are going the way of the ungodly. They know what I mean while I speak it. God grant that they may bear the rebuke, and repent, and turn to the Lord! They are looking one way and rowing another—trying to be the people of God, if they can, and yet at the same time acting as common sinners act. The Lord bless you, beloved, by making you all holy! And if you will not be holy, may he take that great fan into his hand, and blow the chaff away! If it cannot be that this shall be a pure heap lying upon his floor to his honour and glory, then may he still continue that great purgation which is always going on in every church where he is really present! Brethren, *we must be holy*. We must be holy, or else cease to be what we are. God bring us to this—that with every oblation we may offer huge handfuls of salt! May we ever be accepted in Christ, accepted with our sweet savour: holy, acceptable to God, because his Spirit has made us holy, and keeps us right before him. The Lord bless you evermore! Amen.

PORTION OF SCRIPTURE READ BEFORE SERMON—Ephesians iv.

HYMNS FROM "OUR OWN HYMN BOOK"—386, 623, 435.

Metropolitan Tabernacle Pulpit.

LOVE JOYING IN LOVE.

A Short Address

To a few Friends at Mentone, at the Breaking of Bread,

on Lord's-day afternoon, January 9th, 1887, by

C. H. SPURGEON.

"I am come into my garden, my sister, my spouse: I have gathered my myrrh with my spice; I have eaten my honeycomb with my honey: I have drunk my wine with my milk: eat, O friends; drink, yea, drink abundantly, O beloved."—Song of Solomon, v. 1.

No sooner does the spouse say, "Let my Beloved come into his garden," than her Lord answers, "I am come into my garden." "Before they call, I will answer; and while they are yet speaking, I will hear." When we desire our Lord Jesus to come to us, he has already come in a measure; our desire is the result of his coming. He meets us in all our desires, for he waiteth to be gracious. Our "come" is no sooner uttered than it is lost in his "Behold, I come quickly!"

When we perceive that the Bridegroom has come, we perceive also that he has done exactly what he was asked to do. How cheering to find that our mind is in harmony with his mind! Our heart saith, "Let my Beloved come into his garden, and eat his pleasant fruits." His heart replies, "I have gathered my myrrh with my spice; I have eaten my honeycomb with my honey; I have drunk my wine with my milk." "Delight thyself also in the Lord; and he shall give thee the desires of thine heart." The Lord Jesus makes the desires of his saints to be the foreshadowings of his own actions: "The secret of the Lord is with them that fear him." His secret counsel is made known in the believing soul by desires inspired of the Holy Ghost.

Note well that the Bridegroom kindly takes to himself as his own all that is in the garden. His spouse spoke of "his pleasant fruits," and he acknowledges the least and most homely of them to be his own. He repeats the possessive particle—"my": "*my* myrrh, *my* spice, *my* honeycomb, *my* honey, *my* wine, *my* milk." He disdains nothing which the garden of his bride produces. He is fond of the notion of joint-heirship, even as in another place he said, "My Father, and your Father, my God, and your God." Let us also value the personal possessive pronouns: the sweetness of the promises lies in them. These are our arms with which we embrace the promises. Beloved brethren in Christ Jesus, is it not charming to see our Lord appropriating us, and all that we are, and all that we have, and all that grows within us, and all the varied

No. 1,943.

361

forms of his grace, which are the outcome of his own work within our hearts? Within us certain things are bitter, but wholesome; and he saith, "my myrrh." Some things are sweet, though homely; and he saith, "my honey." Some things are of a rarer sort, and he saith, "my spice"; while others are common-place enough; and he saith, "my milk." Our Lord taketh no exception to any one of the true growths of the garden, whether it be myrrh or milk; and he asks for nothing more than the garden may be expected to yield; he is content without the butter of kine, or flesh of fed beasts, satisfying himself with honey fresh from the hive.

I note, with much delight, that matters which seem inconsistent with perfection are not refused by the heavenly Bridegroom. As the Lord did not refuse for an offering the leavened cakes of the first-fruits, so in this instance he saith, "I have eaten my honeycomb with my honey." The honey would be purer without the comb; but as it is incident thereto, he takes the one with the other. He graciously accepts, not only our heart's desire, but the very mode in which our weakness works towards that desire. It is as if he delighted in the words of our prayers as well as in the essence of our prayers, and prized the notes of our songs as well as the meaning of them. Yes, I believe our Lord puts our tears as well as our sorrows into his bottle, and hears our groanings as well as our desires. The honeycomb which contains the honey is precious to him. After he had risen from the grave, he ate a piece of a honey-comb, and I doubt not that he had a reason for choosing that food: sweet gathered from sweets, yet not without wax. Our Lord accepts our services without nicely noting and critically rejecting the infirmity which goes with them.

I note also that he himself gathers what he enjoys: "I have gathered my myrrh with my spice." Many a holy thing, which we have not in detail offered to him in set form, he knows to have been given in the gross; and so he takes with his own hand what he knows we have by a com-prehensive covenant made over to him. How sweetly does he fill up our blanks, and believe in our consecration, even when we do not repeat the form of it!

Moreover, he makes mixtures out of our fruits, for he gathers myrrh with balsam, and drinks wine with milk; thus taking the rarer with the more common. He knows how to make holy compounds out of the graces of his people; thus increasing their excellence. He is the best judge of what is admirable, and he is the best fashioner and com-pounder of character: he is using his skill upon us. Often by our mingled experiences he accomplishes an increase of virtue in us. Some graces are the result of work and wisdom, as wine which must be trodden from the grapes; others are natural, like milk which flows from living fountains without art of man: but the Lord accepts them both, and so combines them that they are pleasant to him to a high degree. Simple faith and experimental prudence make up a sacred milk and wine; and the like may be seen in rapturous love and calm patience, which blend most deliciously. The Lord loves us, and makes the most of us. He is pleased with all that is the true produce of his grace, and finds no faults with it; on the contrary, he says, "I have eaten my honeycomb with my honey."

Having made these observations upon the Lord's fulfilling the prayer of the spouse, I should like to deliver the following remarks upon the text :—

It is evident that *the Lord Jesus is made happy by us.* These poetical sentences must mean that he values the graces and works of his people. He gathers their myrrh and spice because he values them ; he eats and drinks the honey and the milk because they are pleasant to him. It is a wonderful thought that the Lord Jesus Christ has joy of us. We cost him anguish, even unto death, and now he finds a reward in us. This may seem a small thing to an unloving mind, but it may well ravish the heart which adores the Well-beloved. Can it be true that we afford joy to the Son of God, the Prince Emmanuel ? The King has been held in the galleries, he has been charmed by us. Our first repentance made him call together his friends and his neighbours ; the first gleam of faith he ever saw in us made his heart rejoice ; and all that he has seen in us ever since of his own image, wrought by his grace, has caused him to see of the travail of his soul. Never has a husbandman taken such pleasure in the growth of his choice plants as our Lord has taken in us. "The Lord taketh pleasure in them that fear him · in those that hope in his mercy." That is a thought to be rolled under the tongue as a sweet morsel. Yes, the Lord's church is his Hephzibah, for, saith he, "my delight is in her."

The second thought is that *the Lord Jesus will not and cannot be happy by himself : he will have us share with him.* Note how the words run—"I have eaten "; "Eat, O friends ! " "I have drunk" ; "Drink, yea, drink abundantly, O beloved ! " His union with his people is so close that his joy is in them, that their joy may be full. He cannot be alone in his joy. That verse of our quaint hymn is always true :—

> "And this I do find, we two are so joined,
> He'll not be in glory and leave me behind."

He will not be happy anywhere without us. He will not eat without our eating, and he will not drink without our drinking. Does he not say this in other words in the Revelation—"If any man hear my voice, and open the door, I will come in to him, and will sup with him, and he with me"? The inter-communion is complete : the enjoyment is for both. To make our Lord Jesus happy we must be happy also. How can the Bridegroom rejoice if his bride is sad ? How can the Head be content if the members pine ? At this table of fellowship his chief concern is that we eat and drink. "Take, eat," saith he ; and again, "Drink ye all of it." I think I hear him now say—"I have eaten, and I have drunk ; and although I will drink no more of the fruit of the vine until that day that I drink it new in the kingdom of God ; yet eat ye, O friends : drink, yea, drink abundantly, O beloved ! " Thus we have seen, first, that Christ is made happy by us ; and, secondly, that he insists upon our sharing his joy with him.

If we have already enjoyed happy fellowship with him, *the Lord Jesus calls upon us to be still more happy.* Though we may say that we have eaten, he will again say, "Eat, O friends ! " He presses you to renew, repeat, and increase your participation with him. It is true we have drunk out of the chalice of his love ; but he again invites us, saying,

"Drink, yea, drink abundantly, O beloved!" Of other wines it would be ill to say, " Drink abundantly;" but of this wine the Lord says, with an emphasis, "Drink abundantly, O beloved!" Oh, for grace to renew all former enjoyments with greater zest, and deeper intensity! It has been sweet even to taste and sip; what must it be to eat and drink abundantly?

Must it not mean that, though we know the Lord Jesus, we should try to know more of him, yea, to know all that can be known of that love which passeth knowledge? Should we not labour to realize more of HIM, taking in the whole truth concerning his person and love by meditation, contemplation, understanding and reverent simplicity? Let nothing lie by : let us eat and drink all the stores of the banquet of love.

As the mouth with which we eat is faith, does not the Saviour seem to cry, " Believe on me. Trust me. Confide in me abundantly"? Eat and drink with large appetite, by receiving into your heart's belief all that can be received. Oh, for grace to appropriate a whole Christ, and all the love, the grace, the glory that is laid up in him !

Does it not also mean—have greater enjoyment of divine things? Partake of them without stint. Do not restrict yourself as though you could go too far in feeding upon the Lord Jesus. Do not be afraid of being too happy in the Lord, or of being too sure of his salvation, or of having too much assurance, or too much devout emotion. Dread not the excitements which come from fellowship with Christ. Do not believe that the love of Jesus can be too powerfully felt in the soul. Permit the full sweep and current of holy joy in the Lord to carry you away : it will be safe to yield to it. " Rejoice in the Lord alway : and again, I say, Rejoice."

Beloved, let us now take our fill of Christ. Since we believe, let us believe more unreservedly : if we enjoy, let us enjoy more thoroughly. If we have life, let us have it more abundantly. In this case we may eat, and our soul shall live; we may drink, and not only forget our misery, but drink again, and enter into bliss. Our Lord beckons us from the shore to the sea : he calls us from the lower seat to come up higher. He would have us gladder, stronger, fuller, holier. He presses the provisions of his love upon us, like a host whose joy lies in seeing all his guests feasting. Do not hold back. Be not satisfied with little believing, and scant enjoying, and cool feeling : but let us enter fully into the joy of our Lord.

True, we are unworthy, but he invites us. We shall be wise to yield to his loving pressure. We may not have such another feast just yet ; and possibly we may have to go for forty days into the wilderness, on the strength of this meal ; wherefore let us keep the feast heartily. Our Lord, in his invitation, challenges our friendship and our love. He says—" Eat, O *friends !* " Prove yourselves friends by being free at his table. " Drink, yea, drink abundantly, O *beloved !* " If this be his way of testing us, let us not be slow in accepting it. Let us show our love by joying in him as he joys in us. Amen.

Metropolitan Tabernacle Pulpit.

MIGHT HAVE BEEN, OR MAY BE.

A Sermon

INTENDED FOR READING ON LORD'S-DAY, JANUARY 30TH, 1887,

DELIVERED BY

C. H. SPURGEON,

AT THE METROPOLITAN TABERNACLE, NEWINGTON,

ON THURSDAY EVENING, SEPTEMBER 9TH, 1886.

"And some of them said, Could not this man, which opened the eyes of the blind, have caused that even this man should not have died?"—John xi. 37.

"*JESUS WEPT:*" it does not mean that he shed a tear or two, but that his tears flowed freely. Such is to be gathered from the original word. He wept copiously and continuously, till he became the observed of all observers. He was deeply affected, and his tears were the fit expression of his intense emotion. *Love made him weep:* nothing else ever compelled him to tears. I do not find that all the pains he endured, even when scourged or when fastened to the cruel tree, fetched a single tear from him; but for love's sake "Jesus wept." At first I feel inclined to say "Behold, how he wept!" and then I check myself, and borrowing my language from the bystanders, I cry, "Behold, how he loved him!" The Jews recognized, even with their unfriendly eyes, that his tears were drawn from him by love alone. From this Rock of our salvation no rod but that of love could bring forth water-floods.

So when we have noticed the tears, and the power of love which brought forth the tears, let us observe how, being such as we are, *tears are towards us a fit expression of his love.* When you look upon your children with love, your eyes flash joy. When they are in health and strength, your love expresses itself fitly in delight in them. But love in Christ towards us most fitly shows itself in tears. When he thinks of what we are, and how we have become subject to death, and how sin has brought us under this bondage, since he loves us, he must weep; nay, he must die; for even his tears cannot suffice to manifest his love. Jesus must pour out his soul, not only unto tears, but unto death, that all may see how deeply he loves us.

I should like to begin my sermon with that thought deeply fixed upon our spirits, if we are indeed the people of God—that Jesus loves us— loves us unto tears. Inasmuch as he loved Lazarus when Lazarus was dead and in the tomb, let us herein behold how he loved us when we were dead in trespasses and sins. See how he loves us though, perhaps,

No. 1,944.

our spirits may be dull and dead; and how he will love us even when we come to die. " Precious in the sight of the Lord is the death of his saints." He loves us so that he will love us when we die, even as he loved Lazarus at the grave's mouth.

Let us turn away from our preface, which we have found in the context, to look at the text itself. While there were some who thought only of the love of Christ when they beheld his tears, there were others standing by more full of reasoning, who argued, " Could not this Man, which opened the eyes of the blind, have caused that even this man should not have died ?"

Placing my text in various lights, I see, first, *a vain argument;* secondly, *a vile argument;* thirdly, *a fair argument;* and, fourthly, if read in connection with the verses which succeed it, *a full and faithful argument.*

I. But, first, I see in the text A VAIN ARGUMENT. It is an argument about what might have been if such-and-such a thing had been. It is a very common thing to hear people thus talk :—" If so-and-so, then so-and-so." Such talk is always vain, because *it leads to no practical result.* What was the use of saying, " If Jesus had been here, then Lazarus would not have died," when Lazarus was already dead ? The thing is done, and cannot be undone: what is the use of asking about what once might have been but now cannot be ? Yet have I seen strange sorrows wrung out of these suppositions. Perhaps the bitterest griefs that men know come not from facts, but from things which might have been, as they imagine ; that is to say, they dig wells of supposition, and drink the brackish waters of regret. The sisters of Lazarus did this. Each said, " Lord, if thou hadst been here, my brother had not died." In a more unbelieving way the Jews did it, and said, "Could not this Man, which opened the eyes of the blind, have caused that even this man should not have died ?" Yes, and so you say, " Now, if I had gone to so-and-so, this would not have happened ; and then the other might have happened ; and a third thing probably would have occurred ; and then how different it would have been from what it is now !" You blame yourself for steps which were not only innocent, but wise and right ; but now that you see the consequences of them, you begin to imagine that they were not innocent, and not wise, and not right, and you fret to think that you took such steps.

I have known some go a great deal further than vainly accusing themselves ; they have even accused God. They say, " Why was moral evil admitted into the world ? Why were men and women constituted as they are ? Could not God, who is omnipotent, have so arranged things that there should have been no sin and no sorrow ?" What a fine mess we get into when once we begin arguing over those points, and conjecturing what might have been under other circumstances ! You see, dear friends, these things will not be, and cannot be ; and, therefore, what is the good of our worrying over what is not, and cannot be? I will plough, but if there be no field, excuse me. I shall not plough the sea, or the mist. I will get to work on anything that is practical, but I will not break my heart over fancies.

If it is to be done, and it is right to do it, let us go at it at once ; but if it cannot now be done, but is only a thing that might have been, let us leave it. You may go to the "might have beens," I have better work to do. This was David's method about his child, as it should be yours about all your sick ones, and those that have already departed. David fasts, and prays, and cries to God as long as his child is alive, but when his child is dead, he washes his face, and eats bread, because he says, "Can I bring him back again? I shall go to him, but he shall not return to me." It is done, and cannot be undone; and what is the use of fretting over it now? Oh, that you would have grace to leave this foolish chopping of logic with yourself and providence, and use your reason for something better! Lazarus is dead; and what is the use of saying that he might not have died if Jesus had interposed?

I call this a vain argument, in the next place, because, even though we raise the question about what might have been, and we push it until we begin to think that it ought to have been, still *unbelief will never get an explanation of it from the Lord*. In the chapter there is no explanation given to the Jews of why Jesus, being able to open the eyes of the blind man, and able to keep this person from dying, yet did not keep him from dying. An explanation was given by the Lord to his disciples by his assurance that it was for the glory of God. That explanation you will get. You have received it already. If you are God's child, and he has denied to you what you think he might as well have given you, if he has permitted you to suffer under a calamity which you think he might have averted, he will give you no other explanation than this which he gives you now without any pressure at all, namely, that it is for his glory. If it be for his glory, is it not for your advantage? What can more advantage a servant than the glory of his master? What can more profit our loving hearts than to see God glorified? If you are not satisfied with that answer, do not expect any other. "Why have I been bereaved of my children?" "Why have I been ill so many years?" "Why did I fail when I hoped to reach wealth?" "Why did I break down in the examination when I might have obtained a degree?" It is an idle piece of business to demand the reasons of unavoidable trials. It is mere dreaming to guess what would have been if such another thing had been. "What thou knowest not now, thou shalt know hereafter;" let that content thee.

Once again, I call this a vain argument, because *it cannot benefit you to pry into this thing which the Lord has hidden from you*. You are fostering self-conceit in calling God's providence to your bar. You are practically sitting upon a throne, and making God to be the prisoner at your bar. You are weighing over again what he has already weighed in the scales of wisdom. This will never do. A child-like spirit is infinitely healthier as it is infinitely holier than the spirit of questioning. Brothers, we should not even thirst to know all the things that are, for if it be the glory of God to conceal a thing, let it be concealed; but as for the things that might have been, what have we to do with them? If we begin lifting up these curtains, we cannot tell what we may one day see. I have known persons intrude into this sphere until at last they have stumbled on a horror which they were never intended to see, and which indeed they never would have seen if their own unhallowed imaginations had not created it for themselves. They were ambitious to alter providence, and change the times and seasons which God had ordained, and at last they fell into such a morbid condition that, if they were not positively mad, they might have been happier if they had been; for there is a state of mind, bordering on insanity, which has still a guilt about it, and is therefore worse than if responsibility had been destroyed. I shall beg you, therefore, brethren, to forbear from prying into those secret things which belong to God only. Your profit lies in the direction of abstaining from such speculations. Do not talk about what might have been, and should have been, interfering with the good which God has given you by pining after what he has denied. Oh, could you know as he knows, and then love as he loves, you would act as he acts! Believe in him, and sit still at his feet, and talk no more about what he could have done, or might have done, or what you fancy he should have done, lest evil come of it.

II. Secondly, as I have spoken upon a vain argument, I will now speak of A VILE ARGUMENT; for I believe these Jews intended a piece of evil argument against the Christ of God. They put it thus: this Man says that he opened the eyes of the blind, and all the people think that he did; but if he did so, why did he not prevent his friend, whom he evidently loved, from dying? Either he has a want of power, which will prove that he did not open the eyes of the blind after all, but that it was an imposture; or else, if he has such power, and does not use it for his friend, he does not love him, and these tears are a mere pretence. He could have saved this man's life, and now he stands here and weeps because he is dead. Thus the adversary would put the believer in our Lord upon the horns of a dilemma. We are not gored by either horn, for we know a way of escape therefrom. Still you see the drift, and this is often the drift of Satan's arguments. Your brother, your mother, your child, your friend—these are dead. You sent to Jesus, you cried to God, you importuned for the precious life: and yet they are dead. Well, then, there must have been a want of power on the part of God to save life. Peradventure that conversion of yours, in which you have rejoiced, and of which you have said, "One thing I know, that, whereas I was blind, now I see"—perhaps, after all, that was not a work of divine power, but a delusion; for he that saved your soul could have saved the life of your beloved; and as he did not do so, has he any power at all, and have you ever been the subject of that power?

You see the drift of the specious reasoning; is it not a vile argument? Let us unveil the falsehood of it. Suppose that Jesus is willing to open the eyes of the blind, and does open them; is he therefore bound to raise this particular dead man? If he does not see fit to do so, does that prove that he has not the power? If he lets Lazarus die, is it proven therefore that he could not have saved his life? May there not be some other reason? Does Omnipotence always exert its power? Does it ever exert all its power? May there not be some great reason why Christ should open the eyes of the blind, and yet should not step in to prevent the death of Lazarus? We can see that there may be many such reasons; but it is easy, when you wish to argue against Christ and the gospel, to forget a good deal. You can shut your eyes where it is inconvenient to see, and then you can rush on blindly like a mad bull.

On the other hand, if they say, "If Christ can prevent Lazarus dying, and he does not do so, there is a want of love in him;" is it so? Is that fair argument? It is not true as a matter of fact; nor will it be thought to be true by our faith. It may be infinite love that wounds, that chastens, that afflicts. There is as much love in the Father when he wields the rod as when he gives the kiss: as much love in the Saviour when he permits Lazarus to die as when he raises Lazarus from the grave. Ay, and it is possible that the less pleasing deed may be the more greatly charged with love! The greatest blessings come to us in the guise of sorrows. I should not wonder if the death of Lazarus was the passing of Lazarus into a higher state of spiritual life than he had ever enjoyed before. I doubt not that he was a converted man before his death; but, certainly, that wonderful passing into the region of death-shade, (which I will not picture because the Bible does not picture it,) and that coming back again, must have given him such a vivid consciousness of the power of Christ that the spiritual life that was within him must have become more strong, more clear, more supreme than ever it had been before. I should have liked to meet that man after he had been raised from the dead by him who said, "I am the resurrection and the life." I think he could have preached from that text very wonderfully. He would have understood it by an experience unknown to us. I should think that Lazarus rose into the higher life in the very highest degree; and so it was Christ's love to Lazarus that let Lazarus die, and it was a calumny altogether that he died because Jesus had a want of love towards him. It is Christ's love that has let some of you be ill and poor. It is Christ's love that has suffered you to be despised and down-trodden. It is Christ's love that has let you remain in affliction, because the divine benefit that has come of it is more to your profit than the thing itself could ever be to your loss. So the vile argument may well be driven away, whatever shape it takes in our minds.

There is no justification for our distrust as to what God has done for us in the way of grace: it has been real, and no dream. And there is no justification for any doubt as to what God can do for us and will do for us in the future: he that has helped us so far will help us to the end. He that has done so much for us will withhold no good thing from us, but bestow all that is needful for this life and godliness, and for the life to come and glory.

III. We shall now proceed very briefly to notice what is A VERY FAIR ARGUMENT. If you take the text, and press the malice out of it, it is true. "Could not this Man, which opened the eyes of the blind, have caused that even this man should not have died?" Yes, it is true. Jesus Christ, by what he has done, has proved his power to do anything. I need not enlarge upon the point, but I will put it before you. There is not a life which he cannot preserve. You may cry to him about your sick ones. You are permitted to do so. Even if they are given over by the physician, I counsel you to go to Jesus about them, though it is far better to go to Jesus before you consult the physician. We often make a mistake about the use of medicines by using medicine first. We should first go to the Lord, that we may be guided as to what medicine shall be used, and what means shall be employed, and trust in God to bless the means made use of for restoration.

We may make idols out of physicians as much as the heathen make idols out of blocks of wood. Medicines are right enough in their place for healing, even as bread is right for nourishment: but as men live not by bread only, so are they not healed by medicine only. Before we eat bread, we ask God's blessing on that bread; let us seek a blessing on medicines whenever we use them. We are not healed by the physician, but by that God who works according to his own will and pleasure. Let us then believe that the Christ, who has done this and that for other sick folk, can do the same for those whom we bring to him, and let us leave their cases in his hands.

But take the text spiritually. I want you to believe that Christ can preserve us spiritually from death. Are we forced by our employments into the society of the ungodly? Does providence call some of you working-men to toil side by side, or even at the same bench, with infidels? The Lord Jesus can cause that you shall not be injured by them. He can give you spiritual health and strength, even when you seem to be under the most deadly influences. He that opened your eyes, when you were blind, can keep you alive now that you can see. Trust in him for your final perseverance with the same unquestioning faith with which you trusted in him for the pardon of your sin. I say again, he that opened your eyes, when you were in darkness, can cause that you should not die even though the deadliest influences from the world, the flesh, and the devil, should be set in operation against you. Because he lives you shall live also. Fly to him in the time of your temptation. Cry to him in the hour of your need, and he will help you, and deliver you. You shall not die, but live and declare the works of the Lord.

Beloved, what a mercy it is that we can look back upon Christ's having opened the blind man's eyes, and see the same thing in ourselves! Here is a blind man whose eyes Christ opened. It is yourself. He was able to give *you* sight, and can you not transfer the argument to others? If the Lord Jesus Christ could give *you* sight, he can give others sight. If he opened *your* blind eyes, he can open the blind eyes of your children, of your unconverted father, your unsaved brothers, your unsaved sisters. Believe about your friends, and cry to God about them. Take the text at once, and read it so: "Could not this Man, who opened my blind eyes, open the blind eyes of those about whom my heart is heavy?" Remember that the man who was blind, whose eyes Christ opened, was born blind. Christ can deal with original sin, and constitutional sin. Some seem to have inherited a nature more wild than common; their heart does not appear to be a heart of flesh, but a heart of stone; yet Jesus, who dealt with this strangely blind man—blind from his birth—can deal with those strange sinners, those sinners of a scarlet hue, who develop in their lives more of desperate viciousness than you see in others. Christ can deal with the blackest of the blacks. Take them to him, believe on account of them, and be fully convinced that no case is beyond the power of the living Saviour.

For my part, I never can or will despair of the salvation of one of my fellow-creatures now that I am myself saved. I know that there were certain traits in my character, and certain elements in my disposition, which make my conversion to Christ to be more remarkable than that of the conversion of anybody else, and so I shall have hope concerning the most blasphemous, the most obstinate, the most unbelieving. This glorious Man who, in the days of his flesh, opened the eyes of one born blind, which thing had never been known before, can come and deal with the very chief of sinners—ay, with sinners that are dead in sin—with sinners that lie rotting in their lusts, and he can make them to be saints! This is a fair argument : I am sure it is.

IV. But, now, lastly, they had never thought of THE FULL AND FAITHFUL ARGUMENT from the text. All they said was—This Man, who has opened the eyes of one born blind, could have prevented Lazarus from dying. That was fair argument, but it was not full argument, and it never occurred to them to go further, and enquire, "Now that Lazarus is dead, cannot this Man raise him from the dead?" The first piece of argument did not go far enough to yield any comfort, because it only dealt with what might have been, and what could not be. I fear a great deal of our religion is of that kind. But what a mercy it would be if God would give some Christians sixpennyworth of common-sense! Oh, if some people could but believe what I am sure is true—that true religion is sanctified common-sense—that there is about the religion of Jesus Christ that which is just as practical as if our life were to be spent in keeping shop! True, it is spiritual and divine, celestial and sublime, but yet it is as accurate as if we were to be nothing but arithmeticians, calculating and estimating through all our days. There is a mathematical truthfulness about our holy faith as well as a lofty, eagle-winged aspiration. So then they should have argued thus: "Jesus Christ, who opened this blind man's eyes, has come to a corpse in its grave, and he is able to make it live." Friend, is there laid upon your mind at this time some poor sinner who is dead in trespasses and sins ? You cannot get at him. You do not know how to make him feel or think. There does not seem to be a vital spark anywhere about him, and you know not how to deal with him. Believe that the gospel is meant for such a case as this, and that the living God, in Jesus Christ, by the Holy Spirit, can meet with this clay-cold dead heart. "Oh, it is worse than that," say you, "it is worse than that. The person I am thinking of is put out of society, and is too corrupt to be spoken with." Yes, I know what you mean. Perhaps you speak of a fallen woman. We are always more eager to bury the fallen women than the fallen men. A man, of whom we must say with Martha, "By this time he stinketh," may still be tolerated in society; but if it happens to be a woman that sins, they cry, "Bury her out of sight. Roll the stone to the mouth of the tomb. We never speak to her, or mention her." If you have an anxiety on your soul about a person who is thus shut out from society, I want you to believe that Jesus can bring out the buried and corrupt. "Oh!" say you, "but it is not merely that the person I think of is buried away, but the case is really one which may not be described. He hath been dead four days. He has gone so far that his crime is un-mentionable." I know the case. Yet you may mention it before the Lord ; in his presence no harm will come of it. I do not read in the gospel narrative of anybody being distressed by the odour when the sepulchre of Lazarus was opened. When Jesus said, "Take ye away the stone," he knew that he had divine disinfectants ready to hand.

He knew what he did. When you seek after gross sinners, prudent people say, "Well, if you go after such people as that, your own character will be injured before long." The Lord will prevent any harm coming from it, for he can speak to the most corrupt sinner, and say, "Live," and he shall live, and then the corruption is no more. Wherefore let us drive out of our minds the notion that any sinner is too far gone for Christ to save him. I used to hear in my youth about a "day of grace," and about persons having passed that day of grace; but I do not believe it. As long as you are in this world I am bidden to preach to you, for the gospel message is to be proclaimed to every creature, and I dare not draw vain distinctions about a day of grace. If you have a disease about you that will carry you off before the clock strikes twelve to-night, I still bid you believe in the Christ of God, and live. If you are so bad in your own esteem that there never lived a worse man or a worse woman out of hell, yet still believe in Jesus Christ. My Lord loves to save great sinners, even as he delighted to bring from the grave the long-dead Lazarus, that he might be received into the bosom of his family, to be the joy of the house, and the glory of Christ.

I have not gone too far : I am sure that I have not. Nay, I could not go too far. The shoreless, bottomless love of my great Lord—I wish I had the tongues of men and angels to tell of it. You have not sinned beyond his power to save you. He is a great Saviour, a mighty Saviour, and his precious blood can remove all your death and corruption. When I think of those whom he has saved, I argue, "Could not my Lord Jesus, who opened the eyes of the blind, make these dead sinners live?"

I will tell you something else. If you yourself to-night are that dead sinner, I say to you, in the name of Jesus Christ of Nazareth, "Thus saith the Lord, believe in the Lord Jesus Christ, and thou shalt be saved." "I cannot," says one, "I am dead." I know that you are, but if the Lord speaks to you, you will live : *and he does speak to you by this voice of mine.* I speak to you *in his name.* Thou careless sinner, in the name of Jesus Christ of Nazareth, consider thy ways! Thou dead sinner, in the name of Jesus, live! His Spirit has gone with the word which I have spoken. The thing is done in some who have heard me, and will be done in others who will read these words. Glory be to the Father, and to the Son, and to the Holy Ghost, for ever and ever! Amen.

PORTION OF SCRIPTURE READ BEFORE SERMON—John xi.

HYMNS FROM "OUR OWN HYMN BOOK"—319, 844, 631.

Metropolitan Tabernacle Pulpit.

THE HEART: A GIFT FOR GOD.

A Sermon

INTENDED FOR READING ON LORD'S-DAY, DECEMBER 11TH, 1887,

DELIVERED BY

C. H. SPURGEON,

AT THE METROPOLITAN TABERNACLE, NEWINGTON.

" My son, give me thine heart."—Proverbs xxiii. 26.

THESE are the words of Solomon speaking in the name of wisdom, which wisdom is but another name for the Lord Jesus Christ, who is made of God unto us wisdom. If you ask, " What is the highest wisdom upon the earth ?" it is to believe in Jesus Christ whom God has sent—to become his follower and disciple, to trust him and imitate him. It is God, in the person of his dear Son, who says to each one of us, " My son, give me thine heart." Can we answer, " Lord, I have given thee my heart"? Then we are his sons. Let us cry, " Abba, Father," and bless the Lord for the high privilege of being his children. "Behold, what manner of love the Father hath bestowed upon us, that we should be called the sons of God."

I. Let us look at this precept, " My son, give me thine heart "; and notice, first, that LOVE PROMPTS THIS REQUEST OF WISDOM.

Only love seeks after love. If I desire the love of another, it can surely only be because I myself have love toward him. We care not to be loved by those whom we do not love. It were an embarrassment rather than an advantage to receive love from those to whom we would not return it. When God asks human love, it is because God is love. As the sparks mount toward the sun, the central fire, so ought our love to rise toward God, the central source of all pure and holy love. It is an instance of infinite condescension that God should say, " My son, give me thine heart." Notice the strange position in which it puts God and man. The usual position is for the creature to say to God, " Give me"; but here the Creator cries to feeble man, " Give me." The Great Benefactor himself becomes the Petitioner—stands at the door of his own creatures, and asks, not for offerings, nor for words of praise, but for their hearts. Oh, it must be because of the great love of God that he condescends to put himself into such a position; and if we were right-minded, our immediate response would be, " Dost *thou* seek my heart? Here it is, my Lord." But, alas ! few thus respond, and none

Nos. 1,995-6-7.

do so except those who are, like David, men after God's own heart. When God says to such, " Seek ye my face," they answer at once, " Thy face, Lord, will we seek " : but this answer is prompted by divine grace. It can only be love that seeks for love.

Again, *it can only be supreme love which leads wisdom to seek after the heart of such poor things as we are.* The best saints are poor things; and as for some of us who are not the best, what poor, poor things we are ! How foolish ! How slow to learn ! Does wisdom seek us for scholars ? Then wisdom must be of a most condescending kind. We are so guilty, too. We shall rather disgrace than honour the courts of wisdom if she admits us to her school. Yet she says to each of us, " Give me thy heart. Come and learn of me." Only love can invite such scholars as we are. I am afraid we shall never do much to glorify God ; we have but small parts to begin with, and our position is obscure. Yet, common-place people though we are, God says to each one of us, " My son, give me thine heart." Only infinite love would come a-wooing to such wretched hearts as ours.

For what has God to gain ? Brothers and sisters, if we did all give our hearts to him, in what respect would he be the greater ? If we gave him all we have, would he be the richer ? " The silver and the gold are mine," says he, " and the cattle on a thousand hills. If I were hungry, I would not tell thee." He is too great for us to make him greater, too good for us to make him better, too glorious for us to make him more illustrious. When he comes a-wooing, and cries, " Give me thine heart," it must be for our benefit, and not for his own. Surely it is more blessed for us to give than for him to receive. He can gain nothing : we gain everything by the gift. Yet he does gain a son : that is a sweet thought. Everyone that gives God his heart becomes God's son, and a father esteems his children to be treasures ; and I reckon that God sets a higher value upon his children than upon all the works of his hand besides. We see the Great Father's likeness in the story of the returning prodigal. The father thought more of his re- turning son than of all that he possessed besides. " It was meet," said he " that we should make merry, and be glad : for this thy brother was dead, and is alive again ; and was lost, and is found." Oh, I tell you, you that do not know the Lord, that if you give your hearts to him you will make him glad ! The Eternal Father will be glad to get back his lost son, to press to his bosom a heart warm with affection for him, which heart aforetime had been cold and stony towards him. " My son, give me thine heart," says he, as if he longed for our love, and could not bear to have children that had forgotten him. Do you not hear him speak ? Speak, Spirit of God, and make each one hear thee say, " My son, give me thine heart " !

You who are sons of God already may take my text as a call to give God your heart anew, for—I do not know how it is—men are wonder- fully scarce now ; and men with hearts are rare. If preachers had larger hearts, they would move more people to hear them. A sermon preached without love falls flat and dead. We have heard sermons, ad- mirable in composition, and excellent in doctrine, but like that palace which the Empress of Russia built upon the Neva of blocks of ice. Nothing more lustrous, nothing more sharply cut, nothing more charming; but oh, so cold, so very cold! Its very beauty a frost to the soul! "My son," says God to every preacher, "give me thine heart." O minister, if thou canst not speak with eloquent tongue, at least let thy heart run over like burning lava from thy lips! Let thy heart be like a Geyser, scalding all that come near thee, permitting none to remain indifferent. You that teach in the school, you that work for God anyhow, do it thoroughly well. "Give me thine heart, my son," says God. It is one of the first and last qualifications of a good workman for God that he should put his heart into his work. I have heard mistresses tell servants when polishing tables that elbow-grease was a fine thing for such work; and so it is. Hard work is a splendid thing. It will make a way under a river, or through an Alp. Hard work will do almost everything; but in God's service it must not only be hard work, but hot work. The heart must be on fire. The heart must be set upon its design. See how a child cries! Though I am not fond of hearing it, yet I note that some children cry all over: when they want a thing, they cry from the tips of their toes to the last hair of their heads. That is the way to preach, and that is the way to pray, and that is the way to live: the whole man must be heartily engaged in holy work. Love prompts the request of wisdom. *God knows that in his service we shall be miserable unless our hearts are fully engaged.* Whenever we feel that preaching is heavy work, and Sunday-school teaching after six days' labour is tiresome, and going round a district with tracts is a terrible task—then we shall do nothing well. Put your heart into your service, and all will be joyful; but not else.

II. Now, I turn my text another way. WISDOM PERSUADES US TO OBEY THIS LOVING REQUEST. To take our hearts and give them up to God is the wisest thing that we can do. If we have done it before, we had better do it over again, and hand over once more the sacred deposit into those dear hands which will surely keep that which we commit to their guardian care. "My son, give me thine heart."

Wisdom prompts us to do it; for, first, *many others crave our hearts*, and our hearts will surely go one way or other. Let us see to it that they do not go where they will be ruined. I will not read you the next verse, but many a man has lost his heart and soul eternally by the lusts of the flesh. He has perished through "her that lieth in wait as for a prey, and increaseth the transgressors among men." Happy is that young man whose heart is never defiled with vice! There is no way of being kept from impurity except by giving up the heart to the holy Lord. In a city like this, the most pure-minded are surrounded with innumerable temptations; and many there are that slip with their feet before they are aware of it, being carried away because they have not time to think before the temptation has cast them to the ground. "Therefore, my son," says wisdom, "give me thine heart. Everybody will try to steal thy heart, therefore leave it in my charge. Then thou needest not fear the fascinations of the strange woman, for I have thy heart, and I will keep it safe unto the day of my appearing." It is most wise to give Jesus our heart, for seducers will seek after it.

There is another destroyer of souls. I will not say much about it, but I will just read you what the context saith of it—"Who hath woe? Who hath sorrow? Who hath contentions? Who hath babbling?

Who hath wounds without cause ?   Who hath redness of eyes ?   They
that tarry long at the wine.   They that go to seek mixed wine.   Look
not thou upon the wine when it is red, when it giveth his colour in the
cup, when it moveth itself aright.   At the last it biteth like a serpent,
and stingeth like an adder.   Thine eyes shall behold strange women,
and thine heart shall utter perverse things."   Read carefully the rest
of the chapter, and then hear the voice of wisdom say, " My son, if thou
wouldst be kept from drunkenness and gluttony, from wantonness and
chambering, and everything that the heart inclineth to, give me thy
heart."

It is well to guard your heart with all the apparatus that wisdom can
provide.   It is well totally to abstain from that which becomes a snare
to you: but, I charge you, do not rely upon abstinence, but give your
heart to Jesus; for nothing short of true godliness will preserve you
from sin so that you shall be presented faultless before his presence with
exceeding great joy.   As you would wish to preserve an unblemished
character, and be found honourable to the end, my son, I charge thee
give to Christ thy heart.

Wisdom urges to immediate decision because *it is well to have a heart
at once occupied and taken up by Christ.*   It is an empty heart that the
devil enters.   You know how the boys always break the windows of
empty houses; and the devil throws stones wherever the heart is empty.
If you can say to the devil when you are tempted, " You are too late ;
I have given my heart to Christ, I cannot listen to your overtures, I
am affianced to the Saviour by bonds of love that never can be broken,"
what a blessed safeguard you have !   I know of nothing that can so
protect the young man in these perilous days as to be able to sing " O
God, my heart is fixed; my heart is fixed !   Others may flit to and fro,
and seek something to light upon, but my heart is fixed upon thee for
ever.   I am unable to turn aside through thy sweet grace."   " My son,"
says the text, " give me thine heart," that Christ may dwell there, that
when Satan comes, the One who is stronger than the strong man armed
may keep his house, and drive the foeman back.

Give Jesus your hearts, beloved friends, for wisdom bids you do it at
once, because *it will please God.*   Have you a friend to whom you wish
to make a present?   I know what you do : you try to find out what that
friend would value, for you say, " I should like to give him what would
please him."   Do you want to give God something that is sure to please
him?   You need not build a church of matchless architecture—I do not
know that God cares much about stones and wood.   You need not wait till
you shall have amassed money to endow a row of almshouses.   It is well to
bless the poor, but Jesus said that one who gave two mites, which made
a farthing, gave more than all the rich men who cast in of their wealth
into the treasury.   What would God my Father like me to give?   He
answers, " My son, give me thine heart."   He will be pleased with that,
for he himself seeks the gift.

If there are any here to whom this day is an anniversary of birth, or
of marriage, or of some other joyful occasion, let them make a present
to God, and give him their hearts.   It is wonderful that he should
word it so.   " My son, give me thine heart."   I should not have dared
to say such a thing if he had not said it, but he does put it so.

This will please him better than a bullock that hath horns and hoofs, better than smoking incense in the silver censer, better than all you can contrive of art, or purchase by wealth, or design for beauty. " My son, give me thine heart."

For notice, again, that *if you do not give him your heart, you cannot please him at all.* You may give God what you please, but without your heart it is all an abomination to him. To pray without your heart is solemn mockery; to sing without your heart is an empty sound; to give, to teach, to work, without your heart is all an insult to the Most High. You cannot do God any service till you give him your heart. You must begin with this. Then shall your hand and purse give what they will, and your tongue and brain shall give what they can; but first your heart—first your heart—your inmost self—your love—your affection. You must give him your heart, or you give him nothing.

And does he not deserve it? I am not going to use that argument, because, somehow, if you press a man to give a thing, at last it comes not to be a gift, but a tax. Our consecration to God must be unquestionable in its freeness. Religion is voluntary or else false. If I shall prove that your heart is God's due, why, then, you will not give, but rather pay as though it were a debt; so I will touch that string very gently, lest, in seeking to bring forth music, I snap the chord. I will put it thus: surely it were well to give a heart for a heart. There was One who came and took human nature on him, and wore a human heart within his bosom, and that human heart was pressed full sore with sorrow till, it is written, that he wept. It was pressed still more with anguish till, it is written, "He sweat, as it were, great drops of blood, falling to the ground." He was still further overwhelmed with grief, till at last he said, "Reproach hath broken my heart, and I am full of heaviness;" and then it is written, "One of the soldiers with a spear pierced his side, and forthwith came there out blood and water." A heart was given for you, will you not give your heart? I say no more.

I was about to say that I wished I could bring my Master here to stand on this platform, that you might see him; but I know that faith comes by hearing, not by seeing. Yet would I set him forth evidently crucified among you, and for you. Oh, give him, then, a heart for a heart, and yield yourself up to him! Is there not a sweet whisper in your spirit now that says, "Yield thy heart"? Hearken to that still small voice, and there shall be no need that I speak farther.

Believe me, beloved friends, *there is no getting wisdom except you give your heart to it.* There is no understanding the science of Christ crucified, which is the most excellent of all the sciences, without giving your heart to it. Some of you have been trying to be religious. You have been trying to be saved, but you have done it in an off-handed sort of style. "My son, give me thine *heart.*" Wisdom suggests to you that you should do it, for unless your whole heart is thrown into it you will never prosper in it. Certain men never get on in business; they do not like their trade, and so they never prosper. And, certainly, in the matter of religion, no man can ever prosper if he does not love it, if his whole heart is not in it. Some people have just enough religion to make them miserable. If they had none, they would be able to enjoy the world; but they have too much religion to be able to enjoy the world, and yet not enough to enjoy the world to come. Oh, you poor betweenities—you that hang like Mahomet's coffin, between earth and heaven—you that are like bats, neither birds nor beasts—you that are like a flying fish, that tries to live in the air and water too, and finds enemies in both elements—you that are neither this, nor that, nor the other, strangers in God's country, and yet not able to make yourselves at home with the devil—I do pity you. Oh, that I could give you a tug to get you to this side of the border-land! My Master bids me compel you to come in; but what can I do except repeat the message of the text? "My son, give me thine heart." Do not be shilly-shallying any longer. Let your heart go one way or the other. If the devil be worth loving, give him your heart, and serve him; but if Christ be worth loving, give him your heart, and have done with hesitation. Turn over to Jesus once for all. Oh, may his Spirit turn you, and you shall be turned, and his name shall have the praise!

III. And now I close with the third observation. LET US BE WISE ENOUGH AT ONCE TO ATTEND TO THIS ADMONITION OF WISDOM. Let us now give God our heart. "My son, give me thine heart."

When? At once. There is no intimation that God would have us wait a little. I wish that those persons who only mean to wait a little would fix a time when they will leave off waiting. They are always going to be right to-morrow. Which day of the month is that? I have searched the calendar, and cannot find it. I have heard that there is such a thing as the fool's calendar, and that to-morrow is there; but then, you are not fools, and do not keep such a calendar. To-morrow, to-morrow, to-morrow, to-morrow, to-morrow, to-morrow; it is a raven's croak of evil omen. To-day, to-day, to-day, to-day, to-day; that is the silver trumpet of salvation, and he that hears it shall live. God grant that we may not for ever be crying out, "to-morrow," but at once give our hearts to him!

How? If we attend to this precept, we shall notice that it calls upon us to act *freely.* "My son, *give* me thine heart." Do not need to have it led in fetters. It might, as I have already said, prevent a thing from being a gift if you too pressingly proved that it was due. It is due, but God puts it, as it were, upon free-will for once, and leaves it to free agency. He says, "My son, *give* me thine heart. All that thou hast from me comes as a gift of free grace; now give me back thy heart freely." Remember, wherever we speak about the power of grace, we do not mean a physical force, but only such force as may be applied to free agents, and to responsible beings. The Lord begs you not to want to be crushed and pounded into repentance, nor whipped and spurred to holy living. But "My son, give me thine heart." I have heard that the richest juice of the grape is that which comes with the slightest pressure at the first touch. Oh, to give God our freest love! You know the old proverb that one volunteer is worth two pressed men. We shall all be pressed men in a certain sense; but yet it is written, "Thy people shall be willing in the day of thy power." May you be willing at once!

"My son, give me thine heart." It seems a pity that a man should have to live a long life of sin to learn that sin does not pay. It is a sad case when he comes to God with all his bones broken, and enlists in the divine army after he has spent all his youth in the service of the devil, and has worn himself out. Christ will have him whenever he comes; but how much better it is, while yet you are in the days of your youth, to say, " Here, Lord, I give thee my heart. Constrained by thy sweet love, I yield to thee in the dawn of my being " !

Now, that is what the text means : give God your heart at once, and do it freely.

Do it thoroughly. " My son, give me thine heart." You cannot give Christ a piece of a heart, for a heart that is halved is killed. A heart that has even a little bit taken off is a dead heart. The devil does not mind having half your heart. He is quite satisfied with that, because he is like the woman to whom the child did not belong : he does not mind if it be cut in halves. The true mother of the child said, " Oh, spare the child ! Do not divide it;" and so Christ, who is the true Lover of hearts, will not have the heart divided. If it must go one way, and the wrong way, let it go that way : but if it will go the right way, he is ready to accept it, cleanse it, and perfect it, only it must go all together, and not be divided. " Give me thine heart."

Did I hear somebody say, " I am willing to give God my heart ? " Very well, then, let us look at it practically. *Where is it now?* You cannot give your heart up till you find out where it is. I knew a man who lost his heart. His wife had not got it, and his children had not got it, and he did not seem as if he had got it himself. " That is odd," say you. Well, he used to starve himself. He scarcely had enough to eat. His clothes were threadbare. He starved all who were round him. He did not seem to have a heart. A poor woman owed him a little rent. Out she went into the street. He had no heart. A person had fallen back a little in the payment of money that he had lent him. The debtor's little children were crying for bread. The man did not care who cried for hunger, or what became of the children. He would have his money. He had lost his heart. I never could make out where it was till I went to his house one day, and I saw a huge chest. I think they called it an iron safe : it stood behind the door of an inner room; and when he unlocked it with a heavy key, and the bolts were shot, and the inside was opened, there was a musty, fusty thing within it, as dry and dead as the kernel of a walnut seven years old. It was his heart. If you have locked up your heart in an iron safe, get it out. Get it out as quickly as ever you can. It is a horrible thing to pack up a heart in five-pound notes, or bury it under heaps of silver and gold. Hearts are never healthy when covered up with hard metal. Your gold and silver are cankered if your heart is bound up with them.

I knew a young lady—I think I know several of that sort now—whose heart I could never see. I could not make out why she was so flighty, giddy, frothy, till I discovered that she had kept her heart in a wardrobe. A poor prison for an immortal soul; is it not? You had better fetch it out, before the moth eats it as wool. When our garments become the idols of our hearts, we are such foolish things that we can hardly be said to have hearts at all. Even such foolish hearts as these, it were well to get out of the wardrobe, and give to Christ.

Where is your heart? I have known some leave it at the public-house, and some in places that I shall not mention, lest the cheek of modesty should crimson. But wherever your heart is, it is in the wrong place if it is not with Christ. Go, fetch it, sir. Bring it here, and give it into the hand of him that bought it.

But in what state is it? "Ay, there's the rub." For, as I told you, that the miser's heart was musty and fusty, so men's hearts begin to smell of the places wherein they keep them. Some women's hearts are mouldy and ragged through their keeping them in the wardrobe. Some men's hearts are cankered through keeping them among their gold; and some are rotten, through and through, through keeping them steeped in vice. Where is the drunkard's heart? In what state must it be? Foul and filthy. Still God says, "Give me thine heart." What! such a thing as that? Yes, did I not tell you that when he asked for your heart it was all for love of you, and not for what he should get out of you: for what is such a heart as yours, my friend, that has been in such a place, and fallen into such a state? Yet, still give it to him, for I will tell you what he will do: he will work wonders for your heart. You have heard of alchemists who took base metal, so they say, and transmuted it into gold: the Lord will do more than this. "Give me thine heart." Poor, filthy, defiled, polluted, depraved heart!—give it to him. It is stony now, corrupted now. He will take it, and in those sacred hands of Christ, that heart shall lie, till, in its place you shall see a heart of flesh, pure, clean, heavenly. "Oh," say you, "I never could make out what to do with my hard heart." Give it now to Christ, and he will change it. Yield it up to the sweet power of his infinite grace, and he will renew a right spirit within you. God help you to give Jesus your heart, and to do it now!

There is going to be a collection for the hospitals. Stop, you collectors, till I have said my last word. What are you going to give? I do not mind what you are going to put into the boxes; but I want to pass round an invisible plate, for my Lord. I desire to pass it round to all of you; and please will you say to yourself when you drop your money into the box, "I am going to drop my heart into the invisible collection, and give it up to Jesus. It is all that I can do." Collectors, pass round the boxes, and thou, O Spirit of God, go from man to man, and take possession of all hearts for Jesus our Lord! Amen.

PORTION OF SCRIPTURE READ BEFORE SERMON—Proverbs viii.

HYMNS FROM "OUR OWN HYMN BOOK"—428, 522, 797.

Metropolitan Tabernacle Pulpit.

PUBLIC TESTIMONY: A DEBT TO GOD AND MAN.

DELIVERED BY

C. H. SPURGEON,

AT THE METROPOLITAN TABERNACLE, NEWINGTON.

"Then they said one to another, We do not well: this day is a day of good tidings, and we hold our peace: if we tarry till the morning light, some mischief will come upon us: now therefore come, that we may go and tell the king's household."—2 Kings vii. 9.

You are not surprised to find that, when those four lepers, outside the gate of Samaria, had made the great discovery that the Syrian camp was deserted, they first satisfied their own hunger and thirst. And quite right too. Who would do otherwise? It is true that they were bound to go and tell other hungry ones; but they could do that with all the louder voice, and they were the more sure of the truth they had to tell, when they had first refreshed themselves. It might have been a delusion: they were prudent to test their discovery before they told it. Having refreshed and enriched themselves, they bethought them of going to tell the besieged and starving citizens. I would advise every soul that has found Christ to imitate the lepers in this matter. Make sure that you have found the Saviour. Eat and drink of him; enrich yourself with him; and then go and publish the glad tidings. I shall not object to your going as early as possible; but still, I would prefer that you should not go to assure others until you are quite certain yourself. I would have you go with a personal witness, for this will be your chief power with others. If you run too soon, and do not first taste and see that the Lord is good, you may say to others, "There is abundance in the camp"; and they may reply, "Why have you not eaten of it yourself?" Thus your testimony will be weakened, if not destroyed; and you will wish you had held your peace. It is better that you first of all delight yourself in fatness before you proclaim the fact of a festival. It is good that your faith should grasp the exceeding great and precious promises; and then, when you run as a tidings-bearer, you will testify what you have seen. If any say to you, "Are you sure that it is true?" you will answer, "Ay, that I am, for I have tasted and handled of the good word of life." Personal enjoyments of true godliness assist us in our testimony for truth and grace.

But the point I desire to bring out is this: if those lepers had stopped in the camp all night, if they had remained lying on the Syrian couches,

singing, "Our willing souls would stay in such a place as this";
and if they had never gone at all to their compatriots, shut up and
starving within the city walls, their conduct would have been brutal
and inhuman. I am going to talk to some at this time (I do not know
how many of the sort may be here) who think that they have found the
Saviour, who believe that they are saved, who write themselves down as
having truly enjoyed religion, and who imagine that now their sole
business is to enjoy themselves. They delight to feed on the word, and
to this I do not object at all ; but then, if it is all feeding and nothing
comes of it, I ask to what end are they fed ? If the only result of our
religion is the comfort of our poor little souls ; if the beginning and the
end of piety is contained within one's self, why, it is a strange thing to
be in connection with the unselfish Jesus, and to be the fruit of his
gracious Spirit. Surely, Jesus did not come to save us that we might
live unto ourselves. He came to save us from selfishness.

I am afraid that some of my hearers have never yet confessed the
work of God in their souls. They feel that, whereas they were once blind,
now they see ; but they have never declared what the Lord has done
for their souls. Has all this work been done in a corner for their personal delectation ? I want to have a drive at them, and at all others
who have not yet considered that the object of their receiving grace
from the Lord is that God may, through them, communicate grace to
others. No man liveth unto himself. No man should attempt so
to live.

My subject will be this : first, *to hide the great discovery of grace is
altogether wrong ;* in the second place, *if we have made that discovery we
ought to declare it;* and, thirdly, *this declaration should be continually
made.* It should not be a matter of one solemn occasion, but our whole
life should be a witness to the power and grace which we have found in
Christ.

I. First, then, dear friends, TO HIDE THE DISCOVERY OF DIVINE
GRACE WOULD BE WRONG.

Let me ask you to remember the connection of my text. God had
come to the Syrian camp, and had by himself alone routed the whole
Syrian host : they had every man of them fled. Though the starving
citizens of Samaria did not know it, the Lord had made provision in
abundance for all their hunger ; and there it was, within a stone's throw
of the city gates. The Lord had done it: his own right hand and his
holy arm had gotten him the victory, and had provided for Israel's needs,
though they did not know it. These lepers found out the joyful facts,
and had utilized their discovery by entering into possession of the
treasure : they were appointed to make known the joyful facts ; and
if they had concealed them they would have been guilty men.

For, first, *their silence would have been contrary to the divine purpose in
leading them to make the discovery.* Why were these four lepers led into the
camp that they might learn that the Lord of hosts had put the enemy
to the rout? Why, mainly that they might go back, and tell the rest
of their countrymen. I fear that the doctrine of election has too often
been preached in such a way that thoughtful minds have objected to it
upon the ground of its tendency to selfishness. Men do not like the
doctrine anyhow ; but there is no use in putting it in a needlessly ugly

shape. Election is a fact, but a fact which relates to other facts. The Lord calls out of the world a people, a peculiar people, whom he makes to be his own ; but the ultimate end of the election of these men is that they may gather in others. As Israel was chosen to preserve the light for the nations, so has the Lord chosen his believing people that they may bring in the other sheep which are not yet of the fold. We are not to get within four narrow walls, and sit and sing—

> " We are a garden walled around,
> Chosen and made peculiar ground :
> A little spot enclosed by grace
> Out of the world's wide wilderness."

Or if we do so sing, we are not to bless ourselves over and over again as being the end and climax of the Lord's work and wisdom. No, but since we are a garden walled around, we are to bring forth fruit to him who owns us. We are to be a nursery ground. I know a piece of ground upon which some millions of young fir trees were grown, which were afterwards planted out upon a range of Scotch hills. Such should our churches be. Though comparable in our feebleness to a handful of corn upon the top of the mountains, we expect that the fruit thereof shall shake like Lebanon, and they of the city shall flourish like grass of the earth. We are chosen unto salvation that afterwards we may go and be lights to those that sit in darkness, and spiritual helps to those that are ready to perish. These four men were allowed to see what God had done on purpose that they might run home with the cheering news. If they had not gone to Samaria with the tidings they would have been false to the divine purpose; and so will you be, my brother, if you continue to hold your tongue ; so will you be, my sister, if you never say, " The Lord has done great things for me, whereof I am glad." Let the purpose of God, for which you ought to adore him every day, be plenteously fulfilled in you, and let it be seen that he has chosen you to know Christ that you may make him known to others.

These people would not only have been false to the divine purpose, but *they would have failed to do well.* They said one to another, " We do not well." Did it ever strike some of you, dear friends, that it is a very serious charge to bring against yourselves, " We do not well " ? I am afraid that many are content because they can say, " We do not drink. We do not swear. We do not gamble. We do not lie." Who said you did ? You ought to be ashamed of yourselves if you did any of those things. But is this enough ? What are you actually doing ? " To him that knoweth to do good, and doeth it not, to him it is sin." I have heard of perfect people, but I have not seen any such. If it came to acts of positive commission of sin, I could possibly compare notes with such brethren ; for I endeavour to be blameless, and I trust I am : but when I remember that sins of *omission* are really and truly sins, I bid " good-bye " to all notions of perfection, for my many shortcomings overwhelm me. No man has done all the good he could have done, and ought to have done. If any man assures me that he has done all the good that might have been possible to him, I do not believe him. I will say no more; but let us labour to avoid sins of omission. Dear friend, if you know the Lord, and you have never confessed his name, then you have not done well. If you have been in company, and you have not spoken up for Christ, you have not done well. If you have had opportunities of telling out the gospel even to children, and you have not done so, you have not done well. It is a heavy charge, after all, for a man's conscience to bring against him when it forces him to join with others in saying, "We do not well." That is the reason why the barren fig-tree was cut down. He that kept the vineyard did not say, "Cut it down, it bears such sour fruit." It bore no fruit at all. There was the point: it cumbered the ground. Take heed, oh, take heed, of a religion which does not make you positively do well! If all that your religion does is to keep you from doing mischief, it has too small an effect to be the religion of Jesus Christ. He asks, "What do ye more than others? Do not even publicans so?" God help us then to make an open declaration of what his Spirit has secretly taught to us!

Besides this, had those lepers held their tongues, *they would actually have been doing evil.* Suppose that they had kept their secret for four-and-twenty hours, many hundreds might have died of starvation within the walls of Samaria: had they so perished, would not the lepers have been guilty of their blood? Do you not agree with that? May not neglect be as truly murder as a stab or a shot? If, in your street, a man shall perish through not knowing the Saviour, and you never made an effort to instruct him, how will you be guiltless at the last great day? If there be any within your reach who sink down to perdition for want of the knowledge of Christ, and you could have given them that knowledge, will your skirts be free from blood in the day when the great inquest shall be held, and God shall make inquisition for the blood of men? I put it to the consciences of many silent Christians, who have never yet made known to others what God has made known to them—How can you be clear from guilt in this matter? Do not say, "Am I my brother's keeper?" for I shall have to give you a horrible answer if you do. I shall have to say, "No, Cain, you are not your brother's keeper, but you are your brother's killer." If, by your effort you have not sought his good, by your neglect you have destroyed him. If I were able to swim, and I saw any of you in a stream, and I merely looked at you, and greatly regretted that you should be so foolish as to tumble in, but never stretched out a hand to rescue you, your death would lie at my door; and I am sure it is so with those who talk about enjoying religion, and yet keep it all to themselves, and never rescue the perishing. Stern truths these. Let them go home where they ought to go home, and may God the Holy Ghost bless them!

Again, these lepers, if they had held their tongues, *would have acted most unseasonably.* Note how they put it themselves: they say, "We do not well: this day is a day of good tidings, and we hold our peace." O brother, has Jesus washed your sins away, and are you silent about it? I remember the day when I first found peace with God through the precious blood; and I declare that I was forced to tell somebody about it: I could not have stifled the voice within me. What, my dear brother! are you saved in the Lord with an everlasting salvation, and can you keep the blessing to yourself? Do you not wonder that all the timbers in your house do not groan at you, and that the earth itself does not open her mouth to rebuke you? Can you be such an ungrateful wretch as to have tasted of amazing mercy, and yet to have no word to say by way of confessing it? Come, brother, come, sister, overcome that retiring spirit of yours, and cry—"I cannot help it; I am driven to it; I must and will bear witness that there is a Saviour, and a great one." Personally, *I* cannot hold my tongue, and never will while I can speak.

> " E'er since by faith I saw the stream,
>   His flowing wounds supply ;
> Redeeming love has been my theme,
>   And shall be till I die ! "

Oh, that God would stir up every silent Christian to speak out for his Lord ! We have had enough of the dumb spirit. Oh, for the Spirit in the form of tongues of fire !

One thing more : *silence may be dangerous.* What said these men ? " If we tarry till the morning light, some mischief will come upon us." That morning light is very close to some of you. If you tarry till to-morrow morning before you have spoken about Christ, some mischief may come upon you. I might put it farther off on a grander scale. There is a morning light which will soon be seen over yon gloomy hills of darkness ; how soon we cannot tell, but our Master has bidden us to be always on the watch for it. In such an hour as we think not, he will come ; and when he comes, it will be to reward his faithful servants. There is a text which speaks of our not being ashamed at his coming. What a wonderful text that is ! What if he were to come to-night : should we not be ashamed ? He may come ere the unformed word has quitted my lip, or reached your ear ; the shrill clarion of the archangel may startle the dead from their graves, and the Christ may be among us on his great white throne ! Suppose he should come to-night, and you, who have thought that you knew him and loved him, should never have sought to win a soul for him—how will you face him ? How will you answer your Lord, whom you have never owned ? You knew the way of salvation, and you concealed it. You knew the balm for the wounds of sinners, and you let them bleed to death. They were thirsty, and you gave them no draught of living water ; they were hungry, and you gave them no bread of life. Sirs, I cannot venture to his judgment-seat with such a blot upon my soul ! Can you ? Brother, can you ? Sister, can you ? What ! your own dear children—your own flesh and blood—have you never prayed with them, nor sought to bring them to Jesus ? What ! the servants of your house—have you never spoken of the Saviour to them ? Your wife, your husband, your old father, your brother—and you have never yet opened your lips to say, " Jesus has saved me ; I wish you were saved too " ! You might have done as much as that. You have said bolder things than that to them about worldly matters. Oh, by the love of God, or even by a lower motive, by the love of your fellow-men, do burst your bands asunder, and speak out for Christ ; or else, if your profession be true, you do not well ; indeed, there is reason to question your religion.

Thus much upon the first point—to hide the blessed discovery would have been wrong in the lepers, and it would be wrong in us.

II. Secondly, if we have made the blessed discovery of Christ's gracious work in routing our enemies, and providing for our needs, and if we have tasted of the fruit of that glorious victory ourselves, WE OUGHT TO MAKE A VERY EXPLICIT AVOWAL OF THAT DISCOVERY. It ought to be confessed very solemnly, and in the way which the Lord himself has appointed. How can we better show forth all righteousness than by being buried with Christ in baptism, according to his command? We ought, also, to unite with the church of the Lord Jesus Christ, and to co-operate therewith in holy service. This ought to be done very decidedly, because *our Lord requires it.* Our blessed Lord Jesus Christ couples always with faith the confession of it. He that with his heart believeth, and with his mouth maketh confession of him, shall be saved. "He that believeth and is baptized shall be saved." We constantly find the two together. The faith that saves is not a sneaking faith, which tries to get to heaven by keeping off the road, and creeping along behind the hedge. The true faith comes into the middle of the road, feeling, "this is the King's highway, and I am not ashamed to be found in it." This is the faith which Jesus expects of you, the faith which cries, "I have lifted my hand unto the Lord, and I will not go back."

Next, if you have found Christ, *the man who was the means of leading you to Christ has a claim upon you that he should know of it.* Oh, the joy of my heart, the other day, when I saw some four-and-twenty who were my spiritual children! I felt then that I was receiving large wages at the Master's hands. Many get good from the minister, and yet they never let him know of it. This is not doing as they would be done by. It is rather like cheating us of the reward of our ministry. To know that God is blessing us is a great comfort and stimulus. Do not muzzle the mouth of the ox that treadeth out the corn.

Next, I think *the church of God has a claim upon all of you* who have discovered the great love of Jesus. Come and tell your fellow-Christians. Tell the good news to the King's household. The church of God is often greatly refreshed by the stories of new converts. I am afraid that we who get over fifty come by degrees to be rather old-fogeyfied, and it is a great blessing to us to hear the cries of the babes in grace, and to listen to the fresh and vivid testimony of new converts. It stirs our blood, and quickens our souls, and thus the church of God is benefited. If some of you old folks had been at the church-meeting the other Monday evening, and heard some five little children, one after the other, telling what the Lord had done for their souls, you would have agreed with me that you could not have done it so well yourselves. You may know more, but you could not have stated what you know so simply, so sweetly, so charmingly, as those dear children did. One of them was but nine years old, or younger, and yet she told of free grace and dying love as clearly as if she had been eighty or ninety. Out of the mouth of babes and sucklings the Lord ordaineth strength. Some of you have known the Lord for many years, and yet you have never confessed him. How wrong it is of you! How much you injure the church!

Besides that, a decided testimony for Christ *is due to the world.* If a man is a soldier of the cross, and does not show his colours, all his comrades are losers by his want of decision. There is nothing better for a man when he is brought to Christ than for him decidedly to express his faith, and let those about him know that he is a new man. Unfurl your standard. Decision for Christ and holiness will save you from many dangers, and ward off many temptations. Compromise creates a life of misery. I would sooner be a toad under a harrow than be a Christian man who tries to conceal his Christianity. It is sometimes difficult, in this age, for a man to follow his conscience, for you are expected to run with a party ; but I am of this mind—that I would sooner die than not live a free man. It is not life to have to ask another man's permission to think. If there be any misrepresentation, if there be any scorn, if there be any contempt for being a Christian, let me have my share of it, for a Christian I am, and I wish to be treated like the rest.

If all Christians came out, and declared what the Lord has done for their souls, the world would feel the power of Christianity, and would not think of it as men now do, as though it were some petty superstition, of which its own votaries were ashamed. If indeed ye be soldiers of the cross, bear your shields into the light of day, and be not ashamed of your Captain! What can there be to make us blush in the service of such a Lord ? Be ashamed of shame, and quit yourselves like men !

Your open confession is due all round, and it is specially *due to yourself*. It is due to your spiritual manhood that, if the Lord has done anything for you, you should gratefully acknowledge it. It is also due to your love of others—and love of others is of the very essence of Christianity—that you should explicitly declare that you are on the Lord's side. What more shall I say? What more need I say? I would sound the trumpet, and summon to our Lord's banner all who are good men and true.

III. THIS DECLARATION SHOULD BE CONTINUALLY MADE. Here I speak of many who have confessed Christ publicly, and are not ashamed of his name. Beloved, we ought always to make Christ known, not only by our once-made profession, but by frequently bearing witness in support of that profession. I wish that we did this more amongst God's own people. Miss Havergal very admirably says, " The King's household were the most unlikely people to need to be instructed in this good news :—So it seems at first sight. But, secondly, the lepers were the most unlikely persons to instruct the King's household ; and yet they did so." You and I might say—Christian people do not require to be spoken to about our Lord and his work; they know more than we do. If they do require it, who are we, who are less than the least of all our Master's household, that we should presume to instruct them ? Thus even humility might check our bearing testimony in certain companies. If you were in the midst of uninstructed people, to whom you could do good, you might feel bound to speak ; but among Christians you are apt to be dumb. Have you not said to yourself, " I could not speak to that good old man. He is much better instructed in the faith than I am"? Meanwhile, what do you think the aforesaid good old man is saying ? He says to himself, " He is a fine young man, but I could not speak to him, for he has so much more ability than I have." Thus you are both as mute as mice when you might be mutually edified. Worse still, perhaps you begin talking upon worthless themes : you speak of the weather, or of the last wretched scandal, or of politics. Suppose we were to change all this, and each one say, " I am a Christian man, and next time I meet a brother Christian, whether he is my superior or not, I shall speak to him of our common Master." If two children meet, they will do well to speak of father and mother. If one is a very little child, he may know but little about his father compared with the knowledge possessed by his big sister ; but then he has kissed his father last, and has of late enjoyed more caresses from his father than his grown-up sister has. The elder can tell more of father's wisdom and providence, but the younger has a more vivid sense of his tenderness and love ; and so they can unite in fervent admiration.

Why should Christian people so often meet and part without exchanging five words about the Lord Jesus ? I am not condemning any of you : I am censuring myself more than any one else. We do not bear enough testimony for our Lord. I am sure I felt quite taken aback the other day when a flyman said to me, " You believe that the Lord directs the way of his people, don't you, sir ? " I said, " That I do. Do you know anything about it ? " " Why," he said, " Yes. This morning I was praying the Lord to direct my way, and you engaged me ; and I felt that it was a good beginning for the day." We began talking about the things of God directly. That flyman ought not to have been the first to speak : as a minister of the gospel, I ought to have had the first word. We have much to blame ourselves for in this respect. We hold our tongues because we do not know how a word might be received; but we might as well make the experiment. No harm could come of trying. Suppose you were to go into a place where persons were sick and dying, and you had medicine about you which would heal them ; would you not be anxious to give them some of it ? Would you say nothing about it because you could not tell how it might be received ? How could you know how it would be received except by making the offer ? Tell poor souls about Jesus. Tell them how his grace healed *you,* and perhaps they will answer, " You are the very person I need ; you have brought me the news I have longed to hear."

There are districts in London, to my knowledge, in the suburbs especially, where, if a man knocks at the door, and begins to say a word about Christ, the poor people answer, "No one ever calls upon us to do us any good. We are left to perish." It is shameful that it should be so, but so it is. Men live and men die in this Christian country as much lost to the knowledge of the gospel as if they had lived on the Congo. If they lived on the Congo, we should all subscribe to send a missionary up the river to tell them of Jesus and his love : even at the risk of his dying of fever, we should send a missionary to them ; and yet those who live next door to our homes, or are even in our employ, are left in ignorance of salvation. The woman that comes in charing, the man who sweeps up the mud from the street—these may know no more of Christ than Hottentots, and yet we do not speak about Christ to them. Is not this shocking ? We have satisfied our own hunger, and now we allow others to starve ! If I should persuade any brother here, or any sister here, who has tasted that the Lord is gracious, to shake off sinful lethargy, I should have done good service. Dear friends, do let us quit indifference, and get to work for Jesus. It is not enough to me that I should myself preach the gospel ; I would fain turn you all out to proclaim it. Oh, that the thousands here assembled would go through London proclaiming Christ ! The result of such a crusade eternity alone could reveal. I spoke from this pulpit once about Christian young men who were great hands at cricket, but could not bowl straight at a sinner's heart. A gentleman who was present that day, and heard me, said, "That is true about me, I am a Christian man, but yet I am better known as a cricketer than as a worker." He began to serve his Lord with his whole heart, and he is at this day in the front rank of usefulness. Oh, that I could win another such ! The multitudes of London are dying in the dark. I beseech you bring them all the light you have ! Myriads are perishing all over this United Kingdom. Hasten to their rescue ! The world also remains under the power of evil. I beseech you to reclaim it !

"I do not know anything," says one. Then do not say what you don't know. "Oh ! " cries another, "I hope I am a Christian." Tell others how you became a believer, and that will be the gospel. You need not study a book, and try to make a sermon with three heads and a tail; but go home, and say to your biggest boy, "John, I want to tell you how your father found a Saviour." Go home to that sweet little daughter of yours, and say, "Dear Sarah, I want to tell you how Jesus loves me." Before the morning light you may have had the joy of seeing your dear children brought to the Saviour if this very evening you talk to them out of the fulness of your heart.

Only this I say to you : if you do not love my Master, then turn you from your evil ways. If you have not trusted Jesus, trust him at once, and find salvation full and free. When you have found that salvation, then publish the tidings of it. By the love of him that bled upon the cross—by every drop of blood from his pierced heart, arouse yourselves to serve him with all your might. Either with tongue or with pen tell of the love of Jesus.

> "Tell it out among the heathen,
> That he reigneth from the tree."

Sound it forth everywhere beneath yon arch of heaven that Jesus Christ came into the world to save sinners; and add, "He has saved me." God bless you !

PORTIONS OF SCRIPTURE READ BEFORE SERMON—2 Kings vii. 3—16, and Psalm xxxiv.

HYMNS FROM "OUR OWN HYMN BOOK "—228, 246, 632.

GOD'S LONGSUFFERING: AN APPEAL TO THE CONSCIENCE.

DELIVERED IN THE AUTUMN OF 1886, BY

C. H. SPURGEON,

AT THE METROPOLITAN TABERNACLE, NEWINGTON.

"And account that the longsuffering of our Lord is salvation."—2 Peter iii. 15.

JESUS is well called "our Lord," let us at the commencement adore him. Let us each one cry to him, "My Lord, and my God." It is a long, long time since our Lord went up to heaven, and he said that he would come again. Evidently, some of those who best understood him *mis*understood him, and thought that he would surely come again even in their lifetime. He said that he would come, and faithful ones in all ages have looked for him, and it is not possible that our Lord can have deceived us. Because he is so sweetly our Lord, our brethren have made sure that he will keep his word; and he will. But certain of them have gone beyond our Lord's promise, and have felt sure that they knew *when* he would come; and they have been bitterly disappointed because the hour which they fixed passed over, and he did not appear. This does not prove that he will not come. The day is certainly nearer, and every hour is hastening his coming. "Behold, he cometh with clouds, and every eye shall see him."

But why are his chariots so long in coming? Why does he delay? The world grows grey, not alone with age, but with iniquity; and yet the Deliverer comes not. We have waited for his footfall at the dead of night, and looked out for him through the gates of the morning, and expected him in the heat of the day, and reckoned that he might come ere yet another sun went down; but he is not here! He waits. He waits very, very long. Will he not come?

Longsuffering is that which keeps him from coming. He is bearing with men. Not yet the thunderbolt! Not yet the riven heavens and the reeling earth! Not yet the great white throne, and the day of judgment; for he is very pitiful, and beareth long with men! Even to the cries of his own elect, who cry day and night unto him—he is not in haste to answer, for he is very patient, slow to anger, and plenteous in mercy.

But his patience sometimes greatly puzzles us. We cannot make it out. Eighteen, nineteen centuries, and the world not converted! Nineteen centuries, and Satan still to the front, and all manner of iniquity still wounding this poor, bleeding world! What meaneth it? O Son of God, what meaneth it? Seed of the woman, when wilt thou appear with thy foot upon the serpent's head? We are puzzled at the longsuffering which causes so weary a delay.

One of the reasons is that we have not much longsuffering ourselves. We think that we do well to be angry with the rebellious, and so we prove ourselves to be more like Jonah than Jesus. A few have learned to be patient and pitiful to the ungodly, but many more are of the mind of James and John, who would have called fire from heaven upon those who rejected the Saviour. We are in such a hurry. We have not the eternal leisure of God. We have but to live, like ephemera, our little day, and therefore we are in hot haste to see all things accomplished ere the sun goes down. We are but leaves in the forest of existence; and if something is not done soon, and done quickly, we shall fade, and pass away amid unaccomplished hope; and so we are not patient. We are staggered when the Master tells us to forgive unto seventy times seven. When he forgives unto seventy times seven, and still waits, and still holds back his thunders, we are amazed, because our mind is not in harmony with the mind of the Infinitely-patient God.

We are all the more puzzled, again, because the ungodly so sadly misuse this longsuffering of God as a reason for greater sin, and as a motive for denying that there is a God at all. Because he gives them space for repentance, they make it into space for iniquity; and because he will not deal out his judgments immediately, they say, "Where is the promise of his coming?"

We have impatiently wished that he would break the silence. Have I not in my heart of hearts cried out, "O Lord, how long? Can this go on much longer? Canst thou bear it? Wilt thou not come with the iron rod, breaking thy foes before thy face, most mighty Son of God?" It is hard to have the days of blasphemy and rebuke multiplied upon us, and to hear the adversary say in every corner, "Where is now their God?" Yet, dear friends, we ought not to be affected by the hissing of these serpents. Surely we would not have our God change his purposes because of the foolish taunts of men. One said, "If there be a God, let him strike me dead"; but God did not smite him, and from this he argued that there was no God: from the same fact I argue that there is a God, and that this God is truly God; for, if he had been less than divine, he might have struck him dead; but, being infinitely patient, he bore with him still. Who was that speck that he should cause God to move hand or foot even to crush him? God is not easily moved, even by the blasphemies of the ungodly. He may be provoked one of these days, for longsuffering has its end, but for a while the Lord pauseth in pity, not willing that any should perish, but that all should come to repentance.

Beloved brethren, God's longsuffering with a guilty world he may never explain to us. There are many things which we must not ask to have explained. We get into deep waters, and into terrible troubles, when we must have everything explained. For my part, I like to believe great truths which are beyond my reason. A religion without mysteries seems to me to be false on the face of it. If there be an Infinite God, it is not possible that poor I, with my finite mind, shall ever be able to understand everything about him. If the Lord chooses to tarry till thousands of years have passed away, yea, till millions of years have elapsed, yet let him do as he wills. Is he not infinitely wise and good ; and who are we that we should put him to the question ? Let him tarry his own time; only let us watch, and wait, for he will come, and they that wait for him shall have their reward.

At this time I am going to speak a little upon this point. First, *let us admire the longsuffering of God.* And, secondly, *let us make a right account of it* by accounting it to be salvation.

I. First, I would conduct your minds hurriedly over a few points that may help you to ADMIRE THE LONGSUFFERING OF GOD.

Admire the longsuffering of God as to *peculiar sins.* Look, brethren, they make images of wood or stone, and they say, "These are God," and they set up these things in the place of him that made the heavens and the earth. How does he endure to see reasonable beings bowing down before idols, before fetishes, before the basest objects ? How does he bear that men should even worship emblems of impurity, and say that these are God? How does he bear it—he that sitteth in the heavens, in whose hand our breath is, and whose are all our ways ?

Others, even in this country, blaspheme God. What an amount of profanity is poured out before God in this city ! One can scarcely walk the streets to-day without hearing horrible language. An oath has often chilled me to the marrow—an oath which was not excused by any special circumstance, but rolled out of the man's mouth as a customary thing. We have to-day some among us that might match the devil in blasphemy, so foully do they talk. And oh, how is it that God bears it when they dare imprecate his curse upon their bodies and their souls ? O Father, how dost thou bear it ? How dost thou endure these profane persons, who insult thee to thy face ?

Besides, there are those who use fair speech, and yet blaspheme most intolerably. Men of education and of science are often worse than the common folk because they blaspheme with fearful deliberation, and solemnly speak against God, and against his Son, and against the precious blood, and against the Holy Ghost. How is it that the Thrice-holy One bears with them ? Oh, wondrous longsuffering of a Gracious God !

And then there are others who wallow in unmentionable impurity and uncleanness. No, I will not attempt any description, nor would I wish to take your thoughts to those things whereof men may blush to think, though they blush not to do them. The moon sees a world of foulness, fornication, and adultery: and yet, O God, thou bearest it ! This great blot upon the face of the world, this huge city of London reeks in its filthiness, and yet thou holdest thy peace !

And then, when I turn my thoughts another way, to the oppression of the poor, to the grinding down of those who, with the hardest labour, can scarcely earn bread enough to keep body and soul together, how does the Just God permit it ? When I mark the oppression of man by man—for among wild beasts there is none that equals the cruelty of man to man—how doth the All-merciful bear it ? Methinks the sword of the Lord must often rattle in its scabbard, and he must force it down, and say, "Sword of the Lord, rest and be quiet!"

I will not go further, because the list is endless. The wonder is that a Gracious God should continue to bear all this! Think of the sin involved in false teaching. I stood one day at the foot of Pilate's staircase, in Rome, and saw the poor creatures go up and down, on their knees, on what they are taught was the very staircase on which the Lord Jesus Christ stood before Pilate. I noticed sundry priests looking on, and I felt morally certain that they knew it to be an imposture. I thought that if the Lord would lend me his thunderbolts about five minutes, I would make a wonderful clearance thereabouts: but he did nothing of the kind. God is not in haste as we are. Sometimes it does suggest itself to a hot spirit to wish for speedy dealing with iniquity : but the Lord is patient and pitiful.

Especially notice, next, that this longsuffering of God is seen in *peculiar persons*. In certain persons sins are greater than the same sins would be in other people. They have been favoured with a tender conscience, and with good instruction, so that when they sin they sin with a vengeance. I have known some who have stood at God's altar, and have gone forth from his temple to transgress; they have been Levites of his sanctuary, and yet first in villanies. Yet the Lord spares the traitors, and lets them live.

It is wonderful that God should have such longsuffering when we look at the *peculiar circumstances* under which some men sin. Some men sin against God wilfully, when they have no temptation to it, and can plead no necessity. If the poor man steals, we half forgive him ; but some do so who have all that heart could wish. When the man driven to extremity has said the thing that was not true, we have half excused him; but some are wilful liars, with no gain or profit therein. Some sin for the sheer love of sin, not for the pleasure they gain by it, nor for the profit they hope from it, but for mere wantonness. Born of godly parents, trained as you were in the very school of godliness, made to know, as you do know in your own conscience, the Lord Jesus to be the Son of God, when *you* sin against him, there is a painful emphasis in your transgressions. I speak to some who may well wonder that they are yet alive after having sinned with such gross aggravations.

Some manifest the longsuffering of God very wonderfully in the length of time in which they have been spared to sin. Many men are provoked by one offence, and think themselves miracles of patience if they forget it. But many have provoked God fifty, sixty, seventy, perhaps eighty years. *You* could not stand eighty minutes of provocation, and yet the Lord has put up with you throughout a lifetime. You tottered into this house to-night. You might have tottered more if you had remembered the weight of sin that cleaves to you. Yet the mercy of God spares you. Still, with outstretched arms, infinite mercy bids you come and receive at the hand of God your pardon bought with the blood of Jesus Christ. This longsuffering of God is marvellous.

Remember that it would be easy on God's part to be rid of you. There is a text where he says, "Ah! I will ease me of mine adversaries." Some men bear because they cannot help it. They are obliged to submit ; but God is not in that condition.   One wish, and the sinner will never provoke him any more, nor refuse his mercy again.   He will be gone out of the land of hope.   Therefore, I say, the longsuffering of God is enhanced in its wonderfulness by the fact that he is under no necessity to exercise it except that which springs out of his own love.

I beg all of you who are unconverted to think earnestly upon God's longsuffering to you in permitting you to be here, still to hear from the cross of Christ the invitation, " Look unto me, and be ye saved, all the ends of the earth."

II.   Secondly, let us take THE RIGHT ACCOUNT OF THE LONG-SUFFERING OF GOD.   " Account that the longsuffering of our Lord is salvation."   What does this mean ?

Does it not mean, first, as *to the saving of the many ?*   The Lord Jesus Christ is, as I believe, to have the pre-eminence.   I think that he will have the pre-eminence in the number of souls that will be saved as com-pared with those that will be lost ; and that can scarcely be effected except by a lapse of time in which many will be brought to Christ.   I am not, however, going into any speculations.   I look at it this way.   As long as this old hulk keeps beating up against the rocks, as long as she does not quite go down into the sea of fire, it means man's salvation.   It means, " Out with the lifeboat !   Man the lifeboat, and let us take off from her all that we can, and bring them to shore."   God calls upon us, until the world is utterly destroyed with fire, to go on saving men with all our might and main.   Every year that passes is meant to be a year of salvation.   We rightly call each year " the year of our Lord "; let us make it so by more and more earnest efforts for the bringing of sinners to the cross of Christ.   I cannot think that the world is spared to increase its damnation.   Christ came not to destroy the world, but that the world through him might be saved; and so, as every year rolls by, let us account it salvation, and spend and be spent in the hope that by any means we may save some.

And if we can indulge a brighter hope still that the kingdom of Christ shall come, and that multitudes shall be converted, and that the earth shall be filled with the knowledge of God as the waters cover the sea, so let it be.   But ever let this be to the front—that this longsuffering of God means salvation, and at that we are to aim.

So, dear friends, in the second place, the next meaning of this is *to any of you who are unconverted.*   I want you to account that the long-suffering of God in sparing you means to you salvation.   Why are you here to-night ?   Surely it is salvation.   I met years ago a soldier who had ridden in the charge of Balaclava.   He was one of the few that came back when the saddles were emptied right and left of him.   I could not help getting into a corner, and saying to him, " Dear sir, do you not think that God has some design of love to you in sparing you when so many fell ?   Have you given your heart to him ? "   I felt that I had a right to say *that.*   Perhaps I speak to some of you who were picked off a wreck years ago.   Why was that ?   I hope it was that you might be saved.   You have had a fever lately, and have hardly been out before.   You have come hither to-night, still weakly, scarcely recovered.   Why were you saved from that fever when others were cut down ?   Surely it must mean salvation.   At any rate, the God who was so pitiful as to spare you, now says to you, "Call upon me in the day of trouble : I will deliver thee, and thou shalt glorify me." When Master Bunyan was a lad, he was so foolhardy that, when an adder rose against him, he took it in his hand, and plucked the sting out of its mouth, but he was not harmed. It was his turn to stand sentinel at the siege of Nottingham, and as he was going forth, another man offered to take his place. That man was shot, and Master Bunyan thus escaped. We should have had no "Pilgrim's Progress" if it had not been for that. Did not God preserve him on purpose that he might be saved ? There are special interpositions of divine providence, by which God spares ungodly men, whom he might have cut down long ago as cumberers of the ground : should we not look upon these as having the intention that the barren tree may be cared for yet another year, if haply it may bring forth fruit ? Some of you who are here to-night are wonders to yourselves that you are still in the land of the living —I pray you account the longsuffering of God to be salvation. See salvation in it. Be encouraged to look to Christ, and, looking to him, you shall find salvation, for "there is life in a look at the Crucified One." Account God's longsuffering to be salvation to you if to no one else.

God's longsuffering is one of the great means by which. he works for the salvation of his elect. He will not let them die till first they live to God. He will not suffer them to pass into eternity till first his infinite love has justified them through the righteousness of Christ.

Thus I have said what I hope may be embraced by some here present. But I must finish. This text seems to me to have a bearing upon *the people of God.* Indeed, it is for them that it is written. "Account that the longsuffering of God is salvation."

I must turn the text to give you really what lies in it. God hears the cry going up from his own elect, and it is written, "Shall not God avenge his own elect, though he bear long with them ? " That long forbearance of God brings to his own people much of trouble, pain, sorrow, much of amazement and soul distress. Brother, you must learn to look upon that as salvation. I hear you say, "What mean you ? " I mean this. The very fact that you are made to groan and cry by reason of God's longsuffering to guilty men gives you sympathy with Christ, and union with Christ, who endured such contradiction of sinners against himself. Reckon that in being brought into harmony, sympathy, oneness with Christ, through enduring the result of the divine longsuffering, you find salvation. It is salvation to a man to be put side by side with Christ. If you have to bear the jests and gibes of the ungodly—if God spares them, and permits them to persecute you, be glad of it, and reckon it as salvation, for now you are made partaker of Christ's sufferings. What more salvation do you desire ?

Remember, too, that when the ungodly persecute the righteous, they give them the mark of salvation, for of old it was so. He that was born after the flesh persecuted him that was born after the spirit. If you were never reviled, if you were never slandered or traduced, who would know that you are a Christian? But when, through the longsuffering of God with the ungodly, you are made to suffer, account it to be a mark of your salvation. "Rejoice, and be exceeding glad : for great is your reward in heaven: for so persecuted they the prophets which were before you."

Once more: reckon the longsuffering of God, when it permits the ungodly to slander and injure you, as salvation, because it tends to your salvation by driving you nearer to the Lord. It prevents your making your home in this world. It forces you to be a stranger and a foreigner. It compels you to go without the gate bearing Christ's reproach, and so, in this way, that which seemed so hard to bear brings salvation to you.

Wherefore, comfort one another, dear children of God. Be not over cast-down and troubled because of your Lord's delaying his coming, for he will yet help you, and you shall be delivered.

If the Lord has shown longsuffering to any of you, and yet you have never repented or turned to him, do so to-night. "The harvest is past, the summer is ended, and you are not saved." But, oh, that you might be saved ere this service ends! The leaves are falling from the trees thick and fast, and ere you fall from the tree of this mortal life, think of your God, and turn to him, and live. "Believe in the Lord Jesus Christ, and thou shalt be saved." May he snatch you from the burning! Amen, and amen.

PORTION OF SCRIPTURE READ BEFORE SERMON—2 Peter iii.

HYMNS FROM "OUR OWN HYMN BOOK"—174, 529, 513.

Metropolitan Tabernacle Pulpit.

THREE DROPS OF HONEY FROM THE ROCK CHRIST.

THE MIRACLES OF OUR LORD'S DEATH.

A Sermon

INTENDED FOR READING ON LORD'S-DAY, DECEMBER 30TH, 1888,

DELIVERED BY

C. H. SPURGEON,

AT THE METROPOLITAN TABERNACLE, NEWINGTON,

On Lord's-day Evening, April 1st, 1888.

"Jesus, when he had cried again with a loud voice, yielded up the ghost. And, behold, the veil of the temple was rent in twain from the top to the bottom; and the earth did quake, and the rocks rent; and the graves were opened; and many bodies of the saints which slept arose, and came out of the graves after his resurrection, and went into the holy city, and appeared unto many."—Matthew xxvii. 50—53.

OUR Lord's death is a marvel set in a surrounding of marvels. It reminds one of a Kohinoor surrounded with a circle of gems. As the sun, in the midst of the planets which surround it, far outshines them all, so the death of Christ is more wonderful than the miracles which happened at the time. Yet, after having seen the sun, we take a pleasure in studying the planets, and so, after believing in the unique death of Christ, and putting our trust in him as the Crucified One, we find it a great pleasure to examine in detail those four planetary wonders mentioned in the text, which circle round the great sun of the death of our Lord himself.

Here they are: *the veil of the temple was rent in twain; the earth did quake; the rocks rent; the graves were opened.*

I. To begin with the first cf these wonders. I cannot, to-night, enlarge. I have not the strength. I wish merely to suggest thoughts.

Consider THE RENT VEIL, or *mysteries laid open.* By the death of Christ the veil of the temple was rent in twain from the top to the bottom, and the mysteries which had been concealed in the most holy place throughout many generations were laid open to the gaze of all believers. Beginning, as it were, at the top in the Deity of Christ, down to the lowest part of Christ's manhood, the veil was rent, and everything was discovered to every spiritual eye.

1. *This was the first miracle of Christ after death.* The first miracle of Christ in life was significant, and taught us much. He turned the water into wine, as if to show that he raised all common life to a

Nos. 2,059-60-61.

higher grade, and put into all truth a power and a sweetness, which could not have been there apart from him. But this first miracle of his after death stands above the first miracle of his life, because, if you will remember, that miracle was wrought in his presence. He was there, and turned the water into wine. But Jesus, as man, was not in the temple. That miracle was wrought in his absence, and it enhances its wonder. They are both equally miraculous, but there is a touch more striking about this second miracle—that he was not there to speak and make the veil rend in twain. His soul had gone from his body, and neither his body nor his soul was in that secret place of the tabernacles of the Most High; and yet, at a distance, his will sufficed to rend that thick veil of fine twined linen and cunning work.

The miracle of turning water into wine was wrought in a private house, amidst the family and such disciples as were friends of the family; but this marvel was wrought in the temple of God. There is a singular sacredness about it, because it was a deed of wonder done in that most awful and mysterious place, which was the centre of hallowed worship, and the abode of God. See! he dies, and at the very door of God's high sanctuary he rends the veil in twain. There is a solemnity about this miracle, as wrought before Jehovah, which I can hardly convey in speech, but which you will feel in your own souls.

Do not forget also that this was done by the Saviour after his death, and this sets the miracle in a very remarkable light. He rends the veil at the very instant of death. Jesus yielded up the ghost, and, behold, the veil of the temple was rent in twain. For thirty years he seems to have prepared himself for the first miracle of his life; he works his first miracle after death in the moment of expiring. As his soul departed from his body our blessed Lord at that same moment laid hold upon the great veil of his Father's symbolical house, and rent it in twain.

2. This first miracle after death stands in such a place that we cannot pass it by without grave thought. *It was very significant, as standing at the head of what I may call a new dispensation.* The miracle of turning water into wine begins his public life, and sets the key of it. This begins his work after death, and marks the tone of it. What does it mean?

Does it not mean that *the death of Christ is the revelation and explanation of secrets?* Vanish all the types and shadows of the ceremonial law;—vanish because fulfilled and explained in the death of Christ. The death of the Lord Jesus is the key of all true philosophy: God made flesh, dying for man—if that does not explain a mystery, it cannot be explained. If with this thread in your hand you cannot follow the labyrinth of human affairs, and learn the great purpose of God, then you cannot follow it at all. The death of Christ is the great veil-render, the great revealer of secrets.

It is also the great opener of entrances. There was no way into the holy place till Jesus, dying, rent the veil; the way into the most holy of all was not made manifest till he died. If you desire to approach God, the death of Christ is the way to him. If you want the nearest access and the closest communion that a creature can have with his God, behold, the sacrifice of Christ reveals the way to you. Jesus not only says, "I am the way," but, rending the veil, he makes the way. The veil of his flesh being rent, the way to God is made most clear to every believing soul.

Moreover, *the cross is the clearing of all obstacles.* Christ by death rent the veil. Then between his people and heaven there remains no obstruction, or if there be any—if your fears invent an obstruction—the Christ who rent the veil continues still to rend it. He breaks the gates of brass, and cuts the bars of iron in sunder. Behold, in his death "the breaker is come up before them, and the Lord on the head of them." He has broken up and cleared the way, and all his chosen people may follow him up to the glorious throne of God.

This is significant of the spirit of the dispensation under which we now live. Obstacles are cleared; difficulties are solved; heaven is opened to all believers.

3. *It was a miracle worthy of Christ.* Stop a minute and adore your dying Lord. Does he with such a miracle signalize his death? Does it not prove his *immortality?* It is true he has bowed his head in death. Obedient to his Father's will, when he knows that the time has come for him to die, he bows his head in willing acquiescence; but at that moment when you call him dead, he rends the veil of the temple. Is there not immortality in him though he died?

And see what *power* he possessed. His hands are nailed; his side is about to be pierced. As he hangs there he cannot protect himself from the insults of the soldiery, but in his utmost weakness he is so strong that he rends the heavy veil of the temple from the top to the bottom.

Behold his *wisdom,* for in this moment, viewing the deed spiritually, he opens up to us all wisdom, and lays bare the secrets of God. The veil which Moses put upon his face Christ takes away in the moment of his death. The true Wisdom in his dying preaches his grandest sermon by tearing away that which hid the supremest truth from the gaze of all believing eyes.

Beloved, if Jesus does this for us in his death, surely, we shall be saved by his life. Jesus who died is yet alive, and we trust in him to lead us into "the holy places made without hands."

Before I pass on to the second wonder, I invite everyone here, who as yet does not know the Saviour, seriously to think upon the miracles which attended his death, and judge what sort of man he was who, for our sins, thus laid down his life. He was not suffered by the Father to die without a miracle to show that he had made a way for sinners to draw near to God.

II. Pass on now to the second wonder—"THE EARTH DID QUAKE." *The immovable was stirred by the death of Christ.* Christ did not touch the earth: he was uplifted from it on the tree. He was dying, but in the laying aside of his power, in the act of death, he made the earth beneath him, which we call "the solid globe," itself to quake. What did it teach?

Did it not mean, first, *the physical universe fore-feeling the last terrible shake of its doom?* The day will come when the Christ will appear upon the earth, and in due time all things that are shall be rolled up, like garments worn out, and put away. Once more will he speak, and then will he shake not only the earth, but also heaven. The things which cannot be shaken will remain, but this earth is not one of them: it will be shaken out of its place. "The earth also and the works that are therein shall be burned up." Nothing shall stand before him. He alone is. These other things do but seem to be; and before the terror of his face all men shall tremble, and heaven and earth shall flee away. So, when he died, earth seemed to anticipate its doom, and quaked in his presence. How will it quake when he that lives again shall come with all the glory of God! How will you quake, my hearer, if you should wake up in the next world without a Saviour! How will you tremble in that day when he shall come to judge the world in righteousness, and you shall have to face the Saviour whom you have despised! Think of it, I pray you.

Did not that miracle also mean this?—that *the spiritual world is to be moved by the cross of Christ.* He dies upon the cross and shakes the material world, as a prediction that that death of his would shake the world that lieth in the wicked one, and cause convulsions in the moral kingdom. Brothers, think of it. We say of ourselves, "How shall we ever move the world?" The apostles did not ask that question. They had confidence in the gospel which they preached. Those who heard them saw that confidence; and when they opened their mouths they said, "The men that have turned the world upside down have come hither unto us." The apostles believed in shaking the world with the simple preaching of the gospel. I entreat you to believe the same. It is a vast city this—this London. How can we ever affect it? China, Hindostan, Africa—these are immense regions. Will the cross of Christ tell upon them? Yes, my brethren, for it shook the earth, and it will yet shake the great masses of mankind. If we have but faith in it, and perseverance to keep on with the preaching of the Word, it is but a matter of time when the name of Jesus shall be known of all men, and when every knee shall bow to him, and every tongue confess that he is Christ, to the glory of God the Father. The earth did quake beneath the cross; and it shall again. The Lord God be praised for it.

That old world—how many years it had existed I cannot tell. The age of the world, from that beginning which is mentioned in the first verse of the Book of Genesis, we are not able to compute. However old it was, it had to shake when the Redeemer died. This carries us over another of our difficulties. The system of evil we have to deal with is so long-established, hoary, and reverent with antiquity, that we say to ourselves, "We cannot do much against old prejudices." But it was the old, old earth that quivered and quaked beneath the dying Christ, and it shall do so again. Magnificent systems, sustained by philosophy and poetry, will yet yield before what is called the comparatively new doctrine of the cross. Assuredly it is not new, but older than the earth itself. It is God's own gospel, everlasting and eternal. It will shake down the antique and the venerable, as surely as the Lord liveth; and I see the prophecy of this in the quaking of the earth beneath the cross.

It does seem impossible, does it not, that the mere preaching of Christ can do this? And hence certain men must link to the preaching of Christ all the aids of music and architecture, and I know not what beside, till the cross of Christ is overlaid with human inventions, crushed and buried beneath the wisdom of man. But what was it that made the earth quake? Simply our Lord's death, and no addition of human power or wisdom. It seemed a very inadequate means to produce so great a result; but it was sufficient, for the " weakness of God is stronger than men, and the foolishness of God is wiser than men "; and Christ, in his very death, suffices to make the earth quake beneath his cross. Come, let us be well content in the battle in which we are engaged, to use no weapon but the gospel, no battle-axe but the cross. Could we but believe it the old, old story is the only story that is needed to be told to reconcile man to God. Jesus died in the sinner's stead, the just for the unjust, a magnificent display of God's grace and justice in one single act. Could we but keep to this only, we should see the victory coming speedily to our conquering Lord.

I leave that second miracle; wherein you see the immovable stirred in the quaking of the earth.

III. Only a hint or two upon the third miracle—THE ROCKS RENT.

I have been informed that, to this very day, there are at Jerusalem certain marks of rock-rending of the most unusual kind. Travellers have said that they are not such as are usually produced by earth-quake, or any other cause. Upon that I will say but little; but it is a wonderful thing that, as Jesus died, as his soul was rent from his body, as the veil of the temple was rent in two, so the earth, the rocky part of it, the most solid structure of all, was rent in gulfs and chasms in a single moment. What does this miracle show us but this—*the insensible startled?* What! Could rocks feel? Yet they rent at the sight of Christ's death. Men's hearts did not respond to the agonizing cries of the dying Redeemer, but the rocks responded: the rocks were rent. He did not die for rocks; yet rocks were more tender than the hearts of men, for whom he shed his blood.

> " Of reason all things show some sign,
> But this unfeeling heart of mine,"

said the poet; and he spoke the truth. Rocks could rend, but yet some men's hearts are not rent by the sight of the cross. However, beloved, here is the point that I seem to see here—that obstinacy and *obduracy will be conquered* by the death of Christ. You may preach to a man about death, and he will not tremble at its certainty or solemnity; yet try him with it. You may preach to a man about hell, but he will harden his heart, like Pharaoh, against the judgment of the Lord; yet try him with it. All things that can move man should be used. But that which does affect the most obdurate and obstinate is the great love of God, so strangely seen in the death of the Lord Jesus Christ. I will not stay to show you how it is, but I will remind you that it is so. It was this which, in the case of many of us, brought tears of repentance to our eyes, and led us to submit to the will of God. I know that it was so with me. I looked at a thousand things, and I did not relent; but when

> " I saw One hanging on a tree
> In agonies and blood,"

and dying there for me, then did I smite upon my breast, and I was
in bitterness for him, as one that is in bitterness for his first-born.   I
am sure your own hearts confess that the great rock-render is the
dying Saviour.

Well, now, as it is with you, so shall you find it with other men.
When you have done your best, and have not succeeded, bring out
this last hammer—the cross of Christ.   I have often seen on pieces of
.cannon, in Latin words, this inscription, "The last argument of kings."
That is to say, cannons are the last argument of kings.   But the cross
is the last argument of God.   If a dying Saviour does not convert you,
what will?   If his bleeding wounds do not attract you to God, what
will?   If Jesus bears our sin in his own body on the tree, and puts it
away, and if this does not bring you to God, with confession of your
sin, and hatred of it, then there remains nothing more for you.   "How
shall we escape if we neglect so great salvation?"   The cross is the
rock-render.   Brothers and sisters, go on teaching the love of the
dying Son of God.   Go on preaching Christ.   You will tunnel the
Alps of pride and the granite hills of prejudice with this.   You shall
find an entrance for Christ into the inmost hearts of men, though they
be hard as adamant; and this will be by the preaching of the cross
in the power of the Spirit.

IV.   But now I close with the last miracle.   These wonders
accumulate, and they depend upon each other.   The quaking earth
produced, no doubt, the rending of the rocks; and the rending of the
rocks aided in the fourth wonder.   "THE GRAVES WERE OPENED."
The graves opened, and *the dead revived.*   That is our fourth head.
It is the great consequence of the death of Christ.   The graves were
opened.   Man is the only animal that cares about a sepulchre.   Some
persons fret about how they shall be buried.   That is the last concern
that ever would cross my mind.   I feel persuaded that people will
bury me out of hatred, or out of love, and especially out of love to
themselves.   We need not trouble about that.   But man has often
shown his pride by his tomb.   That is a strange thing.   To garland
the gallows is a novelty, I think, not yet perpetrated; but to pile
marble and choice statuary upon a tomb—what is it but to adorn a
gibbet, or to show man's great grandeur where his littleness is alone
apparent.   Dust, ashes, rottenness, putridity, and then a statue, and
all manner of fine things, to make you think that the creature that goes
back to dust is, after all, a great one.   Now, when Jesus died, *sepulchres
were laid bare, and the dead were exposed:* what does this mean?

I think we have in this last miracle "the history of a man."   There
he lies dead—corrupt, dead in trespasses and sins.   But what a
beautiful sepulchre he lies in!   He is a church-goer; he is a dissenter
—whichever you please of the two; he is a very moral person; he is a
gentleman; he is a citizen; he is Master of his Company; he will be
Lord Mayor one day; he is so good—oh, he is so good! yet he has
no grace in his heart, no Christ in his faith, no love to God.   You see
what a sepulchre he lies in—a dead soul in a gilded tomb.   By
his cross our Lord splits this sepulchre and destroys it.   What are
our merits worth in the presence of the cross?   The death of Christ is
the death of self-righteousness.   Jesus' death is a superfluity if we can

save ourselves. If we are so good that we do not want the Saviour, why, then, did Jesus bleed his life away upon the tree? The cross breaks up the sepulchres of hypocrisy, formalism, and self-righteousness in which the spiritually dead are hidden away.

What next? *It opens the graves.* The earth springs apart. There lies the dead man: he is revealed to the light. The cross of Christ does that! The man is not yet made alive by grace, but he is discovered to himself. He knows that he lies in the grave of his sin. He has sufficient of the power of God upon him to make him lie, not like a corpse covered up with marble, but like a corpse from which the grave-digger has flung away the sods, and left it naked to the light of day. Oh, it is a grand thing when the cross thus opens the graves! You cannot convince men of sin except by the preaching of a crucified Saviour. The lance with which we reach the hearts of men is that same lance which pierced the Saviour's heart. We have to use the crucifixion as the means of crucifying self-righteousness, and making the man confess that he is dead in sin.

After the sepulchres had been broken up, and the graves had been opened, what followed next? *Life was imparted.* "Many of the bodies of the saints which slept arose." They had turned to dust; but when you have a miracle you may as well have a great one. I wonder that people, when they can believe one miracle, make any difficulty of another. Once introduce Omnipotence, and difficulties have ceased. So in this miracle. The bodies came together on a sudden, and there they were, complete and ready for the rising. What a wonderful thing is the implantation of life! I will not speak of it in a dead *man*, but I would speak of it in a dead *heart*. O God, send thy life into some dead heart at this moment while I speak! That which brings life into dead souls is the death of Jesus. While we behold the atonement, and view our Lord bleeding in our stead, the divine Spirit works upon the man, and life is breathed into him. He takes away the heart of stone, and gives a heart of flesh that palpitates with a new life. This is the wondrous work of the cross: it is by the death of our Lord that regeneration comes to men. There were no new births if it were not for that one death. If Jesus had not died, we had remained dead. If he had not bowed his head, none of us could have lifted up our heads. If he had not there on the cross passed from among the living, we must have remained among the dead for ever and for ever.

Now pass on, and you will see that those persons who received life, in due time *quitted their graves.* It is written that they came out of their graves. Of course they did. What living men would wish to stay in their graves? And you, my dear hearers, if the Lord quickens you, will not stay in your graves. If you have been accustomed to strong drink, or to any other besetting sin, you will quit it; you will not feel any attachment to your sepulchre. If you have lived in ungodly company, and found amusement in questionable places, you will not stop in your graves. We shall not have need to come after you to lead you away from your old associations. You will be eager to get out of them. If any person here should be buried alive, and if he should be discovered in his coffin before he had breathed his last, I am sure that, if the sod were lifted, and the lid were taken off, he would not need prayerful entreaties to come out of his grave. Far from it. Life loves not the prison of death. So may God grant that the dying Saviour may fetch you out of the graves in which you are still living; and, if he now quickens you, I am sure that the death of our Lord will make you reckon that if one died for all, then all died, and that he died for all, that they which live should not live henceforth unto themselves, but unto him that died for them and rose again.

Which way did these people go after they had come out of their graves? We are told that "*they went into the holy city.*" Exactly so. And he that has felt the power of the cross may well make the best of his way to holiness. He will long to join himself with God's people; he will wish to go up to God's house, and to have fellowship with the thrice-holy God. I should not expect that quickened ones would go anywhere else. Every creature goes to its own company, the beast to its lair, and the bird to its nest; and the restored and regenerated man makes his way to the holy city. Does not the cross draw us to the church of God? I would not wish one to join the church from any motive that is not fetched from the five wounds and bleeding side of Jesus. We give ourselves first to Christ, and then to his people for his dear sake. It is the cross that does it.

> " Jesus dead upon the tree
> Achieves this wondrous victory."

We are told—to close this marvellous story—that they went into the Holy City "*and appeared unto many.*" That is, some of them who had been raised from the dead, I do not doubt, appeared unto their wives. What rapture as they saw again the beloved husband! It may be that some of them appeared to father and mother; and I doubt not that many a quickened mother or father would make the first appearance to their children. What does this teach us, but that, if the Lord's grace should raise us from the dead, we must take care to show it? Let us appear unto many. Let the life that God has given us be manifest. Let us not hide it, but let us go to our former friends and make our epiphanies as Christ made his. For his glory's sake let us have our manifestation and appearance unto others. Glory be to the dying Saviour! All praise to the great Sacrifice!

Oh, that these poor, feeble words of mine would excite some interest in you about my dying Master! Be ready to die for him. And you that do not know him—think of this great mystery—that God should take your nature and become a man and die, that you might not die, and bear your sin that you should be free from it. Come and trust my Lord to-night, I pray you. While the people of God gather at the table to the breaking of bread, let your spirits hasten, not to the table and the sacrament, but to Christ himself and his sacrifice. Amen.

PORTION OF SCRIPTURE READ BEFORE SERMON—Matthew xxvii. 35—54.

HYMNS FROM "OUR OWN HYMN BOOK"—300, 280.

THE MESSAGES OF OUR LORD'S LOVE.

DELIVERED BY

C. H. SPURGEON,

AT THE METROPOLITAN TABERNACLE, NEWINGTON,

On Lord's-day Evening, August 5th, 1888.

"Go your way, tell his disciples and Peter that he goeth before you into Galilee: there shall ye see him, as he said unto you."—Mark xvi. 7.

SEE, brethren! Jesus delights to meet his people. He is no sooner risen from the dead than he sends a message by an angel to say that he will meet his disciples. His delight is in them. He loves them with a very tender love, and he is happiest when he is in their midst. Do not think that you will have to entreat and persuade your Lord to come to you; he delights in near and dear fellowship. The heavenly Bridegroom finds solace in your company, if you be indeed espoused to him. Oh, that you were more anxious to be with him!

Our Lord knows that, to his true people, the greatest joy they ever have is for him to meet them. The disciples were at their saddest. Their Lord, as they thought, was dead. They had just passed the dreariest Sabbath of their lives, for he was in the tomb; and now, to comfort them, he sends no message but this—that he will meet them. He knew that there would be magic in that news to cheer their aching hearts. *He would meet them:* that would be all-sufficient consolation: "Go into Galilee; there shall ye see *him*."

If all the sorrows of God's people could be poured out in one vast pile, what a mountain they would make! How varied our distresses! How diverse our depressions! But, beloved, if Jesus will meet us, all the sadness will fly away, and all the sorrow will grow light. Only give us his company, and we have all things. You know what I mean, many of you. Our Lord has made our hearts to leap for joy in sorrowful times. When we have been filled with physical pain, his company has made us forget the body's weakness; and when we have newly come from the grave, and our heart has been ready to break through bereavement, the sight of the Saviour has sweetened our bitter cup. In his presence we have felt resigned to the great Father's will, and content to say, "It is the Lord: let him do what seemeth him good." Until the day break, and the shadows flee away for ever, we want nothing but our Well-beloved's company. "Abide with me! Abide with me!"—this is our one prayer; and if we have that fulfilled, all other desires may wait their turn.

My subject is chosen with a view to our coming, as we always do on the first day of the week, to this table of communion. I want every child of God here to seek after, nay, to gain, full fellowship with Christ. I long to enjoy it myself, that I may preach a Saviour in whose presence I live. I long for you to enjoy it that you may hear, not my voice, but his voice, which is sweeter than the music of angels' harps. Oh, that those who do not know our Lord may now be set a-hungering after his surpassing sweetness! He is willing to come to you. A prayer will find him; a tear will draw him; a look of faith will hold him fast. Cast yourself on Jesus, and his open arms will joyously receive you.

But now to the text. I shall take it just as it stands, and make five observations upon it.

I. The first is: JESUS, THAT HE MAY MEET HIS PEOPLE, ISSUES INVITATIONS, AND THE INVITATIONS ARE VERY GRACIOUS—"Go, tell his disciples and Peter." "*Tell his disciples.*" The invitation is most gracious as directed to them, for "they all forsook him, and fled." On that night, that doleful night, when he most needed company, they slept; and when he woke, and was taken off to the hall of Caiaphas, they fled—yes, every one of them; there was not a steadfast spirit among them. They all fled. "Shame on them!" say you? Yes, but Jesus was not ashamed of them; for in one of the first speeches of his glorious life on earth he specially mentions them. "Tell my disciples": not picking and choosing, here and there, a heart more faithful than the rest, but mentioning the whole coward company, he says, "Tell my disciples." Brethren, disciples of Christ, Jesus would meet us now; let us hasten to his presence. Not one among us dares plume himself upon his fidelity; we have all at times played the coward. We may each one of us hide our faces when we think of our Lord's most faithful love to us. We have never acted towards him according to his deserts. If he had banished us: if he had said, "I will no more acknowledge this dastard company," we could not have wondered; but he invites us all, all who are his disciples—invites us to himself. Will you stay away? Will any of you be satisfied without beholding that dear countenance, more marred than that of any man, and yet more lovely than the face of angels? Come ye, all who follow him, for he bids you come. Hear the address of the message—"Tell my disciples."

But the bounty and beauty of his grace lay in this—that one had been worse than the rest, and, therefore, for him there is a special finger to beckon him, a special word to call him: "Tell my disciples AND PETER." He that denied his Lord, he that cursed as he denied, he who, after boisterous self-confidence, trembled at the jest of a maid, is he to be called? Yes, "Tell my disciples *and Peter.*" If any of you have behaved worse to your Master than others, you are peculiarly called to come to him now. You have grieved him, and you have been grieving because you have grieved him. You have been brought to repentance after having slidden away from him, and now he seals your pardon by inviting you to himself. He bids you not to stand in the background, but to come in with the rest and commune with him.

Peter, where art thou? The crowing of the cock is still in thine ear, and the tear is still in thine eye, yet come and welcome, for thou lovest him. He knows thou dost. Thou art grieved that a doubt should be put upon thy love. Come, he has forgiven thee; he has given thee tokens of it in thy broken heart and tearful eye. Come, Peter! Come thou, if nobody else should come. Jesus Christ invites thee by name before any other. In this place may be believers who have acted strangely, and have even forsaken the Lord, and they are now bemoaning themselves. Go on with your holy sorrow, but come to your Lord. Be not content till you have seen him, till you have laid hold upon him by a fresh grip of faith, and till you can say, "My beloved is mine, and I am his."

Most tender, then, are the invitations which Jesus issues. Part of the tenderness now lies in *the lips which deliver the message* on the Lord's behalf. The women came, and said—Jesus has said to us, by an angel, he will go before us into Galilee, and there shall ye see him. I am always thankful that God has committed the ministry of the Word, not to angels, but to us poor men. As I told you a little while ago, you may grow tired of me and my stammerings; but yet they are more suitable for you than nobler strains might be. I have no doubt that if you had an angel to preach to you, there would be a very great crowd, and for a time you would say, "It is wonderful"; but it would be so cold from lack of human sympathy, that you would soon weary of the lofty style. An angel would try to be kind, as became his heavenly nature, but he would not be *kinned*, and you must necessarily miss the kindness which comes of kinship. I speak to you as bone of your bone, and flesh of your flesh: I speak to you, teacher, for I am a teacher. I speak to you, disciple, for I am a disciple, and I dare not think myself greater than the least of you. Let us come hand in hand to our dear Saviour, and all together let us pray him to manifest himself to us as he doth not unto the world. This, then, is my first point—his invitations are gracious.

II. Secondly, we see in our text that JESUS KEEPS HIS TRYST. "I will go before you into Galilee." If you turn to Mark xiv. 27, 28, you will see that he told them before he died, "All ye shall be offended because of me this night: for it is written, I will smite the shepherd, and the sheep shall be scattered. But after that I am risen, I will go before you into Galilee." He will be where he says he will be. Jesus never breaks a promise. It is a great vexation, especially to us who are very busy, when somebody says, "Will you meet me at such and such a place?" "Yes; at what hour?" The hour is appointed. We are there. Thank God, we never were a half minute behind time when it was possible to be punctual; but punctuality is a lesson which very few persons as yet have learned. We wait, and wait wearily, and perhaps we leave the place to let our dilatory friends know that if they are in eternity we are in time, and cannot afford to lose any of it. Many people make an engagement and break it, as if it were just nothing at all to be guilty of a practical lie. It is not so with Jesus: he says, "I will go before you into Galilee"; and into Galilee he will go.

xx

When he promises to meet his people he will meet with them without fail, and without delay.

Let us dwell on this appointment for a minute. Why did our Lord say that he would go to Galilee? Was it because *it was his old haunt*, and being risen from the dead, he desired to go back to the spot where he had been accustomed to be—to the lake, and to the hillside? Surely there is something in that. It was *their* old haunt, too: they were fishermen on that lake, and he would take them back to the place where a thousand memories would be awakened by their voices, like echoes which lie asleep among the hills. Besides it would provide witnesses to his identity, for the Galileans knew him well: since there he had been brought up. He would go where he was known, and show himself in his former places of resort.

Perhaps, too, it was because *the place was despised*. He has risen, and he will go to Galilee. He is not ashamed to be called the Galilean and the Nazarene. The risen One does not go to the halls of princes, but to the villages of peasants and fishermen. There was no pride in Jesus: not even the smell of that fire had passed upon him. He was ever meek and lowly in heart.

Did he not also go to Galilee, because *it was some little distance* from Jerusalem, that those who would meet him might take a little trouble? Our Beloved would be sought after. A journey after him will endear his society. He will not meet you at Jerusalem, perhaps— at least, not the whole company of you; but he will show himself by the sea in distant Galilee.

Do you think he went to Galilee because *it was " Galilee of the Gentiles,"* that he might get as near to us Gentiles as his mission allowed? He was sent as a preacher only to the lost sheep of the house of Israel; but he travelled to the very edge of his diocese to get as near to the Gentiles (I mean to ourselves) as he could. Oh, happy word for us aliens!—"I will go before you into Galilee." So he said; and when he left the tomb, he kept his word.

Now, beloved, we have his word for it, that he will come and meet us where we are met together. "Where two or three are gathered together in my name, there am I in the midst of them"; and does he not keep his word? How many times in our assemblies, great and small, have we said, " The Lord was there"! How frequently have we forgotten preacher and fellow-worshippers, feeling ourselves in the presence of a greater than mortal man! Our eyes of faith have seen the King in his beauty, revealing his love to us. Oh, yes! he keeps his tryst. He comes to his people, and he never disappoints them. I think this is particularly true of the table of communion. How often he has met us there! I am compelled to repeat my personal testimony. I have never omitted being at the Lord's table on any Sabbath of my life for many years past, except when I have been ill, or unable to attend; and I am therefore able to answer the question—Does not frequency diminish the solemnity of the ordinance? I have not found it so; but the rather it grows upon me. That broken bread, that poured out wine, the emblems of his flesh and blood—these bring him very near. It seems as if sense lent aid to faith; and through these two windows of agates, and gates of carbuncles, we come very near to our

Lord. What have we here but himself, under instructive emblems? What do we here but remember him? What is our business here but to show his death until he come? And so, though we may not have seen him in converse by the way, for our eyes have been holden, yet we have seen him in the breaking of bread. May it be always so! May we prove that Jesus keeps his pledge. He will be with us even now. Suppose Jesus had said that he would come into this place to-night in literal flesh and blood, you would be all sitting in expectation, and saying to each other, "When will he come?" The preacher would be waiting to drop back, or fall upon his knees in adoration, while his Master stood in the front. You will not see him *so;* but may your faith, which is much better than eyesight, realize him as the present Christ, near to each one of you. If he were here in the flesh, he might stand *here,* and then he might be near to me, but far off from my friends yonder; but coming in spirit he can be equally near to us all, and speak to each one of us personally, as though each one were the only person present.

III. My third observation·is, JESUS IS ALWAYS FIRST AT EVERY APPOINTED MEETING. So runs the text: "*He goeth before you* into Galilee." Remember that promise, "Where two or three are gathered together in my name, there *am I*"—not "there will I be." Jesus is there before his disciples reach the place. The first to reach the house is he who is first in the house. We come to him: it is not that we meet, and then he comes to us; but he goes before us, and we gather to him.

Does it not teach us that *he is the shepherd?* He said, "Smite the shepherd, and the sheep shall be scattered; but after I am risen, I will go before you into Galilee." He would take up the shepherd's place again, and go before the flock, and the sheep would take up the position of the flock again, no longer scattered, but following at the Shepherd's heel. Great Master, come to-night; call thy sheep to thyself! Speak to us, look upon us, and we will arise, and follow thee.

Is he not first, next, because *he is the centre?* We gather to him. You must choose a centre before you can mark the circumference. When Israel travelled through the wilderness, the first place to pitch upon for an encampment was the place where the tabernacle and the ark should rest, and then the tents were set around it. Jesus is our centre; he must therefore be first, and we rejoice to hear him say, "I will go before you into Galilee." He will take the first place, and we will cluster about him as bees around their queen. Do you always gather to the name of Christ, beloved? If you gather to the name of any minister, or any sect, you gather amiss. Our gatherings must be unto the Lord Jesus: he must be the centre, and he alone; let us take care of that.

Next, he goes before us naturally, because *he is the host.* If there is to be a feast, the first person to be there is the one who provides it —the master or mistress who sits at the head of the table. It would never do for the guests to be there first, and then for the master to come hurrying home, crying, "Excuse me: I quite forgot that you were to be here at six o'clock!" Oh no, the host must be first! When Jesus bids us come to him, and says he will sup with us, and we with him, he will be sure to be first, so as to prepare the feast. He goes before us into Galilee.

But surely, the reason why he is first is this—that *he is more ready for us than we are for him.* It takes us time to get ready for communion, to dress our souls, and collect our thoughts. Are you all ready for the Lord's Supper to-night? Some of you, perhaps, have come carelessly here, and yet you are members of the church, and mean to stay to the Supper. Beloved, try to come with a prepared heart, for the communion will be to you very much what you make it; and if your thoughts and desires are not right, what can the outward emblems be to you? On our Lord's part all things are ready, and he waits to receive you, and to bless you. Therefore he is first at the appointed meeting-place.

I may also add that *he is much more eager to have fellowship with you than you are to have fellowship with him.* It is a strange thing that it should be so, but so it is. He, the great lover of our souls, burns with a passionate desire to press his people to his heart; and we, the objects of such a matchless love, start back, and reward the ardour of his affection with lukewarmness. It must not be so on this occasion. I have said to my Lord, "Let me either feast upon thee or hunger after thee." I pray that you may have such a burning thirst for Jesus at this hour that you *must* drink of his cup or pine with thirst for him.

IV. The fourth observation is this: THE LORD JESUS REVEALS HIMSELF TO HIS PEOPLE. How does the text run? "He goeth before you into Galilee. *There shall ye see him.*" The main object is to *see him.* He will go to Galilee on purpose that he may reveal himself to them. My dear brethren, this is what they needed beyond all else. Their sorrow was because they thought him dead; their joy would be because they saw him alive. Their griefs were multiform, but this one consolation would end them all. If they could but see Jesus, they would look their fears away. What have you come here for to-night, children of God? I trust that you can answer, "Sir, we would see Jesus." If our Master will come, and we shall feel his presence, it will not matter how feebly I speak, or how poor the service may be in itself; you will say, "It was good to be there, for the Lord drew near to us in all the glory of his love." *His presence is what you want.*

And *this is what he readily gives.* Jesus is very familiar with his people. Some worship a Saviour who sits enthroned above in the stately dignity of indifference; but our Lord is not so. Though reigning in heaven, he is still conversant with his people below. He is a brother born for adversity. Spiritually he communes with us. Do you know what the company of Christ is? Are you altogether taken up with doctrines about him, or with ceremonies that concern him? If so, yours is a poor life; but the joy of the inner life is to know, and to speak with, and to dwell with the Lord Jesus. Do you understand this? I charge you, be not satisfied till you come to personal and intimate intercourse with your Lord. Short of this, you are short of the privilege which he sees you need, for this is his great promise, "There shall ye see me."

What is more, this sight of him *is what our Lord effectually bestows.* Jesus not only exhibits himself, but he opens our eyes, that we may enjoy the sight. "There *shall* ye see me." He may be manifest, and yet blind eyes will not see him. Blessed Master, come and take the scales away and make our hearts capable of spiritual perception! It is not everybody that can see God, and yet God is everywhere. The eye must first be cleansed. Jesus says, "There shall ye see me"; and he knows how to open our eyes, so that we do see him. Our Lord can make this to be the absorbing occupation of his people. "He goeth before you into Galilee"—and what then? "There shall ye see him." Why, they went fishing, did they not? Yes, but they were called off from that. "There shall ye see him." They took a great haul of fish, did they not? Yes, yes, yes; but that was a mere incident: the grand fact was, that they *saw him.* I pray the Lord to make the one occupation of our lives the seeing of HIM. May all the lower lights grow dim. Where are the stars at midday? They are all in their places, but you only see the sun. Where are a thousand things when Christ appears? They are all where they should be, but you only see *him.* May the Lord cause all other loves to vanish, and himself alone to fill our hearts, so that it may be true of us, "There shall ye see him"!

I have thus far proceeded, crying to the Holy Ghost for help, and now comes the fifth observation, with which we close.

V. OUR LORD REMEMBERS HIS OWN PROMISES. It was before he died that he said he would go before them into Galilee, and now that he has risen from the dead, he says, by the mouth of his angel, "There shall ye see him, *as he said unto you.*" The rule of Christ's action is his own word. What he has said he will perform. You and I forget his promises, but *he* never does. "As he said unto you" is the remembrance of all that he has spoken. Why does our Lord remember and repeat what he has so graciously spoken?

He does so because *he spoke with foresight,* and forethought, and care. We make promises and forget them because we did not consider well the matter before we spoke; but if we have thought, calculated, weighed, estimated, and come to a deliberate resolve before we speak, then we earnestly remember what we resolved upon. No promise of our Lord Jesus has been spoken in haste, to be repented of afterwards. Infinite wisdom directs infinite love; and when infinite love takes the pen to write a promise, infallible wisdom dictates every syllable.

Jesus does not forget, because *he spoke the promise with his whole heart.* It is not every tongue that represents a heart at all; but even though true people, we say many things which we mean, but there is no depth of feeling, no potent emotion, no stirring of the heart's centre. Our Lord, when he said, "Ye shall be scattered; but after that I am risen, I will go before you into Galilee," spoke with a heavy heart, with many a melting sigh; and his whole soul went with the promise which closed the mournful scene. He has purchased what he promised, purchased it with his blood, and therefore he speaks most solemnly, and with his whole heart. There is no trifling on Christ's part with one to whom he makes a promise, and therefore he never forgets.

And, once more, *his honour is bound up with every promise.* If he had said that he would go to Galilee, and he had not gone, his disciples would have felt that he had made a mistake, or that he had failed. Brethren, if Christ's promise were to fail, what should we think of it? But he will never jeopardize his faithfulness and veracity.

> "As well might he his being quit,
> As break his promise or forget,"

Let the words of man be blown away like the chaff; but the words of Jesus must stand, for he will not tarnish his truth, which is one of the choicest of his crown-jewels.

I want you to turn over this thought in your quietude. Jesus remembers all that he has spoken; let not our hearts forget. Go to him with his covenant bonds and gracious promises: he will recognize his own signature. He will honour his own promises to the utmost, and none that trust in him shall complain of his having exaggerated.

I have done when I have said just this. I am very anxious that at this time we should come into real fellowship with Christ, at the table. Jesus, thou hast made us hunger after thee; wilt thou not feed us? Thou hast made us thirst after thee; wilt thou not supply that thirst? Do you think that our Beloved means to tantalize us? Our hunger is such that it would break through stone walls; shall we find his heart hard as a stone wall? No; he will clear the way, and we on our part will burst through all obstacles to come to him. "But," says one, "how can *I* come to him, poor, unknown, unworthy one that I am?" Such were the disciples at the lake. They were fishermen; and when he came to them, they had been toiling all night. Are you working for him? Then he will come to you. Expect him now. "Ah!" says one, "I have been working without success"—you are a poor minister whose congregation is falling off, whose church is not increased by conversions —you have toiled all the night, and taken nothing. Or you are a Sunday-school teacher, who cannot see her girls converted; or a brother who mourns that his boys are not coming to Christ. Well, I see who you are; you are just the sort of people that Jesus came to, for they had toiled all night in vain. Are you hungry? Jesus cries, "Children, have you any meat?" He comes to you and enquires about your hunger; while on the shore he has a fire of coals, and fish laid thereon, and bread. "Come and dine," says he. The table is spread. Come to himself! He is your food, your hope, your joy, your heaven. Come to him; give him no rest till he reveals himself to you, and you know of a surety that it is your Lord who embraces you. So may he do, to each of us just now, for his sweet love's sake! Amen.

PORTION OF SCRIPTURE READ BEFORE SERMON—Mark xvi. 1—14.

HYMNS FROM "OUR OWN HYMN BOOK"—385, 784, 785.

THE EVIDENCE OF OUR LORD'S WOUNDS.

A Sermon

DELIVERED BY

C. H. SPURGEON,

AT THE METROPOLITAN TABERNACLE, NEWINGTON,

On Lord's-day Evening, December 2nd, 1877.

"Then saith he to Thomas, Reach hither thy finger, and behold my hands; and reach hither thy hand, and thrust it into my side: and be not faithless, but believing."—John xx. 27.

AMONG us at this day we have many persons who are like Thomas— dubious, demanding signs and tokens, suspicious, and ofttimes sad. I am not sure that there is not a slight touch of Thomas in most of us. There are times and seasons when the strong man fails, and when the firm believer has to pause a while, and say, "Is it so?" It may be that our meditation upon the text before us may be of service to those who are touched with the malady which afflicted Thomas.

Notice, before we proceed to our subject in full, that *Thomas asked of our Lord what he ought not to have asked.* He wanted to put our risen Lord to tests which were scarcely reverent to his sacred person. Admire his Master's patience with him. He does not say, "If he does not choose to believe he may continue to suffer for his unbelief." But no; he fixes his eye upon the doubter, and addresses himself specially to him; yet not in words of reproach or anger. Jesus could bear with Thomas, though Thomas had been a long time with him, and had not known him. To put his finger into the print of the nails, and thrust his hand into his side, was much more than any disciple had a right to ask of his divine Master; and yet see the condescension of Jesus! Rather than Thomas should suffer from unbelief, Christ will let him take great liberties. Our Lord does not always act towards us according to his own dignity, but according to our necessity; and if we really are so weak that nothing will do but thrusting a hand into his side, he will let us do it. Nor do I wonder at this: if, for our sakes, he suffered a spear to be thrust there, he may well permit a hand to follow.

Observe that *Thomas was at once convinced.* He said: "My Lord, and my God." This shows our Master's wisdom, that he indulged him with such familiarity, because he knew that, though the demand was presumptuous, yet the act would work for his good. Our Lord sometimes wisely refuses—saying, "Touch me not; for I am not yet ascended"; but at other times, he wisely grants, because, though it be too much for us to ask, yet he thinks it wise to give.

The subject for our present meditation is just this: *the cure of doubts.* Thomas was permitted to put his finger into the print of the nails for the curing of his doubts. Perhaps you and I wish that we could do something like it. Oh, if our Lord Jesus would appear to me for once, and I might thrust my hand into his side; or, if I might for once see him, or speak with him, how confirmed should I be! No doubt that thought has arisen in the minds of many. We shall not have such proofs, my brethren, but we shall have something near akin to them, which will answer the same purpose.

I. The first head of my discourse shall be this: CRAVE NO SIGNS. If such signs be possible, crave them not. If there be dreams, visions, voices, ask not for them.

Crave not wonders, first, because *it is dishonouring to the sacred Word to ask for them.* You believe this Bible to be an inspired volume —the Book of God. The apostle Peter calls it "A more sure word of prophecy; whereunto ye do well that ye take heed." Are you not satisfied with that? When a person, in whose veracity you have the utmost confidence, bears testimony to this or that, if you straightway reply, ",I would be glad of further evidence," you are slighting your friend, and casting unjust suspicion upon him. Will you cast suspicion upon the Holy Ghost, who, by this word, bears witness unto Christ? Oh, no! let us be content with his witness. Let us not wish to see, but remain satisfied to believe. If there be difficulties in believing, is it not natural there should be, when he that believes is finite, and the things to be believed are, in themselves, infinite? Let us accept the difficulties as being in themselves, in some measure, proofs of the correctness of our position, as inevitable attendants of heavenly mysteries, when they are looked at by such poor minds as ours. Let us believe the Word, and crave no signs.

Crave no signs, because *it is unreasonable that we should desire more than we have already.* The testimony of the Lord Jesus Christ, contained in the Word, should alone suffice us. Beside that, we have the testimony of saints and martyrs, who have gone before us, dying triumphant in the faith. We have the testimony of many still among us, who tell us that these things are so. In part, we have the testimony of our own conscience, of our own conversion, of our own after-experience, and this is convincing testimony. Let us be satisfied with it. Thomas ought to have been content with the testimony of Mary Magdalene, and the other disciples, but he was not. We ought to trust our brethren's word. Let us not be unreasonable in craving after proofs when already proofs are afforded us without stint.

Crave no signs, because *it may be you will be presumptuous in so doing.* Who are you, to set God a sign? What is it he is to do before you will believe in him? Suppose he does not choose to do it, are you therefore arrogantly to say, "I refuse to believe unless the Lord will do my bidding"? Do you imagine that any angel would demean himself to pay attention to you, who set yourself up to make demands of the Most High? Assuredly not. It is presumption which dares to ask of God anything more than the testimony of himself which he chooses to grant us in his Word.

It is, moreover, damaging to ourselves to crave signs. Jesus says, "Blessed are they that have not seen, and yet have believed." Thomas had his sign, and he believed; and so far so good, but he missed a blessing peculiar to those who have not seen, and yet have believed. Do not, therefore, rob yourselves of the special favour which lights on those who, with no evidence but the witness of the Spirit of God, are prepared at once to believe in the Lord Jesus unto eternal life.

Again, crave no signs, for *this craving is highly perilous.* Translated according to many, and I think translated correctly, our Saviour said, "Reach hither thy finger, and put it into the print of the nails; and *become* not faithless, but believing," intending to indicate that Thomas, by degrees, would become faithless. His faith had grown to be so little that, if he continued insisting upon this and that, as a sign or evidence, that faith of his would get down to the very lowest; yea, he would have no faith left. "Become not faithless, but believing." Dear friends, if you began to seek signs, and if you were to see them, do you know what would happen? Why, you would want more; and when you had these, you would demand still more. Those who live by their feelings judge of the truth of God by their own condition. When they have happy feelings, then they believe; but if their spirits sink, if the weather happens to be a little damp, or if their constitution happens to be a little disordered, down go their spirits, and, straight-way, down goes their faith. He that lives by a faith which does not rest on feeling, but is built upon the Word of the Lord, will remain fixed and steadfast as the mount of God; but he that craves for this thing and that thing, as a token for good at the hand of the Lord, stands in danger of perishing from want of faith. He shall not perish, if he has even a grain of living faith, for God will deliver him from the temptation; but the temptation is a very trying one to faith.

Crave, therefore, no sign. If you read a story of a person who saw a vision, or if you hear another declare that a voice spake to him—believe those things, or not, as you like; but do not desire them for yourself. These wonders may, or may not, be freaks of the imagination: I will not judge; but we must not rely upon them, for we are not to walk by sight, but by faith. Rely not upon anything that can be seen of the eyes, or heard of the ears; but simply trust him whom we know to be the Christ of God, the Rock of our salvation.

II. Secondly, when you want comfort, crave no sign, but TURN TO THE WOUNDS OF YOUR LORD. You see what Thomas did. He wanted faith, and he looked for it to Jesus wounded. He says nothing about Christ's head crowned with glory. He does not say that he must see him "girt about the paps with a golden girdle." Thomas, even in his unbelief, is wise; he turns to his Lord's wounds for comfort. When-ever your unbelief prevails, follow in this respect the conduct of Thomas, and turn your eyes straightway to the wounds of Jesus. These are the founts of never-failing consolation, from which, if a man doth once drink, he shall forget his misery, and remember his sorrow no more. Turn to the Lord's wounds; and if you do, what will you see?

First, you will see *the tokens of your Master's love*.   O Lord Jesus,
what are these wounds in thy side, and in thy hands?   He answers,
"These I endured when suffering for thee.   How can I forget thee?
I have graven thee upon the palms of my hands.   How can I ever fail
to remember thee?   On my very heart the spear has written thy name."
Look at Jesus, dead, buried, risen, and then say, "He loved me, and
gave himself for me"!   There is no restorative for a sinking faith like
a sight of the wounded Saviour.   Look, soul, and live by the proofs
of his death!   Come and put thy finger, by faith, into the print of
the nails, and these wounds shall heal thee of unbelief.   The wounds
of our Lord are the tokens of his love.

They are, again, *the seals of his death*, especially that wound in his
side.   He must have died; for "one of the soldiers, with a spear,
pierced his side, and forthwith came there out blood and water.   And
he that saw it bare witness."   The Son of God did assuredly die.
God, who made the heavens and the earth, took to himself our
nature, and in one wondrous person he was both God and man; and
lo! this wondrous Son of God bore sufferings unutterable, and con-
summated all by his death.   This is our comfort, for if he died in our
stead, then we shall not die for our sins; our transgression is put
away, and our iniquity is pardoned.   If the sacrifice had never been
slain, we might despair; but since the spear-wound proves that the
great Sacrifice really died, despair is slain, hope revives, and confidence rejoices.

The wounds of Jesus, next, are *the marks of identity*.   By these we
identify his blessed person after his resurrection.   The very Christ
that died has risen again.   There is no illusion: there could be no
mistake.   It is not somebody else foisted upon us in his place; but
Jesus who died has left the dead, for there are the marks of the
crucifixion in his hands and in his feet, and there is the spear-thrust
still.   It is Jesus: this same Jesus.   This is a matter of great comfort
to a Christian—this indisputably proven doctrine of the resurrection
of our Lord.   It is the keystone of the gospel arch.   Take that away,
or doubt it, and there remains nothing to console you.   But because
Jesus died and in the selfsame person rose again, and ever lives,
therefore does our heart sweetly rest, believing that "them also which
sleep in Jesus will God bring with him"; and also that the whole of
the work of Jesus is true, is completed, and is accepted of God.

Again, those wounds, those scars of our Lord, were *the memorials of
his love to his people*.   They set forth his love so that his chosen can
see the tokens; but they are also memorials to himself.   He conde-
scendingly bears these as his reminders.   In heaven, at this moment,
upon the person of our blessed Lord, there are the scars of his
crucifixion.   Centuries have gone by, and yet he looks like a Lamb
that has been slain.   Our first glance will assure us that this is he of
whom they said, "Crucify him; crucify him."   Steadily look with the
eyes of your faith into the glory, and see your Master's wounds, and
say within yourself, "He has compassion upon us still: he bears the
marks of his passion."   Look up, poor sufferer!   Jesus knows what
physical pain means.   Look up, poor depressed one!   he knows what a
broken heart means.   Canst thou not perceive this?   Those prints upon

his hands, these sacred stigmata, declare that he has not forgotten what he underwent for us, but still has a fellow-feeling for us.

Once again, these wounds may comfort us because in heaven they are, before God and the holy angels, *the perpetual ensigns of his finished work.* That passion of his can never be repeated, and never needs to be: "After he had offered one sacrifice for sins for ever, he sat down on the right hand of God." But the memorials are always being presented before the infinite mind of God. Those memorials are, in part, the wounds in our Lord's blessed person. Glorified spirits can never cease to sing, "Worthy is the Lamb that was slain"; for every time they gaze upon him they perceive his scars. How resplendent shine the nail-prints! No jewels that ever gemmed a king can look one-half so lustrous as these. Though he be God over all blessed for ever, yet to us, at least, his brightest splendour comes from his death.

My hearer, whensoever thy soul is clouded, turn thou to these wounds which shine like a constellation of five bright stars. Look not to thine own wounds, nor to thine own pains, or sins, or prayers, or tears, but remember that "with his stripes we are healed." Gaze, then; intently gaze, upon thy Redeemer's wounds if thou wouldest find comfort.

III. This brings me to my third point, whenever faith is staggered at all, SEEK SUCH HELPS FOR YOUR FAITH AS YOU MAY. Though we cannot literally put our finger into the print of the nails, and may not wish to do so, yet let us use such modes of recognition as we do possess. Let us put these to their utmost use; and we shall no longer desire to put our hand into the Saviour's side. We shall be perfectly satisfied without that. Ye that are troubled with doubts and fears, I give you these recommendations.

First, if you would have your faith made vivid and strong, *study much the story of your Saviour's death.* Read it: read it: read it: read it. "*Tolle: lege,*" said the voice to Augustine, "Take it: read it." So say I. Take the four evangelists; take the fifty-third chapter of Isaiah; take the twenty-second psalm; take all other parts of Scripture that relate to our suffering Substitute, and read them by day and by night, till you familiarize yourself with the whole story of his griefs and sin-bearing. Keep your mind intently fixed upon it; not sometimes, but continually. *Crux lux:* the cross is light. Thou shalt see it by its own light. The study of the narrative, if thou pray the Holy Ghost to enlighten thee, will beget faith in thee; and tnou wilt, by its means, be very greatly helped, till, at last, thou wilt say, "I cannot doubt. The truth of the atonement is impressed upon my memory, my heart, my understanding. The record has convinced me."

Next, if this suffice not, *frequently contemplate the sufferings of Jesus.* I mean by that, when you have read the story, sit down, and try and picture it. Let your mind conceive it as passing before you. Put yourself into the position of the apostles who saw him die. No employment will so greatly strengthen faith, and certainly none will be more enjoyable!

> "Sweet the moments, rich in blessing,
> Which before the cross I spend,
> Life and health and peace possessing
> From the sinner's dying Friend."

An hour would be grandly spent if occupied in turning over each little detail, item, and incident in the marvellous death by which you are redeemed from death and hell. You will be surprised to find how this familiarizing of yourself with it, by the help of the Holy Spirit, will make it as vivid to you as if you saw it; and it will have a better effect upon your mind than the sight of it would have done; for probably the actual sight would have passed away from your mind, and have been forgotten, while the contemplation of the sorrowful scene will sink deep into your soul, and leave eternal lines! You will do well, first, to read and know the narrative, and then to contemplate it carefully and earnestly—I mean, not to think of it for a minute or two at chance times, but to take an hour or two that you can specially set apart on purpose to consider the story of your Saviour's death. I am persuaded, if you do this, it will be more helpful to you than putting his finger into the print of the nails was to Thomas.

What next? Why, dear friends, the Lord has a way of *giving his people wonderful realizations.* I hope I shall not say anything incorrect when I remark that there are times with us when the Lord is present with us, and we are strongly impressed with that fact, and therefore we act under a sense of that presence as if the divine glory were actually visible. Do you know what it is to write a letter to a friend feeling as if the Lord Jesus were looking over your shoulder? I know what it is at times to stand here and preach, and feel my Lord so near me that if I had literally seen him it would not have surprised me. Have you never, in the watches of the night, lain quiet when there was no sound but the ticking of the watch, and thought of your Lord till, though you knew there was no form before you, you were just as certain that he was there as if you could see his sorrowful countenance? In quiet places all alone—you scarcely like to tell the story—in the lone wood, and in the upper chamber—you have said, "If he spake I should not be more certain of his presence; and if he smiled upon me I should not be surer of his love." These realizations have sometimes been so joyfully overwhelming that for years you have been lifted by them beyond all power of doubt. These holy summer days banish the frosts of the soul. Whenever a doubt is suggested to me about the existence of my Lord and Master, I feel that I can laugh the tempter to scorn, for I have seen him, and spoken with him. Not with these eyes, but with the eyes of my inner life, I have beheld my Lord, and communed with him. Wonder not that I am not among the crew of the black, piratical ship of "Modern Thought."

Nor is it merely in seasons of enjoyment that we get these helps, but in times of *deep distress.* Prostrate with pain, unable to enjoy any comfort, unable even to sleep, I have seen the soul of the believer as happy as if all sounds were marriage peals. Some of us know what it is to be right gleesome, glad, and joyous in hours of fierce trial, because Christ has been so near. In times of losses and bereavements, when the sorrow stung you to the quick, and you thought, before it came, that you never could bear it, yet have you been so sustained by a sight of the sacred head once wounded, and by fellowship with him in his sufferings, that you have said, "What are my griefs compared with his?" You have forgotten your sorrows and sung for joy of heart, as those that make merry. If you have been helped in this way, it will have all the effect upon you that ever could have come of putting your finger into the print of the nails. If, perchance, you have been given up to die, and have, mentally, gone through the whole process of dying, expecting soon to stand before the bar of God, and have been happy, and even exultant, then you could not doubt the reality of a religion that bore you up above the surging billows. Now that you are again restored to life for a little longer time, the recollection of your buoyant spirits, in what you thought to be your dying hours, will answer all the purpose to you, I think, of putting your finger into the nail-prints.

Sometimes the strengthening influence may be afforded under the stress of *temptation.* If ever, young man, you have had a strong temptation hurling itself against you, and your feet have almost gone —ay, let me not say "young man"; but if ever a man or a woman of any age has had to cry out, "God, help me: how shall I escape out of this?" and you have turned your eyes and seen your Lord and beheld his wounds; and if you have felt at that moment that the temptation had lost all power, you have had a seal from the Lord, and your faith has been confirmed. If at the sight of your Lord you have exclaimed, in presence of the temptation, "How can I do this great wickedness, and sin against God?" after that, you have had the best proof of your Redeemer's power to save. What better or more practical proof could you desire?

In these times, when the foundations of our faith are constantly being undermined, one is sometimes driven to say to himself, "Suppose it is not true." As I stood, the other night, beneath the sky, and watched the stars, I felt my heart going up to the great Maker with all the love that I was capable of. I said to myself, "What made me love God as I know I do? What made me feel an anxiety to be like him in purity? Whatever made me long to obey my God cannot be a lie." I know that it was the love of Jesus for me that changed my heart, and made me, though once careless and indifferent to him, now to pant with strong desires to honour him. What has done this? Not a lie, surely. A truth, then, has done it. I know it by its fruits. If this Bible were to turn out untrue, and if I died and went before my Maker, could I not say to him, "I believed great things of thee, great God; if it be not so, yet did I honour thee by the faith I had concerning thy wondrous goodness, and thy power to forgive"? and I would cast myself upon his mercy without fear. But we do not entertain such doubts; for those dear wounds continually prove the truth of the gospel, and the truth of our salvation by it. Incarnate Deity is a thought that was never invented by poet's mind, nor reasoned out by philosopher's skill. Incarnate Deity, the notion of the God that lived, and bled, and died in human form, instead of guilty man, it is itself its own best witness. The wounds are the infallible witness of the gospel of Christ.

Have you not felt those wounds very powerful to you in the form of *assistance in times of duty?* You said, "I cannot do it, it is too hard for me." You looked to Jesus wounded, and you could do anything. A sight of the bleeding Christ has often filled us with enthusiasm, and so with power : it has rendered us mighty with the omnipotence of God. Look at the church of Christ in all ages. Kings and princes did not know what to do with her. They vowed that they would destroy her. Their persecuting edicts went forth, and they put to death thousands upon thousands of the followers of Christ. But what happened? The death of Jesus made men willing to die for him. No pain, no torture, could keep back the believing host. They loved Jesus so that though their leaders fell by bloody deaths, another rank came on, and yet another, and another, till despots saw that neither dungeon, nor rack, nor fire could stop the march of the army of Christ. It is so now. Christ's wounds pour life into the church by transfusion : the life-blood of the church of God is from Jesus' wounds. Let us know its power and feel it working within us to will and to do of his good pleasure.

And as for those who do not trust him, what shall I say? The Lord help you to do so at once ; for as long as you do not trust him, you are under an awful curse, for it is written, "If any man love not the Lord Jesus, let him be Anathema Maranatha "—cursed at the coming of the Lord. May it not be so with you ! Amen.

PORTION OF SCRIPTURE READ BEFORE SERMON—John xx. 18—31.

HYMNS FROM "OUR OWN HYMN BOOK"—785, 937, 282.

WITNESSES AGAINST YOU.

A Sermon

INTENDED FOR READING ON LORD'S-DAY, JANUARY 19TH, 1890,

DELIVERED BY

C. H. SPURGEON,

AT THE METROPOLITAN TABERNACLE, NEWINGTON.

"I set a great assembly against them."—Nehemiah v. 7.

THE facts are these. At the time when certain of the Jews returned with Nehemiah to Jerusalem, many of them were in very straitened circumstances; and, contrary to the Jewish law, the richer Jews lent them money upon usurious interest, amounting to the hundredth per month, or twelve per cent. per annum. They took from their poorer brethren their lands, or put a heavy mortgage upon them; and in some cases took the men themselves to be slaves for debts which they had unavoidably incurred. Now, as you know, every Jew was a land-holder, and his land, if mortgaged for a time, must return free to him in the fiftieth year; and, though a Jew might for a while become a servant to his Jewish brother, yet he must go out free at the end of the seventh year. He could only be bound for a short period of servitude. Nehemiah called to him, therefore, the elders, and nobles, and rulers of Jerusalem, and showed them how wrong they were to hold their poorer brethren in bondage. "Ye exact usury, every one of his brother," he says; and he rebukes them sharply for it. When he found that his own words were scarcely powerful enough with them, he gathered together the people, and let them all have a voice, and in the many voices there was power. "I set," said he, "a great assembly against them." Some persons are deaf to the voice of justice until it is repeated loudly by thousands of their fellow-men. The silent voice of principle and right they will not hear, and the gentle rebuke of some one faithful friend they will despise; but when righteousness enlists public opinion on its side, when many are seen to be its advocates, then these very persons will show that they have relics of conscience left, and they yield to right demands, because they see them not only to be just, but to be popular. This is the main point with those of the feebler sort; and we turn the scale, if, like Nehemiah, we "set a great assembly against them."

Now, it struck me to-night that I could most properly, without any

Nos. 2,123-4-5.

difficulty whatever, set a great assembly against every unconverted person here; and, in addition to calling upon him in the name of God, and by the claims of truth, to consider his ways and turn to God, I might summon a great assembly who should testify against the evil course which the unconverted are pursuing.

I shall try to act upon this plan to-night, in reference *to those who remain unconverted.* I would set a great assembly against you. You have not repented of your sins; you have not accepted the salvation which is provided in Christ Jesus; you live without prayer; you seek your own, instead of seeking God.

I set against you the great assembly of all the godly that are upon the earth. They all testify against you. They look upon you with love and anxiety, and desire to see you converted; but, while you are as you are, they are against you. Does not *the consistent life* of every true Christian rebuke you? When you see humble persons devout, gracious, though nothing be said, and though they be not eloquent in speech, is not their life eloquent? Do you not feel it? Have you never felt, even in your most careless moods, that it would be better for you if you were as they are? And when you have seen them remain true and upright under temptation, have you not said within yourself, "After all, there is something in them which I admire, and I wish that I possessed the same strong principles to keep me right in the hour of trial"? Every man, after all, in the bottom of his soul, feels the power of godliness: he cannot help it. In the assembly of the righteous God is greatly feared. The wicked know God's presence among his people, and they do fear it, whether they confess it or not. In fact, slander, ridicule, and persecution are a form of homage which rebellion pays to obedience, which sin pays at the footstool of righteousness. The evil hate the good, because it condemns their evil; they try to make themselves despise it because it makes them despise themselves.

The righteous do not only stand against you in the consistency of their character, but *their joy in God* rebukes you. If you happen to be an unconverted man, and to have had a godly mother, the subject of much weakness and pain, you cannot have forgotten the sacred cheerfulness with which she bore her life-long affliction. Or, if you have lost a Christian wife, who enjoyed but little comfort in her life with you, you cannot but remember that pale yet happy face when it bade you adieu, and entered into its rest. You know there was a calm about that woman in the time of trouble which you could not imitate; that she took patiently pain which would have startled you into madness, for the power of grace was in her, and made her strong. She, and such as she was, children of God, made calm, and peaceful, and happy— I set them in an assembly against you, and they bear witness against you, because you obey not the living God.

Moreover, they do not only bear witness, but *their very horror at your sin* and at your state is a witness against you. I often think that, if I really could know the condition of my unconverted hearers (thoroughly know it), it might be impossible for me to address them. I do try to realize the position of some of you, and to project my mind into the future which awaits you if you die without God, and without hope. I am not about to give any terrible descriptions of the world to come; but, remember, the most terrible I could give would fall infinitely short of what the reality must be. If I could realize that dreadful future more fully, this tongue might be silent through the horror of my heart's emotions. I pray you, therefore, by that terror which we experience in speaking to you, let it stand as a witness against the sin which will bring upon you such misery. We cannot bear to think of that which awaits you. Holy Whitefield, when he began to touch upon that subject, would, with the tears streaming down his cheeks, cry "The wrath to come! The wrath to come!" It was too much for him. He could but repeat those words, and there cease. *We* feel for you, if you will not feel for yourselves. There are those present who never bow the knee at night without praying for the unconverted with great burden of spirit. I know some here, strong men, whom I have seen overcome with sacred passion when they have agonized for you, and for the souls of the ungodly. It has not been merely a plentiful stream of tears bedewing their manly cheeks, but their hearts have heaved within their bosoms, and their whole being has been convulsed with agony of spirit, lest, peradventure, you should perish.

All the praying people in the world I set as an assembly against you. Shall they pray for you, and will you never pray for yourselves? Shall horror seize them on account of your sins, and shall no horror ever seize you? Shall a godly mother waste—no, it is not waste, shall she spend nights in tears for your soul, and will you never weep the tear of repentance? Shall we plead with you with all the eagerness our heart is capable of, and search for words with which to plead with you, and feel that we have done all too little when we have done our best to persuade you—shall we do all this, and yet will you say, "It is nothing to me. It is nothing to me"? Well, then, if it must be so, I can only say that I set the whole assembly of the living saints upon earth against you. Let them have some influence over you.

"Ah!" say you, "but there are many hypocrites amongst them." Very well, they shall go over to your side: you shall be welcome to them; but all the sincere I set against you.

"But it is not the sincere only that pray." Very well, you shall have all the insincere. Poor company! I wonder you should claim them; but still, every sincere believer does, as it were, when he pleads with God, protest against you that your knees are never bent, and your hearts never cry to God as the Father of spirits. Some live week after week, and month after month, and year after year, without prayer. The very Mahometans and heathen rebuke you: they dare not live a single day without their prayers. You are worse than they are. The little chick, as it drinks at the stream, lifts its head as though to thank God. You are worse than the poor fowls. You have become like the swine under the oak, which search for the acorns, but never think of the tree. You receive the mercies of God, but never give thanks to the Giver. O conscience, if there be conscience left, cry shame upon the man who dares to live without God! I set the prayerful, then, against you.

But next, I have another mighty squadron to call. I set against

unconverted men *all the inspired writers of the Old and New Testaments.*
Let them come up, one by one, and speak as they were wont to
do. Not one has a word of comfort for a man that will not repent of
his sins. "Mercy," they will all cry, to the man that accepts the
atoning sacrifice; but if he will not believe in Jesus, with one chorus,
all the prophets, and the apostles too, will say, "Woe, woe, woe,
woe unutterable to the man that lives and dies without Christ!" The
universal consent of all the men that ever spake as the Spirit moved
them is against the ungodly.

But I mention a larger host than either of these, and that is, *the
departed saints.* Oh, could you see them this day in their white robes,
could you hear their sacred song, it were a sight worth dying to behold; and the sound—it were worth losing all the voices of earth in
the silence of death to hear! But suppose you, an unconverted person,
should seek a friend amongst that blood-washed host. I will picture
you beholding them as they stand in their glorious ranks, and you
say, "I am an enemy to God, I am prayerless, I am impenitent, I
am graceless, and I intend to remain so; which among you all will be
a friend to me?" Not an eye will glance upon you, except with
indignation; not a hand will be put out to grasp you. There! March
down that long file, look into those joyous faces, and see if you can
find among them all a trace of sympathy with your obstinate rebellion.
Ask them; conjure them to come and assist you in your sins, or to
comfort you in your impenitence. Is there one that will do it? I
set the whole assembly against you. And there stands one—you
remember her, for though she is strangely changed, and the beatific
vision makes every part of her to shine so gloriously, yet you know
her. It was your mother, who wept over you in childhood, and who
died with prayers for you upon her lips. Ask her whether, if you live
and die unconverted, she will be your friend; and that face, which
you have often gazed upon with affection, and which was always full
of love to you, is turned from you. What has she to do, even with
her child, if that child is an heir of wrath? She loves the Saviour
too much to side with the Saviour's enemies. On earth she could
weep and pray for you: in heaven she has other work to do, and has
undergone such an absorption into the will of God that, if your spirit
should pass into another world unrenewed, she, with those dear lips,
would say, "Amen!" most solemnly to your condemnation. She, too,
will confess, with all the army of the faithful, that the sentence would
be just. There is not one of all you knew on earth who is now in
heaven who can love you, unless you are renewed and changed in
heart. I have sought with many of you, many times, to put the truth
as plainly as I could, and to speak as earnestly as I could; but, once
past the portal, and you are gone into another world, no preacher shall
ever trouble you there. Go down to the shades of death and hell, and
no earnest voices shall ever plead with you there. You shall have
nobody to ridicule as a fanatic there. You shall hear no sermons of which
you can say, "How the man seems to rave!" Ah, no! you shall
have other company, and other engagements, but all God's ministers
will be against you; and, as long as you remain ungodly here, they
are against you. I set the whole host of the redeemed in heaven

before you now, and challenge you, by all their glory, to turn from the error of your way, lest that glory should only increase your misery by contrast.

I have to add to all these saints on earth, and glorified spirits in heaven, *the whole company of the angels.* They are the friends and companions of the saints, but they are by no means the friends of the ungodly. They would rejoice over you if you repented ; but, while you do not repent, it seems to me as if full often the angels, as they fulfil their errands among us, must feel tempted to cry, "Great God of vengeance, let us draw our swords, and let us smite these rebels !" There stands a man who the other day cursed God, and dared him to blast his limbs. If there had been an angel passing by, and doubtless it might have been so, I wonder he did not pause, suspended in mid-air, in very horror. I should not wonder if he felt in his soul that it was poison to him to be near to such a man, and would fain have drawn the mighty sword, which seraphs wield, to cut the man down. The angels are against you. No one of the sacred host is friend to the man who is the foe of God.

The worst is to come : *God is against you.* "The face of the Lord is against them that do evil, to cut off the remembrance of them from the earth." He would fain have you saved. He has sworn with an oath, "As I live, saith the Lord God, I have no pleasure in the death of the wicked ; but that the wicked turn from his way and live." But if you will not turn, you must burn. If you will not repent, you must perish. God has said it, and he will not lie. Justice demands it, and the Judge of all the earth must be just.

And, to crown all, *Jesus Christ, the Son of God, is against you* if you resolve to be the enemy of God. He loves sinners : he died for sinners : he is ever willing to receive them ; but as long as they remain impenitent and unbelieving, he cannot love their sin, he cannot love them, viewing them in the light of wilful, persistent rebels. And when he comes in the latter days, you know what will happen to those that loved not Christ : they will be *Anathema Maranatha*—cursed at his coming. He himself will say it ; and it appals me to have to remind you of the fact—he himself, whose gentle lips were like lilies dropping sweet-smelling myrrh, tender as a woman's—he himself, when he comes, will say, "Depart from me, ye cursed, into everlasting fire, prepared for the devil and his angels !" You will find no friend in Christ in that last tremendous day. He will break you in pieces with a rod of iron, as potters' vessels are broken into shivers. So, then, I set this great assembly against you : saints on earth and saints in heaven, the angels, and God, and Christ himself against you.

Who is there for you ? Who is there on your side, O enemies of God ? It is as dreadful to think of those who are for you as of those who are against you ; for those who are for you, and on your side, are the ungodly, like yourselves ; and the lost in hell, who are now what you must be, except you escape ; and the devil and his angels, themselves punished for their sins. A grim assembly, surely, those that are for you ! Methinks a man should start up and say—"I cannot abide in such company as this ! Do I sail in this pirate's vessel, with such a dreadful crew on board, and Satan for captain ? In God's name I will jump overboard, and swim to another ship, for in this vessel I will never stay, and under this black flag I will never fight, let the bribe be as high as it may. I cannot serve Satan, and I will not." Friends, if such be your language, I stand here, as a servant of Jesus, and hold above you the blood-stained banner of Christ's cross. Oh, ye who will take the enlisting-money, here it is: come and take it, for whosoever receives Christ—receives him by trusting him—to him is given power to become a servant of Christ, and a soldier of the cross; and then I shall have no assembly to set against him, but the same august assembly shall be on the side of the man saved by faith in Jesus! God grant that these words may be found useful, and Christ shall have the glory!

For a few minutes I will vary the strain, but keep closely to the same idea. *Some say that sin is a very pleasant and profitable thing:* indeed, many profess to be of that opinion nowadays. I may have some here, particularly some young men just commencing life, who are fascinated by the charms of London life, and have begun to sip of the dangerous wine which is vended in the house of the strange woman. To them it seems that vice is pleasure. O young man, I wish I had thee in a room alone, that I might speak to thee, for some things that I would say earnestly to thee in private I must but hint at in a public assembly. The results of sin are not such as I can speak of here. Thou art under great delusions. If thou thinkest sin will give thee pleasure, I will set an assembly against thee concerning this dream. Oh, what an assembly it would be if I could bring up from the hospitals the wretches who are suffering an earthly hell from their sins! Have I not seen them? Have I not seen them crawling through the earth, creatures that dare not look up, broken down with hypochondriasis, desponding and despairing, with that despair which nothing but vice ever brings on man? Have I not seen them when their very bones have rotted through their sin? There are diseases which are the stamp and seal of the curse of the Eternal upon transgression. There are diseases which are the big first drops of the everlasting rain of hell's tremendous tempest. If there were a physician or a surgeon here, he could tell you that there are sins which are commonly practised, which bring on men, even in this life, a penalty most terrible. The furnace of hell devours; but, like Nebuchadnezzar's guards, men in this life are made to fall down, slain by the powerful heat that glows from the eternal burnings, when God suffers a portion of the results of sin to come upon them in this life. Could I not bring up here to-night, if it were fit and proper, spendthrifts, who squandered their early days in all manner of dissoluteness, and who have brought themselves to rags and disease? Go over the casual ward, enter the union-house, spend an evening in a low lodging-house, and sit down and hear the tales of sons of ministers, of sons of gentlemen, of sons of noblemen, of men that once were merchants, traders, lawyers, doctors, who have brought themselves down by nothing else than their own extravagance and sin, to eat the bread of pauperism, and to know the lack even of that bitter fare. Tell me sin is pleasure! If it be, you can have too much of it; but it is bitterness before long, and they are wise who flee from it.

"Well, well," cries one, "we are not all lovers of that kind of sin." Indeed, I hope you are not: I, too, refused such sins, but I had other sins—the world would not call them sins, but they were such—and when, before I found the Saviour, I began to discover what sin was (I speak what I do know), my sins, to me in my consciousness, were a little hell. I know that men who are not saved, sometimes on a dark night, or in sickness, or in trouble, or when alone, will permit conscience to work, and they feel dreadfully uneasy. Have I not seen your cheek blanch when you have been told that your friend was dead? When the funeral knell has been tolling, have you not wished yourself in the depths of the forest, that you might not hear it? When you have been compelled to sit a little while alone, you feared to allow your mind to meditate upon eternity; but you tried to fly off again to the frivolities of time, though you felt there was nothing in them. Sin is a wretched thing, unsatisfying at best. Even painted sins, with their Jezebel faces, are not truly beautiful. What men call immoralities are wretched in themselves, upon the outside; and a grain of common-sense will enable a man to see that their misery far exceeds their pleasure. I set an assembly against the man who declares that there is pleasure in iniquity.

On the other hand, *it is said that true religion makes people miserable.* I would set an assembly against anybody who dares to say that. It was in my mind to ask you who are unhappy through being Christians, to bear witness to-night against Christianity; and then I thought perhaps I would put it the other way; and let those of you who love the Saviour, and find consolation and happiness in him, sing with me one of our joyous hymns; and I warrant you, sirs, we would make this great dome resound with hearty music. Unhappy! Unhappy through being Christians! I have suffered as much of bodily pain as most here present, and I know also about as much of depression of spirit at times as anyone; but my Master's service is a blessed service, and faith in him makes my heart leap for joy. I would not change with the most healthy man, or the most wealthy man, or the most learned man, or the most eminent man in all the world, if I had to give up my faith in Jesus Christ—tried as it sometimes is. Ah! it is a blessed thing to be a Christian, and all God's people will tell you so. It is ofttimes our lot to go to see the sick, but sick believers usually cheer our heart. There is a seat just below that used to be occupied by a beloved sister, well-known to you, whom I went to visit in her sickness; and I do assure you, when she was in a consumption, and near to death, I never spent a happier hour than I did with her. And only last week, or ten days ago, when I sat down with her, and she could scarcely speak, yet what she did say was as full of sacred joy as words could compass. She is in heaven now, and heaven was in her then. "So much farther on have I got," said she, "to the better land—so many the fewer of these hard breaths to fetch, and so many the fewer of these hard pains to bear. I shall soon be where Jesus is;" and she talked as freely about dying, and going home, as I should talk of going to my own house when this service is ended. Before she fell asleep yesterday, about twelve o'clock, she said to those about her she felt strangely as if she were going through a river. At one time she said she was in the midst of it, the floods were round about her;

and soon she said, in intervals of consciousness, "I am going up the other side; the waters are shallower: I am mounting the other bank." At length she cried, "Jesus is coming for me! I can hear the music of heaven!" Her heart seemed to be overpowered with some sweet mystic melody, which, if it did not enter her soul by the ear, at any rate reached her inmost spirit by some other channel. "I can hear them sing! I can hear them sing!" she said, "and when Jesus comes, don't keep him waiting for me; don't wish me to stop. Let me go." She is gone. Never one I think suffered more in dying, and never had a consumptive more difficulty in breathing. Thank God, they do not often suffer as much as she did; yet there was never one more calm, more comfortable, and more joyous on the bed of death than this daughter of affliction.

I believe in God without any evidence except himself, and his own revelation of himself to my soul; but yet I thank God for evidences, and among those most helpful to me are the death-beds of believers. It does my soul great good to see the Lord's people depart this life. I grieve that you should be taken away to heaven, for we want you here; but ah! if the departure of any of you shall be so sweet as those I have been privileged to witness of late, I shall come to my pulpit boldly. If the religion that I teach makes men and women die like this, I am not ashamed to preach it. If the faith that I have delivered to them, by the power of the Holy Ghost, makes them so triumphant in the last article of death, I will deliver nothing else, but still continue to tell them to trust simply in the substitutionary sacrifice of Jesus Christ, and rest wholly and only there. I say, then, by the living saints that do rejoice, and by the dying saints who die without a fear, I set an assembly against the man who dares to slander true religion by saying that it does not make men happy.

I had many other things to say, but it were well to leave you where you are, only praying you, by the shortness of time, by the suddenness of death, by the certainty of judgment, by the terrors of hell, by the glories of heaven, by the value of your own souls, by the blood of Jesus, and by the glory of the eternal God, to cease being his enemies. Seek ye his face. "Let the wicked forsake his way, and the unrighteous man his thoughts: and let him return unto the Lord, and he will have mercy upon him; and to our God, for he will abundantly pardon." "Believe on the Lord Jesus Christ, and thou shalt be saved;" for "he that believeth and is baptized shall be saved; but he that believeth not shall be damned." From that, God save you! Amen.

PORTION OF SCRIPTURE READ BEFORE SERMON—Isaiah i. 1—20.

HYMNS FROM "OUR OWN HYMN BOOK"—387, 34, 514.

HELP FOR YOUR SICKNESS.

A Sermon

DELIVERED BY

C. H. SPURGEON,

AT THE METROPOLITAN TABERNACLE, NEWINGTON.

"When the even was come, they brought unto him many that were possessed with devils: and he cast out the spirits with his word, and healed all that were sick: that it might be fulfilled which was spoken by Esaias the prophet, saying, Himself took our infirmities, and bare our sicknesses."—Matthew viii. 16, 17.

It was the evening: in all probability it was the evening of a Sabbath-day. The Jews were so tender not to break the Sabbath that they did not even bring forth the sick to the Saviour until the even was come. The Saviour would gladly have healed them on the Sabbath-day, for that was to him a high day for holy work, but they did not think it right, and so they kept back their sick till the day was ended. If any of you have thought that the time has not come for you to approach the Saviour, you have laboured under a great error, for he would not have you delay for a single hour; but I hope you are now satisfied that you have waited long enough, and that at last the evening is near in which you should come to Jesus. God grant that any superstition which has kept you back may be removed; and may this be the set time, the hour of grace to your souls!

Whether it was a Sabbath-evening or not, the day had been spent by the Saviour in diligent labour; for our Saviour took care, when the people would listen to him on the seventh day, to preach with all his might. As soon as the sun was up, he began to tell out saving truth. He was tired when evening was come, and he might have sought rest; but instead of that, they brought out the sick to him to heal, and he must close up a weary day by a yet more arduous task. Until darkness had covered the earth, he must continue still to scatter blessings right and left. At this hour our blessed Master has laid aside all weariness; and now at eventide he is waiting to bless. Whatever has been done during the day, yet if some poor, weary soul has spurned the voice divine through all the former hours, he is waiting still to save, ere yet the sun has quite gone down. When even was come, they brought unto him those that were sick. We are in like case. Let us put up this prayer to him, "O thou who didst bless the sick in the evening, come now and bless us while all is cool and still, and let us find thy salvation!"

What a strange sight that evening saw! They brought forth to the Saviour those that were possessed of evil spirits, and those that were sick. They brought them on their mattresses, and laid them in the streets. It must have been a very difficult thing to bring out some that were possessed, because they struggled and raved; but nevertheless they brought them. The streets were turned into a hospital, and in the still evening air you could hear the cries of those poor creatures who were possessed of evil spirits, and the moans of those in acute pain. It was a sad sight, a piteous sight, to look upon; and as far as Christ's eye could see, every nook and corner were occupied with these sick people. But what a glorious thing it must have been to see him, the divine Physician, with tears of pity in his eyes, and yet with beaming joy on his countenance; suffering intensely all the while because of their suffering, and yet joyous because he was able to bless them. You see him go along, and lay his hand on one sick man, and he leaped up from the bed; and you hear him speak to another, and the foul spirit fled, and he that was madness itself became calm and rational. See him cast a look over yonder, and with that glance he expels the fever. Hear him speak a word to one far away, and, with that word he dries up dropsy, or opens a blind eye. It was grand to see the Saviour thus fighting with Satan and with foul diseases, and everywhere victorious. That was one of the happiest evenings that ever ended day in Palestine. I want you to feel that we can have its parallel to-night. We have Jesus here. We have been seeking him. There are some here who dwell with him. Jesus is here, and the sick folk are here, and he is just as able to heal to-night as he was in days gone by.

I am going to speak about *his works of healing,* and to draw encouragement therefrom; and then we shall go into *the explanation of his power to heal,* which is given us in the second verse of our text: "Himself took our infirmities, and bare our sicknesses."

I. Let us notice, first, OUR LORD'S WORKS OF HEALING. On that occasion, and on many others, he cured *all sorts of sickness.* I think I am right in saying that there is not in the whole list of diseases one which the Saviour did not heal. They may be known by new names, for they say the doctors have invented a dozen new diseases lately; but they are only old diseases to which they have given new names. Our great grandfathers died of diseases the names of which they never knew, or else they had other names than those which are given to them now. But as man has always been much the same, most diseases have continued as long as the human race. We have to be very grateful that leprosy, which was the great scourge of the Jews, is almost extinct now; but in our Saviour's day it seems to have been exceedingly common. But leprosy and all forms of disease came under the Saviour's power, and fled at his word.

Now the parallel of that is this—Jesus Christ can forgive sins of all sorts. There are different grades of sin. Some are exceedingly defiling and loathsome. Other sins are scarcely hurtful to the general commonwealth, and so are often almost unnoticed. Yet any sin will ruin a soul for ever. It may be thought to be little, but as a little prick with a poisoned arrow will heat all the blood, and bring on death, so is sin such a venomous disease that the least of it is fatal. But from whatever kind of sin you are suffering, I would encourage you to come to Jesus with it, be it what it may. Is yours an extreme case? Have you been grossly guilty? Come with it, then, for our Lord healed the worst diseases. On the other hand, have you been kept out of gross sin from your early youth? Have you been preserved from outward vice? It may be that your chief sin is the forgetting of God, and living without love to Christ—a deadly sin, let me tell you; but bring it to the Saviour. Have you been idle? Have you been proud? Have you been lascivious? Have you been untruthful? Have you been profane? Have you been malicious? I cannot tell; but God knoweth—who can read your heart as readily as we read a book. But whatever the sin may be, remember that all manner of sin and of blasphemy shall be forgiven unto men. "The blood of Jesus Christ his Son cleanseth us from all sin." Oh, hear this, and look up to the Saviour, and pray him of his great mercy to exercise the healing art of his redeeming love on you, this evening, now that the sun has set! They brought to Jesus all sorts of diseases.

Note, next, that Jesus can deal with *special cases of devilry*. Possession with evil spirits was probably peculiar to that age. I sometimes think that, when the Saviour came down on earth, the devil had the impudence to ask to be let loose, that he and all his servants might come on earth, and in person might meet the Saviour. Satan is still busy, going about, seeking whom he may devour; but not exactly in the particular way in which he raged in Christ's day. He cannot take possession of men's bodies as he did then. So the Saviour met Satan foot to foot, and face to face; but the devil made a poor fight of it, for whenever the Lord Jesus made his appearance, the devil wanted to be off; and if he did not want to go, the Saviour soon moved him by saying, "Come out of him." Like a whipped dog, he did not dare to make a sound, but fled. A whole legion of demons were glad to get into a herd of swine, and ran violently down a steep place into the sea, to escape from the frown of our Lord. Satan had found somebody that was more than a match for him. The parallel to that is this. There are some men that we meet with, in whom the devil evidently reigns; and there are such women too—for when women are bad, they can be bad, and there can be no mistake about it. The devil can make more mischief out of a woman than out of a man when he thoroughly gets possession of her. Well, whether men or women, there are some who might be called "the devil's own." One man is a drunkard: there is no holding him; he must drink on; he seems to be infatuated by it. He takes the pledge, and abstains for a little while; but by-and-by the devil gets hold of him again, and he goes back to his taps. Though he has drunk himself into delirium tremens, and to death's door, yet still he gives way to this loathsome vice. Others are possessed with the devil of lasciviousness, and it does not matter what they suffer; they will be always defiling themselves, ruining body and soul by their iniquity. We know persons who seem to have a devil in them in the matter of passion. They are but a little provoked, and they lose all command of themselves, and you would think that they ought to be put in a padded room in Bethlehem Hospital, and kept there till they cooled down. Otherwise, they might do mischief to themselves and to others. Surely some men, who can scarcely speak without swearing, have the devil in them. How one's blood runs chill, in going down our streets, to hear how commonly our working-men degrade themselves with filthy conversation! It is not exactly cursing: it is less honest, and more vile! Is there any hope for such? These are the very people in whom Jesus Christ has often displayed his healing power. I could tell you to-night of lions that have been turned to lambs, men of furious passions who have become gentle, and quiet, and loving, men of profane speech who would be shocked at the very remembrance of what they once said, and whose voices have been often heard in prayer: men and women, too, who loved the wages of iniquity, and lost their character, and defiled themselves; but they are washed, and they are sanctified. I have blessed the name of God when giving the right hand of Christian fellowship to ransomed ones to whom we could not have given our right hand a little while ago, for it would have been wrong to join with them in the wickedness of their pursuits. Oh, yes, my Master still casts devils out of men! If there are any such here to-night, let your cry for help go up to our blessed Master. Come again, great Lord, and cast out the evil spirit from men, and get to thyself the victory in many a heart, to the praise of the glory of thy grace!

The remarkable point about this miracle-working was that *all were healed, and there was no failure.* When a man brings out a patent medicine, he publishes verifications of the efficacy of his physic. He gets a number of cases, and he advertises them. I suppose they are genuine. I should not like to be hanged if they were not. I suppose, therefore, they are all accurate and authentic. But there is one thing which you never knew a medicine advertiser do: he never advertises the failures of the medicine. The number of persons that have been induced to buy the remedy, and have derived no good from it: if these were all advertised, it might occupy more room in the newspaper than those who write of a cure. My Lord Jesus Christ is a Physician who never had a failure yet—never once. Never did a soul wash in Christ's blood without being made whiter than snow. Never did a man, besotted with the worst of vice, trust in Jesus without receiving power to conquer his evil habits. Not even in the lowest pit of hell is there one that dares to say, "I trusted Christ, and I am lost. I sought his face with all my heart, and he cast me away." There is not a man living that could say that, unless he dared to lie; for not one has with heart and soul sought the Saviour, and trusted in him, and then had a negative from him. He must save you if you trust him. As surely as he lives he must save you, for he has put it, "Him that cometh to me I will in no wise cast out." I will repeat it, "Him that cometh to me I will in no wise cast out." You have never come if he has not received you; for he must save those who trust in him.

Notice, that *his word was the sole medicine he used:* "He cast out the spirits with his word." No other medicine, no charms, no long performances, no striking of his hand over the place; but he spake, and it was done. He said to the devil, "Come out of him"; and it came out. He said to the disease, "Go"; and away it went. In that way the Lord saves men to-day—by his word. While I am speaking it to-night, or when you shall be reading it, his word will be the power of God unto salvation. I am glad that you are here to hear it, for faith cometh by hearing. I shall be glad if you diligently read it, for reading is a kind of hearing, and many are brought to the Saviour thereby. Jesus Christ does not need to put you through a long purgatory, and keep you for months getting ready to be saved. He has only this night to open your ear to hear his word, and when you hear it he can bless it to your soul so that you shall live, and your sin shall die; and you shall become changed and renewed by his matchless grace.

I speak his word to-night, praying that he will make it effectual, as he has done aforetime; and to him shall be the praise.

We have the same medicine to-night that Jesus used, for we have his word. We have got himself here in answer to the prayers of his people, and we have the same sort of sick people here; and therefore we expect to see the same wonders wrought.

II. May God give you a hearing ear, and save you while I speak, secondly, of OUR LORD'S PERSONAL POWER TO HEAL! Whence came it that he was able to save? We are pointed to the secret of his power by these words, "That it might be fulfilled which was spoken by Esaias, the prophet, saying, Himself took our infirmities, and bare our sicknesses."

Christ was able to heal the diseases of men, because he bare them himself. Do not think that our Lord Jesus was actually diseased: he suffered greatly, but I read not that any disease was upon him. Probably there was no man in whom there was less tendency to natural disease than in him. His pure and blessed body was not subject to the diseases which are brought upon men through sin being in them. How, then, did he take upon him our sicknesses and our sorrows?

First, *he bare our sicknesses by intense sympathy.* When Christ looked at all those sick people, he did, as it were, take all their sicknesses upon himself. You know what I mean. If you talk with a person who is very ill, and you feel for him, you seem to lay his pains upon yourself, and then you have power to comfort him. When I am seeing troubled people, I enter into one sorrowful case after another till I am more sad than any of them. I try as far as I can to have fellowship with the case of each one, in order to be able to speak a word of comfort to him; and I can say, from personal experience, that I know of nothing that wears the soul down so fast as the outflow of sincere sympathy with the sorrowing, desponding, depressed ones. I have sometimes been the means in God's hand of helping a man who suffered with a desponding spirit; but the help I have rendered has cost me dearly. Hours after, I have been myself depressed, and I have felt an inability to shake it off. You and I have not a thousandth part of the sympathy that was in Christ. He sympathized with all the aggregate of human woe, and so sympathized that he made his heart a great reservoir, into which all streams of grief poured themselves. My Master is just the same now. Though he is in heaven, he is just as tender as he was on earth. I never heard of anybody losing tenderness by going to heaven. People get better by going there ; and so is Christ, if it were possible, even more tender than when on earth. Think of this. Somebody might not sympathize with you, poor sinner, but Jesus does. You would not like to tell some people what you have done, for they would turn upon their heel, and give you a wide berth, but it is not so with Jesus. He looks upon sin, not with the eye of a judge, but with the eye of a physician. He looks at it as a disease, and he deals with it that he may heal it. He has great sympathy with sinners, though he has no sympathy with sin. He takes the sinner's sorrows to himself.

"Ah!" says one, "no man careth for my soul." Dear friend, man or woman, whoever you may be, One greatly cares for you, and he speaks to you to-night by these lips. Oh, that these lips were better fitted to be used by him! He says, "Come unto me, and I will give you rest." He bids you take of the water of life freely. He is ready at this moment to bestow salvation.

"Nobody knows my case," cries one. But Jesus knows it. He knows that dark spot in it. He knows that hard core which will not come away. He knows that filthy thing which you remember to-night, and shiver as you remember it. He knows it all, and yet he says, "Return, thou backsliding daughter." He bids the vilest of the vile come to him, for he has sympathy with them still.

Jesus Christ took upon himself our sicknesses by his championship of our humanity. Satan misled our first parents, and the powers of darkness held us captive. In consequence of sin we have become sick and infirm, and liable to suffer.

Now, when our Lord Jesus came on earth, he as good as said, "I am the Seed of the woman ; and I have come to bruise the head of men's adversary." So Christ, in that respect, took upon himself all the consequences which come of sin. He stood forth as the Champion of fallen manhood, to fight Satan, and cast him out of men's bodies ; to battle with disease, and to overthrow the evil which lies at the root of it, that men might be made healthy.

He is our Champion still. I delight to preach him to you, ye suffering, ye sorrowing, ye sinful, ye lost, ye castaways! One has come who has taken up your cause, the sinner's Redeemer, next-of-kin to man, who has come to avenge him of his adversary, and to buy back his lost inheritance. Behold in Jesus the Champion of sinners, the David who comes and defies the Goliath that has long afflicted men. Oh, I wish you would trust our glorious Champion! Remember how he met the adversary alone, and vanquished him. "'Twas on that dark, that dreadful night." The enemy sprang upon him in the garden like a lion, and the Saviour received him on his breast. He brought the Saviour to his knees ; but there he grasped the lion, hugged him, crushed him, rent him, and flung him from him. Our Samson sweat as it were great drops of blood falling down to the ground; and though he had won that victory, he afterwards bowed his head, and gave up the ghost. He lives, however, now again, the Champion of the cause of all the suffering, the sorrowing, and the sinful, if they will but come and put their case into his hands. He himself took our sicknesses and our infirmities, by championing our cause, and standing in our place to fight our battles. Give him *your* cause, trust *your* soul in his hands, and he will redeem *you* out of the jaw of the lion, yea, out of the very mouth of hell.

But here is the pith of the whole matter. The reason why Jesus is able to heal all the mischief that sin has wrought is this—because *he himself took our sin upon him by his sacred substitution.* Sin is the root of our infirmities and diseases; and so, in taking the root, he took all the bitter fruit which that root did bear. Oh, tell it out again, and tell it out again, and tell it every day, and tell it in the dead of night, and tell it in the glare of noonday, and tell it in the market, and tell it in the street, and tell it everywhere, that God took sin from off the back of sinners, and laid it on his innocent and only-begotten Son! O mystery divine, never to be known if God had not revealed it; and not even now to be believed if God himself had not assured us of it! He laid sin upon Christ. "All we like sheep have gone astray; we have turned every one to his own way; and the Lord hath laid on him the iniquity of us all." Hearken, then, ye guilty ones! Hear how freely God can forgive, and yet not injure his justice. If you trust Christ, you may be sure that you are among the number of those whose sins were laid on Christ. He was punished in your room, and place, and stead. Now, it is not just that, if another was punished in your stead, you should be punished too; and therefore the very justice of God requires that, if Christ suffered in your stead, you should not suffer. See you that?

"But did he suffer in my stead?" I must answer this question by another, "Dost thou believe that Jesus is the Christ? Wilt thou trust thy soul with him?" Well, if thou dost, thy transgressions are not thine, for they were laid on him. They are not on thee, for, like everything else, they cannot be in two places at one time; and if they were laid on Christ, they are not laid on you. But what did Jesus do with the sins that were laid on him? Can they not come back to us? No, never; for he took them to the sepulchre, and there he buried them for ever. And now, what saith the Scripture? "In those days, and in that time, saith the Lord, the iniquity of Israel shall be sought for, and there shall be none; and the sins of Judah, and they shall not be found." "I have blotted out, as a thick cloud, thy transgressions; and, as a cloud, thy sins." "Thou wilt cast all their sins into the depths of the sea." Our sins are gone. Christ has carried them away. "As far as the east is from the west, so far hath he removed our transgressions from us." Believers are the seed for whom the victory has been gained. They are the seed to whom the promise is sure. It is not to those who are of works, but to those who are of faith. Those that are born again, of the Spirit of God, through faith which is in Christ Jesus—these are "redeemed from among men." Suppose I owed ten thousand pounds: if a dear friend should call on my creditor, and pay that ten thousand pounds for me, I should then owe the creditor nothing. I could meet him with a smiling face. He may to-morrow morning bring his account-books if he likes, and say, "There, you see, there are ten thousand pounds down there against you." I would joyfully answer, "Yes; but look on the other side. You have been paid. Here are the words at the foot of your bill, 'Received in full of all demands.'" Now, when Jesus took the sins of believers upon himself, he discharged them by his death; and every man that believes has the receipt in full in our Lord's resurrection. "Therefore being justified by faith, we have peace with God." Yea, those that believe in Christ have the complete forgiveness of every sin. As for me, I like to sing with Kent—

> "Here's pardon for transgressions past,
> It matters not how black their cast;
> And O my soul, with wonder view,
> For sins to come here's pardon too!"

All blotted out at once with one stroke of the sacred pen—obliterated once for all. God does not again lay to the charge of men what he has once forgiven them. He does not forgive them half their sins, and visit them for the rest; but, once given, the blessing is irrevocable; as it is written. "The gifts and calling of God are without repentance." He never draws back, nor repents of what he has done. He saves, and the salvation which saves is everlasting salvation.

Now I see why Christ can heal. Dear heart, you have come here to-night full of the disease of sin, and you are saying, "Will he heal me?" Look to him! Look to him! Look to him! The morning that I found Christ I did not think to find him. I went to hear the word as I had heard it before; but I did not hope to find Jesus there and then. Yet I did find him. When I heard that there was nothing to be done but simply to look to Jesus; and when the exhortation came so sharp, and shrill, and clear, "Look! look! look!" I looked, and I bear witness to the change that passed over me—such a change as though I died and rose again. And such a change, my hearer, shall pass over thee if thou believest.

> "There is life for a look at the Crucified One;
> There is life at this moment for thee."

God give thee the look, and give thee the life, even now, for Jesus Christ's sake! Amen.

Portion of Scripture read before Sermon—Isaiah liii.

Hymns from "Our Own Hymn Book"—410, 568, 296.

HOPE FOR YOUR FUTURE.

A Sermon

DELIVERED BY

C. H. SPURGEON,

AT THE METROPOLITAN TABERNACLE, NEWINGTON.

"I will settle you after your old estates, and will do better unto you than at your beginnings."—Ezekiel xxxvi. 11.

THESE words were spoken to the mountains, and valleys, and rivers of Judah; and we know that the Lord careth not for hills and rivers, but he speaketh altogether for the sake of his people. The blessing to the land was intended to be a blessing to the people. We shall do no violence to the text if we take the promise as belonging to ourselves, and plead it before the mercy-seat, trusting that the Lord will do this unto us, and that our latter end may be better than our beginning.

Have you ever noticed that when nations fall they seldom rise again? Babylon and Nineveh become mountains of rubbish. If the Medo-Persian kingdom falls, the throne is never revived. If Greece and ancient Rome cease from their eminence, we see no more of them than their ruins. But God's people are not numbered amongst the nations, so that when Israel falls she revives again. Though for many centuries the ancient people have been scattered and peeled, derided and despised, yet every Israelite may put down his foot with joyous tread, and say, "No, Israel, thou shalt never perish!" Even in her ashes live her wonted fires, and the days shall come when Israel shall own her Messiah, and her God will fulfil the promise of the text, "I will settle you after your old estates, and will do better unto you than at your beginnings; and ye shall know that I am the Lord." I believe that to be the first sense of the passage; but since all the blessings of the covenant, which belong to the seed according to the flesh, do spiritually belong to all those who are in that covenant according to the spirit, we shall take this word as spoken to all believers.

If a hypocrite falls, he falls like Lucifer, never to hope again. He is a meteor, that flashes across the sky and disappears; a wandering star, for whom is reserved the blackness of darkness for ever. Let Judas fall from his apostleship, and there is no restoring the son of perdition. But how different is the case of God's own, when they fall! Alas, that they should do so! Yet of them it is said, "Rejoice not against me, O mine enemy: when I fall, I shall arise." Peter, at a look from his Master, wept bitterly, and lived to say, "Thou knowest that I love thee." There is hope of a tree, if it be cut down, that it will sprout again, for there is life in it; and where there is life there is hope. If Mordecai be of the royal seed, the enemy shall never prevail against him. There may come dark times of backsliding, but surely the redeemed of the Lord shall come again with mourning and repenting, and they shall seek unto him from whom they have wandered.

I am not, however, going to dwell much upon the dark side of the subject of declension; but I shall invite your attention to the gracious promise that God will make things better for us than they were at our beginnings. First, I shall answer the question, *what is there, then, so good in our beginnings?* In the second place, *if so good, can anything be better?* And, in the third place, *how can we secure these better things,* so that our life shall verify the statement of the text, "I will do better unto you than at your beginnings"?

I. WHAT IS THERE, THEN, SO GOOD IN OUR BEGINNINGS? Let us look back. Some of us have been converted to God for a good number of years now; and all that while we have enjoyed spiritual life. Others are young beginners, but their present enjoyment will assist them to answer the question—What is there so good about those first days? We read of our first love as "the love of our espousals"; and we all know there was something specially charming about those first hours when forgiving love was precious to us, and we rejoiced in the Lord.

One choice enjoyment was our *vivid sense of pardon.* We knew that we were forgiven: we had not the shadow of a doubt of it. We were black so lately that, being washed from our stains, we saw the change. It would not have been possible for Satan then to make us doubt it. When we stood at the cross-foot, and said, "Thus my sins were washed away," then things went well with us. When substitution was a novelty to us, and when we seemed to hear a voice like that of the angels before the throne, singing, "There is therefore now no condemnation to them which are in Christ Jesus,"—we all knew then that we had looked to Jesus, for we felt that we could look nowhere else. We were newly-cleansed sinners, and we knew it. Oh, that blessed period! Our earthly comforts were forgotten in the greater sweetness, and our earthly sorrows ceased because guilt was gone. Taken out of the bonds of iniquity, our hearts danced at the very sound of the redeeming name. You sang, "I am forgiven: I am forgiven." You wanted to tell the angels this strange wonder of almighty love. That was one of the good things of your beginning.

You recollect very well, too, that you had then *a delicious enjoyment of the good things of the covenant of grace.* You did not know a tenth of what you know now, but you intensely enjoyed what you did know. When the Israelites first of all came into Canaan, they found it to be a land that flowed with milk and honey. It became afterwards a stony land through their sins, but rare clusters then grew in Eshcol, and the wild bees made honey plentifully, even in such a strange place as the carcase of a lion. When we first came to Christ, it was so with us as to the things of God; they were all sweets. We saw one covenant blessing, then another, and then another; and we were enraptured with each one. Whether in the body or out of the body we could scarcely tell; for we did not look then without tasting, and we did not taste then without feasting, and we did not feast then without feasting again. We grudged the world the hours we spent in business : we wanted to get back to our Bibles, or to the assembly of the saints. Our Lord was a precious Christ then, and exceeding lovely in our eyes, that had been so newly opened. Everything about him, and his people, and his Word, and his day, and his cross was astonishing to us, and filled us with an intensity of delight. It was "happy day" indeed with us then. That was another blessed point in our beginnings.

And, at that time, we were like the children of Israel in a third matter, namely, that *we had repeated victories.* Do you recollect when your Jericho fell down—when a high walled-up sin, that you feared would never yield to you, was brought down suddenly? As Israel went from victory to victory, and slew king after king, so in those early days did you. As quickly as conscience revealed a sin, you smote it as with a two-edged sword. You sometimes wondered at professors that they could live as they did. You felt *you* could not. Your hand was in for fighting; and, like Joshua, you did not stay it. The day was not long enough for you in which to slay your sin; you felt inclined to bid the sun stand still, and the moon to rest, that you might make full work of blessed carnage in putting sin altogether to the sword. You have had a good many defeats since then, it may be, for which you cannot excuse yourself; but then "Victory !" was your watchword, and you went on to realize it in the name of the eternal God. From day to day, though attacked by the uprising of corruptions, you said, "In the name of the Lord will I destroy them," and you sometimes cried like her of old, "O my soul, thou hast trodden down strength!" You marvelled to see how the adversary was subdued beneath the foot of your faith. Those were good times, were they not—those beginnings?

In those days, you had *great delight in prayer.* When alone with Christ, it was heaven below; and in the prayer-meetings, when God's people were warm at heart, how you delighted to unite with them! The preaching was marrow and fatness to you. You did not mind walking a long way on a wet night to hear about your Lord and Master then. It may be there was no cushion to the seat, or you had to stand in the aisle. You did not mind that. You are getting wonderfully dainty now; you cannot hear the poor preacher whose voice was once like music to you. You cannot enjoy the things of God as once you did. Whose fault is that? The kitchen is the same, and the food the same : the appetite has gone, I fear. How ravenous I was after God's Word— how I would wake early in the morning to read those books that are full of the deep things of God! I wanted none of your nonsensical novels, nor your weekly tales, for which some of you pine, like children for sugar-sticks. Then one fed on manna that came from heaven, on Christ himself. Those were good times in which everything was delightful. You heard a gospel preacher, and perhaps he spoiled the Queen's English; but you did not care a bit about that. You were hungry, and you minded not the knives, and the table-cloths: you wanted meat, and plenty of it, and so long as it was good spiritual meat, your souls were delighted therewith. That is one of the good things of our beginnings.

In those days we were *full of living fruitfulness*. I hope we have not lost it. Just as the mountains of Judæa dropped with wine, and ran with milk, through the abundance of the soil, so was it with us then. We could do anything. Sometimes, in looking back, we wonder how we ever attempted so much. We were not so anxious to keep up our spiritual life as we were to spend what we had got. We thought then we would push the church before us, and drag the world behind us. What marvels we were going to do; ay, and we did many of them by God's good grace!

Then, if we had but little strength, yet we kept the Lord's Word. If we had but one talent, we made as much use of it, perhaps, as some do with ten. I love to see you young Christians as active as ever you can be; and I am going to put my hand on young heads, and say "This is right. Do all you can. You may not be so lively by-and-by." If you are not earnest when you begin, what will you be soon? I want you to maintain that earnestness, and to let it increase, for no man is doing too much for Jesus. No one is too consecrated, no one too self-denying, no one too enthusiastic. There has never been seen on the face of the earth yet a man who has laid himself out too much for the cause and kingdom of our Master. That will never be. But it is one of the good points of our beginnings that we were full of fruitfulness for the Lord our God.

This is because the saints begin generally with *abounding love*. Oh, how we loved the Saviour when first we discovered how he had loved us with an everlasting love! When we see that the dunghill is never to be our portion again, but yon bright glory at the right hand of the Eternal—oh, then we love our Saviour with all our hearts! I am not saying that we do not now love even more; but it is a good beginning when we overflow with love to our Lord Jesus.

II. I could thus keep on reminding you of the days gone by; but I do not care to do so. I am going now, in the second place, to answer the question, CAN ANYTHING BE BETTER THAN THIS?

Well, it would be a very great pity if there could not be, because I am sure we, when we were young beginners, were not much to boast of; and all the joy we had was, after all, but little compared with what is revealed in the Word of God. We ought to get to something better; and it would be a miserable thing if we were to get "small by degrees, and miserably less." It would not look like Christian perseverance if our light were to shine less and less unto the perfect darkness. No, but it is to shine more and more unto the perfect day; and in the beginning our day is only twilight. In coming to God at first we are only in the outer courts: we have not yet entered the holy of holies of inward experience: we stand in the outer court. We are wheat in the blade as yet. Ask the farmer whether he thinks that the green blade is the best thing on the farm. He says, "Yes, for the present"; but if it is a green blade next July, he will not think so. There is something better on before. All the good that God gives us draws something better behind it. And let me whisper it: there is a best thing yet to come, not yet revealed unto eye or ear of saint, but it will be ours by-and-by when our Lord cometh.

In what respects, then, can our future be better than that which is behind? I answer very readily, *faith may be stronger*. By the grace of God it will be firmer and more robust. At first it shoots up like the lily, very beautiful, but fragile; afterwards it is like the oak with great roots that grip the soil, and rugged branches that defy the winds. Faith in the young beginner is soon cast down, and doubts and fears prevail; but if we grow in grace, we become rooted and grounded. In these days, when it is fashionable to sneer at the doctrines of Scripture, and nobody is thought to be sensible who believes anything, the young believer is apt to be staggered; but it would take a great many of the critics and divines of the present day, with all their scepticisms, to shake some of us. We have tasted, and handled, and lived upon these things; and being established in them, we are not to be moved from the hope of our calling. Though all the wiseacres in the world should dip their pens in tenfold darkness, and write it down as proven that there is no such thing as light, we have seen it with our eyes, and we live in it, and we are not to be moved from the eternal verities.

This is something better than early faith, is it not? Go on, and obtain it.

Again, God gives to his people, as they advance, *much more knowledge*. At first they enjoy what they know, but they hardly know what they enjoy. As we grow in grace we know more. We are surprised to see that what we thought to be one blessing is fifty blessings in one. We learn the art of dissecting truth—taking it to pieces, and seeing the different veins of divine thought that run through it; and then we see with delight blessing after blessing conveyed to us by the person and sacrifice of our exalted Lord. Brethren, if years and experience make us know more, our present is better than our beginnings.

Love to Christ gets to be more constant. It is a passion always, but with believers who grow in grace it comes to be a principle as well as a passion. If they are not always blazing with love, there is a good fire banked up within the soul. You know how you bank your fire up when you come to chapel of an evening, and have nobody at home, and want to keep the fire alight till you get home. That is often the condition of a Christian. Even if we do not talk much about assurance, and say nothing about getting near perfection, yet we lie humbly before God, and do not doubt that we love him. We are sure that we do, for it becomes a daily delight to us to speak with Christ; and, in the speaking, we feel our love glowing. You do not always feel that you love those whom you never see: but when you talk to the dear objects of your love, your heart is moved. As one of the old Puritans used to say, our graces are not apparent unless they are in exercise. You walk through a preserve, and there may be partridges and pheasants and hares all round you: you will not see them till one flies out of its hiding, or a hare starts up before you. You see them in motion; but while they were quiet in the copse, you did not observe them. So may love to Christ and all Christian virtues lie concealed till they are called into action. Our Lord's dear presence attracts them all out of their hiding-places; and then you perceive that love was always there, and there in strength too, though it was not always on your lip, nor even in your thought.

As Christians grow in grace, *prayer becomes more mighty.* If the Lord builds you up into true spiritual manhood, you will know how to wrestle. Why did not Jacob meet the angel the first time when he went to Bethel? He lay him down, and slept, and dreamed a dream. He was a spiritual babe, and a dream suited his capacity. But when he came back, a man who had grown by years of experience, then the angel of God came and wrestled with him. It is one part of the teaching of divine experience that we grow stronger in the art of prayer, and know how to win from God greater things than at the first we ever dreamt of asking. God grant you better things in the matter of prayer than at your beginnings!

So, I think, it is in *usefulness.* Growing Christians, and full-grown Christians, are more useful than beginners. They may not, apparently, be doing so much; but they are doing it better, and there is more result. Their fruit, if not quite so plentiful, is of better quality, and more mellow. If there be fewer fruits, they are larger each one, and each one of a finer flavour.

In fact, this one thing is clear of all believers who have grown in grace—that *the work of grace in them is nearer completion.* They are getting nearer heaven, and they are getting more fit for it. Some of you are sitting very loose by this world. You are expecting very soon to hear the summons which will call you to quit these earthborn things. As ripe fruit comes from the tree with a gentle touch, so is it getting to be with you: the world had a greater hold upon you when you were young than it has now; and your thoughts of departure from it are more frequent, and more full of desire than they used to be. You have come to look at death as though it were only a removal to a neighbouring town, or like stepping across the street. You have looked at it so long that you can say like one I knew, "I have dipped my foot in the river every morning, and I shall not be at all afraid to ford it when the time comes." The Lord has made you to stand on tiptoe, ready to rise. You can say, "The time of my departure is at hand." Your chariot is at the door. Well, now, this is something better than your beginnings.

The old Christian may look back upon the new wine, and say regretfully, "How it sparkled and effervesced! But the old is better." You may think of the days of your youthful vigour when the body kept pace with the spirit; and you were young and full of nerve, and muscle, and enthusiasm. Those animal spirits have now gone from you, and you are sobered, and even slow. You have become old, and, perhaps, forgetful of many things. You go over the old story now instead of inventing new ones; but then, the old story—the old, old story—is as new to you as at the first, and you love it better than ever before. You cannot be driven from it now. I should think Satan himself would hardly like to meddle with some of you; he feels that he cannot shake your faith in the living God; or if he should shake you, you would in turn shake *him*. He has had so many brushes with you during the last fifty years that he begins to know that you carry the true Jerusalem blade, and he had rather deal with other folks who are fond of the "modern thought" wooden sword. You have come to the land Beulah, and you are sitting on the brink of Jordan, waiting to cross over to the Celestial City. Surely, you have realized that God is dealing better with you than at your beginnings.

III. I will end with the last, which is a practical matter. How can we, dear friends, we who are beginning a Christian life, How CAN WE SECURE THAT IT WILL BE BETTER WITH US BY-AND-BY THAN IT IS NOW? Alas! we have seen some start splendidly in appearance. They did run well; but they were soon out of breath, or turned aside. We hear no more of them. Our fear should be lest the like should happen to us. How can we act so as to hold on our way, and go from good to better?

I answer, first, *keep to the simplicity of your first faith*. Never get away from that. You remember the story we used to tell of poor Jack the huckster, who sang—

> "I'm a poor sinner and nothing at all,
> But Jesus Christ is my all in all."

Questioners could not make him doubt. He said that he could not doubt that he was a poor sinner and nothing at all, for he knew he was. And why should he doubt that Jesus Christ was his all in all? The Word of God said so; why should he doubt it? Here he stood, and would not budge an inch. Neither will I. The cony is safe in the rock, and he knows better than to come out. I hide in Jesus, and there I mean to remain, whatever the critics or the cultured may say. Jesus is my all in all, and I am nobody. My life cost him his death, and his death is my life. He took my sin, and died; I take his righteousness, and live. You may laugh, but I win. You may sneer, but I sing. O dear friend, fly to Jesus, and hide in him, and then keep there! Never get an inch beyond the cross; for, if you do, you will have to come back. That is your place till you die: you nothing, and Christ everything. You have to sink lower, and lower, and lower; and in your esteem Christ must rise higher, and higher, and higher. The "nothing at all" must be more emphatic the older you grow, and the "all in all" must be more emphatic too. If you get borrowing wings, and trying to fly up with speculations about what you may be in yourself, you will end in coming down heavily, with a bruised heart, if not with broken bones. Keep you at the foot of the cross, and you will maintain—nay, you will increase—your joy in the Lord.

At the same time, dear friends, *practise great watchfulness*. Many a child of God has to weep for months because he did not watch for minutes. He closed his eye a little while, and said, "It is all right with me"; and in that little while the enemy came and sowed tares among his wheat, and great mischief came of a little nap. We ought to have the eyes of a lynx, and they ought never to be closed. We know not which way the next temptation will come. We need to be guarded on all sides, and remember the words of our Master, "What

I say unto you, I say unto all, Watch." You will not keep your joy and grow in grace unless you watch.

The next advice is *grow in dependence upon God*. For your watchfulness, depend upon his watching. You cannot keep yourself unless he keeps you. You must watch, but still it is he that keepeth Israel, and doth neither slumber nor sleep. Remember that.

Determine, dear friend, at the very beginning, *to be thorough*. I love to see young Christians very scrupulous about the mind of the Lord. I would not have you say, " Oh, that is non-essential! " Obedience to a command may not be essential to your salvation, but it must be essential to the completeness of your holiness. " Whatsoever he saith unto you do it." Safe walking can only come of careful walking. I have known the time when I felt afraid to put down one foot before the other for fear I should go wrong; and I believe I was never so right as when that feeling was on me continually. You young people must cultivate more and more the grace of holy fear. Daily dread lest in anything you should omit to do your Lord's will, or should trespass against him. In this way your joy shall be maintained, and you shall be settled after your old estates; and God will do better unto you than at your beginnings.

Lastly, *seek for more instruction*. Try to grow in the knowledge of God, that your joy may be full. It will be ill for you to say, "I know I was converted, and therefore need not care any further." That will not do. No, no, in conversion you began a race from which you are never to cease. You have been born again, and therefore you need spiritual food. You enjoy spiritual life, and you are to nurture that life till it is conformed to the perfect image of Christ. Onward, brother! Onward, for that which is beyond will repay your labour!

PORTIONS OF SCRIPTURE READ BEFORE SERMON—
Ezekiel xxxvi. 1—15; 23—34.

HYMNS FROM "OUR OWN HYMN BOOK"—675, 889, 867.

A

SKETCH OF THE LIFE

OF PASTOR

CHARLES HADDON SPURGEON,

WITH

THIRTEEN PORTRAITS AND ENGRAVINGS.

LONDON:

PASSMORE AND ALABASTER,
PATERNOSTER BUILDINGS.

1887.

Yours most heartily,

C. H. Spurgeon

A SKETCH OF THE LIFE OF PASTOR

CHARLES HADDON SPURGEON.

His Ancestry.

GODLINESS in the home generally leads to godliness in the hearts and lives of those who form the household. For three centuries, the Spurgeon family can show a record of uninterrupted piety, and the influence of the successive lives of the various branches on their immediate surroundings has been incalculable. Upon the families themselves, the religious conduct has strengthened and deepened with accumulating power; and in these last times, we see, in the lives and actions of those now representing the family, the fulness of blessing which has been the answer to the prayers of many generations.

Those earnest, godly, and heroic men who left the Netherlands two centuries ago, and settled, some in Norfolk, others in Essex, were men who took daily counsel of God, and willingly followed the divine guidance. Their faithful endurance through fierce persecution and trial told of their strong hold on the arm of Omnipotence. The record of their sufferings is a memory their successors will not let die.

"When I spoke, the other day, with a Christian brother," said Mr. Spurgeon, in a recent sermon, "he seemed right happy to tell me that he sprang of a family which came from Holland during the persecution of the Duke of Alva, and I felt a brotherhood with him in claiming a like descent. I dare say our fathers were poor weavers; but I had far rather be descended from one who suffered for the faith than bear the blood of all the emperors within my veins."

There are descendants now living of both the Norfolk and Essex branches, and they are distinguished for their love of liberty, and their love of God. The Pastor of the Metropolitan Tabernacle is a direct descendant of the Essex branch. For more than a century, this family has had representatives in the office and work of the Christian ministry; and the lives of three only of these have covered a period of more than a century, and it has been the writer's privilege to have personal knowledge of, and correspondence with, all three.

The grandfather of Pastor C. H. Spurgeon was named James Spurgeon, a venerable pastor of the Puritan type. He was born at Halstead, in Essex, September 29th, 1776, and was a seriously disposed child from his earliest years, following the godly example set before him by his father. James joined the Independent Church in his native place whilst yet a youth, and during his business career he lived a consistent, useful, Christian life. At the age of twenty-six, feeling himself drawn to the ministry, he yielded to what he believed was the call of God, entered Hoxton Academy in 1802, and two years afterwards began his public ministry at Clare, in Suffolk. The Independent Church there was in a very languishing condition; but under his ministry a tide of prosperity set in, and in 1806 he was elected pastor. In 1810, he was called to the pastorate of the church at Stambourn, in Essex, which had a high reputation for piety, and he entered on the responsible duties of that church in May, 1811. Himself the fourth of a succession of pastors who had presided over that cause during 200 years, he retained the pastorate there more than fifty years, during which period he was peaceful, happy, and successful in his labours. He was a great favourite with the Essex people, and was widely known from his being so frequently invited to preach special sermons. His own chapel held about six hundred people, and on Sunday afternoons it was well filled, the farmers coming from many miles round to hear him, and he lived a beautifully simple and useful pastoral life amongst them. He had a long range of stables erected near the chapel for the shelter of their horses. His grandson preached a memorable sermon in his pulpit when he had completed fifty years of ministerial service, and it is published with the title "The God of the Aged." (See Nos. 81, 82 of the "New Park Street Pulpit"). The aged pastor was able to preach for three years after that time, and retained his influence over the people to the end of his life. The venerable man never preached in any place away from his own church without the satisfaction of hearing that some good had resulted from the service. He had a good voice, and his preaching was very earnest and practical. He was specially attached to the hymns written by Dr. Watts, and could scarcely tolerate any others. He was fond of children, and usually carried in his pocket a packet of sweets, which had an attractive influence for them. His kind and gentle manners made him a general favourite. He died, honoured and beloved, February 12th, 1864, aged 87 years; his funeral was attended by a large number of loving friends. His portrait is on the next page.

John Spurgeon, the father of the Metropolitan Tabernacle Pastor, was born in 1811, and is now six years beyond the limit of life recorded by the Psalmist David, yet he is ten years younger than his father when he died. Old age is honourable, especially in the service of God, and the Spurgeons are born to that distinction : even the Pastor of the Tabernacle, like his two predecessors, is hoping and expecting to celebrate the Jubilee of his ministry at his great Church.

Yrs most affectionately

Stambourn   Spurgeon

John Spurgeon was engaged in business during the week for many years, and on the Sunday preached to a congregation of Independents, at Tollesbury, in Essex, for sixteen years. Retiring from business, he became pastor of the Independent church at Cranbrook, Kent, for five years. He then came to London, and accepted the pastorate of the Independent Church in Fetter Lane, which he afterwards exchanged for a similar position, in a more congenial sphere, in the Upper Street, Islington. The latter charge he resigned in 1876. He has done good service in the cause of his divine Master in each of his pastorates. His preaching has always been plain, earnest, and pointed, and he has ever manifested an affectionate solicitude for all under his care, especially the young people. Although there were many large places of worship in Islington, with preachers of distinction, yet Mr. Spurgeon gathered a large congregation, had a good working church in that locality, his preaching being both acceptable and beneficial. On several public occasions, there have been present as speakers at the Tabernacle and the Orphanage the Revs. John Spurgeon, Charles Haddon Spurgeon, James A. Spurgeon, and Charles (or Thomas) Spurgeon, three generations of preachers in one family. The Rev. John Spurgeon's portrait is on the next page.

The mother of Mr. Spurgeon was the youngest sister of Charles Parker Jarvis, Esq., of Colchester, in which place she and her husband resided many years. She is known and loved for her sincere piety and humility, and was remarkable for her success in works of Christian usefulness, so long as health and strength enabled her to engage in active work for the Saviour. Her son Charles inherits many of the distinguishing characteristics of her devoted, simple, godly life. Mr. and Mrs. Spurgeon made great sacrifices in early life to educate their children well and thoroughly; they now have the reward of their cheerful self-denial. The care bestowed on their home training of their children is abundantly rewarded by the exemplary usefulness of their lives. Mrs. Spurgeon's solicitude about her oldest boy was deep and earnest. One day she said to him, " Ah, Charley ! I have often prayed that you might be saved, but never that you should become a Baptist." To this Charles replied, " God has answered your prayer, mother, with his usual bounty, and given you more than you asked."

Birth and Early Life.

Charles Haddon Spurgeon was born in the village of Kelvedon, in Essex, on June 19th, 1834. In the villages of England, some of the most distinguished men of the country were born, nurtured, and trained, and in those humble localities nature formed and developed their faculties, and there the foundations of future usefulness and greatness were laid. Kelvedon is a small town, with a population of about two thousand. When young Spurgeon was born, the clergyman of the parish was the Rev. Charles Dalton, a godly and useful minister, who lived long enough to celebrate his jubilee as their pastor. Charles H. Spurgeon had a younger brother, James Archer Spurgeon ;

yours very truly

C H Spurgeon

the boys were of different build, and unlike in personal appearance: Charles was the stouter of the two, and the boys of the village gave them characteristic names. There were six sisters in the family, two of whom are said to have resembled Charles in figure and mental energy. When old enough to leave home, Charles was placed under the care of his grandfather, at Stambourn. The venerable grandsire ardently loved his grandson, and as their acquaintance matured, it is hard to say which loved the other most. A maiden aunt at the Stambourn parsonage took charge of Charles, and he soon developed into a thoughtful, serious boy, more fond of his books than play. The pious precocity of the child soon attracted the attention of all around him. He astonished the grave deacons and matrons who called on his grandfather, on Sabbath evenings, by the serious, intelligent questions he asked, and by the pertinent remarks he made. It is said on good authority that before he was six years old, he publicly reproved sinners in the street. The following remarkable instance is said to have occurred while he was under his grandfather's roof. One of the members of the church at Stambourn, named Rhodes, was in the habit of frequenting the public-house to have his "drop of beer," and smoke his pipe, greatly to the grief of his godly pastor, who often heaved a sigh at the thought of his unhappy member's inconsistent conduct. Little Charles had doubtless noticed his grandfather's grief on this account, and laid it to heart. One day he suddenly exclaimed, in the hearing of the good old gentlemen, "I'll kill old Rhodes, that I will!" "Hush, hush! my dear," said the good pastor, "you mustn't talk so; it's very wrong, you know, and you'll get taken up by the police, if you do anything wrong." "Oh, but I shall not do anything bad; but I'll kill him though, that I will." Well, the good grandfather was puzzled, but yet perfectly sure that the child would not do anything which he knew to be wrong, so he let it pass with some half-mental remark about "that strange child." Shortly after, however, the above conversation was brought to his mind by the child coming in and saying, "I've killed old Rhodes; he'll never grieve my dear grandpa any more." "My dear child," said the good man, "what have you done? Where have you been?" "I haven't been doing any harm, grandpa," said the child; "I've been about the Lord's work, that's all." Nothing more could be elicited from little Charles. Before long the mystery was cleared up. "Old Rhodes" called to see his pastor, and, with downcast looks and evident sorrow of heart, narrated the story of how he had been killed, somewhat in this fashion :—"I'm very sorry indeed, my dear pastor, to have caused you such grief and trouble. It was very wrong, I know; but I always loved you, and wouldn't have done it if I'd only thought." Encouraged by the good pastor's kindly Christian words he went on with his story. "I was a-sitting in the public just having my pipe and mug of beer, when that child comes in—to think an old man like me should be took to task and reproved by a bit of a child like that! Well, he points at me with his finger just so, and says, 'What doest thou here, Elijah! sitting with the ungodly; and you a member of a church, and breaking your pastor's

MR. SPURGEON'S BIRTH-PLACE, KELVEDON, ESSEX.

heart. I'm ashamed of you! I wouldn't break my pastor's heart, I'm sure.' And then he walks away. Well, I did feel angry; but I knew it was all true, and I was guilty; so I put down my pipe, and did not touch my beer, but hurried away to a lonely spot, and cast myself down before the Lord, confessing my sin and begging for forgiveness. And I do know and believe the Lord in mercy pardoned me; and now I've come to ask you to forgive me; and I'll never grieve you any more, my dear pastor." It need not be said that the penitent was freely forgiven and owned a brother in the Lord, and the Lord was praised for the wonderful way in which it had all come about. But it must be added that henceforward the godly pastor had no more consistent member or godly helper in the church than "old Rhodes."

At the age of seven, Charles H. Spurgeon removed to his father's home, then at Colchester, that he might have greater educational advantages. In 1844 he spent his summer vacation at the house of his grandfather, and during his brief sojourn there, the following interesting circumstance occurred. It has several times appeared in print in a fragmentary form; but we now give it as told by Mr. Spurgeon himself, while these pages were going through the press, on Sunday morning, July 10th, 1887.

Incident and Prophecy.

" When I was a young child staying with my grandfather, there came to preach in the village Mr. Knill, who had been a missionary at St. Petersburg, and a mighty preacher of the gospel. He came to preach for the London Missionary Society, and arrived on the Saturday at the manse. He was a great soul-winner, and he soon spied out the boy. He said to me, 'Where do you sleep? for I want to call you up in the morning.' I showed him my little room. At six o'clock he called me up, and we went into the arbour. There, in the sweetest way, he told me of the love of Jesus, and of the blessedness of trusting in him and loving him in our childhood. With many a story he preached Christ to me, and told me how good God had been to him, and then he prayed that I might know the Lord and serve him. He knelt down in the arbour and prayed for me with his arms about my neck. He did not seem content unless I kept with him in the interval between the services, and he heard my childish talk with patient love. On Monday morning he did as on the Sabbath, and again on Tuesday. Three times he taught me and prayed with me, and before he had to leave, my grandfather had come back from the place where he had gone to preach, and all the family were gathered to morning prayer. Then, in the presence of them all, Mr. Knill took me on his knee, and said, 'This child will one day preach the gospel, and he will preach it to great multitudes. I am persuaded that he will preach in the chapel of Rowland Hill, where (I think he said) I am now the minister.' He spoke very solemnly, and called upon all present to witness what he said. Then he gave me sixpence as a reward if I would learn the hymn

'God moves in a mysterious way, His wonders to perform.'

I was made to promise that when I preached in Rowland Hill's Chapel that hymn should be sung. Think of that as a promise from a child! Would it ever be other than an idle dream? Years flew by. After I had begun for some little time to preach in London, Dr. Alexander Fletcher had to give the annual sermon to children in Surrey Chapel, but as he was taken ill, I was asked in a hurry to preach to the children. 'Yes,' I said, 'I will, if the children will sing "God moves in a mysterious way." I have made a promise long ago that so that should be sung.' And so it was: I preached in Rowland Hill's Chapel, and the hymn was sung. My emotions on that occasion I cannot describe. Still that was not the chapel which Mr. Knill intended. All unsought by me, the minister at Wotton-under-Edge, which was Mr. Hill's summer residence, invited me to preach there. I went on the condition that the congregation should sing, "God moves in a mysterious way"—which was also done. After that I went to preach for Mr. Richard Knill himself, who was then at Chester. What a meeting we had! Mark this! he was preaching in the theatre! His preaching in a theatre took away from me all fear about preaching in secular buildings, and set me free for the campaigns in Exeter Hall and the Surrey Music Hall. How much this had to do with other theatre services you know.

'God moves in a mysterious way, His wonders to perform.'"

His School Life.

When he settled at home, his father placed him in a school at Colchester, conducted by Mr. Henry Lewis, the head teacher being Mr. Leeding, who afterwards opened a School for young gentlemen at Cambridge. During the four years spent at the Colchester School, Charles H. Spurgeon acquired a fair acquaintance with the Latin, Greek, and French languages: to Mr. Leeding he was indebted for all the knowledge he there obtained. At the examinations he was invariably the prize-winner. In 1848, he spent a few months in an Agricultural College at Maidstone, conducted by one of his relatives. In 1849, being then in his 15th year, he removed to Newmarket, having engaged himself as usher in the School of Mr. Swindell, a Baptist, connected with the Independent Church in that town. While fulfilling with his characteristic thoroughness the duties of his calling, he, nevertheless, was able by the practice of much self-denial to make very considerable progress in his classical and other studies. Here it was that he had a fierce struggle with scepticism; but appealing by prayer to God for help and guidance he conquered, and that pernicious temptation has ever since been subdued. During his residence at Newmarket he competed for a prize: his essay was entitled "Antichrist and her Brood; or, Popery unmasked." There were only three competitors. He did not win the prize, but his essay was returned to him two years afterwards with a handsome gift of money, to encourage him to write again.

Towards the close of 1849, owing to an outbreak of fever, the school was closed, and Mr. Spurgeon returned to his home at Colchester.

The precautions taken against infection were, however, unavailing in his case, for he was attacked by typhus fever, and brought very low. But he, whose name is Jehovah-Rophi, soon not only caused his young servant to say with the psalmist, " Bless the Lord, O my soul, who healeth all thy diseases "; but to add with an emphasis, "Who redeemeth thy life from destruction, who crowneth thee with loving-kindness and tender mercies." Here we must let Mr. Spurgeon tell, in his own inimitable way, the story of

His Conversion.

" It pleased God in my childhood to convince me of sin. I lived a miserable creature, finding no hope, no comfort. My heart was broken in pieces : six months did I pray, agonizingly, with all my heart, and had no answer. I resolved to visit every place of worship in Colchester, that I might find out the way of salvation : I felt willing to be anything, and to do anything, if God would only forgive me."

" At last, one snowy day,—it snowed so much, I could not go to the place I had determined to go to, and I was obliged to stop on the road, and it was a blessed stop to me,—I found rather an obscure street and turned down a court, and there was a little chapel. I wanted to go somewhere, but I did not know this place. It was the Primitive Methodists' chapel. I had heard of these people from many, and how they sang so loudly that they made people's heads ache ; but that did not matter I wanted to know how I might be saved, and if they made my head ache ever so much I did not care So, sitting down, the service went on, but no minister came. At last a very thin-looking man came into the pulpit and opened his Bible and read these words : ' Look unto me, and be ye saved, all the ends of the earth.' Just setting his eyes upon me, as if he knew me all by heart, he said, 'Young man, you are in trouble.' Well, I was, sure enough. Says he, ' You will never get out of it unless you look to Christ.' And then lifting up his hands he cried out, as only I think a Primitive Methodist could do, ' Look, look, look ! ' ' It is only look,' said he. I at once saw the way of salvation. Oh, how I did leap for joy at that moment ! I know not what else he said : I did not take much notice of it, I was so possessed with that one thought. Like as when the brazen serpent was lifted up, they only looked and were healed. I had been waiting to do fifty things, but when I heard this word, ' Look,' what a charming word it seemed to me ! Oh, I looked until I could almost have looked my eyes away, and in heaven I will look on still in my joy unutterable. I now think I am bound never to preach a sermon without preaching to sinners. I do think that a minister who can preach a sermon without addressing sinners does not know how to preach."

In passing, it may interest our readers to learn that the identical pulpit from which that memorable " Look " sermon was delivered is to be seen—shall we say, as a sacred " relic ? "—at the Stockwell Orphanage.

In 1856, on the anniversary of his conversion, Mr. Spurgeon preached from the same text to his own people, when he related what took place on that very day and hour six years previously. The Sermon is No. 60, "New Park Street Pulpit," the title " God's Sovereignty," text Isaiah xlv. 22. In October, 1864, Mr. Spurgeon preached to 500 people in the same chapel in which he was converted, and from the same text.

Mr. Spurgeon returned to his duties at Newmarket full of his new-found joy, and devoted himself, heart and soul, to the service of his Lord and Master. It is scarcely necessary to add here that he determined to embrace the earliest possible opportunity to make a public profession of his faith in Christ, and to join himself to the people of God. On applying to the pastor and members of the Independent Church, they received him into their fellowship, and found him ready to every good work. His duties in the School of which he was assistant master were very onerous, occupying him early and late ; but, constrained by the love of Christ, he seized every opportunity to win souls to the Saviour. Situated as he was, tract distribution seemed to be the best means to attain this end, and whenever he walked out he took a supply of these " Messengers of Mercy " with him, and thoroughly " worked " the neighbourhood.

The Sunday School very soon gained his attention ; and his addresses to the children were so full of interest and instruction, that the children carried glowing reports of them home to their parents, and soon they also came to hear " teacher, " and were held spellbound by his earnest words and racy style.

Next to his conversion, the circumstance which had the most important bearing on Mr. Spurgeon's future course was his conviction of the scripturalness of Believers' Baptism. As we have seen, he was at this period of his history a pedobaptist. Not only by the most tender and sacred associations, but by his own personal choice, his lot was cast among firm believers in the doctrines and practices of the Congregationalist body. But no sooner did he see it to be his duty to be immersed, than he made haste to keep his Lord's command. On May 3rd, 1850, he was publicly baptized at the village of Isleham, Cambridgeshire, by the Rev. W. W. Cantlow, Baptist Minister of that place. He was then under sixteen years of age. Writing to his father on that day, ever memorable to him, he says, " It is very pleasing to me that the day on which I openly profess the name of Jesus is my mother's birthday "; and he expresses a hope that it may be to both a foretaste of many glorious and happy days to come.

He resided one year at Newmarket, after which he became usher in the school of his former teacher and friend, Mr. Henry Leeding, who had but recently opened a school at Cambridge. At Cambridge there was a Society called The Lay Preachers' Association, and young though he was, Mr. Spurgeon was accepted as a member. He readily accompanied some of the preachers, and soon after he had completed his sixteenth year he began himself to preach.

His First Preaching Experience.

As this was one of the most important steps in Mr. Spurgeon's life, the reader will be glad to learn from his own pen the circumstances which lea to his first attempted sermon. In introducing the text, "Unto you therefore which believe he is precious," 1 Peter ii. 7, Mr. Spurgeon remarks, in 1873—"I remember well that, more than twenty-two years ago, the first attempted sermon that I ever made was from this text. I had been asked to walk out to the village of Teversham, about three miles from Cambridge, where I then lived, to accompany a young man whom I supposed to be the preacher for the evening, and on the way I said to him that I trusted God would bless him in his labours. 'Oh, dear!' said he, 'I never preached in my life; I never thought of doing such a thing. I was asked to walk with you, and I sincerely hope God will bless you in your preaching.' 'Nay,' said I, 'but I never preached, and I don't know that I could do anything of the sort.' We walked together till we came to the place, my inmost soul being all in a tremble as to what would happen. When we found the congregation assembied, and no one else there to speak of Jesus, though I was only sixteen years of age, as I found that I was expected to preach, I did preach, and the text was that just given."

He soon became popular in the villages around Cambridge, large numbers being attracted to hear him; and, young though he was, invitations to preach special sermons in towns and villages at a distance rapidly increased in number. At Waterbeach, a village of some 1,500 persons, the little Baptist Church saw in the "Boy Preacher" a young man suitable to their wants, and they promptly secured him as their pastor.

The College Incident.

This is Mr. Spurgeon's account of a circumstance which may well be designated "a remarkable providence":—

"Soon after I had begun, in 1852, to preach the word in Waterbeach, I was strongly advised by my father and others to enter Stepney (now Regent's Park) College, to prepare more fully for the ministry. Knowing that learning is never an incumbrance, and is often a great means of usefulness, I felt inclined to avail myself of the opportunity of attaining it, although I believed I might be useful without a college training. I assented to the opinion of friends that I should be more useful with it. Dr. Angus, the tutor of the college, visited Cambridge, where I then resided, and it was arranged that we should meet at the house of Mr. Macmillan, the publisher. Thinking and praying over the matter, I entered the house at exactly the time appointed, and was shown into a room where I waited patiently for a couple of hours, feeling too much impressed with my own insignificance and the greatness of the tutor from London, to venture to ring the bell and enquire the cause of the unreasonably long delay."

"At last, patience having had her perfect work, the bell was set in motion, and, on the arrival of the servant, the waiting young man of eighteen was informed that the doctor had tarried in another room, and could stay no longer, so had gone off by train to London. The stupid girl had given no information to the family that anyone had called and had been shown into the drawing-room, consequently the meeting never came about although designed by both parties. I was

COTTAGE AT TEVERSHAM, WHERE MR. SPURGEON FIRST PREACHED.

not a little disappointed at the moment; but have a thousand times since then thanked the Lord very heartily for the strange providence which forced my steps into another and far better path."

This point of college training was most seriously considered, both by himself and his parents, as is manifested in several letters written at that period. In one letter he sent to his mother, November, 1852, he says, "I am more and more glad that I never went to college": further on he adds, "I have all that heart can wish for; yea, God giveth more than my desires. My congregation is as great and loving as ever. During all the time I have been at Waterbeach I have had a different house for my home every day. Fifty-two families have thus taken me in, and I have still six other invitations not yet accepted." All that was very encouraging to a youth of eighteen. But a greater change was at hand, one that was to determine all his after life. At the anniversary meeting of the Cambridge Union of Sunday Schools, in 1853, one of the speakers was the young pastor from Waterbeach. Among others, upon whose mind the address delivered by Mr. Spurgeon made a lasting impression, was Mr. Gould, of Loughton. Shortly afterwards, this gentleman met in London one of the deacons of a famous Baptist Church in Southwark, then without a pastor, and ventured the opinion that the youthful Cambridgeshire evangelist possessed just the qualifications for ministering to the New Park Street Church. That church had existed since 1652, and had numbered among its pastors some very eminent men of God. At the time of which we are writing, this once prosperous cause was diminished and brought very low: its glory seemed to have departed. The deacons considered all that Mr. Gould communicated about the young Waterbeach pastor, and an invitation was sent him to preach at New Park Street.

His Call to London.

When Mr. Spurgeon received at Waterbeach the letter inviting him to preach in London, he thought it was a mistake, and that the letter was intended for some other person; but his deacons in that village soon understood the matter, and said that promotion, by him unsought, was awaiting him. He accordingly came to London to supply the pulpit at New Park Street Chapel for one Sunday, in the autumn of 1853. The chapel, which had sitting accommodation for upwards of a thousand persons, presented anything but an encouraging appearance to the preacher; for we have been credibly informed that the congregation, all told, numbered about two hundred on that occasion. But such was the impression made upon the faithful few by the whole service, and especially by the sermon, that in the evening the congregation was nearly doubled, and the people wondered at what they heard. The deacons then invited Mr. Spurgeon for three alternate Lord's-days, and afterwards the church unanimously requested him to occupy the pulpit for six months, with a view to the pastorate. This arrangement, however, was soon superseded by the church unanimously electing him as their pastor. In his letter of acceptance he says, " I give myself into the hands of our Covenant God, whose wisdom directs all things. He shall choose for me, and, so far as I can judge, this is His choice."

NEW PARK STREET CHAPEL.

Before three months had expired, the fame of the young preacher had spread all over London and its suburbs, although he was not quite twenty years old. In the autumn of that year he preached a sermon on " Is it not Wheat Harvest to-day ? " The sermon was printed ; it was the first of the series, and created a demand which has been growing and spreading, till now there are thirty-two large yearly volumes of his sermons published, and they have been circulated by millions, have found their way over the entire globe, and have been translated into many languages. They were first issued with the title " New Park Street Pulpit," but in 1861 the name was changed to " Metropolitan Tabernacle Pulpit," owing to the sermons being then preached there. By the end of the present year the total number of separate sermons issued in succession will (D.V.) be 2,000. Of some of them more than 100,000 copies have been sold ; but the average weekly sale is about 25,000 copies, a result quite unparalleled in the history of sermon literature. No other preacher in any 'and or at any time has realized such a result.

Within one year not only was the chapel in New Park Street filled to its utmost capacity, but every Sunday hundreds were disappointed at not being able to gain admittance. The chapel therefore had to be enlarged, and Exeter Hall was occupied for about three months whilst the enlargement was being made. The crowds being as great as ever when the services were resumed in the enlarged chapel, it was found necessary to hire the very large Music Hall in the Royal Surrey Gardens.

Here occurred, at the first Sunday-evening service, October 19, 1856, a sad calamity. A false alarm of fire having been raised, a panic ensued, resulting in the death of seven persons, twenty-eight others being injured. The preacher himself received so severe a shock to his nervous system that he was utterly prostrated for a time. By the

2

great mercy of God he recovered sufficiently to occupy the pulpit in the chapel on October 31st, and gradually regained his wonted health. To avoid all fear of further panic, it was arranged that the services at the Music Hall should be held in the morning instead of the evening of the Lord's-day. Although that part of the day is least favourable for large congregations, the multitude came Sunday after Sunday, to the number of ten thousand at a service, to listen to the story of redeeming love as they had never heard it told before. Best of all, the slain of the Lord were many.

In December, 1859, the Directors of the Music Hall having determined to open it as a place of amusement on Sunday evenings, Mr. Spurgeon and his friends felt compelled, for conscientious reasons, to vacate the building, and they again were obliged to hold their services at Exeter Hall, and continued to do so until the opening of the Metropolitan Tabernacle. A short time after Mr. Spurgeon left the Music Hall a fire almost destroyed the building, and the relics were for years turned into a hospital.

Such an unusual amount of popularity having arisen, without any desire for it by the young preacher, the question was asked a thousand times, " Who is this Spurgeon ? " He was urged to answer the question by publishing a brief account of his life ; but this he would not do. At length, meeting with a friend in Paternoster Row who was selling his sermons, he consented to his doing so, and gave the required information, with help from his father and grandfather. The result was the publication of " A Sketch of the Life and Ministry of C. H. Spurgeon," with an outline of "The Baptist Confession of Faith," of which nearly ten thousand copies were sold in one year. That work served to satisfy the curiosity as to the early life of the young pastor, since which time the press has abundantly made known the results of his varied and extensive labours.

For several years, both by pen and pencil, he was caricatured almost unmercifully ; sometimes as the result of the bitter animosity of men who did not understand the tendency and value of his work ; at other times the sketches published had in them much of vigorous force and truth. One of these pencil sketches was entitled, " Brimstone and Treacle ; " another, " Catch 'em alive O ! " In the former Mr. Spurgeon is made to represent Brimstone, because he spoke plain truths in his sermons, and said, " The wicked shall be turned into hell, with all the nations that forget God." Treacle was to represent the Rev. J. C. M. Bellew, who was the " Society " or fashionable preacher of the day, and who could only preach smooth and sweet things : it was a true representation of both preachers. The other sketch was intended to set forth, by a figure of flies on a gummed paper, how the people by thousands gathered at every service to hear the popular preacher.

All these things tended to increase the preacher's fame, until it reached every part of England ; and ere long there were but few newspapers of any influence in which some commendatory article had not appeared. Even the *Times* was led to discuss the subject of preachers and preaching, and asked the question, Why St. Paul's Cathedral and

Westminster Abbey should remain comparatively empty, whilst this young Nonconformist preacher could gather around him 10,000 people to hear the Gospel, in the Surrey Music-Hall, every Sunday morning.

All these circumstances tended to add to the attractiveness of Mr. Spurgeon's ministry, and at length it was found to be absolutely necessary to provide a suitable building for his large and rapidly increasing church, and the great numbers desirous of attending his ministry.

His Marriage.

The year 1856 was a remarkable one in the life of Mr. Spurgeon. It was the year of his marriage, the year also in which he preached his grandfather's jubilee sermon, and one of the centenary sermons in Whitefield's Tabernacle, in Tottenham Court Road. We have already referred to the Surrey Gardens' catastrophe which occurred in the October of the same year. It is also noteworthy, we think, that in December Lord Chief Justice Campbell twice attended the services at the Music Hall, and encouraged Mr. Spurgeon with the assurance that by his labours great good was being done amongst the people.

During the first week of the year Mr. Spurgeon was delighting large audiences at Bath. The second week was made memorable by a service held in his own chapel, in which the young people more particularly took a very lively interest. Early in the forenoon of January 8th Mr. Spurgeon was married, by Dr. Alexander Fletcher, to Miss Susannah Thompson, daughter of Mr. Robert Thompson, of Falcon Square, London. An interesting account of the service appeared in the *Christian Cabinet* for January 11th. About two thousand persons were unable to enter the chapel on the occasion. The service was commenced by singing the well known hymn, "Salvation! oh the joyful sound." The One hundredth Psalm having been read, a solemn and affecting prayer was offered, and an appropriate address given. The form of marriage used by Protestant Dissenters was then gone through, after which Ephesians v. was read, and the wedding hymn sung, commencing, "Since Jesus freely did appear." Dr. Fletcher again implored the divine blessing on them. They were both attended by their parents. Never did two persons unite hands and hearts more suited to each other in mind, disposition, and mutual love: twin boys, Charles and Thomas Spurgeon, are the only issue of their marriage. (See page 29.)

The Metropolitan Tabernacle.

The history of the Metropolitan Tabernacle is a theme in itself so full of interest and remarkable incidents, that a long and instructive chapter might be written out of the circumstances attending its origin, growth, completion, and opening free from debt. Such results as were then so fully realized were the source of astonishment alike to both Churchmen and Nonconformists. In October, 1856, the first great meeting was held for considering the steps necessary to be taken for erecting a great Tabernacle. The proposal was very neartily taken up by Mr. Spurgeon's friends, and very soon in every part of the country sympathy was largely shown with the movement by evangelical Christians of every name, and generous gifts attested the Christian love of rich and poor—of Smith the ploughman, and Shaftesbury the peer. It is true that there were many who laughed at the idea of erecting an edifice as a place of worship to seat five thousand persons, and not a few good people shook their heads, and predicted the speedy collapse of the preacher and his plan. But, regardless of these obstructions, the work went on, Mr. Spurgeon travelling all over the land, preaching daily, with the promise of half the proceeds of the collection being devoted to the new Tabernacle. The foundation stone was laid by Sir Samuel Morton Peto, August 16th, 1859. In 1860, a large and enthusiastic meeting was held in the shell of the new building. The opening services were commenced in March, 1861, and were continued daily for five weeks.

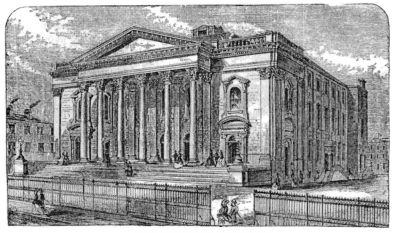

THE METROPOLITAN TABERNACLE.

At the end, the sum of £31,332 had been placed in the hands of the treasurers, the free-will offerings of the people, and the magnificent Tabernacle, to seat 5,500 persons, and with standing room for 1,000 more, was opened free of debt. The church members were 1,178 when the Tabernacle was opened: in December, 1886, the membership stood at 5,351. During the greater part of this period the losses by death have averaged more than 50 per annum; and there has always been a constant exodus of members to outlying districts to form new churches; in most cases these enterprises have been led by students of the Pastors' College. Thousands of members also have left London for distant parts, and many of these have gone to the very ends of the earth.

The Metropolitan Tabernacle is a wonderful edifice. Underneath the large audience room there is a lecture-room which will seat 900 persons, a Sunday school-room in which 1,000 children are taught, several class-rooms, a number of vestries, a kitchen fitted with every convenience for tea-services, store rooms on two stories, and rooms for mothers' meetings and other such agencies.

In connection with the Tabernacle church there are many evangelistic and philanthropic agencies constantly at work, the bare mention of which is all our space will permit.

For Home Missions, there is the Baptist Country Mission, which seeks to evangelize the villages by open-air preaching and cottage services, by which much good has been done. The Evangelists' Association is at work in halls, lodging-houses, street corners and on the Tabernacle steps, and sends helpers to any church needing assistance. The church and Sabbath schools liberally contribute to the work of Foreign Missions. There are also a small Auxiliary Mission for the conversion of the Jews, and a Benefit Society for the working classes, which provides payments in sickness and at the death of members.

There are 28 Mission Stations, and 24 Sunday and Ragged Schools in connection with the Tabernacle, doing an incalculable amount of spiritual and philanthropic work, especially among the poor and the neglected classes. There are also a Young Christians' Association, a Children's and Teachers' Library, a Gospel Temperance Society, and a prosperous Band of Hope. The history of the many good works at Haddon Hall, Bermondsey, and Richmond Street, Walworth, not to mention others in this connection, would require a lengthy chapter.

The ladies take their full share of work : they sustain a Maternal Society, a Benevolent Society for relieving the poor and visiting the sick, and a Poor Ministers' Clothing Society, for supplying boxes of clothing to needy pastors and their families. The ladies have also a flourishing Auxiliary in aid of Zenana work in India and China.

The Pastors' College.

Never was an institution more clearly originated by divine providence than was the College for Theological Students now in connection with Mr. Spurgeon's Tabernacle. It originated from urgent necessity, and its claims were pressed on the young pastor on this wise. Before he had preached in the New Park Street Chapel three months, many young men had been converted, baptized and admitted to church fellowship. Constrained by the love of Christ, and stimulated by the zeal of the pastor, they commenced earnest work for the good of others. One of these, Mr. T. W. Medhurst, began out-door preaching, and, encouraged therein by seeing much good done, he applied to Mr. Spurgeon for instruction to fit him better for the work, and found his pastor heartily willing to assist him in his studies to that end. In this way Mr. Medhurst became Mr. Spurgeon's first student, and really formed his College. Believing in a great and successful future, all Mr. Spurgeon's actions in this department looked for a succession of students whom it would be his joy to help fit themselves for the Lord's work. He had no means, only his own salary, to help forward the work ;

but one day, Mr. Winsor, Mr. William Olney, and the Pastor together contributed the first £20 to buy books for future use, and thus to begin the work of the College. When the writer first visited Mr. Spurgeon in Dover Road, in the Borough, in 1855, his first student was with him at his lessons. It was not long ere Mr. Medhurst was invited to a pastoral charge at Kingston. In 1860, he removed to Coleraine, and in 1862, to Glasgow. From Glasgow he removed, in 1869, to his present sphere at Landport, Portsmouth, where his labours have been greatly owned of God: more than a thousand converts have been added to the Church by baptism, and much good done in many departments of philanthropic and evangelistic work. Such is a sample of the work done by Mr. Medhurst, the first of a long line of 742 students who have been trained for the ministry under Mr. Spurgeon's care.

Considering his own heavy pastoral duties, Mr. Spurgeon waited on the Rev. George Rogers, of Camberwell, and to him he opened his mind with regard to the training of young men for the ministry. Mr. Rogers entered heart and soul into the scheme, and at once accepted the position of Theological Tutor to the applicants. The first students were domiciled in his family. Once every week, all the young men used to meet Mr. Spurgeon at his home, to receive such instruction and direction as he knew would be helpful to them; and this custom was observed for many years. As they completed their course of training, the readiness with which the students found spheres of labour was taken as evidence that the work was of God. Mr. Rogers, now a venerable octogenarian, intensely beloved by the students he has had under his care, for a quarter of a century devoted his best energies to this important work.

As the students increased in number, larger accommodation than the class and lecture-rooms at the Tabernacle was required, and the present College buildings were erected in 1874. From the first Mr. Spurgeon has habitually set apart a large portion of his income to the support of the College.

Many readers of his sermons and other works show their love to him and his "life-work," by pecuniary help, and the weekly offerings of the congregation at the Tabernacle are also devoted to the same purpose: these in 1869 amounted to £1,869, and ever since they have been made to correspond with the year-date: thus last year they amounted to £1,886. At the annual College Meeting held at the Tabernacle, about £2,500 is subscribed. As a rule, those churches whose pastors have been educated in the College make annual collections in aid of its funds. From these sources the College is supported, the annual cost being about £7,000.

During the thirty years the College has been in operation, over 740 young men have been trained, and over 550 are now preaching the gospel: fifty-four have died, and a few are in secular callings. There are about eighty in residence. About 70,000 converts have been baptized and become church-members, as the fruit of the labours of the College students who are or have been pastors.

At one period in the early history of the work Mr. Spurgeon's faith was put to a severe test. He had been contributing a large proportion of the funds needed for its support; his ability to act in this princely fashion being largely due to the popularity of his sermons in the United States. But suddenly the remittances from America ceased: he had dared to champion the cause of the slave: this was the head and front of his offending. (We are bound to add here in a parenthesis, that all this has long been changed, and nowhere is the name of the Tabernacle pastor more honoured, or his many works more highly valued than by our brethren across the water; and the Christian love and esteem are mutual.) Naming this financial difficulty to his congregation, the Weekly Offering was resorted to. A lady gave £200 to the College, and another friend sent £100, and so the work was carried on, and His servant's faith strengthened by His faithful God. When Sermon No. 500 was issued, Mr. Spurgeon's publishers gave a supper at which £500 were raised and given to the College.

THE PASTORS' COLLEGE.

One feature of the College work calls for special note, namely its missionary character; we use the word in its widest sense. From the first Mr. Spurgeon has sought to impress upon the students the duty of "breaking up new ground"; not to be content to build upon another's foundation, or to enter into other men's labours, but to extend the bounds of the Redeemer's kingdom by commencing new interests at home, or taking the message of mercy to the heathen in far-off lands. That this has been done is evident by the long list of pastors and missionaries in foreign lands (about 140 names), and by the statement of the President in the Report, that "in nearly 150 cases those who remain at home have founded new churches, and in many more they have revived interests which were almost defunct."

While this success, which it would be difficult to over-estimate, has been a constant reason for gratitude and praise to the Great Head of the Church, it has brought with it a great burden of care to the President of the College. Each new and growing church has necessitated the erection of a chapel and schools, and this has always meant an appeal to Mr. Spurgeon to give and to get substantial pecuniary help to scores of building funds, and in many cases grants in aid of the ministers' support, until these communities have become self-supporting. Under all these burdens the Lord has sustained his servant hitherto, supplying through him the needs of the churches, in answer to his earnest prayer and childlike trust.

The Loan Building Fund.

This fund was raised with the view of meeting in some measure the needs to which we have referred in the preceding paragraphs. During the past twenty-four years it has been augmented by the gifts of Mr. Spurgeon and many generous donors until it now amounts to a little over £5,000. It is in constant circulation, in sums varying from £100 to £800, lent, without interest, to churches having debts on their buildings, but able to guarantee repayment by regular instalments. It has been of incalculable value to many new causes, though far from sufficient to meet the numerous applications for its benefits.

Co-Pastor James A. Spurgeon.

In connection with the Pastors' College, it is important to notice the invaluable services of the Rev. James Archer Spurgeon. He was born June 8th, 1837, and has consequently just completed fifty years of his life. His many friends at the Tabernacle spontaneously acknowledged the festive occasion by a handsome presentation to him, as a mark of sincere esteem and love. He was educated partly with his only brother, Charles. He was converted in early life, baptized, and joined the Baptist Church. Thirty years ago he began to preach, and his ministry was very acceptable to the people. After passing through the usual curriculum at Regent's Park College, he was called to take the oversight of the church at Portland Chapel, Southampton. This charge he relinquished at the earnest request of Sir S. M. Peto, who had erected a commodious chapel at Notting-hill. Here Pastor J. A. Spurgeon gathered a large congregation, and founded a new Baptist Church, of which he remained Pastor for some years, doing much good amongst the best families in the Westend of London. This charge he resigned in January, 1868, to become co-pastor with his brother at the Metropolitan Tabernacle. In 1860, he married a daughter of that distinguished officer, the late

Yours ever faithfully

James A. Spurgeon

General Sir John Fox Burgoyne, Bart. Lady Burgoyne and her daughter were members of the church at New Park Street, and thus became intimately acquainted with the Spurgeon family. This accomplished and earnest Christian lady was, after a period of severe suffering, called to her heavenly rest in 1881.

Soon after Mr. James Spurgeon's acceptance of the co-pastorate he took up his residence at West Croydon, where he soon established a new Baptist church and erected a chapel. This soon proved too small for the congregations gathered, and ere long a handsome and commodious structure was erected, which has since been supplemented by large school buildings. Two branch chapels also have been erected through the efforts of the pastor and friends of the West Croydon church. Greatly as Mr. J. A. Spurgeon is loved and valued by his people at Croydon, it is as co-pastor with his brother at the Metropolitan Tabernacle that he is best known and most sincerely loved. As Vice-President of the College, his wisdom and sound judgment exercise a most important influence for good on the minds of the young men in training. As Vice-President of the Orphanage he not only manifests an affectionate sympathy with the orphans, but also takes a large share in the onerous work connected with this large institution. As Vice-President of the Colportage Society his business tact in directing the affairs of its many branches is highly appreciated by his co-workers in this important field of Christian service. In all these varied labours he has been and is a great help and comfort to his brother. We must not close this too brief sketch of Pastor J. A. Spurgeon without noting that in 1882 he married the only daughter of James Withers, Esq., of Reading, in whom the West Croydon Church, and the Stockwell Orphanage especially, find an earnest and valued helper.

The Stockwell Orphanage.

For interest and importance, the Stockwell Orphanage is second only to that of Mr. Müller's, at Bristol. Its origin may be briefly stated. Mrs. Hillyard, the widow of an English clergyman (but who had subsequently joined the Baptist denomination) placed the sum of £20,000 at the disposal of Mr. Spurgeon, with which to found an Orphanage for boys. At first, Mr. Spurgeon shrank from such a very heavy responsibility; but in conversation with the lady, found her purpose was unchangeable. The money was accepted, trustees chosen, and the work of founding such an Institution commenced. An estate was purchased at Stockwell, in the Clapham Road, and the foundation stones of several houses were laid in the summer of 1867. The plan of the Orphanage was matured within one year, and many generous friends heartily co-operated with the pastor, and largely supplemented Mrs. Hillyard's gift. Several families contributed £500 each to build a house, and those houses are called after their donors. Never was a more joyous day for Pastor Spurgeon than August 9th, 1867, when the foundation stones of these first houses were laid; for a great concourse of friends gathered to cheer him by their sympathy and liberal gifts on that occasion. The urgent need for the institution was proved by the fact that 200 applications were before the Trustees when the first house was ready for occupation. It was from the first made a fundamental rule that the *most needy* should be accepted, without respect to creed. Girls were first admitted in 1879, and new buildings have been erected for their special use. There are about 240 boys and 230 girls in residence.

BIRD'S-EYE VIEW OF STOCKWELL ORPHANAGE.

The expenses for a year are about £11,000, and God sends the money by his servants in many ways, and often as special providences. The applications are so numerous that only two out of every ten of those for whom its benefits are sought are able to gain admission, therefore only the most needy cases can be accepted. The orphans themselves collect for the funds, and each one after leaving gives the first-fruits of his or her earnings as a thankoffering to the institution. One of the most interesting sights of London is the annual festival in June at the Orphanage, which, once seen, can never be forgotten: it is a scene of real joy.

The Almshouses.

Very near to the Tabernacle, and close to the "Elephant and Castle" railway station, stands a handsome range of buildings, consisting of Schools and Almshouses. The central portion is the

Almshouses, in which are seventeen rooms for as many poor women over sixty years of age, whose names are on the Tabernacle Church Book. There were only six Almshouses in New Park Street. After the removal of the church and congregation to the Tabernacle, and the sale of the New Park Street property, Mr. Spurgeon determined that in the new building there should be accommodation for a larger

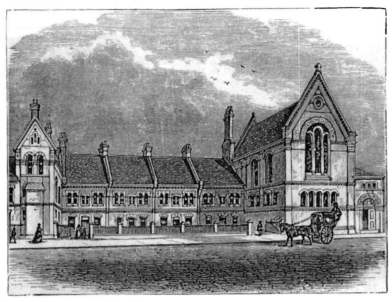

ALMSHOUSES.

number of inmates, with the result we have just recorded. There is a small endowment for the benefit of the occupants. Being near to the Tabernacle, the aged inmates can get to the services without any undue fatigue. When Mr. Spurgeon had completed the twenty-fifth year of his pastorate, his friends gave him £6,233 as a mark of their esteem and affection. The generous impulses of his mind led him to invest the sum of £5,000 as an endowment fund for ever, to increase the weekly allowance to the alms-women. The other portion was given to other agencies.

The Day School adjoining the Almshouses is a valued and prosperous institution, a great boon to the Nonconformists of the neighbourhood and their children : the teaching is very thorough and the fees are very low.

Mr. Spurgeon's Twin Sons.

The two sons of Mr. and Mrs. Spurgeon have been a source of very much happiness to their parents. Many prayers were offered continually for their conversion, and much solicitude manifested for their future usefulness. Just as their minds and judgments were formed, God called them by his sovereign grace ; they joined the church at the Tabernacle, and laid themselves out for Christian usefulness.

Upon leaving school for business they devoted the whole of their available time and energy to evangelistic services, and established a mission-church and schools in the vicinity of their home, which was marked with singular success. They also responded to frequent invitations to preach in other places. In 1879 the first-born, Charles, settled in a pastorate at Greenwich, near London, where he has now a large and important Baptist Church. Thomas, whose health failed him in England, went to Australia, where under God, he has done a great work, built a large tabernacle in Aukland, New Zealand, and was for many years pastor of one of the largest churches in the colony.

CHARLES SPURGEON.   THOMAS SPURGEON.

During the enforced absence of his father through ill-health, or when seeking rest and restoration, his elder son Charles frequently occupied the pulpit at the Tabernacle, where his preaching was very acceptable.

Mr. Thomas Spurgeon, too, when in England, was several times called upon under similar circumstances to take the afflicted pastor's place, and his sermons on those occasions, since published in a neat volume, entitled, "The Gospel of the Grace of God," price 1/6, will well repay perusal. He is also a regular contributor to the pages of *The Sword and the Trowel*, greatly to the pleasure and profit of its readers.

In 1893, Mr. Thomas Spurgeon was elected to the Pastorate of the Metropolitan Tabernacle, which position he still occupies.

Mrs. Spurgeon's Book Fund.

A very pretty volume, published in 1886 and already in the third edition, entitled, " Ten Years of my Life in the Service of the Book Fund, by Mrs. C. H. Spurgeon," describes how Mrs. Spurgeon began to give away books to very needy clergymen and ministers of all religious denominations. It is a record of real Christ-like benevolence, and one of the finest examples in print of the way in which a feeble Christian sufferer can gladden the hearts of thousands, and diffuse new and fresh information to tens of thousands. The book itself is deeply interesting, and of great value, and shows that Mrs. Spurgeon not only possesses great literary ability, but that she is one of England's true heroines. No more touching proof of the pressing necessity for such a mode of Christian service can be found than the extracts given from the letters of thanks sent by the recipients of Mrs. Spurgeon's beneficence, names, of course, being withheld.

A few figures may help the reader to judge of the work involved in this "*labour* of love." During the past nineteen years, many thousand grants of books have been made, the total number of volumes being 154,735. A large number of sermons have been supplied to ministers for village distribution. To Missionaries abroad Mr. Spurgeon's sermons are regularly posted, to the number of nearly 10,000 a year ; and very highly do they prize both the gift and the loving sympathy of which it is an expression.

Colportage Society.

It is now twenty years since Mr. Spurgeon invited his friends and the Christian public in general to assist him in providing a system of Christian Colportage for the villages and hamlets of England similar to the successful association inaugurated a few years previously in Scotland. "The agency of Colportage," wrote Mr. Spurgeon in 1866, "has in past ages been honoured of God in the very highest degree. Sellers of trinkets carried the Bible in their packs, and sold it to noble matrons at the castle-gate as the best of jewels, and thus the way was paved for the Reformation ! Pedlars hawked throughout England the valuable works of the Puritans, and so spiritual truth was preserved in England amid general declension. We feel bound to wield afresh this well-tried weapon, and a committee has been formed . . . to push the work with all their might."

How well and wisely these brethren have worked, and how largely the divine blessing has now been vouchsafed to their well-chosen agents, may be seen in the last Annual Report, from which we can only find space for these significant figures :—In 1866 there were two Colporteurs employed, and 1867 four others were engaged. The gross sales effected by these six good men amounted to nearly one thousand pounds, and they made nearly two thousand five hundred visits to families. Last year the number of Colporteurs was eighty-seven, the sales of Scripture and good books reached nearly ten thousand pounds, and the visits to more than five hundred and sixty thousand. Best of all, many souls have been saved every year, and much service done in the promotion of temperance and vital religion. This is really a Home Missionary work, and should bespeak the generous help and earnest prayer of all Christian people.

Mr. Spurgeon's Publications.

Already Pastor C. H. Spurgeon was one of the most voluminous writers of the nineteenth century. A long chapter might be written to describe the books his pen produced. We have already referred, on page 17, to that marvel of pulpit literature, "The Metropolitan Tabernacle Pulpit," a theological library in itself, which contained up to Mr. Spurgeon's death no less than 2241 consecutive sermons. The publishers have enough manuscript of unpublished sermons to carry them on for about another twelve years. "The Treasury of David," in seven large closely-printed volumes, has been justly called Mr. Spurgeon's *magnum opus;* and it merits the designation not only for its intrinsic value, but for its widespread circulation on both sides of the Atlantic. In America a fac-simile reprint has been produced. This may also be said of most of the author's works. As a pleasing testimony to the value of the "Lectures to my Students," it may be mentioned that one of the Bishops of the Established Church makes a point of asking "candidates for orders" if they have read these Lectures ; and if the answer is in the negative, he strongly advises them to do so. Two other works, unique in their character, viz., "John Ploughman's Talk," and "John Ploughman's Pictures," claim special mention from the fact that they have attained the astonishing circulation of over 500,000 copies in England alone, and have been translated into several languages. A complete catalogue of Mr. Spurgeon's works, which will be found at the end of this book, represents an amount of literature with but few parallels in any country, especially if we consider that it has been the work of one burdened with the duties of the largest pastorate in Christendom, and the direction and care of many other religious and philanthropic works.

Mr. Spurgeon's Long Illness and Departure "to be with Christ."

For many years Mr. Spurgeon was subject to severe and prolonged attacks of rheumatic gout. That he was able, under such conditions, to sustain labours, many arduous, and ever multiplying, was thought to be proof that he had "an iron constitution." This was far from being true ; and there were from time to time indications that he was literally spending and being spent in his loved Lord's service. It required no supernatural prescience to forecast that a heavy penalty would one day be exacted from the man who had preached a thousand sermons before he had attained his majority, and who for years afterwards preached on an average twelve sermons a week : it was in the natural order of things that it should be so.

While the preacher was careful to impress upon his hearers the wisdom and beneficence of the Creator in ordaining a definite proportion of time for rest, and the necessary repair of the " wear and tear " of the body, he disobeyed the law through his very love and zeal for the Lawgiver. It is true he tried to be "as good as his creed" in this particular, by resolving to set apart one day in seven for rest, but much more frequently than not the rest day was given up in response to some importunate request for public service or literary labour.

For obvious reasons he was compelled to leave home for several weeks every winter. Towards the close of 1890, it happened, as on several previous occasions, that he was prostrated by illness just as he was about to leave home for his usual winter resort in the South of France. Later on he was able to travel to Menton, and he returned considerably benefited in health, and resumed his pulpit ministrations on February 8th, 1891. At that time there was a general belief that not a few years of usefulness were in reserve for God's servant, and in this conviction he himself shared. That the All-wise willed far otherwise all the world now knows.

Before his return from Menton Mr. Spurgeon had made an arrangement with his esteemed friend, the Rev. W. Stott, that he should help him in the work at the Tabernacle. " We have many invaluable helpers," wrote Mr. Spurgeon, " but we have need of another minister to lead. The senior Pastor hopes to *preach* none the less frequently, but he wishes more and more to be allowed to spend what strength he has in ministering in word and doctrine, and to be eased in other matters."

In less than three months an incident happened which showed that the relief thus obtained had come too late. From Mr. Spurgeon's own reference to the event, as given in the Memorial Volume,* we gather the following particulars :—" On Lord's-day morning, May 3rd, 1891, Mr. Spurgeon commenced his sermon upon Psalm xl. 7, with the following memorable statement : 'To my great sorrow, last Sunday night I was unable to preach. I had prepared a sermon upon this text, with much hope of its usefulness. . . . I came here feeling quite fit to preach, when an overpowering nervousness oppressed me, and I lost all self-control, and left the pulpit in anguish. . . a circumstance which never happened to me before in the forty years of my ministry.'

" Although probably no one suspected it at the time, this was the beginning of the end of the noble life that closed at Menton on January 31st, 1892. The preacher was at the time terribly overworked, and applications for additional services were continually coming. He struggled on bravely, however, and on May 17th preached a sermon on the text, ' My times are in Thy Hand,' which many people regarded as almost prophetic of the great illness he was about to suffer. He was even then attacked by

---

* *From the Pulpit to the Palm Branch.* A Memorial of C. H. Spurgeon. Passmore & Alabaster.

that terrible scourge 'influenza.' He was, indeed, confined to the house for nearly three weeks; but at the end of that time, on Lord's-day morning, June 7th, he preached from 1 Samuel xxx. 21—25, a most memorable discourse, for it was practically *the Pastor's farewell to the Tabernacle.* He was never inside the building again until all that remained of him was brought from Menton in the olive-wood casket, amid universal mourning."

The next day, Monday, June 8th, accompanied by two friends, he left home for a brief visit to the scenes of his childhood, in Essex, hoping thereby to further his convalescence, and also to obtain additional illustrations for the interesting little book entitled "Memoirs of Stambourne," which was then nearly ready for the press. Unhappily, the weather proved capricious, east winds prevailed, and on the Thursday he took a chill, which (to use his own words) brought on " an overpowering headache, and he had to hurry home on Friday, to go up to that chamber where, for three months, he suffered beyond measure, and was often between the jaws of death."

The public interest in the beloved patient was very great. Not only were representatives of the daily press in almost constant attendance at "Westwood," to glean any and every item of intelligence ; but the four principal telegraphic Press agencies made arrangements for the transmission of the two daily bulletins the world over as soon as they were issued by the physicians. On two occasions the Prince of Wales instructed Colonel Knollys to write to Dr. Kidd for information as to the sufferer's condition, and gave him messages of sympathy to convey to his patient.

Besides very many personal enquiries at "Westwood," letters were received from persons of all classes from different parts of the world.

When the case had evidently passed beyond the power of human aid, and the cloud was darkest, a ray of hope pierced the gloom : the anxious watchers were surprised by signs of improvement; so very slight at first that while they could but rejoice, yet it was "with trembling."

Subsequent weeks saw frequent fluctuations in the sufferer's state, but the balance was happily on the side of improvement, though the doctors could not affirm that the disease had yielded to their skill.

" On October 3rd, Mr. Spurgeon went to Eastbourne, in the hope that a short stay at the seaside might bring to him sufficient strength to enable him to take the journey to Menton. Mrs. Spurgeon also went for a few days ; and the experiment appeared quite satisfactory ; so that when the Pastor returned to "Westwood," he was so much stronger, that the arrangements for starting for Menton were completed.··

" On Monday, October 26th, Pastor and Mrs. C. H. Spurgeon, Pastor and Mrs. J. A. Spurgeon, and Mr. Harrald started on their thousand miles' journey, and arrived at their destination on Thursday, the 29th. Dr. FitzHenry at once took charge of his patient, and aided him greatly by his wise and kindly advice.

" The appearance of Mr. Spurgeon from this time, until a few days before he was called home, led many beside himself to hope that a long rest by the sunny shore of the Mediterranean would complete his restoration. He gradually gained strength . . . . but not until the last day of the old year was he able to conduct a service."

Then, and on the morning of New Year's Day, to a little group of delighted friends, he gave the memorable address which appears in the Memorial Volume under the head of " *Breaking the Long Silence.*"

From Mrs. Spurgeon's beautiful letter of thanks we cull a line here and there descriptive of the last days on earth of this eminent servant of God :—

" One fact has greatly comforted me in my deep grief. It is that the Lord so tenderly granted to us both three months of *perfect earthly happiness* to us here, before He took him to the 'far better' of His own glory and immediate presence! For fifteen years my beloved had longed to bring me here ; but it had never before been possible. Now we were both strengthened for the long journey, and the desire of his heart was fully given him. We took long daily drives ; his enjoyment was intent, his delight was exuberant. He *looked* in perfect health, and rejoiced in the brightest of spirits. Then, too, with what calm deep happiness he sat, day after day in a cosy corner of his sunny room, writing his last labour of love, *The Commentary on Matthew's Gospel !* Up to the last ten days of his sweet life, health appeared to be returning, though slowly, and he himself believed that he should live to declare again to his dear people, and to poor sinners, the unsearchable riches of Christ. But it was not to be. His Saviour wanted him up higher, and could spare him to us no longer. He is gone to his everlasting reward, and the hallelujahs of heaven must hush and rebuke the sobs and sighs of earth."

The removal of the body to England, its reception at the Tabernacle, the wonderful memorial services held on several days previous to the funeral, attended by tens of thousands are circumstances never to be forgotten by those who took part in them. The funeral procession passed through the streets from the Tabernacle to Norwood Cemetery amidst the most profound sorrow, hundreds of thousands of people by their silent and reverent behaviour testifying to the greatness and usefulness of the servant of God whose life on earth was ended. Perhaps the most touching scene along the route was witnessed at the Stockwell Orphanage, where the singing of the orphans was choked by sobs. At the cemetery Students and Pastors, friends from near and far, had assembled round the open grave, and amidst tears and great regrets the service was conducted by the Rev. Dr. A. T. Pierson and the Rev. Archd. Brown. To-day a noble monument is erected on the spot, and many a visitor stands in silence at the grave and thanks God for the life of His servant. But his greatest monument is the work which he did in the strength of God—the building up of souls in the love of Christ, the training of men for the ministry, and the kindly hand which he extended to the orphaned little ones.

Textual Index for Sermons

CPSIA information can be obtained
at www.ICGtesting.com
Printed in the USA
FSOW02n1955271116
27794FS